Finland
a Lonely Planet travel survival kit

Markus Lehtipuu

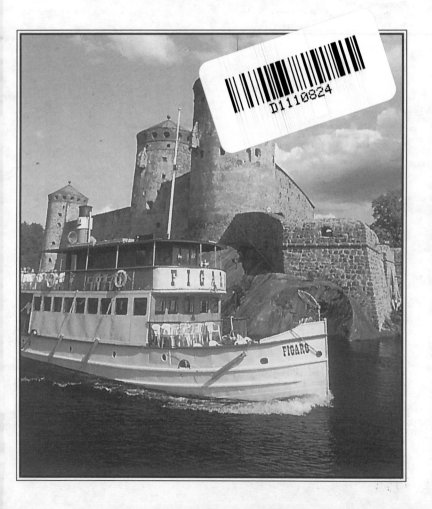

Finland

2nd edition

Published by
Lonely Planet Publications
Head Office: PO Box 617, Hawthorn, Vic 3122, Australia
Branches: 155 Filbert St, Suite 251, Oakland, CA 94607, USA
            10 Barley Mow Passage, Chiswick, London W4 4PH, UK
            71 bis rue du Cardinal Lemoine, 75005 Paris, France

Printed by
SNP Printing Pte Ltd, Singapore

Photographs by
Markus Lehtipuu
Front cover: Museum, Kuusamo

First Published
January 1993

This Edition
May 1996

Although the authors and publisher have tried to make the information as accurate as possible, they accept no responsibility for any loss, injury or inconvenience sustained by any person using this book.

National Library of Australia Cataloguing in Publication Data

Lehtipuu, Markus
   Finland

   2nd ed.
   Includes index.
   ISBN 0 86442 356 X.

   1. Finland – Guide-books. I. Title. (Series: Lonely Planet
   travel survival kit).

914.8970434

Markus Lehtipuu

A native of Finland, Markus has travelled to over 60 countries since 1982, including working spells in Sweden, Norway and Canada, and seven months in India. He has contributed to Lonely Planet's *Scandinavian Europe phrasebook* and *Scandinavian & Baltic Europe*, and authored several guidebooks in Finnish, including guides to Finland, Morocco, Thailand, Malaysia and Singapore. He has guided tourists from Calcutta to Colva, and even read his Malaysia guidebook aloud for the blind. He edited one issue of a glossy travel magazine before it went bust (not his fault), and presented a travel show on a local radio station. He has covered every corner of Finland, hitchhiking (with a broken bicycle) and carrying a laptop computer in his backpack – even travelling in an all-day rainstorm in Lapland. When not trying to figure out how to see tourist attractions outside official opening hours, Markus spends much of his time in various Asian countries, preferably Indonesia.

From the Author

Thanks to every friendly person who helped me out during my research, including good friends with whom I shared some of the best moments on the road. As usual, I am grateful to my parents Irma and Martti Lehtipuu for valuable assistance, as well as my uncle Eero for help with the section on tracing ancestors, and my brother-in-law Kari for last-minute e-mail. Other people whom I want to thank include Leena Rautavaara at the Finnish Youth Hostel Association and the rest of the people there, Matti Oksanen, Matti Siivonen and Raili Pölönen in Enonkoski, Leena Julku, Päivi Vänttinen, Kalevi and Terttu Räisänen in Heinävesi, Teija Kurvinen, Jouni Puruskainen and Tuija Rytkönen in Ilomantsi, Virpi Luostarinen, Risto Matsi, Leena Waismaa-Matsi and Soile Palviainen in Joensuu, Jyrki Teeriaho in Juuka, Raimo Lehtosalo in Karigasniemi, the Puska family in Kauhajoki, Helena Lång in Kuusamo, Kikka Mannersalo in Lahti, Kimmo Kortelainen, Jouni Ortju and Mari Palosaari in Lieksa, Juha Vallin in Mäntyharju, Anne Nurmi in Naantali, Mikko Wikström and Matti Turunen in Nurmes, Janne Hänninen in Punkaharju, Pia Keloneva in Rovaniemi, Pirkko Käck in Savonlinna, Veikko and Tuovi Tepsa in Sodankylä, the Ristimäki family in Solf, Kati Hämäläinen in Sulkava and Päivi Ikonen in Tampere. Thanks also to Taina Kettula at the Finnish embassy in Canberra. Finally, my deepest thanks to Tom Ylkänen from MEK for help in compiling this and the 1st edition.

This Book

The 1st edition of this book was the result of research by Virpi Mäkelä (who covered the South Finland, Turku, Åland, South Häme and West Lapland sections of the book) and Markus Lehtipuu, who did the rest.

Since then, Finland has changed considerably and this second edition has gone through a major rewrite by Markus, with over 100 new destinations covered.

From the Publisher

This edition was edited by Suzi Petkovski, with able assistance from Bethune Carmichael, Liz Filleul, Lyn McGaurr and Mary Neighbour. Janet Austin and Jane Fitzpatrick joined the crew at proofing.

Additional eagle-eyed checking was done by Adrienne Costanzo, Jane Hart and Jane Marks. The incomparable Jacqui Saunders navigated her way around 100,000-odd Finnish lakes, laid out the book and still found time to produce the bulk of the illustrations. Marcel Gaston and Glenn Beanland assisted with mapping, while Tamsin Wilson added her illustrative flair. Julie Young and the readers' letters team supplied useful feedback. Thanks to Jane (The Sage) Fitzpatrick and Steve Womersley for entertaining a string of inane queries. Thanks also to Sharon Wertheim for producing another index in record time. The crowning touch was provided by Simon Bracken and Andrew Tudor, who produced the cover.

Thanks

Thanks to all the following travellers and others who took the time and trouble to write to us about their experiences of Finland:

Kelyn Bacon (UK), Courtenay Francis Raymond Barnet (TC), Marcus Bednarek (Ger), Mario Fernandez Cano (Esp), Howard Clark (UK), John Cox (UK), Penelope Curtis (UK), Kathleen Osgood Dana (USA), Luca Di Vito (Ita), Angela Dyer (UK), Victoria Feldman (USA), Mario Fernandez Cano (Esp), Barbara Gold (USA), Nick Hare (UK), Jennifer Harmsworth (UK), Philipp Hartmann (Fra), Ahmet Incesu (Tur), Manfred Lange (Fin), Olwyn Lanigan (Ire), Debra S Lee (USA), Jonathan Love (UK), Fergal McGirl (Ire), Angel Montoro Martos (Esp), Ana Mulder (Ned), Karl R Newman (USA), Steve Page (UK), Sheila Pankhurst (UK), Marzio Andrea Pistilli (Ita), Frances Pordes (Aut), Bob & Margaret Poutto (Can), Mick Rasmussen (Den), Kerry Rauch (Can), Timo Rautiainen (Fin), Carl Rubino (USA), IJ Rykkvin (Nor), Johan Segers (Bel), Michael Sherman (UK), Pat Silver (UK), Dorothy Smith (UK), Rhona KM Smith (UK), Malcolm Thomas (Aus), Juha Tiainen (Fin), Elina Torvinen (Fin), Erik & Hilde Verbeeck (Bel), Luca di Vito (Ita), Doris & Alec Waldron (UK), Arthur Westerback (USA), Sarah Williams (Can).

Aus - Australia, Aut - Austria, Bel - Belgium, Can - Canada, Den - Denmark, Esp - Spain, Fin - Finland, Fra - France, Ger - Germany, Ire - Ireland, Ita - Italy, Ned - Netherlands, Nor - Norway, TC - Turks & Caicos Islands, Tur - Turkey, UK - United Kingdom, USA - United States of America.

Warning & Request

Things change – prices go up, schedules change, good places go bad and bad places go bankrupt – nothing stays the same. So if you find things better or worse, recently opened or long since closed, please write and tell us and help make the next edition better.

Your letters will be used to help update future editions and, where possible, important changes will also be included in a Stop Press section in reprints.

We greatly appreciate all information that is sent to us by travellers. Back at Lonely Planet we employ a hard-working readers' letters team to sort through the many letters we receive. The best ones will be rewarded with a free copy of the next edition or another Lonely Planet guide if you prefer. We give away lots of books, but, unfortunately, not every letter/postcard receives one.

Contents

INTRODUCTION 11

FACTS ABOUT THE COUNTRY 12

History 12
Geography 24
Climate 24
Flora & Fauna 25

Government & Politics 26
Economy 28
People 30
Education 31

Arts 31
Culture 37
Religion 42
Language 43

FACTS FOR THE VISITOR 52

Visas & Embassies 52
Customs 54
Money 54
When to Go 55
Tourist Offices 56
Useful Organisations 57
Business Hours 57
Festivals & Public Holidays 58
Post & Telecommunications 60

Time 62
Electricity 62
Laundry 62
Weights & Measures 62
Books & Maps 62
Media 63
Film & Photography 64
Health 64
Women Travellers 69

Dangers & Annoyances 69
Work 70
Highlights 70
Accommodation 71
Food 75
Drinks 77
Entertainment 78
Things to Buy 79

ACTIVITIES 81

Trekking **81**
Access 81
Things to Take 82
Transport 83
Where to Trek 83
Free Accommodation 84
Cycling **85**
Bringing your Bicycle 85

Where to Cycle 86
Skiing **87**
Downhill Skiing 87
Cross-Country Skiing 87
Ski Jumping 87
Snowmobile Safaris 87
Rowing & Canoeing **88**
River Routes 88

Where to Row & Paddle 88
Boat Travel 90
Other Activities **90**
Fishing 90
Golf 90
Tracing your Ancestors 90

GETTING THERE & AWAY 92

Air 92

Land 96

Sea 100

GETTING AROUND 105

Air 105
Bus 106
Train 107

Taxi 109
Car & Motorbike 109
Hitching 111

Boat 112
Local Transport 112
Tours 112

HELSINKI 113

Orientation 114
Information 114
Museums 118
Churches 122
Parks & Gardens 122
Architecture 123
Activities 123
Organised Tours 123

Festivals 124
Places to Stay 124
Places to Eat 127
Entertainment 130
Things to Buy 130
Getting There & Away 131
Getting Around 132
Around Helsinki **133**

Suomenlinna 133
Espoo 135
Kirkkonummi 137
Myyrmäki 138
Vantaa 138
Järvenpää 139
Tuusula 139

UUSIMAA 142

West Uusimaa **142**
Hanko 142
Tammisaari 147
Tenala 150

Snappertuna 150
Karjaa 151
Pohja 151
Lohja 152

Karkali Nature Reserve 153
Sammatti 153
Siuntio 153
Mustio 153

Inkoo	153	Around Porvoo	157	Askola	161
Hyvinkää	154	Pernaja	158	Liljendal	161
South-East Uusimaa	**155**	Loviisa	158	Lapinjärvi	161
Sipoo	155	**North-East Uusimaa**	**160**	Orimattila	161
Porvoo	155	Mäntsälä	160		

ÅLAND 162

Mariehamn	**165**	Jomala	174	Brändö	179
Mainland Åland &		Lemland	174	Kumlinge	179
Around	**169**	Lumparland	175	**Southern Archipelago**	**181**
Eckerö	169	Saltvik	175	Föglö	181
Finström	172	Sund	176	Kökar	181
Geta	172	Vårdö	178	Sottunga	182
Hammarland	173	**Northern Archipelago**	**179**		

TURKU & PORI PROVINCE 183

Turku	**183**	**Salo Region**	**203**	**Satakunta**	**212**
Turku Region	192	Salo	203	Pori	212
Northern Turunmaa	**194**	Halikko	204	Yyteri	215
Naantali	194	Angelniemi	205	Reposaari	215
Nousiainen	198	Perniö	205	Irjanne	215
Masku	198	Teijo	205	Ulvila	216
Lemu	198	Kimito	206	Luvia	216
Askainen	198	Dragsfjärd	206	Leineperi	216
Velkua	199	Dalsbruk	206	Kullaa	216
Merimasku	199	Västanfjärd	206	Kankaanpää	216
Rymättylä	199	Kasnäs	206	Kokemäki	217
Turunmaa Archipelago	**199**	Hiittinen	207	Harjavalta	217
Kaarina	199	**Vakka-Suomi**	**207**	Panelia	219
Parainen	200	Mynämäki	207	Lappi	219
Around Parainen	200	Vehmaa	207	Eura	219
Nauvo	200	Taivassalo	207	Köyliö	219
Korppoo	201	Kustavi	208	Puurijärvi & Isosuo National
Houtskär	201	Uusikaupunki	208	Park	220
Iniö	202	Pyhämaa	211	Rauma	220
Historical Routes	**202**	Pyhäranta	211	Vammala	225
Ox Road	202	Kalanti	211	Around Vammala	227
King's Road	203	Laitila	211		

SOUTH-EAST 229

Kotka	**229**	Kouvola	240	Ylämaa	247
Kymi River Valley	**233**	Iitti	241	Lemi	248
Ruotsinpyhtää	233	Kausala	242	Imatra	248
Pyhtää	235	Jaala	242	Ruokolahti	251
Hamina	235	**South Karelia**	**243**	Parikkala	252
Elimäki	238	Lappeenranta	243	Around Parikkala	252
Anjalankoski	239	Luumäki	247	Uukuniemi	253

HÄME 255

Hämeenlinna	**255**	Urjala	264	Forssa	267
Around Hämeenlinna	259	Nuutajärvi	264	Jokioinen	268
South Häme	**261**	**Ox Road**	**265**	**Tampere**	**268**
Iittala	261	Renko	265	**Pirkanmaa**	**278**
Janakkala	261	Liesjärvi National Park	265	Eräjärvi	278
Loppi	262	Tammela	265	Hämeenkyrö	278
Riihimäki	262	Saari Park	265	Ikaalinen	279
Sääksmäki	263	Torronsuo National Park	267	Kangasala	280
Valkeakoski	264	Somero	267	Lempäälä	280

Nokia	280	Korkeakoski	284	Toriseva	285
Vesilahti	282	Kallenautio	284	Virrat	285
Kuru	282	Siikaneva Marshland	284	Perinnekylä	286
Route 66	**282**	Ruovesi	285	Liedenpohja	286
Orivesi	282	Helvetinjärvi National Park	285		

CENTRAL FINLAND 288

Jyväskylä	**288**	Suolahti	298	Vääksy	307
Around Jyväskylä	294	Äänekoski	298	Heinola	307
Western Central	**295**	Saarijärvi	298	Hartola	308
Petäjävesi	295	Pyhä-Häkki National Park	299	Sysmä	309
Himos	296	Karstula	299	Luhanka	310
Keuruu	296	Viitasaari	299	Joutsa	310
Haapamäki	296	Konginkangas	300	Padasjoki	310
Pihlajavesi	297	**Lake Päijänne Region**	**300**	Kuhmoinen	310
Mänttä	297	Lahti	300	Isojärvi National Park	311
Ähtäri	298	Hollola	304	Korpilahti	311
Northern Central	**298**	Asikkala	306		

SAVO 313

Savonlinna	**315**	**Around Mikkeli**	**332**	Suonenjoki	341
Around Savonlinna	**320**	Mäntyharju	332	Varkaus	341
Punkaharju	320	Mouhu	333	**Kuopio**	**343**
Rantasalmi	324	Ristiina	333	**North Savo**	**349**
Linnansaari National Park	324	Juva	335	Siilinjärvi	349
Enonkoski	325	**Central Savo**	**336**	Lapinlahti	349
Around Enonkoski	325	Pieksämäki	336	Iisalmi	350
Kerimäki	326	Heinävesi	337	Around Iisalmi	352
Sulkava	327	Around Heinävesi	337	Sonkajärvi	352
Mikkeli	**328**	Leppävirta	340	Ameriikka	353

NORTH KARELIA 354

Joensuu	**356**	Tiensuu	367	Vaikkojoki River	378
Around Joensuu	**360**	Patvinsuo National Park	369	Nurmes	378
Sailing the Pielisjoki River	360	Ruunaa	369	Around Nurmes	381
Outokumpu	360	Nurmijärvi Area	371	**Ilomantsi**	**382**
Lake Viinijärvi Loop	362	Vuonislahti	372	Hattuvaara	386
South of Joensuu	**363**	**Lake Pielinen**	**373**	Around Hattuvaara	387
Rääkkylä	363	Koli	374	Möhkö	388
Värtsilä	363	Kelvänsaari	375	Petkeljärvi National Park	388
Kitee	363	Juuka	375	Taitajan Taival	389
Heinoniemi	364	Paalasmaa	376	Mutalahti	389
Kesälahti	364	Vuokko	377	Naarva	389
Lieksa	**365**	Nunnanlahti	377	Lake Koitere	390
Lieksa Town	365	Ahmovaara	377		

POHJANMAA 391

Vaasa	**393**	Kauhava	404	Kristinestad	407
Around Vaasa	397	**South Pohjanmaa**	**404**	Around Kristinestad	409
Central Pohjanmaa	**398**	Alavus	404	Kaskinen	410
Seinäjoki	398	Kuortane	404	Närpes	410
Laihia	401	Alajärvi	405	Korsnäs	412
Ilmajoki	402	Lauhavuori National Park	405	Malax	412
Isokyrö	402	Kauhajoki	406	Bergö	413
Tervajoki	403	Kurikka	406	**Central Swedish Belt**	**413**
Ylistaro	403	Jalasjärvi	407	Maxmo	413
Lapua	403	**Swedish Coast**	**407**	Vörå	413
Härmä	403	Sideby	407	Oravais	414

Kimo...414
Nykarleby...............................414
Around Nykarleby.................415
Larsmo....................................415
Kronoby..................................416
Bennäs.....................................416
Pietarsaari..............................416

North Pohjanmaa............ 419
Evijärvi....................................420
Kaustinen................................420
Kokkola...................................421
Lohtaja....................................423
Himanka..................................424
Kalajoki..................................424

Maakalla..................................425
Pyhäjoki..................................425
Raahe.......................................425
Around Raahe.........................426
Vihanti....................................427
Ylivieska.................................427

OULU PROVINCE 428

Oulu.................................. 428
Around Oulu..................... 434
Hailuoto Island.......................434
Haukipudas.............................436
Ii..436
Kempele..................................436
Kiiminki..................................437
Liminka...................................437
Lumijoki..................................438
Siikajoki..................................438
Tyrnävä...................................438
Piippola...................................439
Ruukki.....................................439
Kainuu............................... 439

Kajaani....................................439
Paltaniemi...............................444
Sotkamo..................................445
Vuokatti..................................445
Kuhmo.....................................446
Around Kuhmo........................449
UKK Trekking Route.............449
Hyrynsalmi.............................450
Puolanka.................................451
Kuivajärvi...............................451
Ämmänsaari............................451
Around Ämmänsaari...............452
Hossa.......................................453
Kylmäluoma............................455

Koillismaa 455
Kuusamo Town.......................455
Karhunkierros Trekking
Route...................................458
Juuma......................................460
Käylä.......................................461
Canoeing the Kitkajoki River...461
Canoeing the Oulankajoki
River....................................461
Ruka..462
Julma Ölkky............................463
Taivalkoski..............................463
Pudasjärvi...............................463
Syöte..464

LAPLAND 466

Samis.......................................468
Sami Languages......................469
Rovaniemi.......................... 470
Around Rovaniemi..................475
South-West Lapland........ 476
Tornio......................................476
Around Tornio.........................479
Kemi..480
Kemi to Rovaniemi.................482
North-West Lapland.......... 483
Ylitornio..................................483
Aavasaksa...............................483
Juoksenki................................483
Rovaniemi to Pello.................483
Pello..484
Sieppijärvi...............................484
Lappea.....................................484
Kolari......................................485
Pakasaivo................................485
Ylläs..485
Kittilä......................................486
Around Kittilä.........................486

Sirkka & Levi National Park
Region..................................487
Näkkälä...................................492
Karesuvanto............................492
Lätäseno River........................492
Järämä.....................................492
Kilpisjärvi...............................492
South-East Lapland......... 494
Ranua......................................494
Posio..494
Around Posio...........................496
Kemijärvi................................496
Around Kemijärvi...................498
Pyhä & Luosto........................498
Suvanto...................................500
Salla..501
Savukoski................................501
Martti......................................502
Korvatunturi Fishing Area......502
Sodankylä...............................502
Tepsanniemi............................503
North-East Lapland 503
Ivalo.......................................505

Tulppio....................................505
Around Tulppio.......................506
Vuotso.....................................506
Tankavaara..............................506
Kiilopää...................................507
Saariselkä................................507
Saariselkä Wilderness (Urho
Kekkonen National Park).......509
Nellim.....................................514
Myössäjärvi.............................514
Inari...515
Lemmenjoki National Park.....516
Angeli......................................518
Kaamanen...............................518
Muotkatunturit........................519
Kevo Nature Reserve..............519
Karigasniemi...........................519
Sevettijärvi..............................520
Around Sevettijärvi.................521
Utsjoki.....................................522
Utsjoki to Karigasniemi..........523
Nuorgam.................................523
Nordkapp................................524

GLOSSARY 525

APPENDIX 529

INDEX 530

Maps.....................................530   Text.............................530

Map Legend

BOUNDARIES

▬·▬··▬·▬··▬··	International Boundary
▬··▬··▬··▬··	Regional Boundary
– – – – – –	National Park Boundary
· · · · · · · · · · · ·	Arctic/Antarctic Circle

ROUTES

═══════	Freeway
━━━━━━	Highway
──────	Major Road
– – – – –	Unsealed Road or Track
──────	City Road
──────	City Street
++++++++++	Railway
– – – ·· – –	Four Wheel Drive Track
– – – – – ·	Walking Track
· · · · · · · · · ·	Walking Tour
– – – – – –	Ferry Route
++─+─+─+─+─+─++	Cable Car or Chairlift

AREA FEATURES

	Parks
	Built-Up Area
	Pedestrian Mall
	Market
+ + + + + +	Cemetery
	Glacier, Ice Cap
	Beach or Desert
⌢⌢ ⌒	Mountain Ranges
/////////// Cheap hotels	Key area hatch

HYDROGRAPHIC FEATURES

	Coastline
	River, Creek
→ →	River Flow
»» ─╫─ ⇚	Rapids, Waterfalls
⬭ ⬭	Lake, Intermittent Lake
	Canal
⏄ ⏄ ⏄ ⏄	Swamp

SYMBOLS

✪ CAPITAL		National Capital	✈ ✝	Airport, Airfield
◉ Capital		Regional Capital	🛏 ✿	Swimming Pool, Gardens
🌑 CITY		Major City	◆ 🐘	Shopping Centre, Zoo
● City		City	₽ ╻	Petrol Station, Golf Course
● Town		Town	← A25	One Way Street, Route Number
● Village		Village	🏛 ⚜	Stately Home, Monument
■ ▼		Place to Stay, Place to Eat	🏯 ▣	Castle, Tomb
☕ 🍴		Cafe, Pub or Bar	⌒ ⌂	Cave, Hut or Chalet
✉ ☎		Post Office, Telephone	▲ ☀	Mountain or Hill, Lookout
❶ ⑤		Tourist Information, Bank	🎇 ⚲	Lighthouse, Shipwreck
☻ ℗		Transport, Parking	)(◎	Pass, Spring
🏛 ⚑		Museum, Youth Hostel	🏊 ⚶	Beach, Ski Field
⚏ ⚐		Caravan Park, Camping Ground	⸫	Archaeological Site or Ruins
>		Open sided shelter	Ⓜ	Metro (Underground Station)
✝ ➕		Church, Cathedral		Ancient or City Wall
☪ ✡		Mosque, Synagogue		Cliff or Escarpment, Tunnel
✛ ★		Hospital, Police Station		Railway Station

Baltic word meaning 'an inhabitant of the interior', which is also the original word for Sami, (or Sábme as Lapps call themselves).

During their migration, Hämenites and Karelians were met by Sami tribes, obviously earlier arrivals, who belong to the same ethnic and linguistic group as Finns. The fact that there were earlier European inhabitants of Finland, and a constant flow of other Europeans, especially Scandinavians and Russians, visiting or settling in Finland until today, explains the diversity of today's Finns.

Early Finnish Society

Approximately 2000 years ago south Finland was sparsely inhabited by ethnic Finns and an untold number of other European peoples. The two Finnish tribes, Hämenites (Swedish: Tavastians) and Karelians, lived separately, in the west and the east respectively, but were constantly engaging each other in wars. There were trading contacts with Estonians and Swedish Vikings. The lands around the Kokemäki River and its tributary Vanajavesi in Häme (Swedish: Tavastland) were the most densely populated areas, with a chain of hill fortresses providing defence. In the east, there was a similar chain of defence fortresses in Savo, and along the shores of Lake Lagoda in Karelia (now an autonomous republic within Russia).

Furs were the main export item, and there were trading posts in present-day Hämeenlinna, Teljä (in Kokemäki), Turku, Snappertuna and in Halikko, to name a few. Many burial grounds and hill defences remain. It is probable that there was friendly contact between fortresses, despite each having its own social system. A common law and judicial system existed in each region.

The Åland Islands and coastal regions south-east of Turku were occupied by busy contacts with Viking sailors. One theory places Birka, the main Viking centre during the 10th century, on Åland, although with more elaborate scientific methods, Birka has

---

Why Finland?

Some Americans think Finland is a place where everything costs five bucks. Other people think that it's a *fine* land, especially Swedes, because *fin* in Swedish translates literally thus, and there are several reasons to think so. Or maybe Finland is a country where everything is prohibited, and you get *fined* for doing anything. Another theory: Finns are keen on fishing, and that's why the country is called *Fin*land. But why is Finland Finland, or Suomi, as it is called in Finnish?

French may provide a clue. *Fin* means 'the end', and *fin de lande* could easily be, if not 'the end of the world' (although that's exactly what many Finns think about their recession-struck country), the end of the European land mass in the north. One of the better achievements of the Finnish government in early 1990s was the new international country abbreviation FIN ('The End') that replaced the old SF, often mistakenly read as Soviet Finland.

The early Romans called this land Fennia. In the English dictionary today we find the word *fen*, which means a swampy land. (And *lande* in French is not exactly 'land' but more like a swampy land.) The word fen is mostly used for the watery land in eastern England. But Romans went to England too, and Finland is exactly such a swampy land, and swamp in Finnish is *suo*. A Finn in Finnish is *suomalainen*, whereas *suomaalainen* (with double a) means an inhabitant of a swampy land. Suomi is pronounced 'SWAM-ee'.

The Finnish word Suomi resembles 'suo' too much to be completely ignored, but there is another explanation. An old Baltic word, *zeme* or *seme* means 'an inhabitant of the interior'. Finland is called Somija in Latvian, Suomija in Lithuanian and Soome in Estonian. This word may also be the origin of Sami (they call themselves Sábme), the longtime inhabitants of Lapland, and even Häme, the region in, and the tribe of, the interior of south Finland.

So what's the moral of this story? Finns are not flattered by all these references to inferior interior swampy wetlands. Many Finns would like their country be called Finlandia or Fennica (in Latin) because that sounds more respectable ... but it wouldn't change the facts. ∎

since been located on Björkö Island to the west of Stockholm. Six hill fortresses on Åland date back to the Viking era and indicate the former importance of these islands.

When the Turku region came to be dominated by Catholic Swedish settlers, the pagan hinterland moved its trade to Halikko, which may have been the mythical Portus Tavastorum, the harbour of Häme. But the Swedish presence did not remain confined to coastal regions. An uninterrupted line of bonfires along the chain of fortresses in Häme may have been lit as warning when the Swedish crusades arrived in 1249.

Swedish Rule

To Swedes, Finland was a natural direction of expansion, on a promising eastern route towards Russia and the Black Sea. For Swedes, Finland's history starts in 1155 when Bishop Henry arrived in Kalanti on a mission of the Catholic Church. As the church became established, it moved to Nousiainen, and in 1229, by the order of Pope Gregorius, to today's Turku. The bishops obtained a right to confiscate pagan sacrifice sites for the Church. Twenty years after the establishment of Turku, fortresses in Häme were defeated.

In addition to castles in Turku (started in 1280), Hämeenlinna and Vyborg, the oldest remaining buildings are medieval grey stone churches which bear distant resemblance to Central European cathedrals, although in Finland the style is rougher.

The upper layer of society in Finland was made up of newly arrived Catholic bishops and Swedish nobility, set to govern the eastern province of the Catholic kingdom of Sweden. The Swedish nobility dates back to the 14th century cavalry, consisting of the *frälset*, who enjoyed tax-free status.

It took more than 200 years to define the border between Sweden and Russia (Novgorod). In 1323, the first such border was drawn in a conference at Nöteborg (Finnish: Pähkinäsaari) on Lake Ladoga. Sweden gained control of south-west Finland, much of the north-west coast and,

in the east, the strategic town of Vyborg (Finnish: Viipuri), with its magnificent castle. A suzerainty was established over Karelia by Novgorod and was controlled from a castle at Käkisalmi (Russian: Priodzorsk) that was founded in the 13th century. Novgorod spread the Russian Orthodox faith in the Karelia region, which became influenced by eastern Byzantine culture.

To attract Swedish settlers to the unknown land, a number of incentives were created, such as large estates of land and tax concessions. These privileges were granted to many soldiers of the Royal Swedish Army.

In 1527, King Gustav Vasa of Sweden adopted the Lutheran faith and confiscated much of the property of the Catholic Church. Finland had its own supporters of the Reformation: Mikael Agricola, born in Pernå (Finnish: Pernaja) in 1510, studied literature and religion with Martin Luther in Germany for three years, and returned to Finland in 1539 to translate parts of the Bible into Finnish. More importantly, he was the first to properly record the traditions and animist religious rites of ethnic Finns. Agricola's work changed the religious tradition. Most of the colourful frescoes in medieval greystone churches, for example, were whitewashed with lime (only to be rediscovered some 400 years later in relatively good condition).

Sweden was not satisfied with its share of power in the east. In 1546 King Gustav Vasa founded Ekenäs (Tammisaari) and in 1550, Helsinki. Using his Finnish subjects as agents of expansion, the Swedish king told Finns to 'sweat and suffer' as pioneers in Savo and Kainuu, well beyond the legitimate territory set down in treaties with the Russians. When Finns did what they were told to do (a pattern still evident today), Russians grew alarmed and attempted to throw the intruders out. The bloody Kainuu War raged on and off between 1574 and 1584, with most new settlements destroyed by fire. The Treaty of Teusina (Finnish: Täyssinä) in 1595 expanded Swedish rule to the entire Kainuu region.

Golden Age of Sweden

The 17th century was the golden age of Sweden, then in control of Finland, Estonia, and parts of today's Latvia, Denmark, Germany and Russia.

After 65 years of Lutheranism, the Catholic Sigismund (son of Swede Johan III and Pole Katarina Jagiellonica and grandson of Gustav Vasa) assumed the Swedish throne. Karl IX, Gustav Vasa's youngest son and Sigismund's uncle, was given control over Finland. He encouraged peasants in Pohjanmaa to mutiny in 1596, attacked the Castle in Turku the next year and defeated his nephew Sigismund in 1598 to bring all of Finland under his reign by the end of the century. Karl IX waged territorial wars against Poland, Denmark and Russia. The Treaty of Stolbova in 1617 further expanded Swedish territory to the east. North Karelia, with its Greek Orthodox faith, was ceded to Sweden. Many Orthodox believers, fearing Lutheran persecution, fled into Russian forests.

While Gustav II Adolf (son of Karl IX and king from 1611 to 1632) was busily involved in the Thirty Years War in Europe, political power in Finland was exercised by the General Governor, who resided at the Castle of Turku, capital of Finland. Count Per Brahe, a legendary figure of the local

Sweden's Count Per Brahe
founded many towns in Finland.

Swedish administration, travelled around the country at this time and founded many towns. You will see his statue in places like Turku, Raahe, Kajaani and Lieksa.

After Gustav II Adolf, Sweden was ruled from 1644 to 1654 by the eccentric Queen Kristina, namesake for such Finnish towns as Kristinestad and Ristiina. The queen's conversion to Catholicism and move to Rome marked the end of the Swedish Vasa dynasty. Now Sweden (and Finland) came under the German royal family of Pfalz-Zweibrücken. Karl X Gustav and Karl XI engaged in wars against almost all north European nations, not always successfully. In 1656 Russians attacked eastern Finland and destroyed the town of Brahea (Lieksa).

All this time, Finland was considered an integral part of Sweden. Industrial works were founded in Finland and a chain of castle defences was Sweden's buffer against Russian attack. The official language was Swedish. Åbo Academy, the second-oldest university in Sweden, was founded at Turku in 1640. Stockholm was the de facto capital of Finns, who were subjects of the king (or queen) of Sweden. The Swedish 'caste system', the House of Four Estates, was firmly established in Finland. The highest ranking were knights and the 'nobility'. The Swedish and Finnish 'nobility' maintained their status in the Swedish Riksdagen until 1866 and in the Finnish parliament until 1906. Their privileges were cancelled in 1919. (The Finnish nobility still exists through a registered organisation.)

The Catholic Church, a strong political force in Sweden, enjoyed almost as much power in Finland, until King Gustav Vasa (who became the head of the church), decreed Lutheranism the only accepted form of Christianity. Religion remained a dominant feature of Finnish society in the 17th century – the Bible was translated into Finnish in 1642. The clergy resided in *prästgård* (Finnish: *pappila*) manors (some still do) and conducted moral education and tax collection on behalf of the Church.

The burgher class was also dominated by Swedish settlers, as very few Finns engaged in industrial enterprises. Some of the successful industrialists were central Europeans who settled in Finland via Sweden.

Ethnic Finns were largely farmers, victimised by unfair land division between the privileged nobility and the poor peasantry. As estates grew, more peasants were forced to lease land from Swedish landlords, although Finland never experienced the feudal serfdom typical in Russia. However, Koitsanlahti manor in Parikkala was notorious for such treatment, and the last slaves there were liberated in 1858.

New factory areas were founded in the 17th century. The *bruk* was often a self-contained society, with hydro power stations, ironworks and transport systems for firewood. There were also social institutions such as schools and churches. Some of these old areas have been well preserved, especially Fagervik and Fiskars in western Uusimaa, and Ruotsinpyhtää in the Kymi River valley.

A severe famine in 1696-97 claimed almost a third of the Finnish population. In 1697 Karl XII ascended the throne. Within three years he was sucked into the Great Northern War (1700-1721), which marked the beginning of the end of the Swedish Empire.

The Turbulent 1700s

While the Swedish King Karl XII was busy fighting for his empire elsewhere, the Russians under Peter the Great saw their moment. The Great Northern War saw Vyborg defeated (in 1710) and much of Finland conquered, including the Swedish-dominated west coast. From 1714 to 1721 Russia occupied Finland, a bitter time still referred to as the Great Wrath. Russians destroyed practically everything they had access to. Many administrators fled to Sweden (and remained there). Åland and Pohjanmaa suffered great material damage. The Russians even wreaked havoc on the coast of Sweden. The 1721 Treaty of Uusikaupunki (Swedish: Nystad) brought temporary peace at a cost – Sweden lost south Karelia, including Vyborg, to Russia.

Finland's Foreign Rulers

Up until 1919, when Kaarlo J Ståhlberg became the first president, Finland had had at least 20 royal rulers, none of them Finnish! The kings and two queens (listed below) came from the royal families of Sweden, Germany and Russia.

Swedish kings assumed absolute power in Finland during the Reformation, when the Catholic Church lost much of its property and the Catholic bishops (the closest thing Finland had to rulers) lost their power. Gustav I Vasa, the Swedish king who adopted the Reformation, became head of the Lutheran Church. As well as being Finland's first official monarch, he was the founder of Helsinki, in 1550.

Viking Era to 1060
Stenkil Family 1060 to 1130
Sverker and Erik Families 1130 to 1250
Folkung Family 1250 to 1389
Union Era to 1521

Vasa Family (1521-1654)
Gustav I Vasa (1521-62)
Erik XIV (1562-68)
Johan III (1568-93)
Sigismund (1593-99)
Karl IX (1599-1611)
Gustav II Adolf (1611-32)
Kristina (regency 1632-44)
  (1644-54)

Pfalz Family (1654-1751)
Karl X Gustav (1654-60)
Karl XI (1660-97)
Karl XII (1697-1718)
Ulrika Eleonora (1718-20)
Fredrik I av Hessen (1720-51)

Holstein-Gottorp Family (1751-1809)
Adolf Fredrik (1751-71)
Gustav III (1771-92)
Gustav IV Adolf (regency 1792-1796)
  (1796-1809)

Romanov Family (1809-1917)
Alexander I (1809-25)
Nicholas I (1825-55)
Alexander II (1855-81)
Alexander III (1881-94)
Nicholas II (1894-1917)

To regain its lost territories, Sweden attacked Russia in 1741-43, but with little success. Russia again occupied Finland, for a period called the Lesser Wrath, and the border was pushed further west. The Treaty of Turku in 1743 ceded the Kymi River valley and parts of Savo to Russia. The famous Olavinlinna castle in present-day Savonlinna was Russian property until 1917, and the Pyhtää region was cut in half. The former border bears some reminders of these serious times.

Only after the 1740s did the Swedish government try to improve Finland's socioeconomic situation. Defences were strengthened by the building of fortresses off the coast of Helsinki (Sveaborg, now Suomenlinna) and Loviisa, and new towns were founded. These measures, however, were ultimately unsuccessful in holding back the Russian tide.

Sweden and Russia were to clash once again, in the sea battles of Ruotsinsalmi off Kotka in 1788-89. This time it was King Gustav III who led the Swedish fight, which involved up to 500 vessels in the battle. Sweden won but to no territorial advantage. The 'Gustavian Wars' continued along the eastern border of Finland until the king was murdered by a conspiracy of aristocrats in 1792. Gustav IV Adolf, who reigned from 1796, was drawn into the disastrous Napoleonic Wars and lost his crown in 1809.

Russian Rule

Inevitably, after the Treaty of Tilsit was signed by Russian tsar Alexander I and Napoleon, Russia attacked Finland in 1808. Following a bloody war, Sweden ceded Finland to Russia in 1809 as an autonomous grand duchy, with its own Senate and the Diet of the Four Estates, but all major decisions had to be approved by the tsar. At first, Finland benefited from the annexation and was loyal to the tsar, who encouraged Finns to develop the country in many ways.

The Finnish capital was transferred to Helsinki in 1812, to ensure a closer watch over Finland. Parts of Karelia, Salla and Kuusamo were annexed to Finland, and fortifications on Åland were constructed.

The early 19th century saw the first stirring of indigenous Finnish nationalism. One of the first to encourage independence during the 1820s was Mr A I Arwidsson, who uttered the much-quoted sentence: 'Swedes we are not, Russians we will not become, so let us be Finns'. His ideas didn't attract much admiration; he was advised to move to Sweden in 1823.

As a Russian annexation, Finland was dragged into the Crimean War (1853-56), where Russia fought Turkey and its allies, including Britain and France. British troops attacked Finland in many locations, and destroyed fortifications at Loviisa, Helsinki and Bomarsund. The Finns were successful in Kokkola.

Stirrings of Nationalism

When centuries of western influence gave way to an increasingly unpopular Russian rule, a great number of talented artists, writers, composers and scientists emerged to pave the way to Finnish independence. Although most of the famous names, such as Sibelius, Gallen-Kallela and Edelfedt, spent a considerable time abroad studying their art, their work is mostly known for its use of indigenous traditions.

The cultural framework of Finnish independence was laid by a restless trekker and literature professor, Elias Lönnrot, who created the mammoth Finnish epic, the *Kalevala*, a collection of oral folk songs and poems which were documented in the Finnish language for the first time. No doubt Lönnrot should be dubbed Finland's greatest traveller. He undertook 11 long tours, covering most of Finland, Karelia, Estonia and further afield by foot or on reindeer. The first edition of the *Kalevala* was published in 1833, the final version in 1849. Equally important was Lönnrot's work in creating a standard Finnish by adopting words and expressions from various dialects. This 19th century Finnish has remained very much the same ever since, at least in written form. Places associated with Lönnrot and the Kalevala include Sammatti, Ilomantsi, Kuhmo and Kajaani.

Several artists and composers, including

Elias Lönnrot: creator of the *Kalevala,*
Finland's national epic.

Jean Sibelius, drew much of their inspiration directly from the *Kalevala*, or the source of its poetry, the Karelian wilderness. At last, Finnish culture had an identity and a place among European civilisations. Mr Johan Vilhelm Snellman began the ultimately successful campaign to give the Finnish language equal status with Swedish. Finland issued its first postal stamps in 1856 and gained its own currency, the markka, in 1860.

However, the emergence of Finnish nationalism coincided with the rise of Pan-Slavonic ideas in Russia after 1880, and led to oppression and Russification of the Finns, especially from 1899, during the reign of Nicholas II. After a general strike in Finland in 1905, a new unicameral parliament, the Eduskunta, was introduced with universal and equal suffrage. Finland was the first country in Europe to grant women full political rights (second in the world after New Zealand). Yet new oppression and Russification followed from 1908 and lasted until the Russian revolution in 1917. Many artists, notably Jean Sibelius, were inspired by this oppression, which made Finns emotionally ripe for independence.

Independence

The downfall of the tsar of Russia following the Communist revolution in 1917 enabled the Finnish senate to declare independence on 6 December 1917. Finland was first recognised by the Soviet Union one month later, although some 47,000 Russian soldiers, part of the former tsarist army, remained. Many of them soon switched to the revolutionary army.

Vladimir Lenin, after granting Finland independence, offered 10,000 guns to the Finnish Red cadres. With Russia devastated by WWI, Lenin envisaged a supporting role for the Russian troops; it was really the job of the Finnish Reds to bring about the revolution. The Reds in Finland slowly evolved from semi-military workers' groups. Meanwhile, a number of civil guards groups had been founded in various parts of Finland, all private and only partly equipped with arms.

The Russian troops were problematic because there was no Finnish army. There would have been a power grab unless a Finnish army was quickly created. That seemed impossible. Finnish communists maintained the Russian troops should not leave until a revolution had first taken place in Finland. Civil guards groups, especially in the north and the east, considered driving out the Russians their most important objective.

When Russian troops, helped by the Finnish Reds, attacked the civil guards in Vyborg, the Finnish senate stepped in and equipped the civil guards and appointed them government troops on 25 January 1918. CGE (Gustaf) Mannerheim was appointed to lead the new government troops, who were to disarm Russian troops near Vaasa in Pohjanmaa.

On 28 January 1918, the Civil War flared in two separate locations. The Reds attempted to achieve a revolution in Helsinki. The Whites (as the government troops were now called) clashed with Russian troops in Pohjanmaa. The two separate incidents developed into two theatres of war. During 108 days of a bloody civil war, approximately 30,000 Finns were killed by their fellow citizens.

The Reds, comprising the rising working class (and some of those 47,000 Russian soldiers), aspired to Russian-style socialist revolution while retaining independence. The nationalist Whites dreamed of monarchy and sought models from Germany. The Whites eventually gained victory under Lieutenant General Mannerheim, with help from Germany. The bloody and devastating war ended in May 1918.

The Prince of Hessen, Friedrich Karl, was elected king of Finland by the Eduskunta on 9 October 1918 but the Republicans boycotted the election. When the German Monarchy collapsed just one month later with Germany's final defeat in WWI, Finland faced a dilemma. The Russian presence was a clear security risk, but Germany was a discredited political model because of its war loss. Talks with Britain and France made Finland decide that it should distance itself from Germany, and political changes took place.

Building a Nation

Relations with the Soviet Union were normalised by the Treaty of Tartu in 1920, which saw Finnish territory grow to its largest ever, including the 'left arm', the Petsamo region in the far north-east. The defeat of imperial Germany made Finland choose a republican state model and the first president was KJ Ståhlberg.

But more trouble awaited the new nation. Following WWI bitter language wars between Finnish and Swedish speakers shook the administration, universities and cultural circles. Wounds from the Civil War were devastating – illegal massacres (mostly of Reds by Whites) took place and human rights were grossly violated. These days, people still tell stories that cannot be found in written records.

In 1930, 12,000 right-wing farmers marched from Lapua to demand laws banning communism. A mutiny in Mäntsälä in 1932 tried to prevent socialists from meeting and to make Marxism illegal in Finland. The rising right-wing tide in central Europe attracted many Finns, especially those along the west coast.

Internationally, Finland at this time gained fame as a brave new nation, as the only country to pay its debts to the USA, and as a sporting nation. Paavo Nurmi, the most distinguished of Finnish long-distance runners, won six gold medals in three Olympic Games and became a national figure. With continuing Finnish success in athletics, Helsinki was chosen to host the 1940 Olympic Games (these were postponed until 1952 due to WWII). Meanwhile, the approaching war forced Finland to foster neutrality.

Finnish Presidents

Kaarlo J Ståhlberg	1919-25
Lauri K Relander	1925-31
Per E Svinhufvud	1931-37
Kyösti Kallio	1937-40
Risto Ryti	1940-44
Carl G E Mannerheim	1944-46
Juho K Paasikivi	1946-56
Urho K Kekkonen	1956-81
Mauno Koivisto	1982-94
Martti O K Ahtisaari	1994-

WWII

During the 1930s, Finland developed close ties with Nazi Germany, partly in response to the obvious security threat posed by the USSR. Relations with the newborn communist Soviet Union remained suspicious. Much warmer were relations with the newly independent Estonia.

On 23 August 1939, the Soviet and German foreign ministers, Molotov and Ribbentrop, stunned the world by signing a nonaggression pact. A secret protocol stated that any future rearrangement would divide Poland between them; Germany would have a free hand in Lithuania, the Soviet Union in Finland, Estonia, Latvia and Bessarabia. The Red Army was moving toward the earmarked territories less than three weeks later.

The Soviet Union pressed more territorial claims, arguing its security required a slice of south-eastern Karelia. JK Paasikivi (later to become president) visited Moscow for negotiations (or dictations) on the ceding of the Karelian Isthmus to the Soviet Union. The negotiations failed. The Russians fired shots from their territory at the Finnish village of Mainila and accused Finland of violating peace agreements. A few days later, early on the morning of 30 November 1939, the 'Winter War' began. Finland had little chance in its fight against a world power, but its soldiers nevertheless endured. It was an especially harsh winter, with temperatures reaching -40°C, and soldiers died in their thousands. The war lasted a full 100 days and ended in victory for the Red Army. Finland had to give up the Karelian Isthmus, home to about 12% of the Finnish population, and including Vyborg, the second biggest Finnish town at the time. About half a million Karelian refugees flooded over the new border. Across the country in the south-west, the Soviet army occupied the Hanko Peninsula as a military base.

The Soviet Union continued to pressure Finland for more territory, even after the Treaty of Moscow was signed in March 1940. The 'Continuation War' between Finland and the Red Army started in June 1941. Isolated from Western allies, Finland turned to Germany for help.

The war started successfully for Finland. Its soldiers advanced over the old border to Russian Karelia, inhabited by linguistic relatives of the Finns. Finnish nationalists started to dream of a Greater Finland which would span all of Karelia, although the only stated reason for the war was to regain territory lost during the Winter War. Karelian refugees of the year before were moving back to the once-lost Karelia, which everyone expected to remain Finnish territory.

But in the summer of 1944 the Soviet Union launched an enormous counterattack, with plans to take Helsinki and eventually occupy the entire country. Finland remained independent, but at a price: it was forced to cede territory and pay heavy war reparations to the Soviet Union. The Porkkala Peninsula west of Helsinki was a Soviet military base and off-limits to Finns until 1956. The final bitter phase of the war took place in Lapland, where Finland had to drive German troops out of the country. Before leaving, the Germans left a trail of burned towns and villages.

In all, Finland's war experience was an enormous defeat, not only territorially but financially, materially, politically and most of all emotionally. Until very recently, old drunkards in Helsinki, many of them humiliated war veterans, cursed the Russians.

From Ashes to Prosperity

The Treaty of Paris in 1947 dictated an uneasy coexistence between Finland and the Soviet Union for the next 45 years. The Karelian Isthmus was ceded to the Soviet Union, as well as the eastern Salla and Kuusamo regions and the 'left arm' of Finland in the Kola Peninsula.

Although there was never a foreign military presence in Finland after the war, there was the Treaty of Friendship, Cooperation & Mutual Assistance (Finnish: YYA) with the Soviet Union, signed in 1948. The agreement drew the two countries into an awkward semimilitary relationship, in spite of Finland's claim to neutrality. The agreement remained valid until 1992, when it was replaced by a loose agreement with Russia without reference to military cooperation.

Finland was like a Third World country in the late 1940s, with almost everything rationed and poverty widespread. The vast majority of the population was still engaged in agriculture.

War reparations played a central role in laying the foundations of the heavy engineering industry, which transformed Finland's trade patterns and stabilised the economy. This was also the start of joint projects and profitable trade agreements with the USSR.

Things changed quickly in the following decades, with domestic migration (from the north to the south) especially strong in the 1960s and 1970s. New suburbs appeared almost overnight in and around Helsinki. This later-condemned building pattern largely followed the Swedish ideals of modernism and socialism. However, many people had difficulty adjusting to urban life, and large areas in the north and the east lost most of their young people, often almost half their population.

On 30 October 1961 the Soviet Union blew up a 58 megatonne nuclear bomb on Novaja Zemlja Island, not far from Finland. What shook Finland even more was a short message from Moscow: the Communist Party wanted changes in Finland's domestic politics. It got what it wanted. The Berlin Wall had just been erected and the Cold War was at its height.

The politically turbulent 1960s saw left-wing parties gain enormous popularity, in no small part due to secret Soviet subsidies and anti-American feeling arising from the Vietnam War. In the election of 1966, socialist parties gained 103, or 51.5%, of the seats. On 25 November 1968, the old Student House in Helsinki was occupied by a communist mob. Although little more than a binge of excess drinking, this event was seen as the culmination point; for more than two decades afterward Communists and Social Democrats had an enormous impact on everything from local administration and school reform to churches and mass media. This cultural revolution of the 1970s also loosened traditional values, such as religion, family and nationalism. Although the first centralised wage negotiations in 1968 proved beneficial for all society, hard-line communists and human greed caused instability. Inflation ran high and over 1000 strikes took place in 1973 alone.

The extreme left attracted many recently arrived rural migrants suffering from alienation in an urban society. Another support base was the growing public sector, which provided secure employment for thousands of socialists.

One of the main players in the Soviet infiltration was Viktor Vladimirov, who worked as a ministerial adviser for the Soviet embassy in Helsinki from the 1950s to 1984. Vladimirov provided a direct link between presidents Kekkonen and Koivisto, and the Communist Party of the Soviet Union. He also influenced presidential elections with the help of local politicians.

The Kekkonen Years

In Finland all political parties largely followed the same foreign policy line, known as the 'Paasikivi-Kekkonen line' (named after the two post-war presidents who were its architects). This pragmatic approach to geopolitics was referred to as 'Finlandisation', which implies subservience to pressure from a stronger state, but it was also a formula for survival in a difficult geographical situation.

One of the great leaders of his age, and the brain behind this tightrope foreign policy, Urho K Kekkonen (president from 1956 to 1981) gained fame abroad as an eccentric and witty president. He was also well known for his role as host of the initial Conference on Security & Cooperation in Europe (CSCE) meeting, in Helsinki in 1975. On the home front, however, things weren't all that good. Democracy reached an all-time low during his reign in 1974, when a vast majority of delegates from all major parties decided to postpone presidential elections and extend Mr Kekkonen's term by four years. Political nominations were submitted to Moscow for approval within the framework of 'friendly coexistence'.

Leading Finnish politicians visiting the Soviet Union often received overwhelming attention in Moscow, and the Finnish media afforded lavish coverage to these visits, which in turn boosted the popularity of Finnish politicians at home. Few noticed that Finnish leaders were used as propaganda tools in the West by the Soviet regime, at a time when many Western leaders kept a politically correct distance from Commies.

Although Finland remained a Western democracy (with certain shortcomings), anti-Soviet attitudes were not conducive to advancement. Some right-wing politicians claimed their phones were tapped; this has never been denied. Kokoomus, the popular conservative party, was firmly kept out of government. As recently as the late 1980s, the Soviet Communist Party exercised Cold War tactics by infiltrating Finnish politics, with the aim of reducing US influence in Finland and preventing Finnish membership of the European Community (today's European Union). When Kekkonen became unfit to fulfil his job as president, his true state of health was carefully kept secret. He spent his last years virtually caged in Tamminiemi House, now a museum open to tourists.

As a balance to all this, relations with Scandinavia were always extremely important. Finland was a founding member of the Nordic Council (along with the Scandinavian countries), pursuing a similar social welfare programme to Scandinavia and enjoying the benefits of free movement of labour, passport-free travel, and even common research and educational programmes with its western neighbours.

Many of the rural people who left northern Finland bought one-way tickets to Sweden, which at that time (1970s) welcomed foreign labourers with open arms, thus providing Finland with a valve for the inevitable pressures associated with the drastic social transformation from a rural to modern society.

Recession of the 1990s

Finns were probably the people least excited by the collapse of the Soviet Union, partly because of profitable barter trade arrangements. And the democratisation of Eastern Europe took place exactly when Finnish society no longer could afford its expensive welfare system. This gives the impression that Finland was more closely linked to the Communist Bloc than was actually the case. As a booming free-market economy in the second half of the 1980s, Finland suffered the illnesses that hit most countries in the Western world, only much harder: the bubble economy of the 1980s had burst, the Soviet Union disappeared (its debts unpaid), unemployment jumped from 3% to 20% and the tax burden grew alarmingly. The markka was devalued twice, and the whole society was on the verge of collapse in autumn 1992.

A huge number of individuals and private companies could not pay their debts. When banks were not able to collect interest and money from individuals and companies, they too collapsed. The government stepped in and promised to save all banks. An instant communism was at hand: much private property was about to be confiscated by banks, and all banks were on the verge of becoming government property. At the same time people were governed by a non-socialist government and were complaining about the hard hand of capitalism! Both images were right. Government spending was as high as 63% of GDP in 1993, and much private property was indeed confiscated by authorities. On the capitalist side, the government-subsidised Savings Bank group was sold to four big banks in October 1993, many state subsidies were cut and the government set a low 25% capital income tax to attract foreign capital.

At the same time, over 200,000 Finns were reported starving, and photos of long bread lines were distributed around the world. Probably the saddest incident was when worthless old B&W TV sets were confiscated from poor people in North Karelia who could not pay their debts. The 'welfare state' was striking back.

As many as 90% of Finns polled said they had lost confidence in politics, and little wonder: the Minister of Labour was a populist womaniser who seemed to be more concerned with his image than the 20% unemployment figure. The Minister of Environment was caught smuggling in a stray cat from India. The Foreign Minister's 'merits' included two reported incidents of drunk driving, the first killing one person, the second a hit and run which left a pedestrian wounded. Yet the right-wing coalition government remained·in power a full four years until the 1995 election. This remarkable achievement was due to a majority of the government parties in Parliament. Hardly ever has a government gained so many votes of confidence!

One of the better achievements of the much-hated government was joining the European Union. In the national referendum on 16 October 1994, 57% of voters gave the go-ahead to the EU. From 1 January 1995, food became cheaper and the strict alcohol laws were finally relaxed, but just a little. Only time will tell whether Finland made the right decision.

The parliamentary elections of 16 March 1995 brought to power a surprise government consisting of Social Democrats and four smaller parties, including Communists and the conservative Kokoomus. Finland's economic woes, however, were far from over. Some trade unions started ruthless strikes – nurses didn't work for a month, fire brigades for two months. Arson caused heavy damage in Helsinki. As at June 1995, only three major banks remained in the retail banking sector in Finland. Unemployment showed no signs of improving, and the new government announced a bright solution to the problem: rename some of the unemployed as retired people! In autumn 1995, the government negotiated another centralised wage hike with powerful union leaders, at a time when employers could only afford to pay wages to four-fifths of the working population. At the same time, the government proposed tax deductions for foreigners to attract non-Finnish executives, giving little hope to Finns struggling with the highest tax rate in the world.

GEOGRAPHY

With an area of 338,000 sq km, Finland is the seventh largest country in Europe. It is slightly larger than Italy and Vietnam, and a little smaller than Congo and Japan. The southernmost point, the town of Hanko, lies at the same latitude as Oslo in Norway, Anchorage in Alaska, and the southernmost tip of Greenland. The shape of Finland has been compared to that of a female, holding her right arm up (the 'left arm' was lost to the former Soviet Union after WWII). Finland shares a 1269-km border with Russia in the east; a 716-km border with Norway in the far north; and a 586-km border with Sweden in the west. The Gulf of Finland separates south Finland from Estonia.

Some 70% of Finland is covered by forest. The Finnish bedrock is stable, with few earthquakes recorded. There are few, if any, real mountains; rather, sandy ridges and wooded hills dominate. The highest hills, or *tunturi*, are in Lapland, which borders the mountainous areas of northern Norway and

Sweden. Finland's highest point, the Halti in the north-west corner of the country, rises only 1328 metres above sea level.

Much of the country is lakeland – there are nearly 188,000 lakes in Finland. Together with marshes and bogs, inland water covers about 10% of the country. Finland is shaped by water: lakes and ponds, rivers and creeks, rapids and small waterfalls, islands and islets, bays, capes and straits, and the large archipelagos off Turku, Åland, Helsinki and Vaasa.

CLIMATE

Finland enjoys four seasons. The climate is bearable, and excellent in summer. Because of its inland water, the Baltic Sea and the mild winds from the Gulf Stream along the Norwegian coast, Finland's climate is, on average, much warmer than in other places of similar latitude (Siberia, Greenland and Alaska). Winters *are* cold, but the cold is dry. Indoors, houses are well insulated, with triple windows, and are well heated in winter.

May 1993 was unusually warm and sunny, mostly over 20°C, while June to August was cool and rainy. In 1994, July was hot, with temperatures hovering over 25°C daily, even reaching 30°C occasionally. The rest of the summer was cooler but not as bad as 1993. January 1995 was four degrees warmer than usual, averaging a bearable -4°C in Tampere, and snow didn't cover the entire country until late in January. A sudden snowfall in mid-May blanketed the whole country for two days. Summer 1995 was extremely dry and sunny. Every now and then in summer, Finland is the warmest country in Europe!

Weather in Finland changes from day to day and depends largely on winds, often dry from the east, cold from the north, rainy from the west and warm and humid from the south. Summer sees hot spells and weeks of little rain, although temperatures can be as low as 10°C at any time in summer. It is not unusual to have temperatures of 5°C in January or to get hailstorms or soil frost in June, but yearly averages follow a logical curve: the shorter the nights, the warmer the days, and vice versa.

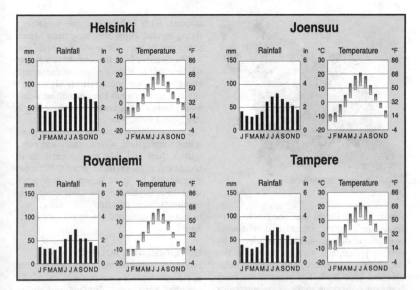

Helsinki

mm Rainfall in	°C Temperature °F

Joensuu

mm Rainfall in	°C Temperature °F

Rovaniemi

mm Rainfall in	°C Temperature °F

Tampere

mm Rainfall in	°C Temperature °F

FLORA & FAUNA

Finnish flora is surprisingly rich and varied, especially during the dynamic period between late May and September. Some low-lying valleys in the south resemble jungles by late July.

Several unique and rare species have been preserved in national parks and nature reserves around the country. The three main types of forest are pine, spruce and birch. Each has a typical accompanying flora. Pine grows generally on dry ground and sand ridges, and there is little vegetation. Spruce forests are dark and dense. Deciduous forests, birch being the typical tree, are the most varied in terms of flora.

There are quite a few mammals in Finnish forests, although you are unlikely to come across them. The largest is the brown bear, which was once so feared that even mentioning its name *(karhu)* was taboo.

Other mammals include elk, fox, lynx, wolf and wolverine, and there are plenty of small animals such as lemming, hedgehog, muskrat, marten, otter and hare. Beavers are quite common. Reindeer *(poro)* abound in north Finland. Elk *(hirvi)* are legally hunted

Climate Table
Winter Gloom & Midnight Sun

Location	Continuous Day*	Continuous Night	Continuous Light** (calendar days)
Helsinki	0	0	0
Tampere	0	0	35
Joensuu	0	0	51
Oulu	0	0	75
Kuusamo	21	0	104
Rovaniemi	33	0	112
Utsjoki	73	52	184

*Continuous day refers to true daylight, that is, the period between sunrise and sunset. Places with continuous day are subject to the true Midnight Sun.
**Continuous light includes twilight, those two times of day (before sunrise and after sunset) when the sun is below the true horizon but the sky is still light and many outdoor activities requiring some light are still possible. ■

every year, because they cause severe road accidents and culling is supposed to keep the stock stable. The lynx *(ilves)*, Häme's 'national' animal, used to be very rare but numbers are increasing. There are practically no home-grown wolves left in Finland, but plenty cross the border regularly from

Brown bear

Russia. Hatred for the wolf *(susi)* is so deep-rooted in eastern Finland that whenever wolves are sighted, friends are alerted by cellular phone, and within a few hours the poor animals are rounded up by 4WD vehicles and shot dead. The viper is the most common poisonous snake, with antivenins readily available in pharmacies.

There are over 300 bird species in Finland. Large species include black grouse, capercaillie, whooper swan and birds of prey, such as the osprey. Chaffinches and willow warblers are the two most common forest species; sparrows are common in inhabited areas. Black woodpeckers, black-throated divers, ravens and many owls are supposed to be 'wilderness birds'. The Siberian jay is a common sight in Lapland because it follows people. Birdlife in winter is still of

Crested-tit

interest, with bullfinches and waxwings flying around. Birds only sing from March to the end of June. Finns who watch migratory birds arrive from the south have a saying on how to determine when summer will come: it is one month from sighting a skylark, half a month from a chaffinch, just a little from a white wagtail and not a single day from a swift.

Less popular creatures include bugs, mosquitoes, horseflies, wasps, gnats and other nasties. June and July are the most active months for these little devils, whereas August can be quite mosquito-free when trekking in Lapland. Some *'Ohvi'* (mosquito repellent), especially the 'Off' brand, will help a great deal, but few insects are really harmful.

GOVERNMENT & POLITICS

Finland is a republic with a president (elected to six-year terms), a government and a 200-member parliament. Presidential duties include overseeing foreign policy, appointing cabinet ministers and acting as the commander in chief of the Finnish army. Legislative power rests with the unicameral parliament, or Eduskunta, whose 200 members are elected to four-year terms. The president has the right to veto a bill. Executive functions are performed by the prime minister and a coalition government of ministers, normally elected members of the parliament. Every citizen over 18 years of age has the right to vote.

Major political parties *(puolue)* in Finland include the Social Democratic Party (which gained 28% of the vote in the 1995 election), the agrarian Centre Party, or Keskusta (20%), the conservative Kokoomus (18%), the ex-communist Left-wing Alliance, or Vasemmistoliitto (11%), the Greens, or Vihreä liitto (6.5%), the Swedish People's Party, or Svenska folkpartiet (5%), and the Christian League, or Kristillinen Liitto (3.0%). Left-wing parties have increased their share of the vote in the last couple of years, one of the changes in Finnish politics in the 1990s.

Most power in the country seems to be

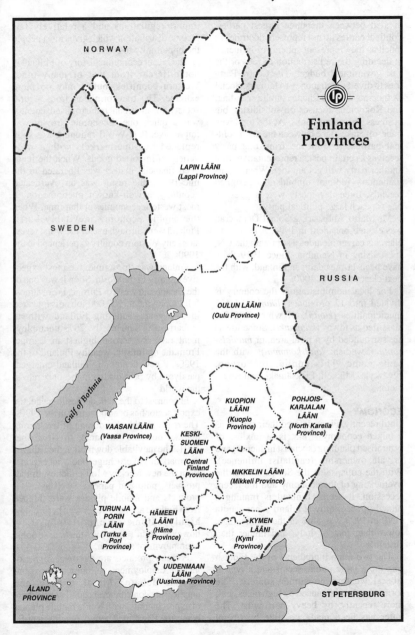

Finland
Provinces

NORWAY

SWEDEN

RUSSIA

LAPIN LÄÄNI
(Lappi Province)

OULUN LÄÄNI
(Oulu Province)

Gulf of Bothnia

KUOPION
LÄÄNI
(Kuopio
Province)

POHJOIS-
KARJALAN
LÄÄNI
(North Karelia
Province)

VAASAN LÄÄNI
(Vaasa Province)

KESKI-
SUOMEN
LÄÄNI
(Central
Finland
Province)

MIKKELIN LÄÄNI
(Mikkeli Province)

TURUN JA
PORIN
LÄÄNI
(Turku &
Pori
Province)

HÄMEEN
LÄÄNI
(Häme
Province)

KYMEN
LÄÄNI
(Kymi
Province)

UUDENMAAN
LÄÄNI
(Uusimaa Province)

ÅLAND
PROVINCE

ST PETERSBURG

divided between the three largest parties. Political parties do not represent doctrines as much as they represent spheres of influence in deciding the redistribution of jobs or the vast government budget. The Centre Party tries to divert much money to farmers, Social Democrats want to finance public spending, and Kokoomus focuses on subsidising big business, including banks. At the top level, trade-offs take place between the main political parties; if someone from one party receives a certain post, a representative from another party will get another. When a parliamentary judicial ombudsman resigned recently, three new posts were suggested: one for each large political party!

Mr Martti Ahtisaari, a Social Democrat, was elected president in 1994. A keen traveller, his career includes a stint with the UN, specialising in Namibia. Since 1919 there have been 11 presidents in Finland, with the next election due in 2000.

For local administration, the country is divided into 12 provinces *(lääni)* and 455 municipalities *(kunta)*, of which 102 are classified as towns *(kaupunki)*. Some towns are surrounded by a rural area, or *maalaiskunta* (Swedish: *landskommun*), with the same name. This applies to Porvoo, Jyväskylä, Mikkeli, Pieksämäki, and Rovaniemi.

ECONOMY

Until recently, Finns defined their system as a mixed economy – that is, a mixture of centralised planning (socialist influence) and private ownership (capitalist influence). With the collapse of the Soviet Union, the overheating of the economy and the recent recession, it seems Finland is running a mixed-up economy. Finland's per capita GNP in 1993 was 88% of the EU average, lower than that of Italy, and higher than Britain's.

The two main ingredients of the Finnish mix are a large public sector and a typical liberal western consumer society. The former has been financed by high taxes, and, more recently, by heavy borrowing. The latter has been made possible by liberal import regulations and a relatively fair income distribution which gives most people the opportunity to consume.

The recent economic history of Finland is not different from that of many other Western countries, but it may be more extreme. The transformation from a rural society to an urban industrialised country was a quick one. Economic growth was impressive. Post-WWII rationing was soon replaced by supermarkets with a wide variety of imported goods. When the regulated financial market was liberated in the mid-1980s, the result was an overheated economy, a well-known phenomenon in most western economies at that time. When the bubble economy inevitably burst, Finland went through one of the worst recessions any Western country experienced in the 1990s.

Finland was, for a time, the most expensive country in the world. Soon it was one of the cheapest in western Europe. From almost full employment, 500,000 jobs disappeared in two years, saddling Finland with an embarrassing and costly 20% unemployment rate, the second highest in Europe. From the optimistic, wealthy Finland of the 1980s, a new depressing Finland emerged, paralysed by perhaps the highest tax rate in the world.

In contrast to the dark domestic scene, the export sector has been booming in the 1990s. The reason is the abandoning of the 'strong markka doctrine' in panic, in November 1991. The inevitable downfall in the value of the markka gave a huge boost to exports. With the new Mickey Mouse money, timber products, pulp and paper as well as metal products and mobile phones were shipped from Finland at a pace never seen before. The highly automated export industries, however, didn't improve the catastrophic unemployment situation.

Forestry products are the main source of income, employment, pollution and environmental debate. Metal mining and engineering contribute an equally large share of export income, with Nokia mobile phones being the flagship. There is much scientific research in several fields, with hundreds of companies based in 'high-tech villages' in Oulu, Espoo, Turku, Lappeenranta, Tampere, Kuopio and Jyväskylä. Hydroelectric power is plentiful, mostly from the Kemijoki River in Lapland, and there are four nuclear power plants.

Trade unions are a powerful force in the Finnish economy. They have a virtual monopoly on the workforce, with over two million members (or 83% of the working population). Wages are centrally determined, and there are strict rules governing working hours, coffee breaks and holidays. The largest trade unions use general strike as a threat in even the smallest disputes.

The average working week is 39 hours and 73% of women are in the workforce. Less than 10% of the population earns a living from agriculture, 32% from industry and 58% from services. In October 1995 there were 448,000 unemployed people, or 18.3% of the total labour force. There are more men than women among the unemployed.

The future of the 'welfare state' is discussed widely, as are the huge farming subsidies. There is overproduction of grain, butter, cheese and eggs, and the prices of most farm products are centrally fixed at an artificially high level.

To make matters worse, some Finns exercise their consumer power by visiting Estonia just to buy cheap food. The system assures that all production is paid for, but to 'save money', the government also pays farmers to have their fields lie fallow or to transform fields into forests.

Finns are not great travellers but some estimates put the figure of 'disappeared' people as high as 150,000 – many residing in Estonia or in EU member countries. This is the result of making it legal for Finns to work in other EU countries but not making it easier for them to work in Finland.

Forestry

Forests are administered by local rangers, who mark stands of trees for cutting. These days, logging sites (*savotta* in Finnish) are taken care of by multi-purpose machines; few down-to-earth lumberjacks still work by hand. Unfortunately, some forests still disappear through clear felling; professionals are more likely to talk about 'forest improvement', trimming or silviculture. They even point out that 'forests rot unless you cut'. Finland lives off its forests, and for each area felled, a similar area is planted with small saplings. As you tour the country, you can see forests of all ages, young and old. Forests are either owned privately or by large timber companies. Timber sales have been based on predetermined prices (some of the highest in the world), but these days there is more pressure for price fluctuation. Paper and pulp industries provide work for thousands but also cause environmental hazards, which are easily seen in areas surrounding factories. To keep everyone happy, the Forest and Park Service (formerly the National Board of Forestry) maintains magnificent trekking and fishing areas, with free accommodation available to everyone.

Tourism

Attracting foreign visitors is not a major industry in Finland. Domestic tourism, however, has been booming for some time, much of it centred around tourist traps created to bring in children and their parents. Theme parks, amusement centres and other artificial attractions are numerous. Not nearly as heavily promoted are Finland's real treasures – its architecture, churches and natural beauty.

Matkailun edistämiskeskus (MEK), or Finnish Tourist Board, is now an independent entity and no longer a government organisation. The recent 'privatisation' changed the purpose of MEK – it now raises money from private companies (ie sells advertisement space in its publications) and no longer serves as a generous godfather to the industry. Yes, enquiries are usually answered promptly and professionally and the lavish pamphlets are free but do expect a highly commercial tone – almost everything printed is there because of the money paid. Tourist traps are therefore well presented, churches and natural attractions seldom so.

Regional tourist offices are emerging as agencies for local companies, and this seems to be working fine. Things are still quiet in some regions, although Lapland is booming. Local companies are usually not involved in international marketing, and are seldom subjected to hordes of tourists. You will be treated with enthusiasm if you contact one of these, either directly or through regional offices.

POPULATION

Finland's population is currently 5,116,000, with an annual growth rate of 0.4%. Only 1.3% (or 67,667) are foreigners and only 19% of the population is under 15 years. The average household size is 2.4 people. Finland has gone through typical demographic phases – 10 children in a family was not uncommon just 50 years ago.

In 1800 the population stood at 800,000; in 1900 it was about two million. Large numbers of Finns have emigrated to other countries: some 250,000 to Sweden, 280,000 to the USA, 20,000 to Canada and 10,000 to Australia. The peak emigration year was 1969, when 54,000 Finns left their country.

Approximately 75% of the population lives in towns. Over half the population lives in the three south-western provinces (around Helsinki, Turku and Tampere), which have 15% of the total land area. The Greater Helsinki area, including Espoo, Vantaa and several municipalities, houses one million people, or 20% of the national total. The next biggest towns, in order of size, are Tampere (population 180,000), Turku (163,000), Oulu (107,000), Lahti (95,000), Kuopio (84,000), Pori (76,500) and Jyväskylä (73,000).

Finland is not a very popular destination for asylum seekers, with only 836 arriving in 1994. Less than 300 were accepted. Somalis, Russians, Iranians and Yugoslavs are the most frequent applicants.

PEOPLE

Nearly 98% of all people living in Finland were born in Finland. There were just 67,667 foreigners living in Finland in 1995, or 1.3%

of the population. This is the lowest percentage of any country in Europe. There are 4000 Somalis, almost half of them in Helsinki, 2500 Vietnamese and a similar number of former Yugoslavs.

The main minority groups are the 300,000 Swedish-speaking Finns (*Finlandssvensk*, or 'Finland's Swede'), the 4000 Sami people of Lapland and the 5000 Gipsies. Finns can be divided into several historical 'tribes', but this distinction has lost much of its significance, to the point where you can now only tell the difference by a person's dialect. In the old days, Savonian people were considered talkative, easy-going and clever, Karelians friendly and hospitable, people of Häme the most reserved and introverted, and Pohjanmaa people proud, cool and sometimes willing to fight. Some of these characteristics can still be observed.

There is no exact evidence of where the original Finns came from. The early Finno-Ugrians were nomadic tribespeople who inhabited much of North Russia. North Asia or the Ural Mountains are generally considered the 'homes' of the Finno-Ugrians, and there are still small Finnic groups living in that area. Linguistic comparisons have found some similarities to Korean grammar, and Hungarian is definitely related to Finnish, though very few similar words remain. Estonians and Karelians are very close relatives of the Finns. During the centuries, however, a substantial Indo-European influence has affected the population of Finland, to the extent that many Finns look very Scandinavian, Baltic or Russian (or vice versa), even though the language is different. You may also see hints of Asian character in some Finnish faces.

An internationally popular guidebook on Europe, now Lonely Planet's rival, once published false information on Finland, stating that Russian soldiers were a common sight in Helsinki. This was never true (they were Finnish soldiers), although a handful of Russians have always been around in Finland. During the Soviet Union era, only the privileged few were allowed to leave the workers' paradise. They visited such interesting sights as Lenin Museum in Tampere. It was customary to see a group of dark-clothed

Russians leaving an electronic shop with each carrying a similar South Korean stereo set. As late as the 1980s, the Helsinki Railway Station foreign exchange booth often received a smelly wad of 1920s US one-dollar bills from Russians, literally carrying their (or their grandparents') life savings, apparently on their first foreign trip! After the break-up of the USSR and the liberalisation of its economy, a new trend emerged: 'Red Squares' at markets throughout Finland, especially in Hamina and Helsinki, where poor Russians sold anything from Lenin medals to sheer junk to illegal stuff. Private enterprise by Russians seems to be bearing fruit. A hotel receptionist recently met with some worried Russians who had earlier checked out of the hotel. They had forgotten something in their room. Under the pillow was an envelope with US$50,000 in cash!

EDUCATION

The literacy rate in Finland is 99% and the number of newspapers and books printed per capita is one of the highest in the world. The nine-year comprehensive school *(peruskoulu)* is one of the most equitable systems in the world – tuition, books, meals and commuting to and from school are free. All Finns learn Swedish and English in school and many also study German or French.

The three-year secondary school *(lukio)* attracts some 30,000 students every year and serves as a stepping stone to universities in Helsinki, Turku, Tampere, Oulu, Jyväskylä, Joensuu, Kuopio, Rovaniemi and Vaasa. Approximately 18,000 new university students start every year.

The first university in Finland was founded in Turku in 1640 and transferred in 1828 to Helsinki, where it now has some 26,000 students. More than half the undergraduates are women. Universities are state-owned and there are practically no fees. State grants, state-guaranteed low-interest loans, subsidised health care, meals and student hostels are available to most students. With these benefits, Finnish students stay an average of seven to eight years at university.

There are more people with a doctorate than ever before. Only 5% of these graduates go on to work in industry. Over 70% are employed by the government.

In addition to higher education, there are several educational institutes, from vocational schools to those specialising in an individual subject or just in 'how to live a happy life'.

ARTS
Architecture

The high reputation of modern Finnish architecture was established by the works of Alvar Aalto and Eliel Saarinen. People interested in architecture make pilgrimages to Finland to see superb examples of modern building. Unfortunately, much great Finnish architecture is overshadowed by supermarkets and other concrete blocks that dominate towns and villages.

The oldest architectural monuments include medieval castles and 75 stone churches, scattered around villages in South Finland. In these Catholic churches, Gothic ideals were emulated but with little success, and as a result, an original Finnish style emerged.

Wood has long been the dominant building material in Finland. Some of the best early examples of wooden architecture include churches on Finland's West Coast. Interesting bell towers can be found in Ruokolahti in the east and Tornio in West Lapland.

Eastern influences date back to 1812, when Finland became an autonomous grand duchy under Russian rule and Helsinki was made the new capital. The magnificent city centre was created by CL Engel, a German-born architect, who combined neoclassical and St Petersburg features in designing the cathedral, the university and other buildings around Senate Square. Engel also designed a large number of churches in Finland. All the largest churches in Finland were built during Russian rule. After the 1850s, National Romanticism emerged in response to pressure from the Russians. The Art Nouveau period, which reached its climax by the turn of the century, combined Karelian ideals with rich ornamentation. Materials were wood and grey granite. The best examples of this style are Hvitträsk and the National Museum (Eliel Saarinen) and the

Cathedral of Tampere (Lars Sonck). After independence was achieved in 1917, rationalism and functionalism emerged, as exemplified by Alvar Aalto's sanatorium in Paimio. Some of the most famous names in Finnish architecture include:

Alvar Aalto – (1896-1976) is the most famous architect produced by Finland. His earliest works can be seen at Alajärvi, but more notable are towns which show his skills in functionalism, including Jyväskylä (museum) and Seinäjoki. There are individual churches in Lahti and Imatra, and other buildings in Paimio, Säynätsalo and Rovaniemi. Several buildings can be seen in Helsinki, and at Otaniemi in Espoo, near Helsinki. See individual towns for details.

Juha Leiviskä was awarded the international Carlsberg prize in 1995 for his works in Helsinki (Vallila Library and much more), Vantaa (Myyrmäki Church) and Kuopio (Männistö Church).

Raili and Reima Pietilä, a married couple, worked together and designed churches and other buildings in Tampere (Kaleva, Hervanta and the library in town centre) and Lieksa (the church).

Eliel Saarinen (1873-1950) designed a great number of attractive town houses in Helsinki, as well as working with two other architects, Herman Gesellius and Armas Lindgren, on projects like the National Museum and the Hvitträsk House, north-west of Helsinki. Town halls in Lahti and Joensuu are his own works, as well as the railway station in Helsinki. Eliel's son Eero Saarinen worked mostly in the USA until he died in 1961.

Lars Sonck (1870-1956) designed some notable stone edifices in National Romantic style, including Kultaranta in Naantali and churches in Tampere, Mariehamn and Helsinki (Kallio)

Josef Stenbäck (1854-1929) designed over 30 churches, most of them Art Nouveau.

Other – Among the most famous post-war architects are Viljo Revell, Aarno Ervi, Heikki Siren, Toivo Korhonen, Timo Penttilä, Aarno Ruusuvuori, Erkki Kairamo and Kristian Gullichsen and Timo and Tuomo Suomalainen (Rock Church in Helsinki).

Regional Styles – Emerging regional schools of architecture include the Oulu School, featuring small towers, porticoes and combinations of various elements, and most evident in the region around Oulu. Mr Erkki Helasvuo, who died in 1995, did plenty of work in North Karelia, providing the province with several public buildings which hint of modern Karelianism.

A Guide to Finnish Churches

Church architecture has always been a playground for Finnish architects. Each municipality has at least one architectural wonder. Following is a guide to the various styles.

Medieval (1200s to 1520s)

Style: Gothic.
Material: Stone, sometimes red brick in the facade.

There are 70 medieval churches in Finland. The oldest ones are on Åland (don't miss Hammarland, Finström, Lemland, Sund, Saltvik or Kumlinge). There are almost 30 medieval churches in Turku & Pori Province (including Nousiainen, Turku, Mynämäki, Korppoo, Parainen, Taivassalo, Rymättylä, Kalanti, Laitila, Sastamala and Rauma). Churches like those in Pyhtää, Hattula, Hollola and Isokyrö were regional centres, and remain historically significant and worth visiting.

In addition to paintings and sculpture, note the facade and the shape of the ceiling.

Wooden (1600s to 1700s)

Style: Often local.
Material: Logs of local wood, painted red.

Remote areas of Finland never enjoyed the privilege of an imposing stone church. Instead, wood was used. Some of the oldest such churches were renovated and the original simplicity was replaced by 19th century style.

The highlight of this style is certainly the Petäjävesi Church in Central Finland. Others include the churches of Irjanne, Keuruu, Maakalla, Paltaniemi, Pihlajavesi, Pyhämaa, Sodankylä, Tervola and Tornio. There are also some colourful churches in the Swedish-speaking Pohjanmaa region, such as Vörå and Nykarleby.

In addition to fine paintings in many of the old wooden churches, look for detailed wood-carving.

Empire & European Gothic (1800s)

Style: Imitations of central European styles, especially neoclassical and neo-Gothic.
Material: Wood, painted various colours.

The 20 largest churches in Finland were all built during the Russian era, between 1815 and 1907. They include imitations of central European Gothic cathedrals. Johannes Church in Helsinki and churches is Pori, Kotka, Forssa and Nurmes are the most notable examples of red brick edifices.

Another feature of the time was large churches made of wood. Communities in

A: Paintings in Kumlinge Catholic Church
B: The main church, Valamo Orthodox Monastery
C: 19th century Orthodox chapel in Tornio
D: Sastamala Church near Vammala
E: The UNESCO-acclaimed church of Petäjävesi

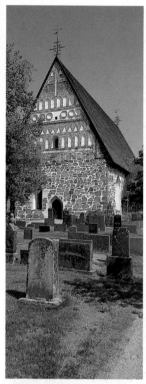

A: Hollola Church
B: 17th century church of Iitti
C: Medieval church of Pernaja
D: The Orthodox Church in Helsinki

Savo and Pohjanmaa are especially famous for building something larger than the neighbouring community. Kerimäki Church in Savo is the largest wooden church in the world, dwarfing even the enormous churches of Mäntyharju, Merikarvia, Mikkeli and Heinävesi.

Many of these churches were built according to a style called Empire, which was influenced by Roman and French architecture. Carl Ludwig Engel was the leading architect of this era.

Orthodox (1700s to 1900s)

Style: Byzantine, Karelian.
Material: Red brick for the old ones; round logs for the more recent tsasounas (chapels).
Most Orthodox churches in Finland date from the Russian era, or independence. The style is clearly Byzantine, with Russian forms most evident.

Although there are fine examples of Orthodox architecture in eastern Finland, such as Ilomantsi, Joensuu, Polvijärvi and Kotka, there are also chapels further west, most notably in Helsinki.

The main feature of Orthodox churches, however, is the wall of icons, rather than the architecture.

National Romantic (late 1800s to early 1900s)

Style: Art Nouveau, Karelian.
Material: Cut granite, oak and other heavy wood, seldom painted.
During the tsarist era, the nationalist movement was clearly visible in several granite churches. Josef Stenbäck designed the greatest number of them, 30 in all, but others, such as Tampere Cathedral, by Lars Sonck, are more famous.

The rich ornamentation, often a reflection of Karelian heritage, is the main feature of these churches.

Modern (1900s)

Style: Art Deco, modern.
Materials: Various, but especially concrete painted white and light wood as interior decoration and/or furniture.
The most famous modern churches in Finland are Alvar Aalto's churches Seinäjoki, Lahti and Imatra, as well as more recent ones in Tampere (Kaleva Church by Pietilä), Myyrmäki (by Leiviskä) and Helsinki's Rock Church (by Suomalainen).

Some of these churches do not look like churches at all, but more like a successful architectural adventure. ■

Design

Finns have created their own design style through their craft tradition, the use of natural materials (wood, glass, ceramics, fabric and metal) and simple but pure forms. Stylistically they combined colourful, geometric, ornamental Karelian (originally Byzantine) design with a more Western European style. Traditional textile art, such as woven *ryijy* rugs and *raanus*, national costumes, as well as wooden furniture and everyday utensils and implements, can be seen in various museums. This heritage is also clearly visible in the works of modern designers.

The products of some early designers, such as Louis Sparre, Gallén-Kallela and Eliel Saarinen, reflected the ideas of Karelianism, National Romanticism and Art Nouveau. In the 1930s Alvar Aalto, the architect, invented wooden furniture made of bent and laminated plywood, as well as his famous Savoy vases, today promoted by Artek. Aalto won a prize for his furniture in the Milan Triennale of 1933.

After WW II, the 'Golden Age of Applied Art' began and in Milan in 1951, Finland received 25 prizes for various designer products. Tapio Wirkkala, Kaj Franck, Timo Sarpaneva, Eero Aarnio and Yrjö Kukkapuro were the most notable designers of the time. Unfortunately, the high quality of Finnish design suffered during the turbulent years of the 1970s, and has had difficulty recovering. Iittala, Nuutajärvi and Arabia are still some of the best brands of Finnish glassware and porcelain, and Pentik is a more recent brand. Aarikka is famous for wooden products, Kalevala Koru for silver designs.

Painting

Of the many prehistoric rock paintings across Finland, those at Hossa and Ristiina are the most famous. Medieval churches in Åland and in South Finland have frescoes, while interesting paintings by Mikael Toppelius and others feature in several 18th century wooden churches, most notably in Paltaniemi, Keuruu and several villages near Oulu, especially Haukipudas. Modern art is alive and well; each large town exhibits paintings that provoke anything from astonishment to despair.

Golden Age Although contemporary art enjoys a high profile in Finland, it is works by National Romantic painters that have been bestowed with Golden Era status. The main features of these artworks are virgin forests and rural landscapes which have since become more scarce.

The following list includes museums that exhibit the best works. The Ateneum and National Museums are in Helsinki; for the rest, the name of the town is mentioned to ease the hunt. Refer to each town for further details.

Brothers von Wright – Magnus (1805-1868), Wilhelm (1810-1887) and Ferdinand (1822-1902). The brothers von Wright are considered the first Finnish painters of the Golden Era, most famous for their paintings of birds. They worked in their home at Haminanlahti near Kuopio (in Savo) and in Porvoo. The Ateneum in Helsinki has devoted one room to their art, and it's worth a close look. There are also superb coffee table books available.

Robert Wilhelm Ekman (1808-1873), one of the founders of Finnish art, worked in Turku and painted mostly altars for churches and Kalevala-inspired works. See Helsinki Cygnaeus, National Museum, Ateneum and Mänttä Serlachius.

Werner Holmberg (1839-1860). The 'Ideal Landscape' is one of the classical paintings of this early Finnish artist, who was able to capture the idyllic Häme landscape in his works. See Ateneum and Helsinki Gyllenberg for these.

Hjalmar Munsterhjelm (1840-1905), one of the most notable landscape painters in Finland, studied in Germany. There are paintings at Ateneum, Turku Art Museum and Turku Ett Hem.

Berndt Lindholm (1841-1914) is mostly known for his paintings of waves hitting a rocky shore. He has also painted Finnish landscape and rural life but unfortunately many of his works are in private collections. Some examples can be seen at Ateneum, Turku Art Museum, and Turku Ett Hem.

Fanny Churberg (1845-1892), one of the most famous female painters in Finland, created landscapes, self portraits and still lives. See Ateneum and Vaasa Hedman.

Gunnar Berndtson (1854-1895). Fine paintings by this artist can be seen at Mänttä Serlachius,

Helsinki Gyllenberg, Ateneum and Turku Art Museum.

Albert Edelfelt (1854-1905), one of the most appreciated of Finnish artists, was educated in Paris, and a number of fine paintings date from this time. Many paintings are photo-like accounts of rural life. His studio in Haikko near Porvoo is simple but worth a visit. Most Edelfelt paintings are to be found at Ateneum and Helsinki Gyllenberg, but there are also a few at Mänttä Serlachius, Hämeenlinna Art Museum, Joensuu Art Museum and Turku Ett Hem.

Victor Westerholm (1860-1919), most famous for his large Åland landscapes, had his summer studio in Önningeby near Jomala (see Åland for details) but there are landscapes from other locations too. Ateneum, Turku Art Museum, Hämeenlinna Art Museum, Mänttä Serlachius and Turku Ett Hem display some of his best works.

Helene Schjerfbeck (1862-1946), probably the most famous female painter of her age, is known for her self portraits, which reflect the situation of Finnish women 100 years ago; Helene didn't live a happy life. There are also landscapes and much more. Go to Ateneum, Mänttä Serlachius, Helsinki Gyllenberg, Vaasa Hedman, Turku Art Museum and Turku Ett Hem.

Eero Järnefelt (1863-1937) was a keen visitor to Koli (See North Karelia for details), where he created over 50 paintings of the 'national landscape'. His sister married Jean Sibelius, the composer. See his work at Ateneum, as well as Mikkeli, Hämeenlinna, Turku, and Kuopio Art Museums.

Akseli Gallen-Kallela (1865-1931), probably the most famous and appreciated Finnish painter, had a distinguished career as creator of *Kalevala*-inspired paintings. His studios in Tarvaspää near Helsinki and Kalela near Ruovesi (see the Route 66 section of the Häme chapter for details) are both places not to be missed. His masterworks can be seen as frescoes in the National Museum in Helsinki, Hämeenlinna Art Museum and at the Jusélius Mausoleum in Pori. The top five art museums are Ateneum, Turku Art Museum, Turku Ett Hem, Mänttä Serlachius and Helsinki Gyllenberg.

Magnus Enckell (1870-1925) is known for his paintings in Tampere Cathedral. His work can be seen at Ateneum, Vaasa Hedman, Joensuu Art Museum, Kokkola Renlund and Jyväskylä Alvar Aalto Museum.

Ellen Thesleff (1869-1954) used strong colours in her landscape paintings. Visit Ateneum and Helsinki Art Museum.

Hugo Simberg (1873-1917) used symbolism in his paintings, some of which were extremely naive, and deliberately so. Visits to Ateneum, Mänttä Serlachius, Vaasa Hedman and Turku Art Museum will prove this.

Juho Rissanen (1873-1950) depicted life among ordinary Finns, and his much-loved paintings at Ateneum, Vaasa Hedman and Turku Art Museum are worth a look.

Pekka Halonen (1865-1933), a popular artist of the National Romantic era, did much of his work at Halosenniemi in Tuusula (see the Around Helsinki section of the Helsinki chapter) although he came from Lapinlahti. His work, mostly devoted to typical winter scenery, is largely privately owned. Some of the best works are displayed in the Ateneum, Turku Art Museum, Kokkola Renlund, Helsinki Gyllenberg and Vaasa Hedman.

Dance

Dance is nurtured in Finland. The Finnish National Opera has its own ballet school, and there are a handful of small dance groups in Helsinki and other large towns. Mr Jorma Uotinen, director of the Finnish National Ballet, is currently the most interesting figure in contemporary dance in Finland. You should try to attend the annual Kuopio Dance & Music Festival to catch the latest trends.

Few traditional folk dances *(kansantanssit)* remain, but they can be seen on ceremonial occasions. In summer you may come across a noisy dance stage in the middle of nowhere. Get ready to experience *lavatanssit*, where local singers and their bands play pop music, and people dance. If the participants are older, the music is *humppa* or *tango*, and instruments include accordion and violin. Younger people demand a contemporary band, so the *lava* (stage) is almost like a disco.

You may be interested in a *naistentanssi*, or 'women's dance', where women propose a dance. This arrangement is generally valid once a week in many local dance restaurants.

Literature

Written Finnish was created by Mikael Agricola (1510-57) who wrote the first Finnish alphabet and covered traditional Finnish culture and religion in his writings. Because Finnish remained a spoken more than written language (although it was emerging in schools), the earliest fiction was written in Swedish.

The most famous of all 19th century writers was Elias Lönnrot, who collected poems, oral runes, folk legends and stories to pen the *Kalevala*, the national epic of Finland, which became the foundation of Finnish culture, literature and history (see The Kalevala). Other notable 19th century writers include JL Runeberg *(Tales of the Ensign Ståhl)*, fairy-tale writer Zacharias Topelius, and Aleksis Kivi, who founded modern Finnish literature with *Seven Brothers*, a story of brothers who try to escape education and civilisation in favour of the forest. Other writers of the era include Minna Canth, Juhani Aho, Teuvo Pakkala, and Eino Leino, the poet.

In the 20th century, Mika Waltari gained fame through *The Egyptian*, and FE Sillanpää received the Nobel Prize for literature in 1939. The national best seller in the postwar period was *The Unknown Soldier* by Väinö Linna. The nearly endless series of autobiographical novels by Kalle Päätalo and the witty short stories by Veikko Huovinen are also very popular in Finland. Another internationally famous author is Tove Jansson, whose children's books on the Moomin family have much to offer adult readers too.

Music

Jean Sibelius is the greatest composer Finland has ever produced, perhaps the greatest in the whole of Scandinavia. Born on 8 December 1865 in Hämeenlinna, Sibelius wrote music for the glorification of his own people and in defiance of the oppressor, Russia. His most famous composition, *Finlandia*, became a strong expression of Finnish patriotism and pride. Sibelius can be said to have composed the *Kalevala* saga, while Gallén-Kallela painted it.

Sibelius' work can be best understood in terms of Finnish nature. Many Finns hear in Sibelius' music a sunrise in summer, the energetic days of springtime or the dark spruce forest before a rainstorm. If you take a Walkman into the wilderness and listen to Sibelius there, you may get the picture. Sibelius' music is dark, almost depressing, but then you should listen to his almost pop-like *Alla Marcia* from the *Karelia Suite*.

After Sibelius, nothing can quite compare. Fredrik Pacius composed *Maamme* (*Nårt Land* in Swedish, Our Land in English), the song that is currently the national anthem of both Finland and the newly independent Estonia. Plenty of popular Finnish songs from the early 1900s are sung in summer or at Christmas time. Although Finnish music has always been influenced from abroad, it has its own aspects, melancholia being the most notable one. These days musical life is very active, from classical music to jazz, pop and rock. Techno music is very much appreciated in Helsinki. Karelian-type folk music is gaining in popularity, and you should try to hear the music of a group called Värttinä, preferably live.

Cinema

Finnish cinema bears a striking resemblance to the better known French film culture. The film elite, which hardly cares about attracting a following, lives in its own microcosm where money is held to be in direct opposition to talent. However, getting government subsidies is the principal concern. According to this establishment, a financially successful film is 'too commercial' and there is no point in seeing it. What sets Finland apart from the French, however, is much more sensitivity for the original soundtrack. Finns do not dub foreign films. Over 10 movies are produced in Finland annually, with some attracting almost 1000 viewers! Many of these films are sold to Norwegian state television (see Finnish Jokes).

Mika and Aki Kaurismäki are currently

The *Kalevala*

Elias Lönnrot was a country doctor who trekked in eastern Finland on a scholarship in order to collect poems, oral runes, folk stories and legends. The results, together with some of his own writing, he put together to form the *Kalevala*, the national epic of Finland.

The first version appeared in 1833, another version in 1835 and yet another, *Uusi-Kalevala* (New Kalevala), in 1849. The *Kalevala* has been translated into almost 40 languages, but as with the Koran, it should really be read in its original language.

Kalevala is an epic mythology which includes stories of creation and the fight between good and evil. Although there are heroes and villains, there are also characters who are not so simply described.

The main story concentrates on the events in two imaginary countries, Kalevala (characterised as 'our country') and Pohjola ('the other place'). Some of the main characters are:

Aino – The bride of Väinämöinen and sister of Joukahainen.
Antero Vipunen – A shaman. In one story, Väinämöinen is looking for the Right Words (which give omnipotence to the user) and ends up in Antero's belly. Eventually, Antero Vipunen has to let him go and give him the Words.
Ilmarinen – One of the main characters, and the husband of the princess of Pohjola. He is a smith who makes the Sampo (a mysterious and powerful machine).
Joukahainen – A youngster who is threatened with drowning in a swamp to the singing of the powerful Väinämöinen. In a vain attempt to be saved, he promises his sister Aino to Väinämöinen.
Kalervo – The father of Kullervo.
Kullervo – The main character of the Kullervo poems; he suffers under a curse.
Lemminkäinen – A hero whose character was created by Lönnrot based on oral tradition.
Louhi – The matron of Pohjola, also called Pohjan Akka or Pohjolan emäntä, the leader of Pohjola.
Väinämöinen – The main character of the *Kalevala*, a god-like, omnipotent figure. He was a bard and probably a shaman, a Santa Claus-type old man and a strong personality.

You'll find an interesting *Kalevala* theme park in Kuhmo and a *Kalevala* exhibition in Parppeinvaara, Ilomantsi. The most notable *Kalevala*-inspired paintings are to be found in the Ateneum Art Museum and in the National Museum, both in Helsinki. ∎

the best known directors. Their success in *film noir* is based on their education in Leningrad (during the USSR era). The American Jim Jarmush is a personal friend of the Kaurismäki brothers, and has also presented his view of Finnish culture in some of his works. Another talented director, Markku Pölönen, has produced some very fine movies on Finnish rural life.

The most successful Finn in Hollywood, Renny Harlin (also known as the husband of actor Geena Davis), directed a strongly anticommunist action movie 'Born American' in the 1980s, portraying an imaginary Soviet prison camp. When the film was banned in Finland and Harlin accused of presenting a 'foreign nation in a hostile manner', the young director found himself directing box-office hits for Hollywood, including 'Die Hard II' and 'Cliffhanger'.

There are several annual film festivals in Helsinki and around Finland, the Midnight Sun festival in Sodankylä being the most interesting.

CULTURE

For Finns, life becomes a *juhla* when you leave *Stadi* and listen to tango on your way to the *mökki* in the middle of a *metsä* at a *järvi*, drink some *viina* after the *sauna* and then watch the *kisat* on TV and drink lots of *kahvi*. To understand Finnish culture, there are a number of five-letter words you should know:

Juhla – Party. With long, dark, cold winters, a history of several less-than-victorious wars and the influence of the rugged and blunt Lutheran faith, Finland is not a likely country for interesting celebrations and festivals. Yet there are juhlas on every occasion: when school ends, birthdays, name days and national holidays. Finns take partying very seriously. When it's official, people dress properly, act muted and look serious. When it's religious, they dress properly, act muted and look serious. When it's unofficial, they dress casually, act light-heartedly and look serious.

Järvi – Lake. Finns have built their towns and villages, factories and hydroelectric plants, transportation systems and timber-floating routes, bridges and road networks along their 188,000 lakes. They have formed their distinctive sports

and recreational habits in close relation to their lake-island-river system. Lakes provide fish and drinking water, and you can cross them by boat to reach other villages. The lake geography has several other important features, such as *saari* (island), *ranta* (shore), *niemi* (cape), *lahti* (bay), *koski* (rapids), *virta* (stream) and *joki* (river). All these words, especially Järvinen, Saarinen, Rantanen, Nieminen, Lahtinen, Koskinen, Virtanen and Jokinen, are some of the most common Finnish family names.

Kahvi – Coffee. Finns consume, on average, nine cups of coffee each day – the world record. It sounds like addiction, and it is, but coffee is much more than just a hot drink. You will seldom visit a house without being served coffee. Traditionally you were supposed to say 'no' three times and then accept, by saying 'OK, just half a cup', which turned out to be four or five. Even now, taking a few long coffee breaks in the office is a must. Coffee is so important that during WWII a substitute was invented to keep people happy. You pour your kahvi into a *kuppi* and add some *maito* (milk) or *kerma* (cream). Finns usually eat some *pulla* (wheat bun) with coffee. After the first cup, you'll have eight more to go.

Kisat – Games. Finns are serious about their sports. Indeed, 'sport' in Finnish translates roughly as 'heroism'. Success in *Olympiakisat* (the Olympic Games) is about the best thing any Finn can dream of; a gold medal means a visit to the President's Palace and innumerable centrefold posters and front-cover photos in magazines. Even the smallest rowing boat competitions are treated with much enthusiasm. Every town right down to the smallest village has sports fields, indoor halls, swimming pools, tennis courts, downhill slopes and jogging and skiing tracks. Lahti and Kuopio are currently dreaming of hosting the Winter Olympic Games one day. Large crowds are attracted to watch a *matsi* (match) of *pesis* (Finnish baseball), *futis* (soccer or football), *koris* (basketball), and especially *lätkä* (ice hockey). National fervour reached fever pitch when Finland defeated Sweden in May 1995 to gain the world ice hockey championship – definitely the biggest event in Finland since the general strike of 1956!

Metsä – Forest. Finns are characteristically forest people who like to listen to the wind humming in trees, either *mänty* or *honka* (pine), *kuusi* (spruce) or *koivu* (birch). Deciduous forests are called *lehto* (from *lehti* which means leaf), while real wilderness is *korpi* or *kaira*. Again, Mäntynen, Honkanen, Kuusinen, Koivunen, Lehtinen, Lehtonen and Korpinen are all fairly common Finnish family names, with or without the *-nen* ending. Other useful metsä words include *marja* (berry), *sieni* (mushroom), *eläin* (animal), *hirvi* (elk) and *lintu* (bird).

Mökki – Cottage. The *kesämökki*, or summer cottage, is an important part of life in Finland. Even if people demand modern amenities in their regular home, the mökki should be basic and definitely in the middle of nowhere. Mökki requirements include a *takka* (fireplace) and a sauna at the *ranta* of a *järvi*. In summer, after a proper sauna bath, you go to the pier at the waterfront, drink some *kalja* (beer) and relax, listen to birds singing and watch the midnight sun approaching the horizon. Then you're a Finn.

Sauna – If you didn't already know, the sauna is a Finnish invention. There are 1.2 million saunas in Finland, which means that practically all Finns have access to a sauna. Usually it's on Saturday evenings that families bathe in their own sauna. It is the ancient *savusauna*, or 'smoke sauna', that has kept the tradition alive and popular; the modern electric sauna stoves don't produce the pleasant *löyly* (steam) you should expect. In towns and in many hotels, you will bathe in an electric sauna, but in the countryside you can expect an authentic, log-heated lakeside sauna. Look for a savusauna and check the price first. Test one while you're in Finland. The sauna was originally a place to bathe, to meditate and even to give birth, but it is not (and never has been) used for making babies; Finns are quite strict about the nonsexual character of the sauna bath, and this point should be respected. These days people go to a sauna to relax, to small-talk and to talk seriously (Finns always talk seriously). For your sauna, you'll use a *kauha* to throw water on the *kiuas*, which then gives off the löyly. At this point, at least in summer in the countryside, you'll take the *vihta* or *vasta* (a bunch of fresh koivu twigs) and hit yourself. This improves your circulation and gives your skin a pleasant smell. After this, you'll go out to the ranta of a järvi to swim.

Stadi – Helsinki. The word stadi is derived from the Swedish *staden*, for 'city'. Although Stadi has just 10% of the entire Finnish population, to the people of Stadi it represents about 99% of the country. The *lande*, or countryside, is the place where you spend the Midsummer weekend. Stadi ends at the *susiraja*, or 'wolf frontier', which is at the Vantaa border, according to the most recent definition.

Tango – Tango. It may surprise some Finns to know that tango is not a Finnish word. No other music could epitomise the melancholic Finn better than this Argentinian music. If Finns lack the electrifying tension that Latin Americans bring to the tango, they lack none of the enthusiasm. Tango is best heard on long bus journeys through the Finnish wilderness, passing by abandoned farm houses; the Finnish lyrics deal with desperation. The best place and time to dance is during the *Tangomarkkinat* in Seinäjoki every July. Many Finns would disagree about tango being the thing; they'd stick to *rokki* or *jatsi* or *tekno* or whatever.

Viina – Aquavit. Finns drink a lot. The expensive bottle of viina is typically purchased in the nearest Alko store on Fridays after work. Yes, yuppies sip their expensive *viini* (wine), and much kalja (beer) is brewed and consumed, but viina characterises the entire hopeless drinking pattern of some Finns; drink until you pass out. An old man from Lapland once summed it all up on a local radio programme: 'You basically travel abroad to buy cheap viina.'

Humour

Finns in general have a great sense of humour although most good jokes relate to peculiarities in Finnish language. If you hear translations of these incomprehensible sentences, try to produce a credible grin. Other than that, Finnish jokes are primitive and mostly deal with alcohol, TV stars dressed in silly clothes, or political imitators.

One peculiar characteristic of Finnish humour is the habit of repeating meaningless words. These come from low quality TV comedies, where the star invents a new jingle. After repeating it on every programme week after week practically all Finns adopt it and use it frequently, way beyond saturation point. Even well-educated Finns seem to find satisfaction in jumping on the band wagon. Some of the recent phrases were *kliffaa hei, tyks tyks, onks viljoo näkyny, diu diu diu,* and *kylä lähtee* but they are all out of fashion by now. These mantras may serve as a collective and egalitarian valve amid social tensions, especially during the Cold War when serious discussion about very much of anything between social groups was next to impossible. For instant success among Finns, do repeat the most popular jingle as often as you can, and there will be great enthusiasm that an *ulkomaalainen* knows Finnish culture so well. Welcome to the club!

Silence

Finns don't go around babbling like noisy

Finnish Jokes

Norwegians have created a fine branch of humour based on Finnish traits. Hundreds of stories are told in Norwegian pubs to anyone who cares to listen. The biggest joke is still the TV show that is said to feature Finnish 'comedy'. Norwegian state television regularly purchased dark, depressing Finnish movies, which Norwegians found extremely amusing!

The Finn in *Finskevitser* (Norwegian for 'Finnish Jokes') is not a loser. The two male heroes, Pekka and Toivonen, are known for their endurance in various challenges, including sexual ability. Once, Pekka returned from battle in the Winter War, and later tells what he did first with his wife. 'What did you do next?' asks the curious listener. 'Then,' replies Pekka, 'I took off my skis.'

Small talk is not common amongst Finns. When Pekka and Toivonen meet again after a long time apart, they go to a sauna in the woods. They drink vodka for a couple of hours. Pekka asks how Toivonen has been doing. Toivonen says nothing, but continues drinking for a couple of hours. Then, slowly, he replies: 'Did we come here to babble, or did we come here to drink?'

A real 'accident' happened once on Lake Inarinjärvi while Pekka and Toivonen were fishing on ice. Both men were wearing thick fur hats. Pekka had a bottle of vodka, and he uttered: 'Toivonen, do you want a sip of vodka?' Because of his thick fur hat, Toivonen did not hear the offer, and was left without. This was the big 'accident' on Lake Inarinjärvi.

Finns in *Finskevitser* have an awkward relationship with the USSR. We learn that Finns use double-ply toilet paper because they had to send a copy of anything they produced to the USSR.

Finskevitser became known among Norwegian soldiers who spent their leave in Finnish Lapland. Liberal consumption of intoxicating liquids on these occasions may give rise to quite a number of new Finnish legends, if you dare set foot in a local pub during the Arctic winter. ∎

southern Europeans. No, they appreciate a cool, sophisticated atmosphere, where each individual is accorded space and privacy. Sounds great? Well, an Australian traveller who spent half a year living in a student apartment in Helsinki gave this comment:

In six months my mate hardly spoke to me more than 10 times. Probably the loudest form of communication I've ever experienced was when, after several weeks of silence, he one morning said abruptly: 'It is your turn to buy toilet paper'.

A Finn can spend days planning how to say something (especially personal criticism). Many Finns don't want to speak unless they've seriously contemplated the issue. Small talk isn't the thing for most Finns. The good thing is you can often trust a Finn, but they will not trust you if you talk too much!

With a little help from intoxicating liquids, a Finn can be most talkative during a long evening in a pub. But the next day, the pale fellow will not even nod to say hello and you may wonder whether you've been

recognised at all. Winter is the most hopeless time, when many people are depressed.

The history of Finns is not a happy one. Colonialisation by Sweden and Russia brought an alien upper class. The strict (some say cruel) Lutheran form of Christianity has not helped either. Finally, the distorted socialist system has worked to discourage individualism and encourage the grey average. A happy, talkative Finn does not inspire admiration among fellow Finns, but rather animosity, jealousy or hostility. Being silent is the way to go.

There are ways to cope with this. One is to accept it as a local custom and just read or meditate more in Finland and leave the merry-making for more vibrant countries. You should not expect to find immediate friends or to crack a joke with a total stranger. Instead, try to present your ideas in a serious, semi-philosophical manner. That may be a way to find a lasting friend (although it may also require a ritual sauna bath). Note that the sauna is another place to maintain silence. Silence should not be interpreted as hostility but rather as contemplation or even respect, although in a small rural shop or pub, silence is similar to that in a theatre: locals wait for the ridiculous actions a visitor is about to perform. One traveller gave this comment:

Most youth hostels were either deserted or else inhabited by some very strange Finns. If you plan to travel north after August, bring some books. I found myself going half nuts at one stage and took to stealing English books from small town libraries to preserve my sanity! I later posted them back from Helsinki.

On the other hand, as most Finns stick to the silence rule, the few foreign clowns who flout the habit may be greatly appreciated, especially by the opposite sex. Another exception to the rule is the manic phase of some Finns, manifested in a sudden burst of activity over the few summer months. (In winter it is considered as a need to visit a mental institution.) A disco or another similar venue can be intolerable because of the unnatural 'fun' people are pretending to have. There are also talkative peoples, such as Savonians and Karelians, who know how to small-talk – in their own dialect, that is.

It is of course dangerous to generalise, but what you actually experience depends on where you stay and whom you happen to bump into. Note that Finns travelling in a group hardly keep silent, proving that a group of people from any nationality will be unbearable, anywhere.

Silence was very much a political virtue during the Soviet Union era. Finland at that time had just one foreign policy – don't offend the Soviets – and no one was to challenge that. Today's taboos: never criticise trade unions, never ever question the right to go on strike and never bash the welfare state.

Sisu

The traditional definition of the Finnish trait *sisu*, often translated as 'guts', is resilience and survival in prolonged hardship. Trying to eke out a living in harsh conditions, resisting the Red Army during WWII and success in long-distance running in Olympic Games are all examples of Finnish sisu. Recently, however, many have come to believe that the generous welfare hand-outs and other modern inventions have killed the initiative and the spirit of sisu among many Finns.

Another interpretation of sisu includes the sense of inevitable, tragic defeat. Finland has won few of its wars. The hard-working Finn may end up ruining his achievements by excessive consumption of alcohol. In sports a bitterly-contested event could be lost at the last minute. But until the final defeat, a Finn will fight like no-one else.

Swedish Culture

'Neither' is the right word to describe the Swedish-speaking minority in Finland. Ethnically, most of them are certainly not Finnish, at least by their own definition and distinction, and centuries of history divide them from the people of Sweden. Some Swedish-speaking people are children of ethnic German, Russian or Jewish families who adopted the Swedish language before learning enough Finnish to deal with daily life.

Many among the Swedish-speaking minority have more wealth than the Finns, and Swedish-speakers are well represented in most cultural, economic and public fields. Although they are usually considered representatives of the 'old money' in Finland, the Swedish minority also has some well-known communists, greens and other influential members in various 'alternative' groups.

Swedish speakers are found mostly in coastal towns and communities, maintaining Swedish literature, newspapers, TV programmes, and a number of cultural traditions different from Finns and even from Sweden. Their small towns and gardens are among the most attractive and well-kept in Finland. Sagalund on the island of Kimito, and Stundars near Vaasa are two museums with plenty of cultural interest, and Åland province is culturally exclusively Swedish.

With a constant presence in the national government, the Swedish party makes sure that everything is fine with the 'most protected minority in the world', as some jealously put it.

Rules Rule

Finns are either the world's worst bureaucrats or the world's most obedient people, judging by the plethora of rigorously-enforced rules and regulations that govern Finnish life.

Road laws in particular are strictly enforced. The government collects hundreds of millions of markaa annually as income from traffic tickets alone. Wearing a seat-belt is compulsory in the back seat of a car. It is compulsory to turn on your headlights on rural roads (or outside urban areas). If you fail to comply, you pay.

A business person recently started a small guesthouse offering catering services. If only it was so simple ... no less than 15 different authorities inspected the building, checking everything from hygiene to plumbing, making sure every word of the law was obeyed.

'In Italy (a member of the EU), only 50% of EU rules are honoured,' remarked the owner of the establishment. 'Finland (at that time not an EU member) already obeys 120% of all EU rules!'

Perhaps the 1990s will bring change now that Finns are showing signs of obedience fatigue. On the other hand, they've always shone in endurance sports. ■

Sami Culture

The unique Sami culture is almost exclusive to Lapland. See the Lapland chapter for coverage.

Romany Culture

The Finnish Gipsies number about 6000 but 2000 live in Sweden. They are descendants of people who emigrated from India from around 500 AD and travelled throughout Europe. As distinct from Romany people in warmer southern European countries, most Finnish Gipsies live in houses.

Horse racing and big cars are two passions of Finnish Gipsies, as is trading at local markets. Many are successful in music, often winning national song competitions. Romany males often raise admiration among Finnish females, and there are many children from interracial relationships. Romany females wear large and colourful costumes. Romany people have their own language (with elements of Indian languages) and distinctive dress. Their values indicate a greater emphasis on the family than those of mainstream Finns.

Finns have a racist term for Gipsies ('black people') and there are constant skirmishes between Finns and Romany people. After 1584 when the first Romany people arrived in Finland, a law was passed in which it was illegal *not* to kill a Gipsy! In Finland today, they have the largest percentage of any ethnic group in prison. No museum in Finland commemorates this colourful culture.

American Culture

If you spend more than a few days in Finland, you may hear that 'Finland is the most American country in Europe'. No, this doesn't mean that Finland is a multicultural, liberal land of opportunity. What people mean is that some aspects of the consumer culture have bitten deep in Finland. F-words, adopted directly from American movies, are not uncommon on the streets, as is the building of enormous supermarkets that can only be reached by private vehicle, and the popularity of American baseball caps and unmatching T-shirts. Finns learn spoken American directly from TV, unlike most Europeans who dub their imported programmes. Perhaps Finns mean they are like Americans because they enthusiastically watch soap operas, such as The Bold and the Beautiful, or music videos on MTV.

Nowadays Finns are said to be becoming more 'European' (whatever that means) in their lifestyle. Recent surveys indicate that Finns increasingly enjoy listening to European pop music (including Finnish and British) and European movies are not rare. Even Latin is booming as a written language and the Finnish Broadcasting Company runs an international news bulletin in spoken

Latin! It is very difficult to believe that Finland is reminiscent of America at all. Yet a traveller from California gave this comment on some young people he saw in Helsinki:

I was disappointed to see all of the young people hanging around the train station who looked like they would be more at home on Telegraph St in Berkeley.

Other Ethnic Cultures
The very few Jews in Finland have kept a low profile because of the Nazis, the pro-Arab sentiments of Finnish leftists, and anti-Semitic voices from the Soviet Union and Russia. Some talented Jews have enriched Finnish cultural life, and there's a very beautiful synagogue and a small kosher shop in Helsinki.

Russians have also kept an extremely low profile (obviously Finns don't value native Russians very highly after what the Soviet Union did to Finland). Russians may have felt uneasy because of the Finnish authorities' notorious former habit of expelling Russian defectors back to the Soviet Union. There is in Finland an ethnic Russian Orthodox Church different from the national Orthodox Church. Russian restaurants are often run by Finns, and their main objective is to make money.

Vietnamese refugees have established a few restaurants and shops, but Somalian refugees, still banned from taking jobs, are yet to create a subculture. A few mosques in Finland attract Mediterranean Arabs and a small number of Tatars who have lived in Finland for over 100 years.

Many Finns are attracted to various imported cultures, and there are ethnic shops, restaurants and clubs in Helsinki and other big cities, where the flavours of foreign cultures can be tasted.

RELIGION
Early Beliefs
In the past, Finns lived in close harmony with nature and made a simple living by fishing, hunting and cultivating land. There were few gods; Finns generally preferred spirits that inhabited both forests (haltija) and back yards (tonttu). These spirits were offered gifts to keep them happy. Deceased relatives were treated with respect. Finns believed that the dead wandered around, especially during festival seasons. The kalmisto (graveyard) was the place for offerings, and conspicuous trees and stones had great significance for local cults.

With the arrival of Catholicism, the animist religion was soon influenced by 'new gods' (Catholic saints), which were incorporated into the polytheistic society, although a handful of old shamans kept the old traditions alive for decades. The Church confiscated all traditional sacrifice sites around the 1230s but perpetuated their religious significance: churches were erected on traditional sacrifice sites or burial grounds.

Today's Finland still bears witness to the distant past. The Midsummer celebration (with bonfires) is a pagan holiday, although it also commemorates John the Baptist. Easter is actually the Finnish version of Halloween, with trick-or-treat-style traditions among kids, and witches and trolls flying above the Nordic forests. The roots of Christmas celebration are also pre-Christian.

Some of the old Finnish gods include Ahti (god of waters and fish), Ilmarinen (god of winds and storms), Tapio (god of forests) and Ukko (god of growth, rain and thunderstorms).

Christianity
The Christian faith was brought to Finland by the Roman Catholic Bishop Henry from England, who arrived in mainland Finland in about 1155 and stayed to tend the church. He met a tragic death on the ice of Lake Köyliö at the hands of a Finnish peasant named Lalli. There were even earlier crusades to Åland, where the oldest churches in Finland are to be found.

The Catholic Church was gradually displaced by the Reformation of Martin Luther, which reflected the rugged individualism typical of Finns. Finland's own reformer was Mikael Agricola, who also created the written Finnish language. The whole Bible appeared in Finnish in 1642. Old stone churches, decorations and ornaments, the bishops' official signs, and popular saints' names and name days are remnants of the Catholic era. The Eastern (Greek or Russian) Orthodox Church is evident in eastern provinces, but there are small chapels (*tsasouna* in Finnish) in many western towns, as many refugees from Soviet-annexed Karelia settled in these towns after WWII. Yet only 1% of Finns belong to the Orthodox Church, which is noted for its beautiful church architecture, old icons and the two monasteries in the municipality of Heinävesi.

Approximately 88% of Finns belong to the national church, the Evangelical-Lutheran Church of Finland. Within the Church are large revivalist groups, such as the Pietists, the Evangelicals and the Laestadians, who all have large summer conventions, with some 20,000 participants in open-air gatherings. One of the most popular modern evangelical movements in Finland is the Tuomasmessu (the Mass of Thomas) which combines medieval Catholic elements and modern gospel rhythms.

The two 'official' churches (Lutheran and Orthodox) still collect taxes and register births, but 10% of the population belong to the civil register. Some of these people were opposed to paying the church taxes, and many women left the church in protest when the battle over women's priesthood was at its fiercest. There are now female priests in the Lutheran Church.

Religious instruction is given in schools, and there are state-supported offices for chaplains serving in the army, hospitals and prisons. Parliament opens and closes its sessions with a church service.

However, services have proved unpopular, with only 5% of members attending regularly. The Church has tried to be active in building new clubrooms, sports facilities and family guidance centres, and in arranging gospel concerts for young people, but with limited success. Evangelical free churches abound. They represent rather outlandish charismatic movements, most of which derive from America. The largest group is the Pentecostals (Helluntaiseurakunta).

Mormon churches are called Myöhempien Aikojen Pyhien Jeesuksen Kristuksen Kirkko, and Jehovah's Witness Halls are called Jehovan Todistajain valtakunnansali, in case you were wondering.

LANGUAGE
Place Names
Finland is officially a bilingual country, with 6% of the population speaking Swedish. In some regions this jumps to 90% or more of the local population.

Of the 470 municipalities in Finland, 24 are designated entirely Swedish-speaking – that is, all signs are in Swedish only. The 24 cases are all in the west – all 16 municipalities of Åland, three in Turku and Pori Province (Houtskär, Iniö, Västanfjärd) and five municipalities in Vaasa Province (Korsnäs, Maxmo, Närpes, Larsmo and Malax).

A further 41 municipalities are officially bilingual, with signs bearing both languages. The majority language always appears first, (which is also the practice throughout this book).

For the purposes of this book, if more than 85% of the local population speaks Swedish, the coverage will use Swedish names for places, hotels, restaurants and things to see. The Finnish name of the town or village is always included, except for Åland province, Västanfjärd, Dragsfjärd, Liljendal, Korsnäs and Iniö, where there is no Finnish version.

Note that even with predominantly Swedish-speaking towns, you might see the Finnish name on all signs outside the town. (See also Appendix 1 – Alternative Place Names.)

Finnish
Finnish, a Finno-Ugric language, is considered difficult to learn. There are 15 cases for nouns, and at least 160 conjugations and personal forms for verbs. There are no articles and no gender, but the word 'no' also conjugates. There are words borrowed from

English, Swedish, Russian, German and Baltic languages. Note that *ä* is pronounced as in 'bat', and *ö* is pronounced 'er', as in 'number'. These letters are the last two in the Finnish alphabet.

Many readers wrote to us about their problems with the Finnish language. One particular reader found a clothes store named 'Farkku Piste' ('Jeans Point') to be especially amusing.

Although local dialects differ from mainstream written Finnish, Finns who speak Finnish to a foreigner usually do so extremely clearly and 'according to the book'.

Lonely Planet publishes a *Scandinavian Phrasebook*, which is a handy pocket-sized introduction to Finnish, Swedish and other languages of the region.

Essentials

Please write it down.	*Voitko kirjoittaa sen.*
Please show me (on the map).	*Näytä minulle (kartalta).*
I understand.	*Ymmärrän.*
I don't understand.	*En ymmärrä.*
Does anyone speak English?	*Puhuuko kukaan englantia?*
Where are you from?	*Mistä olet kotoisin?*
I am from...	*Olen...-sta*
Age?/How old are you?	*Ikä?/Kuinka vanha olet?*
I am...years old.	*Olen...-vuotias.*
Surname	*Sukunimi*
Given names	*Etunimet*
Date of birth	*Syntymäaika*
Place of birth	*Syntymäpaikka*

Map Words

Here is a list of common word endings that you will see on many maps. They are arranged alphabetically for the Finnish. In Swedish, the endings *en* or *et* are often but not always used.

Finnish	Swedish	English
-asema	station	station
-järvi, selkä	-träsk(en)	lake
-joki	-å(n)	river
-katu	-gata(n)	street
-koski	-fors	rapids
-kylä	-by(n)	village
-lahti	-vik(en)	bay
-lääni	-län	province
-maa	-land(et)	land, area
-museo	museum	museum
-mäki	-back(en)	hill
-niemi	-halvö(n), -näs(et), -udd(en)	cape
-ranta	-strand	shore
-saari, salo	-holm(en), -ö(n)	island
-salmi	-sund(et)	strait
-suo	-mosse(n)	swamp, marshland
-talo	-hus(et)	house
-taival, polku	-stig	trail, track
-tie	-väg(en)	road
-tori	-torg(et)	market or square
-tunturi	-fjäll(et)	fell
-vuori	-berg(et)	mountain

Nationality	*Kansallisuus*
Male/Female	*Mies/Nainen*
Passport	*Passi*

Help!	*Apua!*
Go away!	*Mene pois!*
Call a doctor/the police.	*Kutsu lääkäri/poliisi.*
I'm allergic to penicillin/ antibiotics	*Olen allerginen penisilliinille/ antibiooteille*

Entrance	*Sisään*
Exit	*Ulos*
Open/closed	*Avoinna/suljettu*
Prohibited	*Kielletty*
Toilets	*WC*

Greetings & Civilities

Hello.	*Hei.*
Goodbye.	*Näkemiin.*
Good morning.	*Huomenta.*
Good evening.	*Iltaa.*
Thank you (very much).	*Kiitos (paljon).*
You're welcome.	*Ole hyvä.*
Yes.	*Kyllä.*
No.	*Ei.*
Maybe.	*Ehkä.*
Excuse me.	*Anteeksi.*
I am sorry (forgive me).	*Olen pahoillani (anna anteeksi).*
How are you?	*Mitä kuuluu?*
I'm fine, thanks.	*Kiitos hyvää.*

Small Talk

What is your name?	*Mikä sinun nimi on?*
My name is...	*Minun nimeni on... (Mun nimi on...)*
I'm a tourist/ student.	*Olen turisti/ opiskelija.*
Are you married?	*Oletko naimisissa?*
Do you like...?	*Pidätkö...?*
I like it very much.	*Pidän siitä paljon.*
I don't like...	*En pidä...*
Just a minute.	*Pieni hetki.*
May I?	*Saanko?*

How do you say...(in Finnish)?	*Miten sanotaan... (suomeksi)?*

Getting Around

I want to go to...	*Haluan mennä...*
What time does...leave/ arrive?	*Mihin aikaan lähtee/saapuu...?*
Where does...leave?	*Mistä...lähtee?*
it	*se*
the bus/tram	*bussi/raitsikka*
the train	*juna*
the boat/ferry	*vene/lautta*
the airplane	*lentokone*
How long does the trip take?	*Kauanko matka kestää?*
The train is delayed/cancelled	*Juna on myöhässä/peruttu*
Do I need to change?	*Täytyykö minun vaihtaa?*
left-luggage locker	*säilytyslokero*
one-way (ticket)	*yhdensuuntainen (lippu)*
platform	*laituri*
return	*menopaluu (lippu)*
station	*asema*
ticket	*lippu*
ticket office	*lipputoimisto*
timetable	*aikataulu*
I'd like to hire a...	*Haluaisin vuokrata...*
bicycle	*polkupyörän*
car	*auton*
canoe	*kanootin*
rowing boat	*soutuveneen*
guide	*oppaan*

Directions

How do I get to...?	*Miten pääsen...*
Where is...?	*Missä on...?*
Is it near/far?	*Onko se lähellä/ kaukana?*
What...is this?	*Mikä...tämä on?*
street/road	*katu/tie*
street number	*kadunnumero*
suburb	*kaupunginosa*
town	*kaupunki*

(Go) straight ahead. *(Kulje) suoraan eteenpäin.*
(Turn) left. *(Käänny) vasempaan.*
(Turn) right. *(Käänny) oikeaan.*
at the traffic lights *liikennevaloissa*
at the next/second/ third corner *seuraavassa/toisessa /kolmannessa risteyksessä*

up/down *ylös/alas*
behind/opposite *takana/vastapäätän*
east/west *itä/länsi*
here/there *täällä/siellä*
north/south *pohjoinen/etelä*

Accommodation
I'm looking for... *Etsin...*
  the youth hostel *retkeilymajaa*
  the camping ground *leirintäaluetta*
  a hotel *hotellia*
  a guesthouse *matkustajakotia*
  the manager *johtajaa*
What is the address? *Mikä on osoite?*

Do you have a...? *Onko teillä...?*
  bed *sänkyä*
  cheap room *halpaa huonetta*
  single/double room *yhden/kahden hengen huonetta*

  for one night *yhdeksi yöksi*
  for two nights *kahdeksi yöksi*
How much is it per night/per person? *Paljonko on yöltä/ henkilöltä?*
Does that include breakfast/sheets? *Sisältyykö hintaan aamiainen/ lakanat?*
Can I see the room? *Voinko nähdä huoneen?*
Where is the toilet? *Missä on vessa?*
I am/we are leaving now. *Olen/olemme lähdössä nyt.*

Do you have...? *Onko teillä...?*
  a clean sheet *puhtaat lakanat*
  hot water *kuumaa vettä*
  a key *avain*

a shower *suihku*
sauna *sauna*

Around Town
Where is the/a...? *Missä on...?*
  airport *lentoasema*
  bank *pankki*
  bus station *linja-autoasema*
  town centre *keskusta*
  embassy *suurlähetystö*
  entrance/exit *sisäänkäynti/ uloskäynti*

  hospital *sairaala*
  market *tori*
  police *poliisi*
  post office *posti*
  public toilet *yleinen käymälä*
  restaurant *ravintola*
  telephone office *Tele-toimisto*
  tourist informa- tion office *matkailutoimisto*

I want to make a telephone call. *Haluaisin soittaa puhelimella.*
I'd like to change some... *Haluaisin vaihtaa...*
  money *rahaa*
  travellers' cheques *matkashekkejä*

Food
I am hungry/thirsty. *Minulla on nälkä/ jano.*

breakfast *aamiainen*
lunch *lounas*
buffet *seisova pöytä*
dinner *päivällinen*
grocery store *ruokakauppa*
market *tori*
restaurant *ravintola*
food stall *grilli*
café *kahvila*
I would like some... *Haluaisin...*
I don't eat... *En syö...*

Shopping
How much does it cost? *Mitä se maksaa?*
I would like to buy it. *Haluan ostaa sen.*

It's too expensive for me.	*Se on liian kallis minulle.*
Can I look at it?	*Voinko katsoa sitä?*
I'm just looking.	*Mä vain katselen.*
I'm looking for...	*Etsin...*
the chemist	*kemikaalikauppa*
clothing	*vaatteita*
souvenirs	*matkamuistoja*
Do you take travellers' cheques?	*Voiko maksaa matkashekeillä.*
Do you have another colour/size?	*Onko muuta väriä/kokoa?*
big/bigger	*iso/isompi*
small/smaller	*pieni/pienempi*
more/less	*enemmän/vähemmä*
cheap/cheaper	*halpa/halvempi*

Time & Dates

When?	*Milloin?*
today	*tänään*
tonight	*tänä iltana*
tomorrow	*huomenna*
day after tomorrow	*ylihuomenna*
yesterday	*eilen*
all day	*koko päivän*
every day	*joka päivä*
Monday	*maanantai*
Tuesday	*tiistai*
Wednesday	*keskiviikko*
Thursday	*torstai*
Friday	*perjantai*
Saturday	*lauantai*
Sunday	*sunnuntai*
January	*tammikuu*
February	*helmikuu*
March	*maaliskuu*
April	*huhtikuu*
May	*toukokuu*
June	*kesäkuu*
July	*heinäkuu*
August	*elokuu*
September	*syyskuu*
October	*lokakuu*
November	*marraskuu*
December	*joulukuu*

What time is it?	*Mitä kello on?*
It's...o'clock	*Kello on...*
in the morning	*aamulla*
in the evening	*illalla*
1.15	*vartin yli yksi*
1.30	*puoli kaksi*
1.45	*varttia vaille kaksi*

Numbers

1	*yksi*
2	*kaksi*
3	*kolme*
4	*neljä*
5	*viisi*
6	*kuusi*
7	*seitsemän*
8	*kahdeksan*
9	*yhdeksän*
10	*kymmenen*
11	*yksitoista*
12	*kaksitoista*
100	*sata*
1000	*tuhat*
one million	*miljoona*
half	*puoli*

Swedish

Swedish, one of the Scandinavian languages, belongs to the Indo-European group of languages that was separated from the original Germanic some 3000 years ago. *Finlandssvenska*, or 'Finland's Swedish', is very similar to the language spoken in Sweden, but local dialects have many Finnish words, so if you have learned Swedish in Sweden, you'll have some more learning to do!

Dialects Mainland Åland speakers use a language not dissimilar to the Swedish of mainland Sweden. Fishers and farmers in the Åland and Turunmaa archipelagos have their own dialect, and isolated communities along the Swedish Coast in Pohjanmaa have very different dialects, especially in Närpes. In Helsinki, an archaic, almost awkward form of Swedish is used for the purposes of the bilingual administration. Many Swedish speakers in Helsinki use an incomprehensible mix of Swedish and Finnish, often using Finnish terms to express things within Swedish frame language. *Kiva*, or 'nice' is probably the most common Finnish word among Swedish speakers. In villages and towns around Helsinki, other dialects are to be found.

Most Swedish-speakers will talk to you in *högsvenska*, or 'high Swedish'. The Närpes dialect considered the most difficult, being as distant from Swedish as many Norwegian dialects. Another difficulty is that there isn't a written form of the Närpes dialect as yet. Thus, *Kva häitär et?* (meaning 'what is your name?') is written *Vad heter du?*. *Hör yee?* ('How do you do?') is written *Hur mår du?*.

Essentials

Please write it down.	*Kan du skriva den.*
Please show me (on the map).	*Visa det åt mig (på kartan).*
I understand.	*Jag förstår.*
I don't understand.	*Jag förstår inte.*
Does anyone speak English?	*Talar någon engelska?*
Where are you from?	*Var är du ifrån?*
I am from...	*Jag är från...*
How old are you?	*Hur gammal är du?*
I am...years old.	*Jag är...år gammal.*
Help!	*Hjälp!*
Go away!	*Gå härifrån!*
Entrance	*In*
Exit	*Ut*
Open/closed	*Öppet/stängt*
Prohibited	*Förbjudet*
Toilets	*WC*

Greetings & Civilities

Hello.	*Hej.*
Goodbye.	*Hej då.*
Good morning.	*God morgon.*
Good evening.	*God kväll.*
Thank you (very much).	*Tack (så mycket).*

You're welcome.	*För all del.*
Yes.	*Ja.*
No.	*Nej.*
Maybe.	*Kanske.*
Excuse me.	*Ursäkta.*
I am sorry (forgive me).	*Förlåt mig.*
How are you?	*Hur mår du?*
I'm fine, thanks.	*Jag mår bra, tack.*

Small Talk

What is your name?	*Vad heter du?*
My name is...	*Jag heter...*
I'm a tourist/ student.	*Jag är en turist/ student.*
Are you married?	*Är du gift?*
Do you like...?	*Tycker du om...?*
I like it very much.	*Jag tycker om det mycket.*
I don't like...	*Jag tycker inte om...*
Just a minute.	*En stund.*
May I?	*Får jag?*
How do you say...(in Finnish Swedish)?	*Hur säger man... (på finlandssvenska)?*

Getting Around

I want to walk to...	*Jag vill gå till...*
I want to drive to...	*Jag vill åka till...*
What time does...leave?	*När går...?*
arrive?	*kommer?*
Where does...leave from?	*Var avgår...från?*
it	*den*
the bus/tram	*bussen/ spårvagnet*
the train	*tåget*
the boat/ferry	*båten/färjan*
the airplane	*flygplanet*
How long does the trip take?	*Hur länge tar resan?*
Do I need to change?	*Måste jag byta?*
left-luggage locker	*förvaringsboxar*
one-way (ticket)	*enkel (biljett)*
platform	*spår*
return	*retur (biljett)*
station	*station*

ticket	*biljett*
ticket office	*biljettbyrån*
timetable	*tidtabell*
I'd like to hire a...	*Jag ville hyra en...*
bicycle	*cykel*
car	*bil*
canoe	*kanot*
guide	*guide*

Directions

How do I get to...?	*Hur kan jag åka till...*
Where is...?	*Var är...?*
Is it near/far?	*Är det nära/långt bort.*
What...is this?	*Vilken...är detta?*
street/road	*gata/väg*
street number	*gatunummer*
suburb	*stadsdel*
town	*stad*
(Go) straight ahead.	*(Gå) rakt fram.*
(Turn) left.	*(Vänd) till vänster.*
(Turn) right.	*(Vänd) till höger.*
at the traffic lights	*vid trafikljus*
at the next/second/ third corner	*vid nästa/andra/tredje*
up/down	*upp/ned*
behind/opposite	*bakom/mitt emot*
east/west	*öst/väst*
here/there	*här/där*
north/south	*norr/syd*
northern/southern	*norra/södra*

Accommodation

I'm looking for...	*Jag letar efter...*
the youth hostel	*vandrarhemmet*
the camping ground	*campingplatsen*
a hotel	*ett hotell*
a guesthouse	*ett resandehem/ gästhem*
the manager	*direktör*
What is the address?	*Vad är adresset?*
Do you have a...available?	*Finns det...?*
bed	*en säng*

cheap room	*ett billigt rum*
single room	*ett rum for en*
double room	*ett rum for två*
for one night/two nights	*för en natt/två nätter*
How much is it per night/per person?	*Vad kostar det per natt/per person*
Does that include breakfast/sheets?	*Ingår priset frukost/lakan?*
Can I see the room?	*Får jag se ett rum?*
It is very dirty/ expensive.	*Det är mycket orent/dyrt.*
Where is the toilet?	*Var är toaletten?*
I am/we are leaving now.	*Jag är/vi är på väg nu.*
Do you have...?	*Har ni...?*
hot water	*varmt vatten*
a key	*nyckeln*
a shower	*dusch*
sauna	*bastu*

Around Town

Where is the...?	*Var finns...?*
town centre	*centrum*
entrance/exit	*ingång/utgång*
hospital	*sjukhuset*
market	*torget*
police	*polis*
post office	*postbyrån*
public toilet	*toaletten*
restaurant	*restaurang*
telephone office	*Tele-byrån*
I want to make a telephone call.	*Jag ville använda telefon.*
I'd like to change some...	*Jag ville växla lite...*
money/travellers' cheques	*pengar/resande- sheckar*

Food

I am hungry/thirsty.	*Jag är hungrig/törstig.*
breakfast	*frukost*
lunch	*lunch*
buffet	*smörgårsbord*
dinner	*middag*

grocery store	*butik*
market	*torg*
restaurant	*restaurang*
food stall	*grill* or *gatukök*
café	*kaffestuga*
I would like some...	*Jag ville gärna ha lite...*
I don't eat...	*Jag äter inte...*
beef	*biff*
beer	*öl*
bread	*bröd*
bread roll	*sämla*
cabbage	*kål*
carrot	*morot*
cheese	*ost*
chicken	*kyckling*
coffee	*kaffe*
drinking water	*drycksvatten*
egg	*ägg*
fish	*fisk*
herring	*sill*
ham	*skinka*
meat	*kött*
milk	*mjölk*
minced meat	*köttfärsk*
mushroom	*svamp*
oats	*havre*
omelette	*omelett*
open sandwich	*smörgås*
onion	*lök*
pea	*ärt*
pepper	*peppar*
pie	*paj*
pork	*svinkött*
porridge	*gröt*
potato	*potatis*
reindeer (meat)	*ren (kött)*
rice	*ris*
rye	*råg*
salad	*salad*
salmon	*lax*
salt	*salt*
sauce	*sås*
sausage	*korv*
soup	*soppa*
steak	*biff*
stew	*låda*
sugar	*socker*
tea	*te*

vegetable	*grönsak*
vegetarian	*vegetarisk*
water	*vatten*

Shopping

How much does it cost?	*Vad kostar det?*
I would like to buy it.	*Jag ville gärna köpa den.*
It's too expensive for me.	*Den är för dyr för mig.*
Can I look at it?	*Får jag se den?*
I'm just looking.	*Jag bara tittar.*
Do you take travellers' cheques?	*Kan jag betala med resecheckar?*
big/bigger	*stor/större*
small/smaller	*liten/mindre*
more/less	*mer/färre*
cheap/cheaper	*billig/billigare*

Time & Dates

When?	*När?*
today	*idag*
tonight	*på kvällen*
tomorrow	*i morgon*
day after tomorrow	*övermorgon*
yesterday	*igår*
all day/every day	*hela dagen/varje dag*

Monday	*måndag*
Tuesday	*tisdag*
Wednesday	*onsdag*
Thursday	*torsdag*
Friday	*fridag*
Saturday	*lördag*
Sunday	*söndag*

What time is it?	*Vad är klockan?*
It's...o'clock.	*Klockan är...*
in the morning	*morgon bitti*
this morning	*i morse*
in the evening	*på kvällen*
1.15	*kvart över ett*
1.30	*halv två*
1.45	*kvart i två*

Numbers

1	ett or en	14	fjorton
2	två	15	femton
3	tre	16	sexton
4	fyra	17	sjutton
5	fem	18	aderton
6	sex	19	nitton
7	sju	20	tjugo
8	åtta	21	tjugoen
9	nio	30	trettio
10	tio	100	hundra
11	elva	1000	tusen
12	tolv	one million	miljon
13	tretton	half	halv

Facts for the Visitor

VISAS & EMBASSIES

Temporary residency visas *(oleskelulupa)* are generally required only for stays of more than three months in Finland. In theory, Norwegians, Icelanders, and citizens of the European Union can come and go without a passport (an identity card is required), but in practice it is still advisable for EU citizens to carry a passport. Most Western nationals, including Americans, Australians, Canadians and New Zealanders, don't need a tourist visa for stays of less than three months. This also applies to most South Americans, with the exceptions coming from Guyana, Surinam, Peru and Venezuela. A visa is required of Indians, most Eastern Europeans, some Africans (including Nigerians) and some Asians (including Chinese and Hong Kong residents). Malaysians and Singaporeans don't need one.

Finnish Embassies

Visas and information can be obtained at Finnish diplomatic missions, including:

Australia
  10 Darwin Ave, Yarralumla, Canberra, ACT 2600 (☎ 06-273 3800)
Austria
  Gonzagagasse 16, 1010 Wien (☎ 1-531 590)
Belgium
  rue de Trèves 100, 1040 Brussels (☎ 02-287 8411)
Canada
  55 Metcalfe St, Suite 850, Ottawa, Ontario K1P 6L5 (☎ 613-236 2389)
  1188 West Georgia St, Suite 1100, Vancouver BC V6E 4A2 (☎ 604-688 4483)
China
  Tayuan Diplomatic Office Building 1-10-1, Liangmahe nanlu 14, Beijing 100600 (☎ 01-532 1806)
Denmark
  Sankt Annas Plads 24, 1250 Copenhagen K (☎ 3313 4214)
Estonia
  Liivalaia 12, EE0001, Tallinn (☎ 311 444)
France
  2 rue Fabert, 75007 Paris (☎ 01-4705 3545)

Germany
  Friesdorferstrasse 1, 5300 Bonn (☎ 0228-382 980)
India
  Nyaya Marg 5, Chanakyapuri, New Delhi 110021 (☎ 011-611 5258)
Indonesia
  Bina Mulia Building, Jalan H R Rasuna Said Kav 10, Jakarta 12950 (☎ 021-520 7408)
Ireland
  Russell House, St Stephen's Green, Dublin 2 (☎ 01-478 1344)
Israel
  Beth Eliahu, 8th floor, 2 Rehov Ibn Gvirol 64077 Tel Aviv (☎ 03-695 0528)
Italy
  via Lisbona 4, 00198 Rome (☎ 06-854 8329)
Japan
  3-5-39 Minami-Azabu, Minato-ku, Tokyo 106 (☎ 03-3442 2231)
Kenya
  International House, 2nd floor, Mama Ngina St, Nairobi ☎ 02-334 777)
Malaysia
  15th floor, Plaza MBF, Jalan Ampang, 50450 Kuala Lumpur (☎ 03-261 1088)
Mexico
  Monte Pelvoux 111, piso 4, Lomas de Chapultepec, Delegacion Miguel Hidalgo, 11000 Mexico DF (☎ 05-540 6036)
Namibia
  Sunlam Centre, 5th floor, 154 Independence Avenue, Windhoek (☎ 61-221 355)
Netherlands
  Groot Hertoginnelaan 16, 2517 KH The Hague (☎ 070-346 9754)
New Zealand
  Consulate General, Unisys House, 44-52 The Terrace, Wellington (☎ 04-499 4599)
  Consulate, 10 Heather St, Parnell, Auckland (☎ 09-309 2969)
Norway
  Thomas Heftyes gate 1, 0244 Oslo 2 (☎ 2-243 0400)
Philippines
  BPI Building, 14th floor, Ayala Ave, corner Paseo de Roxas, Makati, Metro Manila (☎ 02-816 2105)
Russia
  Polstovo Finlandii, Kropotkinskij Pereulok 15/17, 119034 Moskva G-34 (☎ 095-246 4027)
Singapore
  101 Thomson Rd 21-03, United Square, Singapore 1130 (☎ 254 4042)

South Africa
  628 Leyds St, Muckleheuk Ext 2, Pretoria 0002
  (☎ 12-343 0275 or 12-343 0901)
Sweden
  Jacobsgatan 6, 6tr, 11152 Stockholm (☎ 08-676 6700)
Thailand
  16th floor, Amarin Plaza, 500 Ploen Chit Rd, Bangkok 10330 (☎ 02-256 9306)
UK
  38 Chesham Place, London SW1X 8HW, (☎ 0171-838 6200)
USA
  3301 Massachusetts Ave NW, Washington DC 20008 (☎ 202-298 5800)
  1900 Ave of the Stars, Suite 1025, Los Angeles, CA 90067 (☎ 213-203 9903)
  866 UN Plaza, Suite 250, New York, NY 10017, (☎ 212-750 4400)

Foreign Embassies in Finland

The following is a full list of foreign government representatives in Helsinki. Use the Helsinki area telephone code (09 from October 1996) if calling from elsewhere.

Argentina
  Bulevardi 5 A (☎ 605 249)
Austria
  Keskuskatu 1 A (☎ 171 322)
Belgium
  Kalliolinnantie 5 (☎ 170 412)
Brazil
  Itäinen Puistotie 4 (☎ 177 922)
Bulgaria
  Kuusisaarentie 2 B (☎ 458 4055)
Canada
  Pohjoisesplanadi 25B (☎ 171 141)
China
  Vanha kelkkamäki 11 (☎ 684 8976)
Colombia
  Ratakatu 1 (☎ 680 2799)
Czech Republic
  Armfeltintie 14 (☎ 171 051)
Denmark
  Keskuskatu 1 (☎ 171 511)
Egypt
  Munkkiniemenpuistotie 25 (☎ 458 2299)
Estonia
  Fabianinkatu 13A (☎ 622 0280)
France
  Itäinen Puistotie 13 (☎ 171 521)
Germany
  Krogiuksentie 4 (☎ 458 2355)
Greece
  Maneesikatu 2 (☎ 278 1100)

Hungary
  Kuusisaarenkuja 6 (☎ 484 144)
India
  Satamakatu 2A 8 (☎ 608 927)
Indonesia
  Kuusisaarentie 3 (☎ 458 2101)
Iran
  Bertel-Jungin tie 4 (☎ 684 7133)
Iraq
  Lars Sonckin tie 2 (☎ 684 9177)
Ireland
  Erottajankatu 7 A (☎ 646 006)
Israel
  Vironkatu 5A (☎ 135 6177)
Italy
  Itäinen Puistotie 4 (☎ 175 144)
Japan
  Eteläranta 8 (☎ 633 011)
Korea
  Annankatu 32 A (☎ 694 0966)
Latvia
  Bulevardi 5A (☎ 605 640)
Lithuania
  Rauhankatu 13 A (☎ 608 210)
Mexico
  Simonkatu 12 A (☎ 694 9400)
Netherlands
  Raatimiehenkatu 2A 7 (☎ 661 737)
North Korea
  Kulosaaren puistotie 32 (☎ 684 8195)
Norway
  Rehbinderintie 17 (☎ 171 234)
Poland
  Armas Lindgrenin tie 21 (☎ 684 8077)
Portugal
  Itäinen Puistotie 11B (☎ 171 717)
Romania
  Stenbäckinkatu 24 (☎ 241 3624)
Russian Federation
  Vuorimiehenkatu 6 (☎ 661 876)
South Africa
  Rahapajankatu 1A 5 (☎ 658 288)
Spain
  Kalliolinnantie 6 (☎ 170 505)
Sweden
  Pohjoisesplanadi 7 (☎ 651 255)
Switzerland
  Uudenmaankatu 16A (☎ 649 422)
Turkey
  Puistokatu 1 B (☎ 655 755)
Venezuela
  Mannerheimintie 14A (☎ 641 522)
UK
  Itäinen Puistotie 17 (☎ 661 293)
Ukraine
  Vähäniityntie 9 (☎ 228 9000)
USA
  Itäinen Puistotie 14A (☎ 171 931)

CUSTOMS

If you are entering Finland from another EU country, there are restrictions on the importation of duty-free cigarettes (200), coffee (500 grams), tea (100 grams) and alcohol. Two litres of wine, one litre of strong alcohol and 15 litres of beer may be imported duty free. If you're coming from countries outside the EU, the allowances are much higher but goods must be for personal use. There could be changes to these restrictions in the near future.

MONEY

Currency

The Finnish unit of currency is the *markka* (MAHRK-kah, plural markkaa, often abbreviated as mk), which is equal to 100 *penniä*. Paper currency comes in denominations of 20, 50, 100, 500 and 1000 markkaa. Coins include 10 and 50 penniä pieces and 1, 5 and 10 mk coins. All banknotes issued before 1980 (and 1, 5 and 20 penniä coins), are now void, and can be changed only at Suomen Pankki (Finland's Bank) offices until 31 December 2003. Five mk is often called *vitonen*, 10 mk *kymppi* and 100 mk *satanen*.

The Swedish *krona* (including coins) is accepted on Åland and in western Lapland. The Norwegian krona can be used near the Norwegian border in northern Lapland. For Trans-Siberian travellers, the Russian rouble is slowly gaining acceptability at currency exchange centres.

Exchange Rates

The following table shows exchange rates:

A$1	=	3.19 mk
C$1	=	3.16 mk
DM1	=	3.01 mk
Ekr	=	5.52 mk
FF	=	0.87 mk
Nkr	=	0.68 mk
NZ$1	=	2.82 mk
Skr	=	0.66 mk
UK£1	=	6.66 mk
US$1	=	4.33 mk
¥100	=	4.25 mk

Costs

Finland was declared the world's most expensive country in 1990, right before it plunged into a deep recession. In 1993, the depth of the recession, the markka was very weak and Finland was a cheap country to visit. Since then the markka has appreciated and the country has become more costly again, although the inflation rate is practically zero and Finland will probably remain a relatively inexpensive country.

High prices that remain are the result of high labour and transport costs, agricultural policies and cartels in many industries. It is generally possible to stay overnight in a comfortable hotel for less than 200 mk per person, although on average a hotel room in Finland costs 326 mk according to a recent study. An HI-discounted hostel bed costs, on average, 50 mk. A good set lunch (with salad, a drink and coffee) goes for 30 to 40 mk, and a local bus trip costs 9 mk. A train trip of 100 km costs 46 mk, and the same trip by bus costs 60 mk. A discounted return flight within Finland costs 445 to 975 mk.

Budget travellers should be able to get by on 120 mk per day if they watch their expenses. This estimate includes youth hostel accommodation, self-catering and/or lunch specials. To save on drinks, use tap water for drinking; bottled drinks are expensive and alcohol is very expensive. The price tags on some food items include a 'per kg' price, which enables easy price comparisons. Free accommodation is available along most trekking routes, and hitchhiking is easy, especially in summer, when there is nearly 24 hours of daylight each day.

Top 10 Freebies To really keep costs down, consider taking advantage of the free things in Finland. Here are 10 of them:

1. Accommodation in wilderness huts, shelters and at camp sites along trekking routes all over Finland. Firewood also complimentary.
2. Free fishing for anyone under 18 years of age.
3. Abandoned vegetables at many markets in Helsinki after 2 pm.

4. English books and magazines in most public libraries.
5. Excellent town maps of most towns and villages.
6. Use of all roads, bridges, tunnels and *lossi* ferries.
7. Route ferries to/between coastal islands, including Åland, for island-hopping.
8. Church concerts, in most cases.
9. Forest berries and mushrooms (but know what you pick!)
10. Easy hitchhiking across the country.

Top 10 Bargains Here is a selection of Finland's best bargains:

1. Ferries to/from Sweden (transport only), including free transport of bicycles.
2. The Suomenlinna ferry and the 3T tram in Helsinki's HKL transport system.
3. Student restaurants/cafés in all university towns.
4. Sauna and swimming at public indoor pools.
5. Special discount return flight from Helsinki to Ivalo in north Lapland.
6. Cheap grillis throughout Finland.
7. Camp sites on Åland.
8. Many youth hostels around Finland.
9. Student discount tickets for museums and concerts in large towns.
10. Buffet breakfasts in some hotels and hostels.

Tipping

Tipping is generally not necessary in Finland. You will pay service charges in restaurants as percentages; these are generally included in the quoted menu price. You may ask the taxi driver to keep the change (*pidä loput*). One of the strange habits in Finland is giving a few coins to the 'gorilla' who has done his best to bar your entry to a restaurant and left you freezing to death outside. Even though this may make you feel unwelcome, afterwards you are so happy to finally warm up after some two hours' standing in -20°C, that you tip the door attendant, perhaps in the hope of being allowed in quicker next time.

Bargaining

All prices in shops are fixed and clearly displayed. There is no bargaining in supermarkets and similar establishments. When buying electrical appliances, trekking equipment or used bicycles and similar products in small specialist shops, bargaining is useful and recommended. Many shops can easily drop 10% to 20% off the normal price. For best results, bargaining should be done in a subtle and friendly manner.

Consumer Taxes

Finnish sales tax is currently 22% (in some cases 12% or 6%) and is included in marked prices. If you're a permanent resident outside the EU and Norway it is possible to receive a refund on part of this tax by making purchases in designated shops, which provide you with a cheque for a refund of between 12% and 16% if your purchases are over 100 mk. You can cash the cheque by presenting it and the merchandise at your point of departure (airport transit halls, aboard major ferries, overland border crossings).

WHEN TO GO

You should visit Finland in summer. Any time from May to September is OK. Summer is the time of the midnight sun, warm weather and the freshness of nature, and the only time when many youth hostels, camping grounds, museums and attractions are open. It's also when steamboats ply Finnish lakes.

The dark winter is something quite different. Don't plan to cross Siberia in a heated Russian railway carriage, then appear at Helsinki railway station on a dark weekend afternoon in January when everyone seems to be drunk, depressed or ready to kill you.

Nevertheless, winter offers extensive cross-country skiing treks in national parks, and every town has illuminated skiing tracks. Winter is also good for meeting up with local people, who can be very friendly and talkative once you get out of the cold. Cultural life is active in winter. In fact, Helsinki is quieter in summer, especially in July when many offices are closed. Winter is the busiest time for theatre, films and exhibitions. The following list gives an idea of what to expect each month in Finland:

January – Cold, dark and depressing everywhere. The *kaamos* in Lapland may be of interest if you don't want to see the sun at all (the sun never rises above the horizon at this time). There is plenty of snow for skiing but perhaps not enough daylight.

February – Still cold and dark all over Finland. Skiing is increasingly comfortable. Beware of ski holiday rush.

March – Towards the end of March, the days become longer than the nights. In the south, this is the spring thaw, but there is still snow and ice everywhere. A good month for winter sports but check the local ski holidays. The first migratory birds arrive.

April – Snow disappears in most of south Finland. Many migratory birds return in April; forests are full of birdsong. In Lapland, this is the best skiing season: long days and warm sunshine, yet plenty of snow everywhere. Beware of the Easter holiday rush (and inflated prices).

May – Trees acquire foliage, and all migratory birds return by the end of May. Many lakes still have ice in early May, but snow can only be found in Lapland. The ground is still wet everywhere. It is too early for long walks in most of Finland. Some attractions open in May for the summer season.

June – This month sees the longest hours of daylight. The ground dries, snow melts in Lapland, birds sing everywhere, vegetation grows rapidly and flowers bloom. Many youth hostels and open-air museums open on 1 June. School holidays start, resulting in fewer buses on some routes.

July – Another light month, with no darkness at all in north Finland. The growing vegetation has reached its zenith and Finland is at its greenest. Lapland experiences its short but hectic summer and the number of mosquitoes reaches an unpleasant level. All tourist attractions around the country are open in July, the high season. Summer festivals abound. Hotels have summer discounts.

August – The nights get shorter, vegetation continues to grow, some trees turn yellow towards the end of the month, and birds start to move about. Many youth hostels and open-air museums close on 15 or 31 August. Schools resume by mid-August, with many changes occurring in bus timetables. This is the best month for trekking in Lapland, and the most vibrant month in Helsinki.

September – Day and night are the same length. Temperatures may reach freezing point, but can still be pleasant in the south. Rain is not uncommon; in fact the ground is generally wet. Most trees turn yellow and start dropping leaves. Birds start their migration south. You can trek in Lapland but be prepared for sudden snowfall. As isolated cases, some museums stay open until the winter.

October – You can still feel hints of the past summer in south Finland, but temperatures are crisper and snow is not uncommon in north Finland. All migratory birds have left, trees no longer have leaves, it rains often and days become shorter. Lapland usually gets permanent snow cover, which makes walking nearly impossible.

November – The least popular of all months. It is dark and cold. The wet snow seldom stays, so everything is grey, muddy and depressing. Skiing season starts in the north.

December – The darkest month may see heavy snowfall all over Finland, which makes the landscape more attractive. Temperatures range from freezing down to -30°C. Christmas season is increasingly busy in ski resorts, but some hotels and hostels remain closed during Christmas holidays. Make sure you have a place to stay during Christmas, and stock some food, as almost everything is closed.

WHAT TO BRING

You can buy almost anything you need in Finland. Taking a sleeping sheet will save a lot of money at youth hostels and cottages. Bring a sleeping bag for trekking and camping. You won't need one if you stay indoors, as all houses have heating and blankets to keep you warm. Finnish houses in winter must be the warmest in Europe!

Finns are very casual about clothing, although some of the best restaurants require a tie for men. Weather conditions in Finland are less extreme than in Norway but, as the weather can change quickly, it's best to have layers of clothing, such as cotton T-shirts, shirts and warm pullovers. A windproof jacket is a must even in summer.

If you travel in winter, you'll need all of the above plus fur-lined boots and mittens, a woollen cap, a waterproof jacket and either an overcoat, quilted jacket, thermal suit or parka.

TOURIST OFFICES
Local Tourist Offices

Local tourist information offices are very helpful and useful. With few exceptions, all cities, towns and municipal centres have a tourist office (sometimes several). They are open during office hours; in summer also in the evenings and on weekends. Surprisingly, the Finnish Tourist Board is not at all active at the grass-roots level, whereas local offices will provide you with all imaginable information, from local history and attractions to the seating capacity of petrol station cafés and activities in nearby farmhouses, mostly in Finnish or Swedish but increasingly in English.

Visitors are generally greeted with enthusiasm and staff will go out of their way to help meet your needs. If you happen to be travelling at either end of the high season (when there are more people employed and not so many tourists) you may be subject to quite overwhelming offers of help from the bored officer.

Finnish Tourist Offices Abroad

The Finnish Tourist Board has offices in the following countries:

Australia
    Level 14, 33 Berry Street, North Sydney NSW 2060 (☎ 02-959 1982, fax 959 1996)
Denmark
    Vester Farimagsgade 3, 1606 Copenhagen V (☎ 3313 1362, fax 3332 0501)
Estonia
    Pikk 71, 0001 Tallinn (☎ 631 3990, fax 631 4070)
France
    13 rue Auber, 75009 Paris (☎ 01-4266 4013, fax 01-4742 8722)
Germany
    Darmstädter Landstrasse 180, 60598 Frankfurt (☎ 069-961 2360, fax 069-686 860)
Italy
    Via Larga 2, 20122 Milano (☎ 02-8646 4914, fax 02-7202 2590)
Japan
    Imperial Hotel Room 505, 1-1-1 Uchisaiwaicho, Chiyoda-ku, Tokyo 100 (☎ 03-3501 5207, fax 03-3580 9205)
Netherlands
    Johannes Vermeerplein 5, 1071 DV Amsterdam, (☎ 020-671 1121, fax 020-675 0359)
New Zealand
    Eurolynx Tours Ltd, 3rd floor, 20 Fort Street, Auckland (☎ 379 9716, fax 379 8874)
Norway
    Lille Grensen 7, 0159 Oslo 1 (☎ 2241 1070, fax 2233 4082)
Spain
    Fernando el Santo, 27-5 A, 28010 Madrid (☎ 01-319 7440, fax 01-319 6948)
Sweden
    Kungsgatan 4 a 6 tr, 11143 Stockholm (☎ 08-207 570, fax 08-249 594)

Switzerland
    Schweizergasse 6, 8001 Zürich (☎ 01-211 1340, fax 01-211 1119)
UK
    30-35 Pall Mall, London SW1Y 5LP (☎ 0171-839 4048, fax 0171-321 0696)
USA
    655 Third Ave, New York, NY 10017 (☎ 0212-370 5540, fax 0212-983 5260)

USEFUL ORGANISATIONS

The following organisations may assist you with information and support:

AIDS Information & Support Centre – Linnankatu 2B, 00160 Helsinki (☎ 665 081)
Autoliitto – the national motoring organisation, Hämeentie 105A, 00550 Helsinki (☎ 774 761)
Finnish British Society – friendship society for Britons and Finns, Puistokatu 16A, 00140 Helsinki (☎ 639 625)
League of Finnish-American Societies – friendly contacts between Americans and Finns, Mechelininkatu 10A, 00100 Helsinki (☎ 440 711)
League of Finnish-Australian Societies – friendly contacts between Aussies and Finns, Mariankatu 8, 00170 Helsinki (☎ 631 549)
SETA (Seksuaalinen tasavertaisuus) – The organisation for gay and lesbian equality, Oikokatu 3, 00170 Helsinki (☎ 135 8302)
Suomi-seura – society for people with Finnish roots. Mariankatu 8, 00170 Helsinki (☎ 174 255)
Rullaten ry – disabled travellers organisation which specialises in advice on 'friendly' hotels. A booklet is available. Malminkatu 38, 00100 Helsinki (☎ 694 1155)
Ruohonjuuri – environmental and alternative movements (development centre and book café) Mannerheimintie 13, 00100 Helsinki (☎ 406 927)
Unioni – the national feminist organisation, Bulevardi 11A, 00120 Helsinki (☎ 643 158)

Libraries

Public libraries in Finland are an excellent source for literature in English, although you will have to read inside the library. There are almost twice as many libraries (1025 in all) as hotels in Finland and they also stock plenty of maps.

BUSINESS HOURS

Banks are open Monday to Friday from 9.15 am to 4.15 pm; general office hours are

Monday to Friday from 9 am to 5 pm. People choose their own lunch time and in many companies coffee and lunch breaks can amount to quite a long time, so reaching people at their offices may be a bit of a problem.

Shop hours are somewhat variable, but generally you can visit department stores and supermarkets Monday to Friday from 9 am to 8 pm and on Saturday from 9 am to 6 pm. Specialised shops generally stay open until 5 pm Monday to Friday and until 1 or 2 pm on Saturdays.

Few places are open at night, except some petrol stations. Sunday is still generally considered inappropriate for retail business but this may change soon.

The good news is that many businesses and places of interest officially closed during the off-season (usually from September to May) will be accessible if you try hard enough. Groups especially are always catered to. Contact the tourist (or municipality) office during office hours, explain your interest and enquire about the possibility of getting the door open. Gener-

ally there's a fee on top of the regular price and often the 'compulsory' guide will cost extra. Even some youth hostels have been helpful in putting up travellers in the off-season. You can visit a church whenever someone enters it to clean up or to practise the organ (this is unofficial, so ask politely and don't expect to get permission automatically). You can also enter a church during services. Generally, churches open on Sunday morning after 9 am, and close soon after the service, around 11.30 am. Before a church concert is another time when historic churches can be seen.

The bad news is that any opening hours included in this book, or printed on any pamphlet, may be wrong. Opening hours for the summer season are determined every year as if this had never been done before, and quick changes are always possible. If the day has been quiet, a place can suddenly close; conversely doors may stay open if there are large crowds. Good luck.

FESTIVALS & PUBLIC HOLIDAYS

The term 'festival' in Finland commonly refers to an annual cultural event that concentrates on a certain theme, such as opera in Savonlinna, chamber music in Kuhmo or contemporary music in Viitasaari. These events are arranged by the Finland Festivals

---

Festivals of Finland

Following are the 57 annual festivals held throughout Finland. For further information contact: Finland Festivals, Mannerheimintie 40 B 49, 00100 Helsinki (☎ 445 686, fax 445 117).

January
Työväen näyttämöpäivät – Mikkeli, political theatre.
March
Tampereen elokuvajuhlat – Tampere, short films.
Kemin sarjakuvapäivät – Kemi, cartoons.
April
Oulun Musiikkijuhlat – Oulu, chamber music.
Hetan Musiikkipäivät – Enontekiö, chamber music.
April Jazz Espoo – Espoo, jazz.
May
Kainuun Jazzkevät – Kajaani, jazz.
June
Naantali Music Festival – Naantali, chamber music.
Riihimäen kesäkonsertit – Riihimäki, chamber music.
Jyväskylän Kesä – Jyväskylä, lectures, music, visual arts.
Tampereen Sävel – Tampere, choral music.
Midnight Sun Film Festival – Sodankylä, films.

Ilmajoen Musiikkijuhlat – Ilmajoki, opera.
Joensuu Festival – Joensuu, music, Studia Generalia lectures.
Korsholm Music Festival – Vaasa, Korsholm, chamber music.
Avantiln suvisoitto – Porvoo, chamber music.
Provinssirock – Seinäjoki, rock music.
Kalenat – Lappeenranta, folk music, dance.
Nummirock – Kauhajoki, rock music.
Jutajaiset – Rovaniemi, music, dance, Lapp traditions.
International Kalottjazz & Blues Festival – Tornio, Haparanda, jazz, blues.
Puistoblues – Järvenpää, blues, jazz.
Mikkeli Music Festival – Mikkeli, classical music.
Sata-Häme Soi – Ikaalinen, accordion music.
Kuopio Tanssii ja Soi – Kuopio, modern dance, ballet.
July
Imatra Big Band Festival – Imatra, big band music.
Baltic Jazz – Dalsbruk, jazz music.

organisation, which at last count controlled 57 events throughout the country. (See the boxed information on Festivals of Finland.) Most events take place in summer. In July alone, there are 24 cultural festivals throughout Finland!

Refer to each town section for details of individual festivals. A cultural festival is no doubt the best time to visit a particular place.

The following days are either public holidays or other important events:

January

New Year's Day – Public holiday.

Loppiainen – 'The end of Christmas' on 6 January is a public holiday.

February

Runeberg Day – On 5 February, people eat 'Runeberg cakes', available in all shops, to commemorate the national poet.

Penkinpainajaiset – The last day of school for secondary school students, who dress in funny clothes, stand in the back of decorated trucks and drive around town, throwing candies to children. This event, known as *penkkarit*, generally takes place on the third Thursday in February.

Laskiainen – Seven weeks before Easter, this two-day event (Sunday and the next Tuesday) is devoted to downhill skiing and other winter sports in the countryside and in schools. People eat *laskiaispulla*, a wheat bun with whipped cream and hot milk.

April

Pääsiäinen – Easter is celebrated over several days. Thursday evening has church concerts, Good Friday is a public holiday, and on Sunday people go to church or paint eggs and eat *mämmi* with sugar and milk. Mämmi is made of rye and malt; it looks and tastes weird. The following Monday is a public holiday.

May

Vappu – May Day, traditionally a festival of students and workers, also marks the beginning of summer, and is celebrated with plenty of alcohol and merrymaking. The 'official' celebration starts on 30 April at 6 pm, especially in Helsinki, where people gather in Esplanade Park, around the 'Manta' statue, which receives a white 'student cap'. On 1 May everyone comes out onto the streets. People drink *sima* mead and eat *tippaleipä* cookies.

Äitienpäivä – Mothers' Day sees buffet lunch settings in all restaurants, where families go to eat so that mothers don't have to prepare food at home.

Naisten kymppi – This extremely popular jogging event, held in Helsinki towards the end of May,

---

Tangomarkkinat – Seinäjoki, tango music.

Ruisrock – Turku, rock music.

Kajaanin Runoviikko Sana ja Sävel – Kajaani, poetry, theatre.

Sysmän suvisoitto – Around Lake Päijänne, classical and popular music.

Kangasniemen musiikkiviikot – Kangasniemi, classical songs.

Savonlinna Opera Festival – Savonlinna, opera.

Musiikin Aika (Time of Music) – Viitasaari, modern music, fringe music.

Kuhmon Kamarimusiikki – Kuhmo, chamber music.

Pori Jazz Festival – Pori, jazz.

Kaustinen Folk Music Festival – Kaustinen, folk music, theatre.

Lieksan Vaskiviikko – Lieksa, brass music.

Bomban juhlaviikot – Nurmes, Finno-Ugrian theatre, exhibitions.

Rääkkylä Folk Music Festival Kihaus – Rääkkylä, folk music.

Joutsa Folk Festival – Joutsa, traditional Finnish summer festival.

Kuusamo Natura – Kuusamo, events relating to nature and clowns.

Kymenlaakson kansankulttuuri ja pelimannipäivät – Miehikkälä, folk music, traditions.

Harrastajateatterikesä – Seinäjoki, amateur theatre.

Työväen Musiikkitapahtuma – Valkeakoski, workers' music, political songs.

August

Crusell-viikko – Uusikaupunki, chamber music, especially clarinet.

Lahden urkuviikko – Lahti, organ music.

Spelit – Teuva, folk music, dances.

Turku Music Festival – Turku, classical music.

Pentinkulman päivät – Urjala, Finnish literature.

Hämeen Linna Lastentapahtuma – Hämeenlinna, children's theatre.

Tampereen Teatterikesä – Tampere, theatre.

Helsingin Juhlaviikot – Helsinki, music, theatre, fringe art.

October

Pispalan Sottiisi – Tampere, folk dancing.

Oulaisten Musiikkiviikot – Oulainen, music.

November

Tampere Jazz Happening – Tampere, jazz.

Oulun lastenelokuvien festivaali – Oulu, children's films. ■

attracts thousands of women, who form teams to run 10 km. There are similar events in other towns too.

June

Juhannus – Midsummer is the most important annual event for Finns. People leave cities and towns for summer cottages to celebrate the longest day of the year. It is also the day of the Finnish flag, as well as the day of John the Baptist. Bonfires are lit on the waterfront and people swim and row boats. Much alcohol is consumed (to the point that, every Midsummer, several people drown). Juhannus is celebrated on the Saturday between 20 and 26 June, but the most important time is the Friday night.

Praasniekka – These Orthodox celebrations are day-long religious and folk festivals held in North Karelia and in other eastern provinces between May and September, most notably at the end of June.

July

Kalas – An old-fashioned feast held in Stundars, in the municipality of Korsholm.

Sleepyhead Day – On 27 July the laziest person in the towns of Naantali and Hanko is thrown into the sea.

August

Venetian Nights – The end of the summer cottage season is celebrated on the west coast at the end of August. There are bonfires, fireworks, concerts and exhibitions.

Taiteiden yö – This night of art is held in Helsinki and other towns by the end of August. It features a whole series of street performances, fringe art, open book stores and concerts.

November

All Soul's Day – The first Saturday of November sees people visit the graves of deceased friends and relatives.

December

Itsenäisyyspäivä – Finland celebrates independence on 6 December, which is typically a cold, dark day. There are illuminated windows, students march in procession carrying burning torches, and in some towns there are fireworks. Churches have concerts and ordinary people watch TV to see what kind of clothes the rich and famous wear on the visit to the President's Castle. This is a public holiday.

Pikkujoulu – To celebrate 'Little Christmas', companies and schools organise private parties. In the month of December, much alcohol is consumed and much questionable conduct occurs. Foreign visitors are often welcomed, to experience something wild.

Joulu – Christmas is a public holiday. All traffic comes to a halt on Christmas Eve and resumes only on 26 December, or *Tapaninpäivä*. Families get together and stay together over the holidays.

New Year's Eve – Offices and shops are open till early afternoon. The night sees fireworks and much celebration.

POST & TELECOMMUNICATIONS

Post offices are open Monday to Friday from 9 am to 5 pm, but smaller offices close at 4.30 pm or even earlier. *Posti* in Finnish and *Post* in Swedish, they sell packing material of various sizes, and often provide tape and wrapping material free of charge if you ask politely.

Postal Rates

Current postal rates within Finland are incredible; in Helsinki it's more expensive to send a postcard across the street than to airmail it to Albania or Malta.

Anything under 50 grams within Finland costs 2.80 mk. A postcard or a letter under 20 grams to an EU country costs 3.20 mk, the same to other European countries costs 2.70 mk, and to other continents, 3.40 mk. Mail within the EU is subject to Finland's 22% VAT.

Sending Mail

The Finnish postal system is both reliable and efficient. Letters posted before 5 pm Monday to Friday will reach their destination in Finland the next working day. Letters to Scandinavia take a few days, to Australia less than a week, to North America almost two weeks.

Letter boxes are yellow and usually cleared between 4 and 5 pm Monday to Friday (earlier in Lapland). All stamp counters at post offices will take your letters for immediate forwarding. Some shops, especially R-kioskis, sell stamps of the most common denominations.

Receiving Mail

There are *poste restante* services in all main post offices. The best way to address such mail is as follows:

Name
Poste restante
Postcode and town

The postcodes are five-digit numbers that follow this logic: the first two numbers indicate towns and areas, the next two identify the post office in the town or area, and the last number is always 0, except when you are sending mail to a post office box or poste restante, in which case the last number is 1. The main post office is always '10' in all large towns, so the postcode for the main post office in Helsinki is 00101, for Turku 20101, for Tampere 33101, for Savonlinna 57101, for Vaasa 65101, and for Rovaniemi 96101.

Telephone

Some public telephones take coins and some take phone cards. You can use any telephone booth to make domestic or international calls. Use 5 mk coins (in coin-phones) for international calls. Most booths have a minimum 2 mk fee these days, so dial carefully!

Telephone companies know how to make money; generally you can talk locally for approximately one minute per mk, which makes phone conversations an expensive hobby.

It is cheapest to call Europe, North America or Australia between 10 pm and 8 am (Finnish time). At other times, a one-minute call to Europe costs 3.50 mk, to North America and Australia 5.40 mk and to other countries 9.10 mk per minute.

When calling abroad from Finland, dial 00, 990, 994 or 999 for the International Access Code. When calling from abroad, dial 358 for Finland's country code.

Phone Cards

Currently there are three phone-card systems in Finland, but the Tele company has the widest network of card phones. A 30-mk Tele card is highly recommended, and the only way to make a phone call at many railway stations. Phone cards can be purchased at many newsstands and kiosks; make sure you get one.

New Telephone Codes

From 12 October 1996 all 75 long-distance codes will be replaced by 13 new regional codes. All codes start with a zero, which you disregard when calling from outside Finland. The regions are almost identical to Finnish provinces, and to the chapters of this book. The regions and their corresponding codes are listed below.

02 – Province of Turku and Pori
03 – Häme (including southern Päijänne region)
05 – Province of Kymi (South-East)
06 – Province of Vaasa (Pohjanmaa)
08 – Province of Oulu
09 – Helsinki region
013 – North Karelia
014 – Central Finland
015 – Province of Mikkeli (south Savo, excluding Päijänne region)
016 – Lapland
017 – Province of Kuopio (north Savo)
018 – Åland
019 – Uusimaa (excluding Helsinki region)

Collect Call

Ask your telephone company prior to departure whether there is a Country Direct telephone number. With this number, you can make a call which is paid by the receiver or billed to your credit card, though this may be more expensive than if you pay in Finland.

Australia – (Optus) 0800 11 0611
Australia – (Telstra) 0800 11 0610
Canada – 0800 11 0011
France – 0800 11 0330
Ireland – 0800 11 0353
New Zealand – 0800 11 0640
Norway – 0800 11 0470
Singapore – 0800 11 0650
Sweden – (Telia) 0800 11 0460
Sweden – (TELE2) 0800 11 0461
UK – (BT) 0800 11 0440
UK – (MCL) 0800 11 0289
USA – (AT&T) 0800 11 0010
USA – (MCI) 0800 11 0280

Fax, Telex & Telegraph

Tele offices also have telefax, telegram and telex services.

Electronic Mail

You can continue travelling on the information highway while visiting Finland. Most main libraries in big towns have at least one terminal that you may use free of charge (unless there's a long queue). You must reserve it and don't be late – some libraries limit the usage to one hour. Some universities have Internet access for their own students, but if you get to know one well enough, you might be able to send a message or two. There are also a few Internet cafés.

President Martti Ahtisaari's Internet address is presidentti@tpk.fi.

TIME

Finnish time is two hours ahead of GMT/UTC in winter. Daylight Saving Time is from late March to late September, when Finnish time is three hours ahead of GMT. Noon in Finland is 2 am in Los Angeles, 5 am in New York, 10 am in London and 8 pm in Sydney.

ELECTRICITY

Outlets in Finland are 220 volts, 50 cycles AC. All plugs are of the two-pin Continental European type, so take appropriate conversion plugs if you're bringing any electrical equipment with you. There is electricity in almost every house, including most private summer cottages, but not in wilderness huts along trekking routes. Approximately 16,000 households in Finland lack electricity. Most of them are in Åland, Kainuu, south Savo or Central Finland.

LAUNDRY

There are no self-service laundrettes, except for the odd, overpriced rip-off in each town, meant for company laundry rather than the jeans and underwear of individual travellers. Nor are there many washing machines in youth hostels, not to mention hotels. Hotel laundry price lists would be good jokes if they were not true. This unhappy situation forces the traveller to use laundry machines when available and to do laundry manually at other times. To make things more difficult, shops don't have small packs of laundry powder, so you either have to waste most of the pack or carry the open pack around with you. Or just bring your own.

WEIGHTS & MEASURES

Finland uses all the standard metric weights and measures (see the conversion table at the back of this book).

Beer is sold by *tuoppi* in restaurants and bars. Small, or *pieni* tuoppi is 0.3 litres, *iso* (big) tuoppi, or the *pitkä* is 0.5 litres. Potatoes can be bought at markets by *kappa*, a wooden box which comes in various sizes.

Most clothes follow the S, M, L and XL symbols but inches are also common for pants and shirt necks. Be prepared to learn a new system or two when buying clothes in Finland.

BOOKS & MAPS

Even though Finland produces quite a lot of serious literature, there is not an enormous supply available in English, although the number of translations is increasing. You can see what is available at Akateeminen or Suomalainen bookshops in Helsinki, in their 'Fennica' sections. Naturally you'll see a selection of glossy coffee table books with magnificent nature photography and prohibitive price tags.

The most renowned classical literature dates back to the 19th century. The *Kalevala*, the national epic translated by Keith Bosley, is available in soft cover from Oxford University Press, as is *The Kanteletar*, a new title printed in 1992. The WSOY publishing company has produced several hard-cover translations of the works of notable Finnish authors, such as *The Egyptian* and *The Dark Angel* by Mika Waltari, and *The Unknown Soldier* by Väinö Linna. These books cost around 150 mk.

History

Finnish history is constantly unfolding, especially with the opening of Russian archives dating back to the postwar decades of the Soviet Union era, as well as former president UK Kekkonen's archives. If you want to read about general history, you should find *A Short History of Finland* (F Singleton, Cambridge University Press, 1991), *Finland at Peace and War* (HM Tillotson, Michael Russell 1993) and *Let Us Be Finns* by Matti Klinge, of interest. The books of Mr Klinge give a reliable insight into the forces that shaped the growth of the Finnish nation. *Finland: Myth and Reality* by Max Jacobson deals with postwar history. *Blood, Sweat and Bears* by Lasse Lehtinen is a parody of a war novel and deals with Soviet relations.

Travel Guides

The glossy *Insight Guide Finland* is currently the only other English language guidebook published in the 1990s and solely devoted to Finland. There are, of course, several Scandinavian titles. *Facts about Finland* (Otava, Helsinki) contains plenty of background information on the history, economy and society of Finland, written by Finns. This book comes in several languages and costs around 100 mk.

Maps

Excellent maps in various scales are available for every region of Finland. Free maps are handed out with a smile in all tourist offices, so town maps, some regional maps and most local bus maps will cost you nothing. For extensive treks, for canoeing or sailing tours and for driving and bicycling, however, you should buy a map. Karttakeskus (☎ 154 5655), at Unioninkatu 32 in central Helsinki, produces and sells the largest variety of Finnish maps.

Road Maps There are 19 GT brand maps covering all Finland, available in a scale of 1:200,000. These maps are very clear and show practically all the places that you might be interested in, including youth hostels and wilderness huts. Each sheet costs 50 mk, and is updated every four years or so. Karttakeskus published a handy atlas version of these maps in 1994 (unfortunately Lapland is covered in a scale of 1:400,000). It now seems the book will have annual updates (look for old editions at a discount).

Outdoor Maps A detailed map is absolutely necessary if you plan to do extensive trekking. Karttakeskus has produced approximately 40 titles for trekking areas,

including walking-track presentations of town areas (in 1:25,000 to 1:50,000 scale) and national park maps (1:50,000 to 1:100,000). Prices are usually 50 mk per map.

Field Maps For more detail and accuracy, there are 1:20,000 maps available covering *all* Finland, a full 3730 sheets in all. They cost a hefty 45 mk per sheet. You can also consult them in public libraries, especially in provincial capitals. The complicated numbering system will take you some time to master! These maps also come in a scale of 1:50,000, with several sheets printed in one, available at 65 mk per sheet.

Sailing Maps Accurate coastal maps cost 187 mk per series. Maps for lakes and waterways are approximately 50 mk each.

MEDIA
Newspapers & Magazines

Should you want imported newspapers or magazines, try Akateeminen and Suomalainen bookshops and R-kioski shops. R-Kioski usually stocks an amazing variety of imported magazines, and is often the only outlet for such publications in smaller towns.

Many local newspapers regularly publish an English summary of international and local news, but it often takes a while to find these columns inside the paper. The *Helsingin Sanomat*, the largest daily in Finland, doesn't have a word in English.

Some major European dailies, including the Paris edition of the *Herald Tribune*, are stocked by libraries.

Radio & TV

Finland has had free airwaves since the first commercial radio station, Radio City of Helsinki, set up its rock station. Since then, dozens of local stations have sprung up, and many have already disappeared. The government still has to approve a station application, and there are certain regulations on how much local news there must be, or the minimum number of commercials allowed. Naturally, most of the talk is Finnish, but it seems that some of the private channels are actually trying to play good music! There are four national (non-commercial) radio stations. Radio Mafia, the popular youth channel, plays pop music and a wide variety of 'world music'.

Television in Finland is well endowed with American soap operas, TV series and Hollywood movies. All programmes on Finnish TV have the original soundtrack, with Finnish (sometimes Swedish) subtitles. There are currently three national TV channels. TV1 and TV2 are government channels with no commercials and a good number of films and series in English, but often reruns or depressing Finnish talk shows. MTV3 is the colourful commercial station, with some excellent imported programmes and many Finnish versions of imported shows (try to watch *Wheel of Fortune* if you can). A Finnish cable channel offers local programmes in some of the larger towns, but mostly shows imported series in English. In Helsinki it's called PTV.

Many hotels and hostels are connected to the local cable network. You can watch satellite channels, such as NBC Super Channel, MTV, EuroSport, the French TV5 and sometimes the pay-channels too.

FILM & PHOTOGRAPHY

North Finland offers 24 hours of sunshine around midsummer and there are beautiful summer days all over Finland. Shadows are very long in the mornings and evenings, as well as on short winter days. Taking photos in Finnish forests is much easier than in tropical forests, but there are tricky shadows and reflections which may result in underexposed photos.

Film prices vary considerably between retail outlets, so shop around. Anttila department stores generally have lower prices than most others, and there are small companies selling cheap film when bought in bulk, such as Hertell in Tampere. Processing film is not too expensive and can be done in all towns.

HEALTH

You are not likely to have health problems in Finland unless you engage in endurance tests in the wilderness. There is one species of dangerous snake and a few poisonous mushrooms, berries and plants in Finnish forests.

Travel health depends on your predeparture preparations, your day-to-day health care while travelling and how you handle any medical problem or emergency that does develop. With a little luck, some basic precautions and adequate information, few travellers experience more than upset stomachs.

Travel Health Guides

There are a number of books on travel health, including the following:

Travellers' Health, Dr Richard Dawood, Oxford University Press. Comprehensive, easy to read, authoritative and highly recommended, although it's rather large to lug around.

Travel with Children, Maureen Wheeler, Lonely Planet Publications. Includes basic advice on travel health for younger children.

Predeparture Planning

Health Insurance A travel insurance policy to cover theft, loss and medical problems is a wise idea. There are a wide variety of policies and your travel agent will have recommendations. The international student travel policies handled by STA Travel or other student travel organisations are usually good value. Some policies offer lower and higher medical-expense options but the higher one is chiefly for countries like the USA, where medical costs are extremely high. Check the small print:

- Some policies specifically exclude 'dangerous activities' which can include motorcycling and even trekking. If such activities are on your agenda you don't want that sort of policy. A locally acquired motorcycle licence may not be valid under your policy.
- You may prefer a policy which pays doctors or hospitals direct rather than you having to pay on the spot and claim later. If you have to claim later make sure you keep all documentation. Some policies ask you to call back (reverse charges) to

A	D
B	
C	E

A: Raseborg Castle near Tammisaari
B: Manor house near Lohja
C: Hvitträsk House near Helsinki

D: Church on the island of Maakalla
E: Traditional windmill in Virrat

A	B
C	D	E
F	G

A: Fly Agaric mushrooms
B: Autumn colours, Kuusamo
C: Autumn hues
D: View from the Punkaharju Ridge, Savo
E: Lily of the Valley
F: Taitajan taival trekking route, Ilomantsi, North Karelia
G: Reindeer, Lapland

a centre in your home country where an immediate assessment of your problem is made.

- Check if the policy covers ambulances or an emergency flight home. If you have to stretch out you will need two seats and somebody has to pay for them!
- It may be possible to obtain sickness benefits during a temporary stay – check with your health insurer.

Medical Kit It's wise to carry a small, straightforward medical kit. A kit should include:

- Aspirin or Panadol – for pain or fever.
- Antihistamine (such as Benadryl) – useful as a decongestant for colds and allergies, to ease the itch from insect bites or stings, and to help prevent motion sickness. Antihistamines may cause sedation and interact with alcohol so care should be taken when using them.
- Antibiotics – useful if you're travelling well off the beaten track. They must be prescribed and you should carry the prescription with you.

    Some individuals are allergic to commonly prescribed antibiotics, such as penicillin or sulpha drugs. It would be sensible to always carry this information when travelling.

    Ideally, antibiotics should be administered only under medical supervision and should never be taken indiscriminately. In Finland, antibiotics are quite expensive and available only with a doctor's prescription.
- Kaolin preparation (Pepto-Bismol), Imodium or Lomotil – for stomach upsets.
- Rehydration mixture – for treatment of severe diarrhoea. This is particularly important if travelling with children, but is recommended for everyone.
- Antiseptic such as Betadine, which comes as impregnated swabs or ointment, and an antibiotic powder or similar 'dry' spray – for cuts and grazes.
- Calamine lotion – to ease irritation from bites or stings.
- Bandages and Band-aids – for minor injuries.
- Scissors, tweezers and a thermometer (note that mercury thermometers are prohibited by airlines).
- Insect repellent, sunscreen, suntan lotion, chap stick and water purification tablets.

Health Preparations Make sure you're healthy before you start travelling. If you are embarking on a long trip make sure your teeth are OK before you go.

If you wear glasses take a spare pair and your prescription. Losing your glasses can be a real problem. Although in many places you can get new spectacles made up quickly and competently, new spectacles are not cheap in Finland.

If you require a particular medication take an adequate supply, as it may not be available locally. Take the prescription or, better still, part of the packaging showing the generic rather than the brand name (which may not be locally available), as it will make getting replacements easier. It's a wise idea to have a legible prescription with you to show you legally use the medication.

Immunisations No immunisations are necessary for Finland, unless you arrive from an infected area.

Basic Rules
Care in what you eat and drink is the most important health rule; stomach upsets are the most likely travel health problem, but the majority of these upsets are relatively minor. Don't become paranoid; trying the local food is part of the experience of travel, after all.

Water You can drink the tap water in all Finnish towns and villages, although it is not always tasty. In Lapland and in many places in the eastern provinces, the water in lakes and rivers is fresh and pure, and most trekkers end up relying on it. Note that the brownish colour of lake or river water does not necessarily indicate pollution.

The simplest way to purify water is to boil it thoroughly. Vigorously boiling for five minutes should be satisfactory.

Food In Finland take care with wild mushrooms and berries. Eat only blueberries, elderberries, cloudberries and cranberries in forests. Some red berries may look attractive but can cause you stomach problems, so it's advisable to avoid berries you don't know. Don't pick mushrooms you don't know. If you're determined to try wild mushrooms, seek knowledgeable advice.

Nutrition If your diet is poor or limited, if

you're travelling hard and fast and therefore missing meals, or if you simply lose your appetite, you can soon start to lose weight and place your health at risk. Make sure your diet is well balanced.

During treks and hot spells make sure you drink enough – don't rely on thirst to indicate when you should drink. Not needing to urinate or very dark yellow urine is a danger sign. Always carry a water bottle with you on long treks.

Everyday Health Normal body temperature is 98.6°F or 37°C; more than 2°C higher indicates a 'high' fever. The normal adult pulse rate is 60 to 80 per minute (children 80 to 100, babies 100 to 140). You should know how to take a temperature and a pulse rate. As a general rule the pulse increases about 20 beats per minute for each °C rise in fever.

Respiration (breathing) rate is also an indicator of illness. Count the number of breaths per minute: between 12 and 20 is normal for adults and older children (up to 30 for younger children, 40 for babies). People with a high fever or serious respiratory illness (like pneumonia) breathe more quickly than normal. More than 40 shallow breaths a minute usually means pneumonia.

Medical Problems & Treatment
Potential medical problems can be broken down into several areas. Firstly there are the problems caused by extremes of temperature, altitude or motion. Then there are diseases and illnesses caused through poor environmental sanitation, insect bites or stings, and animal or human contact. Simple cuts, bites and scratches can also cause problems.

Self-diagnosis and treatment can be risky, so wherever possible seek qualified help. Medical advice should be sought where possible before administering any drugs.

An embassy or consulate can usually recommend a good place to go for such advice. So can five-star hotels, although they often recommend doctors with five-star prices. (This is when that medical insurance really comes in useful!)

Costs If you are from Australia, the UK, Scandinavia, Germany, France, Spain, Portugal, Belgium, Netherlands, Italy, Austria, Ireland, Greece, Luxembourg or Hungary and can produce a passport (or sickness insurance card or form E111 for those from EU countries) then medical treatment will cost you the same as it costs the Finns, that is, about 50 mk for a visit to a doctor, 125 mk a day for hospitalisation. Otherwise you'll be charged the full cost of the treatment.

Climatic & Geographical Considerations
Sunburn In June and July in Finland, you can get sunburnt because of long hours of intense sunshine. Use a sunscreen and take extra care to cover areas which don't normally see sun – eg your feet. A hat provides added protection. Calamine lotion is good for mild sunburn.

Cold If you are trekking in Lapland or simply staying outdoors for long, particularly in winter, be prepared. In fact, if you're out walking or hitching, be prepared for cold, wet or windy conditions even in summer.

Hypothermia occurs when the body loses heat faster than it can produce it and the core temperature of the body falls. It is surprisingly easy to progress from very cold to dangerously cold due to a combination of wind, wet clothing, fatigue and hunger, even if the air temperature is above freezing. It is best to dress in layers; silk, wool and some of the new synthetic fibres are all good insulating materials. A hat is important, as a lot of heat is lost through the head. A strong, waterproof outer layer is essential, as keeping dry is vital. Carry basic supplies, including lots of fluid and food containing simple sugars to generate heat quickly. A space blanket is something all travellers in cold environments should carry.

Symptoms of hypothermia are exhaustion, numbness (particularly toes and fingers), shivering, slurred speech, irrational or violent behaviour, lethargy, stumbling, dizzy spells, muscle cramps and violent bursts of energy. Irrational behaviour may take the form of sufferers claiming they are warm and trying to take off their clothes.

To treat mild hypothermia, first get the person out of the wind and/or rain, remove their clothing if it's wet and replace it with dry, warm clothing. Give them hot liquids – no alcohol – and high-kilojoule, easily digestible food. Do not rub victims; allow them to slowly warm themselves. This should be enough to treat the early stages of hypothermia. The early recognition and treatment of mild hypothermia is the only way to prevent severe hypothermia, which is a critical condition.

Heat Exhaustion Too much heat is just as dangerous as too much cold. Dehydration or salt deficiency can cause heat exhaustion. If you take a sauna bath after a hot day or a long trek, make sure you get sufficient liquids. Warm summer weather, with long days and strenuous activity, may cause problems you never expected near the Arctic circle. Wear loose clothing. Do not do anything too physically demanding.

Salt deficiency is characterised by fatigue, lethargy, headaches, giddiness and muscle cramps; in these cases adding salt to your food may help.

Fungal Infections Hot weather fungal infections are most likely to occur on the scalp, between the toes or fingers (athlete's foot), in the groin (jock itch or crotch rot) and on the body (ringworm). You get ringworm (which is a fungal infection, not a worm) from infected animals or by walking in damp areas, like shower floors. Public saunas in Finland are risky. To prevent fungal infections wear loose, comfortable clothes, avoid synthetic fibres, wash frequently and dry carefully. If you do get an infection, wash the infected area daily with a disinfectant or medicated soap and water, and rinse and dry well. Apply an antifungal powder like the widely available Tinaderm. Try to expose the infected area to air or sunlight as much as possible and wash all towels and underwear in hot water as well as changing them often.

Motion Sickness Eating lightly before and during a trip will reduce the chances of motion sickness. If you are prone to motion sickness try to find a place that minimises disturbance – near the wing on aircraft, close to midship on boats, near the centre on buses. Fresh air usually helps; reading and cigarette smoke don't. Commercial motion-sickness preparations, which can cause drowsiness, have to be taken before the trip commences; when you're feeling sick it's too late. Ginger is a natural preventative and is available in capsule form.

Jet Lag Jet lag is experienced when a person travels by air across several time zones (each time zone usually represents a one-hour time difference). It occurs because many of the functions of the human body (such as temperature, pulse rate and emptying of the bladder and bowels) are regulated by internal cycles called circadian rhythms. When we travel long distances rapidly, our bodies take time to adjust to the 'new time' of our destination, and we may experience fatigue, disorientation, insomnia, anxiety, impaired concentration and loss of appetite. These effects will usually be gone within a few days of arrival, but there are ways of minimising the impact of jet lag:

- Rest for a couple of days prior to departure; try to avoid late nights and last-minute dashes for travellers' cheques, passport etc.
- Try to select flight schedules that minimise sleep deprivation; arriving late in the day means you can go to sleep soon after you arrive. For very long flights, try to organise a stopover.
- Avoid excessive eating (which bloats the stomach) and alcohol (which causes dehydration) during the flight. Instead, drink plenty of non-carbonated, non-alcoholic drinks such as fruit juice or water.
- Avoid smoking.
- Make yourself comfortable by wearing loose-fitting clothes and perhaps bringing an eye mask and ear plugs to help you sleep.

Infectious Diseases
Diarrhoea A change of water, food or climate can all cause the runs; diarrhoea caused by contaminated food or water is

more serious. Despite all your precautions you may still have a mild bout of travellers' diarrhoea, especially during visits to Russia.

A few rushed toilet trips with no other symptoms is not indicative of a serious problem. Moderate diarrhoea, involving half a dozen loose movements in a day, is more of a nuisance. Dehydration is the main danger with any diarrhoea, particularly for children where dehydration can occur quite quickly.

Fluid replacement remains the mainstay of management. Weak black tea with a little sugar, soda water, or soft drinks allowed to go flat and diluted 50% with water are all good. With severe diarrhoea a rehydrating solution is necessary to replace minerals and salts. Commercially available ORS (oral rehydration salts) are very useful; add the contents of one sachet to a litre of boiled or bottled water. In an emergency you can make up a solution of eight teaspoons of sugar to a litre of boiled water and provide salted cracker biscuits at the same time. You should stick to a bland diet as you recover.

Sexually Transmitted Diseases Sexual contact with an infected partner spreads these diseases. While abstinence is the only 100% preventative, using condoms is also effective. Gonorrhoea and syphilis are the most common of these diseases; sores, blisters or rashes around the genitals, discharges or pain when urinating are common symptoms. Symptoms may be less marked or not observed at all in women. Syphilis symptoms eventually disappear completely but the disease continues and can cause severe problems in later years. The treatment of gonorrhoea and syphilis is by antibiotics.

There are numerous other sexually transmitted diseases, for most of which effective treatment is available. However, there is no cure for herpes and there is also currently no cure for AIDS.

HIV/AIDS HIV, the Human Immunodeficiency Virus, may develop into AIDS, Acquired Immune Deficiency Syndrome.

Exposure to blood, blood products or bodily fluids may put individuals at risk.

In industrialised countries transmission is mostly through contact between homosexual or bisexual males, or via contaminated needles shared by IV drug users. Apart from abstinence, the most effective preventative is always to practise safe sex using condoms. It is impossible to detect the HIV-positive status of an otherwise healthy-looking person without a blood test.

HIV/AIDS can also be spread through infected blood transfusions (mainly in developing countries) or by dirty needles – vaccinations, acupuncture, tattooing and ear or nose piercing can potentially be as dangerous as intravenous drug use if the equipment is not clean. If you do need an injection, make sure you see the syringe unwrapped in front of you, or better still, take a needle and syringe pack with you overseas – it is a cheap insurance package against infection with HIV.

Fear of HIV infection should never preclude treatment for serious medical conditions. Although there may be a risk of infection, it is very small indeed. The incidence of AIDS in Finland is not high but there *are* risks.

Bites & Stings

Mosquitoes These are a nuisance in most parts of Finland in summer. Finns are usually immune to any problems arising from bites but if you are not, bites may even become infected. Primary prevention must always be in the form of mosquito-avoidance measures. From June to August travellers are advised to:

* wear light-coloured clothing
* wear long pants and long sleeved shirts
* use mosquito repellent
* avoid highly scented perfumes or aftershave
* use a mosquito net if you have one

There are also net hats, useful for treks and outdoor activities, available in sport shops.

Bees & Wasps Bee and wasp stings are

usually painful rather than dangerous. Calamine lotion will give relief and ice packs will reduce the pain and swelling. Local advice is often the best.

Snakes The *kyy* (viper) is the only dangerous snake in Finland. Antivenins are readily available in pharmacies; just ask for *kyypakkaus*. To minimise your chances of being bitten always wear boots, socks and long trousers when walking in areas where snakes may be present. Don't put your hands into holes and crevices, and be careful when collecting firewood.

In case of snake bite, keep the victim calm and still, wrap the bitten limb tightly, as you would for a sprained ankle, and attach a splint to immobilise it. Then seek medical help. Tourniquets and sucking out the poison are now comprehensively discredited.

Women's Health

Gynaecological Problems Poor diet, lowered resistance because of the use of antibiotics for stomach upsets, and even contraceptive pills can lead to vaginal infections when travelling in hot weather. Maintain good personal hygiene and wear skirts or loose-fitting trousers and cotton underwear to help prevent infections.

Yeast infections, characterised by a rash, itch and discharge, can be treated with a vinegar or lemon-juice douche, or with yoghurt. Nystatin suppositories are the usual medical prescription. Trichomoniasis is a more serious infection; symptoms are a discharge and a burning sensation when urinating. Male sexual partners must also be treated, and if a vinegar-water douche is not effective medical attention should be sought. Metronidazole (Flagyl) is the prescribed drug.

Pregnancy Most miscarriages occur during the first three months of pregnancy, so this is the most risky time to travel as far as your own health is concerned. Miscarriage is not uncommon, and can occasionally lead to severe bleeding. The last three months should also be spent within reasonable distance of good medical care. A baby born as early as 24 weeks stands a chance of survival, but only in a modern hospital. Pregnant women should avoid all unnecessary medication, but vaccinations should still be taken where possible. Additional care should be taken to prevent illness and particular attention should be paid to diet and nutrition. Alcohol and nicotine, for example, should be avoided.

Women travellers often find that their periods become irregular or even cease while they're on the road. Remember that a missed period in these circumstances doesn't necessarily indicate pregnancy. There are health posts or Family Planning clinics in many urban centres, where you can seek advice and have a urine test to determine whether or not you are pregnant.

WOMEN TRAVELLERS

Finland is a relatively easy country for women travellers to negotiate. Most Finnish women consider themselves to be 'liberated', and the country as a whole is liberal and sexually tolerant. Nevertheless, women hitchhiking should take the usual precautions.

DANGERS & ANNOYANCES

Finland is generally a very safe country for visitors. Lately, however, the social and political changes in Eastern Europe have contributed to a rise in Finland's crime rate. Higher levels of unemployment have also driven more Finns to criminal activity. Travellers are unlikely to be affected by this, though the usual care should be taken with money, belongings, passport and so on.

The only real annoyance likely to be encountered by visitors is drunks. Finland has something of an alcohol problem (a significant source of revenue for the government, which derives up to 8% of its income from alcohol taxes). There are many drunkards in Helsinki, most of them homeless, but they are not generally beggars nor particularly offensive. In fact, they can be talkative and amusing, and many speak good English. Amateur drunkards who only drink in the evenings will annoy you by urinating in town centres, especially in Helsinki.

Don't be too boisterous at local pubs in small towns and villages, especially if you enter before local males have drunk themselves into a coma. Males with a dark complexion may encounter harassment from intoxicated Finnish males. As a foreign tourist, you may be left alone as an anomaly but local fights are not uncommon.

For the trekker, mosquitoes can be a real problem. In Finland, the mosquito breeding season is very short (about six weeks in July/August), but the mosquitoes make good use of the time. Insect repellent is absolutely essential.

Be careful with wetlands. A typical swamp may once have been a lake, and the muddy sections can be pretty deep. Follow only the boardwalk to be on the safe side, or stick to elevated sections of wetland.

In winter, slippery pavements due to ice and snow are extremely dangerous. Every year 800 Finnish pedestrians die from falls, 200 of these because of slippery pavements. In comparison, car accidents account for 'only' 500 deaths annually. If you are not accustomed to such winter conditions, be extra careful. Speaking of annual deaths, Finnish citizenship seems to be another danger; almost 1500 Finns commit suicide every year, one of the highest per capita figures in the world.

WORK

There are active work exchange organisations in many universities around Finland. Enquire through student organisations such as AIESEC (economics and commerce), IAESTE (technology and engineering) or ELSA (law). Getting a short-term job is rather difficult because there is chronic unemployment, but getting a low-paid job as a dishwasher might be possible in big towns if you try hard and ask around. The 'grey economy' in Finland is large and growing. To stay on the legal side, some institutions have working-holiday schemes for travellers, most notably in the Valamo monastery in Heinävesi or strawberry picking in Savo.

For any serious career-oriented work, a work permit must be obtained beforehand from the Finnish embassy in your country (except for EU citizens, who can obtain work permits easily in Finland).

Street Performing

Tim Morgan of England has written to us to say that if you have a good voice and/or a musical instrument and are a bit short of cash, you should seriously consider busking (performing on the streets) in Finland.

Finland is undoubtedly one of the best countries in Europe in which to play – even a moderate talent can bring in several hundred markkaa a day. There are good places to play in most of the major towns – Rovaniemi, Oulu, Tampere, Turku and Helsinki, for example – but even better are some of the smaller places, where buskers are rarer and the novelty value greater.

It is simply not the case that the more people there are, the more money you will make – a quiet pedestrian street in somewhere like Tammisaari, for example, will probably be far better than a bustling market in a big town, and you will also be spared any hassle from the police about licences etc (although, in practice, you shouldn't worry about these, even in the larger places, if you are only playing for a day or two – no-one seems to mind much, provided the shopkeepers or market stall holders around you are happy for you to play there). Lunch times and Saturday mornings are the best times to play, and English songs go down very well, especially those of The Beatles. If you have a modicum of talent, gather your courage and give it a go!

HIGHLIGHTS

There are so many things to do in Finland, it is hard to choose a top 20, but we've come up with this one:

1. *Passenger ferries between Finland & Sweden*
    The most luxurious passenger ferries anywhere, these offer a very relaxing way to enter Finland. With discounts available for students and railpass holders, this is an experience not to be missed.

2. *The island of Suomenlinna off Helsinki* With several museums, galleries, dark bunkers and isolated spots, this island is now on the UNESCO World Heritage List.

3. *A bicycle tour on the island of Åland* See the oldest churches in Finland, some castles and unusual flora while cycling on narrow roads. Do some island-hopping on free passenger ferries.

4. *Historical Turku* Modern Finland started in Turku, and a castle, a cathedral and a large open-air museum remain.

5. *Old Coastal Towns* Many attractive seaside towns such as Nykarleby, Kristinestad and Tammisaari come alive in summer. They offer a unique atmosphere, with a Swedish flavour.

6. *Aulanko in Hämeenlinna* This old park has nice pavilions and accommodation in all categories.

7. *The Cathedral of Tampere* Probably the best example of National Romantic architecture, the cathedral also offers some controversial church art.

8. *Pyynikki & Pispala area, Tampere* Enjoy magnificent views of two beautiful lakes while visiting the large park right in the middle of Tampere.

9. *Route 66* Whether you drive or cycle, you'll find plenty of interesting sights in the Ruovesi and Virrat areas, including some fine church paintings in Keuruu.

10. *Rauma Old Town* The first entry on the UNESCO World Heritage List, this old wooden township on the south-west coast has attractive houses, artisans and a unique culture, complete with a dialect that few can understand.

11. *Olavinlinna Castle in Savonlinna* The most dramatic castle in Finland features the best opera performances in Finland. Savonlinna is also a centre for lake cruises, which give you the chance to see the castle from a different angle.

12. *Lappeenranta Fort* Visit the interesting museums and handicraft workshops in what is called the summer capital of South Karelia.

13. *Lake steamship trips* Century-old steamers sail the Finnish lakeland, carrying passengers through lakes, straits and canals. You can bring your bicycle to combine other means of travel with old steamers.

14. *Monasteries & canals in Heinävesi area* Probably Finland's most interesting set of attractions, including Orthodox monasteries, canals, and pleasant places to stay in the most beautiful lakeland of Savo.

15. *Orthodox Museum of Kuopio* A priceless collection of old icons, textiles, and gold and silver artefacts, saved from the Soviet-occupied Orthodox monasteries, make this museum one of the most interesting in Finland.

16. *Ruunaa area in Lieksa* The entire eastern frontier has plenty of appeal. Ruunaa stands out because of its variety; you can fish, trek, shoot rapids and visit a number of more distant attractions.

17. *Trekking in Saariselkä National Park* One of the largest wilderness areas in Europe, the park has an incredible choice of free accommodation in well-equipped huts, but you'll need a week to visit any number of them, as well as a good map and a compass.

18. *Karhunkierros Trek in Kuusamo* Finland's most established trekking route will take you to rugged landscape, roaming waterfalls and unusual flora and fauna. Good paths lead from one free hut to another.

19. *Kilpisjärvi lakes & fells* The highest mountains in Finland can be reached by starting a trek from the north-western village of Kilpisjärvi. There are many free huts for trekkers staying overnight in the region.

20. *Any major summer music festival* Attend one of the Finland festivals. Whether it's opera, jazz, chamber music or accordion, you'll have more of it than you ever dreamed, from a weekend happening to month-long cultural events.

ACCOMMODATION

Accommodation in Finland doesn't necessarily have to be expensive. In a one-month trip you may well spend a week for free in various wilderness huts, a few nights in trains, a night or two in an *aitta* room (a storage shed-cum-guestroom, usually part of a traditional farmhouse and usually only in summer) and, if you hitchhike or cycle, a few nights in isolated barns or abandoned farmhouses dotted around the countryside. Youth hostels are probably a bit cheaper than in the USA or Western Europe on average, and several people can share cottages at camping grounds. With some planning, you will pay, on average, not more than US$10 per night in Finland. Hotels are more expensive but there are discounts in summer.

Camping

In Finland the Right of Public Access (*jokamiehenoikeus*) grants you legal permission to temporarily pitch your tent anywhere, except on private property. Few travellers take advantage of this, but as you become familiar with the geography of Finland, you'll find there are virtually no limits on where and how you can stay overnight for free, as long as you keep a low profile and stay discreet. If you ask permission from the landowner, you may be able to stay longer than one night. There are restrictions on the lighting of campfires, though.

The 360 official camping grounds cater more to caravans than to those carrying their own tents. Except for some cheap places on Åland, camping fees can be anything from 35 mk per person to 75 mk per family per night, but then all facilities can be used.

Cottages

What makes camping grounds so recommendable is the availability of pleasant cottages and bungalows. If you have a group of two to six, prices are comparable to youth hostels, typically starting at 100 mk for two-bed cottages and 150 mk for four-bed cottages. Amenities vary, but a kitchen, toilet and shower are not uncommon. Some even have microwave ovens and TV sets. Enquire about the availability of cottages where you see a camping ground sign.

Wilderness Huts

See the Activities chapter for details on huts, shelters and other options on trekking routes.

Youth Hostels

Hostels in Finland offer the best value for money, in most cases. There are over 150 youth hostels in Finland, yet you won't find two that are similar. Many are cheap yet attractive, they are seldom full and in some places you can really get away from it all. Hostels are run by the Finnish Youth Hostel Association (SRM), which classifies retkeilymajat (youth hostels) as either basic two-star hostels or 'standard' three-star hostels. Summer hotels and hostels are 'superior' hostels, now associated with SRM. They tend to be occupied by students during term, and consequently are open to travellers in summer only. Finnhostels are superior hostels, and may be open all year round or only in summer. In towns they resemble hotels, and in the countryside they may be farmhouses.

Some youth hostels have closed recently in some mid-sized towns. In such cases, alternatives in nearby towns have been mentioned in this book. It makes sense to travel 20 km to another youth hostel if it saves you 100 mk, especially if you have a train pass.

All youth hostels are open to anyone. However, you should purchase a membership card, as it gives a 15 mk discount in all hostels (we quote discounted prices throughout this book). You should also bring your own sleeping sheet, as sheets cost 15 mk extra in most hostels. Breakfast is generally not included in the price, but is available for 25 mk or so (good value when it's a buffet).

Often you may use the kitchen, although youth hostels that are farmhouses or in rural locations seldom have a kitchen. In superior summer hostels, there is usually everything you need. In ordinary town hostels (normally student dormitories), the kitchen may not have any utensils.

Top 15 Youth Hostels We ranked all youth hostels in Finland in terms of friendly management, historical value, relaxed atmosphere and good price and quality to produce a top 15. Most of our choices are of the 'off the beaten track' variety, but we concluded that by staying in these hostels, you would experience and understand something of the best that Finland has to offer. If possible, you should stay at least two nights in these hostels, rent a boat or a bicycle (or do short treks), and bathe in their saunas.

Dragsfjärd
Heinävesi (Pohjataipale)
Joutsa
Kerimäki (Korkeamäki)
Kilpisjärvi (Peera)
Koli
Kotka (Kärkisaari)
Liljendal
Ristiina (Löydön kartano)
Nurmes (Hyvärilä)
Rauma (Poroholma)
Ruotsinpyhtää
Siilinjärvi
Suomussalmi (Domnan pirtti)
Vuonislahti (Herraniemi)

Especially fine town hostels are to be found in Kaskinen and Porvoo. The 'worst youth hostel' award goes to Myllykoski or Lahti.

Guesthouses

Guesthouses in Finland, called *matkakoti* or *matkustajakoti*, are usually slightly run-down establishments meant for travelling salespeople and other more dubious types. Some are exceptionally clean and offer pleasant, homey accommodation in old wooden houses. Guesthouses are in town centres and/or near railway stations. In this book they are listed under the 'middle' category.

Private Cottages

There are thousands of cottages for rent around Finland. No centralised rental agency represents them all, although you may be led to believe so. Make sure you set aside enough time for research before making up your mind.

As a rule, one week is the standard time for rental cottages, although weekend and daily rates are also quoted by some companies. Prices vary from less than 1000 mk per week during the off-season to over 3000 mk during the 'white nights' and the skiing holidays. Midsummer, the peak season, is usually sold out well beforehand. The high season ranges from mid-June to early August. The cheapest season starts as early as mid-August, but rules vary so ask first. Tax is not necessarily included in the quoted prices in sales material.

Lomarengas – The largest company in Finland covers all Finland, except Åland. Malminkaari 23, 00700 Helsinki (☎ 3516 1321, fax 3516 1300), or in central Helsinki, Eteläesplanadi 4, 00130 Helsinki (☎ 170 611, fax 170 668)

Saimaatours – Represents hundreds of cottages mostly in the south-east, one of the most popular areas for lakeside holidays. Kirkkokatu 10, 53100 Lappeenranta (☎ 411 7722, fax 415 6609)

Järvi-Savo – A sister company to Saimaatours, this company has hundreds of cottages in the Savo area, another popular region with thousands of lakes. Hallituskatu 2, 50100 Mikkeli (☎ 365 399, fax 365 080)

Ålandsresor – Represents all cottages around the pretty Åland archipelago, with inexpensive prices and rates by the day. Storagatan 9, postal address Box 62, 22101 Mariehamn (☎ 28040, fax 28380)

Regional tourist offices – Finland has more than 20 regional tourist organisations. Although their services vary, most offer rental services, as well as the best expertise in the region. Check major cities for further details.

Farm Holidays

Some of the most interesting accommodation in Finland is to be found in farm houses (even some youth hostels are in old farm houses). The number of houses available for accommodation is increasing, and it's impossible to keep track. Some farm holiday schemes are promoted by Suomen 4H-Liitto (☎ 645 133, fax 604 612) at Bulevardi 28, 00120 Helsinki, which represents quite a number of farms scattered throughout Finland. The minimum stay is two days, from about 230 mk per person full board, 190 mk half-board. Prices include food, accommodation, sheets and sauna. The company charges 60 mk for each reservation. There is an English brochure available. Another company is Lomarengas, Malminkaari 23, 00700 Helsinki (☎ 3516 1321, fax 3516 1300), or in central Helsinki, Eteläesplanadi 4, 00130 Helsinki (☎ 170 611, fax 170 668).

In addition to the farms represented by these organisations, there are hundreds of others offering accommodation, board and plenty of activities, often at lower prices. Advance bookings are not always necessary. Local tourist offices will have information on individual farms, including prices and services.

Hotels

There are apparently more museums than hotels in Finland, despite the building frenzy of the 1980s. Hotels have had hard times in the 1990s (there have already been 300 bankruptcies recorded) and they are not at all the most popular places to stay in summer. Prices have also fallen considerably since we wrote the 1st edition of this book. A good double room which cost US$200 (780 mk) in 1990 was available for as low as US$80 (480 mk) in 1993. Even cheaper doubles were available in the very best hotels.

Hotels have worked hard to attract guests:

facilities are luxurious, service tends to be good and hotel restaurants have become popular with locals. Although listed prices are definitely out of reach for most budget travellers, there are often summer discounts available (in winter, hotels are used by businesspeople). Beware of roadside ads showing low prices: these are usually per person prices for doubles. Singles are often just a little less than doubles.

Hotels tend to lack local character as most of them belong to a chain and feature similar services throughout the country. Sokos Hotels is the largest group (and growing), and very popular among Finns. Arctia Hotels is a major competitor, owned by Alko, the alcohol monopoly. Cumulus is another large hotel chain. In contrast, some of the private hotels are very attractive, with plenty of local flavour. My special favourite is Yöpuu in Jyväskylä.

A bargain in practically all Finnish hotels is the buffet breakfast. Hotel guests will need no lunch! A nuisance in many of the best hotels is the unnecessary air-conditioning that always seems to be on. It makes the air extremely dry. How you react to this depends on what and how much you have been drinking and eating, but I recommend you bring enough drinking water for the night, and use moisturising lotion for your face to stop the skin from drying out.

Finncheque The Finncheque scheme, available in most chain hotels throughout Finland, allows accommodation in designated luxury hotels at a discounted price. This works out at 195 mk (approximately US$45) per person in double rooms, or 255 mk in singles (there is a single supplement). This price reduction may come in handy if you compare the discounted prices with the ordinary price of a double.

The system is simple to use. You purchase coupons in advance in your country, or in Finland, and use them as a means of payment. All supplements have to be paid in the hotel, so you won't have to make any strict plans beforehand. Enquire at your travel agent or at agents in Finland.

Hotels are divided into three categories for the purposes of the Finncheque system. In I Class, you pay 60 mk extra for each guest. There is no supplement in II Class, except for singles. In III Class, lunch is included in the price. Most hotels are II Class.

In summer most hotels have discounted prices anyway. Check special offers before wasting your Finncheques on discounted hotel rooms. Finncheques are good value only in autumn, winter and spring, and even then only from Monday to Friday.

Hotel Reservations You may use the centralised reservation services of the largest hotel chains, or try Suomen Hotellivaraukset (☎ 499 155, fax 440 383) for a centralised reservation agency. Use the Helsinki telephone code (09 from October 1996) for all reservations:

Arctia – ☎ 694 8022, fax 694 8471
Best Western – ☎ 655 855, fax 655 870
Cumulus & Rantasipi – ☎ 733 5480, fax 733 5399
Finlandia Hotels – ☎ 656 600, fax 656 611
Finnish Travel Association – ☎ 170 868, fax 654 358
Fontana Hotels – ☎ 6138 3210, fax 713 713
Private Hotels – ☎ 680 1680, fax 680 1315
Sokos Hotels – ☎ 131 001, fax 1310 0222

Rental
If you plan to stay in Finland for more than a few months, you could try renting an apartment. Prices advertised in daily newspapers are quite high, starting at something like 2000 mk per month, including utilities. If you are enrolled at the university or some other educational institution, you might be able to gain access to student apartments. The rent may be as low as 500 mk per month, including utilities, for a *solu* room with a shared kitchen and bathroom. Many apartment houses have laundry facilities and common utensils.

When measuring the area in apartments, square metres (*neliö*) are used and all space, including toilets and corridors, is included. The number of rooms excludes toilets, corridors and the kitchen, so *yksiö* (one room) includes one big room, a kitchen, a toilet, a corridor and some additional space for storage. *Kaksio* is the same with two larger rooms.

FOOD

Finnish food has elements of both Swedish and Russian cuisines, but with a lot of variations and local specialities. There are also specialities for Christmas and Easter, for festivals and for each of the four seasons.

Like the *baguette* with camembert cheese and red wine in France, you can find some simple but tasty options in Finland. Take fresh, preferably still warm, brown rye bread, add medium hard butter and plenty of cheese (say, Edam or Emmental), and enjoy with very cold milk or lager beer. Or try the Finnish version of sushi: salmon or herring slices on small new potatoes (available from July). Such fare is relatively cheap and delicious. Finnish sausages may be greasy but they taste excellent after a sauna, especially barbecued. You could go to the other extreme and splurge on a Finnish smorgasbord, which includes a great variety of fish and salads.

Typical inexpensive meals in Finland are pizzas, hamburgers, kebabs or *grilli makkara* (grilled sausages), just like anywhere else in the world. Large towns have international restaurants. Finnish food is generally served as 'home-made' at most restaurants, and it makes an inexpensive lunch.

Originally, Finnish food was designed to nourish a peasant population who did outdoor manual work in cold weather. Consequently it was heavy and fatty, but made of pure, natural ingredients: fish, game, meat, milk and dairy products, oats, barley and dark rye in the form of porridges and bread, with few spices other than salt and pepper. Vegetables were rarely used in everyday meals, except in casseroles. Potato is the staple food, served with various fish or meat sauces. Soups such as pea soup, meat soup, cabbage soup and fish soup are common. Hot and heavy dishes, including liver, Baltic herring, turnip and cabbage, and even carrot casseroles, are served as the main course or as part of it. Typical fish dishes are prepared from whitefish, pikeperch, pike, perch, bream, vendace, Baltic herring and salmon, and trout.

Eating Out

Almost everywhere in Finland there are economical set lunches in hotels, restaurants, department store cafés and even petrol stations. Typically, you'll find a hot meal, a salad buffet, a few slices of bread, a drink (milk, water or malt drink) and sometimes coffee available at self-service counters for 25 to 45 mk. Prices, quality and the number of extras vary considerably, but because à la carte prices are so high, you should always look for lunch specials.

A *kahvila* is a normal café, whereas a *kahvio* serves coffee in say, a petrol station or a supermarket. A *baari* serves snacks, beer and soft drinks (no strong alcohol) and is also called *kapakka*. A pub or *pubi* serves strong alcohol and very little food. Restaurants, *ravintola*, licensed to serve strong alcohol have *A-oikeudet*, or 'full rights'. With *B-oikeudet* you have less choice. *Grilli* is a hamburger stand. *Ruokala* is an inexpensive dining hall of a company or an institution that sometimes caters to outsiders.

In virtually every dining and drinking establishment, the service charge and sales tax is included in the advertised price. Tipping is uncommon, although in upmarket restaurants a small tip is customary.

Self-Catering

Each town and municipality has several

Salmon cutlets

supermarkets with regular special discounts on selected food items. These vary daily or weekly, but as the Finnish retail business is very centralised, daily discounted items are sometimes the same in all shops. The main retail chains include K-Kauppa, T-Market and S-Market, but these also tend to be the most expensive ones. Usually each large village centre has at least one competing discount store. These offer fixed prices, and include Alepa, Ruokavarasto, Sale, Siwa and Säästäri.

Food produced in Finland is still relatively expensive in shops, a result of the no-competition pricing policy of primary production as well as the high profit margins of the retail stores. Shopping at discount stores, keeping your eyes open for special discounts and buying imported food, such as canned tuna fish, pineapple slices, sardines and bananas, are options to stretch the budget. Relatively cheap food for a simple meal includes fresh potatoes, yoghurt, eggs, fresh or smoked fish and canned pea soup *(hernekeitto)* and, in late summer, any market vegetables. Salmon can be bought at reasonable prices if you shop around. Cheese, salami and meat are more expensive.

Finnish Cuisine

Following are some typical snacks and dishes that you may encounter on Finnish menus:

Åland pannkaka – pancake with jam and whipped cream.
Janssonin kiusaus – Swedish Janssons frestelse (Jansson's temptation), potato and herring prepared in the oven.
Jauhelihakastike – minced meat sauce with potatoes or spaghetti.
Kaalikääryleet – cabbage with minced meat stuffing.
Kesäkeitto – vegetable soup.
Lämpimät voileivät – warm sandwiches, usually served with cheese and salami.
Lihakeitto – soup with meat, potatoes, and other vegetables.
Lihamureke – seasoned minced meat prepared in the oven.

Lihapullat – meatballs.
Makaronilaatikko – macaroni stew; oven baked macaroni with milk and minced meat.
Metsästäjänpihvi – minced meat with mushroom sauce.
Makkarakastike – sausage sauce, served with potatoes or macaroni.
Makkarakeitto – sausage soup, a typical home-made dish.
Nakkikastike – sauce with small sausages, with potatoes or pasta.
Paistettu broileri – grilled (broiled) chicken.
Porsaankyljykset – pork chops.
Pyttipannu – the Swedish *pytt-i-panna* is ham and potatoes fried in butter.

Food & Drink Terms

Here is a glossary of food and drink terms you are likely to come across in Finland:

camping – barbecued sausage
graavi lohi – raw pickled salmon
hampurilainen – hamburger
herne – pea
hilla – cloudberry
ituja – bean shoots, mung sprouts, alfalfa
jauheliha – minced meat
juomavesi – drinking water
juusto – cheese
kaakao – hot chocolate
kaali – cabbage
kahvi – coffee
kana – chicken
kananmuna – egg
kala – fish
kalakukko – bread with fish filling
kalja – beer
karjalanpiirakka – rye pie with rice or potato filling
karpalo – cranberry
kastike – sauce
kasvis – vegetarian
katkarapu – shrimp
kaura – oats
keitto – soup
kinkku – ham
kiinankaali – Chinese cabbage
kiisseli – berry or fruit soup
kukkakaali – cauliflower

kukko – rooster
kukko – bread loaf filled with fish and pork, a specialty of Eastern Finland
laatikko – stew with minced vegetables and meat
lakka – cloudberry
lanttu – swede
leipä – bread
liha – meat
lihapiirakka – pie with meat & rice filling
limonadi – soft drink
lohi – trout or salmon
loimulohi – glowfired salmon or trout
lörtsy – thin pancake-shaped doughnut with apple or meat filling
maito – milk
maksa – liver
makkara – sausage
mansikka – strawberry
mehu – berry drink
muikku – whitefish
munakas – omelette
munakoiso – egg plant
mustikka – blueberry
muurinpohjalettu – thin large fried pancake
nakki – small sausage
naudan – beef
olut – beer
pannu – pan-fried food
paprika – capsicum
papu – bean
persilja – parsley
peruna – potato
pihvi – steak
piimä – sour milk
piiras – pie
pippuri – pepper
porkkana – carrot
poron – reindeer
poronkäristys – reindeer stew
porsaan – pork
puolukka – cranberry
puuro – porridge
ranskalaiset – French fries
reissumies – two slices of round rye bread
retiisi – radish
riekko – snow grouse
rieska – thin barley bread (like *chappati*)
riisi – rice
ruis – rye

ruisleipä – rye bread
salaatti – lettuce, salad
selleri – celery
sieni – mushroom
silakka – Baltic herring
silli – herring
simpukka – mussel
sipuli – onion
sokeri – sugar
soppa – soup
suola – salt
sämpylä – roll
tee – tea
tomaatti – tomato
vadelma – raspberry
valkosipuli – garlic
vesi – water
vihannes – vegetable
virvoitusjuoma – soft drink
voileipä – open sandwich

DRINKS
Nonalcoholic Drinks
Soft drinks or even water can easily take a large share of your budget if you are not careful. Half a litre of soda water costs the equivalent of US$3 at railway stations, and bottles of mineral water cost over US$3. However, all tap water is safe to drink (if not very tasty), and in Lapland, river water is pure and fresh. Supermarkets often have special prices for soft drinks in one litre glass bottles (say, under US$2). Local soft drinks include Jaffa, Aurinko, Frisco and Pommac, but international brands are also widely available.

You pay a deposit for all glass bottles of locally bottled soft drink and beer; when you return them to any store, your deposit is refunded. You can easily make a few markkaa by picking up discarded empty bottles.

Alcohol
Beer, wine and spirits are available from licensed bars and restaurants. There is a state monopoly on alcohol retail sales. Coupled with high 'sin taxes', this makes alcohol prices prohibitively high.

Many travellers bring the allowed quota

of alcohol from abroad (plan ahead, as Sweden and Norway are equally expensive), and some make a profit by selling their imports (which, naturally, is illegal). Apart from light beer, alcohol is sold exclusively at Alko liquor stores.

Beer What is served in Finland as *olut* is generally light, lager-type beer. Darker beers, let alone stout, are harder to find. There are several breweries and the variety is staggering.

The strongest beer is called IVA, or *nelos olut*, with some 5% alcohol content. It can only be purchased in Alko stores or in restaurants. Widely available in supermarkets are the lighter types of beer, the very popular and sufficiently tasty III Beer (called *keski kalja*, *keskari*, *kepu*, *kolmonen* or *kolmos olut)*, and the I Beer (called *Mieto Olut*, *ykkös olut* or *pilsneri)*, with less than 2% alcohol. It's a bargain at some inexpensive supermarkets. Prices of beer rise sharply according to alcohol content, so price alone is not a totally reliable indicator of taste.

Also popular is Gin Long Drink, also called *lonkero*. It is readily available in Alko stores and in restaurants.

Wine Alko bottles cheap wine, which provides a budget option (say, under 30 mk per bottle) for self-catering. Alko's supply of high-quality wines reaches gourmet standards, and prices are sky-high. Wine drinking in restaurants, despite its cost, has become more popular in Finland. Restaurants have long wine lists, but even a glass of red wine can cost 20 mk in many restaurants.

ENTERTAINMENT
Cinemas
There are over 330 movie theatres (there were 610 in 1960!) spread over 180 municipalities around the country. Of the 180 or so films shown each year, approximately 100 are American movies. France is the second most popular source of imported movies. Britain is third and Sweden fourth. Finnish movies account for 15% to 25% of films shown.

A single ticket costs approximately 40 mk, with discounts in summer or for early afternoon shows. Check locally.

Theatre & Classical Music
All large towns have their own theatre but all shows are in Finnish. Fringe theatre or comedy groups in Helsinki are also not particularly interesting to visitors due to the language problem.

Good classical concerts can be heard in many towns, often in churches and often for free. Enquire locally.

Discos
Large hotels in most Finnish towns run a disco that opens late in the evening and remains open till 4 am or so. There's always an admission fee. Technically, Finnish discos are sufficiently modern.

Spectator Sport
Sport is well commercialised in Finland, which means any sports event is advertised, attracts a large crowd and is endowed with a number of food and beverage outlets.

In winter, ice hockey is the leading magnet for the masses, with two or three matches weekly. Many indoor sports, including basketball and volleyball, have their season in winter. Skiing events don't offer the same intensity as team sports, but national (and international) competitions provide a thrill worth experiencing.

Summer sports are more accessible for the

Beer lovers won't go thirsty!

A downhill slope or cross-country
track is never far away.

traveller. Football (soccer) has a national league, and is followed by small crowds. Outside big cities, Finnish baseball, called *pesäpallo* or simply *pesis*, is the most popular team sport in summer. The Savo and Pohjanmaa regions have most of the teams in the national league, although Sotkamo in Kainuu is the most feverish place for this exciting game. Athletics (track and field) is very popular in Finland, owing to the country's many successful long-distance runners and javelin-throwers. The national games are called Kalevan Kisat, but there are a number of other national championships during the summer.

Car racing is another national craze, although not many notable races are arranged annually. Jyväskylän Suurajot (the Thousand Lakes Rally) is the main event, held in Central Finland. While visiting some isolated rural areas, you may come to the conclusion that local drivers think they are in a car race.

THINGS TO BUY

Finland was not the world's most exciting country for shopping when we wrote the 1st edition of this book. Since then things have changed dramatically. The frenzy years of the early 90s may be gone forever, but as the markka is still weaker than before, and shopkeepers must count on less profit, you can expect to find bargains in anything from electronics and trekking gear to books and popular CD records. There are so many newly poor people in Finland that bargain shops are everywhere. Markets have also mushroomed – from the popular outdoor markets (especially in Helsinki) which operate from May to September, to Sunday markets and flea markets. Also, as Finland is now a member of the EU, there is less duty on some imported goods.

Handicrafts

Finland has a large variety of handicrafts. Two main things should be kept in mind when looking, namely regional and individual styles. Regional styles are not numerous. The Karelian style is found mainly in North Karelia, in the markets of Joensuu, or shops in Ilomantsi. Lappish, or Sami, products are sold throughout Lapland, but the most interesting goods are in Inari and Hetta (Enontekiö). Duodji are authentic handicrafts produced according to Sami tradition. Expensive but genuine items should carry a Duodji token. Materials used include reindeer bone, hide, wood and metals. Jewellery and knives are popular buys. The wooden Lappish *kuksa* cup is an original item to take home. Pohjanmaa is another area with a culture strong enough to have what could be called an indigenous regional style.

As for individual style, there are so many artists it is impossible to create an exhaustive list. Small paintings on anything that can be carried, and sold, are common. Mugs and other pottery products are popular buys, and often reflect a rugged style, with natural colours and dyes. Objects made of birch bark reflect a very old tradition. Jewellery is also available, although much of it is industrially worked and prohibitively expensive. Spectrolite is the speciality of south-east Finland, and is on sale in Helsinki and elsewhere. Lapland and Upper Savo also have many exotic stones.

Many local artists work on cloth, creating colourful mittens *(lapaset)* or woollen hats *(myssy* or *pipo)*, necessary for winter travel, or woven wall-hangings *(raanu* or *ryijy)* and embroidery.

Where to Buy Markets, including Kauppatori in Helsinki, are treasure troves for innovative pieces of handicraft and art. Many artists only sell in their home studio, often advertised only on roadside signs. Few of these studios are listed in this book, so use your own initiative to visit the ones you spot.

Tehtaanmyymälä, a factory outlet, doesn't sell at large discount but may have quality seconds items at bargain prices. Main road crossings have these roadside shopping centres, and although they don't appear very cosy, the products are cheaper than in posh shops. Local artists usually sell through one or several handicraft shops in larger towns. Käsityökeskus is the central organisation for local handicraft. Independent shops are also numerous, and invariably offer a great variety of unique works. In summer, a large number of sales exhibitions pop up.

If you don't care for other people's work, contact the nearest *Käsityöasema* (there are hundreds of them in Finland) and create your own handicrafts. Many of them are especially geared towards visitors. These places preserve cottage industries and provide free advice. You pay only for the material, plus a small fee for rental of the equipment.

Kitchen Utensils & Glass

It may not sound like a good idea to carry home a cooking pot, cutlery or a dozen coffee cups, but Finns do so on their domestic travels. These utensils are often made by Hackman or Arabia factories, and are available in discount shops as well as department stores. Prices are high but so is quality.

Finland has been world-famous for its indigenous glass production for decades.

The heyday may seem gone, but the Savoy vase (designed by Alvar Aalto) and many stylish Iittala, Nuutajärvi and Humppila vases remain excellent buys. Glass is almost invariably sold at big roadside discount shops, and although most of it is crap, the best designs are always available.

Finnish designer pottery includes several mass-produced brand names that have gained popularity. They include:

Bjarmia – These heavy cups and plates come from a small factory in Kuusamo.
Kerman Savi – Probably the most popular brand in Finland, Kerman Savi comes from Heinävesi but there are several factory sales exhibitions throughout Finland.
Pentik – Originally created by Anu Pentik in Posio. There are factory sales points in Posio, Pello and Kuusankoski. Items are sold throughout Finland.

Books

Look for the biannual *alennusmyynti* (sale) in the three chains: Akateeminen, Suomalainen and Info, or at any *kirjakauppa* for that matter. There are always English books at discount rates. Akateeminen has the widest variety of English and French books, some of them at reasonable rates. Suomalainen has a discount section called Pinkka which has plenty of English books at absolutely bargain prices. Kirjatori is a small chain that sells books at low prices, with some isolated titles in English.

Osto ja myynti denotes 'buy and sell' for books and other items. Books in English may be scarce, but they are seldom pricey.

Trekking Goods

There are a few chains worth looking out for because of their special discounts. Partio-Aitta and Lassen Retkiaitta specialise in outdoor equipment, but many sports shops, such as Intersport, Kesport or Elmo Sport, have almost the same variety of sleeping bags and jackets.

Activities

Finland may be an expensive country to travel in, but many cheap or free activities open up some of the most beautiful and fascinating corners of this northern country. Becoming a part of a country's life, preferably as an active participant, is much more rewarding than remaining an isolated spectator viewing the world through a camera lens or car window.

Travelling in Finland is certainly not like travelling in more densely populated countries. There is no 'next bus' waiting to take you to isolated national parks or small fishing villages. You will have to drive, pedal, paddle or walk to get there, and that's what makes Finland more interesting (it may also be a cheaper way to spend more time in Finland).

There is little to do in terms of arrangements. You have a legal right to walk, cycle, paddle a canoe or even camp almost anywhere in Finland. If you have the appropriate equipment, all you have to do is to make the decision to go.

Finnish wilderness areas are essentially open to anyone. No guides or porters are available, so you'll have to be able to survive on your own. In Lapland the recommendation is to avoid trekking alone, but I trekked solo for five days, all the way to the Russian border, and there's really no problem, as long as you know what you are doing and are careful. For those going solo, it is highly recommended that you sign the trekkers' book as you depart. Write your name and next destination in each hut you visit and finally announce the completion of your trek. Without these arrangements, no-one will know of your whereabouts.

ACCESS

Finland grants trekkers more freedom than most countries. The Right of Public Access (Finnish: *jokamiehenoikeus*, Swedish: *allemansrätt*) gives you the right to walk, ski and cycle anywhere in forests and other wilderness areas; to travel on rivers and lakes in

Trekking

Trekking, or fell-walking, is one of the most popular activities in Finland, both among locals and visitors. It is one of the traditional forms of transport; forests are crisscrossed by walking paths and dirt roads (often used by monster logging vehicles).

Trekking in Finnish forests and wilderness areas requires a map, a compass, good preparation and all-weather trekking gear. In many national parks you can follow marked trails. In exchange, you'll get much freedom and good facilities. Nights are short or non-existent in summer, so you can walk at any hour if you don't find a suitable place to sleep. Water is abundant everywhere, and you can camp practically anywhere (though some national parks have restrictions).

summer, or on ice in winter. You can rest and swim anywhere, and pitch a tent for one night, as long as it's not on private property. You can pick wild berries and mushrooms wherever you go. Fishing is also possible everywhere (see Fishing later in this chapter) but you will need a permit.

Restrictions apply to snowmobiles (allowed on established routes only) and fire (no campfires on private land and when you do light fires, be very careful). Felling trees is forbidden (gather fallen wood for your campfire), and hunting is not allowed unless you have a licence.

Restrictions also apply to strict nature reserves where access is limited to paths only. Generally it is not wise to cut or harm living vegetation anywhere.

FOOD

You will have to carry all food when you walk in wilderness areas. You may be aware of your normal calorie (joule) requirements, but trekking is strenuous exercise and you may have to double the minimum daily amount.

Plan a nutritionally well-balanced daily food allowance and ration it with strict discipline. Vitamins should be carried (in tablet form) to supplement the diet. Buy dry food such as oats, macaroni, *jälkiuunileipä* rye bread slices, raisins, peanuts, chocolate, sugar and other dry food of your choice, plus some salami and soft cheese. Look for Blå Band's trekkers' food packs in sports shops. If you plan to walk from one wilderness hut to another, you will not need a cooking kit, but for unexpected situations it's good to have something to boil water in.

Berries & Mushrooms

Not all berries in Finnish forests are edible. Blueberries, which bring many walks to a halt, come into season in late July. The red cranberry is very sour but contains Vitamin C. Crush it, mix with sugar, and add to trekkers' food. On swamps and bogs, you may encounter larger cranberries. They taste best after the first night frost, and can be had the following spring. Orange cloudberry is

so appreciated by Finns that you probably won't have a chance to sample this slightly sour berry in the wild. Market prices are high.

Edible mushrooms are numerous, as are poisonous ones. Some of them must be boiled first to become edible. Unless you already know everything about mushrooms, you should buy a *sieniopas* (mushroom guidebook) and learn such words as *myrkyllinen* (poisonous), *keitettävä* (has to be boiled first) and *syötävä* (edible). Visiting a local market may give a hint as to what is tastiest but those more expensive mushrooms may be harder to find.

THINGS TO TAKE

Negotiate with a hotel or youth hostel about left-luggage arrangements before leaving for a trek. Carry only what you really need in the wilderness. Conversely, do not leave behind anything that you really do need!

A sheath knife will be essential for making a campfire, but a saw and axe are not necessary. Consider the following:

- binoculars
- bottle (plastic)
- candle
- compass
- cup
- cutlery
- first aid kit
- flashlight (torch)
- knife
- maps
- matches/lighter
- mosquito repellent
- mosquito coil
- mosquito net
- net head cover
- plastic bags
- plate
- sleeping bag

Fuel for Stoves

The most common fuels in Finland are methylated spirits (*spriitä*) and paraffin (*lamppuöljy*). 'Marinol' is a common brand and comes in one litre bottles from petrol stations, camping stores and marine chandlers. Camping Gaz and other butane cartridges are not easily obtainable and you cannot refill the large butane cylinders used by caravans. Coleman fuel is also unavailable but you can buy unleaded petrol from petrol stations if your stove will handle that. Recommended are either a Trangia or Sigg meths stove or an MSR multi fuel stove (which requires more skill).

Lighting a campfire is a commonsense issue on dry summer days, though in practice fires will be forbidden on such days. Don't light campfires away from a lakefront, and preferably use only established campfire places (nuotiopaikka in Finnish). Use at least one bucketful of water even after the fire is out to make sure it doesn't restart. Use too much water rather than too little.

TRANSPORT

Some trekking routes end in the middle of nowhere. Unless you have arranged for someone to meet you on arrival, you will have to walk to the nearest bus stop, which may be another long trek.

If there are private vehicles parked at the end point, you might be lucky enough to get a ride. But don't waste your time waiting. Leave a note under the windscreen wiper. Copy this: 'Saavuin juuri vaellukselta. Aloin jo kävellä tietä eteenpäin. Voitteko antaa kyydin bussipysäkille?' which translates 'I have just finished a trek. I started to walk down the road. Could you please give me a ride to the bus stop?'

Do not forget to write the time, your nationality (maybe a flag will do) and a symbol for the number of people in your party. Don't count on this ploy working but at least other trekkers will have enough time to think about stopping for you.

WHERE TO TREK

You can trek anywhere in Finland, but national parks and established trekking areas will have campfire places, free wilderness huts and boardwalks over the boggy bits.

South Finland

South Finland is not very good for long treks. There's a network of marked routes around the Kuhankuono area north of Turku. There are just a few national parks in southern Finland, including Nuuksio and Liesjärvi, where longer treks are possible.

In the province of Häme, there is some 330 km of marked walking track, mostly in North Häme. Together, the tracks are called Pirkan taival, or 'trail of Pirkka'. Pirkan taival runs between Parkano and Ähtäri, via Seitseminen, Kuru, Ruovesi, Helvetinjärvi and Virrat. The Pirkan taival map, which is sold in the Tampere tourist information office for approximately 25 mk, shows all accommodation options along the tracks.

Central Finland

The Maakuntaura trails zigzag right through Central Finland. Much of the route is still new, but walking tracks are marked with blue plastic string all the way and there are good signs wherever the path forks. With the excellent 1:20,000 topographical sheet maps, available at cost in local tourist offices, trekking is easy.

Eastern Finland

Many long tracks have been set up. There are established trails, with clear signs, in the national parks and recreational areas of North Karelia (free sketch maps are available in tourist and park offices). These include the areas of Patvinsuo, Petkeljärvi and Ruunaa.

Susitaival ('Wolf trail') is a 90 km trail that starts at Möhkö, east of Ilomantsi, and ends at Patvinsuo National Park. From there, it continues as the Bear's Path, or Karhunpolku. This 120 km trail covers the entire Lieksa municipal area, and the best attractions are along the route. At the northern end of the Bear's Path, there's a connecting trail to areas in northern Nurmes (for the Saramo trail) and, further along, there are connections to the UKK Route.

The UKK Route is the longest trekking route in Finland. It was named after president Urho K Kekkonen, and it's been developed for decades. The trail starts at the Koli Hill in the south, continues along the western side of Lake Pielinen and ends at the Iso-Syöte Hill, traversing via Vuokatti, Hyrynsalmi and the Ukko-Halla Hill. Further east in Kainuu, there are more sections of the UKK Route, including the Kuhmo to Lake Peurajärvi leg (connections from Nurmes) and the Kuhmo to Iso-Palonen leg.

There are also two short routes in Ilomantsi, the 26 km Taitajan taival and the 21 km Tapion taival.

Kuusamo & Lapland

The Karhunkierros trail is the most famous of all Finnish trekking routes. It runs through a rugged landscape in the Kuusamo wilderness. Huts provide shelter and free lodging en route, and there are good services and connections at several locations along the route.

Lapland is the main trekking region in Finland. Large national parks with well-equipped (and free) wilderness huts in the Pallas-Ounastunturi, Lemmenjoki, Pyhä-tunturi and Urho Kekkonen National Parks

are popular and well-featured in trekking maps (and in this book). Equally popular (but with only one hut) is the Kevo Gorge Nature Reserve route in the north-east corner of Lapland, where a tent is essential. From Lake Kilpisjärvi in the north-western corner of Finland, another tough route covers much difficult terrain on its way to Halti Fell, the highest in Finland. There are huts where staying overnight costs approximately 35 mk per person. Less-travelled trekking routes connect main roads in Lapland. (See the Lapland chapter for more details.)

FREE ACCOMMODATION
Wilderness Huts

There is a large network of huts throughout Lapland. Most of them have unlocked doors, basic bunks, cooking facilities, leftover dry food, a pile of dry firewood and even a wilderness telephone. You should always leave the hut as it was – replace the used

---

Wilderness Huts

Huts in wilderness areas have different names, according to their different forms and uses.

Autiotupa – A general word for 'desolate hut', with unlocked doors, meagre facilities and hard bunks. You may cook inside.

Kammi – A traditional Lappish hut (that is, made out of earth, wood and branches). It will provide basic shelter for one or two people, but may be hard to find.

Kämppä – This means simply 'a hut'. Kämpät are used by Saame reindeer keepers as a shelter, and are always open and uninhabited. They provide shelter for one to six people. In the south, kämpät are often private and locked.

Rajavartioston tupa – A small hut built for border guards. Most of them have unlocked doors, and sheltering overnight is legal. Keep a low profile, however, as the main users have a serious mission.

Tunturitupa – A 'fell hut'. It has unlocked doors and typical facilities.

Varaustupa – 'A hut to be reserved'. This kind of hut always has a locked door. Some may have an 'open' side too. The reserved side has mattresses and better facilities.

Yksityiskämppä – A private hut. It should not be used for any purpose other than as an emergency shelter when everything else fails. Remember: the Right of Public Access never gives permission to go onto private property.

Other names – Private property. Names given to houses in the wilderness indicate that they are out of bounds to the trekker. ∎

A typical *autiotupa* hut: four-star comfort for free!

firewood and clean the place. Take extra care not to be boisterous or more huts may end up with padlocks on their doors. Finland may now be the only country in the world to provide an extensive network of free, well-maintained huts. Let's keep it that way.

The 'wilderness rule' states that the last one to arrive will be given the best place to sleep. To put it another way: you should not stay more than one night; the first one to arrive will be the first to leave. Huts should not be used by large tourist groups who have paid a travel company for their package tour in advance. If whole huts are occupied by groups like these, you have right to advise them to use their tents (if they carry them) and certainly not to stay longer than one night. This may involve a long discussion, maybe a heated one, but it is to everyone's advantage to keep the hut network as overnight shelters only, not as a way to increase profits of European tour companies.

The tendency at the Forest and Park Service, which maintains most of the huts, is to increase the number of locked huts, which must be reserved beforehand (and which cost money), but most of the huts are still open to tired trekkers at no cost. Some huts have coupons for voluntary payment, which should be arranged after your trek at a post office. Please do pay if you see these coupons. Most huts are shown on maps, even on the 1:200,000 GT brand maps, but finding them might be difficult without a 1:50,000 map.

Shelters

Outside Lapland, trekking routes generally have no free houses, but you may find a simple log shelter, called *laavu* in Finnish. Although the original laavu was a handmade shelter of fresh spruce branches, what you are likely to come across these days is made of solid logs and good timber. A fire outside the laavu makes the inside warmer and keeps mosquitoes away, although that's just the theory. Often there will be smoke inside as well and you'll need insect repellent and a sleeping bag. Some people pitch their tent inside the laavu.

Cycling

Riding a bicycle in Finland is one of the best ways to see the country and to appreciate its nature but it is only recommended in summer.

What sets Finland apart from both Sweden and Norway is the almost total lack of mountains. Main roads are excellent and minor roads have little traffic. Bicycle tours are further facilitated by the liberal camping regulations and the long hours of daylight in June and July. There is also a very good network of cycle paths in and around most major cities and holiday destinations. All petrol stations have free toilets, and their cafés often serve excellent home-cooked lunches, even at 4 pm.

Main roads can be boring and slightly dangerous. Narrow secondary roads offer by far the best views, and they often follow historical walking routes. Most farmhouses are along these roads.

Carry water, as there are few places to fill up along some roads. Weather can be unpredictable, so pack a raincoat. Note that there are small milk-gathering stations along many roads, and they make excellent shelters during rainstorms.

In most towns bicycles can be hired for around 20 to 50 mk per day. Weekly rentals are widely available in many places.

BRINGING YOUR BICYCLE
Air

Most airlines will carry a bike free of charge, so long as the bike and panniers don't exceed the weight allowance per passenger (usually 20 kg/44 lbs). Hefty excess baggage charges may be incurred if you do, and this applies to both international and internal flights.

Inform the airline that you will be bringing your bike when you book your ticket. Arrive at the airport in good time to remove panniers and pedals, deflate tyres and turn handlebars around – the minimum dismantling usually required by airlines.

Bus

Bikes can be carried on long-distance buses for 10 mk if there is space available (and there usually is). Just advise the driver prior to departure. One traveller gave this comment:

When our tandem suffered a serious technical failure on our fifth day, our itinerary was salvaged by the fact that, unlike in the UK, it was transported without difficulty not only on trains but also on buses. One bus office quoted 7.50 mk for this but we were never charged on coaches.

Train

Bikes can accompany passengers on most normal train journeys. Notable exceptions are Inter-City (IC) and Pendolino trains. Take your bike directly to the Konduktöörivaunu carriage, pay the conductor in cash and take the receipt. You must collect your bike from the cargo carriage when you reach your destination.

WHERE TO CYCLE

You are allowed to cycle on all public roads except motorways (there are two types: the typical four lane roads with the green road & bridge symbol and those marked by a green symbol with a car).

Åland

The island province is the most popular region for bicycle tours. Bikes can be rented in Mariehamn and Eckerö, and come with a free island map. Scenic narrow roads are designated as bicycle routes, and marked by green lines on the map. Bikes are transported free on car ferries between the islands, but three special bicycle ferries also operate, charging a flat fee for each bike. Access routes from Turku take you through several islands and ferry routes, all of which are free. See the Åland chapter for details.

South Finland

South Finland has more traffic than other parts of the country, but with careful planning you can find quiet roads that offer more scenic value than busy motorways. King's Road, a historic route between Turku and Vyborg, passes by old settlements, churches and manor houses in Uusimaa and south-east Finland. Even quieter is the Ox Road that runs through rural areas from Turku to Hämeenlinna. There are also some good shorter rides around Turku (via several small villages) Rauma (via Eura and Köyliö), Vammala (via Ellivuori), Lahti (via Asikkala) and Kouvola (via Jaala and Iitti).

In addition to King's Road and the Ox Road, there are theme routes in Häme, such as Klaus Kurjen tie in Vesilahti, south of Tampere, and Route 66 north of Tampere.

Pohjanmaa

This flat region is a biker's dream, except that distances are long. Always follow quiet roads, such as those in central Pohjanmaa along the rivers Kauhajoki, Kyrönjoki, Laihianjoki and Lapuanjoki. Further north, practically all towns and villages lie along rivers that run from south-east to north-west. Bring your bike by train to Seinäjoki, or further north, and continue along the narrow roads.

Eastern Finland

Two theme routes cover the entire eastern frontier area, from the south all the way to Kuusamo in the north. Runon ja rajan tie ('Road of the poem and frontier') consists of secondary sealed roads which pass by several Karelian-theme houses where you can stuff yourself with eastern food. The route ends in northern Lieksa. Some of the smallest, most remote villages along the easternmost roads have been lumped together to create the Korpikylien tie ('Road of Wilderness Villages'). This route starts at the village of Saramo in northern Nurmes and ends at Hossa, in the north-east of Suomussalmi. Some sections are unsealed.

The provincial tourist office has printed a leaflet, *Karjalan kirkkotie*, which guides riders along the 'Karelian church route', from the Heinävesi monasteries to the municipality of Ilomantsi in the far east.

A recommended loop takes you around Lake Pielinen, and may include a ferry trip across the lake (this costs money, though). Following narrow gravel roads you will see attractive Karelian scenery.

Skiing

Skiing is one of the main outdoor activities in Finland. Just make sure you have access to a warm shower soon after exercise. Don't stay out in the cold after sweating on skiing tracks.

DOWNHILL SKIING

Considering how low Finnish hills are, it's surprising how many downhill resorts popped up during the 1980s. Most of the small ones are barely open in winter (beware of the busy winter holiday weeks that are too expensive and crowded to be appreciated) but there are many excellent ski resorts in North Finland. A short list of the best resorts includes Levi, Ruka, Pyhä and Ylläs, although Luosto, Olos, Pallastunturi, Saariselkä and Syöte are also fairly good. South of Kainuu, you could be satisfied with Himos (in Jämsä) or Koli. There are ski lifts in all major towns with a hill taller than the local apartment buildings.

Winter is the high season for all ski resorts. Accommodation is expensive in luxury cottages and apartments (built to satisfy the typical 1980s yuppie from Helsinki) but there are also cheaper options. You can rent all equipment at major ski resorts. If you have your own equipment, all you need is money for the ski lift. You can pay separately for each ride but daily passes are highly recommended. Around 100 mk would be a typical price for a day pass. Finnish slopes are rarely fatal – in fact, they are excellent slopes for learning this addictive activity. There are better slopes across the border in Sweden or Norway.

CROSS-COUNTRY SKIING

Cross-country skiing is one of the simplest things to do in winter in Finland. Practically every town and municipality maintains ski tracks around the urban centre. In many cases, these tracks are illuminated (valaistu latu). Access is always free, and getting lost is impossible on municipal tracks (they are usually loops of a few km).

Once you venture to tourist centres, the tracks get much longer but also better maintained. This means that tracks are in excellent condition soon after a snowfall. You can cover over 100 km of skiing tracks around some of the most popular tourist centres, especially in Lapland. Getting lost is a small but potential risk. Study route maps in advance. The long tracks are never illuminated, so get back well before the sun goes down.

Renting cross-country (nordic) ski equipment is not as simple as obtaining downhill skis, so ask around. Alternatively, purchasing simple skis in a local sports shop would be a good investment if you're staying more than a few days in winter. You also need special skiing shoes, or monot, for cross-country skiing. Flea markets are a safe bet for these.

SKI JUMPING

Although ski jumping is spectacular, it's not recommended for travellers! However, you can watch flying Finns at various centres. Lahti's skyline is dominated by its three ski jumping ramps. Other big ski jumping towns are Kuopio and Jyväskyä, home town and former training ground of Olympic champion Matti Nykänen. You might be fortunate enough to be in town the same time as a competition, although just watching practice can be interesting. Ski jumping events are usually part of general ski tournaments.

SNOWMOBILE SAFARIS

As a modern means of transport across huge snowfields, snowmobile safaris have become common among tour agents, from the Lahti area in the south to Lapland in the north. This noisy activity ain't cheap but it does enable you to reach distant destinations far more quickly than by skiing.

Snowmobile safaris are regulated. Following established snowmobile routes is mandatory (they are clearly marked) and tours include a guide and insurance. Snowmobile safaris are not for everyone but they do offer a professional guide, a warm meal in the wilderness and some interesting fellow travellers. Contact regional or local tourist offices in Lahti, North Karelia, Kainuu, Kuusamo or Lapland. In Kuhmo alone, you'll find 350 km of marked routes. Expect to pay 1000 mk for an all-day tour. The main season is from November to March, in Lapland to April.

Rowing & Canoeing

Finland is best experienced travelling on lakes, rivers and canals.

RENTALS

For independent travel on waterways, you will have to rent a rowing boat or a canoe. The typical Finnish rowing boat is common and will be available everywhere (usually at a cheaper rate than canoes). Your back will be facing the bow of the boat, so you'll have to turn your head to see where you're heading. Controlling a rowing boat is not as easy as canoeing; consequently, rowing boats are never used on rivers with rapids. Use rowing boats on lakes, especially for visits to nearby islands.

It's impossible to provide exact rental prices. A rowing boat is a fairly simple deal; you usually return the same day and there are no hidden extras. Canoe trips usually take several days, so you'll need a waterproof plastic barrel for your gear, and transport to/from either end. Life-jackets are essential, as are waterproof route maps. All these will cost you money (but are certainly worth every markka).

Hiring a canoe is not simple. You should contact a local or regional tourist office and politely refuse a guided tour (unless you want it). Study routes at local libraries (detailed maps are usually available) and enquire about free maps or guidebooks. Try to locate a rental company at both ends of the route, and compare rates (including transport). It would probably be more convenient to rent from the end point so that you will first be transported to the starting point. Thus, the completion of your journey can be more flexible.

RIVER ROUTES

Most Finnish river routes are little travelled. Few 'gateway services' are available; you can't just show up and leave. Fortunately, most routes have been meticulously researched, and a route map with detailed information on all rapids is usually available. In many cases, these maps will be provided free of charge (even if you don't actually go). Waterproof maps usually cost around 25 mk.

Several routes are partly impassable. Obstacles include broken dams, hydroelectric power stations and fatal waterfalls. Studying the route map extremely carefully before and during a canoe trip is essential! Always be prepared to carry the canoe. This could save your life.

All rapids are classified according to a scale from I to VI. I is very simple, II will make your heart beat faster, III is dangerous for your canoe, IV may be fatal for the inexperienced. Rapids classified as VI will probably kill you. Tricky rapids have been researched carefully, and the best route descriptions will tell you exactly how to negotiate them safely (the Lieksa area has such guidebooks). Most route maps are available in English.

WHERE TO ROW & PADDLE
South Finland

Rowing boats are available at most camping grounds and many youth hostels. The southern provinces do not offer extensive canoeing options. You have to travel as north as Vammala or North Häme to find proper canoeing routes.

There are canoes for hire at the Ikaalinen tourist information office. Three routes end in Lake Kyrösjärvi, and you can easily paddle across the lake to the village of Ikaalinen. The Sipsiönjoki River route starts at Lake Liesjärvi, inside Seitseminen

National Park. Beware of the Vaho rapids under the railway tracks (carry the canoe). For the Aurejoki River route, first paddle right across Lake Aurejärvi. The Kallikoski rapids are very tricky, so carry the canoe unless you're experienced. The easiest route to Ikaalinen is the Parkano Route – start from the town of Parkano, or further north in Kihniö. Even though road No 3 is just a few hundred metres away, this is a very quiet route. It is mostly narrow lakes, with no difficult rapids.

The Ruovesi-Virrat area features beautiful wilderness and picturesque waterways. Canoe rentals have to be arranged at least one week in advance through the tourist office at the Haapasaari Holiday Village. The Haukkajoki route starts at Lake Haukkajärvi in Helvetinjärvi National Park and ends near the village of Kuru. Another route goes from Lake Pihlajavesi to Lake Tarjanne. Before you go, contact Pirkanmaan Matkailu in the Tampere tourist office for maps, information and other assistance.

Central Finland

There are two superb canoeing routes in Central Finland. One starts at the village of Karstula and runs through scenic countryside to the town of Saarijärvi. There are several camp sites along the way, and a few demanding rapids, especially the infamous Kalmukoski (which translates roughly as 'rapids of death'). The Wanhan Vitosen route runs from the village of Petäjävesi to the Rasua camping ground, north of the town of Jämsänkoski. There are several camp sites along this route too.

You can a rent rowing boats and canoes for trips on Lake Päijänne, or try some little-travelled routes in Hartola.

Pohjanmaa

The Kyrönjoki River is good for canoeing. Its entire length is 205 km, but you can do shorter trips down the river from Kauhajoki, Kurikka or Ilmajoki. Several historical points of interest are along this route. Get a copy of the *Kyrönjoen Melontareitti* leaflet for further information.

Savo

Savo is by far the most popular region for water travel. Rowing boats are common and can be hired at camping grounds and many youth hostels. Many natural wonders in Savo can only be experienced by canoe or rowing boat, especially the rugged Kolovesi National Park.

The Aquatic Nature Trail from Juva to Sulkava is a 52 km canoeing route. Consult the Juva section for further information. Sulkava hires rowing boats, but its speciality is the unique church longboats. You will have to join a group for the Ulpukka route in Enonkoski.

In North Savo, you'll have several routes to choose from, many of them on large lakes.

North Karelia

North Karelia is one of the best regions for canoe routes. In addition to the tough Ruunaa waterways, and other excellent routes around Lieksa, the Vaikkojoki River between Juuka and Kaavi has been promoted as a good canoeing route. The large municipality of Ilomantsi offers excellent route possibilities on lakes, rivers and rapids.

Kainuu

A most demanding (and rewarding?) canoeing route, between Kuhmo and Kajaani, follows the historic tar route through lakes, rivers and rapids. No longer used for floating tar barrels, the river has been restored to its 'original' state, which has also made water transport more difficult. There is an excellent route guide in English, which may still be available at the Kuhmo tourist office or at other information offices around Kainuu. The detailed route map by Karttakeskus costs about 50 mk.

Another canoeing route runs from Lentiira in the north to Kuhmo in the south.

Kuusamo & Lapland

The two magnificent rivers in Kuusamo, the Kitkajoki and the Oulankajoki, have several dangerous waterfalls. Despite (or because of) this, they are very rewarding routes to take. For anyone not feeling secure about their paddling skills, several operators offer white-water rafting along both rivers. This option may come in handy if you just want to experience the thrill and the beauty.

In north-east Lapland, one of the most interesting canoeing routes starts at the village of Kuttura and finishes in Ivalo, 70 km away. The river is passable all summer, but there are rocks along the route. Of the 30 rapids, the Saarnaköngäs and the Toloskoski are the trickiest. Free leaflets for this route are available in Ivalo. Another good place for canoeing is the Lemmenjoki River.

The Ounasjoki River, which runs from Hetta in the north to Rovaniemi in the south, is one of the longest passable canoeing routes. Contact tour agencies at either end, or at Sirkka (north of Kittilä).

BOAT TRAVEL

The best routes are between Kuopio and Savonlinna, Joensuu and Koli, Tampere and Hämeenlinna and Jyväskylä and Lahti. See Getting Around for ferries, ships and steamers that ply the lakes, and check local information for departure times, prices and other details.

Other Activities

FISHING

Finnish waters are teeming with fish. The best fishing spots are established 'Government Fishing Areas' and the Forest and Park Service puts tonnes of fish in these waters every year. Fishing with a rod or lure always requires a permit. In addition to a local permit, which has time and catch limits (say, two salmon per day and an unrestricted amount of other species), you will need a national fishing permit, which is available from all post offices. Always arrange the national fishing permit beforehand. The waters in northern Lapland require a special regional permit, as do waters in Åland. The local permit can be purchased for three hours, one day, one week, or something in between. You always wonder whether

anyone actually checks these things – well, they do in Finland! The system is enforced by permit checkers, who sneak around fishing areas.

The Forest and Park Service publishes an annual guide to fishing waters. Many tourist offices will give you a guide map for regional waters. Be forewarned, however, that Finland has at least one million enthusiastic (and jealous) domestic anglers. The most popular areas, such as Hossa, Ruunaa, Peurajärvi or Teno, are always full of Finns. Lapland has a great number of excellent fishing spots, but the number of designated places in South Finland is also increasing. You are not allowed to fish in May. Always enquire about local restrictions before buying the daily permit.

GOLF

Golf courses, golf club memberships and the subculture associated with golfing was one of the typical features of the wealthy 1980s. These days many golf courses in Finland are owned by banks (either actual banks or ex-banks trying to figure out how to survive their collapse). The most unusual golf course in Finland is in Tornio (see Lapland).

You need a Green Card to play on most Finnish golf courses, but many courses are open to anyone who knows how to play and how to dress, for 50 to 200 mk per day. At last count, there were approximately 100 golf courses throughout Finland, open from late April to mid-October, but much depends on the weather. On 15 May 1995, all Finland was covered by snow for two days. For information on Finnish golf courses, contact Suomen Golfliitto, Radiokatu 20, 00240 Helsinki (☎ 158 6806, fax 147 145).

TRACING YOUR ANCESTORS

Many visitors to Finland have Finnish ancestors. A trip would be a good chance to find out more about their lives, and you may even find relatives you never knew existed. Before you waste time on futile efforts, try the easiest way of discovering whether your roots are in Finland. It is likely that your ancestors are already mentioned in at least one published book.

Libraries

In provincial capitals and other large cities, public libraries have a special section devoted to the region. With luck, you will find books on surveys of local families there.

The best place to visit first is Suomen Sukututkimusseura (Finnish Genealogical Society) at Mariankatu 7, 00170 Helsinki (☎ 179 189, fax 626 989). There's an extensive library of published books of family surveys, and assistance is provided.

Archives

The best information will come directly from archives, but you will have to pay a fee for the service. If you know for sure where your ancestors lived (and you know they were members of the Lutheran church, which is very likely), go directly to the local Kirkkoherranvirasto (Parochial Archives),

an office usually found near the local Lutheran church. These archives are the best bet for tracing people who lived during the 20th century.

If you're looking for ancestors from the 19th century, or earlier, go to Kansallis-arkisto (National Archives) at Rauhankatu 17, 00170 Helsinki (☎ 228 521, fax 176 302). This place covers all Finland, and there's a section for the Uusimaa region.

If you have several ancestors from various places within a region, go to the regional Maakunta-arkisto (Provincial Archives). These archives have the best information on regional history, and will provide you with invaluable information. The local archive covers a large region, as below:

Turku – South-West
Vaasa – Pohjanmaa
Hämeenlinna – Häme
Joensuu – Eastern Finland
Mikkeli – lost Karelia
Oulu – North Finland, including Kainuu.

Getting There & Away

AIR
Buying a Plane Ticket
The plane ticket will probably be the single most expensive item in your travel budget, and buying it can be an intimidating business. There is likely to be a multitude of airlines and travel agents hoping to separate you from your money, and it is always worth putting aside a few hours to research the current market. Start early: some of the cheapest tickets have to be bought months in advance, and some popular flights sell out early. Talk to other recent travellers – they may be able to stop you making some of their mistakes. Look at the ads in newspapers and magazines, consult reference books and watch for special offers. Then phone around travel agencies for bargains. Find out the fare, the route, the duration of the journey and any restrictions on the ticket. Then sit back and decide which is best for you.

Use the fares quoted in this book as a guide only. They are approximate and are based on the rates advertised by travel agencies at the time of going to press. Quoted airfares do not necessarily constitute a recommendation for the carrier.

Once you have your ticket, write down the ticket number, together with the flight number and other details, and keep the information somewhere separate. If the ticket is lost or stolen, this will help you get a replacement.

It's also sensible to buy travel insurance as early as possible. If you buy it the week before you fly, you may find, for example, that you're not covered for delays to your flight caused by strikes or other industrial action.

Round-the-World Tickets
Round-the-world (RTW) tickets have become popular in the last few years. Many RTW tickets are real bargains, and can work out cheaper than an ordinary return ticket.

Prices start at about UK£850, A$1800 or US$1300, depending on the season.

The official RTW tickets offered by the airlines are usually put together by two airlines, and permit you to fly anywhere you want on their route systems, as long as you don't backtrack. Another restriction is that you (usually) must book the first sector in advance, and cancellation penalties then apply. There may also be restrictions on the number of stops you are permitted. The tickets are usually valid for between 90 days and a year. Finnair has combination routes with Qantas, Cathay Pacific and United. An alternative type of RTW ticket is put together by a travel agency, using a combination of discounted tickets.

Flight Information
Few airlines fly direct to Finland but most European international operators will fly you to Helsinki after a stopover in their respective hub. From outside Europe, you will find that prices are similar to flights to any other European city. Within Europe, there is more variety in fares, depending on which city you want to fly from.

Finnair is the Finnish national carrier, with flights from Bangkok, Beijing, Istanbul, Miami, New York, Osaka, San Francisco, Singapore, Tokyo and Toronto, as well as Amsterdam, Athens, Berlin, Brussels, Budapest, Copenhagen, Düsseldorf, Frankfurt, Geneva, Gothenburg, Hamburg, Hanover, Lisbon, London (Heathrow), Madrid, Milan, Munich, Oslo, Paris, Prague, Rome, Stockholm, Stuttgart, Tallinn, Vienna, Warsaw and Zürich.

There are also direct flights to/from Riga, Vilnius, Kiev, Murmansk, Moscow, St Petersburg and Petrozavodsk.

To/From North America
Because of the shape of the globe, Finland is actually closer to North America than some

destinations in southern Europe, and the flying time is shorter.

To/From the USA Finnair and Delta fly from New York to Helsinki every day except Sunday, and Delta has a wide range of connecting flights to and from other cities in the USA. The normal one-way fare is US$1130, return $1438, but advance purchase return fares start at US$668. There is also a special fare: travel from New York City on a Friday or Saturday, return on Sunday, Monday or Tuesday (maximum stay of four days) for US$548. You should check the discounted trans-Atlantic fares, and the prices of connecting flights to Helsinki, which tend to be relatively low.

The *New York Times*, *LA Times*, *Chicago Tribune* and *San Francisco Chronicle Examiner* all produce weekly travel sections in which you'll find any number of travel agency ads. Council Travel and STA Travel have offices in major cities across the USA. The *Travel Unlimited* newsletter (PO Box 1058, Allston, MA 02134) publishes details of the cheapest airfares and courier opportunities from the USA to destinations all over the world.

From Helsinki, you can fly to New York for as little as 1295 mk one-way, and to Los Angeles for 1690 mk one-way. Prices are for students and people under 26 years of age, as quoted by Kilroy (the main student travel agent in Finland and Scandinavia).

To/From Canada Finnair flies from Toronto to Helsinki, and you will find any number of North American and European airlines with connecting flights all the way to Helsinki. Most airlines fly over Greenland on the way. Travel CUTS has offices in all major cities. The Toronto *Globe & Mail* and *Vancouver Sun* carry travel agency ads. You will also find the magazine *Great Expeditions* (PO Box 8000-411, Abbotsford BC V2S 6H1) useful for airfare information.

To/From the UK
The published one-way fare from London to Helsinki is £279. Not many of these are sold,

however, and cheap return fares start from £209 (with a minimum stay of a Saturday night, maximum stay one month). Student and youth fares from STA Travel London start at £97 one-way, £192 return, with few conditions. The cheapest three month ticket is £275 return, and must be paid for instantly upon booking.

From Helsinki, Kilroy (the student travel bureau) offers return flights to London for 1390 mk.

You may find even cheaper options. Local travel agencies offer flights to Finland – look for listings in the magazine *Time Out* for the most attractive prices. Check the ads in the Sunday papers and in *Exchange & Mart*, and look out for the free magazines widely available in London (outside the main railway station, in the city, etc).

Most British travel agents are registered with ABTA (Association of British Travel Agents). If you have paid for your flight through an ABTA-registered agent who then goes out of business, ABTA will guarantee a refund or an alternative. Unregistered bucket shops are sometimes cheaper but riskier.

To/From Europe
Helsinki is well connected to most European capitals and major cities by a number of airlines. If you live in Europe, you will probably know how to find your way to Finland. If not, you will find busy flight markets in cities such as Amsterdam, Athens, Berlin and Paris. In other towns, consult local telephone directories first. (Travel agency is *reisebüro* in German, *agence de voyages* in French, *reisbureau* in Dutch and *rejsebureau* in Danish.)

In Amsterdam, most inexpensive travel agencies, such as Malibu Travel and NBBS, are to be found along Damrak. In Athens, there are many agents near Syntagma Square. In Berlin, consult the magazines *Zitty* and *TIP* for travel agency ads. In Paris, there are several discount travel agencies on Avenue de l'Opéra, as well as around the Latin Quarter, including the large agency Nouvelles Frontieres.

From Helsinki, the Kilroy travel bureau

Air Travel Glossary

Apex Tickets Apex stands for Advance Purchase Excursion fare. These tickets are usually between 30 and 40% cheaper than the full economy fare, but there are restrictions. You must purchase the ticket at least 21 days in advance (sometimes more) and must be away for a minimum period (normally 14 days) and return within a maximum period (90 or 180 days). Stopovers are not allowed, and if you have to change your dates of travel or destination, there will be extra charges to pay. These tickets are not fully refundable – if you have to cancel your trip, the refund is often considerably less than what you paid for the ticket. Take out travel insurance to cover yourself in case you have to cancel your trip unexpectedly – for example, due to illness.

Baggage Allowance This will be written on your ticket; you are usually allowed one 20-kg item to go in the hold, plus one item of hand luggage. Some airlines which fly transpacific and transatlantic routes allow for two pieces of luggage (there are limits on their dimensions and weight).

Bucket Shops At certain times of the year and/or on certain routes, many airlines fly with empty seats. This isn't profitable and it's more cost-effective for them to fly full, even if that means having to sell a certain number of drastically discounted tickets. They do this by off-loading them onto bucket shops (UK) or consolidators (USA), travel agents who specialise in discounted fares. The agents, in turn, sell them to the public at reduced prices. These tickets are often the cheapest you'll find, but you can't purchase them directly from the airlines. Availability varies widely, so you'll not only have to be flexible in your travel plans, you'll also have to be quick off the mark as soon as an advertisement appears in the press.

Bucket-shop agents advertise in newspapers and magazines and there's a lot of competition – especially in places like Amsterdam and London which are crawling with them – so it's a good idea to telephone first to ascertain availability before rushing from shop to shop. Naturally, they'll advertise the cheapest available tickets, but by the time you get there, these may be sold out and you may be looking at something slightly more expensive.

Bumped Just because you have a confirmed seat doesn't mean you're going to get on the plane – see Overbooking.

Cancellation Penalties If you have to cancel or change an Apex or other discount ticket, there may be heavy penalties involved; insurance can sometimes be taken out against these penalties. Some airlines impose penalties on regular tickets as well, particularly against 'no show' passengers.

Check In Airlines ask you to check in a certain time ahead of the flight departure (usually two hours on international flights). If you fail to check in on time and the flight is overbooked, the airline can cancel your booking and give your seat to somebody else.

Confirmation Having a ticket written out with the flight and date on it doesn't mean you have a seat until the agent has confirmed with the airline that your status is 'OK'. Prior to this confirmation, your status is 'on request'.

Courier Fares Businesses often need to send their urgent documents or freight securely and quickly. They do it through courier companies. These companies hire people to accompany the package through customs and, in return, offer a discount ticket which is sometimes a phenomenal bargain. In effect, what the courier companies do is ship their freight as your luggage on the regular commercial flights. This is a legitimate operation – all freight is completely legal. There are two shortcomings, however: the short turnaround time of the ticket, usually not longer than a month; and the limitation on your luggage allowance. You may be required to surrender all your baggage allowance for the use of the courier company, and be only allowed to take carry-on luggage.

Discounted Tickets There are two types of discounted fares – officially discounted (such as Apex – see Promotional Fares) and unofficially discounted (see Bucket Shops). The latter can save you more than money – you may be able to pay Apex prices without the associated Apex advance booking and other requirements. The lowest prices often impose drawbacks, such as flying with unpopular airlines, inconvenient schedules, or unpleasant routes and connections.

Economy Class Tickets Economy-class tickets are usually not the cheapest way to go, though they do give you maximum flexibility and they are valid for 12 months. If you don't use them, most are fully refundable, as are unused sectors of a multiple ticket.

Full Fares Airlines traditionally offer first class (coded F), business class (coded J) and economy class (coded Y) tickets. These days there are so many promotional and discounted fares available that few passengers pay full fare.

Lost Tickets If you lose your airline ticket, an airline will usually treat it like a travellers' cheque and, after inquiries, issue you with a replacement. Legally, however, an airline is entitled to treat it like cash, so if you lose a ticket, it could be forever. Take good care of your tickets.

MCO An MCO (Miscellaneous Charges Order) is a voucher for a value of a given amount, which resembles an airline ticket and can be used to pay for a specific flight with any IATA (International Air Transport Association) airline. MCOs, which are more flexible than a regular ticket, may satisfy the irritating onward ticket requirement, but some countries are now reluctant to accept them. MCOs are fully refundable if unused.

No Shows No shows are passengers who fail to show up for their flight for whatever reason. Full-fare no shows are sometimes entitled to travel on a later flight. The rest of us are penalised (see Cancellation Penalties).

Open Jaw Tickets These are return tickets which allow you to fly to one place but return from another, and travel between the two 'jaws' by any means of transport at your own expense. If available, this can save you backtracking to your arrival point.

Overbooking Airlines hate to fly with empty seats, and since every flight has some passengers who fail to show up (see No Shows), they often book more passengers than they have seats available. Usually the excess passengers balance those who fail to show up, but occasionally somebody gets bumped. If this happens, guess who it is most likely to be? The passengers who check in late.

Promotional Fares These are officially discounted fares, such as Apex fares, which are available from travel agents or direct from the airline.

Reconfirmation You must contact the airline at least 72 hours prior to departure to 'reconfirm' that you intend to be on the flight. If you don't do this, the airline can delete your name from the passenger list and you could lose your seat.

Restrictions Discounted tickets often have various restrictions on them, such as necessity of advance purchase, limitations on the minimum and maximum period you must be away, restrictions on breaking the journey or changing the booking or route etc.

Round-the-World Tickets These tickets have become very popular in the last few years; basically, there are two types – airline tickets and agent tickets. An airline RTW ticket is issued by two or more airlines that have joined together to market a ticket which takes you around the world on their combined routes. It permits you to fly pretty well anywhere you choose using their combined routes as long as you don't backtrack, ie keep moving in approximately the same direction east or west. Other restrictions are that you (usually) must book the first sector in advance and cancellation penalties then apply. There may be restrictions on how many stopovers you are permitted. The RTW tickets are usually valid for 90 days up to a year.

The other type of RTW ticket, the agent ticket, is a combination of cheap fares strung together by an enterprising travel agent. These may be cheaper than airline RTW tickets, but the choice of routes will be limited.

Standby This is a discounted ticket where you only fly if there is a seat free at the last moment. Standby fares are usually only available directly at the airport, but sometimes may also be handled by an airline's city office. To give yourself the best possible chance of getting on the flight you want, get there early and have your name placed on the waiting list. It's first come, first served.

Student Discounts Some airlines offer student-card holders 15% to 25% discounts on their tickets. The same often applies to anyone under the age of 26. These discounts are generally only available on ordinary economy-class fares. You wouldn't get one, for instance, on an Apex or an RTW ticket, since these are already discounted.

Tickets Out An entry requirement for many countries is that you have an onward or return ticket, in other words, a ticket out of the country. If you're not sure what you intend to do next, the easiest solution is to buy the cheapest onward ticket to a neighbouring country or a ticket from a reliable airline which can later be refunded if you do not use it.

Transferred Tickets Airline tickets cannot be transferred from one person to another. Travellers sometimes try to sell the return half of their ticket, but officials can ask you to prove that you are the person named on the ticket. This may not be checked on domestic flights, but on international flights, tickets are usually compared with passports.

Travel Periods Some officially discounted fares, Apex fares in particular, vary with the time of year. There is often a low (off-peak) season and a high (peak) season. Sometimes there's an intermediate or shoulder season as well. At peak times, when everyone wants to fly, both officially and unofficially discounted fares will be higher, or there may simply be no discounted tickets available. Usually the fare depends on your outward flight – if you depart in the high season and return in the low season, you pay the high-season fare. ■

offers return flights to Brussels (1440 mk), Frankfurt (1990 mk), Rome (2190 mk), Copenhagen (990 mk), Paris (1900 mk), Amsterdam (1850 mk) and Zürich (2160 mk). These are winter prices; fares are apparently lower in summer. For one-way flights from Helsinki to European cities, Kilroy quotes the following prices for students and people under 26 years of age:

Destination	Price
Amsterdam	925 mk
Frankfurt	995 mk
London	695 mk
Paris	950 mk
Zürich	1080 mk

To/From Russia & Estonia Finnair and Aeroflot fly daily between Helsinki and St Petersburg as well as Helsinki and Moscow. Finnair, Estonian Air and Aeroflot fly twice a day from Tallinn to Helsinki. There are also flights to Helsinki from Riga and Kiev.

To/From Asia

Flights from Asia to Europe tend to be cheaper than flights in the other direction, so it's worth purchasing the return flight in places like Bangkok, Penang (Malaysia), Hong Kong, New Delhi or even Kathmandu. In Hong Kong, the *South China Morning Post* carries travel agency prices, but in most other cities, you will have to shop around. In Bangkok, Khaosan Road has more bucket shops than other areas; the reliable ETC is also on soi Ngam Duphli. Agents along or near Silom Road are usually more expensive. In Penang, try Lebuh Chulia agents. In Singapore, shop around Bencoolen Street. In New Delhi, Connaught Circus is the standard hunting area, but the Main Bazaar area has become increasingly popular for cheap flights.

As you will find out, it makes little difference whether you want to fly to Helsinki or Paris – most airlines sell a standard European fare, regardless of the distance flown from the first stop. Bangladesh Biman and Airlanka offer the cheapest European fares but don't fly to Helsinki. It's worth shopping around first. Aeroflot (via Moscow), Lot (via

Warsaw) and ČSA (via Prague) are among the cheapest airlines offering the general European fare all the way to Helsinki, but some airlines (such as Thai or SAS) will sometimes promote special fares for students or young people.

Finnair flies to Helsinki from Singapore, Bangkok, Tokyo and Beijing. (Finnair aircraft from Japan feature the popular Moomin figures.) Its prices are no cheaper than other West European airlines but flights are generally nonstop and convenient. From Helsinki, there are flights to several Asian cities, including Bangkok (1825 mk one-way) and Tokyo (2830 mk one-way). Prices are for students and people under 26.

To/From Australia

Flying from Australia is a two stage journey (at least), with likely stopovers in either Singapore or Bangkok, or cities in Europe. Qantas flies to Frankfurt, and British Airways, KLM, Lufthansa and a few other European airlines fly to Helsinki from Australia via London, Amsterdam, Frankfurt, or other cities, respectively. In Australia, STA and Flight Centres International are major dealers in cheap air tickets. Check the travel agency ads in the newspapers and the Yellow Pages and shop around.

To/From New Zealand

Air New Zealand flies to London and Frankfurt. British Airways, Lufthansa and the French airline UTA will fly you to Europe, with frequent connections available to Helsinki. The cheapest way to visit Finland from New Zealand, on the opposite side of the globe, might be an inexpensive round-the-world ticket which allows you to stop in Helsinki.

As in Australia, STA and Flight Centres International are popular travel agencies.

LAND
To/From Sweden

There are six crossings from northern Sweden to northern Finland across the rivers Tornionjoki (Swedish: Torneälv) and Muonionjoki. Many of these crossings are handy if you are coming from the Norwegian harbour town Narvik via Kiruna, a popular route because of its train and road connections.

Crossing the border involves no hassle. There is usually one joint border post near the bridge across the river. Take the green lane if you have nothing to declare.

Further south in Sweden, there are trains and buses to the Swedish town of Haparanda, from where you can easily walk to the Finnish town of Tornio. (See the Tornio map in the Lapland chapter.) From Tornio, you will have to pay for the bus ride to the nearest railway station, in Kemi.

Further north, there are five additional crossings (see the West Lapland map in the Lapland chapter). The Swedish road No 400 and the Finnish road No 21 are parallel to the Tornionjoki and Muonionjoki rivers but some of the crossings are far from the towns or the main road, especially on the Swedish side.

At Övertorneå, a beautiful bridge links Sweden to Aavasaksa, a tourist centre below Aavasaksa hill.

From the small Swedish settlement of Pello, several km from road No 400, there is a bridge to the larger Finnish centre of Pello.

From the Swedish township Pajala further north, there is a narrow road (about 30 km long) which makes the crossing south of Kolari. A new pedestrian bridge across the river near Lappea is planned.

From Muodoslompolo, it is 13 km to the border bridge, which is just 2 km south of Muonio.

Finally, Karesuando, the northernmost town in Sweden and at the end of road No 400, has direct access to the Finnish Karesuvanto on road No 21.

If you just want to cross the border for the heck of it, there are a few places further north of road No 21 that take you to small Swedish settlements. One is at Keinovuopio, a small Swedish Sami settlement across the river near the Peera youth hostel, some 25 km south of Kilpisjärvi. There is no border control whatsoever. There are several walks on the Swedish side. If you walk north, you will eventually reach the joint border post of Sweden, Norway and Finland. (See the North-West Lapland section for further details.)

Bus Buses along the Swedish east coast drive from Stockholm to Haparanda, and further north along the border. Pick a bus stop from where you can walk to Finland. Haparanda, Övertorneå and Karesuando are the most convenient.

Train The typical route to Finland from any point in Europe goes via Denmark to the Swedish town of Helsingborg, from where there are regular trains to Stockholm. It may be best to do this journey in stages. There are also direct long-distance trains to Stockholm from various big cities in Europe (although the journey through southern Sweden is probably one of the most boring train trips in the whole of Europe). Train passes give discounts on most ferry routes across to Finland.

If you don't like the idea of a ferry ride, you can continue by train to the Swedish town of Haparanda in the far north, and transfer there by bus to the Finnish town of Tornio.

To/From Norway

There are six border crossings along roads from the Norwegian Finnmark to Finnish Lapland plus a few legal crossings along wilderness tracks (otherwise crossing the border is a serious violation of the law). This is a real no-hassle border, with no formalities in normal cases. In fact, some border stations actually close in the early evening, after which you can cross the border with no control at all.

Finnish buses run between Rovaniemi and the Norwegian border post, and some buses continue on to the first Norwegian town, which is usually along Norwegian bus routes. Free timetables (ask bus drivers or at stations) usually list these connections. With a car, crossing is often very simple, although a brief check takes place occasionally.

Hitchhiking is only recommended

between June and August (May and September if the weather is fine). Carry waterproof gear and expect long waits. Being positive also helps: getting stuck at the bottom of an Arctic Sea fjord may be a unique experience that you will never forget. There's the midnight sun, fresh winds and abundant bird life.

The north-western route takes you through very beautiful scenery from Kilpisjärvi to Skibotn in Norway. Some buses run from Rovaniemi all the way to Skibotn. The border station is on the Finnish side. If you start hitching from Skibotn, you will have to walk up the road until it forks. Best of luck!

To reach the Norwegian coastal town of Alta from Hetta (also called Enontekiö), take the road north to Kautokeino. This is a Sami town. The route is popular with those making their way to Nordkapp. Some buses will take you from Hetta to Kautokeino, which is connected to Alta and Karasjok by Norwegian companies.

The main Nordkapp route (see Finland map) goes from Rovaniemi via Inari and Kaamanen to Karigasniemi and across the border to Karasjok and Lakselv. The border station is in Karigasniemi. Lakselv is fairly simple to pass through but Karasjok occupies a larger area so you may have to walk a long way to find the way out if you are hitchhiking.

There is a bridge crossing into Norway at Utsjoki over the Teno River (Norwegian: Tana). There is not much on the Norwegian side here, but buses run between Karasjok and Kirkenes on this road.

The road from the northernmost point of Finland, at Nuorgam, will take you to Tana Bru (literally, 'bridge over the Tana river'). There are further connections to various parts of Finnmark. Buses take you to the border, four km from Nuorgam. Polmak is the first Norwegian settlement, two km across the border.

To reach Kirkenes from Finland, drive north from Inari and turn east at Kaamanen to reach Sevettijärvi. Cross the border at Näätämö to reach Neiden, 10 km away. There are further bus connections to

Kirkenes and to other centres in Finnmark. You may have to hitchhike from Näätämö to Neiden as there is hardly any public transport available. There are border stations at both sides of the border but a long distance apart.

Bus Buses between Hammerfest and Kirkenes are very useful because they will drop you off at Karasjok, Levajok, Skipagurra and Neiden, with further connections to Finland available. There are several daily buses from Kirkenes to Neiden, but you may have to hitchhike on to Näätämö, stay there overnight, and catch the morning post bus to Ivalo via Sevettijärvi. For Nuorgam, you can catch the nightly bus from Skipagurra via Polmak. There are also Norwegian buses from Vadsø to Nuorgam at 10.20 am; you can catch the morning bus from Kirkenes and change in Varangerbotn to these buses. There are also two daily departures from Polmak for Rovaniemi. From Lakselv, there are buses to Karigasniemi and Ivalo daily from 10 June to 20 August, and several buses from Karasjok to Ivalo, via Karigasniemi. For Kilpisjärvi (the 'arm of Finland'), there are buses from Skibotn daily from 15 June to 15 August, with very early departures on weekdays. You can reach Skibotn daily from Tromsø, on the Norwegian coast. For Kivilompolo and Enontekiö, catch the bus from Kautokeino; there are four buses per week. To get to Kautokeino from Norway, you have a choice of buses from Alta or Karasjok.

To/From Russia

A border zone that runs along the Russian frontier is still out of bounds to all visitors except those holding a visa or a special permit granted by Finnish border guards. The issuing of permits is more relaxed nowadays.

Along the heavily travelled Helsinki-Vyborg-St Petersburg corridor there are one rail and two road crossings. New crossings may open in the region. The rail crossing is at Vainikkala (Russian side, Luzhayka). Highways cross the border at the Finnish posts of Nuijamaa (Russian side, Brusnichnoe) and Vaalimaa (Russian side, Torfyanovka), just north of Vainikkala. See Eastern Finland map.

Further north, you may be able to drive from Joensuu to the Finnish border post of Niirala at Värtsilä (Russian side, Vyartsilya) and 500 km on to Petrozavodsk. In Kainuu, there is an open border from Vartius to the mining town of Kostomuksha (Finnish: Kostamus). From Salla in Lapland, there is road across the border to Alakurtti, and from Ivalo, a road goes to Murmansk, via the Finnish border post of Raja-Jooseppi (see Finland map). Roads on the Russian side are generally horrible, resembling potato fields, so you will want to have a 4WD vehicle or good nerves, preferably both.

If you drive, you'll need an international licence and certificate of registration, passport, visa and insurance. The Ingosstrakh, Salomonkatu 5C, 00100 Helsinki (☎ 694 0511), is the only Russian insurer in Helsinki. It will cover you in Russia but not in other republics of the former Soviet Union.

Bus There are several bus connections from Helsinki and other towns in south Finland to St Petersburg. There are buses between Joensuu and Sortavala, Joensuu and Petrozavodsk (Finnish: Petroskoi), and from Rovaniemi to Ivalo to Murmansk. To qualify for bus travel, you need a passport and a visa and you must pay for the journey beforehand at a post office. The receipt of your payment is your ticket. New routes may be available so check the current situation at the Helsinki bus station or in Russia.

Train There are two trains a day between St Petersburg and Helsinki, and a daily train to/from Moscow. You can buy Russian rail tickets in Helsinki (at the special ticket office in the central station) and cross the border at Vainikkala.

Trans-Siberian Railway

The Trans-Siberian Railway connects Europe to Asia. Its popularity has declined in recent years due to the general state of chaos in Russia, as well as rising prices. There are also plenty of enterprising Chinese and Russians selling merchandise and blocking practically all carriages. Nevertheless, it's an option worth considering.

There is some confusion of terms relating to the TSR as there are, in fact, three railways. The 'true' Trans-Siberian line runs from Moscow to the eastern Siberian port of Nakhodka, from where one can catch a boat to Japan. This route does not go through China or Mongolia. The Trans-Manchurian line, which crosses the Russia-China border at Zabaikalsk-Manzhouli, also completely bypasses Mongolia. The Trans-Mongolian line connects Beijing to Moscow, passing through the Mongolian capital city, Ulan Bator.

See Lonely Planet's *Russia, Belarus & Ukraine* for more information.

From Helsinki The international ticket counter at the Helsinki railway station has a quota of four seats for a four-bed compartment on the weekly train but the ticket is only valid to the Chinese border. The going rate of 1800 mk includes the Helsinki to Moscow leg. You can apply for Russian and Chinese visas once you have a receipt for your ticket. Enquire locally, as the telephone number is currently an expensive 'service' number that will consume plenty of your money.

From Moscow Anyone already in Moscow can buy Trans-Siberian tickets from the building at ulitsa Krasnoprudnaya 1, next door to Yaroslavl Station. The office is on the 1st floor, marked *zheleznodorozhnoye kassy* (railway ticket office). Tell the staff (who only speak Russian) your destination, what train you want, the date and class of travel. They also need to know your name and passport number. If you don't speak Russian, write it all out. It can be a laborious process, particularly in summer when the queues are long. In summer you should try to come a few weeks in advance to be sure of getting a ticket on the train you want.

Visas The burning question many travellers ask is: 'Can I stop off along the way?' The answer is essentially no. No such thing as a stopover ticket exists. If you are travelling from Moscow to Beijing, spending a night or two in Irkutsk and Ulan Bator, then you'll need three separate tickets: Moscow-Irkutsk, Irkutsk-Ulan Bator and Ulan Bator-Beijing. All your tickets will be for a specific berth on a specific train on a specific day. Generally, ticket offices can only sell places on trains leaving from that particular station.

You can get a few days in Moscow on a transit visa, but stopping off in China and Mongolia requires another visa, either transit or tourist.

Visas can take several days to issue, even longer if you can't show up at the embassy in person and apply instead through the post. Transit visas are valid for a maximum of 10 days; tourist visas are required if the journey is broken. It makes life easier if you can make do with a transit visa because the paperwork is much simpler and quicker – you just require proof that you are leaving the country, such as a visa for the next destination or your rail ticket. In practice you can extend a transit visa but extending a tourist visa is much more expensive – in Russia, the hotel 'service bureau' will do it for you through Intourist, but only with expensive hotel bookings.

In Russia, a transit visa can be issued in three working days for US$40; same day express service for US$60.

Then there is the bizarre 'consular fee' for certain nationalities. There is no logic here – citizens of the UK, USA, Australia and New Zealand are exempt; Belgians pay a consular fee of US$12 for transit visas and US$33 for tourist visas; the French pay US$12 for both kinds of visas. The Swiss pay US$18 for a transit visa but get the tourist visa for free. These fees go up and down like a toilet seat – we can't make any predictions how much you'll actually have to pay.

It's safer to obtain all visas in your home country before setting out. Some tour operators arrange visas as part of their Trans-Siberian packages.

Black Market Tickets If you are approached in either Moscow or Beijing by people plugging black market tickets on the Trans-Siberian, chances are 90% certain that you will be ripped-off. Most likely, you will be sold a rouble-denominated ticket which only Russian nationals can use.

Problems & Precautions Bring plenty of cash (US dollars) in small denominations for the journey – only in China can you readily use the local currency. In China, food is plentiful and readily available from both the train's dining car and vendors in railway stations. In both Russia and Mongolia, food quality is poorer, but meals are available on the train. Once you get off the train it's a different story – food can be difficult to buy in both Russia and Mongolia, especially once you get away from the capital cities. Bring plenty of munchies like biscuits, instant noodles, chocolate and fruit.

Showers are only available in the deluxe carriages. In economy class, there is a washroom. You can manage a bath with a sponge but it's best to bring a large metal cup (available in most Chinese railway stations) and use it as a scoop to pour water over yourself from the washbasin.

There is much theft on the train, so never leave your luggage unattended, even if the compartment is locked. Make sure at least one person stays in the compartment while the others go to the dining car. A lot of theft is committed by Russian gangs who have master keys to the compartments.

SEA

To/From Sweden

Stockholm is the main gateway to Finland, due to the incredibly luxurious passenger ferries that travel regularly between Stockholm and Turku/Helsinki. Before you get confused, remember that Åbo is the Swedish word for Turku. Many travellers have left Stockholm for Åbo, only to find out the next morning that they have actually arrived in Turku! It is the same place.

There are several reasons for the high quality of the ferries. To attract customers,

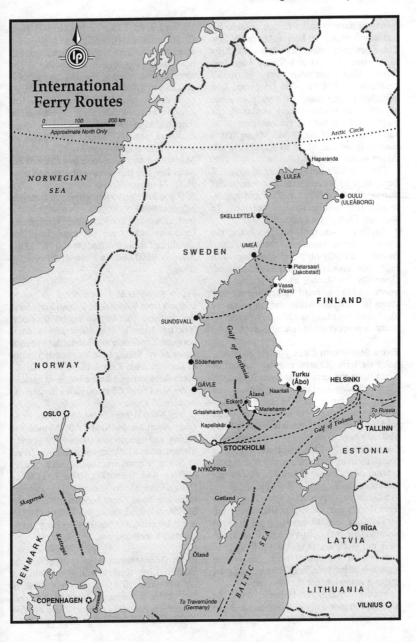

International
Ferry Routes

0   100   200 km
Approximate North Only

NORWEGIAN
SEA

Arctic Circle

Haparanda

LULEÅ

OULU
(ULEÅBORG)

SKELLEFTEÅ

SWEDEN

UMEÅ

Pietarsaari
(Jakobstad)

Vaasa
(Vasa)

FINLAND

SUNDSVALL

Gulf of Bothnia

Söderhamn

GÄVLE

Turku
(Åbo)

HELSINKI

Åland   Naantali

NORWAY

Eckerö

To Russia

Mariehamn

OSLO

Grisslehamn

Gulf of Finland

TALLINN

Kapellskär

STOCKHOLM

ESTONIA

NYKÖPING

Gotland

RĪGA

Skagerrak

LATVIA

Kattegat

Öland

BALTIC
SEA

DENMARK

Öresund

LITHUANIA

COPENHAGEN

To Travemünde
(Germany)

VILNIUS

operators have to make ferries suitable for luxurious cruises, yet keep ticket prices low. There are two competing operators, Silja Line (white ferries) and Viking Line (red ferries). Silja is considered better in overall performance, but its listed prices are also slightly higher (though it does give some attractive discounts). Viking used to be the budget option, but its present fleet is as superb as that of Silja, and Viking has a monopoly on the Åland to Kapellskär and Åland to Naantali routes.

The dramatic sinking of MS *Estonia* on 28 September 1994 caused heavy cancellations during the following months, and ridiculously low prices were advertised. In summer discounts are rare.

Another reason for low prices is that the major source of income for these two companies is actually duty-free shopping; with high sales taxes in both Sweden and Finland, especially for alcohol and cigarettes, ferry operators offer some of the leading tax-free shops in the whole world, though prices for alcohol on board are much higher than those in the supermarkets of central Europe.

From Stockholm Once you get to Stockholm by train (Central railway station) or flight (take the airport bus from Arlanda to Cityterminalen, next to the train station), you should transfer to the Tunnelbana underground train, which will take you to Gärdet for Silja Line, or to Slussen for Viking Line. You may have to walk from these stations to the ferries. Silja Line traditionally gives a complimentary ferry ride to anyone in possession of an Eurail ticket. Check first for current rules.

Silja ferries depart daily from Värtan (bus from Ropsten, or walk from Gärdet) at 6 pm for Helsinki, and at 8 am and 8 pm (9 pm in summer) for Turku. Silja departs from Turku at 8 pm – earlier than Viking (except in summer, at 10 pm). Unfortunately, the regular 6.38 pm train from Helsinki to Turku harbour is too late for the Silja ferry.

Viking departs for Helsinki from the Statsgården pier daily at 6 pm, and at 5 pm on Tuesdays, Thursdays and Saturdays.

Viking has the 15 krona bus No 975 from Cityterminalen (Gate 23) and Slussen. Departures for Turku are at 8.10 am and 8.15 pm (times vary; check in advance). The morning ferry stops at Mariehamn on Åland at 2.25 pm. Be warned, though, that Friday night departures on Viking Line in the low season are considerably more expensive than other nights of the week.

Birka Line's MS *Birka Princess* leaves the Statsgården pier in Stockholm for Mariehamn each afternoon from Monday to Saturday. The trip takes six hours and costs about 24 mk (or 40 kr).

If you have up to four people in a car, the MS *Sea Wind* is the best value, with transport, cabins and breakfast for 900 mk return (one-way tickets are not available). You should call ahead toll-free (☎ 020 795 331 in Sweden, 9800 6800 in Finland) for reservations.

From Kapellskär If you want to sail to Finland from Kapellskär, a small harbour in the northern part of Stockholm province, Viking Line's MS *Ålandsfärjan* sails between Kapellskär and Mariehamn several times a day. Viking Line also has departures in summer from Kapellskär to Naantali. To catch these ferries, take the bus from upstairs at the Stockholm Cityterminalen for approximately 35 krona.

Bus No 631 runs every two hours or so from Norrtälje to Kapellskär Monday to Friday, and three to four times on weekends. The trip takes a little less than an hour. To get to Norrtälje from Stockholm, catch bus No 640 or 644 from Tekniska högskolan (*tunnelbana* Metro station). The journey takes one hour. These buses will accept the SL (Stockholm Länstrafile) Tourist Card or any other SL ticket, unlike the direct Stockholm to Kapellskär bus.

From Grisslehamn Even cheaper are the Eckerö Line ferries from Grisslehamn, another small village in the very north of Stockholm province. Ferries run to Eckerö in western Åland. In summer there are five departures daily. The trip takes two hours and costs 30 to 36 mk (one-way or return). Norrtälje is the gateway town to this harbour. Take bus 637 which runs four to six times a day. The trip takes one hour. See Kapellskär for connections to Norrtälje from Stockholm. There are also direct Eckerö Line shuttle buses to/from Stockholm.

From Sundsvall Further north, Silja Line operates ferries between Vaasa and the Swedish town of Sundsvall. There are daily departures in summer, at 8.30 pm from Sundsvall and at 11.30 pm from Vaasa. One-way tickets cost 110 mk (180 mk in summer) but there are discounts.

From Umeå Silja Line has ferries between Umeå and Vaasa from 1 April to 30 September. There are one or two departures daily from both ends. The trip takes four hours (shorter than the Sundsvall-Vaasa crossing) and costs 95 mk (115 mk in summer) but there are discounts. There are also departures from Umeå to Pietarsaari (Swedish: Jakobstad) on Silja Line ferries.

From Skellefteå Silja Line operates daily ferries between Skellefteå in northern Sweden and Pietarsaari in Finland. The trip costs approximately 80 mk, although there are discounts.

To/From Estonia

The Baltic States have become increasingly popular countries to visit. They are an alternative transit route to Finland and further afield. Lonely Planet publishes two titles which cover these three countries, *Scandinavian & Baltic Europe on a shoestring* and *Baltic States & Kaliningrad*. See these titles for further details.

There are currently a large number of ferries plying between Tallinn and Helsinki, two interesting capital cities just 80 km apart. There is heavy traffic throughout the year. In winter there are fewer departures, and the traffic is slower due to ice. Cancellations occur if the sea is rough.

The following information reflects the situation in summer and is subject to change.

The trip between Helsinki and Tallinn costs roughly 100 to 130 mk one-way, but there are occasional discounts and return packages. Car ferries cross in three to four hours whereas catamarans do it in little more than one hour. Car ferries feature live shows, sumptuous buffets and tempting duty free shops. Express boats have a limited choice of tax-free shopping, and passengers sit on aeroplane-style seats. It is usually possible to get tickets just prior to departure but express boats may be fully booked in July. Booking ahead is a good way to avoid disappointment.

Tallink operates three ferries between Tallinn and Länsisatama in Helsinki. MS *Tallink* departs from Helsinki every morning, and from Tallinn usually at 5.30 pm. MS *Georg Ots* departs from Helsinki at 10 am and from Tallinn in the evening. MS *Vana Tallinn* departs from Helsinki on afternoons, and from Tallinn earlier in the morning. For reservations call ☎ 2282 1211 or buy your ticket at the terminal before departure.

Eestin Linjat run the car ferries MS *Alandia* and MS *Apollo* with daily morning departures from Helsinki Länsisatama terminal. They return from Tallinn in the evening. Tickets are available from their office at Fabianinkatu 9 (☎ 669 944) or prior to departure.

The fast *Tallink Express* boats have four daily departures from Helsinki and Tallinn in summer. For reservations in Helsinki call ☎ 2282 1277.

Estonian New Line runs two fast catamarans, with four daily departures from Helsinki and Tallinn in summer. For reservations call Helsinki ☎ 680 2499.

Silja Line runs a daily car ferry from the Kanavaterminaali in central Helsinki. The ferry departs from Helsinki at 11 am, and returns the next night.

Viking Line has one or two super-fast catamarans, departing from the Makasiinilaituri harbour in central Helsinki.

Day Trips to Tallinn Convenient day tours are available from most ferry companies.

Prices are very cheap, well below 100 mk for some companies. The Tallinn town centre is well within walking distance of the passenger harbour terminal (there are also public buses) and you can reach Raekoja plats (the central square), the Toompea Hill and the entire old town within minutes. Free maps are widely available from ferry companies and in free leaflets. Most Western nationals don't require a visa for Estonia. *Head reisi!*

To/From Germany

Silja Line sails to Helsinki a few times a week from the Skandinavienkaj in the German town of Travemünde on the MS *Finnjet*, reputedly the longest passenger ferry in the world. There are nine to 12 departures each month, and one-way prices start around DM 260 in the low season. Small discounts are available for students. The trip takes 24 hours.

The Finnlines *Poseidon* sails from Lübeck to Helsinki. This trip takes up to a day longer than Silja.

For a real adventure, travel on a container ship. There are very few passengers, and each will have their own cabin. The price is similar to the latter two ferry journeys. Contact Mr Rolf Tubenthal, Hamburger Süd Reiseagentur GmbH, Ost-West Strasse 59-61, Hamburg, ☎ 49 40 3705 2593, fax 3705 2420.

To/From Poland

There are currently no passenger ferries between Poland and Finland. Check the current situation if you desperately need a ride. Overland travel via the Baltic States is probably safer, faster and cheaper.

To/From Russia

Connections exist between Russia and Finland, although at the time of writing the situation was too volatile to offer specific information. Ask around when you get to Finland, especially in Helsinki. Most international ferries dock just near Helsinki's fish market.

WARNING

The information in this chapter is particularly vulnerable to change: prices for international travel are volatile, routes are introduced and cancelled, schedules change, special deals come and go, and rules and visa requirements are amended.

Airlines and governments seem to take a perverse pleasure in making price structures and regulations as complicated as possible. You should check directly with the airline or a travel agent to make sure you understand how a fare (and the ticket you may buy) works. In addition, the travel industry is highly competitive and there are many lurks and perks.

The upshot of this is that you should get opinions, quotes and advice from as many airlines and travel agents as possible before you part with your hard-earned cash. The details given in this chapter should be regarded as pointers and are not a substitute for your own careful, up-to-date research.

Getting Around

There is plenty of free travel information available, but if you want just one book that contains accurate details of every train, bus, flight and ferry route in Finland, you should invest approximately 90 mk for *Suomen kulkuneuvot*, which is published four times a year. The summer edition is generally referred to as *Kesäturisti*. It is probably one of the most complicated timetables to use, all in Finnish, but there are summaries in English and a few other languages.

AIR

Finland can offer some of the cheapest domestic flights in Europe if you are eligible for the discounts. The best deal is the discounted return between Helsinki and Ivalo,

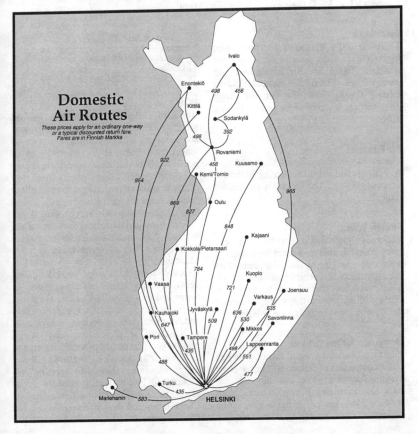

Domestic Air Routes

These prices apply for an ordinary one-way or a typical discounted return fare. Fares are in Finnish Markka.

Ivalo

Enontekiö

498   456

Kittilä

Sodankylä

392

498

Rovaniemi

922   456   Kuusamo

954   Kemi/Tornio

965

869   Oulu

827

848

Kajaani

Kokkola/Pietarsaari

784

Kuopio

721

Vaasa   Varkaus   Joensuu

635

Kauhajoki   Jyväskylä   636   Savonlinna

647   509   530   Mikkeli

Pori   Tampere   Lappeenranta

435   498   551

488   477

Turku

Mariehamn   583   435   **HELSINKI**

which is almost cheaper than taking trains or buses.

There are five domestic airlines in Finland. Finnair (AY) flies DC-9s, Finnaviation (FA) has 34 seater SAABs and Karair (KR) has 66 seater Aeritalia ATR-72s. These three airlines all belong to the same company, in which the government has a majority stake. Usage of various aeroplanes (and airlines) is determined by demand – routes that have few passengers are likely to be using Finnaviation planes. There are also two private airlines: Air Botnia (KF) and Polarwing (WO). Prices and discounts are the same for the three major companies as for most KF and WO flights.

Discounts

There are 50% discounts for prebooked flights (seven days prior to departure), for weekend flights, and for people under 25 years of age. Elderly people and children receive a hefty 70% discount. For group discounts etc, enquire at the nearest Finnair office.

Air Passes

The *Finnair Holiday Ticket* allows 10 one-way flights within Finland during 30 days at a cost of US$425. The flights are on selected routes.

Finnair Tours

Packages comprising a domestic flight and three to seven nights in a hotel are especially good value, judging by the listed prices. City packages include a return flight and a good hotel. Ask for special brochures at any Finnair office around the world, or consult the travel section of *Helsingin Sanomat*.

Domestic Airline Offices

Finnair is the main internal carrier, with two other companies operating within the same system. There are offices in all airport terminals and in many Finnish towns. Call ☎ 9800-3466 for the general reservation office.

Helsinki
  Central Booking Office (☎ 818 800)
  Asema-aukio 3 (☎ 818 7750)
  Töölönkatu 21 (☎ 818 7670)
Enontekiö
  Tunturikuva Ky (☎ 521 399)
Joensuu
  Kirkkokatu 25 (☎ 120 921)
Kajaani
  Pohjolankatu 33 (☎ 120 191)
Kittilä
  Valtatie 41 (☎ 642 072)
Kuopio
  Asemakatu 22-24 (☎ 262 5544)
Kuusamo
  Kitkantie 15 (☎ 852 1395)
Mariehamn
  Skarpansvägen 24 (☎ 19522)
Oulu
  Hallituskatu 21 (☎ 379 033)
Rovaniemi
  Airport (☎ 363 670)
Tampere
  Kyttälänkatu 2 (☎ 222 1200)
Turku
  Eerikinkatu 4 (☎ 251 3600)

BUS

Buses in Finland run efficiently and on schedule. There are public buses in towns and cities and a variety of private buses on longer trips. Buses cover some 90% of all public roads, but on some routes there is only one bus per week. Long-distance buses stop at blue & white stops. In larger towns, yellow & black stops are for regional or local buses. Express buses stop only at *pikavuoro* stops.

Each town and municipal centre has a bus terminal *linja-autoasema*, with timetables displayed. Bus terminals are run by Matkahuolto, another sign to look for. Express buses generally operate on long trips between major towns but always stop in towns and in some villages along the route. Regional buses mainly serve commuters and, in more isolated regions, school children. Schools are closed from early June to mid-August (the period generally referred to as 'summer' in this book), so there are fewer buses available then. Most buses run Monday to Friday, hourly between major towns; there is little bus traffic on Sunday. Check times and days in advance to avoid disappointment.

Bus timetables are almost hopelessly messy collections of colour codes and strange abbreviations. If you are departing, try to locate the *Lähtevät* table. *Saapuvat* stands for arrivals.

Costs

All bus prices are centrally determined according to distance travelled. Express buses charge a supplement of 12 to 15 mk. Bicycles are transported for 10 mk if there is space available. Here are some approximate fares for ordinary one-way, express one-way, return and express return trips:

Distance	one-way	express	return	express
206 km	9 mk	21 mk	18 mk	42 mk
12 km	12 mk	24 mk	24 mk	48 mk
30 km	21 mk	33 mk	42 mk	66 mk
50 km	32 mk	44 mk	64 mk	88 mk
100 km	59 mk	71 mk	106 mk	128 mk
300 km	155 mk	168 mk	279 mk	302 mk
500 km	235 mk	250 mk	423 mk	450 mk
700 km	315 mk	330 mk	567 mk	594 mk

Bus Holiday Tickets

For those on a budget, Matkahuolto has introduced a discount pass, available at most bus terminals and travel agents in Finland. It is valid on all buses (except local buses in the Helsinki, Tampere and Turku regions) and entitles you to cover 1000 km for 340 mk (in 1995), a discount of at least 35%. The pass has coupons for trips of various lengths, in 'denominations' of 250 km, 100 km, 50 km and 10 km; use the appropriate combination of coupons for each journey. You will need to calculate carefully, however, because there's a catch: they don't give change. If you have few coupons left and the journey is, say, 220 km, you will have to use the 250 km coupon and lose 30 km worth of travel. But if you take several short journeys and don't 'lose' too many kilometres, your total saving will approach 50% off the regular fare. This makes bus travel cheaper than buying individual train tickets.

TRAIN

Trains of the State Railways of Finland, or

Valtion Rautatiet (VR), are clean and usually on schedule (hot spells and snow storms are difficult times for the railways). There are three main electric rail lines: the Pohjanmaa line runs between Helsinki and Oulu, and continues to Kemijärvi in Lapland; the Karelian route runs from Helsinki to Nurmes via Joensuu; and the Savonian route runs from Kouvola in the south to Iisalmi in the north, continuing to Kajaani. One of the most popular routes for travellers in a hurry is the triangle between Turku, Helsinki and Tampere. There are several side routes, notably between Tampere and Pori, Seinäjoki and Vaasa, Ylivieska and Iisalmi, Parikkala and Savonlinna, Turku and Joensuu, and Seinäjoki and Jyväskylä. Useful local routes can be found in the Helsinki area. VR operates passenger trains in two classes – 1st and 2nd. Most carriages are open 2nd class carriages with soft chairs. Many trains have just one 1st class carriage, containing small compartments, each seating six passengers. Some trains transport cars from the south to Oulu, Rovaniemi and Kittilä for approximately 500 mk. Finland uses broad gauges, similar to those in Russia, so there are regular trains to/from Russia. Tickets for these trains are sold at Helsinki railway station (see the Getting There & Away chapter).

Bookings

Do buy your ticket in advance, but few trains require a seat reservation. You should book for all Inter-City (IC) trains and some special express (EP) trains. On all other long-distance trains, you can reserve a seat, if you wish, for 20 mk. The conductor does not mark a reserved seat, so you may have to ask someone to move if your seat is already taken. On the other hand, if you don't have a reservation, you can take any free seat but will have to be prepared to give it up if someone with a reservation shows up. Seats can be reserved up to the departure time. Persons with allergies, handicaps, pets or children should contact the reservation office. There are special carriages, including a video carriage, that run on main lines.

Train Passes

Several discounted train passes are available. Both Inter-Rail and Eurail passes give unlimited travel in Finland for Europeans and non-Europeans, respectively. The Scanrail pass, for travel within Scandinavia, is valid for 21 days and can be purchased in any Scandinavian country. For travel within Finland, the Finnrail pass is valid for one month, but the price depends on how many days you want travel. It is available at major train stations in Finland, and costs:

duration	2nd class	1st class
3 days	550 mk	760 mk
5 days	685 mk	1030 mk
10 days	945 mk	1420 mk

Since 1994, new domestic passes for the summer season have been introduced. They are certainly worth buying if available. The general seven day pass with unlimited rides, and hotel vouchers (two people should share a double room) for two nights, costs 888 mk. An even better option is a regional train pass valid for 30 days. There are four routes, each forming a circle, and stopping en route is possible. You will not be allowed to backtrack. These passes cost less than 200 mk each.

Charges & Surcharges

Train tickets are cheaper in Finland than in Sweden or Norway. A one-way ticket for a 100 km train journey costs approximately 46 mk in 2nd class and 69 mk in 1st class. Return fares for the same journey are 88 mk and 132 mk respectively. For a journey of 500 km, fares are 192/288 mk one-way and 366/549 mk return. On overnight trains, sleeping berths are available in one/two/three-bed cabins, at a cost of 200/100/60 mk in addition to the ordinary ticket. Superfast Pendolino trains are a bit more expensive.

As far as discounts are concerned, most of them apply only to Finnish citizens, but then many travellers carry discount passes. If you purchase your ticket from the conductor after boarding from a station where the ticket office was open, a special 5 mk 'penalty' is charged. A regular reservation, which is optional, costs 20 mk. Surcharges apply on certain EP and IC trains, as well as on some rare weekend trains. The surcharge depends on the distance travelled, as shown below:

train type	1-75 km	76-200 km	200+ km
EP train	20 mk	25 mk	30 mk
IC 1st class	35 mk	40 mk	45 mk
IC 2nd class	20 mk	25 mk	30 mk
weekend train	20 mk	25 mk	30 mk

Cargo & Bicycles

Normal long-distance trains carry cargo; IC and Pendolino trains don't. Some large railway stations have a cargo office which takes luggage in advance. Sending cargo anywhere in Finland costs 20 mk. Transporting a bicycle costs 40 mk. You can take your bicycle directly to the cargo carriage (*Konduktöörivaunu*). Our experience is that the self-service system is faster, cheaper and more pleasant. When you leave Finland by train for almost any point in Europe, you can send your luggage at a very low price to the station at your destination. It's worth checking current rates while in Finland.

Food, Drink & Smoking

Most long-distance trains have a restaurant carriage with simple meals, snacks, beer and other drinks. Prices are not cheap. Inter-City trains feature better dining carriages, with a six fingered hand on their doors – a practical joke that very few ever notice. In most cases, the dining room is less congested than the 'drinking side', but the atmosphere in the latter is by far more intense.

Smoking is completely forbidden in local trains near Helsinki. In long-distance trains there are separate smoking rooms (no seats), and smoking carriages are being phased out.

Station Services

VR Matkapalvelu is a travel agency and ticket vendor, whereas VR Lippupalvelu is a normal ticket office which also sells some special products, such as train-bus tickets to Lapland. Toilets are not free at stations (unlike in trains), but there is often a café at the station (you may use their toilet if you buy coffee or something else). Left-luggage service generally costs 10 mk per day, but several stations still have 5 mk lockers available. For complete national timetables, buy the *Taskuaikataulu* booklet for 5 mk at the nearest railway station. For individual routes, there are free pocket timetables available, and every station displays all departures and arrivals. Tourist offices will usually stock a handy train timetable for the appropriate town.

Special Trains

Ask for special trains from Helsinki to Iittala, Helsinki to Porvoo, Turku to Uusikaupunki and Punkaharju to Rantasalmi. Some of these trains only run a few times, in summer. There are old-style reproductions on railway lines from Jokioinen to Humppila and in Kovjoki near Nykarleby. Special steam locomotives are found at Suolahti during a special festival. Train museums are located at Hyvinkää, Pieksämäki and Haapamäki, and old locomotives can been seen outside many railway stations throughout Finland. The largest model railway in Finland is in Kitee, North Karelia.

TAXI

Taxis in Finland are luxurious, expensive and equipped with all kinds of gadgets. In Espoo's taxis, incoming calls are displayed on LCDs and printed by a small fax-like machine. You will feel like the rich and famous, and pay like the rich and famous. Flagfall is 17 mk in the daytime, 29 mk at night, then over 5 mk for each km. If you call a cab, the meter starts ticking when the taxi starts. Taxis are easy to recognise and there are plenty of them in most places, the exception often being Helsinki at night.

Small places usually have a taxi station, very often near the bus or train station. Taxis in small towns are nearly as expensive as in big towns, but they will offer an easy way to continue your journey immediately after arrival by public transport (try to get a small group together).

There is no shared taxi transport available in Finland, the possible exceptions being airport taxis from Helsinki airport, taxis from Turku railway station, and some off-the-beaten-track places in Lapland. However, if you have a group of four people and want to cover a lengthy distance 'in the middle of nowhere', you should be able to negotiate with taxi drivers and end up with an attractive price.

CAR & MOTORBIKE

In Finland, vehicles drive on the right-hand side of the road. Traffic is orderly, and regulations are strict and should always be adhered to. Police checks are frequent and tickets bear unpleasant figures. The wearing of seat belts is compulsory, in front seats and back, and there is a blood alcohol limit of 0.05%. Always drive with your headlights on; even though it's not compulsory in towns, it's easy to forget to turn them back on as you leave inhabited areas. Note that the excellent highway-type roads around Helsinki have speed limits of 70 km per hour, whereas on some narrow dirt roads in other parts of Finland, the limit may be 80 km per hour.

Parking in Helsinki is extremely difficult, except between the Midsummer holiday in late June and the end of July, when most locals are on holiday. Recently, Helsinki introduced a variety of new parking options that few locals feel comfortable with, such as a bulky electronic parking meter that will cost you over 500 mk (US $100) just so that you can control your parking, at your expense. In central Helsinki, every parking space will cost you money, as much as 10 mk per hour. Fortunately, cars with a foreign licence plate will not receive a ticket for parking violations. In other towns, parking is rarely a problem, and much cheaper than in Helsinki. Free parking is always possible in small towns. There are no tow-away zones in Finland.

Petrol is much more expensive than in the USA and the price is generally above average compared with other European countries (around 5 mk per litre at time of writing). The major motoring organisation in Finland is Autoliitto (☎ 774 761, fax 7747 6444), at Hämeentie 105A in Helsinki. The postal address is PL 35, 00551 Helsinki.

Major car rental agencies in Finland include Avis, Budget, Esso, Hertz, Inter-Rent-Europcar and Scandia Rent, but there are also local operators, especially in Helsinki. See the Yellow Pages, under the heading 'Autovuokraamoja', for addresses and telephone numbers. Rates, quoted by the day and with an additional mileage charge, range from 180 to 550 mk per day plus 2 to 5 mk per km. Special weekend and weekly unlimited-mileage rates are available on request. Don't plan on buying a car in Finland, as it's simply too expensive.

You must always give way to elk and reindeer. Elk are dangerous because of their size. In Lapland, reindeer can make motoring somewhat slow and/or hazardous. Expect them to appear at any time.

Roadside Services

Driving through Finland should be no problem. There are petrol stations throughout the country, although in Lapland and in other isolated regions you should be careful and fill up even if the tank isn't completely empty.

Take advantage of roadside services – most petrol stations offer a range of things to buy, from chocolate to motor oil and reserve parts. A café or restaurant is very common, and you may find decent meals, snacks and coffee at surprisingly low prices and at late

---

Reindeer Roadblocks

Some 3000 to 4500 reindeer die annually on Finnish roads. Trains kill an additional 600 reindeer every year. The figures are believed to be artificially inflated because of the high compensation awarded for each accidental reindeer death. One Lappish person told me that some Samis let their older reindeer eat lichen near railway tracks so that they might suffer a fatal accident and bring more money to their owner. Reindeer owners cash $US1 million annually in compensation although material damage is worth over twice as much.

The worst months for reindeer-related accidents are November and December. Also bad are July and August, when the poor animals run amok trying to escape insects.

The worst roads are in the north: Oulu to Kuusamo, Rovaniemi to Kemijarvi and Rovaniemi to Inari, although the problem isn't the quality of the roads – there is a clear relationship between the amount of traffic and the number of accidents. More reindeer-related accidents occur near tourist centres than in uninhabited areas. The best way to avoid an accident is to slow down immediately when you spot a reindeer, regardless of its location, direction or speed. Reindeer move slowly and hardly respond to a moving vehicle.

Reindeer are semi-domesticated and wander freely. Each reindeer is ear-marked and has an owner. Selling a dead reindeer is big business because of the high price – reindeer meat is expensive and greatly appreciated.

When Samis herd their reindeer, they move hundreds of kilometres through Lapland. Thus, a temporary shelter system evolved. The simplest such shelter is a *kammi* but there are also huts. When people from the south travelled north, they were also allowed to stay overnight in these huts. Later, when the Forest and Park Service took over the national parks, they developed the shelters into the free wilderness hut system. All because of the reindeer. ■

hours, especially as shops in Finnish towns close so early. Shell is especially good for meals, and so is Kesoil. SEO, Esso and Neste have cafés, as does Teboil. JET is cheap for petrol but sells nothing else. Roadside stations are growing bigger and often include a small collection of shops, sometimes even a factory outlet or tourist information booth.

When driving at night, you may fill your tank by using *Automaatti* or *Seteli/kortti* automatic petrol pumps. Bank notes and major credit cards (especially Visa) are always accepted. Some stations have instructions in English and also French. If the instructions are in Finnish and Swedish only, you insert bank notes, press *setelikuittaus* after the last note, choose the right pump, choose the right petrol type, and fill the tank.

Municipalities provide drivers with large information maps, which are found at parking areas near municipal borders and scenic locations. These P-marked areas often include a garbage collection point, tables and seats, and toilets.

Road Numbers

Each major road has a number (often referred to in this book). National highways are numbered from one to two digit numbers. Three and four digit numbers are given to less important roads, often gravel ones. There are also plenty of roads with no number at all. The simple road numbering system begins at Helsinki and radiates from west to east as follows:

1 – Helsinki to Turku (E18)
2 – Helsinki to Pori
3 – Helsinki to Tampere to Vaasa (E12)
4 – Helsinki to Jyväskylä to Oulu to Ivalo to Norway (E75)
5 – Helsinki to Mikkeli to Kuopio to Kemijärvi to Sodankylä
6 – Helsinki to Lappeenranta to Joensuu
7 – Helsinki to Kotka to Hamina to Vaalimaa (E18)
8 – Turku to Vaasa to Oulu
9 – Turku to Tampere to Jyväskylä to Kuopio (E63)
10 – Turku to Hämeenlinna
11 – Tampere to Pori
12 – Tampere to Lahti to Kouvola
13 – Jyväskylä to Mikkeli to Lappeenranta

HITCHING

Hitching is never entirely safe in any country, and we don't recommend it. Travellers who decide to hitch should understand that they are taking a small but potentially serious risk. However, many people do choose to hitch; the advice that follows should help to make their journeys as fast and safe as possible.

Finland is reputedly an easy country in which to hitchhike. You should look neat and tidy, stand up and stand out. Relatively few Finns like picking up hitchhikers but the few friendly ones do it with enthusiasm. The best time to hitchhike is Monday to Friday, when lonely travelling salespeople are on the road. They generally like to talk. Most drivers ask *Minne matka?* ('Where are you going?'), so you just tell them your destination. Hitchhiking on motorways (freeways) is forbidden, but there are relatively few motorways in Finland. It is possible to hitch from Helsinki to Turku; more difficult is Helsinki to Tampere or Lahti, where there are longer sections of motorway and continuing a journey after being dropped off may be next to impossible. Walking a few kms from smaller towns along ordinary roads will eventually take you to a good location, such as a bus stop after a road crossing. It is normally not necessary to carry a piece of cardboard with your destination written on it, especially if your route is pretty obvious. Many Finnish drivers engage in vigorous hand signals, often indicating how short their trip is, or that they will soon turn left or right. Quiet roads are not really bad, as drivers seem to be more willing to stop than on busy roads.

Some of the best areas to hitch are Kainuu, North Karelia and Lapland, but all regions outside Helsinki and other big cities are fine, although Lapland may sometimes be very frustrating. Any secondary road, or a crossing at a mid-sized village, will be easy for hitchhiking.

There are occasional rumours of violent Russian Mafia people masquerading as hitchhikers on Finnish roads. Even though they are just rumours, they keep wheels turning fast. The original story centred on a lonely Russian hitchhiker who stabbed a driver and buried him in an open ditch that had been dug beforehand. The next legend involved two ditches, but in Helsinki schoolkids spread the incredible story that there were three ditches for people, and one huge grave for the vehicle! Whenever you hitch, don't use Russian words and don't say anything about graves or spades!

BOAT

Lake & River Travel

Taking a passenger ferry is one of the highlights of a visit to Finland, and there are several good choices.

Finland has almost 188,000 lakes, 179,584 islands and 647 rivers. Several historical canals serve as wharves along passenger routes. Canals connect separate lakes, so that even Nurmes can be reached by yacht from international waters. Not visiting the Finnish lakeland is like missing the pyramids in Egypt. Before the road network was constructed, lake steamers and 'church longboats' provided the main passenger transport in much of Finland. They disappeared until the 1970s, when quite a few of them were brought back into service. Apart from two hour cruises starting from Jyväskylä, Kuopio, Savonlinna, Tampere, Mikkeli and other towns, you can actually cover half of Finland on scheduled boat routes. Many of the steamers now in use were built in the early 1900s and have a lot of character. Most ferries take bicycles, and short-distance travel is also possible.

Ferries only run in summer (June to August). The main lakes that have important traffic include Saimaa (in Savo), Pielinen (in North Karelia), Päijänne (in Central Finland), and Pyhäjärvi and Näsijärvi (in Häme). There is detailed information in the regional chapters.

Sea Ferries

Three kinds of ferries operate between various islands off the coast, and between the islands and the mainland. First, there are the free *lossi* ferries, part of the public road system, which run to a schedule or just continuously, connecting important inhabited islands to the mainland. These simple ferries take all kinds of vehicles, as well as bicycles and even pedestrians. For example, the island of Hailuoto near Oulu is connected to the mainland, over six km away, by a lossi that runs every half hour in the high season. Second, there are ferries that run between several islands to support the livelihood of small fishing villages, especially near Turku and in the province of Åland. Some of these ferries are also free to those who stay overnight on one of the islands, making it possible to island-hop from the mainland to Åland free of charge. Third, there are several cruise companies that run express boats to interesting islands off the coast. From Kalajoki you can visit the historical island of Maakalla, from Kokkola the island of Tankari, and from Helsinki the foremost tour is the short trip to Suomenlinna, to name just a few.

LOCAL TRANSPORT

The most efficient form of local transport is the bus. Most big towns have a local bus network, with departures every 10 to 15 minutes in Helsinki and other large towns, and every half hour in smaller towns. Fares are centrally determined for all Finland, something like 9 mk per ride. The Coach Holiday Ticket coupons (see Bus section earlier this chapter) are also valid for local buses, except in the Helsinki region, Tampere and Turku. Helsinki, however, has some useful local train routes (see Helsinki chapter).

TOURS

Many local tourist offices arrange daily or weekly sightseeing tours around their towns in summer, which may be useful and good value. In addition to regular tours, many small tour operators take groups into the wilderness, for trekking, white-water rafting and all imaginable activities. Local tourist offices will provide information on how to reach these operators. Finnair offers several package tours for those arriving in Finland on Finnair flights. (See Tourist Offices in the Facts for the Visitor chapter.)

Helsinki

Helsinki (Swedish: Helsingfors) is by far the most popular place to visit in Finland. It is both the capital and the centre of cultural, financial and economic activity in Finland. What is less known, however, is that Helsinki is hardly representative of the country as a whole – it's a combination of Swedish, Russian and international influences.

With its green parks and waterways, Helsinki is a pleasant town in summer, with fresh sea winds, seagulls flying over the busy fish market, and many open-air cafés. Summer is also the best time to visit the islands; take some food and go for the day if the weather is fine.

HISTORY

Helsinki is the sixth oldest town in Finland. It was founded in 1550 by King Gustav Vasa who wanted to create a rival to the Hansa trading town of Tallinn (present-day capital of Estonia). An earlier trial at Tammisaari proved unsuccessful, and traders from there, Ulvila and a few other towns were forcibly transferred to the newly founded Helsingfors.

For over 200 years it remained a sleepy market town with wooden houses scattered around the rocky peninsula. When Russia annexed Finland from the decaying Swedish empire in 1809, a capital closer to St Petersburg was needed, to keep a better watch on Finland's domestic politics. Helsinki was chosen, and in 1812 Turku lost its long-standing status as Finland's premier town, something its people still haven't forgiven.

To give the new capital an appropriate look, work soon started on the monumental buildings that comprise what is now known as Senate Square. The square had been the town centre for over a century, but wars and fire had destroyed all its wooden buildings. (The square's oldest surviving building, Sederholm House, which dates from 1757, is made of brick.) Carl Ludvig Engel, a

Highlights

- The fine 19th century architecture of Senate Square.
- Over 30 museums and art galleries.
- Fine markets, including the fish market and the Hietalahti flea market.
- Good value accommodation, from top-end hotels (in summer) to youth hostels.
- The largest bookshop in Scandinavia.
- Suomenlinna islands.
- The biggest shopping district in Finland, at Itäkeskus.
- The 'museum road' around Lake Tuusulanjärvi.
- Art Nouveau studios in Tarvaspää and Hvitträsk.

native of Berlin, was invited to design the new centre. He had earlier worked in St Petersburg, so what you see today in Helsinki looks quite Russian (which may explain why Helsinki is used by Hollywood to shoot 'Russian scenes', such as those in the films *Reds*, *White Nights* and *Gorky Park*). The University of Turku, Finland's oldest university, was relocated to Senate Square in 1828. The statue in the middle of the square, cast in 1894, is of Tsar Alexander II, and symbolises the strong Russian influence in 19th century Helsinki.

Over the following decades, Helsinki grew rapidly in all directions. The fine railway station, finished in 1919, was designed by Eliel Saarinen, who also created an impressive town plan for the entire city of Helsinki. It was never implemented, replaced instead by the somewhat messy town plan of Töölö, in the 1930s. At that time, Helsinki was the only place in Finland to have an intellectual elite and a high society, both of which died during WWII when Helsinki was bombed by the Russians.

The postwar years saw continuing division between the 'haves' and 'have-nots', with the bridge (Pitkäsilta or 'Long Bridge') between Helsinki proper and the suburb of Kallio representing the demarcation line. Helsinki went on, however, to host the Olympic Games in 1952, still the smallest city ever to stage the Summer Games.

In the 1970s, many new suburbs were built around Helsinki, and in 1975 Helsinki enhanced its international reputation when it hosted the Conference on Security and Cooperation in Europe (CSCE). The 'Helsinki Spirit' emerged, a term used for Cold War détente. Since then, Helsinki has served as an international meeting point on numerous occasions.

Despite its international prominence, Helsinki retains a small-town feel; there are no high-rise buildings and the fish market is still surrounded by 19th century architecture. By population, Helsinki remains a clearly Finnish town, with relatively few foreign residents. The population is 520,000, and growing.

ORIENTATION

Helsinki is built on a windy peninsula, with pretty much everything within walking distance of the railway station (or the nearby bus terminal). The main streets include Aleksanterinkatu (department stores and banks), Esplanadi (designer shops and a park) and Mannerheimintie, which takes you from the town centre all the way through Helsinki to the north. The business centre is near the railway station.

The southern suburbs, Eira and Kaivopuisto, are the 'posh' quarters, with villas, embassies and wealthy residents, as is Kruunuhaka with its many historical buildings. Katajanokka, an island east of the centre and connected to the mainland by several bridges, has some interesting architecture. Kallio and Töölö are densely populated residential areas offering relatively little of interest; very much the same applies to all outlying suburbs.

Pasila to the north is the 'New Helsinki', with ugly box-like office buildings and a busy train station. Itäkeskus in the east has probably the largest cluster of supermarkets, shopping centres and boutiques in the whole of Scandinavia, while the nearby areas of Marjaniemi and Vuosaari offer seaside walks and bicycle tours. North-east of Pasila, Kumpula and Käpylä have large areas of refurbished wooden villas; you should tour the area by bicycle if the weather is fine.

Finally, Meilahti, north-west of the centre, gives you access to the museum island of Seurasaari; you can take an attractive scenic loop from Meilahti through Kuusisaari, Lehtisaari, Lauttasaari, and back to the centre.

INFORMATION
Tourist Offices

The city tourist information office (☎ 169 3757) at Pohjoisesplanadi 19 will give you an updated city map and lists of events, restaurants, nightclubs and much more. You can also buy a Helsinki Card here (see later section). The office is open in summer from 8.30 am to 6 pm Monday to Friday and from 8 am to 1 pm on Saturday. In winter, opening hours are 8.30 am to 4 pm Monday to Friday.

Just opposite, across Esplanade Park, is another useful office – the Finnish Tourist Board (☎ 174 631) at Eteläesplanadi 4. Here you'll find brochures about attractions all over the country. The office is open from 9 am to 4 pm Monday to Friday.

Tikankontti (☎ 270 5221, e-mail tikankontti@metsa.fi) at Eteläesplanadi 20 is run by the Forest and Park Service. There is free information on all national parks and many protected areas around Finland, and you can buy maps and fishing licenses or rent wilderness cottages around the country.

Money

The best rates are available at Forex, open daily until 9 pm at the railway station. There are also Forex offices on Pohjoisesplanadi and Mannerheiminkatu, open longer than normal office hours but closed on Sunday. A number of other money exchange booths have sprung up recently. Some charge up to 8% commission and have lousy rates. Check rates and fees first. Banks, department stores and ferry terminals will probably give much worse deals. Hotels serve only their customers, and rates are lousy. American Express (☎ 628 788) is at Mikonkatu 2D. For lost Amex travellers' cheques, call toll-free ☎ 9800-12000. For lost Visa cards, call toll-free ☎ 9800-2400.

Post & Telephone

The main post office (☎ 195 5117) is the large building between the railway station and the bus terminal on the corner of Mannerheimintie and Postikatu. Office hours are 9 am to 5 pm Monday to Friday, but the poste restante (in the same building opposite the railway station) is open from 8 am to 9 pm Monday to Friday, 9 am to 6 pm on Saturday and 11 am to 9 pm on Sunday. Mail is held for one month. The main telephone office is in the same building, at Mannerheimintie 11B. You can use telephone booths from 8 am to 10 pm Monday to Friday, and until 9 pm on weekends.

Yellow Pages for the Helsinki region has an index in English.

Cultural Centres

The British Council (☎ 701 8731) at Hakaniemenkatu 2 has a library. The American Center Library is at Vuorikatu 20. It's a good place to find magazines, books and videos. The Goethe Institute (☎ 641 614) is at Mannerheimintie 20A, and the French Cultural Centre (☎ 622 0330) is at Keskuskatu 3.

Libraries

Helsinki has several public libraries. The most central, at Rikhardinkatu 3, is open from 9.30 am to 8 pm Monday to Friday and from 9.30 am to 3 pm on Saturday. The main library is actually in Pasila, and there is another good branch in Kallio.

The Cable Book (Kirjakaapeli) is a modern computer library at the old Kaapelitehdas factory building (tram 8 or metro stop Ruoholahti). For information, contact http://www.kaapeli.fi.

Travel Agencies

Kilroy travels (☎ 680 7811) at Kaivokatu 10D is the student travel bureau. The Indian-owned Intia-Keskus (☎ 651 066) at Yrjönkatu 8-10 also has cheap flights. Suomi-Seuran Matkatoimisto (☎ 625 155) at Mariankatu 8 sells flights to Australia and North America.

Agencies specialising in travel to Russia are numerous. You can easily arrange trips to the Baltic States, (Russian) Karelia, St Petersburg and beyond. Consult the 'Matkailu' pages of the daily *Helsingin Sanomat* for listings. Estonia is *Viro*, St Petersburg is *Pietari*, and Karelia is *Karjala* in Finnish.

Helsinki Card

This card will give you free travel on all local transport in Helsinki, admission to 48 museums and a number of other attractions, a sightseeing tour, and various discounts and gifts. If you keep busy, the Helsinki Card is definitely good value at 95/135/165 mk for one/two/three days. It is available from tourist information offices, the railway station, some travel agencies and most hotels.

Books & Maps

Akateeminen Kirjakauppa at Keskuskatu 1 is the largest bookshop in Scandinavia. It has an extensive selection of English, German and French magazines, paperbacks and

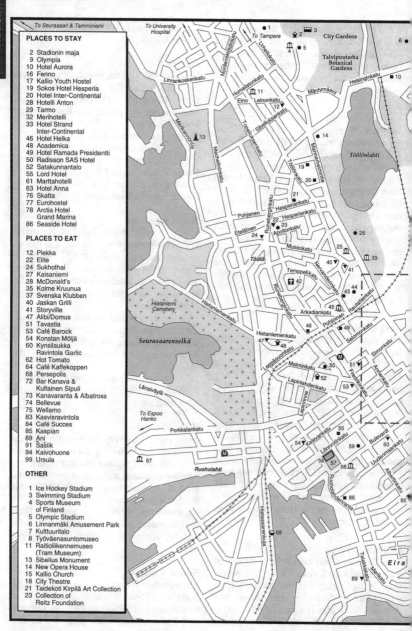

PLACES TO STAY

2 Stadionin maja
9 Olympia
10 Hotel Aurora
16 Fenno
17 Kallio Youth Hostel
19 Sokos Hotel Hesperia
20 Hotel Inter-Continental
28 Hotelli Anton
29 Tarmo
32 Merihotelli
33 Hotel Strand
   Inter-Continental
46 Hotel Helka
48 Academica
49 Hotel Ramada Presidentti
50 Radisson SAS Hotel
52 Satakunnantalo
55 Lord Hotel
61 Marttahotelli
63 Hotel Anna
76 Skatta
77 Eurohostel
78 Arctia Hotel
   Grand Marina
86 Seaside Hotel

PLACES TO EAT

12 Piekka
22 Elite
24 Sukhothai
27 Kaisaniemi
28 McDonald's
35 Kolme Kruunua
37 Svenska Klubben
40 Jaskan Grilli
41 Storyville
47 Alibi/Domus
51 Tavastia
53 Café Barock
54 Konstan Möljä
60 Kynsilaukka
   Ravintola Garlic
62 Hot Tomato
64 Café Kaffekoppen
68 Persepolis
72 Bar Kanava &
   Kultainen Sipuli
73 Kanavaranta & Albatross
74 Bellevue
75 Wellamo
84 Kasvisravintola
84 Café Succes
85 Kaspian
89 Ani
91 Šašlik
94 Kaivohuone
99 Ursula

OTHER

1 Ice Hockey Stadium
3 Swimming Stadium
4 Sports Museum
  of Finland
5 Olympic Stadium
6 Linnanmäki Amusement Park
7 Kulttuuritalo
8 Työväenasuntomuseo
11 Raitioliikennemuseo
   (Tram Museum)
13 Sibelius Monument
14 New Opera House
15 Kallio Church
18 City Theatre
21 Taidekoti Kirpilä Art Collection
23 Collection of
   Reitz Foundation

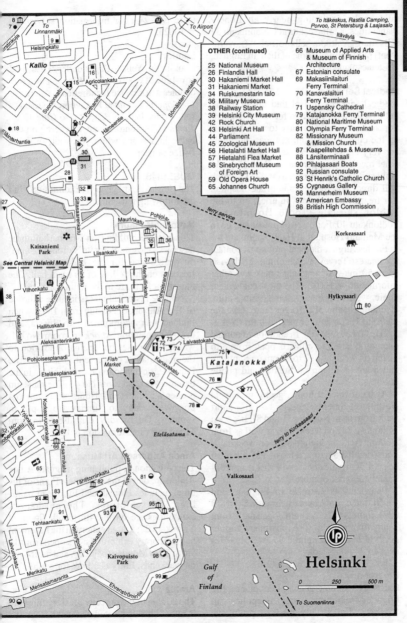

To Linnanmäki

Helsingkatu

Kallio

Agricolankatu

Suoniontie

Pohjantie

Hämeentie

Kalliontnrhantie

Sörnäisten rantatie

To Airport

To Itäkeskus, Rastila Camping, Porvoo, St Petersburg & Laajasalo

Itäväylä

OTHER (continued)

25 National Museum
26 Finlandia Hall
30 Hakaniemi Market Hall
31 Hakaniemi Market
34 Ruiskumestarin talo
36 Military Museum
38 Railway Station
39 Helsinki City Museum
42 Rock Church
43 Helsinki Art Hall
44 Parliament
45 Zoological Museum
56 Hietalahti Market Hall
57 Hietalahti Flea Market
58 Sinebrychoff Museum of Foreign Art
59 Old Opera House
65 Johannes Church

66 Museum of Applied Arts & Museum of Finnish Architecture
67 Estonian consulate
69 Makasiinilaituri Ferry Terminal
70 Kanavalaituri Ferry Terminal
71 Uspensky Cathedral
79 Katajanokka Ferry Terminal
80 National Maritime Museum
81 Olympia Ferry Terminal
82 Missionary Museum & Mission Church
87 Kaapelitehdas & Museums
88 Länsiterminaali
90 Pihlajasaari Boats
92 Russian consulate
93 St Henrik's Catholic Church
95 Cygnaeus Gallery
96 Mannerheim Museum
97 American Embassy
98 British High Commission

Sörnäisten rantatie

ferry service

Maurinkatu

Pohjois-ranta

Kaisaniemi Park

Liisankatu

Unioninkatu

See Central Helsinki Map

Vilhonkatu

Mikonkatu

Kaisaniemenkatu

Fabianinkatu

Keskuskatu

Kirkkokatu

Pohjoisranta

Meritullinkatu

Korkeasaari

Hylkysaari

Hallituskatu

Aleksanterinkatu

Pohjoisesplanadi

Eteläesplanadi

Fish Market

Laivastokatu

Katajanokka

Merikasarminkatu

Kanavakatu

Korkeavuorenkatu

Yrjönkatu

Eerikinkatu

Kasarmikatu

Tähtitorninkatu

Eteläsatama

ferry to Korkeasaari

Valkosaari

Tehtaankatu

Neitsytpolku

Laivurinkatu

Puistokatu

Kaivopuisto Park

Merikatu

Merisatamaranta

Ehrenströmintie

Gulf of Finland

To Suomenlinna

Helsinki

0   250   500 m

(LP)

guidebooks, including nearly all Lonely Planet titles. Karttakeskus at Unioninkatu 32 sells maps. Valtikka sells 'official' (government) publications, some of them in English, at Eteläesplanadi 4.

Medical Services

Medical services in Helsinki are efficient, but exactly where you go for medical attention and how long you have to wait depends on the current situation; at times, hospitals are very congested. For serious injuries or other medical emergencies, call the Helsinki University Central Hospital (☎ 4711), which will direct you to the appropriate hospital. For treatment of serious injuries, go to the Töölön sairaala (Töölö Hospital) at Töölönkatu 40. For cases of poisoning, go to the Meilahti Hospital at Haartmaninkatu 4.

For less urgent medical problems, contact the nearest Terveysasema clinic. Each visit costs 50 mk. For opening times and other information ☎ 10023. The most convenient clinic, with wheelchair access, is in Kallio, at Eläintarhantie 3D. To get there, take the metro to Hakaniemi or catch a tram (Nos 1, 2, 3B, 3T, 6, 7A or 7B). In addition to normal opening hours, this clinic is open from 8 to 11 pm on weekdays, 2 to 11 pm on Saturday and 8 am to 11 pm on Sunday and public holidays.

At inconvenient hours, go to the Kivelä Hospital at Sibeliuksenkatu 12-14 (a short walk from tram Nos 3B, 3T and 8). It's open 24 hours a day on weekends, as well as from 3.30 pm right through to 8 am on weekdays. For specialist doctors, a fee of 125 mk must be paid. A private doctor will charge approximately 200 mk or more.

Pharmacy is *apteekki* in Finnish, and you'll find one at Mannerheimintie 5 (☎ 179 092), right in the city centre, open daily from 7 am to midnight. The pharmacy further north at Mannerheimintie 96 (☎ 241 5778) is open 24 hours a day.

Emergency

Call ☎ 112 for emergencies (ambulance, fire brigade or search and rescue). For police, call ☎ 10022. For strictly medical problems,

there is a 24 hour information service on ☎ 10023.

Laundry

Look in the Yellow Pages under 'Pesuloita' for laundry services. *Itsepalvelupesula* denotes self-service laundrettes.

Rööperin Pesula at Punavuorenkatu 3 is a self-service laundry. Check also *Café Tintin Tango* at Töölöntorinkatu 7, where you can bathe in a sauna while you wait, or drink coffee or beer.

MUSEUMS

The Helsinki Card gives free admission to all the following museums.

National Museum

This notable building on Mannerheimintie deserves a close look for its National Romantic design and for the Kalevala-inspired frescoes on the ceiling of its main hall. The oldest artefacts are in the main hall.

Notable historical pieces include a throne of Tsar Alexander I dating from 1809, when Finland was incorporated into Russia, and the 1899 painting *Attack* in room No 31, which symbolises nationalist opposition to the Pan-Slavic movement. Entry to the Finno-Ugric (ethnographic) exhibition in the basement is from room No 46. The museum is open all year round. Hours are 11 am to 4 pm, Wednesday to Sunday (to 5 pm in summer). On Tuesday, it is also open from 11 am to 8 pm. Admission is 15 mk.

Amos Anderson Art Museum

The collection of publishing magnate Amos Anderson, one of the wealthiest Finns of his time, includes Finnish and European paintings and sculptures. The permanent exhibitions are on the 4th to 6th floors at Yrjönkatu 27; a large gallery in the basement has temporary exhibitions. It's open from 11 am to 5 pm Monday to Friday, and until 4 pm on weekends. Entry is 30 mk for adults.

Arabia

The Arabia brand porcelain factory museum is rather bleakly located on the 9th floor of a suburban factory at Hämeentie 135. Most visitors come for the factory sales downstairs. There are special offers and three price categories. To get there, take tram No 6 to the terminus and walk 200 metres further north. The factory museum is open daily. Admission is 10 mk. Hours are 10 am to 8 pm on Monday, 10 am to 6 pm Tuesday to Friday, and 9 am to 3 pm on weekends. Factory tours are available on request.

Ateneum

This is the most notable art museum in Finland. Its list of painters reads like a 'Who's Who' of Finnish art. Even the building itself is a masterpiece of, well, renovation, finally completed in 1991. More recent works are upstairs in the **Museum of Contemporary Art**. The Ateneum is open daily (except Monday). Hours are 9 am to 6 pm on Tuesday and Friday, 9 am to 8 pm on Wednesday and Thursday, and 11 am to 5 pm on weekends. In summer, the museum opens at 10 am on weekdays, and closes at 9 pm. Tickets cost 10 to 40 mk.

Cygnaeus Gallery

If you're looking for good Finnish art from the 19th century, this is one place to go. The attractive wooden building in Kaivopuisto was built in 1870, and is open from 11 am to 7 pm on Wednesday and from 11 am to 4 pm Thursday to Sunday. Admission is 10 mk.

Helsinki City Museum

Several small museums constitute the Helsinki City museum. All are open from 11 am to 5 pm, Wednesday to Sunday, and each collects a 15 mk entry fee.

Helsinki City Museum This old villa opposite the National Museum has a detailed miniature model of historic Helsinki, giving a glimpse of life in the past. The temporary exhibition is sometimes more interesting than the permanent one.

Ruiskumestarin talo This historic house at Kristianinkatu 12, built in 1818, is the oldest wooden town house in central Helsinki.

Työväenasuntomuseo This museum at Kirstinkuja 4 shows how industrial workers in Helsinki lived earlier this century.

Raitioliikennemuseo This delightful museum, in an old tram depot at Eino Leinonkatu 3, displays almost a dozen old trams, and depicts daily life in Helsinki's streets in past decades.

Sederholmin talo This building, at Aleksanterinkatu 16-18, is the oldest in central Helsinki. It was recently renovated and opened in 1995, but is mostly of local interest.

Tuomarinkylän museo This museum, in the suburb of Tuomarinkylä not far from the airport, shows and explains the lifestyle of a wealthy estate. There's also a children's museum. From central Helsinki take bus No 64 to its terminus and walk one km.

Mannerheim Museum

The interesting home museum of CG Mannerheim, former president and Civil War victor, is at Kalliolinnantie 14 in Kaivopuisto. There are 600 items, including original furniture and a map of Mannerheim's trip to Asia, when he travelled 14,000 km along the Silk Route from Samarkand to Beijing, riding on one faithful horse for two years. Some of the Asian 'souvenirs' can also be seen. The museum is open from 11 am to 4 pm Friday to Sunday. Admission is 30 mk.

CG Mannerheim

Military Museum

This extensive collection of Finnish army paraphernalia has plenty of character. The museum is in Kruunuhaka, at Maurinkatu 1, and is open daily (except Saturday) from 11 am to 4 pm. Admission is 10 mk.

Post Museum

The excellent Postimuseo, right in the middle of town, is one of the best postal museums in the world, and it's all free. You could spend weeks browsing through stamp collections, computerised data banks and other hi-tech exhibits. Don't miss this one. The museum is open from 10 am to 7 pm on weekdays and from 11 am to 4 pm on weekends. It also has a café.

Sinebrychoff Museum of Foreign Art

The largest collection of Italian, Dutch and Flemish paintings in Finland can be found on the premises of the old brewery at Bulevardi 40 (catch tram No 6). It's open daily (except Tuesday) from 9 am to 5 pm. Admission is 10 to 25 mk.

Sports Museum of Finland

The Olympic Stadium houses Finland's 'sporting hall of fame'. There are displays on all Finnish sports heroes, as well as medals and old sporting equipment. The museum is open from 11 am to 5 pm Monday to Friday and from noon to 4 pm on weekends. Admission is 10 mk. Tram Nos 3B, 3T, 4, 7A, 7B and 10 will get you to the stadium. For some of the best views of Helsinki, take a lift to the top of the tower. It's open between 9 am and 8 pm Monday to Friday, and 9 am to 6 pm on weekends. The cost is 10 mk (free with a Helsinki Card).

Museum of Technology

This extensive museum is located in historical Helsinki at Viikinite 1. It's open in summer from 11 am to 5 pm, Tuesday to Sunday, the rest of the year from noon to 4 pm, Wednesday to Sunday. Admission is 15 mk.

Zoological Museum

This museum at Pohjoinen Rautatienkatu 13 doubles as a university department, and there is also a small student restaurant. Exhibits of stuffed animals are on three floors, and include a two headed mutant calf. The museum is open Monday to Friday, from 9 am to 5 pm (to 8 pm on Wednesday), and on

Champion distance runner Paavo Nurmi is featured in the Sports Museum of Finland.

Saturday and Sunday from 11 am to 4 pm. Admission is 20 mk.

Tamminiemi

This park-like area has several museums, each worth a visit. There are also pleasant cafés. From central Helsinki, take bus No 24, or tram No 4 and walk.

Helsinki City Art Museum There are temporary exhibitions in this modern building at Tamminiementie 6, not far from the museum island of Seurasaari. It's open all year round from 11 am to 6.30 pm, Wednesday to Sunday. Admission is 20 mk.

Urho Kekkonen Museum Tamminiemi This large house was a presidential residence for 30 years, right up until Kekkonen's death, when it was turned into a museum. The house is surrounded by a beautiful park. Tamminiemi is open daily all year round. In summer, the hours are 11 am to 5 pm; 11 am to 7 pm on Thursday; in winter it's closed on Monday. Admission is 15 mk.

Seurasaari The large museum island of Seurasaari, just south of Tamminiemi, is a pleasant place to walk and visit the old houses gathered here from around Finland. There's also a 17th century church from Karuna. Most houses have exhibits, and inside them are guides in national costume. Admission is 15 mk, but you can visit the island any time free of charge. There is folk dancing Tuesday to Thursday, normally at 7 pm but you should check actual times (☎ 484 234). Admission to the dances is 20 mk, free with a Helsinki Card. Opening hours are June to August daily from 11 am to 5 pm; in May and September from 9 am to 3 pm Monday to Friday, and 11 am to 5 pm on weekends.

Kaapelitehdas

What was previously a cable factory west of central Helsinki is now full of studios, offices and a number of other features, including a restaurant. There are three museums, one above the other, open from noon to 6 pm Tuesday to Friday (to 8 pm on Wednesday) and to 5 pm on weekends. Each museum carries a 10 mk admission fee, waived for the Helsinki Card. Catch tram No 8, or take the metro to Ruoholahti.

The **Photographic Museum of Finland** has temporary exhibitions of old photos, usually grouped by artist or subject, and invariably of interest. The **Theatre Museum** features temporary exhibitions in its small museum hall, usually involving stage costumes. The **Hotel & Restaurant Museum** on the third floor will be of interest to anyone who likes travelling and visiting hotels and restaurants.

Private Art Collections

The good news is that you can view very extensive art collections in Helsinki, some free of charge. The bad news is that they are hard to find and are open only once or twice a week.

Collection of Reitz Foundation, at Apollonkatu 23 B 64, is open Wednesday and Sunday from 3 to 5 pm. Press the door buzzer.

Taidekoti Kirpilä, at Pohjoinen Hesperiankatu 7, is open Wednesday from 2 to 6 pm, and Sunday from noon to 4 pm.

Didrichsen Art Museum, at Kuusilahdenkuja 1 on the island of Kuusisaari, is open Wednesday from 4 to 6 pm, and Sunday from 1 to 4 pm. Admission is 20 mk.

Villa Gyllenberg, at Kuusisaarenpolku 11, is open Wednesday from 4 to 8 pm, and Sunday from noon to 4 pm. Admission is 20 mk. Take tram No 4 and walk 2 km from its terminus.

Other Museums

Missionary Museum An attractive collection of Chinese and African artefacts, as well as a history of Finnish missionary work in Namibia, can be taken in on Sunday from noon to 3 pm at Tähtitorninkatu 16. Catch tram No 10 from central Helsinki or walk. Admission is 5 mk.

Museum of Medical History This unusual museum at Hämeentie 153C (catch bus Nos 71, 74 or 76) is open from noon to 3 pm on Tuesday and Friday and from 3 to 6 pm on Thursday. Admission is 4 mk.

Museum of Applied Arts If you are interested in Finnish design, this museum has much to offer. It's normally located at Korkeavuorenkatu 23, but temporarily (until 1997) at Laivurinkatu 3. It's open daily (except Monday) from 11 am to 5 pm. Admission is 30 mk.

Museum of Finnish Architecture This large exhibition is at Kasarmikatu 24. It's open daily (except Monday) from 10 am to 4 pm, and until 7 pm on Wednesday. Admission is 20 mk.

Helsinki Art Hall Large temporary exhibitions can be seen at Nervanderinkatu 3. In summer, the hall is open daily (except Saturday) from 11 am to 5 pm; at other times, it's open until 6 pm Tuesday to Sunday. Admission is 25 mk.

National Maritime Museum of Finland

You can reach this interesting cluster of exhibitions only via Korkeasaari. The main building has four floors of exhibits, and there's the MS *Kemi* and two boat shelters. The museum is open daily May to September from 11 am to 5 pm. Admission is 6 mk.

CHURCHES

Helsinki has several churches, including Lutheran, Catholic and Orthodox. As with most Finnish towns, the largest church in Helsinki is Lutheran. There are evangelical interdenominational services every Sunday at 10 am in the Mission Church on Tähtitorninkatu, and at 2 pm in the Rock Church.

Cathedral

Helsinki's landmark Lutheran Cathedral is surprisingly uninteresting inside. Climb the staircase for a good view of old Helsinki. The church is open daily in summer.

Johannes Church

This Lutheran church, with its two spires, is one of the largest in Finland, and the most impressive religious building in Helsinki.

Rock Church

The Temppeliaukio, or Taivallahti Church, designed by Timo and Tuomo Suomalainen and built into solid rock, remains one of Helsinki's foremost attractions. Popular church concerts, both gospel and classical, are given here. The English-language afternoon service at 2 pm on Sunday is followed by an informal coffee hour. The church is in Töölö; the entrance is at the end of Frederikinkatu.

Uspensky Cathedral

This very photogenic red brick church, built in 1868, is one of the foremost Orthodox churches in Finland. The interior is lavishly decorated with icons. Note the calendar icon near the pillar to your right. It is just off the fish market and is open from 9.30 am to 4 pm Tuesday to Friday, 9 am to noon on Saturday and noon to 3 pm on Sunday.

St Henrik's Church

The main Catholic church in Helsinki is at Puistokatu 1. It has English services at 10 am on Sunday. This pleasant, small church keeps its doors open even in winter, unlike Lutheran churches.

PARKS & GARDENS

Botanical gardens at **Talvipuutarha** (literally 'winter gardens'), at Hammarskjöldintie 1, are open daily from noon to 3 pm. The gardens were founded in 1893. Entry is free and there's a café. Take tram No 8 from Ruoholahti metro or Töölö.

Helsinki University overlooks the **Botanical Garden** at Unioninkatu 44. The greenhouses are open daily (except Friday) noon to 3 pm from 1 May to 31 August and on weekends only the rest of the year. Admission to the greenhouses is 10 mk (free with the Helsinki Card) but the garden is open longer, and has free entry.

Linnanmäki

Finland's most popular amusement park is on a hill just north of the suburb of Kallio (take tram Nos 3 or 8). Linnanmäki opens in early May and closes around the end of August. Go in the late afternoon; Linnanmäki closes every night at 10 pm. Admission is 15 mk, free with the Helsinki Card.

Korkeasaari

The main zoo in Finland is on this attractive island. Opened in 1889, it has a large variety of animals from Finland and around the world. There are regular express boats from the fish market, as well as from the pier at the Hotel Strand in Hakaniemi. You can catch bus No 16 to Kulosaari, and walk 1.5 km through the island of Mustikkamaa and onto Korkeasaari. You can also catch bus No 11 from metro stations Kulosaari or Herttoniemi. The zoo is open daily May to September from 10 am to 8 pm; at other times until 4 pm. Admission is 20 mk, free with a Helsinki Card.

Haltiala

North of Helsinki, right at the Vantaa border

and along the Vantaanjoki river, this large rural area contains protected forests and an old farm estate that can be visited at any time, free of charge. The main arterial roads to Hämeenlinna and Tuusula (airport) border Haltiala.

ARCHITECTURE

Helsinki has plenty of interesting buildings. Although there are good examples of modern architecture, many people regard **Senaatintori (Senate) Square** as the purest collection of 19th century houses, including the university main building with its fine library (don't miss it), the Cathedral and the government building.

Behind the square on Snellmanninkatu, **Säätytalo** is a very fine administrative building. Unfortunately, after a recent renovation, it is now closed to mere mortals. Check out the Art-Nouveau wonders on Aleksanterinkatu, as well as the beautiful residential buildings in Katajanokka. Eira has plenty of villas, and Huvilakatu is the finest street in Helsinki.

Finlandia-talo (Finlandia House) is one of the most famous works of Alvar Aalto. Unfortunately, its Italian marble isn't suited to the Finnish climate; architects have been arguing for years about what to do with the awkward marble sheets that unevenly cover the building. Guided tours, available at a cost of 20 mk, are free for those carrying the Helsinki Card.

Some of the finest villas are in Kulosaari (near the metro stop), Kuusisaari (north-west of the centre), Marjaniemi (near metro Itäkeskus) and other suburbs. The small **Library of Vallila** on Mäkelänkatu in Vallila (tram 7) is one of the famous public buildings designed by award-winning architect Juha Leiviskä.

ACTIVITIES
Saunas & Swimming

Helsinki has several public indoor swimming pools with inexpensive admission. The sauna on Yrjönkatu, adjacent to the Forum, has nude swimming (and consequently, separate hours for men and women). There are

swimming pools in Kallio (on Helsinginkatu) and a very large sports complex in Pirkkola in Keskuspuisto park. You can get there by jogging or cycling along the popular tracks that crisscross the forests, but be warned: the park is home to some of Helsinki's more desperate individuals.

The outdoor Swimming Stadium near the Stadionin retkeilymaja (youth hostel) is open daily from 1 May to 31 August. For some authentic bathing in a smoke sauna, catch bus No 20 to Vaskiniemi, on the island of Lauttasaari. The Finnish Sauna Society (☎ 678 677) has a male sauna on Tuesday, Wednesday, Friday and Saturday all year round (except July). For women, hours are 1 to 8 pm on Thursday. Admission is a hefty 70 mk.

Language Courses

Helsinki University, at Fabianinkatu 33, offers regular full-term courses in Finnish, starting mid-September. As a rule, you should be enrolled at the university to qualify for free education. The Helsinki Summer University (☎ 135 4577) at Liisankatu 16A, open all year round from 9 am to 3 pm Monday to Friday, gives Finnish lessons in summer. Expect to pay a few hundred markkaa for a summer course.

ORGANISED TOURS

Use your Helsinki Card for a complimentary sightseeing tour, which otherwise costs 60 mk. The tour takes 1½ hours and starts between the railway station and the post office. There are daily departures at 11 am and 1 pm from June to August, and one departure at 11 am on Tuesday, Thursday and Sunday in May and September. At other times, it's every Sunday at 11 am. There are also several organised walking tours in summer, but usually only once each week. Enquire about the next one when you reach Helsinki.

Cruises

Strolling through the fish market in summer, you won't have to look for cruises – the boat companies will find you. Several companies

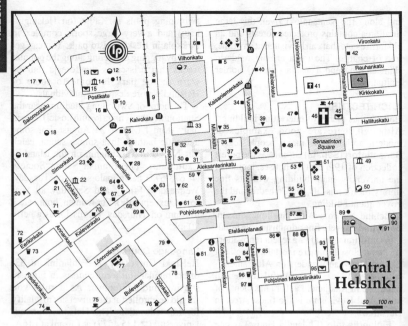

Central
Helsinki

0   50   100 m

can take you around the Helsinki area. Tickets cost around 60 mk, and the trip around the island of Laajasalo, run by Sun Lines, is probably the most interesting. Don't miss the cheapest cruise in Helsinki, to the island of Suomenlinna.

A good day trip destination is the island of Kaunissaari, leaving the fish market daily at 10.30 am and returning some time after 4 pm. One-way tickets cost around 50 mk.

FESTIVALS

Helsinki can seem sleepy in summer, as many locals are touring Finland for festivals. But there is always something going on in Helsinki in summer: concerts, performances and much more. Ask for details at the tourist information office.

The most notable event is the Helsinki Festival, held from late August to early September. (In 1995 this lavish event lost 10 million markkaa.) There are also occasional free concerts on Sunday afternoons in summer. Enquire locally.

PLACES TO STAY – BOTTOM END

Helsinki has an excellent choice of inexpensive accommodation.

Camping

You can pitch your tent anywhere in the large Keskuspuisto (Central Park) if you are discreet. It's legal but not a designated camping ground. There could be traffic in the form of joggers. Camping in public parks or on the islands of Suomenlinna and Seurasaari is not permitted.

Rastila Camping (☎ 316 551), 10 km from the centre, charges 25 mk per person per night for camping, 50 mk per tent if there is more than one person. There are two/four bed cottages for 150/200 mk per night. It is open from 15 May to 5 September. To get there, take the metro to Itäkeskus and change to bus Nos 90, 90A, 96, 96S or 98. At night,

PLACES TO STAY

1	Interpoint & Hotel Arthur & City Apartments
5	Matkustajakoti Pilvilinna & Tähtilinna
6	Omapohja
8	Hotel Booking Centre
16	Sokos Hotel Vaakuna
25	Hotel Seurahuone Socis
34	Matkustajakoti Mekka
36	Sokos Hotel Helsinki
40	Hotel Cumulus Kaisaniemi
42	Kongressikoti
67	Finn
69	Arctia Hotel Marski
70	Sokos Hotel Torni
74	Matkustajakoti Lönnrot
76	Hostel Erottajanpuisto
78	Sokos Hotel Klaus Kurki
94	Hotel Palace
97	Hotel Rivoli Jardin

PLACES TO EAT

2	Taukotupa
3	Croco's
17	Pikkuparlamentti
20	Don't Tell Mama
23	Forum Shopping Centre
27	Zetor
28	Vanha
29	Omenapuu
31	Santa Fé
35	Planet Hollywood
37	Hesburger
39	Porthania
44	Café Krypta
51	Café Engel
55	Ursula
56	Fazer
57	Café Strindberg
58	König
59	Raffaello
60	Café Esplanad
62	Page & Carrols
65	Kosmos
71	Compu Café
72	Corona Bar
73	H2O
75	Café Ekberg
84	Galleria Hariton
85	Cantina West
87	Café Kappeli
91	Margona
93	La Vista
96	Kaarle XII

OTHER

4	Velholinna Shopping Centre
7	Airport Bus No 615
9	Railway Station
10	Sightseeing Tour Departures & Taxis
11	Finnair Terminal
12	Finnair buses
13	Poste Restante
14	Post Museum
15	Main Post Office
18	Bus Terminal
19	Regional Buses
21	Finnish Youth Hostel Association
22	Amos Anderson Art Museum
3.	
32	
33	
38	
41	C...
43	Sä...
45	Pos...
46	Cath...
47	Univer...y Library
48	Helsinki University
49	Sederholmin talo Museum
50	Swedish Embassy
52	Senate Centre
53	Karttakeskus Map Shop
54	City Tourist Information Office
61	Akateeminen Kirjakauppa Bookshop
63	Stockmann Department Store
64	Viking Line
66	Public Sauna
68	Forex Money Exchange
77	Old Church
79	Silja Line
80	Tikankontti
81	Tallink
82	Public Library
83	Savoy
86	Design Forum Finland
88	Finnish Tourist Board
89	Fish Market
90	Suomenlinna Ferry
92	Cruise Boats
95	Post Office

if the metro is not running, bus Nos 90N or 96N from the city centre will take you there. The trip takes 15 minutes by train, a few minutes more by bus.

Hostels

The clean *Kallio Youth Hostel* (☎ 7099 2590), Porthaninkatu 2, has 35 dormitory beds from 1 June to 31 August for 50 mk each. There is a laundry (15 mk), a kitchen with a TV, plus good information. Take the metro to Hakaniemi station (use the northern exit), or tram Nos 1, 2 or 3B. There are also bicycles for rent: 30 mk for eight hours, 70 mk for 24 hours.

The recently renovated SRM hostel *Stadionin maja* (☎ 496 071) at the Olympic Stadium at Pohjoinen Stadionintie 3B, has 130 beds in 20 rooms, with dorm beds from 54 mk, and singles/doubles for 120/150 mk. It is in a quiet location, and there are several walks in the vicinity. The hostel is open all year round, and daily until 2 am. There are bicycles for rent at 50 mk per day, 80 mk for 24 hours, and 250 mk per week. A buffet breakfast costs 25 mk, and there is a well-equipped kitchen, two TV rooms and a laundry (for 15 mk). To get there from central Helsinki, walk through the parks, or take tram Nos 3T, 3B, 7A or 7B.

value is *Academica* (☎ 402
Hietaniemenkatu 14. A student
ment building in winter, it is open to
travellers from 1 June to 1 September. Each
four bed dormitory room has its own kitch-
enette and shower, and there is free morning
swim and sauna. Dormitory beds cost 55 mk,
doubles 180 mk.

Probably the best area to stay in Helsinki
is on Katajanokka island, where *Eurohostel*
(☎ 664 452) at Linnankatu 9 charges only
100 mk per person for a double, including
morning sauna and sheets. It is the nearest
place to the Viking Line terminal. Eurohostel
is an HI youth hostel. There are 135 rooms,
kitchens on each floor (with unique safe
fridges), and a self-service laundrette.
Reception is open 24 hours a day. To get
there, take tram Nos 4 or 2 from the centre.

Very central and also excellent value is
Hostel Erottajanpuisto (☎ 642 169) at
Uudenmaankatu 9, right in the middle of
town. Beds start at 80 mk for HI members,
and there are rooms for 180/250 mk (15 mk
less for HI members).

Satakunnantalo (☎ 695 851) at
Lapinrinne 1A is also a student apartment
building, open to travellers in June, July and
August only. An HI affiliated hostel, it has
dormitory beds from 50 mk, as well as
doubles for 220 mk (less with the HI discount).

Also worth a look is *Interpoint* (☎ 1734
4257) at Vuorikatu 17. Beds are 50 to 60 mk
per night, but you must first purchase a membership card for 16 mk.

PLACES TO STAY – MIDDLE
Guesthouses

There is a cluster of guesthouses near the
railway station. These places defy the typical
'cheap hotel near the station' definition,
charging something like 175 mk for a single
and 220 to 350 mk for a double. It is certainly
cheaper to stay in these than in hotels, but
facilities are quite basic. Small groups get the
best rates per person, and some places will
give a dorm bed to individual travellers.

Omapohja (☎ 666 211), Itäinen Teatterikuja 3,
nearest the station, has rooms from 175/230 mk.

Matkustajakoti Pilvilinna (☎ 607 072), Vilhonkatu 6,
consists of three previously independent guesthouses. Its 44 rooms offer dormitory beds for 70
mk and singles/doubles from 170/230 mk (rooms
with a shower are much dearer). Ask for a room
overlooking the rear courtyard; the main street is
noisy.

Tähtilinna (☎ 627 437), Vilhonkatu 6 on the fourth
floor, just above Pilvilinna, has similar rates.

Matkustajakoti Mekka (☎ 630 265), Vuorikatu 8B,
has 31 rooms near Kaisaniemi metro station.
Rooms start at 200/225 mk, dormitory beds are
85 mk.

Kongressikoti (☎ 135 6839), Snellmanninkatu 15, has
just 10 rooms; singles/doubles are 160/220 mk.

Matkustajakoti Lönnrot (☎ 693 2590), Lönnrotinkatu
16, is central and relatively clean, although there
are common showers. You may use the kitchen.
Singles/doubles cost 160/220 mk, breakfast is 25
mk.

Tarmo (☎ 701 4735), Siltasaarenkatu 11B in
Hakaniemi, has 16 rooms from 170/230 mk.

Hotels

Some hotels in Helsinki offer good deals,
especially in summer (late June to 30 July is
the cheapest period) and on weekends
throughout the year:

Hotel Anna (☎ 648 011), Annankatu 1. Singles/
doubles cost 450/550 mk; 330/420 mk in summer
and on weekends.

Hotelli Anton (☎ 750 311), Paasivuorenkatu 1.
Singles/doubles cost 350/450 mk; 200/300 mk in
summer.

Hotel Arthur (☎ 173 441), Vuorikatu 17. Singles/
doubles cost 320/390 mk; 240/340 mk in summer
and on weekends.

Hotel Aurora (☎ 717 400), Helsinginkatu 50. Singles/
doubles cost 350/420 mk.

City Apartments (☎ 170 255), Vuorikatu 17. Singles/
doubles are 313/403 mk.

Fenno (☎ 773 1661), Franzéninkatu 26 in the suburb
of Kallio. Singles/doubles start at 150/295 mk.

Finn (☎ 640 904), Kalevankatu 3. Singles/doubles
start at 200/250 mk.

Hotel Helka (☎ 613 580), Pohjoinen Rautatiekatu 23.
Singles/doubles start at 300/400 mk; 250/350 mk
in summer.

Marttahotelli (☎ 646 211), Uudenmaankatu 24.
Singles/doubles at this pleasant, small hotel are
410/510 mk; 300/360 mk in summer and on
weekends.

Olympia (☎ 69151), Läntinen Brahenkatu 2. Singles/
doubles are 330/405 mk; 276/340 mk in summer
and on weekends.

Skatta (☎ 659 233), Linnankatu 3. Singles/doubles are 250/300 mk; 200/220 mk on weekends.

PLACES TO STAY – TOP END

Although there are apparently plenty of empty rooms in Helsinki hotels these days, this is not necessarily reflected in special discounts. There are, however, attractive summer prices. For all reservations, including some hostels, contact the Hotel Booking Centre (☎ 171 133) at the train station. From 1 June to 31 August, it's open from 9 am to 7 pm Monday to Saturday and from 10 am to 6 pm on Sunday. At other times, hours are 9 am to 5 pm Monday to Friday.

Hotel Cumulus Kaisaniemi (☎ 172 881), Kaisaniemenkatu 7. A central but noisy location. Singles/doubles are 485/570 mk; 365/365 mk in summer.

Arctia Hotel Grand Marina (☎ 16661), Katajanokanlaituri 7. Located in an old renovated harbour building, this hotel opened in 1992. It has 462 rooms and charges 624/834 mk for singles/doubles; 412/474 mk in summer.

Sokos Hotel Helsinki (☎ 131 401), Hallituskatu 12. Singles/doubles at this centrally located hotel are 420/520 mk; 400/400 mk in summer.

Sokos Hotel Hesperia (☎ 43101), Mannerheimintie 50. Supposedly the best hotel in Helsinki, although many would disagree. Singles/doubles are 1040/1250 mk; 495/495 mk in summer.

Hotel Inter-Continental (☎ 40551), Mannerheimintie 46. With 555 rooms, this is one of the notable international hotels in Helsinki. Singles/doubles are 900/1115 mk; 580/580 mk in summer. Traffic can be a bit noisy.

Hotel Kalastajatorppa (☎ 45811), Kalastajatorpantie 1. Many official visitors have stayed at this legendary hotel outside the town centre. Rooms cost 475 mk in summer and on weekends.

Sokos Hotel Klaus Kurki (☎ 618 911), Bulevardi 2. One of the pleasant hotels in the town centre, Klaus Kurki has singles/doubles for 825/1040 mk; 350/425 mk in summer.

Lord Hotel (☎ 615 815), at Lönnrotinkatu 29, is the finest Art Nouveau hotel in Helsinki. It was previously a technical school. Singles/doubles cost 440/540 mk; 400/440 mk in summer.

Arctia Hotel Marski (☎ 68061), Mannerheimintie 10. This long-appreciated city hotel has singles/doubles for 835/940 mk; 395/395 mk in summer.

Merihotelli (☎ 69121), just off Hakaniemi Square, has singles/doubles for 445/540 mk; 290/390 mk in summer.

Hotel Palace (☎ 134 561), Eteläranta, offers good views of the harbour. Singles/doubles are 905/1070 mk; 480/640 mk in summer.

Hotel Ramada Presidentti (☎ 6911), Eteläinen Rautatienkatu. This centrally located hotel has 495 rooms and a casino. Singles/doubles are 390/390 mk in summer; 594/700 mk at other times.

Radisson SAS Hotel (☎ 69580), Runeberginkatu 2. One of the finest and most expensive hotels in Helsinki. Singles/doubles are 1113/1219 mk; 578/578 mk in summer.

Hotel Rivoli Jardin (☎ 177 880), Kasarmikatu 40. Singles/doubles cost 750/870 mk; 475/475 mk in summer.

Seaside Hotel (☎ 69360), Ruoholahdenranta 3. This fine hotel is near the Hietalahti flea market. Singles/doubles start at 360/6409 mk; 200/360 mk in summer.

Hotel Seurahuone Socis (☎ 69141), Kaivokatu 12. Just opposite the railway station, this hotel has a lot of style and class. Singles/doubles are 519/625 mk. Weekend rates are lower, and in summer all rooms cost 370 mk.

Hotel Strand Inter-Continental (☎ 39351), John Stenbergin ranta 4. Near Hakaniemi Square, this is one of Helsinki's newer hotels, and the most expensive. Singles/doubles are 1208/1367 mk; 664/664 mk in summer.

Sokos Hotel Torni (☎ 131 131), Yrjönkatu. Torni translates as 'tower', and for a long time this hotel was the highest building in the city centre. Singles/doubles are 825/1040 mk; 350/425 mk in summer.

Sokos Hotel Vaakuna (☎ 131 181), Asema-aukio 2. This hotel, opposite the railway station, has singles/doubles at 825/1040 mk; 350/450 mk in summer.

PLACES TO EAT

The basement floor of the Forum shopping centre has a food section, with several pleasant restaurants in one spot. Prices are not especially low, but the kebab restaurant in particular offers good value.

Fast Food

When restaurants close and the late movies end, people queue for hamburgers or *makkara* (sausage) at *grillis*. These true junk-food outlets offer little of nutritious value, but a salty sausage with mustard tastes excellent late at night. *Jaskan Grilli* on Töölönkatu, behind the National Museum, is

HELSINKI

the best grilli in Helsinki. Avoid the overpriced stalls at the railway station.

You will find several simple kebab restaurants, a few taco bars and numerous Hesburger, Carrols and McDonald's restaurants in the centre of Helsinki. Prices are slightly higher compared with similar products in other countries. Also in the budget category are several stalls in market halls on Eteläranta, Hakaniemi Square and Hietalahti Square which serve simple food.

University Eateries

Local students pay between 10 and 15 mk for discounted meals, available in a dozen *Uni* restaurants around central Helsinki. You will have to say 'Ei oo korttia' *(AY OOH KORT-ti-ah)*, meaning 'I don't have a (student) card', and pay the ordinary price of 15 to 20 mk. The price includes three slices of bread, milk and some salad. Coffee and snacks are also inexpensive.

The most pleasant place to eat is *Alibi/Domus* at Hietaniemenkatu 14. It closes at 4 pm, then opens again in the evening as a student bar, often with live music. Opposite the Ramada Hotel, *Eläinmuseo*, Pohjoinen Rautatiekatu 13, is in the Zoological Museum building. *Porthania* serves good food at Hallituskatu 11-13; many foreign students eat there. Finally, *Taukotupa*, at Fabianinkatu 39, is the restaurant of the university's Forestry Department.

Lunch Eateries

Most restaurants around Helsinki offer lunch specials from about 30 mk. The meal usually includes salad, bread, milk or malt drink and sometimes coffee; shop around and ask first. *Suola ja pippuri* ('Salt & Pepper') on Vironkatu is open for lunch only, with cheap meals between 2 and 3 pm. The nearby *Kolme Kruunua* at Liisankatu 5 is a relic of the 1930s. It is famous for its *lihapullat* (meatballs), which can be had for under 40 mk. Lunch is 45 mk.

For an à la carte meal, *Hyvä Ystävä* restaurants have slightly lower prices than others but still can't beat the lunch specials. Other good places are *Omenapuu* at Keskuskatu 6, or the popular *Page* at Keskuskatu 3, complete with Alvar Aalto décor.

Smorgasbords

Konstan Möljä at Hietalahdenkatu 14 is one of the most attractive restaurants in Helsinki, and one of the few to offer a genuine Finnish buffet. Its interior reflects an old Karelian fishing culture from the island of Uuras, annexed by the USSR in 1944. An 'all you can eat' lunch costs 42 mk on weekdays, 50 to 60 mk on weekends. Excellent soups are the speciality, and freshly brewed coffee is available at bargain prices. The place is normally full at noon. Lunch is served from 11 am to 4 pm daily, except on Sunday (noon to 5.30 pm). To get there, take tram No 6 to the end of Bulevardi.

Cantina West is an authentic Tex-Mex bar and restaurant at Kasarmikatu 23. A Mexican-style buffet lunch is available upstairs for a little over 40 mk. The colourful menu has nachos from 27 mk. In the evenings, the bar is often full.

Ani, at Telakkakatu 2, has the best Turkish-Armenian buffet in town, at 38 mk. *Kaspian*, at Albertinkatu 7, offers a Persian buffet for 36 mk. A similar place is *Persepolis*, at Pieni Roobertinkatu 2, which specialises in kebabs and vegetarian food.

Vegetarian

Kasvisravintola, at Korkeavuorenkatu 3, is a simple, informal place with an understanding of vegetarian philosophy.

International Food

Surprisingly, the best Russian food is often found outside Russia, and Helsinki is not a bad place to try some. *Šašlik*, at Neitsytpolku 12, is the top Russian restaurant in Helsinki. Also very good is *Galleria Hariton* at Kasarmikatu 44 (and its annexes nearby) and *Bellevue* at Rahapajankatu 3 in Katajanokka. *Kosmos*, at Kalevankatu 3, a regular haunt of local artists, serves Russian *blini* (pancakes).

The best Indian cuisine is said to be *Namaskaar* at Mannerheimintie 100, but this is also one of the most expensive restaurants in Helsinki. Expect to pay 100 mk for a decent *thali*. *Sukhothai*, at Runeberginkatu 32, is a budget Thai restaurant but there are others too.

Of the Italian restaurants, *La Vista* at Eteläranta 10 has been a local favourite for years. *König*, at Mikonkatu 4, is one of the most popular à la carte restaurants. *Svenska Klubben* at Maurinkatu 17 is an expensive restaurant with plenty of charm and historical value. In summer, you can eat at *Margona*, a boat restaurant at the fish market.

Planet Hollywood at Mikonkatu 9 serves American food at reasonable rates. This is a pet project of 'our man in Hollywood', Renny Harlin. The restaurant was officially opened by Bruce Willis, Demi Moore, Geena Davis and Renny Harlin on 31 August 1995 and has genuine movie paraphernalia from various films, with appropriate explanations.

Croco's, previously known as Crocodile's, is an Aussie bar on Vilhonkatu, near the Interpoint hostel.

Fine Dining

For the pick of Finnish cuisine try *Piekka* at Mannerheimintie 68. It's expensive but the food is superb. Try a game platter, including reindeer and bear meat, fried lake perch with crayfish sauce, and wild raspberries in Arctic bramble liqueur. *Kynsilaukka Ravintola Garlic* at Fredrikinkatu 22 is the best garlic restaurant in town.

There are a few excellent places at the foot of the Orthodox Church on Katajanokka. *Bar Kanava* is a bar, and *Kultainen Sipuli* upstairs offers a fine view of the 'Golden Onion' (as the name translates) dome of the church. This fine restaurant is open for dinner only. Round the corner, *Kanavaranta* and *Albatross* are known for their fine cuisine. Farther along the seashore, *Wellamo* is a small restaurant with inexpensive lunch prices and a colourful clientele.

Cafés

Locals have developed a sophisticated taste for pleasant cafés, where you can also have snacks and small meals. *Café Ekberg* at Bulevardi 9 is probably the oldest café in Finland, known as 'The Pit' when it opened back in 1861. Another historical café is *Fazer*, at Kluuvikatu 3. Founded in 1891, it serves excellent but costly pastries.

There are a number of good cafés around Esplanadi Park. *Café Esplanad* at Pohjoisesplanadi 37 is a shoestring haven with huge wheat buns (only one is required to stuff a big person). The nearby two storey *Café Strindberg* at Pohjoisesplanadi 33 is more chic. Further east, not far from the market, *Ursula* is another popular place, and there's an outdoor section in summer. For historical views and a hint of *haute couture*, *Café Engel* at Senate Square attracts many stylish young things.

Quite different is the café at the fish market. You'll see pictures of the kings and presidents who have visited this simple tent café over the 100 years of its existence, all under the ownership of the same family. *Café Krypta*, eerily located in the crypt of the large Cathedral at Kirkkokatu 18, is open from early June to mid-August daily until 4 pm. It serves coffee and snacks.

In the southern part of town, *Café Kaffekoppen* on Fredrikintori has a pleasant site on a small square. *Café Succes* at Korkeavuorenkatu 2 is run by the same people as Café Esplanad, and there are huge breads and pastries. The seaside café Ursula (a branch of the original Ursula in central Helsinki) is popular all year round; its outdoor section affords good views of Suomenlinna.

Near the island of Seurasaari is *Tamminiementien kahvila*, at Tamminiementie 8. This manor, dating back to the 17th century, retains its old ambience.

CompuCafé at Annankatu 27 is a restaurant and café where you can enjoy a snack while surfing the Internet.

Bars

All bars in Finland serve food. Areas in central Helsinki, such as Aleksanterinkatu, are extremely busy on weekends and you won't find space or quiet in the most popular places, such as *Raffaello* or *Santa Fé*. You can eat in both places and beer is also served outside on warm evenings.

If locals advise you on the 'in' places, it may be best to avoid these, unless you want to wait hours for admission (not very pleasant in winter).

Don't miss *Zetor* at Kaivopiha, just 100 metres off the railway station. This 'redneck' bar, with its tractor-inspired bar and restaurant, is very much a rural person's nostalgic retreat. The interior decoration, not far from sensational, was created by Mato Valtonen and Sakke Järvenpää, two creative rock'n'roll persons who run the Leningrad Cowboys rock group. Their other achievements include *Cantina West* at Kasarmikatu 23, and *Rock'n'roll McDonald's* at Mannerheimintie 53 – not your typical hamburger restaurant.

Café Barock at Fredrikinkatu 42 is in the premises of an old chapel; the building itself is protected.

Elite at Eteläinen Hesperiankatu 22, with its Art-Nouveau décor, is a popular open-air bar in summer. You'll also see a number of others in the city centre, including *Café Kappeli*, *Kaisaniemi*, and *Pikkuparlamentti*. Other names to keep in mind include *Bier-Akademie* at Pohjoinen Rautatiekatu 21, the already-mentioned Cantina West and König, although none beat *Kaarle XII*; it always has long queues outside, and the regulars seem to have first access.

Jazz is a feature at *Storyville*, at Museokatu 8, and at *Hot Tomato*, on Annankatu. *Corona Bar* at Eerikinkatu 11 is famous for its billiard tables.

Opposite, *H2O* is the most famous gay bar in Helsinki. Another is *Don't Tell Mama* at Annankatu 32.

Self-Catering

Alepa, Siwa and Säästäri are the cheapest food chains, with several stores scattered around Helsinki. The most central *Alepa* store, in Asematunneli, below the railway station, is open daily till 10 pm. Check special discount prices.

ENTERTAINMENT
Cinemas

Most cinemas hand out weekly programmes, with a listing in English. Go to the central *Forum* (next door to the Forum Shopping Centre) for a choice of seven cinemas and for the programmes. There are free films on Helsinki at 2 pm on Tuesday and Thursday in *Amanda*, at Sofiankatu 4, just off the fish market.

Nightclubs

Hotels Kaivohuone, Hesperia and Inter-Continental offer some nightlife, as well as the *RAY Casino* in the Ramada Hotel. Locals know the 'in' places, so ask around. Sleazy erotic bars include *Lulu* at Bulevardi 7 and *King's Kakadu* at Iso Roobertinkatu 20-22.

Music

Daily concerts are held in several locations in Helsinki. The tourist information office will help you to find out what is going on, or just keep your eyes open. Rock concerts are regularly held at *Tavastia*, *Botta*, *Vanha* and *Savoy*, to name just a few. The *Jumo Jazz Club* features local and foreign ensembles.

For something more serious, the Symphony Orchestra of the Finnish Broadcasting Corporation (RSO) features popular concerts in the Finlandia Hall, as well as in the Kulttuuritalo.

Theatre

Theatres in Helsinki have shows in Finnish, but there is opera and ballet too. You can get programmes from Lippupalvelu ticket offices or at the tourist information office.

THINGS TO BUY

Helsinki has the largest variety of shops in Finland, but prices are generally higher than in most other large Finnish towns, especially on Pohjoisesplanadi, the main tourist street in town. There are many shops in an underground mall beneath the railway station, and many of them stay open daily until 10 pm. The largest single area for shopping is the eastern suburb of Itäkeskus, which you can reach by metro. In Kallio (metro to

Hakaniemi), you'll find a great variety of small shops, and Porthaninkatu, near the Kallio youth hostel, has several indoor flea markets.

Stockmann, the oldest and largest department store in Finland, is surprisingly reasonably priced for Finnish souvenirs and Sami handicrafts, as well as Finnish textiles, Kalevala Koru jewellery, Lapponia jewellery, Moomintroll souvenirs and lots more. They have an export service whereby they post your goods to you, thus saving you the purchase tax (which more than covers the cost of the packing and postage). Forum and Kluuvi are the two modern shopping centres in central Helsinki. Senate Centre, opposite the cathedral, is worth a visit even if you're not interested in handicrafts and souvenirs.

The notable shopping streets are Aleksanterinkatu, Pohjoisesplanadi (designer shops and galleries) and Frederikinkatu (boutiques). Mariankatu has many antiques shops, and Iso-Roobertinkatu is a pedestrian street. For exhibits on Finnish design, visit the Design Forum Finland at Eteläesplanadi 8, open from 11 am to 5 pm Monday to Friday and from noon to 6 pm on Saturday.

Markets

The famous fish market is a must for anyone visiting Helsinki. Fish, strawberries and makkara (sausages) are on sale, and there is any number of stalls selling local handicraft, hand-painted stones and weird hats, Sami dolls and T-shirts.

Another place that should not be missed is the Hietalahti market (catch tram No 6), where all sellers are local people who generally set up a stall for one week (an official restriction). This is the main second-hand centre in Helsinki: you'll find anything from used clothes to broken electronic goods. Bargain hard, and for really low prices go a little before 2 pm, when the market closes. New people and new goods arrive in the evening.

There are also some interesting indoor markets near the fish market and in Hakaniemi and Hietalahti.

GETTING THERE & AWAY

Air

Helsinki is served by several airlines from the USA, Europe and Asia, and Finnair connects Helsinki to all major cities and towns in Finland. Here is a list of airline companies in Helsinki:

Aeroflot
  Mannerheimintie 5 (☎ 659 655)
Air France
  Pohjoisesplanadi 27C (☎ 625 862)
Air Lithuania
  Eteläesplanadi 24A (☎ 644 066)
Austrian Airlines
  Mikonkatu 7 (☎ 175 300)
Balkan Bulgarian Airlines
  Annankatu 9 (☎ 647 752)
British Airways
  7th floor, Keskuskatu 7 (☎ 650 677)
ČSA (Československé aerolinie)
  Uudenmaankatu 6B (☎ 647 786)
Estonian Air
  Airport (☎ 821 381)
Finnair
  Asema-aukio 3
  Töölönkatu 21
  (☎ 9800-3466)
Iberia
  Annankatu 16B (☎ 640 944)
Icelandair
  Eteläranta 14/6D (☎ 174 775)
JAL Japan Airlines
  Annankatu 29A (☎ 7001 7400)
KLM Royal Dutch Airlines
  Airport (☎ 870 1747)
LOT Polish Airlines
  Keskuskatu 6 (☎ 660 400)
Lufthansa
  Yrjönkatu 29A (☎ 694 9900)
Malév Hungarian Airlines
  Mikonkatu 8 (☎ 660 322)
Qantas Airways
  Museokatu 25B (☎ 447 522)
Sabena World Airlines
  Pohjoisesplanadi 27C (☎ 179700)
SAS Scandinavian Airlines
  4th floor, Keskuskatu 7 (☎ 228 021)
Singapore Airlines (SIA)
  Kalevankatu 13A (☎ 680 2770)
Swissair
  Mikonkatu 7 (☎ 175 300)
Thai International Airways
  Keskuskatu 4 (☎ 602 044)

Bus

The messy bus terminal is located between

Mannerheimintie and the Kamppi metro station. Long-distance buses depart from between the white building on Mannerheimintie and the main bus station. Buses departing from the larger square are local or regional buses which serve the western parts of Helsinki (including Espoo) and Vantaa to the north. To avoid confusion, arrive early and ask around.

Train

The main railway station is right in the middle of Helsinki. All trains also stop at the Pasila station, three km to the north. Helsinki is the terminus for three main railway lines, with regular trains from Turku in the west, Tampere in the north and Lahti in the northeast.

Ferry

Most international ferries arrive just off the central fish market: Viking and Silja from Sweden, Finnjet from Germany and a few companies from Russia. Ferries to Estonia carrying vehicles depart from a new terminal at Länsiterminaali (tram 8 or bus 15). The best places to purchase a ferry ticket are the harbour check-in offices. If you need time-table details or other information, ferry companies do have offices in Helsinki:

Baltic Express Line
      Keskuskatu 1B (☎ 665 755)
Eestin Linjat
      Fabianinkatu 9 (☎ 669 944)
Estonian New Line
      Fabianinkatu 12 (☎ 680 2499)
Silja Line
      Mannerheimintie 2 (☎ 9800-74552)
Tallink
      Erottajankatu 19 (☎ 2282 1211)
Viking Line
      Mannerheimintie 14 (☎ 12351)

An attractive way of leaving or entering Helsinki is on the MS *J L Runeberg*, a former steamship. Catch it from the fish market, to Porvoo, Loviisa or Hanko. There are departures almost daily – check timetables at Ageba (☎ 625 944).

GETTING AROUND
To/From the Airport

Two bus companies serve the airport. Finnair buses are more expensive, at 24 mk; they generally depart every 20 minutes from the city Finnair terminal near the railway station, picking up passengers at the Hotel Inter-Continental bus stop. The local bus No 615 is somewhat slower but also several markkaa cheaper (15 mk). There are also Airport Express minibuses that will take you from the airport to any place in Helsinki for a flat fee of 50 mk. Taxis charge approximately 120 mk for a ride between central Helsinki and the airport.

City Transport System

The city transport system, Helsingin Kaupungin Liikennelaitos (HKL), operates buses, metro trains, local trains, trams and a ferry to the island of Suomenlinna. There are frequent departures on all routes; timetables and route maps are available free of charge from HKL ticket offices, one of which is located in the central Rautatientori metro station. A single journey costs something like 10 mk (price rises are frequent), and you can change transport an unlimited number of times in the (exactly) 60 minutes from the time stamped on your ticket. Bus and tram drivers sell tickets, which you will have to stamp by yourself. For the metro and local trains, you should use the automatic ticket-vending machines. A 10 journey ticket will cost 75 mk.

You can easily get on a tram, train, or the Suomenlinna ferry without a ticket, but there are frequent ticket checks. The penalty for a ticketless ride is currently 260 mk and acting dumb or playing the helpless foreigner won't help. One to three day travel cards are available, and a Helsinki Card gives you unlimited access to all HKL transport, including buses and trains to Espoo and Vantaa.

Bus Most blue HKL buses leave from one of two locations in central Helsinki: the large open area behind the main bus terminal, and Rautatientori (railway square). There are also bus stops near both these places where you can catch other buses. You will need the free bus route map to find your way.

Train The red or grey local trains all depart from the main railway station. If you travel within the municipal area of Helsinki, you can use the HKL ticket. All local trains have carriages where you can buy tickets, and carriages where you can't.

Underground Railway The metro has just one line: from Ruoholahti in the west to Mellunmäki in the east. Trains run every five minutes from Monday to Saturday, every 10 minutes in the evening and on Sunday. There are also fewer trains in summer. The last train leaves the centre at 11.20 pm.

Tram The green-and-yellow or red trams offer slow but pleasant transport in Helsinki. A very popular 'tourist tram' is 3T (or 3B, which goes in the opposite direction). The route takes you past several tourist attractions. A single tram ticket is cheaper than an ordinary HKL ticket but does not allow transfers.

Taxi
A vacant taxi can be hard to come by at certain times. If you need one, join a queue at any of the several taxi stands. All taxis are luxurious, expensive and equipped with all kinds of gadgets. Every taxi driver will use a meter. Prices are fixed in Helsinki.

Car & Motorbike
Cars can be rented at the airport or in the city centre. Some of the more economical rental companies include Lacara (☎ 719 062) at Hämeentie 12 and Budget (☎ 685 3322) at Malminkatu 24. Motorbike rental is not common in Helsinki, and information on rental is not published. You could check the local telephone directory (under the heading 'Moottoripyöriä') for shops that may have second-hand bikes available for rental. It may also be possible to buy a bike and sell it before departure.

Bicycle
There are several bicycle rental places in and around Helsinki, including a few hostels. Cat Sport (☎ 436 1929) has a stall behind the Finlandia Hall, open from 11 am to 8 pm.

Around Helsinki

SUOMENLINNA
Suomenlinna is a UNESCO site, a quiet cluster of islands just south of Helsinki fish market. It is an old Swedish fortress called Sveaborg, or 'Swedish fortress' (in Finnish, Suomenlinna is 'fortress of Finland'). There is plenty to do and see in this still relatively untouched place, a favourite picnic spot for locals. Allow at least five hours to explore properly. If you plan a picnic or a few beers, go for the whole day (avoid Friday and Saturday evenings in summer). Be sure not to miss the sight when the Silja and Viking ferries pass Suomenlinna at 6.30 pm. The strait next to the Walhalla Restaurant is one of the narrowest along the ferry route. There are always dozens of people waving – and more on the ferries.

History
Sveaborg, the greatest fortress of the Swedish empire, was founded in 1748 to protect the eastern part of the empire against Russian attack. At times, Sveaborg was the second largest town in Finland, after Turku. Sveaborg ultimately surrendered to the Russians after the war of 1808. British troops bombed it in 1855, during the Crimean War, but the fortress remained Russian until Finland gained independence in 1917. It continued to have military significance until 1983. These days its population lives both in old barracks and recently built residences. In 1991, Suomenlinna was placed on the UNESCO World Heritage List, making it the most recognised historical landmark in South Finland.

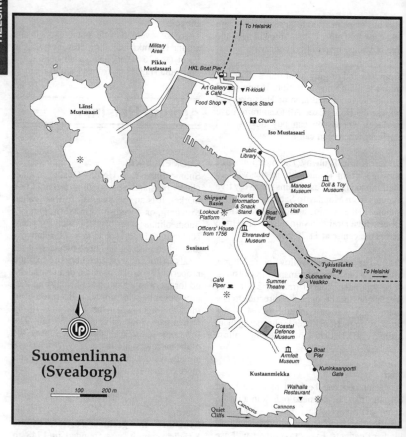

Suomenlinna (Sveaborg)

0   100   200 m

Information

There is an information booth (☎ 668 341) between the two major islands, which are connected by a beautiful bridge. The office is open daily from early May to 31 August between 10 am and 5 pm (often later). There is also a telephone booth.

Things to See

Nordic Art Centre Temporary exhibitions by Finnish and Scandinavian artists are held in old barracks adjacent to a small café opposite the HKL ferry pier. Exhibitions are open daily (except Monday) from 11 am to 6 pm. Admission is 10 mk.

Ehrensvärd Museum Old furniture, paintings, maps and weaponry are displayed in this attractive old museum. Here you will learn about Sweden's heyday, seen from the Finnish point of view. It's open daily from 1 May to 30 September and on weekends in October and November. Hours are 10 am to 5 pm in summer, 10 am to 3.30 pm in September and 11 am to 3 pm on autumn weekends. Entry is 10 mk.

Armfelt Museum Furniture and exhibits for this museum were brought from Joensuu Manor in south-west Finland. The museum has been closed for a few years now but may reopen soon.

Maneesi This war museum commemorates the battles of WWII. There's an aeroplane, a tank and other heavy artillery. Opening hours are similar to those of the Ehrensvärd Museum. Entry is 10 mk.

Coastal Defence Museum Defence equipment is displayed in this bunker-style exhibition. It's open daily 10 am to 5 pm from 12 May to 31 August, and from 11 am to 3 pm in September. Admission is 5 mk.

Submarine Vesikko Because Finland was forbidden by the 1947 Treaty of Paris from possessing submarines, this is one of the very few submarines in Finland (another can be seen opposite the Seaside Hotel in central Helsinki). It dates back to WWII, and is open daily 10 am to 5 pm from mid-May to 31 August, 11 am to 3 pm in September. Admission is 10 mk.

Doll & Toy Museum This delightful collection of old dolls and toys is the personal achievement of Ms Piippa Tandefelt, who runs the place and serves home-made apple pie with coffee. The museum is open daily in summer from 10 am to 5 pm. Admission is 10 mk.

Bunkers There are kilometres of old bunkers and caves all over the place. Bring a torch and enter – it is free adventure. After crossing the bridge to Susisaari Island and passing the information booth, you can start on either side of the fort. The southern end of the island has real bunkers, with cannons and so forth, but the caves there are shorter and well established.

Shipyard Near the information booth is the entrance to a shipyard. The sign prohibits entry but nobody seems to mind. It is a dilapidated yet charming relic from the past.

There is a huge shipyard pool with no water and usually a couple of boats awaiting renovation – quite a sight. Get a legal view from the new platform opposite the Ehrensvärd Museum.

Places to Eat
Suomenlinna has a food store, an R-kiosk and several restaurants and cafés. *Café Piper* is a delightful little wooden villa with a superb sea view from the open-air section. *Walhalla* is the local restaurant; its open terrace offers a good view of passing passenger ships.

Getting There & Away
There are a few ferry connections from the harbour at the fish market. The most useful is the HKL ferry, leaving from opposite the President's Palace. Buy tickets at the pier. If you have only a short time, you can take the ferry, see the island in 30 minutes and return on the same ticket within the 69 minutes that the ticket allows – the cheapest cruise in Helsinki! HKL ferries run every 35 minutes. The trip takes 15 minutes. A less frequent and more expensive express boat takes you a bit further, to the information booth.

ESPOO
Espoo (Swedish: Esbo) is an independent municipality just west of Helsinki. It occupies a large area comprising rural land and a number of *nukkumalähiö* suburbs (sleeping towns), with a large share of its population working in Helsinki. With 190,000 inhabitants, more than Tampere, it ranks as the second largest city in Finland. Espoo Centre is relatively new, although the recently built concrete jungle is near the medieval centre of Espoo. Some of the most famous attractions around Helsinki, such as Tapiola and Otaniemi, are within the city limits of Espoo.

Espoo Church
This church, in the oldest settled part of Espoo, was founded in the 15th century. There are old paintings and sculptures inside, and the immediate vicinity is scenic. Open

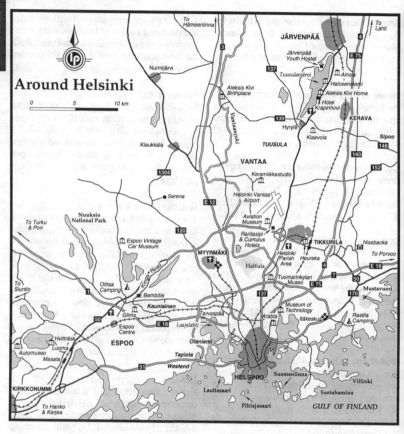

Around Helsinki

0   5   10 km

daily from 10 am to 6 pm, the church is within walking distance of the Espoo railway station.

Glims

This old museum on Glimsintie, some three km north of Espoo church, consists of 19th century buildings and items associated with the estate. The museum is open May to August, from 11 am to 5 pm Tuesday to Sunday (at other times to 4 pm). Nearby, **Bemböle Café** is one of the old, rustic cafés still open in Finland.

Tarvaspää

The magnificent studio of Akseli Gallén-Kallela, one of the most notable of Finnish painters, houses the Gallén-Kallela Museum, and should not be missed. It's just across the Helsinki-Espoo border. The Art Nouveau building itself was designed by the artist. There are paintings and temporary exhibitions, and just having a cup of coffee in the garden is pleasant.

To get there from central Helsinki, take tram No 4 to its terminus and walk the two km seaside path, or catch bus No 33, which runs morning and afternoon, Monday to

Friday. HKL buses won't take you all the way to the museum, as it's in the municipal area of Espoo.

The museum is open in summer Monday to Thursday from 10 am to 8 pm, and Friday to Sunday until 5 pm. In winter, it's open from 10 am to 4 pm Tuesday to Sunday. Admission is 35 mk; free with the Helsinki Card.

Otaniemi

Every architecturally-minded person should get to Otaniemi University campus to see Alvar Aalto's main building and library, the Pietiläs' student building and Heikki Siren's chapel. It is a pleasant area, and getting there from Helsinki is convenient by bicycle via Lehtisaari Island. The canteen in the main building will stuff you for 10 mk. **Kivimuseo**, at Kivimiehentie 1, exhibits rare stones, and is open daily (except Saturday) until 3 pm.

Laajalahti

This large protected bay, north of Otaniemi, is mainly interesting for bird enthusiasts. Visit Villa Elfvik for information on local nature. The villa is more than two km west of Tarvaspää, and is open on Saturday and Sunday from 11 am to 4 pm (in winter only on Sunday). There's a bird observation tower nearby.

Tapiola

This modern shopping centre west of Helsinki was once a masterpiece of Finnish city planning. Now that new buildings mess up the original architecture, it is a somewhat embarrassing detour on several Helsinki bus tours. Tapiola (Swedish: Hagalund) is fine if you get a chance to visit the fringe, not the busy shopping section. There are pools and fountains, and the ample space is a delight.

Suomen Kellomuseo, at Opinkuja 2 north of central Tapiola, is a museum devoted to old clocks and watches. It's open on Sunday from noon to 4 pm.

To the south, **Westend** is the wealthiest area in all Finland, with superb villas at the seaside.

Nuuksio National Park

This national park, at the north-west corner of Espoo, was founded on 1 March 1994. Facilities are still being developed. Contact the Forest and Park Service information office on Eteläesplanadi in Helsinki for current information. Take bus No 85 from Leppävaara (a local train station north-west of Helsinki) to Nuuksionpää, or No 88A to Siikaniemi, or 88T to Siikaranta. From each bus stop, you can walk to the park, which has camp sites by lakes and real wilderness very close to Helsinki.

Espoo Vintage Car Museum

This museum, in Pakankylä, has Finland's largest collection of old motor vehicles. It's open from 11 am to 5 pm Tuesday to Sunday.

Serena

This covered water park in Lahnus, northern Espoo, is a fun place, with a selection of water slides. There's also a Santa Claus tourist trap, and a skiing centre with artificial snow during warm winters. The park is open daily most of the year.

Getting There & Away

Espoo has a local bus network. You can also catch buses to various parts of Espoo from near the bus terminal in Helsinki. Local trains from Helsinki will drop you off at several stations, including central Espoo.

KIRKKONUMMI

Kirkkonummi (Swedish: Kyrkslätt) is a busy commercial centre south-west of Helsinki. The medieval church was founded in the 13th century but it has few remains from medieval times.

Hvitträsk House

North of Kirkkonummi, this fantastic studio in a wilderness setting was the home and working place of three internationally known Finnish architects: Eliel Saarinen, Herman Gesellius and Armas Lindgren. The building was constructed in 1904, and there are furnished rooms with hints of the original

HELSINKI

National Romantic architecture. In some rooms there are modern lamps and other furniture made of synthetic materials. God only knows why such tacky things have been added. The garden and the nearby forests are pleasant on sunny days. Down at the lake there's a beach, and the burial site of two of the architects.

Opposite the beach are cliffs which feature Stone Age paintings. The best way to find the cliffs is to follow the road towards Rauhala and walk from there. The paintings aren't that interesting but the cliff offers fine views. Hvitträsk is open in summer daily from 10 am to 7 pm (on weekends to 6 pm), at other times from 11 am to 6 pm (on weekends to 5 pm). In winter Hvitträsk is closed on Monday. Admission is 15 mk.

Getting There & Away For Hvitträsk, get off in Luoma and walk the final two km (follow the signs). There's also a direct bus, No 166, from platform No 62 at the Helsinki bus station that takes cash only but goes all the way to Hvitträsk. This bus runs three times a day. Your Helsinki Card will give you a free train ride to Luoma (get the ticket in advance from the railway station) and free admission to Hvitträsk House.

Svartvik
The **Automuseo** (vintage car museum) at Svartvik has a collection of old cars, including names such as Auburn, Cadillac and Rolls Royce. It's open from noon to 4 pm on Wednesday, Saturday and Sunday from 1 May to 30 September.

Porkkala
South of Kirkkonummi, the Porkkala peninsula was ceded ('leased') to the Soviet Union from 1944 to 1956. During that time, trains on the Helsinki to Turku route ran with covered windows through the Soviet occupied territory, a humiliation that Finns accepted but never forgot. The whole region was emptied before the Red Army marched in, and it hasn't fully recovered. A large number of Finnish ornithologists swarm all over the cliffs at the southern tip of Porkkala

in May, scanning the southern sky for migrating birds.

Getting There & Away
All local and most long-distance trains from Helsinki and Turku stop at Kirkkonummi railway station. Two buses a day make the 22 km journey from Kirkkonummi to Porkkala.

MYYRMÄKI
The modern **Myyrmäki Church** is the attraction of this residential area north of Helsinki. One of the better modern churches in Finland, it was designed by Juha Leiviskä. Architects certainly should not miss it.

VANTAA
Vantaa may form your first idea of Finland, as this is where Helsinki airport is located. Vantaa has no official town centre; Tikkurila is the de facto centre of the municipality and Myyrmäki is another main concentration. Some 165,000 people live in the area.

Tikkurila
Tikkurila was notorious for its paint factory; there were rumours of children losing their minds because of poisonous leaks from the factory. Tikkurila has since emerged as the centre of Vantaa. There are several museums, the riverside is attractive and it is a good place to shop.

Information The tourist information office (☎ 839 3134) is right next to the Tikkurila train station, at Unikkotie 2. It's open from 9 am to 5 pm Monday to Friday.

Heureka
The most interesting place in Vantaa is Heureka, the science centre. The fun thing is that you can try most things, instead of just looking. Almost all instructions can be obtained in English. Heureka is open daily from 10 am to 6 pm, and until 8 pm on Thursday. In winter it is closed on Monday. Tickets cost 55 mk (20 mk extra for the Omnimax film). Heureka is located close to the train station in Tikkurila, and is worth the trip. Set aside at least half a day.

Vantaa City Museum

This museum is located right next to the railway station in Tikkurila, in Finland's oldest station building (1861). It has special exhibitions relating to local history. The museum is open from 11 am to 4 pm Wednesday to Sunday (to 6 pm on Thursday). Entry is 6 mk (free with the Helsinki Card).

Helsinki Parish Area

The oldest section of the Vantaa area was previously called Helsinki, before the new town was established (in 1550) further south. The area just south of Tikkurila retains an old-world charm. Its grey stone church, dating from 1494, was badly damaged by fire in the 19th century, but has been completely rebuilt and decorated. The interior is still attractive.

It's open in summer from 9 am to noon and 1 to 3 pm weekdays; on Tuesday and Thursday, it's open from 3 to 7 pm. Next to the church is a local museum, which is open summer weekends from 11 am to 3 pm and on Wednesday from 5 to 8 pm.

Getting There & Away Driving north from Helsinki along the Tuusula highway towards the airport, turn right at the 'Tuomarinkylä' sign.

Finnish Aviation Museum

The Finnish Aviation Museum (Ilmailu-museo) near the airport at Tietotie 3 exhibits more than 50 old military and civil aircraft. It's open daily from noon to 6 pm. The entry fee is 20 mk, 10 mk for children and students.

Places to Stay – Tikkurila

Vantaan Retkeilyhotelli (☎ 839 3310) at Valkoisenlähteentie 52, is a nice, clean youth hostel. A dormitory bed costs 30 mk for members. *Asuntohotelli Kuriiri* (☎ 873 4822), at Kuriiritie 35B, has homely singles/doubles for 220/270 mk.

Places to Stay – near the Airport

A number of hotels are located within a few minutes' ride of the airport. There's even a new hotel between the international and domestic terminals.

Bonus Inn (☎ 525 511), Elannontie 9, five km south of the airport, has singles/doubles for 270/320 mk.

Cumulus Airport (☎ 870 600), Robert Hubertintie 6, three km south of the airport, has singles/doubles for 345/345 mk in summer; 450/520 mk at other times.

Airport Hotel Rantasipi (☎ 87051), Robert Hubertintie 4, next to Cumulus. Singles/doubles cost 380/380 mk in summer, 610/690 mk at other times.

Good Morning Hotels Pilotti (☎ 870 2100), Veromäentie 1. Singles/doubles are 250/320 mk in summer; 350/450 mk at other times.

Holiday Inn Garden Court (☎ 870 900), Rälssitie 2, four km south-east from the airport, has singles/doubles for 370/370 mk in summer, 370/470 mk at other times.

Getting There & Away

Local trains and Vantaa buses are by far the most convenient means of transport from Helsinki to Vantaa. Most local trains stop in Tikkurila, but not the long-distance ones.

Getting Around

Vantaa has its own bus system. There are frequent links between the main centres, such as Tikkurila and Myyrmäki.

JÄRVENPÄÄ

Jean Sibelius, the most famous Finnish composer, lived in Järvenpää (Swedish: Träskända), north of Helsinki. The Järvenpää Church is open in summer from Tuesday to Sunday.

Järvenpää Retkeilymaja (☎ 287 775) is a nice youth hostel located on the western shore of Lake Tuusulanjärvi at Stålhanentie 5. Beds are cheap, from 28 to 70 mk. This place is open all year round. There's also a hotel in central Järvenpää.

All Riihimäki-bound local R-trains and H-trains stop in Järvenpää.

TUUSULA

The municipality of Tuusula, north of Helsinki, has a number of interesting sights scattered around Lake Tuusulanjärvi. Tuusula has almost 30,000 inhabitants.

Hyrylä

This modern commercial conglomeration is the centre of Tuusula. There's little of interest in Hyrylä, but you could check out two museums near the main road on Klaavolantie. **Klaavolan museo** is an old estate dating back to the 1880s. Nearby, **Ilmatorjuntamuseo**, the Air Raid Defence Museum, is open in summer Tuesday to Sunday from noon to 6 pm. Entry is 5 mk.

Rantatie Route

The narrow road along Lake Tuusulanjärvi attracted a number of artists during the National Romantic era, ie the early 1900s.

Composer Jean Sibelius, Nobel Prize-winning novelist FE Sillanpää and painter Pekka Halonen, among others, worked here. Today the four km 'museum' road, on the east side of the lake, is protected but there are attractions before and beyond this part of the road.

Working from the south before the actual museum road, **Tuusula Church**, built in 1734, is open daily (except Saturday) in summer, and features interior decoration by Pekka Halonen. Nearby, **Työläiskotimuseo** is a museum displaying the home of a factory worker.

Krapinhovi (the hotel) marks the beginning of the protected road, and less than one km away, on your left, is the small cottage of Aleksis Kivi, the famous 19th century author

---

Jean Sibelius

In 1865 three remarkable artists were born in Finland. Akseli Gallen-Kallela and Pekka Halonen became famous painters. Jean Sibelius became Finland's most acclaimed composer, arguably the greatest in all Scandinavia. Born in Hämeenlinna, Sibelius started playing piano when he was nine and at just 20 years of age composed his first notable work.

Sibelius was greatly inspired by the *Kalevala*, the Finnish epic. During the cultural flowering that inspired Finland's independence, Sibelius provided the would-be nation with music that complemented its literature and visual arts. Later, during the Russian oppression, Sibelius used his music to express his (and his people's) emotions; the well-known *Finlandia* was composed between 1899 and 1901 when Tsar Nicholas II strengthened his grip on Finland. It must be one of the most beautiful protest songs ever composed!

Sibelius married Aino Järnefelt (sister of the famous painter Eero Järnefelt) in 1890 and

together they had six daughters. The family moved to a new home, Ainola, north of Helsinki, in 1904. The house was designed by Lars Sonck. It was here that Sibelius composed five of his seven symphonies.

Sibelius studied in Berlin and Vienna and visited the USA in 1914 as an honorary doctor at Yale University.

Sibelius was creative until 1925 when he retired aged 60. He lived a quiet life in Ainola, although rumours of his heavy drinking persist to this day. Sibelius died in 1957, at the age of 92. His wife Aino lived even longer; she died in 1969 aged 98.

Ainola has been owned by the state since 1974 and is open in summer as a museum. Sibelius' birth home in Hämeenlinna is also open as a museum and there's another museum in Turku devoted to Sibelius and his musical instruments. Sibelius' summer residence in Loviisa has occasional events associated with the composer. ∎

who died here. It's open daily except Monday from noon to 5 pm and admission is 5 mk. A bit further north, **Onnela** has art exhibitions in summer, and you can also stay overnight here. Another old house, **Syväranta**, was renovated in 1995.

Halosenniemi, the Karelian-inspired, log-built National Romantic studio of Pekka Halonen, is the most interesting sight on the Rantatie route. It's open from 1 May to 31 August from 11 am to 6 pm daily except Monday, at other times of the year closing at 4 pm. Entry is 10 mk.

Finally, there's Sibelius' home, **Ainola**, some two km north of the northern end of the Rantatie road. The building was designed by Lars Sonck, and built on this beautiful site in 1904. Ainola is open in summer from 11 am to 5 pm from Tuesday to Sunday. In May and September it's also closed on Tuesday. Entry is 15 mk.

Places to Stay

Krapinhovi (☎ 251 501) on Rantatie is an attractive manor hotel offering a rare chance to experience a traditional smoke sauna. Rooms start from 320/390 mk. *Onnela* (☎ 251 548) at Rantatie 34 has rooms for 230/360 mk, including breakfast.

Getting There & Away

Hyrylä is 28 km north of Helsinki and there are regular buses from the bus station. You could take a local train to Kerava or Järvenpää and proceed from there by bicycle.

Uusimaa

Uusimaa (Swedish: Nyland), like many places on the west coast, has a name that expresses a Swedish point of view; the New Land. The Swedes forcibly settled the southern coast of Finland in medieval times, bringing their language and Scandinavian traditions with them. Prior to these events, Uusimaa was almost empty. It was considered a periphery of Häme, a mere hunting region.

The King's Road, one of the oldest roads in Finland, ran from Stockholm to Turku and, via the first settlements in Nyland, to Vyborg (then a Swedish fortress town). The road exists on tourist maps, and following the route is popular.

Nyland remained predominantly Swedish until 1550 when King Gustav Vasa of Sweden established Helsingfors (Helsinki) at rapids on the Vantaa River, north of today's Helsinki.

Another boost for the region came in 1812 when Finland's capital was transferred from Turku to Helsinki. Only since then have Finns moved to the province in a big way. There are still Swedish pockets on both sides of Helsinki.

Uusimaa today is a treasure trove of historical landmarks. It is one of the regions where bicycle tours are highly recommended.

Highlights
- Historical landmarks along the King's Road.
- Old factory areas dating from the 1600s.
- Medieval churches, especially in Inkoo, Tenala and Lohja.
- The attractive wooden seaside towns of Hanko and Tammisaari.
- The historical town of Porvoo, second-oldest in Finland.
- The eerie castle in Raseborg.

West Uusimaa

HANKO

Hanko (Swedish: Hangö) is the southernmost town in Finland. Once a glamorous retreat for Russian nobles, tsars and artists, Hanko still boasts many beautiful seaside villas.

Even before Hanko was founded, in 1874, the peninsula on which the town lies had been an important anchorage. Hanko has also been a major point of departure from Finland: between 1881 and 1931, approximately half a million Finns left for the USA and Canada via the Hanko docks. During WWII, Hanko was annexed by the Soviet Union for one year.

Hanko is very popular with tourists in summer. Many arrive by boat; Hanko's port is the largest in Finland. Hanko has a population of 11,000 of whom 52% speak Finnish.

Swedish speakers used to constitute a majority; when the situation changed, Finnish speakers demanded that all the official signs in the town be changed so that the

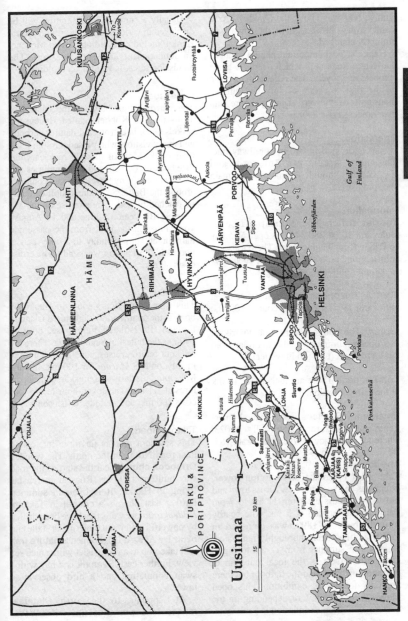

Uusimaa

Finnish text was above the Swedish. As a result, every street sign in the town was promptly changed.

Hanko's most important annual event is the Hanko Regatta in which over 200 boats compete every year. The regatta takes place on the first weekend of July and attracts thousands of viewers. During the regatta many places raise their prices.

Orientation
Hanko is divided in two by a railway line. The main streets are Bulevardi and Esplanaadi, although Vuorikatu is the main shopping street.

Information
Tourist Office The tourist office at Bulevardi 10 (☎ 280 3411) is open Monday to Friday from 9 am to 5 pm. There's also an information booth at the harbour, open daily in summer until almost midnight.

Post & Telephone The post office is at Bulevardi 19. Hanko's post code is 10900.

Library The public library is at Vuorikatu 3-5, open in summer Monday to Friday from 11 am to 7 pm (to 8 pm in winter).

Left Luggage There are lockers for 10 mk at the railway station.

Emergency Services For a general emergency ring ☎ 112; for a doctor call ☎ 10023. There's a pharmacy at Nycanderinkatu 18.

The Town
Take a lift up to the **observation tower**, which has an excellent view across town and out to sea; hours are from 11 am to 7 pm daily, and admission is 5 mk. The nearby **church**, built in 1892, was damaged in WWII and has been thoroughly renovated. It's open in summer from 11 am to 3 pm. **Linnoitusmuseo** is the local museum at Nycanderinkatu 4 near the harbour but there are only temporary exhibitions. It's open daily except Monday, or depending on the current exhibition. Admission is 5 mk.

Usually a summer art exhibition will be displayed in various locations around central Hanko, including buildings called Mekano, Taidemakasiini and Helkama-talo. The admission ticket is valid in all buildings.

Hauensuoli
The narrow strait between the islands of Tullisaari and Kobben, called Hauensuoli (Pike's Gut), is a protected natural harbour, and many visitors who passed through it left their mark. Most of the 600 rock carvings date back to the 16th and 17th centuries and have been made by travellers from countries around the Baltic Sea. Hauensuoli can only be reached by sea. Take a cruise on the MS *Marina*. Between 15 June and 15 August, you can catch the boat from the passenger harbour at 1pm Monday to Friday and at noon and 2.30 pm on weekends. The cruise costs 50 mk.

Bengtskär
This island, two hours south of Hanko by boat, is the southernmost inhabited island in Finland. Its isolated lighthouse, built in 1906, is the tallest in Scandinavia. There are six-hour return cruises, usually on Saturday in July, on MS *Marina* for 100 mk. In July, MS *Anna* sails daily to Bengskär, with departures at 11 am. The seven-hour return tour costs 200 mk, and includes a fish soup.

Täktom Road
This southern road is far more interesting than road No 53 in the north. The wooden **Orthodox church** near the start of the road was built in 1895 by Russian merchants living in Hanko. It is open in summer. Further east, there's a **chapel** in Täktom. *Hiidenkirnut* are wells that have been drilled by powerful water and loose rocks at the end of the Ice Age. At Högholmen a **nature trail** will take you to a rocky islet with a nice sea view. Further east, **Svanvik** is a bay with a swan population and a bird observation tower.

At Lappohja, to the north, **Rintama-museo** is a war museum with WWII

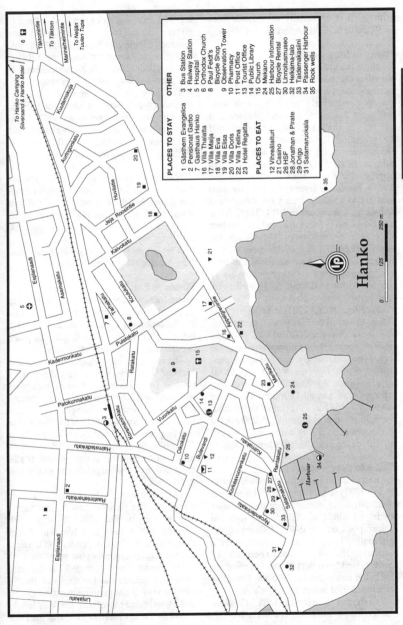

PLACES TO STAY

1 Gästhem Evangelica
2 Pensionat Garbo
7 Gasthaus Hanko
16 Villa Thalatta
17 Villa Maija
18 Villa Eva
19 Villa Elisa
20 Villa Doris
22 Villa Tellina
23 Hotel Regatta

PLACES TO EAT

12 Vihreälaituri
21 Casino
26 HSF
28 Jonathan & Pirate
29 Origo
31 Satamauokala

OTHER

3 Bus Station
4 Railway Station
5 Hospital
6 Orthodox Church
8 Paul Feldt's
9 Bicycle Shop
10 Observation Tower
11 Pharmacy
13 Post Office
14 Tourist Office
15 Public Library
24 Church
25 Mekano
27 Harbour Information
30 Bicycle Rental
32 Linnoitusmuseo
33 Heikama-talo
34 Taidemakasiini
35 Passenger Harbour
   Rock wells

Hanko

0   125   250 m

To Hanko Camping
Silversand & Hanko Motel

To Täktom
To Täktom
To Neljän Tuulen Tupa

Täktomintie
Mannerheimintie

Esplanaadi
Asemakatu
Kadermonkatu
Palokunnakatu
Hallstadinkatu
Raatimiehenkatu
Esplanaadi
Linjakatu
Korsmannkatu
Vuorikatu
Oikokatu
Korkeavuorenkatu
Nycanderinkatu
Statamkatu
Rantakatu
Kulmankatu
Mekano
Appelgrenintie
Puistokatu
Ratakatu
Täktankatu
Kadermonkatu
Kalvokatu
Koulukatu
Jeja Roosintie
Huvilatie
Aurinigonkatu
Koulatamokuja

Harbour

exhibits. It is open daily in summer from 11.30 am to 6.30 pm. Admission is 10 mk.

Places to Stay – villas

A unique feature of Hanko is its selection of old villas that have been meticulously renovated and converted to guesthouses.

One particularly good place is *Villa Tellina* (☎ 248 6356) at Appelgrenintie 2. It was built in 1880, and has a dining hall, and the reception for four other villas. *Villa Thalatta* across the street is a very fine villa built in 1894. *Villa Maija* further east on Appelgrenintie was built in 1888, and has fine verandah windows; there are two smaller houses in the back yard. *Villa Eva* at Kaivokatu 2 was built in 1914. There are at least 64 rooms in four villas and the standard price is approximately 210/340 mk for singles/doubles. If you want cheaper accommodation, it is worth asking for one of their more modest rooms – you may be able to stay here for as little as 100 mk. All four villas are open from 1 June to 20 August.

Villa Elisa (☎ 248 7201) at Appelgrenintie 17 has 15 rooms and is open all year round. Ordinary rooms are 200/250 mk, including breakfast, or ask for the cheaper rooms at the back. The charmingly old-fashioned pensionat, *Villa Doris* (☎ 248 1228) at Appelgrenintie 23, has old furniture from various decades in all 12 rooms. The house was built in 1881 and is open all year round. Prices in summer start from 125/250 mk for singles/doubles, and in winter from 90/180 mk. Prices are negotiable for longer stays.

Places to Stay – other

The best place in Hanko is *Pensionat Garbo* (☎ 248 7897) at Esplanaadi 84. This place is essentially a museum and you stay and dine amidst all kinds of collections, from old Finnish postcards to 1940s Hollywood paraphernalia. Each room commemorates a particular Hollywood star. There are 15 rooms priced from 90/175 mk, but there are also better rooms for 185/340 mk. Breakfast is included, and prices are negotiable.

Nearby at Esplanaadi 61, *Gästhem Evangelica* (☎ 248 6923) is a wooden build-

ing, and serves as an evangelical college in winter. Some rooms have toilets and showers. Singles/doubles cost 180/240 mk, and those without a bathroom are 120/180 mk. *Gasthaus Hanko* at Korsmaninkatu 46 was closed at last visit but may reopen.

The only real hotel in Hanko is *Hotel Regatta* (☎ 248 6491) at Merikatu 1. From one viewpoint the hotel looks really tacky, from another it's not so bad. Singles cost 265 to 370 mk and doubles are 370 to 530 mk. Higher prices apply for rooms with a view of the sea.

Hanko Camping Silversand (☎ 248 5500), about five km from the town centre, has a long beach. The price per family or group is 70 mk, 35 mk if you travel alone. Cottages for four to eight people cost 300 mk.

It is also possible to stay with local families; enquire at the tourist office.

Places to Eat

There are several places to eat at the harbour. The best choice for reasonably priced food is *Satamaruokala* on Satamakatu, with home-style dishes at 20 to 40 mk. The place is open till 5 pm Monday to Friday.

The best gourmet restaurants are near the harbour. *Jonathan* serves meat dishes in a rustic stone-walled room. *Pirate* serves pasta and fish, and has a pizza section upstairs. *Origo* is the best of the bunch, and is especially known for the excellent fish buffet that will be yours for 75 mk. Origo is open from 30 April to 30 September. Don't forget *HSF* in the white building at the harbour. It's in the pavilion of a sailing club, and its lunch is good value.

The summer restaurant *Casino* at Appelgrenintie 10 is the most famous nightspot in Hanko. The place is huge, with dancing and a roulette table. The cover charge is 25 to 30 mk depending on the day, and the food is expensive but good.

Vihreälaituri at Bulevardi 17 is the only restaurant outside the harbour area that is worth a visit. It has genuine maritime decor, and a good salad buffet with the daily lunch. *Neljän Tuulen Tupa*, or House of the Four

Winds, was built in 1910 and during the Finnish prohibition (1919-32) it was called Café Africa and so-called hard tea (alcohol) was served there. Field Marshal CG Mannerheim had his summer cottage next door. He found the merry-making disturbing and solved the problem by buying the whole place. The café is 1.5 km east of the centre, and is open from mid-May to mid-August.

Getting There & Away
Bus Hanko is 132 km south-west of Helsinki, and express buses cover the distance in two hours. Ordinary buses take more than three hours.

Train Catch a Helsinki to Turku train, get off at Karjaa (Swedish: Karis), and change trains to Hanko, via Tammisaari. There are five to seven trains a day from Helsinki or Turku, and a connecting train from each one.

Boat Ask at the harbour for boat connections from Hanko to other harbours further west, including Galtby and Osnäs, with further connections to the Åland islands.

Getting Around
Bicycles can be rented at the eastern harbour (for 50 mk per day), and at Paul Feldt's bicycle shop (cheaper rates still) at Tarhakatu Skvärgatan 4.

TAMMISAARI
Tammisaari (Swedish: Ekenäs), north-east of Hanko, is an attractive seaside town that's especially nice in summer. The beautiful countryside is complemented by the well-preserved old buildings, and parts of the adjacent archipelago have recently been declared a national park.

Tammisaari is one of the oldest towns in Finland. In 1546 Tammisaari was declared a town by King Gustav Vasa who dreamed in vain of founding a rival to the busy Estonian trade centre of Tallinn. The local business people were soon forcibly transferred to the newly founded Helsinki. Despite this, and a devastating fire in 1821, Tammisaari has developed into something of an idyllic little

seaside town. Two previously independent municipalities, Snappertuna and Tenala, have been incorporated into Tammisaari municipality which is now the largest such administrative unit in Uusimaa. The majority of the 14,800 people here speak Swedish, with Finnish the native language of only 17% of the population.

Orientation
Tammisaari is situated on a peninsula, the tip being the oldest part of town. Rådhustorget is the main square. The partly pedestrianised Kungsgatan is the main commercial street. There's a nice view from atop the old water tower; ask for the keys at the tourist office.

Information
Tourist Offices The tourist office (☎ 263 2100) at Rådhustorget is open in summer Monday to Friday from 8 am to 5 pm and on Saturday from 10 am to 2 pm. At other times, it's open during office hours, closing at 4 pm. For information on the natural features of the archipelago, the Ekenäs Archipelago National Park Information Centre will provide free slide shows and information in English. The house at the harbour is open from 10 am to 7 pm in summer, and at other times until 4 pm on Wednesday and Sunday only.

Post & Telephone The post office is at Ystadsgatan 12. Tammisaari's post code is 10600.

Library The library at Raseborgsvägen 6-8, open in summer Monday to Friday from 11 am to 7 pm, has maps in the *läsesal* section. The pleasant café serves meals.

Books & Maps There's a bookshop at Stationsvägen 1.

Left Luggage The railway station closes by 7 pm (1 pm on Saturday) but there are lockers for 10 mk.

Emergency Services For a general emergency ring ☎ 112; for a doctor ☎ 10023.

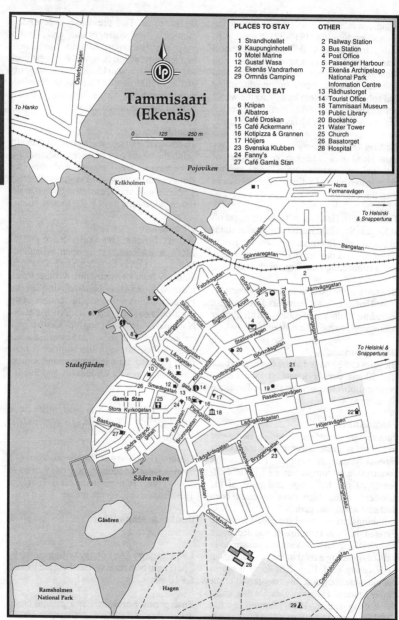

Tammisaari (Ekenäs)

To Hanko

0   125   250 m

Pojoviken

Kråkholmen

Stadsfjärden

Gamla Stan

Södra viken

Gåsören

Ramsholmen
National Park

Hagen

Norra Formansvägen

To Helsinki & Snappertuna

Bangatan

To Helsinki & Snappertuna

PLACES TO STAY

1 Strandhotellet
9 Kaupunginhotelli
10 Motel Marine
12 Gustaf Wasa
22 Ekenäs Vandrarhem
29 Ormnäs Camping

PLACES TO EAT

6 Knipan
8 Albatros
11 Café Droskan
15 Café Ackermann
16 Kotipizza & Grannen
17 Höijers
23 Svenska Klubben
24 Fanny's
27 Café Gamla Stan

OTHER

2 Railway Station
3 Bus Station
4 Post Office
5 Passenger Harbour
7 Ekenäs Archipelago
   National Park
   Information Centre
13 Rådhustorget
14 Tourist Office
18 Tammisaari Museum
19 Public Library
20 Bookshop
21 Water Tower
25 Church
26 Basatorget
28 Hospital

There are pharmacies on Rådhustorget and at Kungsgatan 7.

Tammisaari Museum

Located at Gustav Wasas gata 13, the museum precinct has five buildings. The main building, built in 1802, exhibits the lifestyle of a wealthy artisan family in the 1800s. The modern art museum has temporary exhibitions. Uthuslängan shows how poor workers used to live in the 1930s. In an old studio at the back, Lindbladska huset has an interesting exhibition on photography. Finally, Blombergs hus (1820) was renovated in 1995 and contains temporary exhibitions.

The museum is open daily in summer from 11 am to 5 pm, at other times from Tuesday to Thursday from 6 to 8 pm. Admission is 10 mk, students and children 5 mk.

Gamla Stan

The Old Town has been well preserved. Basatorget square is the starting point of free afternoon walking tours and there are artisans' shops open in summer. The narrow streets are named after hatters, combmakers and other artisans who once worked in the precinct. The oldest buildings on Linvävaregatan date back to the 18th century.

The church tower can be seen from most parts of town. It was built between 1651 and 1680 and was last renovated in 1990. The oldest object is the 1660 frame of the altar painting: the painting was destroyed in a fire in 1821. The church is open daily in summer from 10 am to 6 pm.

Ramsholmen Natural Park

This area, south of the town, consists of the two islands of Ramsholmen and Högholmen and the peninsula of Hagen. The forests are refreshing in summer, and of particular interest to birdwatchers. Free maps are available at the tourist office.

Ekenäs Archipelago National Park

You can explore the beautiful archipelago around Tammisaari but the national park and military areas have restrictions. There are details about these in the free pamphlet available from the information centre.

The best way to visit the park is by the MS *Marina* which departs for Rödjan on the island of Älgö from Tammisaari harbour daily at 1 pm in summer. Departures are subject to a minimum of 12 passengers, but Sunday departures are guaranteed from mid-June to mid-August. Return tickets cost 80 mk.

Once on Älgö, you can see the old fishing house, use the cooking facilities or stay overnight at the camping ground. A two km track provides access to this protected island, and you can swim in Lake Storträsket nearby. There are also camping grounds on the islands of Fladalandet and Modermagan.

The MS *Sunnan II* has daily summer cruises from the Tammisaari passenger harbour.

Places to Stay

Camping *Ormnäs Camping* (☎ 241 4434) is conveniently located at the seaside, next to the Ramsholmen Natural Park. Camping costs 50 mk per tent or 30 mk per individual traveller. There are cottages for two/four for 160/220 mk. The camping ground has boats and bicycles for hire.

Hostel The cheapest place to stay is the *Ekenäs Vandrarhem*, the town's youth hostel (☎ 241 6393), at Höjersvägen 10. It's open from mid-May to mid-August. The modern rooms are neat. For HI members, a dorm bed costs 45 to 55 mk, and singles are 95 mk. As a summer hotel, the place charges 150/270 mk for singles/doubles, including bedclothes and breakfast.

Guesthouse At *Gustaf Wasa* (☎ 241 1551), right in the town centre on Gustav Wasas gata, singles/doubles cost 160/240 mk. There are just nine rooms, all with shared toilets and showers. The guesthouse includes a popular pizza restaurant.

Hotels There are two hotels at the edge of the old town. *Kaupunginhotelli* (☎ 241

3131), Norra Strandgatan 1, is the best in town and has 20 rooms. Singles/doubles cost 300/400 mk.

Motel Marine (☎ 241 3833) at Kammaregatan 4-6 has 29 rooms or apartments. Rooms are neat, and cost 170 to 400 mk for singles, 270 to 500 mk for doubles. Cheaper rooms have no showers.

The imposing seaside establishment beyond the railway line, *Strandhotellet*, went bust in 1995 but it may reopen soon.

Places to Eat

Höijers at Drottninggatan 1 is the best restaurant in town and has an inexpensive and popular lunch until 2 pm that includes a tempting salad buffet. Most regular meals are quite expensive although pasta is reasonably priced.

More Italian-inspired food is available across the street at take-away *Kotipizza* which has an annex, *Grannen,* where meals can be eaten. Another little restaurant, *Fanny's*, on Rådhustorget, serves lunch for 30 to 35 mk. It also has a nice garden.

Albatros is a pavilion at the harbour. Meals are expensive, but beer is available. The finest location in town is to be experienced at *Knipan*, a summer restaurant built on a pier at the harbour. Lunch is served until 3 pm and the place has live music in the evenings. Knipan is open from late April to mid-September.

Another place to eat good food is *Svenska Klubben* at Bryggerigatan 9 built in an old brewery outside the town centre. There is a lunch buffet from 35 mk, and meals from 18 to 98 mk.

Cafés In summer Tammisaari is a fantastic place for cafés. If you only come for a short time, don't miss having a cup of coffee in a fine garden.

A short walk from the tourist office on Gustav Wasas gata, *Café Droskan* serves home-made pies with berries, and there are handicrafts for sale. Even nicer is *Café Gamla Stan* on Bastugatan. The small house has just a few seats, but the garden is superb. Traditional Swiss-style bakery products are

available at *Café Ackermann* at the market square (Rådhustorget).

Getting There & Away

Bus There are 10 buses a day from Hanko, six from Helsinki and five from Turku. Tammisaari is 94 km and 1½ hours west of Helsinki.

Train See Hanko for information.

TENALA

Tenala (Finnish: Tenhola) is a small village north-west of Tammisaari. The imposing **medieval church** was built from stone during the 14th century. It is beautifully decorated with old paintings and coats of arms, and is open from 8 am to 5 pm Monday to Friday. The museum nearby is practically always closed.

Lyktan in the village centre serves lunch, meals and beer.

SNAPPERTUNA

Snappertuna lies east of the town of Tammisaari within the municipality of the same name and has several places of interest to visitors. There is no public transport, so come on foot, by bicycle or in a car. Narrow gravel roads lead to Snappertuna from both Karjaa and Tammisaari.

Raseborg

The ruins of an old castle at Raseborg (Finnish: Raasepori) are the most interesting sight in Snappertuna. The oldest parts probably date from the 13th century. The castle was of great strategic importance in the 15th century, when it protected the important trading town of Tuna. By the mid-1500s, its importance declined, and the castle was left empty for over 300 years. You can visit the area at any time.

When the cafeteria *Slottsknektens Stuga* is open (1 May to 31 August daily from 10 am to 10 pm), tickets should be purchased; they cost 5 mk.

Other Attractions

The museum in Snappertuna is open on

weekends from noon to 4 pm in June and July only. Admission is 5 mk. A short walk from the museum is a wooden church built in 1688. It's open daily in summer from 9 am to 6 pm.

KARJAA

This small town (Swedish: Karis), just north of Snappertuna, is almost like a suburb of Helsinki due to handy train services. It is predominantly a Swedish-speaking region, offering several historical attractions along possible bicycle routes. At last count, Karjaa had almost 9000 inhabitants.

Kroggårdsmalmen

This small spot east of central Karjaa is a monument to a misinterpreted archaeological discovery. A burial ground discovered in 1932 was incorrectly labelled the 'graveyard of the first Finn'. It was later discovered that 10 emigrants from Estonia were buried here approximately 2000 years ago. Nearby,

south of the railway track, Alsätra, another historical site, has burial mounds from 400 to 800 AD.

Karjaa Church

This medieval church, dating from the early 15th century, is in an attractive location near a river a few km north of the centre of town. There are several medieval wooden sculptures, including a pietà. The church is open daily in summer from 10 am to 4 pm.

Grabbacka Ruins

Grabbacka, five km south of Karjaa, is not much of a castle. It was built in the 1490s but is now all in ruins: all that's left is the basement floor.

POHJA

The municipality of Pohja (Swedish: Pojo), just west of Karjaa, has two interesting old ironworks areas, Fiskars and Billnäs, which have become popular tourist attractions. The

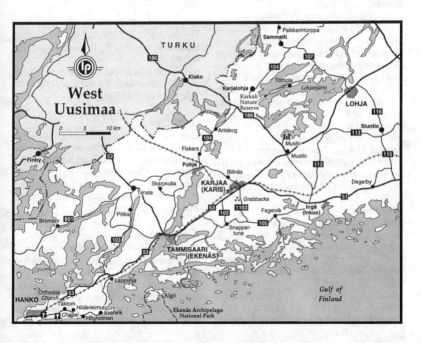

small village of Pohja has a medieval **stone church** that houses sculpture from the Middle Ages.

The tourist information office (☎ 237 041) is in Fiskars and is open from 1 May to 31 August from 10.30 am to 6 pm. Pohja has 5000 inhabitants.

Fiskars
Fiskars (Finnish: Fiskari) is probably the quaintest of all *bruk* (old factory areas). There's a local history **museum**, open daily from 1 May to 30 September from 11 am to 4 pm. Entry costs 10 mk. In the same area, the **Gallery Expohja** is open daily from May to August from 11 am to 7 pm. Admission is 30 mk. The Fiskars area also has a host of shops selling souvenirs and handicrafts.

Getting There & Away Take the hourly bus from Tammisaari or Karjaa. There are also a few direct buses from Helsinki.

Billnäs
In this village (Finnish: Pinjainen), you will find the **Billnäs Ironworks**. Founded in 1641, they were important in the development of Finland's metal industry. The **Power Generating Museum** is really a museum power plant, complete with a turbine house and meter boards. It's open daily from 10 am to 6 pm. The **Axe Museum** next door exhibits axes and other tools manufactured at Billnäs. It's open from 10 am to 7 pm Monday to Friday, 11 am to 4 pm on Saturday and 11 am to 7 pm on Sunday. If you're hungry after all those sights, try the café. It's open for lunch only from 11 am to 3 pm daily. Buses going to Fiskars pass through Billnäs.

Skarpkulla
The local museum in the village of Skarpkulla specialises in old farm equipment. It's open from 15 May to 31 August from 2 to 5 pm on Saturday and Sunday; in July, it's also open on weekdays from 2 to 5 pm.

LOHJA
The area around Lohja (Swedish: Lojo) has

been inhabited for the past 9000 years. Lohja, on the eastern side of Lake Lohjanjärvi, has been a mining town since 1542. There were initially only a few small iron mines, but, since 1897, limestone has been the most important product. Today the town of Lohja has over 15,000 inhabitants and serves a region of over 70,000 people.

Information
Tourist Office The tourist office (☎ 320 1309) is at Sepänkatu 7.

Post & Telephone The post office is in the Lohjantähti shopping centre on Kauppakatu.

Library The public library at Nummentie 6 is generally open from noon to 7 pm Monday to Friday.

Books & Maps Suomalainen Kirjakauppa is in the Lohjantähti shopping centre.

Tytyri Mining Museum
The mine area just north of the town centre is open to visitors. Its museum traces the history of mining in and around Lohja. It is possible to take a tour down the mines at 6 pm daily in summer, and on Friday only from 1 September to 31 May.

Lohja Church
One of the most interesting medieval churches as far as interior decoration goes, Lohja church was built during the 15th century. Its lively murals depict torture, demons and saints. The church is open daily in summer from 9 am to 6 pm and in winter from 10 am to 3 pm.

Lohjan Museo
The local museum behind the church has a historical exhibition in 11 buildings, including the vicarage. The large exhibitions include items from early prehistoric times. It's open from noon to 4 pm Tuesday to Sunday and from noon to 7 pm on Wednesday. There's a café in the garden.

Places to Stay

There are two guesthouses in town. The cheapest is *Matkakoti Linnakangas* (☎ 324 488), conveniently central at Sammonkatu 11, with singles/doubles for 140/190 mk. A little way north of the centre is *Matkakoti Moisio* (☎ 322 405) at Lallinkatu 14, with doubles for 200 to 250 mk.

Hotelli Lohja (☎ 331 244) is right in the town centre at Laurinkatu 34. Rooms cost 450/540 mk. A cheaper hotel to the south of Lohja's centre, *Gasthaus Laurinportti* (☎ 331 771), is at Laurinkatu 1.

Getting There & Away

Lohjan Liikenne and Siuntion Linja run regular buses to Lohja from the Helsinki bus terminal. The 60 km ride takes one hour.

KARKALI NATURE RESERVE

Set on an unusually shaped peninsula in Lake Lohjanjärvi, this park has apparently preserved some unusual flora. The tip of it is now a nature reserve where you *are* allowed to walk but only on a path that loops through the park. July and early August are the best months to see the reserve. On your way to Karkali stop at the sign marking **Torholan luola**. This is a limestone cave, the largest in Finland and said to have been formed 8000 years ago. Karkali is 8 km from road No 107. There's no public transport nor anywhere to sleep or eat, so you will have to carry everything you need.

SAMMATTI

Sammatti, north of Lake Lohjanjärvi, is a northern municipality of the Lohja region offering attractive rural scenery on road No 104 between Lohja and road No 1. Stop at the **timber church**, built in 1755, which has a nice wooden pulpit. A further four km north, **Paikkarin torppa** is the birthplace of Elias Lönnrot, creator of the *Kalevala*. The little grey hut is extremely basic but the setting is marvellous. The hut is open from May to September every afternoon.

A little over 1000 people live in Sammatti.

SIUNTIO

This small place (Swedish: Sjundeå), southeast of Lohja, features a medieval church from 1460. The ceiling is beautifully decorated with medieval frescoes, and the local nobility have left their coats of arms hanging on the wall. The church is open in summer from 9 am to 3 pm, Monday to Friday. The museum nearby is open in summer on Wednesday and Friday from 5 to 7 pm, and on weekends from noon to 3 pm. North on road No 116, the medieval Suitia Manor looks like a haunted house as it's currently not in use.

MUSTIO

At the southern end of Lake Lohjanjärvi, this large estate (Swedish: Svartå, or black river) is now a hotel and congress centre. This should not put you off paying a day visit to see what is reputedly the largest wooden manor house in Europe. The vast building is open from May to mid-August daily from noon to 5 pm, and there's an admission charge of around 15 mk. In addition to the main building, there's a large park with several old buildings, and a church dating from 1761. The estate is north of road No 186. For accommodation in the manor house, call ☎ 348 611.

INKOO

Inkoo (Swedish: Ingå), south of Lohja, is a small, attractive seaside town where locals predominantly speak Swedish. Look for the unusual bell tower atop the **medieval church** that was founded in the 13th century. There are rich paintings on the church walls. It's open daily in summer from 8 am to 4 pm. Nearby, across the river, **Ingå Gammelgård** is the local museum and has red houses that form a ring around grassy grounds.

Fagervik

The most attractive bruk in Finland is on road No 105, west of Inkoo. The factory, established in 1646, was part of the Swedish strategy of founding ironworks in various locations throughout the expanding empire. The Russian army destroyed the area during

Welcome to Karkkila, Comrade

Karkkila, in the north-west of Uusimaa Province, is the only municipality to file for bankruptcy during the economic depression of the early 1990s. It is equally unique for being a communist stronghold. Karkkila was the most left-wing town in all Finland, due to the great bulk of its workforce being engaged in heavy industry.

When the rift between the USSR and China divided international communism into two camps in the early 1960s, the newly-united workers had to take sides. Many Finnish communists towed the Stalinist line; others became Maoists.

Tervetuloa!
Welcome to Karkkila
ПРИВЕТСТВИТЕ В
КАРВИЛЕ
欢迎同志们

Karkkila: a communist stronghold.

As was typical in Finland at that time, each municipality had signs at its borders bearing welcome messages, often in various languages. Karkkila welcomed visitors in Finnish, in several European languages, including Russian, and in Chinese!

Now this was an insult. Chinese was the language of 'those traitors'. Heated discussion ensued and the Chinese characters were painted over, then repainted again!

The controversy escaped the Chinese – not too many people from the People's Republic travelled along road No 2 past Karkkila anyway. ■

---

the Great Northern War in the 1720s, but it was later rebuilt. The factory closed in 1902. There's a wooden church built in 1737, quaint little houses and jungle-like vegetation. A café within the small Fagervik bruk is open daily in summer. There's only one bus each week, on Friday evenings, from Helsinki. A bicycle is very suitable for this narrow road.

HYVINKÄÄ

Hyvinkää, in far north Uusimaa, is one of the booming towns along the Helsinki to Tampere railway line. As a satellite of Helsinki, Hyvinkää has attracted over 41,000 inhabitants. It isn't a very interesting town although Sveitsi Park (Finnish for Switzerland) is an unusually beautiful hill area with thick pine forests.

The tourist information office (☎ 459 1275) is at Hämeenkatu 3D.

Things to See

The **Railway Museum** is the best museum in town, at Hyvinkäänkatu 9. It is open daily in summer from 11 am to 4 pm Tuesday to Sunday. From 1 September to 30 April, it's open from noon to 3 pm Tuesday to Friday

and from noon to 4 pm on weekends. Entry is 10 mk, 5 mk for children.

Hyvinkää Church, a modern triangular building at Hämeenkatu 16, is open daily from 9 am to 4 pm. There are art exhibitions at **Hyvinkää Art Museum** at Hämeenkatu 3D, as well as galleries at Vaiveronkatu 10 and Siltakatu 6. The latter has paintings by children.

Places to Stay

The best place to stay is around Sveitsi Park, where you can enjoy outdoor activities in this hilly *harju* (ridge) area. *Sveitsin maja* (☎ 436 747) is a nice, clean hostel located inside Sveitsi Park. Be sure to call ahead. *Rantasipi Sveitsi* (☎ 45881) at Härkävehmaankatu 4 is a major resort with 195 rooms and all kinds of sports and congress facilities. Rooms cost 450/520 mk.

In central Hyvinkää, *Martina* (☎ 452 400) at Hämeenkatu 2-4 has 39 rooms, from 250/320 mk in summer, or 295/365 mk at other times.

Getting There & Away

In addition to regular buses from Helsinki

and surrounding towns, all Riihimäki-bound local R-trains and H-trains stop in Hyvinkää.

South-East Uusimaa

SIPOO

The municipality of Sipoo (Swedish: Sibbo), east of Helsinki, is inhabited by 14,800 people, most of whom speak Swedish. Its main attraction is a **15th century church** which has fine paintings. You can get to Sipoo by bus from the Helsinki bus terminal.

PORVOO

Porvoo (Swedish: Borgå), 50 km east of Helsinki, makes a good day trip from the capital, or is first stop on the eastern King's Road. The second oldest town in Finland after Turku, Porvoo has officially been a town since 1346, but even before that it was an important trading centre. Porvoo has three distinct sections: the old town, the new town and the 19th century Empire part. The old town is exceptionally large and well preserved. The Porvoo area has 43,000 inhabitants, half of whom live in the town itself.

UUSIMAA

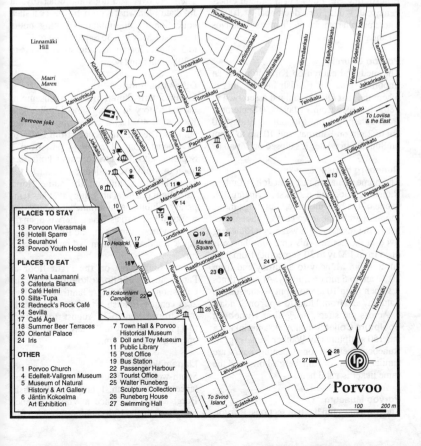

PLACES TO STAY
13 Porvoon Vierasmaja
16 Hotelli Sparre
21 Seurahovi
28 Porvoo Youth Hostel

PLACES TO EAT
2 Wanha Laamanni
3 Cafeteria Blanca
9 Café Helmi
10 Silta-Tupa
12 Redneck's Rock Café
14 Sevilla
17 Café Åga
18 Summer Beer Terraces
20 Oriental Palace
24 Iris

OTHER
1 Porvoo Church
4 Edelfelt-Vallgren Museum
5 Museum of Natural
  History & Art Gallery
6 Jäntin Kokoelma
  Art Exhibition

7 Town Hall & Porvoo
  Historical Museum
8 Doll and Toy Museum
11 Public Library
15 Post Office
19 Bus Station
22 Passenger Harbour
23 Tourist Office
25 Walter Runeberg
  Sculpture Collection
26 Runeberg House
27 Swimming Hall

Porvoo

0   100   200 m

Information

Tourist Office The tourist office at Rauhankatu 20 (☎ 580 145) is open Monday to Friday from 8 am to 4 pm and on Saturday from 10 am to 2 pm.

Post & Telephone The post office is at Mannerheiminkatu 7. Porvoo's post code is 06100.

Library The public library at Mannerheiminkatu 14 is open from 10 am to 7 pm Monday to Friday and from 9 am to 2 pm on Saturday.

Emergency Services For a general emergency call ☎ 112; for a doctor call ☎ 10023. There are pharmacies on Piispankatu at Nos 30 and 34.

Porvoo Church

The medieval church on Kirkkotori has an important place in Finnish history: this is where the first Diet of Finland assembled in 1809. It's open from 1 May to 30 September from 10 am to 6 pm Monday to Friday, 10 am to 2 pm on Saturday and 10 am to 5 pm on Sunday. In winter it's closed on Monday.

Runeberg House

The home of nationalist poet Johan Ludvig Runeberg is located at Aleksanterinkatu 3. It is one of the best-preserved buildings in the Empire part of the town centre. The interior has been preserved as it was when Runeberg lived in the house. This charming house is open from 1 May to 30 September from 9.30 am to 4 pm Monday to Saturday and from 10.30 am to 5 pm on Sunday. At other times it's open from 10 am to 4 pm Wednesday to Saturday and from 11 am to 5 pm on Sunday.

Across the street, the **Walter Runeberg Sculpture Collection** at Aleksanterinkatu 5 has 150 sculptures by Walther Runeberg, JL Runeberg's eldest son. Opening hours are similar to those of Runeberg's home and the same ticket is valid here.

Porvoo Museum

The town museum has two sections. **Porvoo**

Historical Museum, in the old town hall on Vanha Raatihuoneentori, has old furniture and an extensive collection of keys and other paraphernalia. It's open daily from 11 am to 4 pm from 1 May to 31 August; from 1 September to 30 April, it's open from noon to 4 pm Wednesday to Sunday.

Just north-east of the town hall, **Edelfelt-Vallgren Museum** has paintings and sculptures by two of Porvoo's most famous artists. The museum is at Välikatu 11 and has the same opening hours as the historical museum.

Doll & Toy Museum

There are over 800 dolls and other toys at Jokikatu 14 in what is probably the best such collection in all Finland. Opening hours between 1 May and 30 September are 11 am to 3.30 pm Monday to Saturday and noon to 3.30 pm on Sunday.

Other Museums

Luonnontieteellinen museo, a museum of natural history in an old school building at Kaivokatu 40, has a collection of stuffed animals. The museum is open from 1 May to 31 August from 11 am to 4 pm; from 1 September to 30 April opening hours are noon to 4 pm. Admission is 15 mk. In the same building, and on the same floor, **Taidehalli** is a local art gallery that has temporary exhibitions. In summer, it displays the works of local artists. The gallery is open on Tuesday from 5 to 8 pm, and from Wednesday to Sunday from noon to 4 pm. Entry is 5 mk.

Just south-west on the sixth floor at Papinkatu 19, **Jäntin kokoelma** is the art collection of Mr Yrjö A Jäntti. It displays 20th century Finnish art. The collection is open from 1 May to 31 August from 10 am to 4 pm Wednesday to Sunday; in winter the opening time is 11 am.

Linnamäki Hill

South-west of and well within walking distance of the church, Linnamäki (Swedish: Borgbacken) was once a Viking defence post. Later, in the 13th century, a wooden fort was constructed here by Swedish settlers. Today, thick pine trees grow on this hill which offers a fine view of Porvoo.

Places to Stay

Porvoo Youth Hostel (☎ 523 0012), open all year round, is very popular and often full. It is located in a nice wooden building at Linnankoskenkatu 1-3. Dormitory beds cost 40 mk; you should book in advance.

Porvoon Vierasmaja (☎ 524 4454) at Adlercreutzinkatu 29 has just five rooms, at 130/200 mk for singles/doubles.

Hotelli Sparre (☎ 584 455) is a no-nonsense hotel on the third floor at Piispankatu 34. Each room has a TV set, mini-bar and a nice bathroom, and singles/doubles are 350/420 mk. There's also a restaurant.

Seurahovi (☎ 54761) is very central at Rauhankatu 27, near the market square. The hotel is the scene of the local nightlife; it has singles/doubles at 300/350 mk in summer, but is considerably dearer in winter. There are 44 rooms.

If you feel like giving yourself a treat, try *Haikko Manor* (☎ 57601), some seven km south of Porvoo. Rooms in the old house are very classy and so are the prices – expect to pay 500 mk for any room. In summer, rates can be as low as 295/410 mk for singles/doubles.

Motelli Porvoo, another place some distance west of the centre, is close to road No 170, but while the buildings are new, they are not very attractively located. There are 29 rooms priced at 175/210 mk for singles/doubles.

Kokonniemi (☎ 581 967) is a local camping ground at the southern end of Porvoo town. There are five cottages and space for tents and caravans. It's open from late May to late August.

Places to Eat

Iris, at Aleksanterinkatu 20 in the new section of Porvoo, is the restaurant owned and run by the tourism institute. Prices are reasonable but quality can be so-so; there's also a bakery in the same building.

Silta-Tupa, right at the bridge at Mannerheiminkatu 2, is a celebration of rural tackiness, but with more style than the real thing. Meals can be had on its terrace on sunny summer days.

Wanha Laamanni at Vuorikatu 17 is the gourmet restaurant of Porvoo. Game is a speciality and can be had in either floor of this old wooden building with 18th century ambience. Prices are as steep as the alley it is found in.

Cafés are a speciality of Porvoo and at least one should be tested. *Cafeteria Blanca* at the old square on Välikatu 13 has coffee and pastries and is open daily all year round. Nearby, *Café Helmi* at Välikatu 3 may actually be a bit nicer, with home-made pastries and cakes available.

There are more choices in the new centre. The bus station area has several grillis, including *Topkapi*, which serves kebab. *Oriental Palace* is a Chinese restaurant near the market on Lundinkatu. There are a few places on Mannerheiminkatu, such as *Kotipizza*, *Sevilla*, and *Redneck's Rock Café*, an interesting imitation of an American pub that claims to have 'the best beat in town'.

In summer you will find terraces open along the eastern riverfront. *Café Åga* is the place to go when the weather is less friendly, although this nautical pub also has an outdoor terrace.

Getting There & Away

Take a bus from Helsinki (50 km west) – go express if you are using Coach Holiday Ticket coupons. If you are using cash, ordinary buses are cheaper and not too slow. You can catch the same bus at Itäkeskus and end up paying less. Both bus types run every hour or so.

The busy Helsinki to Kotka bus route will come in handy if you need a ride to/from further east. It's 90 km from Kotka to Porvoo.

AROUND PORVOO
Sikosaari

This island south of Porvoo, also known as Ruskis or Svinö, is a protected haven for birds and vegetation. A causeway connects it to the mainland and there are marked trails.

Postimäki

Outside Porvoo at Ilola, some 10 km north on road No 170, this delightful hilltop cluster of houses has been preserved and is open as a museum in summer from 11 am to 5 pm daily except Monday. Continue east from Porvoo along road No 170 for the best scenery.

PERNAJA

Pernaja (Swedish: Pernå) is a primarily Swedish-speaking municipality between Porvoo and Loviisa. The medieval **Pernaja Church**, four km south of road No 7, is decorated with medieval and Swedish treasures. It's open from 15 May to 15 August from noon to 3 pm Monday to Friday. Outside these hours you'll have to call ☎ 636 103 for the keys, and it will cost you 100 mk to see the church.

Stor Sarvlaks Gård, a beautiful manor house almost 10 km east of Pernaja, has a small horse-drawn carriage museum that is open by appointment only.

Rönnäs

The **Archipelago Museum in Rönnäs**, almost 20 km south of road No 7 (or E18) along road No 158, has exhibits relating to the history of the archipelago and to boatbuilding. The museum is open in summer, Wednesday to Sunday.

Places to Stay & Eat

If you go 10 km west of Pernaja, turn south onto road No 158 and continue about 30 km, you'll reach *Kabböle Vandrarhem* (☎ 635 643), a boat hostel with bunks in cabins. HI members pay 50 mk per person, others 65 mk. There are currently only two buses each week, on Tuesday and Thursday, departing from Loviisa at 12.50 pm. The hostel is open from 1 May to 30 September.

The *Kuninkaantie* Esso petrol station on the road to Rönnäs and Kabböle runs a restaurant.

Next to the church in Pernaja, *Café Lillstuga* serves coffee in summer.

LOVIISA

Loviisa (Swedish: Lovisa) is a small, charming town some 90 km east of Helsinki. It was established in 1745 and named after the Swedish Queen Lovisa Ulrika. In the 18th century it was one of the three towns in Finland allowed to engage in foreign trade. In the 19th century Loviisa became an important port and spa town, although the town was devastated by fire during the Crimean War. The population is currently less than 8000.

Information

The tourist information booth (☎ 555 234) at Mannerheiminkatu 4 is open from 9 am to 4 pm Monday to Friday (longer from 1 June to 30 August), and on Saturday from 9 am to 2 pm.

The post office is at Kuningattarenkatu 13. The library is at Itäinen Tullikatu 17. There's a bookshop at Aleksanterinkatu 5. Look for imported magazines at R-kioski just next door.

You'll find a pharmacy at Kuningattarenkatu 15.

Old Town

The old town of Loviisa, south of Mannerheiminkatu, contains the buildings that were saved from the disastrous fire of 1855. The narrow streets around restaurant Degerby Gille are the quaintest in town, but Mariankatu is also attractive.

Loviisa Church

This impressive neo-Gothic church at the western end of Mannerheiminkatu is the first thing you will see on arrival from Helsinki; it's equally impressive from inside. The church is open in summer from 10 am to 7 pm.

Sibelius House

The house at Sibeliuksenkatu 10 was the summer home of the family of Jean Sibelius, the composer. Today it hosts art exhibitions in summer.

Ungern & Rosen

These two fortresses just off the eastern end of Mannerheiminkatu were built in the 18th century to guard the road between Vyborg and Turku. The ruins of the fortresses can be visited any time, free of charge.

Nuclear Plant Tour

If you are interested in nuclear power stations, you'll have a chance to visit one in Loviisa. The operator, Imatran Voima, arranges two-hour tours for the public on Sunday in summer. A bus leaves at 12.30 pm from the bus terminal.

Svartholm Fort

This sea fortress lies on an island 10 km from the town centre. It was established in 1748 soon after Sweden had lost control of the eastern part of Finland. The fort was destroyed by the British during the Crimean War in 1855, but has since been renovated. There are daily morning and noon launches from the Laivasilta passenger harbour in June, July and August (except Friday in June

UUSIMAA

Loviisa

PLACES TO STAY
16 Matkustajakoti Resandehem M Helgas
17 Motelli Z
21 Hotelli Degerby
22 Zilton Hotelli
27 Hotelli Skandinavia

PLACES TO EAT
7 Kappeli
9 Mexmarié
11 Pizzeria & Grill
12 King's Pub
14 Bella
23 Degerby Gille
26 Vaherkylä
28 Saltbodan Café

OTHER
1 Town Museum
2 Rosen
3 Ungern
4 Hospital
5 Orthodox Church
6 Public Library
8 Bus Station
10 Pharmacy
13 Tourist Information Booth
15 Sibelius House
18 Loviisa Church
19 Book Shop & R-kioski
20 Post Office
24 Old Degerby Estate
25 Alexandra
29 Maritime Museum
30 Harbour Information Office
31 Laivasilta Passenger Harbour

and late August). Return tickets cost 45 to 60 mk.

Places to Stay

You can camp for approximately 50 mk at *Casino Camping* (☎ 530 244) at Kapteenintie 1, at the south end of Loviisa by the sea. There are no cottages. The best place to stay in Loviisa is *Matkustajakoti Resandehem M Helgas* (☎ 531 576) at Sibeliuksenkatu 6. It's an attractive old wooden house with pleasant rooms and heaps of olde world ambience. There's a quiet garden. Rooms cost 120/180 mk.

Loviisa has three hotels. *Hotelli Degerby* (☎ 50651) at Brandensteininkatu 17 is the finest in town, with several popular places to eat or drink, and singles/doubles for 340/460 mk. Across the street, *Zilton Hotelli* (☎ 533 191) at Mariankatu 29 is older, with singles/doubles for 200/250 mk. This hotel also arranges accommodation in *Motelli Z* at Sibeliuksenkatu 1 but it's not very pleasant. The oldest is *Hotelli Skandinavia* (☎ 531 725) at Karlskronabulevardi 9-11, where singles/doubles cost 150/250 mk.

Places to Eat

Degerby Gille at Sepänkuja 4 is the most famous restaurant in Loviisa. It is located in a 17th century building on the Degerby estate and has old-fashioned and stylish dining rooms.

Saltbodan Café at the passenger harbour serves coffee in a rustic room and meals in a pleasant dining hall. *Mexmarié* at Mariankatu 20 serves beer, coffee and Mexican and international food. *Kappeli* is an old wooden villa, built in 1865, in Kappelinpuisto Park. It's usually lively in summer evenings and you can dance there.

For local flavour, check the basement *Pizzeria* on Kuningattarenkatu. Nearby, *Grill* is a landmark and serves hamburgers until late, or, around the corner on Itäinen Tullikatu, there's *King's Pub*. *Vaherkylä* on Aleksanterinkatu is a bakery and a pleasant café. *Bella* at Mannerheiminkatu 2 is popular with locals.

Things to Buy

Kuningattarenkatu is the main shopping street, but check Alexandra at Aleksanterinkatu 1 for interesting local handicrafts.

Getting There & Away

There are six to nine buses a day to/from Kotka, Helsinki and Porvoo, and two buses a day from Lahti and Tampere.

North-East Uusimaa

If you travel through this region, blessed with beautiful undulating hills, forests and farmland, you may not believe how close you are to the capital of Finland. There are few world-class attractions but those few are certainly worth a stop. Avoid the busy motorways and choose narrow secondary roads in order to see more.

MÄNTSÄLÄ

Historically significant but presently little more than an oversized cluster of tacky architecture, Mäntsälä offers plenty of hidden gems. There are at least four old estates, some of which keep their gates open all summer. Over 15,000 people live in Mäntsälä.

Sepänmäki

This artisans' museum, or Sepänmäen käsityömuseo, features living handicraft traditions in old houses, some of which date to the 18th century. You will find the museum in the village of Hirvihaara on road No 145, five km south-west of the centre. It is open from mid-May to the end of July, Tuesday to Sunday from noon to 6 pm.

Alikartano

This manor, formerly owned by the wealthy Nordenskiöld family, now houses one of the museums of the National Board of Antiquities. The estate is also known as Frugård, and the main building was built in 1805. The museum has a café called *Hedda Noora*.

Alikartano is nine km south of the centre on road No 149. It is open daily from mid-May to the end of August from 11 am to 5 pm.

Getting There & Away
All long-distance buses from Helsinki to Lahti and beyond stop at Mäntsälä bus station, although the new road, No 4, now passes by the centre.

ASKOLA
Askola, north of Porvoo, has an attractive **church** (built in 1799) with a colourful pulpit. However, the area's main attractions are the 20 **rock wells** (called Hiidenkirnut or 'Devil's Churn') on a pleasant hillside location some 500 metres from the Askola to Pukkila road (No 163). Jättiläisen kuhnepytty is the biggest of them all, 10.3 metres deep and 4.2 metres wide. This is reckoned to be the third largest in the world. Take care at the steep cliff, especially if it's raining.

LILJENDAL
The overwhelmingly Swedish-speaking community of Liljendal (population 1500) is north-east of Porvoo. There is an excellent youth hostel (☎ 616 354) in Embom, two km west of the No 6 Helsinki to Kouvola road. The owners are friendly and the hostel is pleasantly located close to a river. There are two saunas and you'll pay just 45 mk for dormitory beds in the old wooden villa, which is open all year round.

LAPINJÄRVI
This small lakeside town (Swedish: Lappträsk) north-east of Liljendal is named after the Lapp population that dwelt in the region before they were pushed further north by Swedish settlers who arrived during the 13th century. Finns came later. The idyllic, well-preserved centre features two **churches** built side by side in 1744. In 1742,

lightning struck and burnt down both the Swedish and the Finnish church. A fierce two-year construction boom followed. The Finnish church was finished first and became known as 'the small church', as the slower Swedes were able to build a slightly bigger one! The churches are open June to August from 10 am to late afternoon.

The local museum, **Kycklings**, has a tourist information office. In this former residential building there is furniture and the workshops of a shoemaker and a coppersmith. The village also has a number of shops selling handicrafts and pottery. In the nearby village of Porlammi, there is a **museum**, which is open only on Sunday in summer from noon to 1 pm.

To get to Lapinjärvi, take one of the slower buses between Helsinki and Kouvola. There are 10 such buses per day.

ORIMATTILA
Orimattila, south of Lahti, is a town that traditionally has been part of Häme. Most of the attractions are cultural. Its population is 14,000.

Orimattila is known for its art museums. The town art museum, **Orimattilan taidemuseo**, at Lahdentie 65 is generally open from noon to 4 pm, Tuesday to Sunday. Admission is 15 mk. **Taidelinna** at Erkontie 8 has paintings by Ms Soile Yli-Mäyry (see Kuortane in the Pohjanmaa chapter) in an impressive old house. It's open on Sunday from noon to 7 pm and in July daily except Monday from noon to 6 pm. Admission is a hefty 20 mk. **Villa Roosa** at Käkelänraitti 4 has textiles, open daily in summer from noon to 6 pm.

The **local museum** at Pappilantie 4 is open in July daily except Monday. The **Orimattila Church** is open daily in summer from 9 am to 6 pm.

There are daily buses to Orimattila from Helsinki and Lahti.

Åland

The Province of Åland (Finnish: Ahvenanmaa) consists of unique, autonomous islands. The population is entirely Swedish-speaking, and local pride is expressed through the careful protection of nature and historical and cultural heritage, and legislation by the *lagting* (local government). Åland is also the name of the main island. Surprisingly, Åland translates as 'river land', although Åland is better known for its islands and islets, which number more than 6400.

This beautiful island world is perfect for bicycle tours, camping and cabin holidays. Regular ferries connect Åland to both Sweden and the Finnish mainland, and for those interested in island-hopping, free transport is provided by inter-island ferries.

Because nature is so highly prized in Åland, a restrictive outdoor code is in force here. Fishing waters are separately licensed – ask about fishing cards at tourist offices.

History

The first settlers set foot on Åland 6000 years ago, near Orrdals klint (in the north), where a 'prehistoric trail' has been set up. More than a hundred Bronze and Iron Age cemeteries or burial mound areas have been discovered, indicating there was plenty of contact between Swedish and Finnish sailors. All prehistoric sites (*fornminne*) on Åland are clearly signposted. Åland was an important harbour and trade centre during the Viking Age, and six fortresses from that time have been identified. Those in Saltvik municipality (Borgboda and Nääs) are particularly worth a visit.

Christianity arrived here early, well before the first Catholic crusade on mainland Finland. Almost all churches in Åland Province are medieval, dating from the 12th to the 15th centuries. As well as bringing Catholicism to the islands, Swedish administration built defences. Kastelholm Castle was established in the 14th century.

Highlights

- Island-hopping and island scenery.
- Free ferries, especially for cyclists.
- Cycling routes along scenic roads.
- Prehistoric trails and forts.
- Distinctive Swedish-speaking culture.
- Small, isolated, scenic villages.
- Well preserved natural areas.
- Churches dating from the 12th century, notably the Sta Maria Church in Kvarnbo, probably the oldest church in Finland.

During the Great Northern War (1700-21) (nicknamed the 'Great Wrath'), most of the population fled to Sweden to escape the Russians, who were spreading destruction on Åland. The Russians returned during the 1740s (a period known as the Lesser Wrath), and again in 1809 when all of Finland was occupied. The Russians built the impressive 1830s fortifications of Bomarsund but these were destroyed during the Crimean War.

By the time Finland gained its independence in 1917, Ålanders were all too familiar with Russians and feared occupation by the

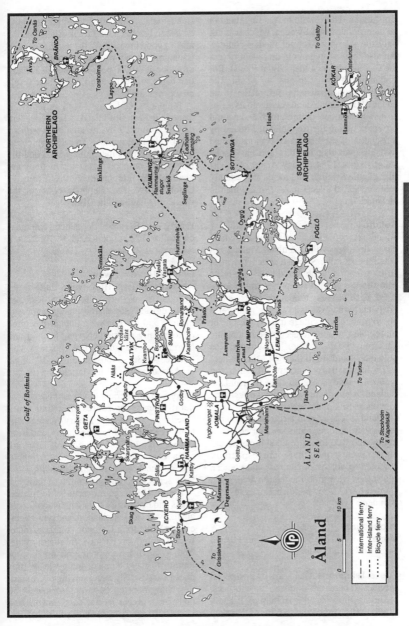

Bolsheviks. There were moves for Åland to be incorporated into Sweden, which was not only the Ålanders' former mother country, but also their source of cultural identity (not the case for the vast majority of Finns). But Finland didn't want to give up Åland. The Swedish-Finnish dispute only came to an end in 1921, when Åland was given its status as an autonomous, demilitarised and neutral province within the Republic of Finland by a decision of the League of Nations. Åland took its own flag in 1954 and has issued stamps since 1984. Today Åland is almost like a Little Sweden, and locals are certainly more aware of events in Stockholm than in Helsinki.

Culture
Åland has its own distinctive culture, which has little to do with mainland Finland but which is not quite Swedish either. The most striking feature in the Åland landscape is the Midsummer pole. It's a long flagpole decorated with leaves, miniature flags, small boats and whatever is available and seems appropriate. Each village usually has one or more poles, which are decorated in a public gathering the day before Midsummer. The pole then stands until the next Midsummer.

Traditional folk dance is still alive and well on Åland, more so than in mainland Finland. Again, Midsummer is the best time to witness folk dancing.

Åland offers little in terms of contemporary urban culture, although Mariehamn is not a bad place to dance on summer weekends. Young men here are especially attracted to old American cars and you can spot a few very fine models on weekends. Gardening is very popular among elderly islanders.

Information
Money You can use both Finnish *markka* and Swedish *krona* in Åland.

Post & Telephone Åland runs its own postal services. There are a dozen post offices, including those on the islands of Brändö, Föglö, Kumlinge and Kökar. On many smaller islands, postal services are provided by general stores. Don't think Åland stamps make a good investment; the number of each issue printed may well be one million, for a province of 20,000 people, although a stamp that has actually travelled somewhere is relatively valuable.

Telephone codes in Åland differ from those in the rest of Finland. To call Sweden, dial 81, followed by the area code *without* the '0', then the number. To call other countries, dial 82 plus the country code and the rest of the number. Exact instructions are available at telephone booths. From 12 October 1996, the telephone code for the whole of Åland will be 018.

Emergency Services For general emergencies call ☎ 112, for police call ☎ 10022, and for medical service call ☎ 10023.

Getting There & Away
Air Skärgårdflyg flies twice daily from Monday to Friday between Stockholm (Arlanda) and Mariehamn, charging approximately 550 mk one-way. Finnair has three or four daily flights between Helsinki and Mariehamn, via Turku. For bookings, call toll-free ☎ 9800-3466. Finnair (☎ 19522) is at Skarpansvägen 24 in Mariehamn.

Ferry See appropriate towns and islands for details on ferry routes. Starting from Sweden, you can take a ferry from Stockholm or Kapellskär to Mariehamn, and from Grisslehamn to Storby in Eckerö. There are Silja Line and Viking Line ferries to Mariehamn from Turku and Naantali, and a ferry service to Långnäs from Naantali.

It's possible to gain free travel for pedestrians and cyclists on the archipelago ferries all the way to mainland Åland via southeastern harbours at Korppoo (southern route, from Galtby) or Kustavi (northern route, from Osnäs), but only if you break your journey to stay on one or more islands (this doesn't necessarily mean staying overnight). Travelling nonstop costs approximately 50 mk, plus a higher fee for cars. For the best views, take a ferry from Galtby to Kökar, and then to Långnäs in mainland Åland. From Osnäs, take a ferry to northern Brändö, and another from the southern tip (20 km overland) to Kumlinge, and then to mainland Åland via Hummelvik on Vårdö. (See also the Turku Region map in the Turku & Pori Province chapter.)

Mariehamn

Mariehamn will seem a bustling metropolis if you've arrived at some of the other entry points in Åland or spent some time in the archipelago. But if you come directly to Mariehamn from either Sweden or mainland Finland, you are in for a pleasant surprise – if you like quiet little towns. Mariehamn is sometimes called the 'town of a thousand linden trees'. It is hectic here in summer, when it becomes the town of a thousand tourists, but in winter the town is quiet, with a population of only 10,400.

Mariehamn was founded in 1861 by Tsar Alexander II, who named the town after his wife, Tsarina Maria. Today, Mariehamn is the administrative and economic centre of Åland. It is the seat of the lagting and *landskapsstyrelse*, the legislative and executive bodies of Åland. Educational and training facilities, foreign consulates, culture and commerce are also centred in Mariehamn.

Orientation
Mariehamn lies on a long, narrow peninsula between busy Östra Hamnen and Västra Hamnen (the East and West harbours). Torggatan is the main street, and features the only pedestrian section in Åland. Most tourists will arrive in Mariehamn by ferry. The main ferry terminals are at the Västra Hamnen. The airport is north-west of the centre.

Information
Tourist Office The Mariehamn tourist information office (☎ 27300) at Storagatan 11, not far from the ferry terminals, has material about the whole of Åland. The tourist office

is open between September and January daily from 10 am to 4 pm, and in June, July and August daily from 9 am to 6 pm.

Post & Telephone The post office at Torggatan 4 is open Monday to Friday from 9 am to 5 pm and Saturday from 11 am to 2 pm and sells Åland stamps.

Library The modern building at the Östra Hamnen is the Mariehamn Municipal Library. It is worth a visit because of its architectural interest and because it subscribes to a fair number of foreign newspapers. There are also free tourist pamphlets available. The library is open from 11 am to 8 pm Monday to Friday and from 11 am to 3 pm on Saturday.

Travel Agencies Ålandsresor (☎ 28040) at Storagatan 9 is a travel agency which specialises in arranging tours of Åland and in renting out summer cottages.

Left Luggage You can store your gear at the ferry terminal for 10 mk per locker.

Emergency Services In a general emergency, ring ☎ 112, for the police ring ☎ 10022 and for a doctor call ☎ 10023. If you need a pharmacy, try Centralapotek, at Skarpansvägen 24, or Provinsial Apotek, at Torggatan 10.

Ålands Museum & Ålands Konstmuseum
Ålands Museum, and the adjoining Art Museum, are well worth a visit. Ålands Museum covers the history of Åland from prehistoric times to the present. It received the 1982 Council of Europe Award for the best new museum. The exhibits are unusually lively and well presented. The Art Museum has a permanent collection of art from Åland, as well as temporary exhibitions. The museums are open 1 May to 31 August from 10 am to 4 pm (Tuesday to 8 pm). At other times of year they are closed on Monday. Admission is 15 mk.

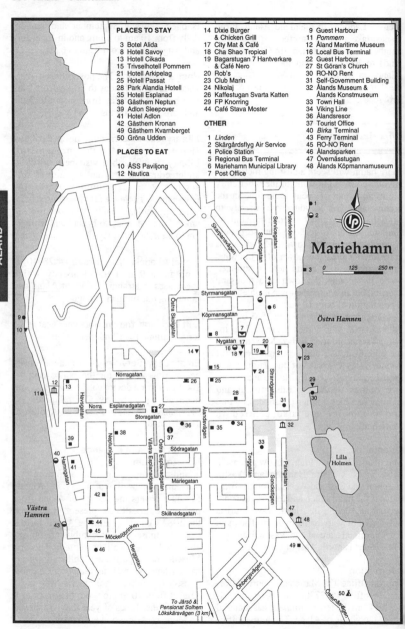

PLACES TO STAY

3 Botel Alida
8 Hotell Savoy
13 Hotell Cikada
15 Trivselhotell Pommern
21 Hotell Arkipelag
25 Hotell Passat
28 Park Alandia Hotell
35 Hotell Esplanad
38 Gästhem Neptun
39 Adlon Sleepover
41 Hotel Adlon
42 Gästhem Kronan
49 Gästhem Kvarnberget
50 Gröna Udden

PLACES TO EAT

10 ÅSS Paviljong
12 Nautica

14 Dixie Burger
    & Chicken Grill
17 City Mat & Café
18 Cha Shao Tropical
19 Bagarstugan 7 Hantverkare
    & Café Nero
20 Rob's
23 Club Marin
24 Nikolaj
26 Kaffestugan Svarta Katten
29 FP Knorring
44 Café Stava Moster

OTHER

1 *Linden*
2 Skärgårdsflyg Air Service
4 Police Station
5 Regional Bus Terminal
6 Mariehamn Municipal Library
7 Post Office

9 Guest Harbour
11 *Pommern*
12 Åland Maritime Museum
16 Local Bus Terminal
22 Guest Harbour
27 St Göran's Church
30 RO-NO Rent
31 Self-Government Building
32 Ålands Museum &
    Ålands Konstmuseum
33 Town Hall
34 Viking Line
36 Ålandsresor
37 Tourist Office
40 *Birka* Terminal
43 Ferry Terminal
45 RO-NO Rent
46 Ålandsparken
47 Övernässtugan
48 Ålands Köpmannamuseum

Mariehamn

0   125   250 m

Östra Hamnen

Lilla Holmen

Västra Hamnen

To Järsö &
Pensionat Solhem
Lökskärsvägen (3 km)

Åland Maritime Museum

This museum on Hamngatan has one of the best presentations of sailing ships in the world. There are heaps of items from old boats, and a few interesting cabins. The museum is open daily from 10 am to 4 pm, except in June and August, when it's open until 5 pm, and in July, when it's open until 7 pm. Admission is 15 mk.

Pommern

The museum ship *Pommern*, behind the Maritime Museum, is one of the symbols of Mariehamn. This four-masted steel barque was built in 1903 and is supposedly unique. Although there are plenty of cabins and stairs to explore, just the sheer size of the ship, best seen on the bottom floor, is worth the effort. The *Pommern* is open pretty much at the same time as the Maritime Museum but it's closed in winter. Admission is 15 mk.

St Göran's Church

The newest church on Åland is not as interesting as the medieval treasure troves in villages. The design is Art Nouveau, by Lars Sonck. It is open Monday to Friday 10 am to 3 pm.

Ålands Köpmannamuseum

This little building on Parkgatan is a house museum of trade and handicrafts. It is open from 15 June to 15 August Monday to Friday from 1 to 3 pm. Admission is free. The nearby red **Övernässtugan** house is the only survivor of the old Övenäs township that was the only settlement here when Mariehamn was founded.

Self-Government Building

This building on the corner of Österleden and Storagatan is an office building. In summer on Friday you can take a free guided tour at 10 pm. The tour ends with a slide show about Åland.

Ålandsparken

This small amusement park close to the Viking Line ferry terminal has rides best suited to small children; indeed the park may turn out to be a disappointment for older kids or grown-ups. For adults, there is the opportunity for small-scale gambling (on coin machines).

Lilla Holmen

South of Östra Hamnen is Lilla Holmen, a park on an island with a little beach. Lilla Holmen's speciality is peacocks, which can be seen walking around.

Järsö

The Järsö recreational area, 12 km south of Mariehamn at the tip of the peninsula, is a good place for short bicycle and walking tours. The area is at its most beautiful in spring and early summer, when wildflowers cover the ground. The narrow scenic road passes over several bridges. Don't forget your camera.

Organised Tours

The traditional sailing ship *Linden* was constructed in 1993 and now sails short tours in summer. The *Linden* departs at 10 am from Östra Hamnen, and at 3 pm from Västra Hamnen. The voyage costs 130 mk per person.

Places to Stay – bottom end

For those with a tent, there is the camping ground *Gröna Udden* (☎ 19041), which is conveniently close to the town centre, between Östernäsvägen and the sea. Camping here is cheap, at 15 mk per person, per tent and per car. The site is pleasant if sometimes a bit cramped, and the beach is good for swimming. There are no cottages.

Nothing in Åland other than camping is cheaper than *Botel Alida* (☎ 13755), which is an independent boat hostel moored at Östra Hamnen quay, not far from the library and the bus station. It's open to any of the few quick ones who can get a vacant bunk here. There are no HI discounts. Rooms are cabins with basic facilities. Beds cost 80 mk, and sheets are 15 mk extra (or bring your own). Sleeping bags are allowed. The restaurant serves cheap meals. Some of the tables are on the deck, which is great on sunny days.

ÅLAND

ÅLAND

Places to Stay – middle

If you're looking for something in this price bracket, check first with *Gästhem Kronan* (☎ 12617) at Neptunigatan 52, close to the ferry terminal. It's open all year round, and has singles/doubles in summer for 195/295 mk, and at other times for 150/230 mk. In summer, there are two other guesthouses that are run by the same company. *Gästhem Kvarnberget* at Parkgatan 28C is a modern house on a quiet street opposite the park, and *Gästhem Neptun*, at Neptunigatan 41, charges 225/330 mk. Reception for all three is at Kronan.

Pensionat Solhem (☎ 16322) is one of the quiet places to stay in Mariehamn, with singles/doubles for 200/280 mk, less outside the summer high season. It is pleasantly situated by the sea on Lökskärsvägen, 3 km south of the centre. Guests can use the rowing boats free of charge, and there's a sauna.

The *Adlon Sleepover* consists of three old buildings across the street from Hotel Adlon. Rooms are bigger than those in the actual hotel and can accommodate up to six people. These are not dormitories, so you pay for each room. Guests may use all the facilities of Hotel Adlon, including the sauna and the swimming pool. Reception is at the Hotel Adlon. In summer, these rooms cost 240/350 mk, including breakfast. At other times, weekday rates are 210/240 mk, while weekend rates are a bit dearer.

Hotell Passat (☎ 15566 or 13260) at Norragatan 7 is a small apartment hotel with only 10 rooms, which should be reserved in advance. The keys can be obtained from a shop nearby. Singles/doubles cost 195/290 mk.

Another cheap hotel in Mariehamn is *Hotell Esplanad* (☎ 16444) at Storagatan 5. It's in need of renovation, but singles/doubles are reasonable at 200/250 mk, although in summer prices rise to 250/350 mk.

Places to Stay – top end

Mariehamn has several good hotels. Prices are highest during the summer high season.

There are restaurants and pubs in hotels, but they are not necessarily good value.

Hotel Adlon (☎ 15300), not far from the Viking Line ferry terminal at Hamngatan 7, is a nice, modern hotel. Singles/doubles cost 440/550 mk in summer but there are discounts.

Hotell Arkipelag (☎ 24020), Strandgatan 31, not far from Östra Hamnen, is the largest hotel in Åland and one of the brighter lights of Mariehamn's nightlife. Singles/doubles in this impressive hotel cost from 450/660 mk, or 360/480 mk during the low season.

Hotell Cikada (☎ 16333) on the opposite side of the peninsula at Norragatan 43 is an imposing building, with 84 rooms that cost from 330/380 to 390/550 mk, depending on the season. There's a swimming pool.

Trivselhotell Pommern (☎ 15555), Norragatan 8-10, has 54 rooms priced from 300 mk in spring and autumn, and 440/550 mk in summer.

Park Alandia Hotell (☎ 14130) is close to the centre at Norra Esplanadgatan 3. There are 80 rooms, with singles/doubles from 380/460 to 450/540 mk during the high season.

Hotell Savoy (☎ 15400), Nygatan 12, is a large hotel with 85 rooms, each costing from 300 mk in the low season to 440/550 mk in summer.

Places to Eat

The restaurant scene is more tempting than the size of Mariehamn would suggest. The superb Ålandspannkaka (pancake) is something not to miss, and can be had in many cafés as well as on the museum premises (you can get into the museum's café free). Make sure, however, that you don't buy one that has been heated in a microwave oven, as this is often a sign that it has been frozen.

Café Stava Moster is opposite the ferry terminal but better is *Kaffestugan Svarta Katten* on Norragatan, a pleasant café where coffee is served in copper pots. Also nice is *Bagarstugan 7 Hantverkare*, which has a handicrafts sales exhibition. There's also *Café Nero* next door, although it isn't the best in town.

Two popular restaurants on Torggatan serve inexpensive lunch packages as daily specials. *Cha Shao Tropical* has a variety of Asian food and *Nikolaj* has huge pizzas. Ordinary meals are dearer.

Nautica, a very fine fish restaurant above

the Maritime Museum, offers a pleasant dinner. A bit north at the western harbour, *ÅSS Paviljong* is the oldest restaurant in town, a nice wooden building with a lunch special for 50 mk, and dinner for 87 mk.

There is a staggering variety of pizzas at *Rob's* at Strandgatan 12. Food here is healthier than it sounds. Similar is *Dixie Burger & Chicken Grill* at Ålandsvägen 40. It has tasty burgers and chicken portions for 20 to 30 mk. Another down-to-earth eatery is *City Mat & Café* on Torggatan, where the home-made food is good value.

The boat restaurant *FP Knorring* is a real treat with costly but classy seafood meals. The pleasant beer terrace on the deck is good when not too crowded. The nearby *Club Marin* is an attractive harbour pavilion that serves beer and meals, and is very popular when there's live music.

Things to Buy

Jussis Keramik and Jussis Glashytta (☎ 13606) at Nygatan 1 sell ceramics and glassware. Visitors can watch the objects being made. The shop and the connected cafeteria are open every day. Fäktargubben (☎ 19603) at Norragatan 13 sells Åland handicrafts. It is open weekdays from 9 am to 5 pm, Saturday from 10 am to 2 pm and, in summer, Sunday from 11 am to 2 pm.

Getting There & Away

Following is information about ferry services to and from Mariehamn. For information about air services, see the main Getting There & Away section earlier in this chapter.

To/From Turku Viking Line ferries depart from Turku harbour at 10 am daily and arrive in Mariehamn at 3.20 pm. A regular one-way ticket costs 60 mk. Silja Line departs Turku at 8 pm (10 pm in summer) and arrives in Mariehamn around 2 am. You can catch the Stockholm ferry back to Turku at about 2 am.

From Naantali Viking Line departs from Naantali at 11 am daily in summer. The trip takes almost six hours and costs 45 mk one-

way. At the time of writing it was not possible to return to Naantali from Åland this way.

To/From Sweden You can catch a Viking Line (departs in the day) or Silja Line (departing at night) ferry from Stockholm. The *Birka Princess* has afternoon departures from Stockholm from Monday to Thursday, returning the next morning. The *Ålandsfärjan* plies three times daily between Kapellskär and Mariehamn.

Getting Around

A local bus services the town, departing from Nygatan. For bicycles, RO-NO Rent, at Västra Hamnen (☎ 12821) and Östra Hamnen (☎ 12820), is the biggest rental firm. There are daily/weekly rates for bicycles (30/150 mk), three-speed models (40/200 mk) and mountain bikes (70/350 mk). RO-NO Rent is open 1 June to 31 August from 9 am to noon and 1 to 7 pm. At other times, arrangements can be made by phone.

RO-NO Rent also rents boating and windsurfing equipment, and scooters can be had for 140 mk per seven hours, including free mileage and full tank.

Mainland Åland & Around

The largest islands of the archipelago form a group which is the most popular destination in the province. This is where many of the oldest historical landmarks in Finland are found. Bicycle tours are popular in summer, and bridges or ferries connect the various islands here to make up a large enough area for an interesting week of touring.

ECKERÖ

The island of Eckerö is in the westernmost municipality (population 820) in Finland, just a two-hour ferry ride from mainland Sweden. This is the area most like a Little Sweden, and vacationing Swedes constitute

ÅLAND

a majority of the population during the summer season. Eckerö has long been popular among tourists, having been a well-known holiday spot in the 1800s. The distance from Mariehamn to Eckerö (40 km) makes this a suitable day trip by bicycle. Eckerö has two main centres: the area around the church and Storby.

Storby

This small village, ironically named 'Big Village', is the de facto centre of Eckerö. Storby has beautiful 19th century wooden buildings, but it's nature that makes it such an attractive place to spend summer evenings.

Eckerö Post och Tullhus The old post and customs office, near the harbour, was completed in 1828, during the era of Tsar Alexander I of Russia. The building was designed by the famous architect Carl Ludwig Engel, who also designed parts of the centre of Helsinki. The building was meant to be a bulwark against the West and, for that reason, is far more grandiose than a post office in a small village should be. The post office here is open from 9 am to noon and from 1 to 4.30 pm Monday to Friday, and includes an art gallery. The main building contains another art exhibition at door B, usually open from mid-June to mid-August from noon to 6 pm. You can also stay in the post office building – contact Hotell Havsbandet for details (see the later Places to Stay section). The large wooden chair, made in 1971, is an artistic creation of designer Zoltan Popovits.

Postrote Muséet This museum is devoted to the old mail route. The communication link across the Baltic has passed through Åland since Viking times. In 1638, the farmers of Eckerö were divided into *rotas*, groups of eight men, who were responsible for maintaining mail services between Eckerö and mainland Sweden. Mail was transported in small boats until 1910. Over the 350 years that the post rota system operated, more than 200 men lost their lives. On the second Saturday in June in odd-numbered years, old-fashioned boats are rowed to Eckerö from Grisslehamn in Sweden. The museum exhibits objects used in the post rota service, including a mail boat. A video film on the mail services and a slide show about the geography and history of Eckerö are also available. The museum is open from 1 June to 15 August daily from 10 am to 4 pm. Admission is 7 mk.

Labbas Museum The local museum of Eckerö has old archipelago houses with local furniture. There is a section devoted to banking history. The museum is on the main road of Storby and is open from late June to early August Wednesday to Sunday (except Friday) from noon to 4 pm.

Käringsund This attractive harbour, complete with old fishing boathouses, is so scenic it's almost unreal (especially on summer evenings). There's an 800 metre *naturstig* (nature path) from the ferry harbour to Käringsund that includes the guest harbour and its services.

Ålands Jakt och Fiskemuseum This large museum building at the Käringsund harbour contains excellent exhibitions on the most typical professions on Åland: hunting and fishing. The museum is open in summer daily from 10 am to 8 pm, from mid-August to mid-September from 10 am to 6 pm (closed on Monday) and until 15 October at weekends from noon to 6 pm. Admission is 20 mk.

Viltsafari Much of the territory north of Storby is fenced, and deer and wild boar roam in the forests. Forty-minute tours are arranged hourly in summer and a few times in autumn, departing from opposite the Ålands Jakt och Fiskemuseum. The tour costs 25 mk per person. Enquire at Käringsundsbyn holiday village for special arrangements. You can see some animals from surrounding paths and roads, too.

Places to Stay Storby has a great variety of places available. Even so, in July you should call ahead to ensure a reservation.

Käringsunds Camping (☎ 38309) is a down-to-earth camping ground with a few three-bed cottages for 150 mk, and 10 four-bed cottages for 200 mk. Camping costs 35 mk.

Gästhem Ängstorp (☎ 38665), on the main road not far from the old post office, is great value. The main house was built in 1778 and served initially as a post office. It's open from 1 May to 30 October, and has rooms for 245 mk, or 170 mk before and after the high season. There are just six rooms, and they're well equipped and attractive.

Opposite the Labbas Museum, *Storby logi* (☎ 38469) is another central guesthouse where 10 rooms are rented for 125/260 mk for singles/doubles, or less during quiet times. There are a few other such guesthouses near Storby, including *Fyra Små Hus* (☎ 38483) with four good cottages for 265/335 mk, and *Granbergs Gästhem* (☎ 39462) with five rooms for 205/260 mk, or less in spring and autumn.

Behind the old post office, *Hotell Havsbandet* (☎ 38200) is a 29-room hotel with a nice restaurant and singles/doubles from 380/475 mk, or less during quiet times. The good news is that this hotel will assist in arranging accommodation in the large post office building. Enquire in advance.

On your way to Käringsund is *Hotell Eckerö* (☎ 38447), which is clearly banking on Swedes. It has 40 rooms for 395/520 mk during the high season and 340/365 mk in winter, and a restaurant with daily specials.

Käringsundsbyn (☎ 38000), at the far end of the road, is the largest and oldest holiday village on Åland. There are 44 cottages from 310 to 415 mk, depending on the season. The cosy *Fyrvaktarstuga* takes 10 people and will be yours from 700 mk per night. There are all kinds of activities available, and the restaurant is busy at weekends with Swedes dancing to their own kind of live music. There is also a cheaper café.

Boasting a dozen cottages, *Alebo stugor* (☎ 38575), 200 metres from the main road, provides the two large companies with further competition but rents by the week in July. Some cabins start from 260 mk per day.

Places to Eat In addition to the restaurants and cafés in the hotels and holiday resorts mentioned in the previous Places to Stay section, you can eat in Storby village at *Pirjo's Café*, which is at the Esso petrol station opposite the Mathis supermarket, or at the *Hem Bagarn* bakery, which is a bit closer to the harbour. There's also a café at the harbour, while *Jannes Bodega* is an attractive little café right at the guest harbour in Käringsund. *Café Lugn & Ro* at the old post office serves sandwiches and hamburgers in historic surroundings.

Degersand

Eckerö has by far the best beach in Åland. Degersand, approximately nine km south of Storby beyond the village of Torp, has long sand dunes and is certainly worth the extra bicycle trip.

Quietly located close to a beach, *Österängens Hotell* (☎ 38356) has rooms at 310/435 mk during the high season, or less during other times. There are also cottages for rent at Degersand.

Kyrkoby

The old centre of Eckerö is now a quiet rural place that boasts a medieval church, a 15-hole golf course, and an adjoining restaurant.

Eckerö Church The St Lars Church of Eckerö stands alone near old burial mounds, some five km west of the harbour. It is a small church from the 13th century, and although there is a 14th century Madonna sculpture, it has more of a 18th century flavour. The church is open Monday to Friday from 10 am to 8 pm, Saturday from 10 am to 6 pm and Sunday from noon to 6 pm.

Places to Stay & Eat *Rusell* (☎ 38499), currently one of the best eateries in the whole province, is in a pink house near the main road. There's a lunch available until 3 pm for 45 mk, but in the evenings, seek local gossip

ÅLAND

downstairs at the pub. You can also stay overnight in one of the rooms upstairs. Enquire within. *Kyrkoby Stugby* (☎ 38610) rents cottages, usually by the week.

Överby

This tiny village serves as a crossing for *Notviken Camping* (☎ 38429), two km south of the Överby. Two-bed cottages cost 140 mk and four-bed ones are 200 to 330 mk. The camping ground also rents boats and fishing equipment.

Skag

In this isolated village on the northern coast, you can stay at *Udden* (☎ 38610), which has cottages for 315 mk per day. (They are rented by the week during the summer high season.)

Getting There & Away

To/From Mariehamn Road No 2 runs from Mariehamn to Eckerö. If you use public transport, take bus No 1. The trip takes 40 minutes and costs 22 mk.

To/From Sweden Eckerö Lines has five connections a day from Grisslehamn during the high season and two or three during the low season. Most of the tours have a bus connection to/from Stockholm and Mariehamn. The boat trip takes two hours, and a combined boat and bus trip from Stockholm to Mariehamn takes five hours altogether. A one-way ticket costs 30 to 36 mk, or 50 to 60 kr.

FINSTRÖM

Finström (population 2250) is the central municipality in Åland, and Godby is the island's second-biggest centre. Godby has a big, well-stocked shopping centre.

Finström Church

The medieval St Mikael kyrka is in a small village five km north of Godby along a picturesque secondary road and is perfect for a stopover on a bicycle tour. The church was probably built during the 13th century and contains a wealth of frescoes and sculptures, including a pietà in the altar, which make a visit here seem like a trip to the Middle Ages. The church is open Monday to Friday from 10 am to 4 pm.

Svartsmara

This village approximately three km south of Finström Church is considered to be one of the best-preserved old villages in Åland.

Godby Arboretum

The Café Uffe på Berget, just before the bridge to Sund, is a good lookout spot. The view from the bridge is great as well. In the immediate vicinity there is the Godby Arboretum, which has both domestic and foreign trees. A walk along the marked trail takes half an hour.

Places to Stay & Eat

Godby Kongresshotell (☎ 41170), an old hospital turned into a hotel, is pleasantly located near the arboretum. Singles cost 265 to 340 mk and doubles are 380 to 445 mk. The place is popular with groups, so phone to check that there are vacant rooms.

Bastö Hotell & Stugby (☎ 42382) on a headland at Bastö, 12 km north-west of Godby, has cottages and hotel rooms for 350/445 mk, a sauna and many kinds of activities.

Grillsnäckan servering, on the opposite side of the road from the shopping centre in Godby, serves tasty hamburgers and other fast food. You should be able to get a fast-food meal for under 30 mk. *Café Uffe på Berget* is a popular place, due to its splendid view over the island. Turn off the main road just before the bridge to Sund.

Getting There & Away

Road No 2 from Mariehamn takes you to Godby. Bus Nos 2, 3 and 4 from Mariehamn all go via Godby. The trip takes 25 minutes and costs 13 mk. To get to other parts of Finström, take bus No 6.

GETA

The northern municipality of Geta (population 460) is quiet and isolated, and it boasts the high 'mountain', Getabergen.

Geta Church

The St Göran Church of Geta is not among the most interesting in Åland, and was probably built in the 1460s. The church is open in summer from 10 am to 6 pm. A cemetery from the pre-Christian era can be found about one km south of the church.

Getabergen

The highest peak of this 'mountain' is 98 metres above sea level – not much, but enough to give a good view. At the top you can follow the two km path to the caves of Getabergen. The path is marked by white arrows. The caves are not much to see, but visiting them is a good excuse for a nice walk.

Dånö Island

There is an open-air museum at the end of the road on the island of Dånö – a quiet little place, with well-preserved old buildings. The museum is in an old house that used to belong to a sailor.

Places to Stay & Eat

Granqvist stugor (☎ 49610) has a group of cottages on the opposite side of the road from the Geta Church. Clean two/four-bed cottages are 160/210 mk. *Soltuna* (☎ 49530), at the top of the Getabergen, is a pleasant, well-located group of cottages. Accommodation costs 170/220 mk in two/four-bed cottages. This is a popular place among cyclists. Breakfast is available at the nearby restaurant for 25 mk.

The restaurant at the top of the Getabergen serves breakfast, lunch and dinner. The kiosk at the Granqvist Allservice, opposite the church, sells hamburgers and sausages for 10 to 20 mk.

Getting There & Away

Road No 4 from Mariehamn via Godby takes you to Geta. A daily bicycle ferry connects Hällö in Geta to Skarpnåtö in Hammarland (see the Hammarland Getting There & Away section for details). To get to Geta from Mariehamn, take bus No 2. The trip to the last stop in Hällö takes 50 minutes and costs 30 mk.

HAMMARLAND

The western parts of mainland Åland form Hammarland (population 1300). This is one of the longest inhabited areas in Åland; almost 40 sites of burial mounds have been discovered.

Kattby is the main village, and that's where the church is. From Skarpnåtö in the north of Hammarland, you can take a bicycle ferry over to Geta.

Hammarland Church

The Sta Catharina Church of Hammarland is an attractive church in the village of Kattby. The geometrically attractive little building was probably built in the 12th century. Unfortunately, few old objects have been preserved – one of the exceptions is a baptismal bowl from the 1250s. The church is open daily from 15 May to 31 August from 9 am to 4 pm. There's an Iron Age burial site to the west of the church; it has over 30 mounds.

Kattby to Skarpnåtö

This pleasant route has several places to stop. **Mörby**, some 1.5 km north off road No 1 to Eckerö, has some old buildings and a wool spinnery called Ålands Ullprodukter. It sells homespun yarn and woollen garments. At **Lillbostad** a bit north, there is a ceramics shop, Lugnet Keramik. All products are handmade. West of the village of Sålis, Bovik is a nice fishing harbour. North of Sålis, **Sålis batteri** was a Russian battery during WWI but it was destroyed in 1919. The old road is still there. The road runs via Gäddviken to Skarpnåtö.

Skarpnåtö

All activities in Skarpnåtö centre around the Södergård Estate (☎ 37212 or 37227). The old main building has been converted into a museum, and there's also a handicrafts shop. The site was chosen as the setting for a TV series that depicted life in the archipelago in the 1800s. The owners of the estate also run the bicycle ferry and have some cottages and boats to rent. For fishing, hire a rowing boat for 50 mk per day or 30 mk an evening.

Places to Stay

There are several places scattered around Hammarland. *Kattnäs Camping* (☎ 37687) is some three km from the main road, a bit west of Kattby. Small cottages cost 150 mk. *Björkliden stugor* (☎ 37800), not far from the main road, before the bridge over Marsund, has 15 cottages, but weekly rentals are a rule in summer. Very fine cottages cost from 355 mk per day outside the high season.

Sålis Gästhem (☎ 37613) in the village of Sålis, has clean but simple rooms for 125/250 mk. A few km north, *Gäddvikens Pensionat* (☎ 37650) has rooms for 155/310 mk. *Kvarnhagens stugor* (☎ 37212) at Skarpnåtö has two/four-bed cottages for 180/230 mk. If you use the bicycle ferry, you can camp in the area free of charge.

Getting There & Away

Bus Bus No 1 from Mariehamn to Eckerö runs through Hammarland.

Ferry In June, July and August, bicycle ferries (☎ 37212) run regularly between Skarpnåtö and Hällö in Geta, leaving at noon and 4.30 pm from Skarpnåtö and at 12.30 and 5 pm from Hällö. The trip takes 25 minutes and costs 30 mk one-way. If you want to travel at another time, phone the ferry operators and make arrangements.

JOMALA

Jomala is a typical drive-through region but there are also reasons to stop. The 3150 inhabitants make it the most populated rural municipality in Åland but its location around Mariehamn makes it a suburb of the capital. Jomala has two centres: the village of Jomala, near the church, and Gottby, a typical Åland village. All places in Jomala are within a short day trip of Mariehamn.

Jomala Church

St Olof's Church of Jomala is one of the oldest in Åland; parts of it were built in the 12th century. The church has been recently renovated, and there is precious little left of the original interior. The back of the church has 13th century paintings and 14th century sculpture. Unless you're passing by, you could give this church a miss. It's open Monday to Friday from 9.30 am to 3 pm.

Ingbyberget

This strange field of rocks, on a hill north of Jomala Church near the main road No 2, can be simply explained: it is evidence of the Ice Age. The narrow gorge that leads to the hill is a bit of an adventure, but be careful, as it is often slippery. There are also paths up on the hill, and a picnic site.

Önningeby

The well-known painter Victor Westerholm had his summer house in Önningeby, on the northern side of the Lemström canal. A group of other painters followed him there, and for two decades around the turn of the century, the area was known as the 'Önningeby colony' of painters. There's a small museum here, open daily except Monday from 10 am to 3 pm. Admission is 10 mk.

Getting There & Away

From Mariehamn, you can catch bus No 3 to Jomala Church, bus No 5 to Önningeby or bus No 1 to Gottby.

LEMLAND

Lemland municipality is between Lumparland and the Lemström canal, which is five km east of Mariehamn along road No 3. It was built in 1882 by POWs. Lemland's population is 1400.

Lemböte Chapel

South of road No 3, just past the canal, there is an old chapel in the middle of the woods. The chapel is open to the public, and a peaceful place worth a visit. Apparently the chapel dates back to the 13th century, and there's a large burial mound site around it.

Lemland Church

One of the more valuable medieval buildings, the Sta Birgitta Church of Lemland has

13th to 14th century wall paintings that were only discovered in 1956. There is also a rare 14th century Madonna. The church is in the village of Norrby, which is Lemland's centre. It is open from 9 am to 3 pm Monday to Friday. There are burial mounds from the Iron Age nearby.

Herrön
This place at the southernmost tip of Lemland is a popular picnic spot. There is a small observation tower for watching birds. Traces of WWI fortifications may be seen in the area.

Places to Stay & Eat
Söderby stugor (☎ 34310) has cottages in the central village of Lemland. You can eat at the café at the road crossing.

Getting There & Away
To get to Lemland from Mariehamn, take bus No 5.

LUMPARLAND
The municipality of Lumparland (population 330) in south-east Åland does not have many sights of note. Despite that, many travellers pass through Lumparland via either of the two popular passenger harbours, Svinö or Långnäs. The St Andreas Church, built in 1720, is one of the newer churches of Åland. This little wooden church, in a beautiful spot at the seaside, is open from noon to 4 pm.

Places to Stay
The cottages of *Långnäsby* (☎ 35557), next to the Långnäs ferry terminal, are a convenient place to stay overnight. Two/four-bed cottages cost 170/220 mk. Another possibility is the cottages of *Svinö stugby* (☎ 35530), in the southern part of Lumparland. The site is just off the main road not far from Svinö harbour. Two-bed cottages are reasonably priced at 120 mk and four-bed cottages cost 200 mk.

Getting There & Away
To/From Mariehamn Take bus No 5. The trip to Långnäs takes 45 minutes. The bus

goes via Svinö, with a connection to the ferry to Föglö.

To/From Sund There is a daily bicycle ferry service between Prästö in Sund and Långnäs. The trip takes 40 minutes and costs 40 mk.

To/From Kumlinge There are one to three ferries a day from Snäckö in Kumlinge to Långnäs in Lumparland. Some of the ferries also call at Överö in Föglö. The trip from Kumlinge takes two hours.

To/From Föglö Two ferry lines travel to Föglö, one from Svinö to Degerby and the other from Långnäs to Överö. Departures on the first route are much more frequent. The Svinö to Degerby trip takes half an hour and the Långnäs to Överö trip takes an hour.

SALTVIK
Was the 10th century Viking capital, Birka, situated in Saltvik? If you visit the national museum of history in Stockholm, you may be convinced that the legendary Viking stronghold was located on the island of Björkö on Lake Mälaren. There is at least one Ålandese archaeologist who will disagree. No doubt this theory is without any further proof, but nowhere else on the Åland archipelago is prehistory as evident as around this north-eastern region of mainland Åland. Much of this is a result of careful preservation of old burial sites. There are several places worth a visit, and many other places that simply remind one of the historical value of the area.

Saltvik is also known for having the highest 'mountain' in Åland, Orrdals klint. The quiet, hilly region offers historical walks and free accommodation. Its population is 1600.

Kvarnbo
The central village of Saltvik has a strongly historical atmosphere. The large Sta Maria Church dates from the 12th century. It is probably the oldest church in Finland. There are some wall paintings and sculptures from the 13th century, but most of the paintings

are from the Lutheran era, from the 1600s. The church is open Monday to Saturday from 10 am to 4 pm. Opposite the church there is a very old *tingsplats* (meeting and cult site), complete with its bogus Birka monument. Along the road, there is a sign, 'fornminne', that points to the Johannisberg burial mounds. There are 180 mounds in this fenced Iron Age site. Use the stairs to enter the area.

Getting There & Away Bus No 3 runs to Kvarnbo from Mariehamn.

Borgboda

The remains of the ancient Viking fortress of Borgboda can be found 600 metres south of the established bicycle route, east of Kvarnbo. Built at the end of the Iron Age (400-1000 AD), Borgboda was the biggest of the six fortresses that were used here during the Viking heyday. Some ruins of the stone parts can be seen today, but otherwise it's just a cow field with a nice view. You will pass the Ängisbacken burial mounds along the path. In 1985, some bronze items were unearthed here.

Orrdals Klint

This is the highest mountain in Åland, a full 128 metres above sea level, yet it is nowhere as crowded as the much lower hill in Geta. One reason for this is its isolation, but this might be a good reason to go there. There is a simple tower with good views, especially to the eastern archipelago. Some rare birds can be heard or even seen. There is a marked walking track from behind the hut that you can follow.

Långbergsöda On your way to the top, there is an artificial prehistoric site and a walking track, complete with dugout canoes and seal-skin tents'on the shores of an artificial pond. If you follow the road up to the parking area, you may complete your 'prehistoric trek' by visiting up to 15 sites, some dating to 4000 BC. Although Långbergsöda is the pride of the locals, it is little to write home about.

Places to Stay The simple hut on top of Orrdals klint has four beds with mattresses and blankets. Few people seem to stay overnight here, but many curious 'early birds' often peep in while you're still snoring. To sleep here, be prepared for a very long bicycle ride and a long walk to the top. Bring sheets or a sleeping bag, a torch (flashlight) and matches. Carry up all water and food you may need. Do not take wood from living trees.

Getting There & Away There is no public transport. Go by bicycle. You can pedal all the way to the Orrdals klint stairway. There is also a car park at the Långbergsöda track, but it's a long walk to the mountain from there.

To find the place, study your map first. The gravel road takes twists and turns, forks many times, and finally gets very narrow. It's also an uphill job at the end. There are occasional signs, though, and it is a scenic route. The stairway takes you to the hill, and there is white paint on the rock to show the way to the top.

SUND

Sund in the east is one of the most interesting municipalities in Åland. There are several places not to be missed, including a medieval castle and a church, the ruins of a Russian stronghold and a large open-air museum. Sund is just 30 km from Mariehamn, which makes it an ideal first overnight stop on a slow-paced bicycle tour. Less than 1000 people live in Sund.

Kastelholm Area

The impressive Kastelholm Castle is one of the most interesting places in Åland. Its exact age is not known, but it was mentioned in writings as early as 1388. Parts of the castle have since been rebuilt. Kastelholm was of strategic importance during the 16th and 17th centuries, and members of the Swedish royal family governed it at that time. In 1634, the legal position of Åland was changed, and the importance of the castle declined. The castle has been under renovation since 1980.

To see it you will have to join one of the several daily guided tours that are arranged in summer. Tours cost 20 mk per person, and tickets are sold at the gate to the Jan Karlsgården Museum.

Vita Björn Jail Museum In the castle area, close to the entrance to the Jan Karlsgården Museum, there is a jail museum called Vita Björn. This little museum is certainly worth a visit. The building was used as a jail from 1784 to 1974, and the exhibition shows how jails have changed over time. The museum is open from 1 May to 30 September from 10 am to 5 pm daily. Admission is free.

Jan Karlsgården Museum This magnificent open-air museum occupies a quaint precinct near Kastelholm Castle. Traditional buildings from the archipelago have been gathered here, and the old Åland culture is alive and well. It's certainly one of the best places in all Finland to witness the Midsummer festival. The museum is open from 2 May to 30 September daily from 9.30 am to 5 pm (in July to 8 pm) and admission is 10 mk.

Golf Åland's first golf course (☎ 43883 or 43723) is a 27-hole test across the bay from Kastelholm Castle. You must have a green card to be allowed to play.

Places to Stay & Eat *Kastelholma Gästhem* (☎ 43841), a guesthouse, gives good value for money. It has a main building, and an old henhouse that has been converted into hotel rooms. If there is room in the main building, stay there – the rooms are excellent. At 150/260 mk for singles/doubles, the price is right. For an extra 25 mk, you can have a good breakfast brought to your room.

The restaurant opposite the Jan Karlsgården Museum serves both light snacks and real meals. The cafeteria side is cheaper than the actual restaurant. This is one of the places to stuff yourself with those incredibly tempting Åland pancakes!

Getting There & Away Bus No 4 from Mariehamn to Vårdö goes via Kastelholma Castle, 23 km from Mariehamn. The area is a bit off the main road (No 2).

Bomarsund

The ruins of Bomarsund Fortress are a memorial to the time when Åland, together with the rest of Finland, was under Russian rule. Åland was of strategic importance to the Russians, and after the war of 1809, Russian troops were sent to Åland. The Russians started to build Bomarsund, a strong fortress against the Swedes. Later, during the Napoleonic Wars, Russia allied itself with England and Sweden against France, and the building of the fortress was discontinued until 1829. The main fortress, finished in 1842, was big enough to house 2500 men. It was destroyed by the French and the English during the Crimean War. The fortress was never rebuilt, and the remaining stones were used to build houses. The ruins of Bomarsund can be seen on both sides of road No 2, between Kastelholm and Prästö. The most impressive area is just before the bridge to Prästö.

Djävulsberget This hill to the north of the road, half a km before the Bomarsund bridge, is an excellent lookout and picnic spot. The hilltop can be reached by car.

Other Attractions Bomarsund covers an amazingly large area, and you will need the entire day to visit all its sights. There are the remains of a 300-metre-long food storage building, the residential area of Nya Skarpans, the unfinished A-Tower, the remains of a hospital and much more. Unfortunately, relatively little of these structures has survived.

Places to Stay & Eat The pleasant *Puttes Camping* (☎ 44036), right next to the Bomarsund area, has a large grass field at the foot of a rocky hill. There are double cottages at 110 to 140 mk, and four-bed ones for 130 to 160 mk. Camping is 10 mk for each tent, person and car, and you can bathe in the sauna for a fee. *Bomarsunds Värdshus* (☎ 44036) has rooms for 155/290 mk.

Prästö Island

This small island is joined to the mainland island by a bridge. It is mostly known for its graveyards, although there is a small **Bomarsund museum** opposite the fortress. The museum is open from May to August Tuesday to Sunday from 10 am to 3 pm. Admission is free. The island of Prästö is also an important entry point to the mainland from the island of Vårdö (and further from mainland Finland on the northern ferry route).

Historic Graveyards There are three separate graveyards on the island of Prästö, all dating back to the Russian occupation. The first graves may be from the 1810s, but the oldest date to be found on a tombstone is 1826. There is a sign near the Prästö Turistservice. Follow the dirt road one km, and turn left to find the old Greek Orthodox graveyard. It's the oldest of them all, an idyllic site near the water. To your right as you enter the old graveyard, a sign will direct you to the Jewish and Muslim graveyards, side by side.

Near the ferry site, there is another road sign, to the Christian graveyard. This is an eerie place, with small fenced sections and plenty of empty space. You should hear a distant thunderstorm in this kind of a place, especially if you're alone.

Places to Stay *Prästö Turistservice* (☎ 44045) on the main road has two/four-bed cottages at 170/220 mk. You can pitch your tent here for a fee, and there's a simple kitchen to test your gourmet cooking skills.

Sund Church

The lonely St Johannes kyrka is the biggest church on Åland. It is 800 years old and has beautiful paintings. Note the stone cross with the text 'Wenni E'. According to researchers, it was erected in memory of the Hamburg bishop Wenni, who died on a crusade in 936 AD. The church is has scenic natural surroundings, and there are a few burial mounds near the main road. The church is open daily in summer from 9 am to 4 pm.

Getting There & Away

Road No 2 and bus No 4 from Mariehamn take you to Sund. The bus goes via Kastelholm, Svensböle and Prästö. A bicycle ferry from Prästö to Långnäs in Lumparland departs from 1 June to 15 August daily at noon. The trip takes 40 minutes and costs 40 mk. To reach the church, you will need a bicycle or a vehicle.

VÅRDÖ

The island of Vårdö (population 400), is connected to mainland Åland by a regular ferry. It is not the most thrilling of those tiny municipal entities of the sparsely populated province, but it's a scenic area and an entry point to Åland. The old mail route from Sweden to Finland passed through Vårdö, and some of the old 'milestones' have been put up again.

The main settlement is Vargata, which has a bank, a shop and a post office. I don't consider Vargata a tourist attraction but you may wish to detour from the main road to visit the quaint village that is famous for its gardens and nice houses.

Vårdö Church

This weird looking 15th century building is one of those lonely churches built apart from the main village. It's not very exciting as there are no medieval treasures inside this one. The unusual roof construction was an eye-sore when it was finished in 1805. The church is 3.6 km from Hummelvik harbour, and it's open daily from 10 am to 6 pm.

Lövö

This village was the scene of a peace conference between representatives of King Karl XII of Sweden and Tsar Peter I the Great of Russia, opened on 20 May 1718, during the Great Northern War. There were up to 1200 participants in this high-class event which saw much French wine and oysters consumed, judging by what has been dug from the earth here. Fine buildings were erected for the occasion but were torn down the following year, when the event ended with few positive results. There was no peace until 1721. There are no monuments from those brave years remaining in the village. **Seffers** is the local museum near the main road, and there is a windmill and a Midsummer pole in the open area behind the museum. Bus No 4 will take you to Lövö from Mariehamn.

Simskäla Island

If you're looking for another quaint island with regular ferry service, this might be your ticket. The island is locally known as the home of Anni Blomqvist who wrote a popular novel on archipelago life. She died in 1990, and her home is now open once a week to visitors.

Getting There & Away Ferries do the 15-minute trip a dozen times daily, sometimes only on request.

Places to Stay

Sandösunds Camping (☎ 47750) has a beautiful seaside location near the bridge that leads to the island of Sandö. This large camping ground is highly recommended and has pleasant two/four-bed cottages for 180/230 mk. You can rent canoes here.

Getting There & Away

To/From Mariehamn Take bus No 4 via Sund. The trip, including a ferry ride from Sund, takes one hour and costs 30 mk. The ferry between Prästö in Sund and Töftö in Vårdö runs whenever needed.

Northern Archipelago Route There are three ferries a day along the northern route. Ferries depart Torsholma on Brändö and call at Kumlinge and Enklinge before arriving at Hummelvik on Vårdö. The trip from Enklinge takes an hour, and the trip from Kumlinge, 1½ hours.

Northern Archipelago

The northern group of Åland islands consists of the archipelago municipalities of Brändö and Kumlinge.

BRÄNDÖ

The municipality of Brändö (population 550) consists of a group of 1180 islands, the most important of which are connected by bridges. Of the villages in the area, Lappo, Asterholma and Jurmo can be reached only by ferry. The special shape of the main island makes it an interesting cycling region – no matter where you go, you will always be riding by the sea.

St Jakobs Church, the wooden church in Brändö, dates from 1893 and is open every day.

Places to Stay

Hotell Gullvivan (☎ 56350) approximately halfway between the two harbours, Åva and Torsholma, has some singles/doubles for 190/350 mk. There are also cottages scattered around the islands, including *Brändö stugby* (☎ 56106) right in the main village.

Getting There & Away

To/From Mainland Finland There are five connections a day from Osnäs in Kustavi to Åva in the northern part of Brändö all year round, and a few more in summertime. The trip takes half an hour.

Northern Archipelago Route There are three connections a day from Vårdö to Torsholma in southern Brändö. The trip all the way from Vårdö takes three hours.

KUMLINGE

If you're pondering whether to take the northern or the southern archipelago route to reach mainland Åland, Kumlinge is your argument in favour of the northern route.

Kumlinge Church

Many consider the Sta Anna Church of

Kumlinge to be the highlight of all Finnish churches. It has the best paintings among Åland churches. The art is not a direct derivative of the 15th century 'People's Bible' as many other medieval frescoes are. This church preserves 500-year-old Franciscan-type paintings with some central European buildings depicted. The church is some two km north of the Kumlinge village and is open in summer daily from 9 am to 9 pm.

Seglinge

It is simple to catch a ferry to this part of the world. The pier you need is eight km from Kumlinge village, on the island of Snäckö, adjacent to Kumlinge, the main island. The ferry is free and will run any time passengers show up. There is no accommodation on Seglinge and no restaurant, only a shop in the main village. There is a relatively charming fishing village near the ferry pier, and the islandscape has its typical charm. It is possible to take the two km walking route to see the rock-drilled wells. In themselves, they are not all that special, but the walk across the empty island is magnificent. There are some picnic tables on the way and at the end.

Enklinge

Three times each day ferries dock at the pier of this picturesque island, north of Kumlinge. Consequently, you have to plan carefully if you want to visit Enklinge, which boasts a museum. **Hermas** has 20 buildings that are all original to this island. The museum (☎ 55334) is 3.5 km from the pier, and is open in June and August from Tuesday to Saturday from 9 am to 4 pm and in July to 7 pm. You should probably not bother the Enklingeites in winter, though.

Places to Stay & Eat

Kumlinge isn't exactly the tourist centre of the world, but there are a few places to stay.
Ledholm Camping (☎ 55662/55647), on the island of Snäckö (it's connected by a bridge), is quite close to the pier for the ferries to Seglinge. It costs 10 mk for each tent, person and car, and you can use the

kitchen and the washing machine in the service building. The site is open from May to September.

The most convenient place for cyclists and those arriving by their own boats is *Remmarina stugor* (☎ 55010) at the guest harbour two km from Kumlinge centre towards Seglinge. There are several clean cottages on a small hill priced at 215/280 mk for two/four. There are showers, a sauna and a small canteen for snacks. The staff may be a bit indifferent, though.

One rather strange place is *Värdshuset Remmaren* (☎ 55402 or 949-529 199), which seems to be closed even during the high season. You should call ahead to reserve a right of admission to this ex-hospital. This is also the only restaurant in the entire archipelago municipality, and although it is often as deserted as the hotel, it is able to put on a pretty impressive buffet for you. Rooms are 300/395 mk, which is a lot for what you actually get, considering what you don't get.

Getting There & Away

Northern Archipelago Route You can visit the Kumlinge archipelago with your own yacht (there are two guest harbours). The only other way to get there is by ferry. MS *Alfågeln* plies between Hummelvik and Torsholma, stopping on both Enklinge and Kumlinge, and MS *Grisslan* leaves from Längnäs in Lumparland. Three ferries a day go from Hummelvik in Vårdö to Enklinge and the northern end of Kumlinge. They then continue on to Lappo and Torsholma. The trip to Enklinge takes one hour, and the trip to Kumlinge takes 1½ hours.

To/From Lumparland One or two ferries a day go from Långnäs in Lumparland to Snäckö in Kumlinge, via Överö, in the Föglö island group. The trip takes two hours.

To/From Sottunga There are ferry connections on Friday, Saturday and Sunday.

Southern Archipelago

The southern group of Åland islands consists of the municipalities of Föglö, Kökar and the tiny Sottunga. It is Kökar that makes this way interesting for those looking for a route between Åland and mainland Finland.

FÖGLÖ

This archipelago municipality can conveniently be visited from mainland Åland. It's also possible to use Föglö as an overland leg on the trans-archipelago boat tour to qualify for a free trip. It would cost you money to take the ferry from Långnäs to mainland Finland. If you catch the same ferry from Överö, another island in the Föglö island group, you are considered a 'long-term' visitor to the archipelago and will be granted a free ride to mainland Finland. Överö also has ferries to Kumlinge.

This unusual island group has only 600 permanent inhabitants, but there are occasional parties in Degerby, the main village, or the dance hall further inland. The church has a terrific location and some of the roads reveal glimpses of that fine seascape.

The island was first mentioned in 1241 by a Danish bishop who landed here en route to Tallinn. An inn was founded in 1745 at Föglö, at the Enigheten Estate. The local population lived by fishing and farming, and were subjected to the taxes and demands of two governments, Swedish and Russian.

Degerby

The 'capital' of Föglö is a small village that is noted for its unusual **architecture**. Most of the Föglöites have traditionally been civil servants, not farmers. There is no specific reason for the houses not to stand close to each other. Some of them have been built in Art Nouveau or Empire styles instead of the traditional archipelago style. In the red building right at the harbour, you will find the local **museum**. It is open from mid-June to early August daily except Monday from noon to 6 pm. Admission is 5 mk.

Places to Stay *Enigheten* (☎ 50310), one km to the left of the ferry terminal of Degerby, is a fine place to stay overnight. The buildings are old and have been maintained in their original form, so there are no toilets or showers in the rooms. The modern facilities are in another building, a few metres from the sleeping quarters. The inn is open in summer. Single rooms cost 90 to 140 mk, doubles are 180 to 220 mk and booking is essential. The good breakfast costs 20 mk.

Seagram (☎ 51092), a small guesthouse with six rooms and a restaurant, has rooms for just over 100 mk, including breakfast.

Föglö Church

The Sta Maria Magdalena Church is located quite a way from Degerby, and getting there is half the fun, as the road is scenic. The church is not very impressive but the way it rises from the plain rock bed is awesome. It was probably built in the 14th century. It is open from 15 June to 15 August weekdays from noon to 3 pm.

Getting There & Away

There are many ways to enter Föglö, but they all involve ferries.

To/From Lumparland A dozen or so ferries a day make the one-hour trip between Svinö and Degerby. They can be crowded during the high season. From Långnäs, there are one or two ferries a day, which continue on to Kumlinge. They stop at Överö, but only if there's demand; there usually is.

To/From Kumlinge One or two ferries a day from Kumlinge stop at Överö, on request, and then continue on to Långnäs.

KÖKAR

Kökar, with its unusual vegetation, barren landscape and quiet pockets of island nature, ranks high among Finland's tourist attractions. Although a glimpse at a map indicates its isolation from the rest of the world, it is not really difficult to reach by free ferry.

Even so, Kökar is not yet overly touristy. Its entire population numbers a staggering

318 individuals, but don't underestimate this figure: in 1994, the growth rate here was 6%, higher than in any country in the world! The main town is Karlby, which has a shop and a very quiet post office.

Hamnö
The main sight in Kökar is this historical island, connected to the main island by a bridge. Since time immemorial, boats have been anchored at its shores, many of them on the Hansa trade route between Germany and Turku. A small Jesuit Franciscan community settled here in the 14th century. The monastery has had 13 members at most. The main building is long gone, but the present church, from 1784 has been built on the same site. The original basement storage was converted into a chapel and consecrated in 1979. There is a small exhibition inside, and the door is always open. The church is open in summer from 9 am to 9 pm. If you have more time, scan the surroundings for more historic remains. Near the church is an area map.

Kökar Museum
There is a small museum on the opposite side of the island, in the village of Hellsö. The museum in open from mid-June to mid-August from 1 to 5 pm daily. Entry is 10 mk.

Places to Stay
Antons Gästhem (☎ 55729) is a red building along the road from the harbour towards the church. It is open from 1 June to 15 August. It has simple singles/doubles for 190/280 mk, or a little more during the high season. Breakfast costs 25 mk extra.

Kökar logi (☎ 55889), a homestay between the harbour and Karlby, has five rooms and is open from Midsummer to the end of July.

Hotell Brudhäll (☎ 55955) is the top establishment of Kökar right in the middle of Karlby. The hotel has 20 rooms, a restaurant and an impressive location at the waterfront. Singles/doubles cost 270/370 mk.

Beyond Karlby is *Österlunds Camping*

(☎ 55782), a small cottage business in the middle of potato fields. It has eight mid-priced doubles in houses, and a café in a barn.

Getting There & Away
From mainland Finland, there are only one or two launches daily, from Galtby. To get there, you will need to pass through the islands of Kuusisto, Parainen and Nauvo to the island of Korppoo. The problem with this route is its popularity. Expect extra hours on Friday going to Galtby and on Sunday going to Turku. Buses will drive straight to ferries, though. It is also possible that the ferry from Galtby will be full. Then you will understand the benefits of a bicycle (or hitchhiking). The trip from Galtby to Kökar takes two hours, and there is usually food available.

It is much easier to get to Kökar from Åland. There are three to five connections a day from Långnäs to Kökar, via Överö (on Föglö) and Sottunga. The ferry also stops at the small island of Husö. Travel time is 2½ hours from Långnäs.

SOTTUNGA
Sottunga (population 129) is the smallest municipality in Finland. There are more cows than people on the island. Despite the small population, the island has its own bank, shop, school, health care centre, library and church.

The wooden Sta Maria Magdalena Church in Sottunga was built in 1661 and renovated in 1974. The best thing to see on Sottunga, it's open from 10 am to 6 pm, and services are held at 11 am on Sundays. The fishing harbour is at the northern end of Sottunga. A short walking route starts at the harbour.

Places to Stay
HE-övernattningsstugor at the harbour has two-bed cottages for 170 mk per night.

Getting There & Away
Ferries on the southern archipelago route, as well as occasional ferries from Kumlinge, will take you to Sottunga.

Turku & Pori Province

The south-west of Finland is often called 'Finland Proper', a description that may well derive from early Swedish settlers. Once you've toured the country, you may decide that the *real* Finland is nowhere near Turku & Pori Province. Whatever you think, this *is* the most historic part of Finland, with medieval stone churches in every other village. The Turku area, along with Åland, also has some of Finland's most beautiful islands. You can do some of the finest island-hopping in Europe, and if you plan ahead it may all be for free.

Turku

Turku (Swedish: Åbo) is by far the most popular gateway to Finland, due to the inexpensive ferries (free with some rail passes) from Sweden. The oldest town and the first capital of Finland, Turku (population 163,000) has much to offer the visitor.

History
The Turku area has been inhabited for several thousand years. Turku was named Åbo because it was a settlement (bo) at the Aura River (å). The Finnish name Turku is derived from the word for marketplace. In 1229 a Catholic settlement was founded at Koroinen, near the present centre. Work soon started on the new church (consecrated in 1300) and the castle. At times Turku was the second largest town in Sweden. Both the early Catholic Church and the Swedish administration ran what is present-day Finland from Turku. During the 17th century, Count Per Brahe lived in the castle. The university of Turku, the first in Finland and the second-oldest in Sweden, was founded in 1640.

Fire destroyed Turku several times over the centuries, but the biggest blow to the town was the transfer of the capital to

Highlights
- Historical Turku, the oldest town in Finland.
- Turku Cathedral, the most notable church in Finland.
- Decorative medieval churches, including Mynämäki Church, the largest medieval church in Finland.
- Naantali, the most popular summer town in Finland.
- The old wooden town of Rauma.
- The Pori jazz festival every July.
- Satakunta Museum in Pori, among the four best regional museums in Finland.
- The Sagalund Museum on Kimito Island, the best local museum of the Swedish-speaking regions.

Helsinki in 1812. Turku still has still a unique flavour, but locals still haven't forgiven Helsinki, or 'the town in the east', as it is called around Turku.

Today, Turku is a substantial city with fine attractions, though locals sometimes joke that after Turku spread culture to the rest of Finland, it never returned. Much of this is due to unscrupulous developers after a quick

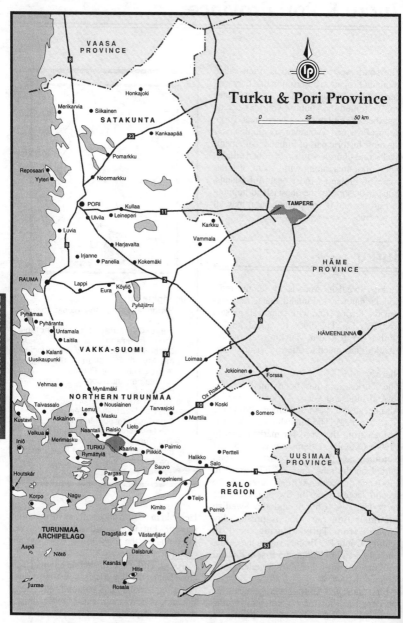

markka, with little appreciation of aesthetics or history. This phenomenon is called 'Turku Sickness' by the rest of Finland. Recently, however, there has been a renaissance of the historical past. New museums have opened, and some traditional restaurants have re-opened.

Orientation

The city centre is a few km from Turku harbour, and accessible by train or bus from each arriving ferry. The city centre is on both sides of the Aurajoki River, and everything is well within walking distance. Aurakatu, Kauppiaskatu, Eerikinkatu and Yliopiston-katu around the market square are the main streets.

Information

Tourist Office The main tourist office Kaupungin Matkailutoimisto, at Aurakatu 4 is open to 7.30 pm and in summer on week-ends from 10 am to 5 pm. The Tourist Association of South-West Finland, at Läntinen Rantakatu 13, is open from 8 am to 3.30 pm on weekdays and handles cottage bookings and tours.

Youth Travel Information Café (☎ 253 5749) at Läntinen Rantakatu 47 is open most of July and August. It offers a meeting place, a left-luggage service and somewhere to take a shower. The centre is open daily 9 am to 9 pm. Bicycles can be hired for 10 mk per day.

Money Suomen Matkavaluutta has an exchange booth near the market at Eerikinkatu 12, with better rates than banks. It is open weekdays 9 am to 6 pm, weekends 9 am to 4 pm. Exchange rates on the ferries are lousy.

Post & Telephone The main post office, at Eerikinkatu 21, 20100 Turku, is open from 9 am to 5 pm, Monday to Friday. The Tele company is nearby at Humalistonkatu 7.

Travel Agencies Kilroy Travels (☎ 233 7033) is at Hämeenkatu 14. WK Matkatoimisto (☎ 233 5333) at Linnankatu

35 is an agent for some cargo ships that sail between Helsinki and Germany.

Library The fine library building is open from 10 am to 7 pm, Monday to Friday. Käsikirjasto on the second floor houses maps, guidebooks, imported magazines in several languages and an Internet terminal.

Books & Maps Akateeminen Kirjakauppa and Suomalainen Kirjakauppa, both within Hansa Shopping Arcade, sell a wide choice of imported magazines. You can find news-papers also at R-kioski at Eerikinkatu 2, and at the railway station.

Left Luggage There are 10-mk lockers at the railway station.

Emergency Services For a general emer-gency dial ☎ 112; for a doctor call ☎ 10023. There's a 24-hour pharmacy at Aurakatu 10.

Turku Castle

The castle, near the ferry terminals, is a must for everyone visiting Turku. It houses an interesting historical museum, with many rooms decorated to resemble a specific decade or century. There are two prisons, a prehistoric section and a room where Count Per Brahe (founder of many towns in Finland) lived in the 17th century. Founded in 1280 at the mouth of the Aurajoki River, the castle has been growing ever since, with recent renovations making it the most notable historic building in Finland. It's open mid-April to mid-September daily from 10 am to 6 pm, at other times to 3 pm. Admis-sion is 20 mk.

Luostarinmäki

This open-air handicrafts museum on the southern slopes of Vartiovuori Hill is the most interesting such museum in Finland. Many carpenters, stonemasons and other workers bought plots in the area after 1779, when the first plots were allotted. When the great fire of 1827 destroyed most of Turku, the settlement in Luostarinmäki survived. Since 1940, it has served as a museum. There

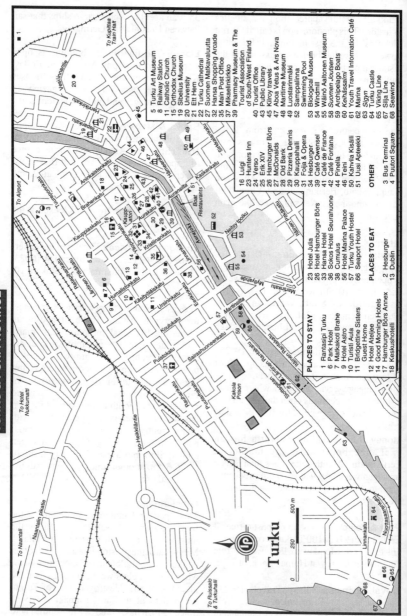

PLACES TO STAY

1 Rantasipi Turku
6 Park Hotel
7 Matkakoti Brahe
9 Hotel Astro
10 Turist Aula
11 Bridgettine Sisters
    Guest Home
12 Hotel Ateljee
14 Good Morning Hotels
17 Hamburger Börs Annex
18 Keskushotelli
23 Hotel Julia
26 Hotel Hamburger Börs
33 Hansa Hotel
36 Sokos Hotel Seurahuone
38 Cumulus
56 Hotel Marina Palace
57 Turku Youth Hostel
66 Seaport Hotel

PLACES TO EAT

2 Hesburger
13 Dublin
16 Luigi
23 Hunters Inn
24 Verso
25 Erik XIV
26 Hamburger Börs
27 McDonalds
28 Old Bank
29 Pizzeria Dennis
30 Kauppahalli
31 Folja & Opera
34 Hesburger
39 Café Qwensel
41 Café de France
42 Café Fontana
44 Pinella
46 Teini
50 Kahvila Kisälli
51 Uusi Apteekki

OTHER

3 Bus Terminal
4 Puutori Square
5 Turku Art Museum
8 Railway Station
15 Catholic Church
19 Orthodox Church
20 Sibelius Museum
21 University
21 Ett Hem
22 Turku Cathedral
27 Suomen Matkavaluutta
32 Hansa Shopping Arcade
35 Main Post Office
37 Mikaelinkirkko
39 Pharmacy Museum & The
    Tourist Association
    of South-West Finland
40 Tourist Office
43 Public Library
45 Kilroy travels
47 Aboa Vetus & Ars Nova
48 Maritime Museum
49 Luostarinmäki
52 Samppalinna
    Swimming Pool
53 Biological Museum
55 Wäinö Aaltonen Museum
58 Suomen Joutsen
59 Archipelago Boats
60 Keihässalmi
61 Youth Travel Information Café
62 Marina
63 Sigyn
64 Turku Castle
65 Viking Line
67 Silja Line
68 Seawind

Turku

are about 30 workshops altogether, representing different trades, and you can always find people working in them. The museum is open daily in summer from 10 am to 6 pm; at other times to 3 pm, Tuesday to Sunday. Admission is 15 mk. Free maps with English text are available.

Turku Cathedral

This medieval cathedral, the most notable of all Finnish churches, is the national shrine of the Evangelical-Lutheran Church of Finland. Its oldest parts date back to the 13th century (it was consecrated in 1300). In the Middle Ages, the cathedral was extended by the addition of side chapels for Catholic bishops. These side chapels became resting places for Swedish war heroes after the Lutheran reformation. In one chapel rests Catherine Månsdotter, Queen of Sweden, wife of Erik XIV, who was exiled to Finland after he went nuts. Frescoes depict other Swedish kings meeting bishops. The cathedral museum displays models showing different stages of the cathedral's construction, as well as medieval sculptures and other religious paraphernalia.

The cathedral is open daily in summer from 9 am to 8 pm. From 1 September to 31 May, it's open 10 am to 4 pm on weekdays, 10 am to 3 pm on Saturday and 2.30 to 4.30 pm on Sunday. Admission to the museum is 10 mk.

Other Churches

Mikaelinkirkko The Church of Michael is an enormous church overshadowed by the more famous Turku Cathedral. The church is not open to visitors so you must become more accustomed to Lutheranism and attend a Sunday service, or better yet, come for a concert. The Art-Nouveau church, designed by young Lars Sonck, resembles Tampere Cathedral on the inside. Many consider this church a mixture of several styles, especially as the exterior is neo-Gothic. The glass windows were added after WWII.

Katariina Church This medieval church, now inside the Turku city area, dates from the mid-14th century. It's open daily from noon to 3 pm. There are subtle frescoes visible inside and the cemetery outside has a great number of old mausoleums.

Maaria Church There are simple paintings in this medieval church, north of the town centre on Maunu Tavastinkatu. Call ☎ 261 7111 for opening hours.

Ylösnousemuskappeli The Chapel of Resurrection at the Turku Cemetery, east of town on the Turku to Helsinki road, is an example of modern architecture in concrete. Get there before 3 pm, Tuesday to Friday.

Orthodox Church This central church, at the market, is open daily from 10 am to 3 pm.

Catholic Church This modern church at Ursininkatu 15, open daily 7 am to 5 pm, is associated with Bridgettine Convent.

Pharmacy Museum

This cute riverside museum at Läntinen Rantakatu 13 is located in the oldest wooden house in Turku. You can see an old laboratorium with aromatic herbs, a fine 18th century interior with hints of 'Gustavian' (Swedish) style, and an exhibition of bottles and other pharmacy items. It's open at the same times as the Turku Castle. Admission is 10 mk, with discounts available. The building also houses a fine café and a herb shop, *Yrttitupa*.

Biologinen Museo

Many reckon that the Biological Museum in Turku is the best of its kind in Finland. The 1907 building is in Art Nouveau style, and contains 13 landscapes from various parts of Finland, complete with stuffed birds and mammals displayed in their natural settings. The museum is on Neitsytpolku behind the theatre, with opening hours similar to the Pharmacy Museum. Ask for a free guidebook in English. Entry is 10 mk.

Maritime Museum

This museum, on Vartiovuori Hill, is in an observatory building designed by CL Engel, the architect. On display are scale models of ships, paintings of ships and navigation equipment. There is also a good view from the 2nd floor. Opening hours are the same as for the Castle, and entry costs 10 mk.

Sibelius Museum

Jean Sibelius is considered the national composer of Finland, and this museum is the most extensive musical museum in Finland. The building itself is a modern adventure in concrete – you could call it ugly – but it's impressive from inside. The main exhibition is on musical instruments from all over the world, but there is a room with exhibits relating specifically to the life and works of Sibelius. You can listen to his music on record, or even better, select your choice from a CD Rom. The museum, near the Cathedral at Piispankatu 17, is open Tuesday to Sunday from 11 am to 3 pm (Wednesday also from 6 to 8 pm). In spring and autumn, there are concerts on Wednesday and occasionally on Sunday. Admission is 15 mk.

Ett Hem

The name of this museum means 'a home'. Ett Hem features a wealthy 18th century home at Piispankatu 14, including old furniture of various styles, a valuable collection of Finnish art from the 'Golden Age', and exhibits of china and glass. It's open daily (except Monday) from noon to 3 pm. Admission is 15 mk.

Wäinö Aaltonen Museum

Wäinö Aaltonen was a leading sculptor in the 1920s, soon after independence. He believed in the idealistic West European notion of a human being, opposing the National Romantic tradition of seeking Finnish roots in the east. The museum also has temporary exhibitions that act as a magnet to both locals and visitors. There is a café on the premises. Near the river at Itäinen Rantakatu 38, the museum is open Tuesday to Sunday from 11 am to 7 pm. Entry is 30 mk.

Turun Taidemuseo

Turku Art Museum, inside a conspicuous Art-Nouveau building, is certainly worth a look if you have an interest in Finnish art. The leading names of the National Romantic era are all here, along with modern art and paintings from other Nordic countries. The museum is on a hill at the northern end of Aurakatu, at No 26. It is open Tuesday to Saturday from 10 am to 4 pm; Sunday from 11 am to 6 pm. There are extended hours in summer on Wednesday and Thursday until 7 pm. Entry is 30 mk, with discounts available.

Aboa Vetus & Ars Nova

These Latin names refer to the archaeological discoveries done of 1994 and 1995 near the Rettig Palace, and a modern art collection in the building itself, located near the river at Itäinen Rantakatu 4-6. The covered area houses a museum on an excavated housing plot from the 14th century, and there are vaulted constructions from later centuries too. This fine museum is open daily from 8.30 am to 7 pm. Tickets are 60 mk for both wings, or 35 mk individually. Ask for the leaflet *A Tour of Aboa Vetus* in English.

Museum Ships

Suomen Joutsen The white 'Swan of Finland' was built in 1902. The Finnish navy bought the ship in 1930 to use as a training ship. During WWII, it served as a mother ship for submarines and as a hospital. After the war it became a training school for sailors until 1988. You can visit the *Suomen Joutsen* from 15 May to 15 August daily from 10 am to 6 pm. Admission is 10 mk.

Sigyn This ship is the world's only surviving barque-rigged, wooden, ocean-going cargo vessel. Launched in the Swedish town of Gothenburg in 1887, it has sailed all over the world. Located on the river near the castle, *Sigyn* is open daily in summer from 10 am to 6 pm. Admission is 10 mk.

Keihässalmi This mine-layer dating from WWII is open daily in summer from 10 am to 6 pm. Admission is 10 mk.

Historic Towns
Three of Finland's five oldest towns are in Turku & Pori Province. The oldest towns are as follows:

Turku (1200) - The oldest town in Finland is dotted with medieval landmarks.
Porvoo (1346) - An attractive seaside town, in Uusimaa Province, featuring fine 19th century wooden sections, several museums and a medieval church.
Rauma (1442) - A Unesco-protected town on the south-west coast, Rauma has a medieval church, ruins and several museums.
Naantali (1443) - The most popular summer town in Finland has a medieval convent church and an attractive wooden 'old town' by the seashore.
Tammisaari (1546) - A Swedish-dominated wooden town in Uusimaa Province, Tammisaari boasts a beautiful seaside location. ■

Activities
Spectator Sports Turkuhalli is also the venue for ice hockey matches. Turku is a hot town as far as ice hockey is concerned.

Swimming & Sauna Samppalinnan Maauimala, an outdoor swimming stadium on the Samppalinna Hill, charges only 12 mk for admission, and this includes a sauna. The 50-metre pool was recently renovated, and though heated, it's only open between late May and late August. Students get a discount and towels and swimwear can be hired. There's a café near the pool. In winter, you have to go to Impivaara indoor pool for swimming and sauna.

Festivals
The Turku Music Festival, in the second week of August, offers traditional classical music. Quite different is the very popular Ruisrock, probably the oldest annual rock festival, held since 1969. Both Finnish and international bands play in Ruissalo Park, near the town centre. For further information on both festivals, contact the Turku Music Festival Foundation (☎ 251 1162, fax 231 3316), Uudenmaankatu 1, 20500 Turku. Down By The Laituri is a town festival in June with music and street performances. Laituri translates as 'pier'.

Places to Stay – bottom end
Turku has one of the best-kept youth hostels in Finland, *Turun Kaupungin Retkeilymaja*

(☎ 231 6578) which is close to the Aurajoki River, at Linnankatu 39, and is open all year round. The staff is friendly and there are all kinds of services, including free use of the laundry, a well-equipped kitchen and lockers for your gear. The hostel is sort of midway between the railway (and bus) station and the harbour so you can walk to it from anywhere in Turku. Beds cost 40 to 60 mk depending on the size of the room.

Bed & Breakfast (☎ 373 902) at Littoistentie 27, less than one km from Kupittaa train halt, has singles/doubles for 100/150 mk.

Places to Stay – middle
Hotel Astro (☎ 251 7838), closest to the railway station at Humalistonkatu 18, has singles/doubles for 210/260 mk, but there are only 38 rooms. Cheaper still, *Matkakoti Brahe* (☎ 231 1973), directly opposite Astro, has 15 simple rooms for 130/180 mk. *Turisti Aula* (☎ 233 4484), another place near the railway station at Käsityöläiskatu 11, has 23 clean but not-so-stylish rooms for 160/220 mk. Each room has a TV; some have a shower.

Also in the same area, *Bridgettine Sisters Guest Home*, or Birgittalaisluostarin vieraskoti (☎ 250 1910), at Ursininkatu 15A, is a guesthouse kept by nuns at this Catholic convent. There are 30 clean but simple singles/doubles at a very reasonable 180/280 mk, including breakfast. This is a rare place – rates are lower from 1 October to 30 April.

But you have to respect the lifestyle of the convent which was re-established in Finland in 1986 – 400 years after the convent in Naantali closed.

Places to Stay – top end

Prices in Turku have come down considerably since the first edition of this book and summer prices are even lower. The summer season varies, but usually applies from mid-June to early or mid-August.

Hotel Ateljee (☎ 336 111) at Humalistonkatu 7 is probably the most interesting hotel in Turku. The building was designed by Alvar Aalto, and now features art exhibitions and two studios always inhabited by local artists (and open to visitors). Several rooms have been decorated by the artists and there's an exhibition on Aalto's architecture. There are also live jazz concerts. Singles/doubles are 390/500 mk; in summer all rooms cost 360 mk.

Cumulus (☎ 263 8211), at Eerikinkatu 28, has 310 rooms, two saunas, a pool and a restaurant. Singles/doubles cost from 420/475 mk in winter; in summer all rooms are 345 mk.

Hotel Hamburger Börs (☎ 637 381), is at Kauppiaskatu 6. The oldest hotel in town, it was demolished in the 1970s but one old Art-Nouveau building remains (rooms in this building are not very modern and could be a bargain if you ask). Rooms in the modern building are 425 mk in summer; 520/605 mk at other times). Then there's the annex *Hotel City Börs* across the street, where rooms are cheaper (350 mk in summer).

Hansa Hotel (☎ 417 000), at Kristiinankatu 9, has singles/doubles for 390/450 mk; 100 mk less in summer.

Hotel Julia (☎ 336 311), at Eerikinkatu 4, is one of the finest hotels in Turku. Food is a feature – the main chef, Antti Vahtera, has won several awards. There are 118 rooms, with singles/doubles at 490/610 mk. In summer all rooms are 360 mk.

Good Morning Hotels (☎ 232 0921), at Yliopistonkatu 29A, was previously known as Kantri. It is now owned by the hotel chain of the same name (in plurals!). There's ample parking space and the hotel is very centrally located. Singles/doubles are 280/370 mk; 50 mk off in summer.

Keskushotelli (☎ 469 0469), at Yliopistonkatu 12A, has singles/doubles for 330/360 mk; in summer for 250/290 mk.

Hotel Marina Palace (☎ 336 300) is an enormous edifice near the river at Linnankatu 32.

Singles/doubles cost 590/760 mk. In summer all rooms cost 430 mk.

Park Hotel (☎ 251 9666), at Rauhankatu 1, is an Art-Nouveau building from 1904 that became a hotel in the mid-1980s. There are 21 individually decorated rooms (although brown is the main colour), with singles/doubles at 600/800 mk; 450/550 mk in summer.

Rantasipi Turku (☎ 376 111), at Pispalantie 7, has 150 rooms and a number of other facilities. Singles/doubles are 420/475 mk; 300/345 mk in summer. The hotel is two km from the centre.

Seaport Hotel (☎ 302 600), at the harbour, has singles/doubles for 360/480 mk; in summer for 290/390 mk.

Sokos Hotel Seurahuone (☎ 637 301), at Humalistonkatu 2, has a rustic decor and the popular Memphis pub. Singles/doubles are 390/475 mk; in summer all rooms cost 375 mk.

Hotelli Nukkumatti (☎ 260 8111), at Satakunnantie 177, a few km out of the centre, has rooms for 260/320 mk; 240/290 mk in summer.

Places to Eat

Despite its long history, south-west Finland lacks a local cuisine (or whatever there is, such as *klimppisoppa* soup, is not worth bothering with). However, Turkuites maintain a certain sophistication in their dining habits – fine dining is very evident. Nonetheless, you should start your food-hunting at *Kauppahalli* indoor market, to sample something of a local flavour.

Cafés *Pinella*, opposite the Cathedral on Porthaninpuisto, is an attractive wooden villa with coffee and set lunches at 35 to 40 mk. Another fine place to sample pastries, including lemon pie, is *Café Qwensel* at the back of the Pharmacy Museum. The quiet backyard is the quaintest in town. *Café Fontana*, on the corner of Aurankatu and Linnankatu, is an Art-Nouveau café with pastries but unfortunately often closed since it was purchased by a wealthy family not in need of petty cash. *Kahvila Kisälli* is a large café in an 1851 building at the entrance to Luostarinmäki precinct.

Fast Food *Hesburger* is the local favourite, now spreading all over the country. Their beef and sauces are juicy and delicious. Prices are similar to those of other hamburger restaurants in Finland. Hesburger is at Hansa Shopping Arcade on Eerikinkatu, as well as near the bus station and several other locations. Centrally located at the market on Eerikinkatu, *McDonald's* is yet to provide Hesburger with a rival. *Pizzeria Dennis* is a reputable pizza and pasta restaurant at Linnankatu 17.

University Eateries Turku is a university city, so it is always possible to get a lunch for 15 mk at one of the university cafeterias.

Lunch Eateries *Teini*, at Uudenmaankatu 1, is a reborn Turku institution, well worth a visit. Its first life lasted from 1924 to 1963; since 1994 it has offered an enormous choice of dining halls and smaller rooms. Food is not extremely expensive, and you can just try starters, and wash it down with beer or wine. *Foija* at Aurakatu 10 is a very popular place. Food is good, portions are big and prices are OK at 40 to 60 mk. Check out also the nearby *Opera*. A very quiet spot on Läntinen Rantakatu offers a few interesting choices, such as *Café de France* at the French consulate and *Verso*, a vegetarian restaurant with hot dishes as well as salads and home-made bread, open until 5 pm, Monday to Friday. Lunch is from 34 mk, including bread and salad.

Boat Restaurants Turku is more of a river town than any other Finnish town, and a boat restaurant is a must in summer. Every summer a new boat pops up, complete with plastic chairs and brewery-sponsored rain shelters, while sometimes old boats disappear. Working south from Auransilta Bridge, closest to the Cathedral, the *Donna* is one of the most popular and established ones. The more recently opened *Svarte Rudolf* has a bar terrace on the upper deck, and its fine restaurant on the lower deck is well worth a visit. Also recently opened, the *Papa Joe* serves American-inspired meals at reasonable prices. The once-sunken boat was found and rescued in the first half of the 1990s and has been renovated with care. The *Lulu* on the other side of the river is associated with the

monster Marina Palace Hotel. Finally there's the *Majland*, which serves beer and barbequed steak.

Bars For an evening beer, *Old Bank* on the corner of Aurankatu and Linnankatu is worth a visit. The place was previously an attractive bank, hence the name. The summer terrace of *Hotel Hamburger Börs* at Kauppiaskatu 6 is usually the most popular in town. The interior is partly Art Nouveau, partly something else. On Eerikinkatu you have a choice of *Erik XIV* or *Hunter's Inn*, both with a pleasant, British-style decor. *Uusi Apteekki* at Kaskenkatu 1 used to be a pharmacy. Now it's a rather smoky pub. *Dublin*, on the corner of Humalistonkatu and Puutarhakatu, is more like a neighbourhood pub and has a fine decor.

Luigi is an underground restaurant and pub next to the Orthodox Church at the market.

Entertainment
Nightclubs Most locals flock to large hotels for chic nightlife. Erotic bars are new in Turku and there are a few of them. If you have an interest in this kind of entertainment, be prepared to pay a hefty admission fee.

Music The vast Turkuhalli near Ruissalo is the main venue for big events, especially concerts.

Things to Buy
Hansakortteli is the largest shopping centre in Turku, right at the market square. Two large bookshops, Stockmann department store and many fashion and electronic shops will help you find the things you need.

Luostarinmäki sells handicraft in the museum shop. Look for more modern Finnish handicraft at the riverside Galleria Joella at Läntinen Rantakatu 21.

Getting There & Away
Air There are flights from Helsinki to Turku throughout the day. There are also flights to/from Mariehamn and Pori, and direct connections from Stockholm and Hamburg.

TURKU & PORI PROVINCE

Bus The bus terminal has regular departures to all towns and villages around Turku, and several express buses a day to towns in south Finland. It's 143 km and two hours to Pori, 113 km and 1¾ hours to Vammala, 95 km and three hours to Houtskär, and 149 km and three hours to Hanko. Each destination has its own platform.

Buses to Naantali, Raisio, Vahto and other nearby towns depart from Puutori square, not far from the bus station.

Train Turku harbour is the terminus for the south-eastern railway line. There are regular trains from the city railway station to Helsinki, Tampere and beyond. You can also get off at the Kupittaa train halt east of the centre.

Ferry Turku is the major gateway to mainland Finland from Sweden and Åland. The harbour has three terminals, for Silja Line, Viking Line and Seawind. See the earlier Getting There & Away chapter.

Getting Around
To/From Airport Bus No 1 from Eerikinkatu will take you to the airport every 15 minutes for 8 mk. After midnight, a shared taxi is the cheapest transport.

Bus The local bus network is fairly extensive – timetables can be obtained from the tourist information office. A one-day tourist ticket costs 20 mk.

TURKU REGION
Ruissalo
The large island of Ruissalo, just outside Turku (see the Turku Region map), has a large number of attractive old wooden villas with restaurants and cafés, signposted walking tracks and large botanical gardens (entry 10 mk for the greenhouses). It is a nice area to explore with a bicycle or vehicle, or take bus No 8 to the camping ground and walk back through the forest.

Information Tammenterho (☎ 623 471) is an information centre that mostly deals with the natural environment of Ruissalo. A slide show can be seen and suggestions for walking tours are given. A free map is available. The place is open daily in summer from noon to 6 pm.

Places to Stay & Eat *Ruissalo Camping* (☎ 258 9249) charges 65 mk for a family, 35 mk for an individual. It is a high-quality camping ground on a peninsula in the farthest corner of the island. Bus No 8 will take you there. *Hotel Ruissalo Spa* (☎ 44540) at Ruissalo 115 is a superb spa and hotel; singles/doubles are 480/680 mk.

Honkapirtti is a Karelian log-house six km from the bridge. Home-made food, coffee and snacks are available until 5 pm daily except Monday and Friday.

Kuralan Kylämäki
If you want to learn about farming in south-west Finland, this place is worth the effort. Four farm estates contain 20 buildings that preserve a traditional rural lifestyle. The main building, Iso-Kohmo, is a farmhouse from the 1950s. There's a café, a shop and an archaeological workshop. The place is open June to August daily from 10 am to 6 pm. To get there, take bus No 28, or drive four km east along road No 10 towards Hämeenlinna.

Kuhankuono Trekking Routes
Although the Turku area has traditionally been fertile farmland, there are pockets of wilderness near Turku. Kuhankuono itself is a unique border point of seven south-western municipalities (one of which is Turku). From the parking place on the Turku to Yläne road No 204 north-east of Turku, there's a path to the Kuhankuono border post, and tracks to the north, south and west. A free *Kuhankuonon retkeilyreitistö* map is available at the Turku tourist office.

Raisio
The town of Raisio (population 22,000), with its landmarks of agricultural business, is merely a busy suburb of Turku and offers little reason to stay. There is a medieval church near the centre, just at the edge of the

Top: Kaivopuisto Park, Helsinki
Bottom: The Cathedral, Helsinki

Top: Kastelholm Castle, Åland
Bottom: Porvoo riverfront, Porvoo

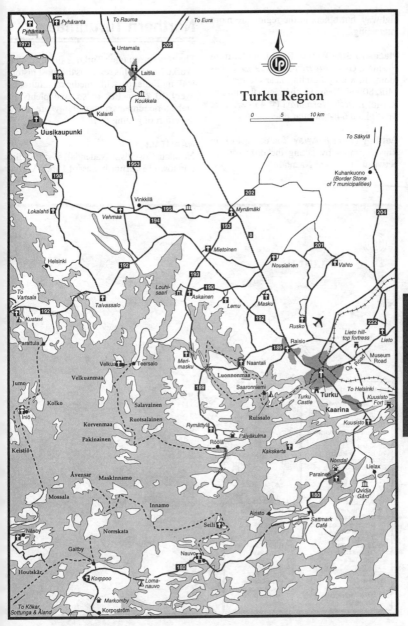

Turku Region

highway, but others in the region are more interesting.

Places to Stay West of Raisio, not far from Naantali, *Gasthaus Henri* (☎ 439 7976) has rooms in a grey building near the road for 240/280 mk. Near the commercial centre of Raisio, *Hotelli Martinhovi* (☎ 438 2333) at Martinkatu 6 has similar prices.

Getting There & Away You can get off in Raisio simply by taking the ordinary bus between Turku and Naantali.

Northern Turunmaa

The area surrounding Turku is simply called 'Turku Land'. This region is the most historical in Finland, with medieval churches every 10 kilometres or so, and plenty of prehistoric remains, although few are worth the effort of getting there.

NAANTALI
Naantali (Swedish: Nådendal) is an idyllic port town 13 km north-west of Turku. Viking

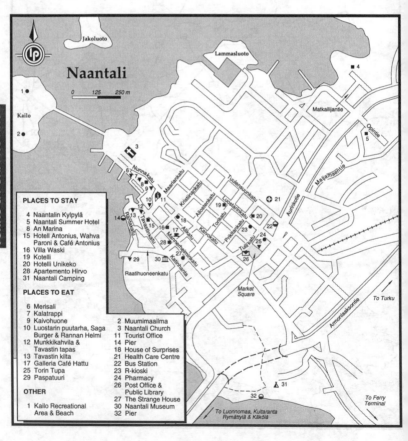

PLACES TO STAY
4 Naantalin Kylpylä
5 Naantali Summer Hotel
8 An Marina
15 Hotell Antonius, Wahva Paroni & Café Antonius
16 Villa Waski
19 Kotelli
20 Hotelli Unikeko
28 Apartemento Hirvo
31 Naantali Camping

PLACES TO EAT
6 Merisali
7 Kalatrappi
9 Kaivohuone
10 Luostarin puutarha, Saga Burger & Rannan Helmi
12 Munkkikahvila & Tavastin tapas
13 Tavastin kilta
17 Galleria Café Hattu
25 Torin Tupa
29 Paspatuuri

OTHER
1 Kailo Recreational Area & Beach
2 Muumimaailma
3 Naantali Church
11 Tourist Office
14 Pier
18 House of Surprises
21 Health Care Centre
22 Bus Station
23 R-kioski
24 Pharmacy
26 Post Office & Public Library
27 The Strange House
30 Naantali Museum
32 Pier

Line ferries from the Swedish town of Kapellskär arrive here. Naantali is a popular day trip from Turku and a typical summer town, lively from June to mid-August and very quiet the rest of the year. The population is 12,500.

History

Naantali grew around a Catholic convent, the Convent of the Order of Saint Birgitta, which was founded in 1443. After Finland became Protestant, the convent was dissolved and Naantali had to struggle for its existence; the convent had been important not only spiritually but also economically. When the pilgrims no longer came to town, people had to find other means of making a living, notably by knitting socks, which became Naantali's main export!

Orientation

Naantali sprawls on both sides of the channel Naantalinsalmi. The town centre is on the mainland, on the north-eastern side of the channel. The island of Luonnonmaa is on the western side. The modern town centre is around the bus terminal, but the old part of Naantali, one km to the west, is by far the most interesting place to visit.

Information

Tourist Office Naantalin Matkailu is the tourist information office (☎ 850 850) at Kaivotori 2, near the guest harbour. In addition to free tourist literature, the office serves as a reservation centre and a travel agent for regional tours.

Post & Telephone The post office is at Tullikatu 11, 21100 Naantali.

Travel Agencies Naantalin Matkailu will arrange regional tours.

Library The library, at the market, is open from noon to 7 pm, Monday to Thursday, and to 3 pm on Fridays. There's also a bookshop at the market.

Emergency Services For a general emer-gency call ☎ 112; for a doctor dial ☎ 10023. There's a pharmacy at Luostarinkatu 25.

Old Town

The old town of Naantali is like a big open-air museum. The town grew around the convent, without any regular town plan, and new buildings were always built on the sites of older ones. Thus, the medieval town plan can still be seen in Naantali. Only the old windmills and storehouses along the shore have disappeared, replaced by the modern guest harbour.

Naantali Church

The massive Naantali Church dominates the harbour area. It was completed in 1462, the tower in 1797. Until this century, the wooden clock face had painted hands which always showed 11.30. People used to say that the end of the world would come when the clock of Naantali Church struck 12.

Inside the church are several valuable items, such as *hostiarum* (tapering monstrance) and several medieval sculptures, the most important of which is Christ's Head on the altar (age unknown). On summer evenings at 8 pm, vespers are played by a trumpet from the church tower. The church is open 2 May to 15 August daily from noon to 7 pm daily, and from noon to 3 pm daily between 16-30 April and 16 August to 30 September. At other times, the church is only open on Sunday and holidays, from noon to 3 pm.

Muumimaailma

The Moomin World of Naantali is a large theme park which is actually located in several parts of this small town. The main attractions are on the island of Kailo, but there are also buildings on the mainland, such as House of Surprises at Kaivokatu 5, and the Strange House at Mannerheiminkatu 21.

A very popular attraction among Finns, Moomin World filed for bankruptcy in 1995, despite almost half a million visitors in its first two years of operation. The town of Naantali stepped in to save the park, and

TURKU & PORI PROVINCE

Ms Moomin

Ms Tove Jansson, creator of the much-loved Moomin children's books, was born on 9 August 1914 in Helsinki to Swedish-speaking parents. Her first drawings were published in a magazine when she was only 14. Her first book on Moomintrolls was published in 1945, and a new title followed every two years or so.

More than 40 years elapsed before the Moomin figures attracted world-wide attention – through a Japanese-made cartoon which has been shown on TV in several countries.

Tove has lived most of her life on various islands off the Finnish south coast. When she tired of the journalists who frequently visited her studio, she moved to a more isolated island. Tove's original drawings are displayed in Tampere, while the tourist trap Moomin World is in Naantali. ■

today it is booming in summer, with Finnish and Scandinavian families crawling all over the place.

Muumimaailma is open mid-June to mid-August daily from 10 am to 8 pm, and is almost solely responsible for the high season in Naantali. At other times in June and August, it's only open on weekends. Admission is 70 to 75 mk; 40 to 45 mk for children.

Naantali Museum

The large museum area features a huge oak that provides shade for the garden. The main building shows how old houses were adapted to shapes in the rock (houses were built straight onto rock as the rocks were too large to be removed). There is old furniture and exhibitions on spa traditions in rooms dating back to 1650. A separate red house can be seen by walking through a nice rose garden. The museum is open 15 May to 31 August daily from noon to 6 pm. Tickets are 6 mk.

Luonnonmaa

There are a few attractions on this island just west of Naantali centre.

Kultaranta The summer residence of the president of Finland, a 56-hectare estate with large rose gardens, can be visited at particu-

lar hours with a guide (the information is at the tourist office), or on Friday from 6 to 8 pm without a guide. The castle is closed to the public.

Farm Museum of Käkölä This old farmhouse is run by a man in his 80s, who tends the garden, and his son, who found hundreds of old farming tools and other items in the barn that now constitutes a charming little museum. You can also purchase woodwork made with a chainsaw. It's open on Sunday from noon to 6 pm and entry is free. To get there, cross the bridge to the island of Luonnonmaa, follow the sign to Käkölä and turn left onto Käköläntie.

Festivals

Sleepyhead Day (27 July) has become a local festival in Naantali. The annual tradition involves the townspeople waking early in the morning to select a well-known person as the 'sleepyhead', who is then woken up by being thrown into the sea. This tradition goes back over 100 years.

The Naantali Music Festival, held in June, features chamber music.

Places to Stay

Naantali is one of the few towns in Finland to offer accommodation in small guesthouses but they are invariably expensive, especially in summer. For budget travellers, Naantali is essentially a day trip from Turku. Some places are not very welcoming, especially after they've hung the *täynnä*, or 'full', sign on the door.

Closest to the harbour, *An Marina* (☎ 435 6066) at Nunnakatu 5 has six clean rooms for 300/400 mk.

On Mannerheiminkatu, *Apartemento Hirvo* (☎ 435 1619) at No 19 is the best value, with a few rooms at 200/350 mk. Staff are friendly, the garden is quiet and you can use the kitchen.

Heading down towards the harbour, *Villa Waski* (☎ 435 1767) at No 10 is another friendly place but its three rooms are usually full in July.

Hotell Antonius (☎ 435 1938) at No 9 has 10 individually decorated rooms (with hints of Art Nouveau) from 380 mk in summer. There are a few cheaper rooms at Luostarin puutarha, their annex restaurant.

Next door to Antonius, *Wahva Paroni* (☎ 435 3722) at No 7 hardly bothers even if you ring the bell; it has a few cottages on the hill for 350 mk. There are also other possibilities – look for signs that say *Huoneita*, *Rum* or *Zimmer*.

The very fine villa at Luostarinkatu 13 is *Kotelli* (☎ 435 1419), with four rooms for 200/250 mk (breakfast is 50 mk). The dining room has heaps of style and the garden is cosy.

A proper hotel nearby at Luostarinkatu 20 is *Hotelli Unikeko* (☎ 436 2852). There are 50 rooms priced at 270/320 mk; a bit less in winter. The price includes breakfast and a sauna bath.

Naantali Camping (☎ 435 0855), on Kuparivuori Hill, is 800 metres from the town centre, between Naantali centre and the Viking Line ferry terminal. This is an exceptional camping ground, with a superb location and good facilities. Camping costs 69 mk per family or 34 mk per person. Two-bed cottages are 160 mk; four-bed cottages cost 210 to 420 mk.

The modern *Naantali Summer Hotel* (☎ 435 6969), at Opintie 1, is open from June to mid-August. Singles/doubles are 200/290 mk.

The top-end establishment is the huge spa, *Naantalin Kylpylä* (☎ 44550), on Matkailijantie, a few hundred metres north of the bus station. Naantali's spa traditions go back as far as 1723, when people began taking health-giving waters from a spring in Viluluoto.

The new spa, opened in 1984, is one of the finest in Finland. All rooms are superb and well equipped, and the whole establishment will pamper you in a way that is unusual in Finland.

If you're not staying in the hotel, use of the spa will cost you 85 mk. This includes several pools and a Turkish bath.

Places to Eat

Naantali caters well to tourists, with a great variety of places to sample good food. However, prices are higher than in other Finnish towns.

Merisali at Nunnakatu 1, right at the harbour, is where everybody who is anybody wants to be seen. The terrace is really nice and there's the popular smorgasbord for lunch (45 mk) and dinner (55 mk), including salads and a great variety of fish.

Kalatrappi at Nunnakatu 3 is a fish restaurant and *Kaivohuone* at Nunnakatu 7 is a nightclub which frequently charges an admission fee.

Luostarin puutarha at Fleminginkatu 6 has a basement pub and an open-air pizzeria for summer days. *Saga Burger* is probably exactly as you would expect it to be. *Rannan Helmi*, another place in the same block but much cosier, has succeeded in attracting a regular clientele due to the 50-mk lunch offer.

Across the narrow street, *Munkkikahvila* is a Moomin-café with doughnuts. *Tavastin tapas* is a large summer restaurant and pub with plenty of style, a nice garden, Red Army-inspired decor and live jazz on Tuesday.

Tavastin kilta at Mannerheiminkatu 1 has meat and fish dishes with prices not too high but not cheap either. A bit further but still at

TURKU & PORI PROVINCE

the waterfront, *Paspatuuri* at Rantakatu 20 is a nice wooden villa with art exhibitions, coffee and meals.

Café Antonius, in the Hotel Antonius at Mannerheimintie 9, is certainly the cosiest place on chilly winter days due to its warm atmosphere. In summer, you will have to endure the combination of style, kitsch and erratic service, but the excellent pastries are hard to beat. There is also *Galleria Café Hattu* at Mannerheimintie 12, a tiny space upstairs from an art gallery.

Torin Tupa is a popular eatery at the market square. Lunch is served until 4 pm for 28 to 38 mk, or choose something from the menu until late. Nearby, *Hesburger* serves its tasty burgers.

Getting There & Away
Bus Virtually all routes to Naantali go via Turku, 13 km away. There are buses to Naantali every 15 minutes from Puutori in Turku.

Ferry The SS *Ukkopekka* sails from 16 June to 11 August daily between Turku and Naantali. This pleasant trip takes either 1½ or three hours (depending on which of the two routes you take), and costs 80 mk one-way, 100 mk return. There are also other boats from Turku.

Viking Line operates a daily ferry in summer between Kapellskär in Sweden and Naantali. The ferry departs Naantali at 11 am and stops at Mariehamn en route. Catch a bus to Kapellskär from Stockholm's central Cityterminalen. There's also a car ferry that sails in summer between Naantali and Långnäs, on Åland.

NOUSIAINEN
Nousiainen Church, built in the 1300s and restored in the 1960s, is where the first (Catholic) Bishop of Finland, St Henry, lies buried. His sarcophagus was made in Flanders in 1430. The church is a triple-aisled hall design, with chalk murals from the early 15th century. It is open from noon to 6 pm, Tuesday to Sunday.

The church is three km from road No 8.

Nousiainen is 21 km north of Turku and there are buses almost every hour.

MASKU
The church in Masku, a few km south of Nousiainen, is from the 14th century. There are plenty of old paintings, a wooden 13th century St John, and weird wall frescoes, which are obviously making an effort to imitate curtains.

LEMU
There is also an old church in this village (the name of which translates as 'bad smell') but it has less appeal than other churches in the region. The building is from the 1460s and is open in summer from 11 am to 5 pm.

Lemu is 16 km north of Raisio and 10 km south-west of Nousiainen. Three to four buses drive daily from Turku via Lemu to Velkua.

ASKAINEN
West of Lemu, Askainen is another small place with scenic countryside, including a white-washed stone church. It was completed in 1653 and includes a great number of coats of arms of the local nobility and a fine pulpit. The church is open 15 May to 31 August daily from 11 am to 5 pm.

Louhisaari
One of the most stunning places to visit in Finland, Louhisaari was a private estate from the 15th century, possibly even earlier. The imposing five-storey manor, built by mid-17th century, was purchased by the Mannerheim family in 1795. The famous former president CG Mannerheim was born here but the family soon lost the property, which later was acquired by the National Board of Antiquities. There are lavishly decorated rooms, including a church and a 'ghost room'. The garden, with very old trees, complements the manor. The museum is two km from Askainen Church, and is open 15 May to 31 August daily from 11 am to 5 pm.

Places to Eat

You can buy some snacks and coffee at *Askaisten Kahvitupa* in the tiny centre. Near the manor, *Kartanon kahvila* serves coffee and food daily until 5 pm in summer.

Getting There & Away

Askainen is 17 km south-west of Mynämäki, 12 km north of Merimasku and seven km west of Lemu. Three to four buses drive daily from Turku to Velkua, via Lemu and Askainen.

VELKUA

Velkua, west of Naantali, is one of the smallest municipalities in Finland, with just 235 inhabitants. Three to four buses drive daily from Turku to Teersalo (the commercial centre of Velkua), via Lemu and Askainen. There are several inhabited islands and a few daily ferries connect the islands to Teersalo. The church from 1793 is on the island of Palva.

MERIMASKU

A free ferry connects Merimasku to Askainen in the north, but you can also get to Merimasku from Naantali. The wooden church was built in 1726 and has plenty of treasures, including a colourful pulpit.

Coming from Naanatali, you can buy a meal at *Särkänsalmi*, at the crossing just past the bridge, five km before Merimasku.

Merimasku is five km off road No 189, 12 km west of Naantali. There are buses from Turku and Naantali every two hours or so, until late afternoon.

RYMÄTTYLÄ

One of the most colourful of all Finnish medieval church interiors is to be found on this quaint archipelago island. The church, located in the middle of the modern village, is open May to August from 9 am to 4 pm.

This heavily indented island group has almost 2000 inhabitants.

Places to Stay

There is the excellent youth hostel *Päiväkulma* (☎ 252 1894) in a large wooden house at the seafront. It charges a mere 35 mk (50 mk for HI nonmembers) per bed. You will need a map to locate this house three km from the village.

Getting There & Away

Rymättylä is 20 km south-west of Naantali. There are buses from Turku every two hours or so. Some continue to Röölä (which has ferry connections to the islands) and further south.

Turunmaa Archipelago

One of the most rewarding routes to Åland runs via islands south of Turku. Free ferries can be taken all the way (especially for those travelling by bicycle or bus), and there are several historical attractions.

GETTING AROUND

All passenger boats and ferries that ply between the islands are free of charge. On some routes, especially between Parainen, Nauvo and Korppoo, there's continuous traffic. Smaller ships that serve inhabitants of the small islands may run only once a day, or even less frequently. The free timetable *Saaristomeri Liikenneyhteydet* is published annually and has accurate information in Finnish and Swedish. See also Kökar (in the Åland chapter) for further information.

KAARINA

This town is kind of a southern suburb of Turku. Its small commercial centre is one of the least attractive in Finland. Kaarina serves as a gateway; it's from here that the trip through the archipelago starts.

Kuusisto Fort

The Swedish Catholic bishops, who actually ran the country in medieval times, built this stronghold in 1317 to defend their power. When King Gustav Vasa of Sweden made up his mind in favour of Lutheranism in 1527, the fort was defeated and demolished, stone by stone. Restoration work has partly saved the fort, although the trip to this easternmost tip of Kuusisto Island (just south of Kaarina centre) is at least half the fun. Turn off road No 180 when you see the sign that says 'Kuusisto kko'. Proceed past Kuusisto church and the manor. You can visit the site anytime.

PARAINEN

Parainen (Swedish: Pargas), south of Kaarina, is sometimes called 'the capital of the archipelago'. It has 740 km of coastline, including nearby islands. To get further out in the archipelago, you will pass through Parainen. Among the population of about 12,000 are many Swedish speakers.

Information

The tourist office (☎ 458 5944) at Fredrikanaukio 1 is open weekdays from 9 am to 4 pm.

Things to See

There are paintings and old treasures in the medieval church, open in summer from 10 am to 8 pm. The nearby chapel houses a church museum. The old town is behind the church. Parainen is also known for its limestone. Visitors can see the biggest limestone quarries in Scandinavia at Partek's site, almost in the middle of Parainen.

Places to Stay

Solliden is the seaside camping ground of Parainen, some 1.5 km north of the centre. There are four-bed cottages for 190 mk. Within the same precinct, *Norrdal* (☎ 458 5955) is a youth hostel in a rustic old building, with beds for only 40 mk, a kitchen and a TV room.

Gasthaus Alvar (☎ 458 5400) is at Kauppiaskatu 2. *Hotel Pargas* (☎ 458 9300) at Rantatie 1 has singles/doubles for 265/320 mk, including breakfast.

Places to Eat

At the seaside, close to the centre, you will find *Hesburger*. Behind the church, *Museokahvila Fredriikantupa* is, as its long

name suggests, a museum café with plenty of historical ambience.

Half-way between Parainen and the island of Nauvo, *Sattmark* is always worth a stop. It is a small 1780-built red wooden cottage with plenty of charm and home-made wheat buns and cakes.

Getting There & Away

There are one to three buses an hour from Turku to Parainen, and five to six buses a day from Helsinki. For further connections, see Korppoo and Kökar.

AROUND PARAINEN
Qvidja Gård

The very fine castle-like stone manor dates from medieval times. Qvidja (Finnish: Kuitia) is in an isolated spot near the village of Lielax (Finnish: Lielahti), off road No 1805, on an island east of Parainen. The oldest parts date back to the 1490s, when it was the property of Catholic bishops. These days the privately owned castle (☎ 886 946) is shown to groups by appointment.

Airisto

One of the oldest holiday resorts, and one of the sunniest places in Finland, this beautiful spot is at the far end of Stormalö island, west of Parainen. *Airisto* (☎ 881 301) is the top-end resort that overlooks the guest harbour.

NAUVO

Nauvo (Swedish: Nagu) is an idyllic island between Parainen to the east and Korppoo to the west. It is connected to both by free ferries which run continuously, without a timetable. Nagu Church dates back to the 14th century and exhibits the oldest Bible in Finland. It is open June to 15 August daily from 10 am to 6 pm, and from 16 to 30 August from 10 am to 4 pm.

Nauvo Archipelago

The MS *Harun* (☎ 949-320 093) sails from the harbour of Pernäs (at Lomanauvo) to the islands of Nötö, Aspö and Jurmo and Utö, which are all within the South-West Archipelago National Park. The boat takes 160 passengers and sails daily except Monday and Wednesday. The trip is free.

The MS *Bastö* sails more regularly between the islands north of Nauvo, departing from Nauvo harbour. The ferry takes two passenger cars and 60 passengers.

The MS *Fiskö* busily sails from the harbour at Kirjais (south of Nauvo) to islands south-east of Nauvo.

Places to Stay & Eat

Lomanauvo (☎ 465 7111) is a large camping ground well hidden in the forest at the Pernäs ferry jetty in the Korppoo (west) end of the island. The cheapest two-bed cottages are 120 mk; there are bigger ones for four at 200 mk.

Much dearer is *Strandbo* (☎ 465 1611) at the Nauvo guest harbour. It is a stately home type building with enough pomp to keep the prices relatively high, say 400/500 mk. *Nagu Marthahem* (☎ 465 1409), right in the main village, has cheaper rooms and a buffet lunch.

Next to Strandbo is *l'Escale*, a French-style restaurant, mainly catering to wealthy sailors visiting the guest harbour. You could give it a miss and instead buy the tasty sandwiches at the Esso *kahvila* right in Nauvo centre.

KORPPOO

Korppoo (Swedish: Korpo) is the most distant island that can be reached without a long car trip. It is connected to Nauvo by a car ferry which operates continuously. The population of Korppoo is 1080.

One of the highlights in the Turunmaa Archipelago is the medieval **Korppoo Church** built in the late 1200s. Treasures in this church include naive paintings on the ceiling and a statue of St George fighting a dragon. The church is open in summer from 9 am to 8 pm.

The MS *Finnö* takes 36 passengers and two cars through the **Korppoo Archipelago**. The harbour of Verkan near Korppoo village is the departure point for several small islands to the south-west, with three daily departures on weekdays, just one on weekends.

Places to Stay & Eat

Forellen (☎ 463 1202), right in the village centre, has four rooms at 100/200 mk. Meals and snacks are also served. The youth hostel *Markomby*, five km south of Korppoo, may be closed; check listings.

Getting There & Away

Korppoo is one of the end points for the Saaristotie buses that run regularly from Turku. Galtby is the passenger harbour, four km north-east of Korppoo centre. A number of free ferries depart from Galtby for Houtskär and Åland. See the Åland chapter for details.

HOUTSKÄR

A cluster of islands off Turku, this municipality (population 710) offers interesting scenery and an old church on the island of Houtskär (Finnish: Houtskari). Up to 94% of the local population speaks Swedish, the highest number in the region.

Näsby on the main island is the main village of Houtskär municipality. The main feature is the **local museum**, with several buildings and a windmill. It's open June and July only, on Tuesday, Thursday, Saturday and Sunday from noon to 3 pm. The old wooden **church**, dating from 1703, has plenty of religious paraphernalia from the 18th century. It's open May to August daily from 9 am to 9 pm.

The MS *Bergö* sails around the Houtskär Archipelago, including an unusual entry point to Åland via the harbour of Torsholma on Brändö. The typical route goes between Näsby and the island of Själö in the north.

Places to Stay & Eat

You'll have to take other ferries to the islands of Mossala or Björkö to find an established place to stay. There's a *folkhögskola* (school) in Näsby that might be able to put you up if you speak to the people in charge. Other than that, pitching your tent for one night, keeping a low profile and not damaging the fragile environs would be the only option. And it's free.

The ship restaurant *Astrea* is moored near the village of Medelby, halfway between the pier and Näsby. In Näsby itself, *Svarte Rudolf* is the local centre of activity, with meals, coffee and beer.

Getting There & Away

There are direct Saaristotie buses from Turku to Näsby. Alternatively, you can choose a route that goes to Mossala or Hyppeis a few times a week, but you may have to change buses after a ferry trip. The simplest way to do it on your own is to take the ferry from Galtby (Korppoo) to Houtskär and pedal your way through the island. The ferry trip takes just 30 minutes and is free.

INIÖ

The isolated island world of Iniö, a municipality of 250 inhabitants, offers some of the most desolate archipelago scenery. At Norrby, the main settlement on the main island, you'll find a stone church from 1801. You can stay overnight in a guesthouse at the harbour.

Getting There & Away

The passenger harbour of Parattula, on the island of Kustavi, is the jumping-off point for the oversized ferry that could transport all Iniöites at one time. You can expect to catch the ferry up to five times a day from 1 June to mid-August. The ferry makes stops at the islands of Jumo, Kolko, Perkala and Iniö (Norrby).

Historical Routes

Because Turku was settled so early, some of the oldest roads in Finland emanate from there. Amidst the concrete and asphalt, little of the old roads remains today. But two old roads can be identified. Ox Road runs to Hämeenlinna in Häme. King's Road, an international route, runs from Oslo to St Petersburg, via Stockholm, Turku and Helsinki.

OX ROAD

The old Ox Road of Häme runs from Turku to Hämeenlinna, as it did before the first crusades in the 1200s. Refer to the Häme chapter for a route description of the South Häme section of the route. The first leg of any interest is at the Lieto fortress.

Lieto Fortress

Some five km north-east of Turku off road No 10 is a museum road that takes you to the rocky hill, Liedon Vanhalinna, or the 'old fort of Lieto'. This is not a building, although it has been estimated that it was here during the 13th century that bricks were used for the first time in Finland. The hill today offers a fine view of the Aurajoki River, plus interesting flora. A **museum** at Vanhalinna Manor at the foot of the hill features archaeological discoveries. The museum is open just on Sunday from 1 to 4 pm, but occasionally also Tuesday to Friday during office hours.

Lieto to Marttila

The **medieval church** in Lieto centre dates from 1336 but most of its treasures are now in the Turku Art Museum. The actual Ox Road continues as road No 223 to **Tarvasjoki**. It is here that the archaic atmosphere of the narrow winding road can be experienced. The Paimionjoki River follows the road and sometimes cows seem to be the only living creatures visible. Many houses have been left empty and traffic is just a fraction of that on the nearby road No 10. **Härkätien museokahvila**, an old museum café, has fallen into decline and is no longer worth a stop. In **Marttila**, the church from 1765 has wooden statues and is open on Sunday only. There's also a large **ox statue**.

Marttila to Somero

The riverside road continues on to **Koski**, with its old bell tower. The road eventually takes you to the long Lake Pitkäjärvi, before reaching Somero. See the Häme chapter for further details.

KING'S ROAD

The equally old and important King's Road is no longer as intact as the Ox Road. The main point with King's Road is not to follow the actual road but to find the old attractions along the route.

Pukkilan Kartano

This manor house, dating from 1755, has belonged to the Rabbe and Rehbinder families. Today it is a National Board of Antiquities museum with an emphasis on old carriages. There is also a herb garden. The museum is on Littoistentie in Piikkiö, and is open mid-May to the end of August daily from 11 am to 5 pm.

Piikkiö

This small village has a stone church but it was built as lately as 1755. Featuring a large hall with plenty of paintings, it is open in summer from 9 am to 4 pm.

Paimio

Another commercial centre, Paimio offers a wide range of services. The church here, similar to the one in Piikkiö, is from 1689, and equally as colourful. A bit north of the centre, the Paimio Sanatorium was designed by Alvar Aalto, the famous Finnish architect, and was to symbolise the beginning of functionalism in architecture. From Paimio, the King's Road initially follows road No 2352, but turns soon to road No 2351 towards Halikko.

Trömperin Kestikievari

The last landmark before approaching the Salo Region, this old roadhouse is one of the two remaining *kestikievari* cafés in Finland. The other one is Kallenautio on road No 66. The word kestikievari is an adaptation of the Swedish word *gästgivare*, which translates as 'guest giver'. This one has coffee and snacks, a home museum and a nice little garden. The last resident died here at the end of the 1960s. The home museum is open

daily (except Monday) in summer from noon to 6 pm; admission is 5 mk. It is 15 km from here to Halikko, 20 km to Salo.

Salo Region

Plenty of prehistoric discoveries and traces of the wealthy Swedish lifestyle await in this region, as well as the archipelago of Kimito where Swedish is still predominantly spoken.

SALO

The industrial town of Salo, south-east of Turku, is the namesake of the relatively well-known Salora television sets, but busier is the Nokia cellular phone factory. Salo has 22,000 inhabitants, but the population of surrounding areas easily doubles that figure. Salo serves as an excellent jumping-off point for tours to historical areas nearby.

Information

Tourist Office The tourist office in the Sininen Talo building at Rummunlyöjänkatu 2 (☎ 733 1274) is open daily from 10 am to 6 pm (to 3 pm on Fridays). The building also houses a café, exhibitions and handicraft shops.

Post & Telephone The main post office is at Turuntie 6, 24100 Salo.

Library The modern public library is at Vilhonkatu 2.

Emergency Services In a general emergency call ☎ 112; for a doctor call ☎ 10023. There are pharmacies on Vilhonkatu at Nos 4, 8 and 14 and at Helsingintie 6.

Things to See

The CL Engel-designed **Uskela Church** was built in 1832. Situated on a hill, the church is open daily from 10 am to 6 pm but is not as interesting as the view from the outside. Despite its name, it's the main church of Salo.

Salo town council manages **Vuohensaari Island**, to the south of the centre. On your way, there's a sewage purification facility with a pool that attracts plenty of birds during migration time. There's an observation tower. The island itself has a nature path and a camping ground.

For a little-known place to visit, follow the Salo to Teijo road 3.5 km from the centre, until you see the small 'Viitan Kruunu' sign on your right. Yellow poles mark the path, which takes you to a high hill with a spectacular view of the fjord. The rock formation is probably a prehistoric burial mound but has never been researched. Don't you do it either.

Places to Stay

Laurin koulu (☎ 308 4400) is a local youth hostel in a school building at Venemestarinkatu 37. Beds start as low as 28 mk and you can use the kitchen. The place is open in summer soon after school ends and closes before school restarts. To get there, turn left at the railway station.

Leirintäalue Vuohensaari (☎ 731 2651), a camping ground five km from the centre on the island of Vuohensaari (with road access), has cottages from 145 to 230 mk.

The cheapest hotel in town is *Hotel Martina* (☎ 731 7474) at Turuntie 2, with rooms from 200/250 mk. Its nightspot Life is popular with the young crowd. *Sokos Hotel Rikala* (☎ 774 4100) at Asemakatu 15 is the largest hotel in town, with rooms for 470 mk, including breakfast. Its Night Club is popular with the older set. *Hotelli City Rikala* at Asemakatu 5 is run by the former; singles/doubles start at 300/385 mk.

Places to Eat

Penan Saluuna at Helsingintie 10 is an honest down-to-earth restaurant with good beef dishes. The Plaza shopping centre has the popular *Antonio* with Tex-Mex food and drinks. You will also find *Hesburger* at the Plaza. For fine dining, *Hoffi* in Hotel Rikala is the ticket. *Krassi* is a vegetarian restaurant upstairs at Helsingintie 3.

Getting There & Away

All buses and trains in the area stop at Salo. The bus station, on the street level in the Anttila building, close to the train station, has clear timetables and half a dozen departures daily to various destinations in the region, including Teijo, Perniö, and Kimito Island. The information booth inside gives away timetables.

HALIKKO

This historical centre, now overshadowed by the nearby hi-tech Salo to the east, is close enough for rewarding bicycle tours from the Salo bus and train stations. All elements of Finland's past are present: prehistoric forts, a medieval church, remains of the nobility and more recent handicraft.

The long and narrow Halikonlahti Bay, almost like a fjord, was an important trading port well before the Swedish crusades. It is believed this was the mysterious Portus Tavastorum, a free port for pre-Christian fur traders from Häme. This situation didn't last long. It is also likely that the Christian influence was strong in Halikko even before the Swedish crusades to the region.

There are three old estates that have belonged to just two families, first the Horns and later the Armfelts. Vuorentaka, from the 14th century, is the oldest of them. Its unusual tower is visible from the main road. Originally established in medieval times, Joensuu estate has a manor dating from 1780s. It is from here that the Armfelt Museum on Suomenlinna near Helsinki obtained its furniture. Viurila, from early 19th century, now includes the Viurila Golf course, with public access. The club houses, with their distinctive columns, were designed by CL Engel, the famous Empire style architect.

Halikko Church

This church, probably erected in 1440, is a legacy of the wealth of the Swedish nobility in the area. The Horn and Armfelt families have their crests hanging on the walls here. The adjoining graveyard has plenty of mausoleums. The nearby **Halikon museo**, a local museum, is certainly worth a visit. Count CG Armfelt has donated his gun collection, which is unusually extensive for a local museum. Next to the museum, **Taitojen tupa** has a café, a gallery and handicraft for sale. Unfortunately the opening times are not visitor-friendly: the church is open weekdays from 7 am to 4 pm, the museum and Taitojen tupa are only open on Sunday from 11 am to 5 pm.

Halikon Rikala

The Rikala Hill of Halikko was discovered in the 1950s to be a prehistoric defence post. The nearby Kärävuori Hill was probably a site of local tribunals. There's a walking track with explanations in Finnish, but you can just enjoy the local scenery if you don't want a history lesson. To find the hill, look for the clear sign on road No 1, to the west of Halikko crossing. You can also reach the hill from the old Turku Road, aka King's Road.

    Kreivinmäen ulkomuseo, the open-air museum on Kreivinmäki Hill, is not especially interesting or extensive. The wolf trap, albeit recently constructed, is a speciality.

Getting There & Away

There are buses from Salo to Halikko every 30 minutes on weekdays; every hour on weekends.

ANGELNIEMI

A visit to the island of Kimito, just southwest of Salo, is recommended. You can take the road from either Sauvo or Perniö, or the free ferry to Angelniemi, at the northern tip of the island. The church here, dating from 1772, is situated on a beautiful spot near the water, and is a good place for birdwatching.

    From Salo, take road No 1835 to the ferry. From Kimito centre, it's 25 km on a good road.

PERNIÖ

Perniö, south of Salo, is full of historical landmarks. It was never as busy as Halikko with its harbour, but there are old wealthy estates, factories and plenty of prehistoric discoveries. Perniö today is a quiet rural municipality that has suffered from the deviating of the new train route away from its villages. The tourist office in Salo will give full details of various places to research but the central village, as well as Teijo, are certainly the highlights of Perniö.

Perniö Church

The medieval Perniö Church dates from 1480 although there was a wooden church on the site at least 100 years earlier. The church ceiling is covered by paintings that were probably created by Petrus Henriksson in 1480, in a style similar to the fine paintings of Kalanti. There are sculptures from the 14th century. The church is open daily except Monday, but just from 4 to 7 pm on weekdays.

Perniön Museo

The local museum displays an ancient dress, reconstructed according to archaeological discoveries. The museum is open from noon to 6 pm on Sunday in summer (in July also on Wednesday and Thursday).

Getting There & Away

Vainion Liikenne runs buses from Salo to Perniö every hour or so.

TEIJO

A factory was founded on the old Teijo estate in 1686. The historically wealthy Teijo, south-west of Salo, was recently divided into three areas. The actual village has a number of small companies, including a restaurant. A wealthy investor from Oulu took care of a golf course, a downhill skiing facility and a number of other facilities at Mathildedal. Finally, the National Board of Forestry acquired the 2.3 sq km wilderness area that has facilities for trekkers. In the village of Teijo, the information centre (☎ 736 6480) for the wilderness area is open in summer from 10 am to 5 pm on weekdays, 10 am to 2 pm on weekends.

Places to Stay & Eat

Meri-Teijo (☎ 736 3801) has superb cottages

and apartments. *Puistoravintola* serves lunch in Teijo, while *Plattapoffi* is a restaurant and pub in Mathildedal.

Getting There & Away
Every three hours, a bus from Salo runs south to Teijo. Some buses continue to Mathildedal.

KIMITO
Kimito (Finnish: Kemiö) is the main village on the island of the same name. The church is worth a look for its grandiose interior, although there are few treasures. Its construction began at the end of 14th century on. The church is open mid-May to mid-August daily from 8 am to 8 pm. There's a museum within the church.

Sagalund
This excellent museum, two km west of Kimito Church, has over 20 buildings, most of which could qualify as local museums on their own. There's a large school museum, a gun museum and the Sagalund Villa exhibits thousands of old items. The museum is open Tuesday to Sunday from noon to 5 pm. Admission is 15 mk and there are guided tours every hour.

Places to Eat
There's a hamburger restaurant in Kimito.

Getting There & Away
To get to Kimito, take one of the three to five buses a day from Turku, or from Salo, 50 km away.

DRAGSFJÄRD
Dragsfjärd (population 3800), in the southwest of Kimito Island, boasts an excellent youth hostel and some unusual villages. The old church dates from the 1700s and has a blueish interior with old paintings. Nearby, the youth hostel (☎ 464 553) gives probably the best value for money in Finland. A hostel of hotel standard, the rooms cost only 40 to 60 mk for HI members.

Söderlångvik
This manor house was once the summer residence of newspaper magnate Amos Anderson, who died in 1961. There are paintings, furniture and special exhibitions in this beautiful manor, as well as an extensive garden and a café. The museum is open daily in summer from 11 am to 6 pm. Admission is 20 mk.

Getting There & Away
Take a bus from Salo, Turku or Kimito. There are several buses a day.

DALSBRUK
This seaside village (Finnish: Taalintehdas) in southern Dragsfjärd is dominated by industrial monsters, with some of the early industrial areas preserved as a museum. A popular destination for sailboats, Dalsbruk is also worth a visit by bicycle, car or bus. At the guest harbour, you will find a tourist information office, open daily. There's a choice of two restaurants.

VÄSTANFJÄRD
This Swedish-speaking community (population 880) in the south-eastern corner of the Kimito Island is spectacularly attractive in summer, with tidy farmhouses and flowers in blossom. The main village, Lammala, has two churches. The newer one, a massive grey-stone construction, has little of interest, but the old red wooden church, dating from 1755, reflects the original subtle church architecture. Both churches are open daily in summer.

KASNÄS
This harbour, south of Kimito Island, is the main jumping-off point for regional archipelago ferries. Visit **Sinisimpukka** (☎ 466 6290) in summer daily from 10 am to 6 pm for information on the South-West Archipelago National Park. The centre, also known as Naturum, organises tours to some of the islands in June, July and August, depending on demand. There's also a nature trail from Sinisimpukka.

Getting There & Away

There are just one or two bus connections from Dalsbruk (Taalintehdas) to Kasnäs, the only useful one being the 11.15 am departure.

HIITTINEN

This small island group (Swedish: Hitis), previously a struggling fishing municipality, is now part of Dragsfjärd to the north. Its history begins well before the recorded era. In 1995, an extensive archaeological excavation revealed a Viking Age trading place at **Kyrksundet**, on the main island. The colourful archipelago **church** from 1686 ranks among the oldest wooden churches in Finland. The main community is **Rosala**, which offers accommodation in small huts.

Getting There & Away

To get to the main island, take a bus or drive to Kasnäs, then take the large MS *Aura* ferry which runs every one to two hours. The ride is free. If you want to visit any of the other islands, get aboard the MS *Falkö* , which takes 110 passengers and nine cars, and plies between the islands, including Högsåra, with its old fishing village and houses from the 18th century.

Vakka-Suomi

The region north of Naantali is known as Vakka-Suomi, and refers to the wooden bowls (vakka) that have been typical local products for centuries. Uusikaupunki is the largest town in the region, which also boasts idyllic islands.

MYNÄMÄKI

This busy little village boasts the largest medieval stone church in Finland, with almost 1000 seats. There are numerous wooden statues, miniature ships, tomb stones and coats of arms of the local nobility. The church is also one of the oldest in the region, dating from the early 14th century.

It's open May to August daily, from 8 am to 3 pm; to 5 pm on Sunday.

Places to Eat

All eateries are around the church, including *Bisse* for beer, *Mynä Grilli* for junk food and *Jounin Pakari* for bakery products but not coffee. Esso petrol station has a café. Supermarkets are to the south of the church.

Getting There & Away

The bus station is at the northern end of the village. There are buses from Turku, Uusikaupunki and Rauma every two hours or so.

If you're visiting other churches near Turku, Mynämäki is 17 km north-east of Askainen, 15 km north-west of Nousiainen.

VEHMAA

This extremely small village west of Mynämäki is dominated by a medieval church which is open daily in summer from 8 am to 4 pm. In addition to some fine wooden houses, there's *Kesäkahvila,* which serves coffee in summer daily except Monday.

If you desperately need something else, proceed four km east to the village of Vinkkilä. There's a post office, a bank, a restaurant, a café and some shops. *Kiinteistö Oy Lahtivuo* (☎ 433 2252) in Vinkkila rents a few inexpensive rooms. Further east on road No 195 towards Mynämäki, there are small museums at Lahdinko (open daily except Monday and Saturday from noon to 4 pm) and Korvensuu (open on Sunday in summer from 11 am to 1 pm).

Getting There & Away

Ordinary (non-express) buses between Uusikaupunki and Turku usually pass through all the places mentioned above.

TAIVASSALO

A scenic route towards Kustavi Archipelago takes you through the wealthy rural landscape of Taivassalo. The main attraction is the 1325 church. The interior is lavishly decorated with medieval paintings depicting saints. The church is open daily in summer from 10 am to 6 pm.

Getting There & Away
There are regular buses from Turku, 52 km south-east. It is 18 km from Vehmaa south to Taivassalo.

KUSTAVI
The municipality of Kustavi (Swedish: Gustavs) has a population of just over 1000. It's a beautiful area with scenic seascapes.

The wooden church built in 1783 features the miniature ships common in coastal churches. Sailors offered them to churches in exchange for divine blessings. The church is open early June to mid-August daily from 10 am to 5 pm.

Places to Stay & Eat
There are a few places north and south of the main village. *Kustavin lomakeskus* (☎ 876 230) is a large holiday village to the south of Kustavi with over 50 rooms in cottages and a host of activities. To the north at Kevo, there are two cottage businesses on road No 1924. *Lomavalkama* (☎ 877 814) is larger than *Lomapalvelut* (☎ 876 420).

In the main village, you can eat lunch at *Retari Messi*, more simple meals at *Arjan Kahvila* or *Punainen Tupa*. At the harbour of Osnäs, eat and unwind at *Matsalong Boris & Maris*.

Getting There & Away
Most people pass through Kustavi on their way further west. Near the church, there's a free ferry to the island of Vartsala. Some 8.5 km further west is the passenger pier of Osnäs (Finnish: Vuosnainen), with free ferries to the island of Brändö (See the Åland chapter). Direct buses from Turku will continue to Osnäs, some to Brändö. If you have a private vehicle, expect delays during the high season. Taking a car by ferry to Brändö will cost money; bicycles travel free.

UUSIKAUPUNKI
Uusikaupunki (Swedish: Nystad) is an idyllic seaside town to the north of Turku. It is best known for its windmills and its car factories. The name translates as 'New Town' – ironic because Uusikaupunki is now one of the oldest towns in Finland, having been founded in 1617 by Gustav II Adolf, the King of Sweden.

Uusikaupunki's main claim to fame is the treaty of 1721 which brought an uneasy peace between Sweden and Russia after the devastating Great Northern War. Today, almost nobody in the town speaks Swedish and Nystad is merely a historical name – use Uusikaupunki!

The population of 17,800 suffers from one of the highest unemployment figures of any Finnish town. This is due to problems in the local auto industry, hit hard during the economic depression. Some new businesses have been established, one of which is the mysterious Bonk exhibition. Don't miss it!

Orientation
Uusikaupunki is built beside the sea, on both sides of the narrow Kaupunginlahti Bay. The town centre is on the northern side of the bay, and the market square is the centre of the centre. Alinenkatu is the main street.

Information
Tourist Office The tourist office at Levysepänkatu 4 (☎ 1551) is open weekdays until 3 pm but it is inconveniently located outside the town centre. In summer until mid-August, a booth (☎ 842 1225) at the park near the bus station is open until 5 pm on weekdays and until 3 pm on Saturday.

Post & Telephone The post office, on the corner of Rauhankatu and Alinenkatu (23500 Uusikaupunki), is open weekdays from 9 am to 5 pm.

Library The extensive public library at Alinenkatu 34 includes a newspaper room that subscribes to *Time*. There are regional maps in scale 1:20,000 in the käsikirjasto section. The library is open weekdays from 11 am to 7 pm.

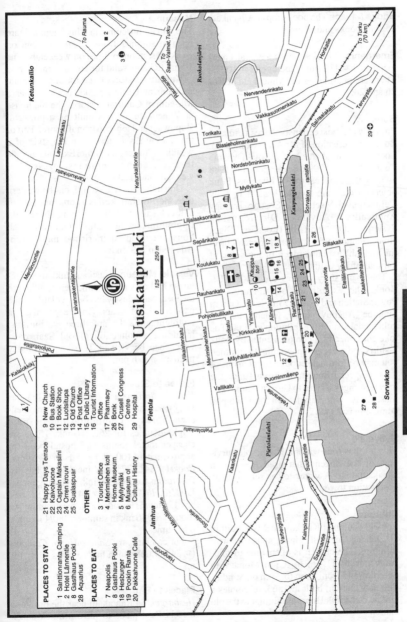

PLACES TO STAY
1 Santtionranta Camping
2 Hotel Lännentie
8 Gasthaus Pooki
28 Aquarius

PLACES TO EAT
7 Neapolis
8 Gasthaus Pooki
18 Hesburger
19 Pookin Ranta
20 Pakkahuone Café

21 Happy Days Terrace
22 Kaivohuone
23 Captain Makasiini
24 Orren krouvi
25 Sualaspuar

OTHER
3 Tourist Office
4 Merimiehen koti
Home Museum
5 Myllymäki
6 Museum of
Cultural History

9 New Church
10 Bus Station
11 Book Shop
12 Luotsitupa
13 Old Church
14 Post Office
15 Public Library
16 Tourist Information
Office
17 Pharmacy
26 Bonk
27 Crusell Congress
Centre
29 Hospital

Uusikaupunki

TURKU & PORI PROVINCE

Books & Maps The bookshop at Alinenkatu 25 sells books and maps.

Emergency Services In a general emergency call ☎ 112; for a doctor call ☎ 10023. There are pharmacies on Alinenkatu at Nos 26 and 28.

Bonk

Probably the most expensive joke in Finland, Bonk is the creation of Mr Alvar Gullichsen. Located at Siltakatu 2 in an old Dynamo Centre (built in 1909), Bonk opened in 1988 as an exhibition centre of hilarious Bonk objects which are 'world leaders in fully Defunctioned Machinery, Cosmic Therapy Applications, Advanced Disinformation Systems (ADS) and LBH (Localised Black Hole) technology'. The text for each object (in English) explains much of the sense of humour of Mr Gullichsen.

The main story centres around Mr Per Bonk who established an Anchovy Oil Power Station and made a fortune on 'Garum Superbe' Anchovy spice, which fetched a gold medal at a Paris exhibition in 1900. The joke goes on, and is complemented by Bonk T-shirts and other paraphernalia. In summer, you may be fortunate enough to catch one of the few special Bonk trains from Turku, the only passenger service to Uusikaupunki. The museum is open daily from 11 am to 6 pm, admission is 25 mk.

Myllymäki

This hill has four windmills, the sole survivors of the dozens that used to exist in Uusikaupunki. A water tower serves as an observation tower.

Churches

The old church at Kirkkokatu 2 was built in 1629. It has fine wall paintings and colourful furniture. The church is open June to mid-August from 11 am to 3 pm Monday to Saturday and from noon to 4 pm on Sunday. The new church, built in 1863, resembles a Gothic cathedral. Hours are similar to the old church.

Museums

The three museums in Uusikaupunki are open in summer from 11 am to 3 pm on weekdays, noon to 3 pm on weekends. The 10 mk ticket is valid for all three museums.

Kulttuurihistoriallinen museo, the main museum of Uusikaupunki, is defined as a Museum of Cultural History. The old house at Ylinenkatu 11 was built by a powerful shipowner and tobacco manufacturer. Part of the museum is furnished in the style of a wealthy 19th century home. Exhibits include textiles, coins, ceramics, glassware, weapons and nautical items.

Down the Myllymäki hill, on the western side, **Merimiehen koti** is a home museum of a local sailor. Admission is three mk. **Luotsitupa**, on the Vallimäki hill, is a small house devoted to maritime navigation. Admission is 3 mk.

Vehicle Museum Uusikaupunki manufactures Opel cars for the time being, although the local car industry has been volatile in the past couple of years. On the premises at Autotehtaantie 14 are three exhibitions, including a collection of old Saab cars, which can be viewed Tuesday to Sunday from noon to 6 pm.

Places to Stay

Hotel Lännentie (☎ 841 2636) at Levysepänkatu 1 provides basic, inexpensive hotel accommodation in neat singles/doubles for 260/370 mk. There are cheaper motel rooms and hostel beds for approximately 100 mk per person. *Gasthaus Pooki* (☎ 841 2771) at Ylinenkatu 21 has just four rooms for 290/330 mk, including breakfast. *Hotelli Aquarius* (☎ 841 3123), the best hotel in town, includes a cultural centre. All rooms are 350 mk in summer, 380/440 mk at other times.

For camping, try *Santtionranta Camping* (☎ 842 3862) which has cottages from 150 mk.

Places to Eat

Hesburger, on Rantakatu near the bridge, is the cheapest place to have a quick snack.

There are seafront places on Rantakatu, such as *Pookin Ranta* (in weird silos) and *Pakkahuone Café* at the guest harbour (winner of the award as Finland's best guest harbour in 1995).

If you want to have just one proper meal in Uusikaupunki, there are four options. All are in old wooden buildings on Sorvakon rantatie, across the bridge from the centre. *Sualaspuar* , the most traditional of them, is open until 11 pm. *Orren krouvi* is a pub associated with the latter restaurant, while *Captain Makasiini* is a sea-inspired place, with a nicer atmosphere upstairs. This place serves pizzas. Further west, *Kaivohuone* is a large establishment which serves food but is best for evening dancing and live music.

Back in the centre, *Gasthaus Pooki* at Ylinenkatu 21 has a nice restaurant, serving good meals at reasonable prices. You can also sit on the pleasant terrace and have a beer or two. Next door, *Neapolis* serves pizza.

Getting There & Away
Buses from Turku, 74 km south, run once or twice per hour on weekdays, less frequently on weekends. There are five to eight buses per day from Rauma. Buses from Helsinki run via Turku.

PYHÄMAA
The scenic coastal routes north of Uusikaupunki could take you to this small village, where you will find a very special church. Built on an old cult site, it has since the 1600s been the foremost sacrificial shrine in Finnish Christianity. It looks modest outside, but the interior is richly decorated with paintings. The church is open on Sunday, after the service. For other possible opening times, enquire at the Uusikaupunki tourist office. The neighbouring new church is from 1804.

Places to Eat
Pyhämaan ruori is not a bad place to eat typically oily restaurant food; it is also the only place to do so. Coffee and snacks are also served.

Getting There & Away
There are buses from Uusikaupunki to Pyhämaa.

PYHÄRANTA
This very small place, across the strait from Pyhämaa and north of Uusikaupunki, is very pretty and features an Art-Nouveau church from 1909. It's open in summer from 9 am to 6 pm.

KALANTI
Kalanti is a small rural village that is now part of Uusikaupunki municipality. It was here that Finland's history started. In 1155, Bishop Henry arrived in Kalanti on a crusade.

The medieval **Kalanti Church** dates back to the late 1300s. It's notable because the paintings, by Per Henriksson, are the oldest signed works of art in Finland. The paintings depict, among other scenes, Bishop Henry meeting a pagan on the Finnish coast. The church is open daily in summer from 9 am to 5 pm.

Kalanti is a few east of Uusikaupunki. Catch an Uusikaupunki to Laitila bus.

LAITILA
The region of Laitila, north-east of Uusikaupunki, is well endowed with prehistoric sites, churches and nice old houses. The busy little town of Laitila is a regional centre. There is an interesting church from 1483 with extensive frescoes and a number of wooden statues, also from the Catholic era. Hours vary in summer. Get there early, as doors close by early afternoon. On Sunday it's open until 8 pm. Laitila centre serves over 9000 people who live in the area. There are several restaurants and other eateries. You won't go hungry.

Untamala
This village, just five km north of Laitila on road No 8, is one of the oldest in the region. It has a church from 1785, a museum and a prehistoric trail to a cemetery that is 2000 years old.

Koukkela

Another little village, five km south of Laitila, Koukkela features a well-preserved home museum with original buildings from the 17th century. The museum is open in summer from noon to 3 pm, Wednesday to Saturday, and to 6 pm on Sunday. Admission is 5 mk.

Places to Stay

Laitilan Kievari (☎ 5020) at Keskuskatu 20 has just eight rooms, priced at 200/300 mk, including breakfast. Less central is *Asuntohotelli Hartikkala* (☎ 56900) at Garpintie 5, with 28 apartments.

Getting There & Away

Laitila is 20 km east of Uusikaupunki along road No 198. There are buses from Turku and Uusikaupunki.

Satakunta

This is one of Finland's most historical areas. Much of its heritage is prehistoric and consequently it's less suitable for commercial exploitation than many other regions in Finland – maybe this is why it's not as popular with tourists and travellers. Perhaps this is a good reason to go there.

PORI

Pori (Swedish: Björneborg) is one of the most important harbours in Finland, and industries are the town's major employers. However, Pori has more recently become famous for its annual jazz festival in July, recognised as one of the best in Europe, and July is the best time to visit Pori.

Pori has a very limited number of Swedish speakers. The Swedish name Björneborg translates as Fort of Bear.

History

In 1558, Duke Juhana of Finland decided to establish a strong trading town on the eastern coast of the Gulf of Bothnia. As a result, Pori was founded at the mouth of the Kokemäenjoki River. Ulvila, the previous centre east of Pori, was abandoned. Since then, Pori has been a regional centre for trade, shipping and industry. The population is 76,500.

Orientation

Yrjönkatu, the main street, leads to the market square in the north. There's a pedestrianised section on Yrjönkatu and Itäpuisto.

Information

Tourist Office The tourist office at Hallituskatu 9A (☎ 633 5780) is open in summer on weekdays from 8 am to 6 pm, and on Saturday from 9 am to 1 pm. At other times of the year it's open on weekdays only until 4 pm.

Post & Telephone The main post office is at Yrjönkatu 8, 28100 Pori.

Library The public library at Gallen-Kallelankatu 12 is open in summer Monday to Friday from 9 am to 7 pm.

Books & Maps Suomalainen Kirjakauppa at Yrjönkatu 13, on the pedestrian street, has the widest choice.

Emergency Services For general emergency phone ☎ 112 and for a doctor ring ☎ 10023.

Satakunta Museum

This excellent regional museum at Hallituskatu 11 focuses on local history and also has temporary exhibitions. On the 2nd floor, there is an interesting miniature of Old Pori. The museum is open daily (except Monday) from 11 am to 5 pm. Admission is 10 mk.

Pori Art Museum

This former warehouse on Eteläranta was turned into a museum in 1981. It has temporary exhibitions and is open daily (except Monday) from 11 am to 6 pm. Admission is

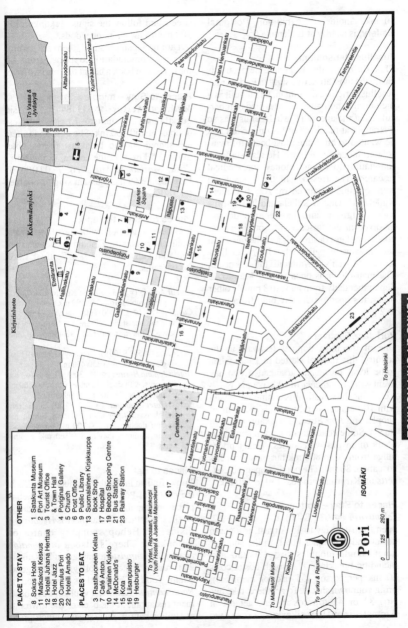

TURKU & PORI PROVINCE

PLACE TO STAY

8 Sokos Hotel
11 Matkakoti Keskus
12 Hotelli Juhana Herttua
18 Hotel Jazz
20 Cumulus Pori
22 Hotelli Amado

PLACES TO EAT

3 Raatihuoneen Kellari
7 Café Anton
10 Punainen Kukko
14 McDonald's
15 Kota
16 Liisanpuisto
19 Hesburger

OTHER

1 Satakunta Museum
2 Pori Art Museum
3 Tourist Office
  & Town Hall
4 Poriginal Gallery
5 Church
6 Post Office
9 Public Library
13 Suomalainen Kirjakauppa
  Book Shop
17 Hospital
19 Bebop Shopping Centre
21 Bus Station
23 Railway Station

Pori

ISOMÄKI

0   125   250 m

10 mk. Another art exhibition, **Poriginal Gallery**, is nearby at Eteläranta 6.

Juselius Mausoleum

This shrine at the Käppänä Cemetery is easily the most attractive sight in Pori. Mr FA Juselius, a rich businessman, had it built as a memorial to his daughter, who died of tuberculosis at the age of 11. Mr Juselius was so distraught at the death of his only child that he wanted to build the most beautiful mausoleum money could buy. He also started a foundation to donate money for medical research. The frescoes in the mausoleum were originally painted by Akseli Gallen-Kallela. Mr Gallen-Kallela had just lost his own daughter, and he became deeply involved in the frescoes. The original frescoes were later destroyed, and the ones you see now were painted by Jorma Gallen-Kallela, Akseli's son, after his father's death. The mausoleum is open from 1 May to 15 September daily from noon to 3 pm. At other times, it's open on Sunday only from noon to 2 pm.

Pori Jazz Festival

One of the most popular festivals in the country, this festival started in 1966, when some local musicians arranged a two-day event with an audience of 1000 people. Nowadays, the July festival is a nine-day event with 100 concerts and tens of thousands of people, and Jazz Street (Eteläkatu) is full of stands. Some concerts are held in tents, outdoors or in old warehouses. Ticket prices range from 20 to 800 mk but most concerts cost about 80 mk. The popular open-air concerts on Kirjurinluoto cost 130 to 170 mk.

Places to Stay – bottom end

Tekunkorpi (☎ 637 8400) at Korventie 52, open from 15 May to 15 August, is a youth hostel and a summer hotel. In the summer hotel, singles/doubles cost 180/250 mk, including breakfast. The youth hostel costs 70 mk per person (55 mk for members); bring your own sheets. To get there, take bus Nos 32 or 42 towards Yyteri, get off at Ammatillinen kurssikeskus, cross two

streets and follow the signs. Tekunkorpi is 200 metres away, in the woods.

During the jazz festival, there are several cheap accommodation options (from 55 mk). You can book a bed at the tourist office.

Places to Stay – middle

Matkakoti Keskus (☎ 633 8447), a basic guesthouse at Itäpuisto 13, has singles/doubles at 150/200 mk. Showers and toilets are shared and no breakfast is available. Some 3.5 km from the centre, in the Musa area, *Matkakoti Musa* (637 0100) at Putimäentie 69 has pleasant singles/doubles for 180/270 mk.

Places to Stay – top end

Pori has seven hotels, with one of the lowest occupancy rates in Finland – though they tend to fill up during the Jazz Festival. Look for bargains.

Hotelli Amado (☎ 633 8500) at Keskusaukio 2, has singles/doubles from 240/290 mk.

Cumulus Pori (☎ 828 000) at Itsenäisyydenkatu 37 is near the bus station. There are 109 rooms that cost 325 mk in summer, or 395/450 mk at other times.

Hotel Jazz (☎ 552 9300) at Itsenäisyydenkatu 41 has singles/doubles from 350/450 mk.

Hotelli Juhana Herttua (☎ 845 300) at Itäpuisto 1 has 57 rooms, with singles/doubles from 300/360 mk in summer, or 380/460 mk at other times.

Sokos Hotel Vaakuna (☎ 552 8100) at Gallen-Kallelankatu 7, right in the town centre, has singles/ doubles for 300/400 mk on weekends and in summer; they're 430/560 mk at other times.

Places to Eat

You'll find an incredible number of grillis in the centre of Pori. There's a popular kebab place on Itäpuisto, opposite the Matkakoti Keskus. Another popular place is *Hesburger*, inside the Bebop shopping centre on Yrjönkatu. There's also a *McDonald's* nearby. *Liisanpuisto* restaurant at Liisankatu 20 is run by a catering college and has good, cheap food. The food is also good at *Raatihuoneen Kellari*, a vaulted, cosy basement restaurant at the back of the town hall at Hallituskatu 9, with special lunch prices and good steaks. Lunch at *Café Anton* near the market is also good value. *Kota* at Liisankatu 12 is located in a little white house. It serves pizza and good meals in a cosy dining room.

Getting There & Away
Air There are daily flights between Pori and Helsinki. There are also daily flights to/from Turku.

Bus There are 16 buses daily between Helsinki and Pori. There are 12 buses a day between Rauma and Pori on weekdays and seven on weekends. There are also a few buses from Turku and Tampere.

Train All trains to Pori go via Tampere, where you often have to change. There are five or six trains a day between Tampere and Pori, all of which have good connections with trains from Helsinki.

Getting Around
Bus An extensive bus service operates in the town area; route maps are available at the tourist office. Most buses pass the market square.

Bicycle Ask at the tourist office about special deals for bicycle rental.

YYTERI
Yyteri beach is still something of a playground in summer, though all Finnish beach resorts have been in a decline ever since charter flights to Spain were invented. Yyteri has monster hotels offering all kinds of activities, and the white sand stretches quite a distance.

Immediately after you turn off the main road to Yyteri, there is an observation tower with a café. It's open Monday to Friday from noon to midnight and on weekends from 10 am to midnight.

Places to Stay & Eat
Matkustajakoti Tiira (☎ 343 792) is an old guesthouse near the water tower but hopelessly far from the beach.

Yyterin kievari (☎ 343 922) near the beach offers rooms and cottages at 240/290 mk. Their *aitta* accommodation is the cheapest option. Just opposite, *Yyterin leirintä* (☎ 638 3778) is a camping ground with cottages from 350 mk. This place is open only from June to August.

Hotelli Merimaailma Yyteri (☎ 345 300) deserves a look – it's an oversized concrete castle to the north of the main beach centre. It has a spa and the cheapest singles/doubles cost 350/390 mk.

Getting There & Away
To get to Yyteri, take bus No 32 from the market square in Pori.

REPOSAARI
This fishing village is at the end of the northwest peninsula of Pori. It's located on an island which was connected by bridge to the mainland in 1956. Reposaari has wooden houses and well-kept parks, and it is hard to believe that it is primarily an industrial village.

Places to Stay & Eat
Siikarannan leirintäalue (☎ 344 120) is smaller and quieter than Yyteri. The camping fee is 65 mk per family or 35 mk per individual camper, and there are two/four-person cottages for 175/190 mk.

For excellent fish, try *Reposaaren Ravintola* at Satamapuisto 34. The buffet, with several main courses, is 65 mk. The buffet is served daily in July and August, and on Sunday at other times.

Getting There & Away
Reposaari is 30 km north-west of Pori, and bus Nos 30 or 40 will take you there.

IRJANNE
This tiny little village is unknown to most Finns, let alone foreign tourists. Yet, it offers three museums, an old church and several old houses, all in a rural setting.

Kalle Antinpoika Killainen built the red wooden church in 1731, and it is considered one of the best examples of churches built by

Finnish peasantry (the one in Petäjävesi tops the list). The museums exhibit items associated with local life, farming and firefighting. The museums' opening times are Monday to Thursday between 2 and 7 pm, or Sunday from 6 to 7 pm. Most Pori to Rauma buses will go via Irjanne, but check first.

ULVILA

Although Ulvila (population 12,700) today is just a suburb of Pori, it was here that the great Kokemäki River culture flourished after Teljä (in today's Kokemäki) was abandoned in 1365. Ulvila was abandoned in 1550 in favour of the newly-founded Helsinki, which took away almost all of Ulvila's trade. Eight years later, Pori was founded.

The 14th century stone church of Ulvila is a highlight of the town, and it is the second oldest church in Satakunta after the one in Sastamala. There are regular buses from Pori to Ulvila. The church is on road No 244, outside the main centre of Ulvila.

LUVIA

This small village lies south-west of Pori and has some attractive buildings and a 1910 Art-Nouveau church, designed by Josef Stenbäck. All buses going south from Pori to Rauma travel via Luvia.

LEINEPERI

This fine village received the 1993 Europe Nostra award for careful preservation of 18th century buildings. Today it is a lively village with artisans, a few museums and an attractive natural landscape. The place was first known as Fredriksfors when it was a *bruk* for Swedish iron in 1771, and manufactured household items. The huge **Masuuni**, now renovated, used Finnish ore for smelting. Its heyday was during the 1860s; all work with iron ended in 1902.

Free town maps are available at most attractions. The Kullaanjoki riverside's scenic attractions include Masuuni and a blacksmith's shop. Many workers' houses have been renovated, and have been given individual names. **Sacklen** is a tiny museum depicting a smith's home. **Museo Kangasniemi** is devoted to Kaarlo Kangasniemi, the 1968 Olympic weight-lifting champion. The museum is open daily in summer from 10 am to 6 pm. Entry is 5 mk. On weekends you may be lucky enough to meet the champion.

Try to visit Leineperi on a summer weekend. At other times some places will be closed.

Places to Stay & Eat

Gasthaus Matinliisa (☎ 591 566) is the nearest accommodation available; it's 7.5 km from Leineperi if you drive via road No 11. There's a short-cut via Kiviniemi. It's in an old school building which has been turned into a restaurant and a guesthouse. There are four rooms from 120 to 150 mk, including breakfast and sauna, but you can negotiate. Those travelling with children might like to stay here as it lays on activities to keep them amused.

In Leineperi itself, there are two places called *Kahvila*. One is in a red building and is a stylish café with exhibitions and tourist information. The other one is a food store.

Getting There & Away

Leineperi is on a bad road, which runs parallel to the Tampere to Pori road No 11. If you don't have your own wheels, the only way to get there is to take the bus that runs at least twice a day Monday to Friday between Pori and Kullaa. Departures are at 1 and 4 pm from Pori. You can negotiate a price for a taxi from Kullaa to Leineperi.

KULLAA

The centre of Kullaa is quite small, with a café, post office, pharmacy, taxi rank and some other services. The church is near the main road, not far from Neste petrol station, which has a café. At least three buses between Pori and Tampere stop daily at Kullaa, and more come from Pori, Monday to Friday.

KANKAANPÄÄ

The name of this surprisingly large town

translates roughly as 'end of pine forest' and refers to the Hämeenkangas forest through which one of the oldest regional roads runs. Kauppatori (the market square) is in the centre of town.

Places to Stay & Eat

Hotelli Reissupoika (☎ 578 1688) at Kauppatori 5 B is cheaper than *Hotelli Kantri* (☎ 578 3000) at Linnankatu 2, which has rooms for 370/470 mk, including breakfast. In summer, until early August, you can stay at *Finnhostel Kankaanpää* (☎ 572 2373) at Neuvoksenkatu 2. Beds start from 60 mk per HI member. Come before 5 pm.

Restaurants in town include *Siili* at the market, and *Susanna* at Keskuskatu 36. *Makasiinikahvio* at the market serves coffee.

Getting There & Away

There are regular buses from nearby towns. If you're driving, an interesting way to get to Kankaanpää is on the historical Hämeenkangas gravel road which runs north of Ikaalinen. Drive first along road No 2594 towards Suodenniemi, until you reach the old Vehuvarpeen kestikievari roadhouse, then take the right-hand turn-off to Hämeenkankaantie. Almost ten km east from Kankaanpää, Kuninkaan lähde (King's Spring) is a natural spring which was named after king Adolf Fredrik of Sweden who visited here in 1752. It has cold, fresh water.

KOKEMÄKI

Kokemäki is an unimpressive little town which is located at the site of one of the oldest places in Finland, Teljä. With a population of almost 10,000 people, Kokemäki has a few attractions for the traveller. The main street, Tulkkilantie, has a number of old wooden townhouses – a rare sight in today's Finland, unfortunately.

Things to See

Kokemäki has some medieval buildings. The wooden house which is now protected by bricks is believed to have been used by Bishop Henry in the 12th century. The large **church** dates from 1786. The nearby stone

building dating from 1838 houses **Maatalousmuseo**, or the Agricultural Museum. This misleading name doesn't give credit to the more than 8000 items (not all of them agricultural) that have been collected since 1936. It's open in summer only. **Ulkomuseo** is the local museum two km to the north along the Kokemäki to Kauvatsa road, past the bridge. The Kokemäenjoki River, one of the most historical waterways in Finland, runs through the town, and you can watch the rapids here.

Places to Stay & Eat

Hotelli Henrik (☎ 546 0864) is currently the only hotel in Kokemäki. *Hotelli Seurahuone* (☎ 546 4211) on Teljänkatu has been closed for some time, but it has a good location so could reopen soon.

Tulkkilantie, the main street, has a pub, *Sateenkaari* for lunch, and a grilli that serves big portions of inexpensive junk food.

Getting There & Away

Kokemäki has a train station, but it is located three km from central Kokemäki in the village of Peipohja. If you're on your way to Rauma, the bus at the railway station will wait for the train to arrive, and will take you to Rauma at no extra charge if you have a valid train pass. For those making train connections, most buses stop at Matkahuolto on Kiikunkatu, practically in the centre of town.

HARJAVALTA

Harjavalta (population 8400) is an industrial town with the reputation of being the most polluted in Finland. A gas leak in July 1995 created local panic and national attention. On the plus side, the region is well endowed with historical places, some of which are worth a visit. The small centre near the river has the typical small-town range of services.

Emil Cedercreutzin Museo

This large museum is devoted to Emil Cedercreutz (1879-1949) who was a sculptor, silhouette artist, writer and eccentric. He spent his summers here. Some of the houses he built, including the church-like

Maahengen Temppeli (Temple of Earth Spirit) are not open to the public, but there are several buildings which now house temporary exhibitions, silhouettes, Finnish art, Emil's own sculpture and an extensive two-storey ethnographic collection. Emil's home, Harjula, which carries the motto 'Memento Vivere' (Remember to Live) contains the artist's furniture and a range of items including European art and polar bear furs. The museum is three km east of the centre on Satakunnantie, the secondary Harjavalta to Kokemäki road. It is open in June to August daily from 11 am to 6 pm (on Saturday until 4 pm), and in other times daily from noon to 4 pm (Thursday and Sunday until 6 pm). Tickets are 10 mk. Ask for an English guidebook.

Bronze Age Mounds

Harjavalta is along the historic Kokemäenjoki River region. There are four main Bronze Age burial mounds, comprising at least 45 marked sites – presumably the final resting places of some Bronze Age nobles. They are located along a loop which can be done in a few hours, even by bicycle.

Juti is nearest to Harjavalta, but consists only of three smallish piles with public access. The one at the Matomäki crossing is impressive. Kaunismäki has 12 mounds, but just a few are visible from the main road. The biggest one is over three metres high. Kuumonmäki, not far from Juti, has 20 ruins on a forested hill. Mound No 32 is 26 metres wide and three metres high. Kivitie is in the woods, with nine sites scattered around. Mound No 3 is the second largest in Finland (see Panelia), with a width of 33 metres, and a height of two metres. Mound No 1 spans 22 metres.

In each location, a site map has been set up to assist with searching. All mounds are protected and should not be touched. Some of the mounds at Juti and Kaunismäki are on private property, and should not be visited. The mounds are not excessively thrilling but provide an excuse for a pleasant tour around the rural landscape.

Getting There & Away Head south from central Harjavalta along road No 219 towards Eura and Kiukainen, and turn right (1.3 km from the bridge over road No 11) towards Hiirijärvi on road No 2173. Proceed 2.2 km and turn right to Niitynrinnantie towards Juti, 3 km away. From Juti, turn left towards Matomäki, and proceed 1.5 km to Kaunismäki. Return to Juti, and continue 600 metres to Kuumonmäki. Continue the loop through the flat fields. When the road curves right to a forest, look for the road sign 'Seiväsojantie' on your right. Just 20 metres beyond this crossing, on the same side, is a small dirt road with no sign. This is Kivitie (Stone Road) which leads towards the sites.

Places to Stay & Eat

Paroninlahti right at the Emil Cedercreutz museum is a camping ground where you can pitch a tent or plug in your caravan. There are no cottages. Contact the reception inside the precinct on arrival.

Hotelli Marilyn (☎ 742 760) on the corner of Harjavallankatu and Siltatie right at the centre, contains lots of pictures of Marilyn Monroe, but otherwise it's just like any other small town hotel!

Hotelli Hiittenharju (☎ 354 111) is outside the town centre but near the main Helsinki to Pori road (No 2) and in a recreational area. It's the top-end establishment, with singles/doubles from 260/330 mk – more on weekdays unless you bargain. You can ski here, and there's a public indoor swimming pool nearby. The gravel road leads to the top of the hill with a 7000-year-old shoreline, but it is not really an attraction to write home about.

Harjavalta has a number of bars, hamburger joints and fast-food outlets. The museum has a café, and the two hotels serve meals.

Getting There & Away

Harjavalta has a railway station where Tampere to Pori trains stop regularly. All buses stop at the bus station.

PANELIA

Panelia is one of the earliest inhabited places in Finland. It is another commercial centre for the municipality of Kiukainen. Rivimylly is a renovated water-mill, from which you can admire the rapids. The small church dates from 1908, and follows the National Romantic style. Nearby, the dairy Panelian Osuusmeijeri also dates from 1908, and is built in the same style. The main sight in Panelia is **Kuninkaanhauta**, the largest burial mound in Finland. It's at the southern fringe of Panelia, and is impressive considering it's over 3000 years old.

Places to Stay & Eat

There are no places to stay in Panelia. *Merjan kioski* is open daily, and serves snacks. *Systeri Pub* is where locals gather to heal the world's ills while they ruin their own health. There are supermarkets in Panelia.

Getting There & Away

From Monday to Friday, Panelia is served by twice-daily buses from Harjavalta and Rauma. Driving from Harjavalta, follow road No 2173 towards Hiirijärvi, proceed 10.6 km until you hit road No 2172, and continue a few km.

LAPPI

This small village is particularly pleasant, with the Lapinjoki River running through it. An old stone bridge survives, and *Joki-Pub* serves food and beer right by the river. There's a café at the bus station and another at the Kesoil petrol station on the main road. The church across the river dates from 1760, and has medieval sculpture and a separate bell tower. There are also historical stables nearby.

The main attraction in Lappi (Finnish for Lapland) is the prehistoric site by the name **Kirkonlaattia** (Church Floor) which is a plain stone tableau in a seemingly Lappish setting. There are also burial mounds in the area.

Getting There & Away

Buses between Helsinki and Rauma run through the village, as do regional buses. The prehistoric site is four km from the main road No 42 – turn north to Eurajoentie (No 207) and turn left at the sign. It's a long drive along a gravel road.

EURA

Eura is a small roadside settlement with an imposing red-brick church dating from 1898. The commercial centre is across the main road (No 42) and includes *Euran Parkki* and *Haukkapala*, which serve junk food, and *Armis*, which serves inexpensive lunches at the bus station. Taxis depart from opposite the bus station.

Kauttua

The main attraction in Eura is this historical area which includes an imposing 1902 manor house which serves food only by appointment. The bell tower is unusual. The ironworks was founded in 1689, and the modern factory is still busy, though it won't disturb the visitor. Information is available at *Kyöpeli* (☎ 865 1520) which also serves coffee and snacks.

Alvar Aalto has designed two of the buildings. The Terrace House is from 1939 and Villa Aalto from 1943. Down at the lakeside, Villa Ahlström is a fine manor house, unfortunately not open to visitors, but Villa Mäntylä nearby has art exhibitions, and is open on weekday evenings, and on weekends from noon onwards. Old workers' houses on Sepäntie date back to the 19th century. Kautta is on the shores of Lake Pyhäjärvi, four km south of Eura centre.

Prehistoric Sites

Eura is rich in archaeological sites, including **Luistarin Muinaispuisto** three km southwest from the centre, and **Käräjämäki** east from Eura.

Getting There & Away

Buses from Rauma are your best bet. Bring a bicycle for regional tours, or hire a taxi.

KÖYLIÖ

The main attraction in this place is its name,

which serves as a good introduction to tongue-twisting spoken Finnish – ask a local to tell you how to pronounce it. In 1156 a local peasant, Lalli, killed the British-born Catholic Bishop Henry on frozen Lake Köyliönjärvi. This event has created a special type of Catholic art where Lalli is depicted under the foot of the saint, his inevitable fate in the afterlife. Köyliö was an important estate in medieval times, and today serves as the finishing point of Catholic pilgrimages from Turku. Cross the causeway to the island on Lake Köyliönjärvi where the church is located. This is a pleasant tour by car or bicycle; use Eura as a base and don't forget to visit Kauttua on the same trip.

Getting There & Away
Köyliö is just 10 km from Kauttua, or 14 km from Eura. There are no buses.

PUURIJÄRVI & ISOSUO NATIONAL PARK
One of the best birdwatching lakes in western Finland, Lake Puurijärvi is now protected, as are several marshland areas nearby. The location has always been isolated as the Kokemäenjoki River cuts practically all connections from the south, the east and the west. In the north, the Kauvatsa area is rural. The area has been protected since 1993, and includes Lake Puurijärvi and its immediate shoreline; the Korkeasuo (marshland) behind it; the partly open Isosuo marshland on the same side of the main river; and, across the Kokemäenjoki River, the inaccessible Aronsuo, Kiettaneensuo and Ronkansuo marshlands.

Lake Puurijärvi is the highlight, and can be reached by a 800-metre-long track from the main road. The Näköalapaikka (a viewing cliff) offers a good general view. It's easy to descend to the fields here and to follow the dirt road in either direction along the shoreline, or you could splash through the water if you have waterproof boots.

Isosuo is accessible along a new boardwalk which makes a loop to the fringe of the open marshland. There's an observation tower here.

This national park doesn't have much in the way of tourist services. Camping must be on private land, because the national park is either water or wetland. You will have to bring your own food, your own cooking kit and even your own water.

Getting There & Away
There are currently two areas which can be reached via public roads. The more accessible one, for Lake Puurijärvi, is on the Kauvatsa to Äetsä road No 2481. For Isosuo, head 3.1 km south from the Lake Puurijärvi parking area, and turn right following the Karhiniemi signs. (The road No 2481 from here leads to Äetsä and could be taken on your way from the park). Proceed 1.2 km towards Karhiniemi and turn right to Mutilahdentie following the Ala-Kauvatsa signs. The national park boundary (with the boardwalk path) is 2.2 km away.

RAUMA
Rauma (Swedish: Raumo) is one of the most interesting old wooden towns in Finland. Its main attraction, the old town, was recently placed on the UNESCO World Heritage List as Finland's first entry. Although it is the largest wooden town preserved in the Nordic countries, Rauma's old town is not a museum but a living centre, with many artisans, lace makers and goldsmiths working in small studios. Yet another feature of Rauma is its dialect, which is almost a separate language.

Rauma is also destined to become a scorned tourist destination, as a huge pulp factory, Finland's largest, is being finished near the protected old town. An enormous paper factory is now due to be built. Over 38,000 people in Rauma will be adversely affected.

Orientation
Rauma can be roughly divided into the old town and anything that's new. Valtakatu is the main street, running north-west from the old town, and it includes the tourist office, hotels and shops. A nice canal offers walking tours, as do the pleasant recreational areas at Poroholma and Fåfänga.

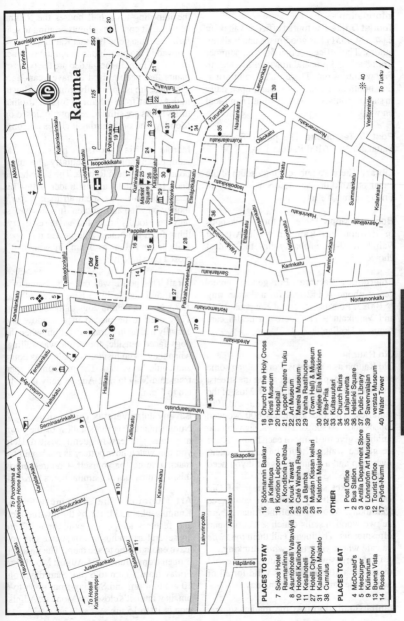

TURKU & PORI PROVINCE

PLACES TO STAY

7   Sokos Hotel
    Raumanlinna
8   Asuntohotelli Vaittaväylä
10 Hotelli Kalliohovi
11 Kesähotelli
27 Hotelli Cityhovi
31 Kalatorin Majatalo
38 Cumulus

PLACES TO EAT

4   McDonald's
5   Hesburger
9   Kulinarium
13 Buena Vista
14 Rosso

15 Söömannin Baakar
    ja Kaffetupa
16 Kontion Leipomo
    & Konditoria Peltola
24 Kruuk Tawast
25 Café Wanha Rauma
26 La Bamba
28 Mustan Kissan kellari
31 Kalatorin Majatalo

OTHER

1   Post Office
3   Bus Station
3   Anttila Department Store
6   Lönnström Art Museum
12 Tourist Office
17 Pyörä-Nurmi

18 Church of the Holy Cross
19 Kirsti Museum
20 Hospital
21 Puppet Theatre Tiuku
22 Art Museum
23 Marela Museum
29 Vanha Raatihuone
    (Town Hall) & Museum
30 Ateljee Ella Minkkinen
32 Pits-Priia
33 Kultasuutari
34 Church Ruins
35 Lahjanavetta
36 Helsinki Square
37 Public Library
39 Savenvalajan
    verstas Museum
40 Water Tower

Information

Tourist Office The tourist office at Valtakatu 2 (☎ 834 4551) has good maps and walking guides. The office is open daily in summer from 8 am to 3 pm, and in winter Monday to Friday until 4 pm. There's also an information booth at the market square, open daily in summer only, on weekdays until 6 pm, and on weekends till 3 pm.

Post & Telephone The post office is at Valtakatu 15, 26100 Rauma.

Library There's a public library south of the canal at Ankkurikatu 1, open Monday to Friday from 10 am to 7 pm.

Books & Maps There are three bookshops in Rauma, but Rauman Kirja-Aitta at Valtakatu 9-11 probably has the widest choice.

Emergency Services For general emergency phone ☎ 112 and for a doctor, ring ☎ 10023. Pharmacies are at Kauppakatu 11 and Valtakatu 9-11. There's a health care centre at Uotilantie 2.

Old Rauma

Old Rauma as a whole is worth taking some extra time to explore. Walk along the streets, visit shops and stop at cafeterias. Most of the buildings were erected in the 18th and 19th centuries. The old town has 600 wooden houses and 180 shops. The oval signs on the buildings give the name of each house. There are guided walking tours but the excellent town map and a sunny day are all you need to appreciate the old town.

The market square is the heart of Old Rauma and a lively centre for commerce even today. At one end of the square, there are two wooden stalls which sell coffee and refreshments. The locals call them *pystcaffe* – a café where you stand while drinking.

There are several museums in the old town, and a 10 mk ticket is valid for all of them on the same or following day.

Vanha Raatihuone At the market square,

the imposing town hall houses the Rauma Museum. It contains exhibits relating to seafaring and the good life that Raumaites have enjoyed in the past. It has an annual summer display of lace. In the garden are the types of plants that people used to have years ago. The museum is open daily from mid-May to mid-August from 10 am to 5 pm. At other times hours are similar, except it's closed on Monday, and on Saturday it closes at 2 pm.

Marela This house museum at Kauppiaankatu 24 is actually the most popular museum in Rauma. The large house once belonged to a rich trader. After his death, his two sons spent all their father's money on wine and women. In a few years, they were totally broke and had to sell everything from the house. The museum is open daily from 10 am to 5 pm. In winter, it's closed on Monday.

Kirsti This house was once the home of a sailor, and people lived here as recently as 1972. Note the china dogs in the bedrooms. They used to be placed in a window and actually had an important function: when the dogs faced outside, the sailor was sailing; when they faced inside, the sailor was home and could be visited. The museum is open from mid-May to mid-August daily from 10 am to 5 pm.

Savenvalajan Verstas This small pottery at Nummenkatu 2 is the smallest of the town museums, and least frequently visited. Here you can watch how pottery is made and try making some for yourself. Children enjoy this. The museum has similar hours to Kirsti.

Art Museum The art museum at Kuninkaankatu 37 is run by the town council and features temporary exhibitions. There are several art studios nearby; make sure you leave enough time to see them. The museum is open from 1 June to 31 August Monday to Friday from 10 am to 6 pm, Saturday from 10 am to 4 pm and Sunday from noon to 6 pm. In winter, it's closed on Monday. Admission is 10 to 15 mk.

Church of the Holy Cross The Pyhän Ristin Kirkko at Luostarinkatu 1 is a 15th century Franciscan church. A Catholic monastery functioned here until 1538, when the Lutheran reformers closed it, forcing the monks out.

The church can be visited from 1 June to 31 August Monday to Friday from 9 am to 6 pm, on Saturday from 9 am to 1 pm and on Sunday from noon to 6 pm. In September, it is open Monday to Friday from 10 am to 4 pm, on Saturday from 9 am to noon and on Sunday from noon to 3 pm.

Church Ruins Next to Kalatorin Majatalo, the park contains the ruins of the Church of the Holy Trinity. It was built during the 14th century, but was destroyed by a fire in 1640.

Helsinki Square This small square in the middle of the old town is a landmark and especially worth a visit for the attractive flower display in the nearby park on Vähämalminkatu. The statue is devoted to bobbin-lace makers.

Lönnström Art Museum

This attractive townhouse at Valtakatu 7 was renovated in 1993 and became an art museum for the Lönnström foundation. The foundation is independent from, say, the bureaucratic whims of the town council, and features highly unconventional forms of art. Having said this, you should enquire locally first whether the 25 mk ticket is good value for the current exhibition. There are three floors of exhibition space in the main building, and two floors in the smaller building. The museum is open daily except Monday from noon, and closes at 4 pm on weekends, and at 6 pm on other days.

Lönnström Home Museum

A particularly interesting place to visit is this mansion which belonged to wealthy industrialists Teresia and Rafael Lönnström, who created their fortune by selling ammunition and other military material. They also founded a munitions factory in Rauma in 1936 – this perfect timing led to their becoming wealthy. The pleasant location at Syväraumankatu 41 includes a large garden. In addition to old furniture and guns, this museum exhibits a great selection of Finnish and international art, and the modern annexe is devoted to the collection of modern paintings that were acquired by Teresia, who died in 1986 at the age of 91. Although the museum is more than two km north from the centre, it's worth the effort. It's open on Wednesday and Sunday from noon to 4 pm. Opening hours are longer during the Lace Week.

Water Tower

This tower, which also functions as an observation tower, is open daily in summer from 10 am to 8 pm.

Reksaari

The holiday island of Reksaari is owned by Rauma's town council. You can get there by boat, leaving from Syväraumanlahti. The boat runs twice a day in summer, at 10 am and 5 pm, and the return trip costs 30 mk. If you want to take the same boat back, you'll have 30 minutes in Reksaari. You are allowed to camp on the island free of charge. There are also cottages.

Festivals

Rauma Lace Week is the town's biggest annual event. It starts on the last weekend of July and includes a host of exhibitions and events. The whole weekend starts with the 'Night of Black Lace', a small-scale carnival during which shops and restaurants are open until 3 am and there are masses of people on the streets. Hotel prices tend to inflate during the festival.

Places to Stay – bottom end

Poroholma (☎ 822 4666), by the sea on Poroholmantie, is a youth hostel within a camping ground. Standards have declined although the old villa is still attractive. Reception is at the entrance of the camping ground, not inside the old building. For HI members, beds cost from 45 mk in a separate house. There are also four-bed cottages from 190 mk. There's a café in the old villa.

Kesähotelli (☎ 824 0130) at Satamakatu 20 is a summer hotel and a youth hostel, open from 1 June to late August. The rooms are student apartments; quite OK but not particularly attractive. Singles/doubles cost 135/185 mk, including breakfast, or ask for hostel rooms for 85/110 mk.

Places to Stay – middle

Hotelli Cityhovi (☎ 822 3745) is a small town hotel at Nortamonkatu 18, with discounted rooms for 240/280 mk on weekends and in summer. Ordinary rates are 290/350 mk.

Asuntohotelli Valtaväylä (☎ 822 4144) at Valtakatu 3 is a small hotel with rooms from 200/300 mk in summer. At other times rates are 240/320 mk.

Hotelli Kuntosumppu (☎ 822 1639) at Karjalankatu 29 on the western edge of town is a sports centre and offers a host of activities. There are singles/doubles for 230/300 mk.

Places to Stay – top end

Kalatorin Majatalo (☎ 822 7111) at Kalatori 4 in Old Rauma is the most pleasant hotel in town. It is in a beautifully renovated old Art-Deco warehouse. The owners are very friendly and know a lot about the history and sights of Rauma. Singles/doubles are 350/400 mk in summer, 370/500 mk at other times.

Sokos Hotel Raumanlinna (☎ 822 1111) at Valtakatu 5 is a chain hotel close to the bus station. Rooms cost 450/570 mk but on weekends and during much of summer, discounted rooms cost 390 mk.

Another nice hotel, a bit farther from the old town, *Hotelli Kalliohovi* (☎ 822 2811) at Kalliokatu 25 has rooms for 430/490 mk but in summer and on weekends, rooms cost 360 mk.

Cumulus (☎ 37821) at Aittakarinkatu 9 is a very clean hotel, and the location near the canal is superb. There are 103 rooms, three restaurants and a number of other facilities.

In summer and on weekends, rooms cost 345 mk; at other times they're 420/475 mk.

Places to Eat

Unless you eat at the market, the cheapest option is the local student cafeteria *Kulinarium* on the corner of Seminaarinkatu and Satamakatu. In summer, it's open for lunch Monday to Friday until 2 pm and slightly longer in winter.

For a decent lunch, locals prefer *Buena Vista* at Kanalinranta 5, by the canal. *La Bamba* in the market serves huge pizzas in a cosy dining room. Another place in the old town is *Kruuk Tawast* at Kauppakatu 22. Nearby, *Kalatorin majatalo* has good food, especially fish.

Rosso at Savilankatu 1 is a typical chain restaurant but serves pizzas in a nice old building. *Mustan Kissan kellari*, a basement restaurant at Anundilankatu 8, has a popular terrace.

Finally, Rauma also has fast-food restaurants for the modern locals. *Hesburger* is at Nortamonkatu 3, and *McDonald's* at Karjalankatu 1.

Cafés Cafés are abundant in Rauma and, probably due to the competition, are excellent value.

Kontion Leipomo at Kuninkaankatu 9 is particularly attractive, and includes an attractive garden. *Konditoria Peltola*, just next door at No 11 is also good. If you're at the market and fancy a coffee, *Café Wanha Rauma* is new and large, but has a quiet garden. A typical example of Rauma dialect, *Söömannin Baakar ja Kaffetupa* (adapted from the Swedish *Sjömannens Bageri & Kaffestuga*) at Kauppakatu 8 has bakery products and coffee, and a quiet garden.

Things to Buy

One of the things for which Rauma is famous is its bobbin lace. The best place to buy lace is the Pits-Priia at Kauppakatu 29, where you can see the bobbin lace being made. The laces are not cheap – you can't really get anything for less than 200 mk – but the makers argue that if they charged a decent

A: Harbour and old church, Naantali
B: Frozen windmill, Uusikaupunki
C: Mail boxes near Ellivuori, not far from Vammala
D: Kimito ferry

Top: Locomotive Museum, Haapamäki
Left: Old church, Keuruu
Right: Head of Valamo Orthodox Monastery

hourly wage, the prices would at least double.

Among the more interesting handicraft shops in Rauma are Ateljee Eila Minkkinen at Vanhankirkonkatu 20 (for jewellery and metal reliefs) and Lahjanavetta at Kulmakatu 6. Kultasuutari at Kalatori 4 is a goldsmith's shop where you can watch the goldsmith at work and buy locally made jewellery.

Getting There & Away

Bus There are daily direct buses between Helsinki and Rauma; they take one 250-km Coach Holiday Coupon. The 7.30 am departure is especially handy. Between Rauma and Pori, there are buses every hour or so. From the south, Turku and Uusikaupunki are connected by buses every two hours or so.

Train Get off the Tampere to Pori train at the Kokemäki railway station, and transfer to a connecting bus. Your train pass will be valid on the bus.

Getting Around

You can rent old bicycles at the tourist office for 10 mk per hour or 40 mk per day. Compare prices and quality at Pyörä-Nurmi at Kuninkaankatu 26. The tourist office will provide you with a free bicycle map for the surrounding region where you can visit farmhouses, prehistoric sites and natural attractions.

VAMMALA

This small historic town (population 15,790) offers the visitor a number of attractions. Most shops and restaurants are along or near the main street, Puistokatu.

Information

The main tourist office is in the town centre. In addition, from 1 June to 15 August, the tourist information booth (☎ 519 8255) on Rautavedenkatu, at the harbour, is open every day from 10 am to 5 pm.

Things to See

Tyrvää Museum This museum at Jaatsinkatu 2 has a collection of old objects from around Vammala. Because the area has been inhabited for a very long time, the museum also has archaeological items. It's open Sunday to Friday from noon to 4 pm. Tickets cost 5 mk.

Tyrvää Church The church at the northern end of Puistokatu was the first one in Finland to have two towers. It's open in summer every day from 10 am to 6 pm.

Jaatsi This old house on Asemakatu is the childhood home of Akseli Gallen-Kallela, probably the most famous Finnish painter of all time. It houses the art collection of the town of Vammala. Jaatsi House is open from 10 am to 3 pm every day. Admission is free.

Vehmaanniemi At Vehmaanniemi, three km east of the town centre along Tampereentie, there is a nature path along the little peninsula, protected by the World Wide Fund for Nature. The path runs through a preserved area in which Iron Age graves have been found. The path is approximately two km long and is marked by signs along the way.

Places to Stay

Tervakallio (☎ 514 2720) is a small camping ground on the northern shore of the river at the end of Uittomiehenkatu. It's open from 1 May to 15 August.

Three tiny huts at 160 mk could theoretically house four people each, but larger ones are available for 250 mk. Pitching a tent costs 65 mk per family, 35 mk for an individual. You should take advantage of late opening hours to see the small Traktorinäyttely (Tractor Exhibition) in a house next to Tervakallio. The reception will lend you the keys for a 10 mk deposit per person.

Gasthaus Liekoranta (☎ 514 3662) at Asemakatu 34 is directly opposite the railway station, and has singles/doubles from 180/240 mk.

Also in the northern part of town, *Kesähotelli Tyrvää* (☎ 514 2720) at Varikonkatu 4 is a summer hotel that is open from early June to early August. There are 27 rooms, and each group of three rooms has a common kitchen, bathroom and TV lounge. Singles/doubles are 120/185 mk.

Hotelli Nukkumatti (☎ 514 2623) at Onkiniemenkatu 6 offers a quiet, homely place to stay. Some of the decoration is rather old-fashioned, but the rooms are neat and clean. Singles/doubles cost 240/350 mk.

Hotelli Vammalan Seurahuone (☎ 51941) at Puistokatu 4 is where locals spend their evenings, but there are also 20 rooms at 350/450 mk – they're at least 100 mk less in summer.

Places to Eat

Gasthaus Liekoranta at Asemakatu 34 serves an 'all you can eat' buffet lunch for 34 mk. At the same side of the river, *Rautavesi* serves inexpensive meals with extras all day in a small lakeside house on your way to the camping ground. In the town centre, you can eat at hotels, or try *Rosso* at Puistokatu 1 for standard meals. *Herkku-Tuote* at Onkiniemenkatu 6, near the market square, is a pleasant place for coffee or snacks.

Getting There & Away

Bus The bus terminal is on Puistokatu. There

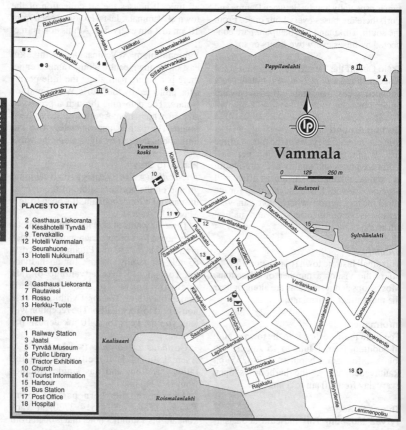

PLACES TO STAY
2 Gasthaus Liekoranta
4 Kesähotelli Tyrvää
9 Tervakallio
12 Hotelli Vammalan Seurahuone
13 Hotelli Nukkumatti

PLACES TO EAT
2 Gasthaus Liekoranta
7 Rautavesi
11 Rosso
13 Herkku-Tuote

OTHER
1 Railway Station
3 Jaatsi
5 Tyrvää Museum
6 Public Library
8 Tractor Exhibition
10 Church
14 Tourist Information
15 Harbour
16 Bus Station
17 Post Office
18 Hospital

Vammala

are regular buses from Tampere and Turku as well as from some smaller places in the region.

Train The railway station can be found on the other side of the bridge that crosses the Vammaskoski River. Trains between Tampere and Pori stop at Vammala, and there are five or six trains each day.

Getting Around

In the town centre, you can reach everything on foot. If you want to travel further afield, catch a bus from the bus terminal. To get to the Ellivuori, take the twice-weekly boat. Tervakallio rents out rowing boats at 30 mk, and can be used to travel to at least one nearby medieval church. If you're fit, you can row as far as Ellivuori.

AROUND VAMMALA

The region around Vammala – especially some of the places along the Kokemäenjoki River – is among the most historic in Finland. There are two top-class medieval churches, and a number of natural attractions. The loop via Ellivuori is highly recommended, and can be done by bicycle.

Tyrvää St Olav's Church

This medieval church, from the 15th century, is just 5 km from Vammala on a headland. The church was left idle from 1855, and features old wooden benches. The location is idyllic, and while getting there, the road almost touches old farmhouses. There's a sign on road No 249. The church is open in summer daily from 10 am to 4 pm; on Sunday till 6 pm. The sign says 'Tyrvään vanha kirkko'.

Sastamala Church

This church was the *emäkirkko*, or 'mother church' of the entire Satakunta region from the late 13th century, meaning that people would come from quite far away to attend services here. The church was built on a former sacrificial site for pre-Christian Finns, and thus was to maintain its significance. The huge church seems quite empty today, although there is a 14th century Madonna statue to the left of the altar. The separate bell tower dates from 1792. There are too few signs from road No 249, but the church is not hard to find. It is open Monday to Thursday from 10 am to 4 pm, and on Sunday from 11 am to 6 pm. The sign says 'Sastamalan vanha kirkko'.

Karkku

This formerly independent municipality is now part of Vammala town, and has consequently lost much of its prestige. It's a very pretty little village with a number of impressive farmhouses. There are a number or historical places around here. The grey stone church dates from 1913 and is one of the National Romantic churches; it's three km from the actual village. You will travel via Karkku between Sastamala Church and Ellivuori, following road No 249.

Ellivuori

Situated on Salonsaari Island on Lake Rautavesi (part of the Kokemäenjoki River system), this small mountain is one of the main attractions in the region, although the downhill skiing is rather seasonal. Summer activities include sweating uphill with a bicycle on narrow gravel roads, while enjoying some really pretty waterscape. The downhill slope and the upmarket hotel are in separate locations. The actual peak, Pirunvuori (Devil's Mountain), rising 100 metres above water level, has been a cult site and a fearsome place for locals. The scenery inspired a Finnish painter, Emil Danielsson (1882-1967) to build a studio on the top of it in 1906. Now the Kivilinna (Rock Castle) can be reached by walking the 1.5 km track from the hotel; ask for the keys at reception.

Places to Stay & Eat *Hotelli Ellivuori* (☎ 51921) is a top-end resort with everything from après-ski activities to chic restaurants. You can also play tennis and golf here. Singles/doubles are 260/365 mk in summer and around Christmas; 470/600 mk at other times.

Situated at the Ellivuori crossing on the

Tampere to Turku road (No 41), *Kiskokabinetti* is a roadhouse with coffee and meals at a Shell petrol station. The adjacent **Marskin salonkivaunu** is an old railway carriage which was the venue of a meeting between Marshal CG Mannerheim and Adolf Hitler on 4 June 1942. There's also an old locomotive.

Getting There & Away Ellivuori can be reached by bus. For those who have their own wheels, the loop between roads No 41 and 249 is recommended for its attractive rural scenery – the distance is over 10 km. In summer, enquire about boat services from the pier in Vammala.

South-East

The south-east corner of Finland, officially the Province of Kymi, consists of the industrial Kymi River Valley and the narrow slice of South Karelia that the Soviet Union let Finland keep after WWII. The northern part has some interesting unspoiled nature.

After reading this chapter, and visiting some of the extreme places in the region, you may think that this is the most polluted and least attractive area of Finland. Certainly someone has got rich at nature's expense here, but it is the history that makes this province so intriguing. There are remains of battles between Sweden and Russia, and any number of forts, ruins and alien architectural styles. This is where Russian influence is at its strongest in Finland.

Highlights
- Towns and villages along the King's Road.
- Islands off Kotka and Hamina.
- Cruises on and around Lake Saimaa from the pleasant town of Lappeenranta.
- Fortified old towns with Russian-inspired architecture in Kotka, Hamina and Lappeenranta.
- The oldest Orthodox church in Finland.

Kotka

Kotka, 132 km east of Helsinki, is Finland's most important port and is sometimes called the Sea Town. For a traveller, Kotka has a lot to offer – interesting museums, small islands in the Gulf of Finland and one of the most pleasant youth hostels in the country.

The population figure of 56,000 includes residents of nearby Karhula, now a suburb of Kotka. Massive industries, the large harbour and oil tanks are features of Kotka. A visit to the pleasant archipelago may be the best way to escape the occasional industrial stench.

Orientation

Kotkansaari is the island on which the actual town of Kotka is situated. Keskuskatu and Kirkkokatu are the two main streets in the centre. The island of Mussalo to the west is a suburb – a more rural area with a camping ground and youth hostel. Karhula to the north was previously an independent entity and is now a regular stop along all bus routes.

Information

Tourist Office The tourist office at Keskuskatu 17 (☎ 274 424) is open Monday to Friday from 9 am to 4 pm and Saturday from 10 am to 2 pm.

Post & Telephone The main post office, 48100 Kotka, is at Kapteeninkatu 16 and is open Monday to Friday from 9 am to 5 pm.

Library An excellent variety of literature and magazines can be read at Kirkkokatu 24.

Emergency Services In a general emergency, ring ☎112. For a doctor, call ☎ 10023.

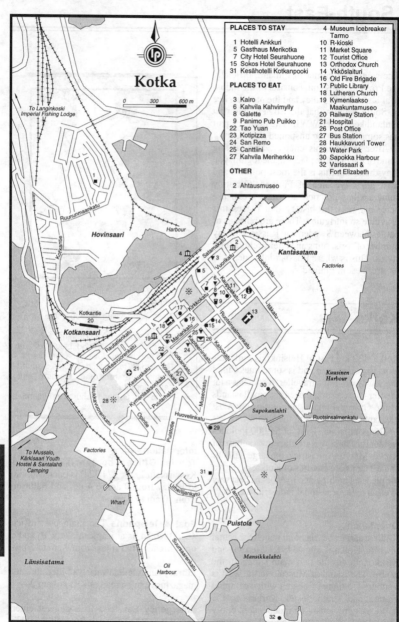

Kotka

0   300   600 m

PLACES TO STAY

1 Hotelli Ankkuri
5 Gasthaus Merikotka
7 City Hotel Seurahuone
15 Sokos Hotel Seurahuone
31 Kesähotelli Kotkanpooki

PLACES TO EAT

3 Kairo
6 Kahvila Kahvimylly
8 Galette
9 Panimo Pub Puikko
22 Tao Yuan
23 Kotipizza
24 San Remo
25 Canttiini
27 Kahvila Meriherkku

OTHER

2 Ahtausmuseo

4 Museum Icebreaker
   Tarmo
10 R-kioski
11 Market Square
12 Tourist Office
13 Orthodox Church
14 Ykköslaituri
16 Old Fire Brigade
17 Public Library
18 Lutheran Church
19 Kymenlaakso
   Maakuntamuseo
20 Railway Station
21 Hospital
26 Post Office
27 Bus Station
28 Haukkavuori Tower
29 Water Park
30 Sapokka Harbour
32 Varissaari &
   Fort Elizabeth

To Langinkoski
Imperial Fishing Lodge

Ruununmaankatu

Hovinsaari

Harbour

Kantasatama

Factories

Kotkantie

Kotkansaari

Kuusinen
Harbour

Sapokanlahti

Ruotsinsalmenkatu

To Mussalo,
Kärkisaari Youth
Hostel & Santalahti
Camping

Factories

Wharf

Puistola

Mansikkalahti

Länsisatama

Oil
Harbour

SOUTH-EAST

32

There are pharmacies at Kirkkokatu 10 and on Keskuskatu at Nos 25 and 31.

Kymenlaakso Maakuntamuseo

This regional museum at Kotkankatu 13 is an excellent introduction to the colourful history of the Kymi River Valley. It's open Tuesday to Friday from noon to 6 pm and at weekends from noon to 4 pm. Admission is 10 mk.

Churches

The Orthodox Church of St Nicholas is the oldest building in Kotka. It was the only building in Kotka to survive the Crimean War of 1853-56. According to legend, this was due to the courageous actions of a 100-year-old lady, Maria Feodorovna Purpur, a colonel's widow. Most of the church's treasures were taken to Hamina, where some of them remain. The church is located in Isopuisto Park and is open from May to August daily (except Monday) between noon and 3 pm.

The Lutheran church was built in the Gothic style in 1898, and houses 1600 people. The altarpiece was painted by the famous Pekka Halonen. The church is open in summer daily from noon to 4 pm.

Langinkoski

The Imperial fishing lodge at the Langinkoski rapids (see the Kymi River Valley map) is the most interesting building in Kotka. It was built in 1889 for Tsar Alexander III. The tsar came to Langinkoski frequently, to live like the common people. Most of the furniture has been retained, so the rooms look as they did at the turn of the century. The area around the lodge is protected. Fishing is allowed with a permit, which can be obtained locally. The lodge is open from 1 May to 30 September daily from 10 am to 7 pm. In October, it's open on weekends from 11 am to 4 pm. Admission is 15 mk. You can get almost all the way to Langinkoski on bus No 13 or 27. Alternatively, get off at the sign at the *pikavuoro* (express) bus stop and walk 1.2 km.

Islands

Several interesting islands off the Kotka coast rank among the most interesting island day trips in Finland. See the Kymi River Valley map for locations.

Varissaari Fort Elisabeth on Varissaari was built by the Russians as part of a fortification to defend the coast against the Swedes. When Russia took over the rest of Finland early in the 19th century, shifting Russia's western border to the Gulf of Bothnia, the fort lost its military significance. Since the end of the 19th century, Fort Elisabeth has been used for nonmilitary purposes. It is a popular venue for festivals, dances and open-air performances, and a favourite picnic spot. If you do not wish to bring a picnic, there is a restaurant.

From May to August, there is an hourly boat connection between Varissaari and Sapokka Harbour in Kotka. Return tickets cost 20 mk. The trip takes just a few minutes.

Kukouri The Fortress of Honour, also known as Fort Slava, is accessible from mid-June to 30 July approximately five times per day. Return tickets are 35 mk. The fort was built by Russians and was finished in 1794, before it was destroyed by the British in 1855. It was renovated in 1993.

Lehmäsaari This island has beautiful beaches. There are three to four boat connections between Sapokka and Lehmäsaari each day. Boats operate in July daily and in June and August four days a week. One-way tickets for the half-hour trip cost 20 mk.

Kaunissaari There is a fishing village and a local museum on this island, a one-hour boat trip from Kotka. There are one to three connections a day between Sapokka and Kaunissaari (35 mk one-way). There is a restaurant on the island, and you can stay overnight in a cottage.

Other Attractions

Sapokka, the pleasant harbour area, includes a large park. Puistola is a residential

SOUTH-EAST

area on a hill, and offers good sea views. On Haukkavuori hill, a water tower will give even better views. Among interesting architecture, check the 100-year-old Fire Brigade building at Kirkkokatu 13.

Festivals
The biggest event in Kotka is the Kotkan meripäivät, or Kotka Maritime Festival, which is held annually at the beginning of August. Events include boat racing, concerts, cruises and a market.

Places to Stay – bottom end
For the locations of places in this section, see the Kymi River Valley map.

Santalahti Camping in Mussalo has a good location by the sea. Camping costs 70 mk per family or 35 mk per person. There are also four-bed cottages for 350 mk. Bus Nos 13 and 14 will take you to Santalahti. Camping in tents is also possible on the island of Kaunissaari, which can be reached by boat from Sapokka Harbour.

Kärkisaari (☎ 604 215), at the northern end of the island of Mussalo, must be one of the nicest youth hostels in Finland. It is an old wooden building on a small island, and there are no neighbours. Guests can go swimming, use the small seaside sauna or have a barbecue on the terrace. Kärkisaari hostel is open from 2 May to 30 September. It is the only survivor of the three hostels that were previously open in Kotka. Summer weekends are hopeless due to weddings. There are a few doubles (80 mk per person) and two big dormitories (55 mk per person). You can hire bicycles and boats for 10 mk per three hours or 40 mk per day. To get to Kärkisaari, take bus No 13 (longer route) or 27 from Kirkkokatu bus stop at the church. There is an 800 metre walk from the bus stop to the hostel. Call in advance to make sure there's a vacancy.

Koskisoppi (☎ 285 555) at Keisarinmajantie 4, close to the Imperial Fishing Lodge at Langinkoski, is no longer a youth hostel, but it opens as a summer hotel. Rooms cost from 120/180 mk.

Places to Stay – middle
Kesähotelli Kotkanpooki (☎ 181 945) at Urheilijankatu 2B is a summer hotel, open from mid-June to mid-August. There are apartments with two/three rooms from 200/300 mk, but individual rooms start at 115 mk. You are advised to call ahead, and negotiate how you will be put up.

Gasthaus Merikotka (☎ 15222) at Satamakatu 9 is a modest but nice hotel. Singles/doubles are 240/320 mk. There are 15 rooms, each with a TV and a bathroom. *Hotelli Ankkuri*, a bit out of the centre in Hovinsaari district at Merenkulkijankatu 6, has rooms for 200/280 mk.

Places to Stay – top end
Sokos Hotel Seurahuone (☎ 186 090) is the finest hotel in town and the most popular night spot. There are 100 rooms, each costing 390 mk in summer. At other times, singles/doubles cost 475/560 mk. You can also stay at *City Hotel Seurahuone* at Kirkkokatu 14, an annex of the Sokos Hotel, with rooms for 270/300 mk.

Out in Karhula there are several hotels along the bypass road. *Innotel Cumulus Kotka* (☎ 693 100) has 100 well-equipped rooms for 265/310 mk; *Karhu* (☎ 63466) on Karjalantie has doubles from 200 mk in summer (from 250 mk at other times); and *Hotelli Leikari* (☎ 227 8111, see the Kymi River Valley map), at Rantahaka, has 103 rooms from 330 mk.

Places to Eat
Kotka is not bad when it comes to dining; you can find pizzas and hamburgers in several places, including *Kotipizza* at Kotkankatu 14. Kotkankatu has a great number of pubs if you want to go bar-hopping with locals. Around the corner, *Tao Yuan* at Mariankatu 24 is a Chinese restaurant. *Canttiini* at Kaivokatu 15 serves pasta and other, more substantial meals, and is quite popular among locals. Also good is *San Remo* at Keskuskatu 27, where you will be served large portions.

The fabled *Kairo* at Satamakatu 7 is a sailors' pub, its walls covered with paintings of nudes. Even though there are more tourists than sailors among its clientele these days, the old atmosphere is still there. Don't miss it; come in the evening when it's open. *Panimo Pub Puikko* at Ruotsinsalmenkatu 14 translates as a brewery but, no, they don't have their own home brew. Both these pubs also serve meals.

Kahvila Kahvimylly at Kirkkokatu 12 has good salads for vegetarians, and a selection from the salad bar can also be combined with a meal. More traditional is *Galette* at Kirkkokatu 9. *Kahvila Meriherkku* is a good café at the bus station.

Getting There & Away

Bus Kotka serves as a base for visiting south-east Finland, although all buses stop at Karhula near road No 7. There are regular express buses from Helsinki, via Porvoo, Loviisa, and Pyhtää. Hourly buses make the 45-minute trip to Hamina, 26 km east.

Train Taking a train from Kotka is not your regular experience. The ticket office closes at 4.10 pm, and the ticket vending machine probably won't take your credit card. The public phone takes only Tele cards. The 'stations' between Kotka and Kouvola to the north are little more than concrete shelters. So if you get on the train at one of these concrete shelters or at Kotka after 4.10 pm, you will have to buy your ticket on the train. There are between four and six trains a day to Kouvola and they take 40 minutes to cover the 50 km.

Kymi River Valley

RUOTSINPYHTÄÄ

If you are looking for somewhere quiet yet exotic to stay for a day or two, this place is for you. The long name means 'Pyhtää of Sweden', as it was here that the Swedish-Russian international border cut Pyhtää into two. The western, oddly shaped section was Swedish property; Pyhtää proper was to become Russian for some time. The munic-

ipal and provincial border follows the river, and nobody has had the courage to unite these areas. Perhaps locals think that Finns are not supposed to unite what Swedes and Russians have separated. Ruotsinpyhtää has a very interesting old industrial milieu; the Strömfors Ironworks area from the 1700s has many attractions which make it a popular place to unwind in summer.

Administratively, Ruotsinpyhtää (population 3200) is part of Uusimaa Province.

Ruotsinpyhtää Ironworks

The Workshop Museum consists of an old smith's workshop and equipment. It's open 1 June to 15 August from 10 am to 7 pm daily. The octagonal wooden church dates from 1770; its altarpiece was painted by Helene Schjerfbeck, a famous Finnish painter. The ironworks area has several craft workshops. You can find pottery, a silversmith, textile makers and painters. One of the buildings serves as an art gallery in summer.

Ahvenkoski

This part of the Kymi River, with rapids and a hydroelectric power station, marked the Sweden-Russia border from 1743 until 1809. Just off road No 7 at Ahvenkoski, Savukosken silta is a 'museum bridge' over the Savukoski rapids. Built in 1928, it represented the new technology of its time. There are ruins of an old Swedish fort, from 1743-90, on the western side of the bridge. On the eastern side is the Ahvenkoski Mansion, which is privately owned but worth a quick look from a distance along the narrow road.

Places to Stay & Eat

Two renovated buildings in the ironworks area serve as youth hostels (☎ 618 474). Both are open all year round. Accommodation costs 110 mk in *Lukkarinmäki* and 125 mk in *Krouvinmäki*. The hostels are in good shape and have heaps of style and class.

There's a restaurant in the Workshop Museum building.

Getting There & Away

To get to Ruotsinpyhtää, take a bus from

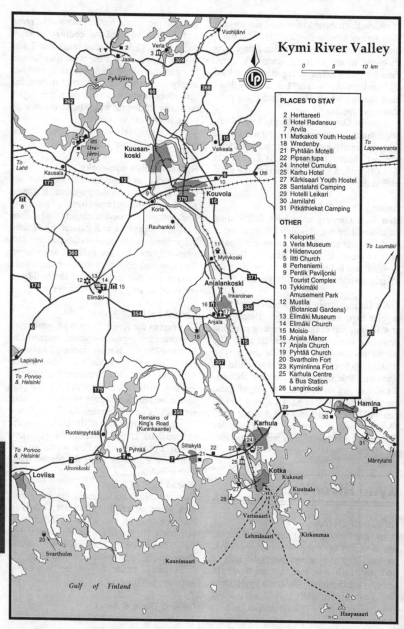

Kymi River Valley

0   5   10 km

PLACES TO STAY

2   Herttareeti
6   Hotel Radansuu
7   Arvila
11 Matkakoti Youth Hostel
18 Wredenby
21 Pyhtään Motelli
22 Pipsan tupa
24 Innotel Cumulus
25 Karhu Hotel
27 Kärkisaari Youth Hostel
28 Santalahti Camping
29 Hotelli Leikari
30 Jamilahti
31 Pitkäthiekat Camping

OTHER

1   Kelopirtti
3   Verla Museum
4   Hiidenvuori
5   Iitti Church
8   Perheniemi
9   Pentik Paviljonki
    Tourist Complex
10 Tykkimäki
    Amusement Park
12 Mustila
    (Botanical Gardens)
13 Elimäki Museum
14 Elimäki Church
15 Moisio
16 Anjala Manor
17 Anjala Church
19 Pyhtää Church
20 Svartholm Fort
23 Kyminlinna Fort
25 Karhula Centre
    & Bus Station
26 Langinkoski

SOUTH-EAST

Helsinki, Loviisa or Kouvola. There are one or two connections a day from Helsinki via Porvoo, three to five from Loviisa and one to three from Kouvola.

PYHTÄÄ

Pyhtää (Swedish: Pyttis), near the Uusimaa border, is the historical centre of the region. In the past it controlled much of the river valley. Pyhtää was annexed by Russia in 1743, when the western part was named Ruotsinpyhtää (the Swedish Pyhtää).

Part of the original King's Road remains between Pyhtää Church and the village of Siltakylä. It is certainly worth choosing to take it instead of the main road No 7.

Pyhtää Church

The medieval stone church is the highlight of the municipality. In addition to the typical coats of arms, miniature boats and wooden statues, the highlight is the huge and weird painting 'St Kristoforus carrying Baby Jesus'. The church is open in summer daily from 9 am to 3 pm.

Places to Stay & Eat

If you are driving, there's the tacky *Pyhtään Motelli* in the village of Siltakylä, close to road No 7. Farther east along the same road, *Pipsan tupa* is a small guesthouse with mid-range prices.

In the village of Pyhtää, near the church, *Keihässalmi* is a restaurant, while *Jussin kulma* is more of a pub.

Getting There & Away

Pyhtää is 115 km east of Helsinki and one km off main road No 7. Most long-distance buses visit the village.

HAMINA

Farther east is Hamina (Swedish: Fredrikshamn), probably the most Russian town in Finland in terms of architecture. It was founded in 1653, when Finland was a part of Sweden, and its unique circular plan and ramparts date from 1722, when work began on the fortifications. The Russian period began as early as 1742. Since then, Hamina has been an important garrison town. The cadet school of imperial Finland was here, and today Hamina is known as the home of the Finnish Reserve Officer School. For a visitor, Hamina is interesting because of its unique town plan and its pleasant small-town atmosphere.

As Hamina is close to the eastern border of Finland, it has become a favourite place for Russians to visit. Its population is 10,000. Every two years in July, Hamina celebrates military music during the one-week Hamina Tattoo, an international event.

Information

Tourist Office The tourist office in the library at Rautatienkatu 8 (☎ 749 5251) is a bit difficult to find, as the entrance is at the back. The office is open Monday to Friday from 8 am to 4 pm. Much easier to find is the tourist office in the tower near the market, which is open from 1 June to mid-August Monday to Friday from 9 am to 5 pm and Saturday to 1 pm.

Post & Telephone The post office is at Maariankatu 4, 49400 Hamina.

Travel Agencies Vilkas Matkat (☎ 344 6800) at Maariankatu 16 is a regular travel agency which runs buses to St Petersburg, although you should arrange your visa in advance.

Library A legacy of the free-spending 1980s, the public library at Rautatienkatu 8, near the bus station, is open Monday to Friday from 1 to 7 pm and Saturday from 10 am to 2 pm. Here you can see maps of the region at the scale of 1:20,000, or read books and magazines in English.

Books & Maps Suomalainen Kirjakauppa, near the market square, is the only bookshop in Hamina. R-kioski at Kaivokatu 10 sells imported magazines and newspapers.

Left Luggage You can leave your luggage at the bus station for 12 mk, but you must pick it up before 6 pm.

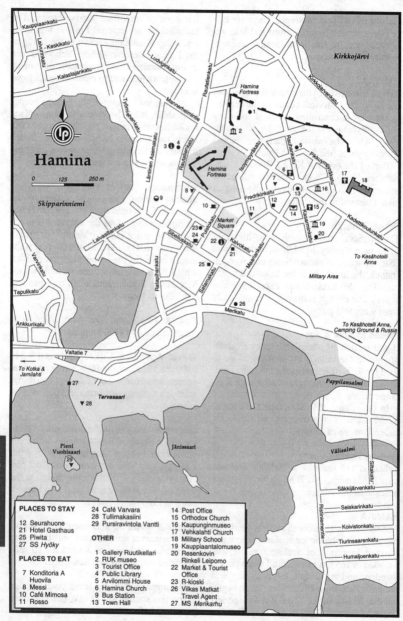

Hamina

0 125 250 m

Kirkkojärvi

Skipparinniemi

Hamina Fortress

Hamina Fortress

Military Area

Tervasaari

Pieni Vuohisaari

Jänissaari

Pappilansalmi

Välisalmi

To Kesähotelli Anna

To Kesähotelli Anna, Camping Ground & Russia

To Kotka & Jamilahti

Valtatie 7

Market Square

PLACES TO STAY

12 Seurahuone
21 Hotel Gasthaus
25 Piwita
27 SS *Hyöky*

PLACES TO EAT

7   Konditoria A Huovila
8   Messi
10 Café Mimosa
11 Rosso

24 Café Varvara
28 Tullimakasiini
29 Pursiravintola Vantti

OTHER

1   Gallery Ruutikellari
2   RUK museo
3   Tourist Office
4   Public Library
5   Arvilommi House
6   Hamina Church
9   Bus Station
13 Town Hall

14 Post Office
15 Orthodox Church
16 Kaupunginmuseo
17 Vehkalahti Church
18 Military School
19 Kauppiaantalomuseo
20 Resenkovin Rinkeli Leipomo
22 Market & Tourist Office
23 R-kioski
26 Vilkas Matkat Travel Agent
27 MS *Merikarhu*

Emergency Services In a general emergency, ring ☎ 112. For a doctor, ☎ 10023. There are pharmacies at Isoympyränkatu 13 and Sibeliuskatu 36.

Churches

There are three churches in a cluster near the town hall. The neoclassical **Hamina Church** was built in 1843. The miniature ship from 1763 was brought from Koivisto, now in Russian Karelia. The church is open in summer from 10 am to 5 pm. Directly opposite, behind the town hall, the round-shaped Orthodox **Church of Saints Peter & Paul** from 1837 has several old icons, including some from the 18th century. It's open Tuesday to Sunday from 11 am to 3 pm. The nearby **Vehkalahti Church** at Pikkuympyräkatu 34 is the oldest building in the Province of Kymi, but it has been completely rebuilt and absolutely nothing remains from the 14th century. It's open in summer from 9 am to 6 pm.

Museums

All three museums are open May to August Wednesday to Saturday from 11 am to 3 pm and Sunday from noon to 5 pm. Admission is 10 mk.

Kaupunginmuseo at Kadettikoulunkatu 2 is the town museum of Hamina. There are old restored rooms and local history exhibits. King Gustav III of Sweden and Catherine II (the Great) of Russia held negotiations in one of the rooms in 1783.

Kauppiaantalomuseo is a former merchant's store and residence at Kasarminkatu 6, and one of the best house museums in Finland. The shop itself is full of interesting details, and all the storehouses, sheds and stables are also part of the museum. Nearby is the **Resenkovin Rinkeli Leipomo**, owned by the Resenkovs who came from Russia. They still run this bakery at Kasarminkatu 8, which has a 100-year tradition. The building was erected at the beginning of the 20th century.

RUK museo at Mannerheimintie 7 is devoted to the local Reserve Officer School.

On display are military uniforms and weapons.

Hamina Fortress

Although most of the 18th century fortress is within a military area, you can walk freely in the western section. **Gallery Ruutikellari**, an old gunpowder warehouse on Roopertinkatu, has been renovated into an art gallery.

Museum Ships

The harbour at Tervasaari has two museum ships open March to October from 9 am to 10 pm. The SS *Hyöky* is also open as a hotel, and the MS *Merikarhu* is a harbour icebreaker. Admission is 10 mk per person for a guided tour. The museum ships serve coffee and beer.

Architecture

You go to Hamina to see Russian-inspired architecture, not modern achievements. The only modern building of real note is the library, which is enormous. The central town hall is Hamina's landmark, and the three churches are located around it. Opposite the town hall is an old blue wooden house, **Aladinin talo**, dating from 1889. On the corner of Rauhankatu and Pikkympyränkatu, **Arvilommin talo** is from 1849 and represents a unique neo-rococo style in Finland. Note also the huge main building of the **military school** on Kadettikoulunkatu. A free pamphlet on Hamina's old town is available at the tourist office.

Tammio & Ulkotammio Islands

There are regular cruises to the fishing harbour on the island of Tammio. Departures from Tervasaari take place from late May to late August on Tuesday, Saturday and Sunday, and cost 60 mk. You can also reach Ulkotammio, an island farther south, from mid-June to the end of July at weekends. Expect to pay 75 mk. You should check current departure times at the tourist office.

Places to Stay

Leirintäalue Pitkäthiekat (☎ 344 8014) is a camping ground six km east of Hamina at

Vilniemi, open May to September. Pitching a tent costs 55 mk per family. Cottages cost 150 to 370 mk.

You can rent a cabin in the SS *Hyöky* (☎ 354 3600), which is moored in Tervasaari Harbour. There are 16 cabins, with singles/doubles at 150/200 mk. There's a café, and a sauna.

Kesähotelli Anna (☎ 344 7747) at Annankatu 1 is open from 1 June to 15 August and has singles/doubles for 150/250 mk. It is associated with the Finnish HI, and a discount is available. There's a sauna, a canteen and a laundry.

Singles/doubles cost 220/330 mk at *Hotel Gasthaus* (☎ 354 1434) at Kaivokatu 4, opposite the information tower. The entrance, through a restaurant, looks horrible, but the rooms are OK.

The best of the bunch in town is *Seurahuone* (☎ 497 263), at Pikkuympyränkatu 5. Full of olde world ambience, it has a dozen rooms, available from 350 mk.

Then there's *Piwita* (☎ 344 9098) at Sibeliuskatu 32, which provides all kinds of services, including a few rooms for rent. It certainly won't hurt to check this place out.

On the western side of Haminanlahti, *Jamilahti* (☎ 344 6040), or Jamilahden kansanopisto, two km from the town centre, offers accommodation in summer for groups. The place is an old mansion beautifully located by the sea. There are 30 rooms, priced at 150 mk.

Places to Eat

Hamina has a great variety of *grillis*, pubs and cafés, and several restaurants, including those in hotels. The following are worth a try.

Konditoria A Huovila at Fredrikinkatu 1 is the best place to enjoy coffee and tempting cakes. It's closed on Sunday. *Café Mimosa* at Puistokatu 8 is a pleasant place to eat lunch for 25 to 40 mk, Monday to Saturday. Also on offer are ice cream, salads and bakery products. *Café Varvara* at Puistokatu 2 offers good home-baked buns and cakes, as well as snacks and beer. It closes at 5 pm, and on Sunday. *Rosso* at Isoympyräkatu is a popular restaurant where locals eat until late.

Restaurant Gasthaus at Kaivokatu 4 is a popular nightspot, with dancing. Not far from the library, *Messi* at Vallikatu 2 is more of a pub, with a terrace in summer. On summer weekends, *Pursiravintola Vantti*, on the island of Pieni Vuohisaari, is the place to go for dining and dancing to live music. To get to the island, take one of the special boats from Tervasaari Harbour (5 mk per person). There's also a quaint restaurant at Tervasaari, *Tullimakasiini*, located in an old customs house. Fresh fish is a speciality.

Getting There & Away

You can reach Hamina hourly by bus from Kotka, 26 km to the south-west. Express buses from Helsinki make the 153 km trip in less than three hours; ordinary buses take 3½ hours.

ELIMÄKI

Elimäki is a green little village north of Pyhtää, surrounded by a rural municipality along road No 6. It is some 115 km east of Helsinki and 25 km south-west of Kouvola. In 1608 the whole area became the property of the Wrede family, and there are several historical landmarks. Many visitors stop to see the Arboretum Mustila and other sights. The population is 8500.

Mustila

The botanical gardens of Mustila were founded in 1902 when State Secretary AF Tigerstedt planted the first foreign trees in the Mustila Estate area. In the 1920s both woody and perennial ornamental species were introduced. The original purpose of the arboretum was to gain information about the economic value of exotic tree species in the Finnish climate. In 1981, Arboretum Mustila became a national conservation area. The arboretum is at its most beautiful in June, when literally thousands of rhododendrons blossom, and in September during the *ruska* (autumn). There are walking routes of 1.5, 2.5 and three km in the arboretum area. The entry fee of 15 mk can be paid in the cafeteria. Mustila is on road No 6.

Elimäki Village

The **Elimäki Homestead Museum** in Elimäki village, half a km west of road No 6, consists of half a dozen old farm buildings, and items used on a farm. It's open in summer Tuesday to Friday from 2 to 7 pm, Saturday from 1 to 6 pm and Sunday from noon to 7 pm. A **school museum**, which is on the opposite side of the road, has the same opening hours. The **Elimäki Church**, built in 1638, is one of the oldest wooden churches in Finland still in regular use. There is also a church museum.

Places to Eat

There are a few places on road No 6 to eat and buy things: *Alppiruusu*, a collection of pyramid-shaped glass structures at a petrol station, serves food and sells handicrafts. Across the road, *Piika ja Renki* is an attractive red house, previously a granary. In addition to coffee and snacks, there's a handicrafts shop and an art exhibition. There are also other places nearby, such as *Makeistehdas*, a confectionery. The Arboretum has a café.

In Elimäki village, *Lounas Kaari* at the bus station serves simple meals from Monday to Friday. *Japan Tupa* is a local pub, but 'Japan' refers to a genitive form of a proper noun, not to an island nation in East Asia.

East of the village, *Moision kartano* is a manor house with a café open in summer from 11 am to 6 pm.

ANJALANKOSKI

Anjalankoski, north of Kotka, has over 18,000 inhabitants, and its historical section, Anjala, is one of the highlights of the Kymi River Valley route. Unfortunately, greater Anjalankoski is an industrial centre, and while visiting Anjala village you will have to put up with the huge pulp factories that mar the riverscape.

The two main commercial centres of Anjalankoski are Inkeroinen, just across the river from Anjala, and Myllykoski farther north. Both offer hellish industrial vistas, box-like supermarkets and other such novelties. The artificial centre of Anjalankoski is at Keltakangas, but nobody likes it there.

Anjala Church

The old church (1756) in Anjala has an unusual bell tower. Take the dirt road from behind the church to the hill, and climb the tower for a view. On the other side of the hill in the forest, there is the unusual graveyard chapel of the wealthy Wrede family.

Anjala Manor

The large estate of the influential Wrede family dates back to 1606, but the wooden main building is from the late 18th century. It houses a museum with extensive coverage of local history and school traditions. The mansion has played an important role in regional history, as well as improving school and prison conditions, mostly through the work of the women of the Wrede family. The museum is at the riverside on road No 359, and is open from mid-May to mid-August daily from 11 am to 5 pm. Admission is 10 mk. There is a gallery-cum-café in the precinct.

Places to Stay

The school (☎ 367 4654) at Anjala Manor has accommodation in summer from 120 mk per person, including breakfast.

Across the bridge in Inkeroinen, a little more than one km from Anjala, *Hotelli Kantri* (☎ 317 1901) has 32 rooms, priced at 300/500 mk.

West of Anjala, *Wredeby* (☎ 367 5177) is a private stately home with accommodation available at 300/460 mk.

If you are taking the train between Kouvola and Kotka, Myllykoski has a plus side: its youth hostel *Matkakoti*, also called *Rauhala*, (☎ 365 6061), which is next to the railway station. It is a messy place with five smoky rooms and old furniture but you could stay there if you are having trouble finding bottom-end accommodation in Kotka or Kouvola. HI members pay only 35 to 65 mk.

Punainen Mylly (☎ 365 65619) at Kenraalintie 6, close to the factory in

SOUTH-EAST

Myllykoski, has singles/doubles for 200/240 mk.

Places to Eat
In Myllykoski, walk south from the hostel near the railway station, turn right and proceed through the tunnel. The commercial centre has two supermarkets, open Monday to Friday until 8 pm and Saturday until 6 pm. *Simpukka* at the Shell petrol station has huge pizzas with coffee and salad for less than 40 mk. Meals are served until 9 pm (7 pm on weekends). Esso has a café, and *R-kioski* is open daily until 9 pm. Behind the post office, *Pub Wildcat* is a scene for local heroes.

Getting There & Away
There are regular buses from Kouvola and Kotka to Anjala, while the train from Kouvola to Kotka passes the youth hostel in Myllykoski.

KOUVOLA
Kouvola, north of Kotka, is the only provincial capital in Finland that you could skip yet miss almost nothing. The reason for this is that it is barely 100 years old, and when its landmarks were built, the ideas on how a town should look are now those that prescribe how a town should *not* look. Kouvola has one old area, Kaunisnurmi, near the railway station, which has been recently renovated as a cultural centre.

Administratively, Kouvola (population 32,000) is the capital of the Province of Kymi. Founded in 1875, it was originally a small village along the Riihimäki to St Petersburg railway line but has since become the economic and administrative centre of the surrounding area. The railway is still important : Kouvola is one of the busiest rail junctions in Finland. A busy shopping area near the station is surrounded by a green belt where most attractions are to be found.

Information
Tourist Office The tourist office (☎ 829 6561) at Torikatu 10 is open Monday to Saturday in summer (to Friday at other times).

Post & Telephone There's a post office on the main street, at Kauppalankatu 13.

Library The public library at Salpausselänkatu 33 is open from 10 am to 7 pm, Monday to Friday.

Books & Maps Suomalainen Kirjakauppa is at Kauppalankatu 12. For magazines, check also the kiosks at the railway station.

Left Luggage At the railway station, you can find lockers for only 5 mk per day.

Emergency Services In a general emergency, ring ☎ 112. For a doctor, call ☎ 10023. There are pharmacies near the post office at Kauppalankatu 15, and at Torikatu 5.

Architecture
Kouvola has an unusual **kaupungintalo** (town hall) that was designed by award-winning architect Juha Leiviskä. Surrounded by a nice park, **Keskuskirkko** (Kouvola Central Church) is modern to the point of being ugly. The façade is made of aluminium and painted steel, and the interior features whitish tile walls and a ceiling made of steel and concrete.

Speaking of churches, the Orthodox **Church of the Holy Cross** was built in 1915 for the Russian army. Long used as a Lutheran church, it was only in 1982 that it turned back into an Orthodox church. The icons are beautiful. The church is on Sakaristonkatu near the Keskuskirkko and Hotel Vaakuna, and is open from 1 June to early August, Tuesday to Sunday from 11 am to 3 pm.

Kaunisnurmi
The old town area near the railway tracks includes several museums and the modern **Kouvola-talo**, which has an art museum with modern paintings. The museum is open Tuesday to Friday from 11 am to 6 pm and on weekends from noon to 5 pm. Admission is free. Nearby, the **Apteekkimuseo** (Pharmacy Museum) at Varuskuntakatu 9

recreates the interior of an old pharmacy. It's open on Sunday from noon to 5 pm. Admission is 10 mk.

Putkiradiomuseo is devoted to old radios, and is open only by appointment (☎ 949-550 459). **Rautatieläiskotimuseo** is a small red house which was the home of a railway worker. It's open Sunday from noon to 5 pm. Several artisans live in other houses, and their shops are open Monday to Saturday.

Tykkimäki Amusement Park

This park, five km east of the town centre, has the rides and games typical of amusement parks, as well as a terrarium with snakes, crocodiles and turtles. Tykkimäki is open from late May to mid-August daily from noon to 8 pm.

Places to Stay

Käyrälampi Camping (☎ 321 1226), five km east of the town centre along road No 6, is pleasant and well kept. It is also close to the Tykkimäki Amusement Park. The camping fee is 60 mk per family or 30 mk per person. There are cottages from 205 mk. There are tennis courts, and you can rent boats and canoes.

Kouvola has a youth hostel, *Kouvonpesä* (☎ 375 1778) at Utinkatu 39 (two km northeast of the station), open from 1 June to 15 August. The listed price is 85 mk for members, including sheets. You can rent bicycles there.

The cheapest place in central Kouvola is *Turistihovi* (☎ 311 5661) at Valtakatu 23, with singles/doubles at 145/210 mk.

Kymenhovi (☎ 375 8770) at Keskikatu 9 has just 19 rooms, at 150/250 mk, but it's mostly a smoky bar with live music almost every night.

Puistokartano (☎ 375 3440) at Oikokatu 4 has 47 rooms, with singles/doubles at 160/320 mk.

Hotel Cumulus (☎ 28991) at Valtakatu 11 is centrally located and has 107 nice rooms, four restaurants and two saunas. Singles/doubles are 270/390 mk on weekends and 425/570 mk on weekdays.

Sokos Hotel Vaakuna (☎ 2881) at Paimenpolku 2 is a modern structure near the Keskuskirkko Church that shares the church's bad luck with architecture. There are 172 rooms, with rates starting at 400 mk.

Places to Eat

You can buy hamburgers and coffee outside the railway station at *Onnipussi*.

Kauppalankatu has several pleasant cafés, including *Manner kahvila* at No 3. Another place to look for a decent meal is the market, on Poikkikatu. *Wiener Café* has wonderful pastries, and *Sip Pub* downstairs has a meal package at 40 mk, including salad, coffee and more. The decor draws its inspiration from the railway. *Torikahvila* is another place nearby.

Getting There & Away

Bus Most eastbound buses from Helsinki stop at the Kouvola bus terminal, which is right in the centre of town, and next to the railway station. Buses from the east will also take you to Kouvola.

Train Kouvola is one of the busiest railway junctions in Finland, with hourly trains from Helsinki, Riihimäki and Lahti. The journey from Helsinki generally takes less than two hours. Trains from the north and the east stop in Kouvola.

Trains to Kotka are small electric ones, and you can buy your ticket on the train.

IITTI

The municipality of Iitti (population 7700) is on the main Lahti to Kouvola road No 12. The old village of Iitti, seven km north of that road and just west of Kuusankoski, has just 100 inhabitants. It was elected the best-kept village in Finland in 1990, and in 1991 it won fourth prize in a Europe-wide competition. The buildings date from the 19th and early 20th centuries. Some of the villagers have given permission for visitors to enter their yards to look at the houses. A map of these houses can be obtained at the Iitti Summer Café.

The 1693 **church**, the pride of Iitti, is open

from 1 June to mid-August, Wednesday to Sunday from 10 am to 5 pm. There's also a museum open in the afternoons daily except Monday.

There are no restaurants in the village itself, but the café is open in summer.

Places to Stay & Eat
See the following Kausala section for details.

Getting There & Away
There are a few daily buses from Helsinki to Kouvola that go via Iitti. Iitti is 142 km from Helsinki, 28 km west of Kouvola, and seven km north of Kausala.

KAUSALA
This modern commercial conglomeration is the de facto centre of Iitti municipality. Information (☎ 750 2461) on services in Iitti municipality can be obtained at the post office at Rautatienkatu 18, near the bus station.

Places to Stay & Eat
Accommodation possibilities are scattered around the countryside. Five km north of Kausala, *Arvila* (☎ 366 3815) has cottages from 80 mk per person, as well as horse-riding. The nearby *Hotel Radansuu* (☎ 366 3838) is a quiet lakeside place which offers accommodation in three buildings for 75 to 155 mk per person. The cheapest accommodation is in the old mansion, where rooms do not have facilities.

Perheniemi (☎ 366 3071), 10 km south of Kausala, is an evangelical school that arranges courses on non-religious subjects and may accommodate individual visitors. The main building, an imposing manor house, is worth a visit. Look for the *B&B place* of Ms Kaarina Pylkäs nearby.

Ravintola Tensikka at Kauppakatu 13 is the main restaurant, and there are a number of grillis and cafés around Kausala.

Getting There & Away
Kausala is a jumping-off point for the more interesting northern loop around Lake Pyhäjärvi via Iitti and Jaala, which can be done on bicycle. Only a few daily trains stop at the station in Kausala, but all long-distance buses will stop here.

JAALA
From Kausala, it's possible to do a scenic loop around Lake Pyhäjärvi via Iitti and Jaala, a rural municipality to the north of Kouvola. Jaala village has a superb location, with a nice view of Lake Pyhäjärvi. The earliest known inhabitants were Hämenites who settled here 1000 years ago, although in 1995 a golden bracelet was discovered in a lake north of Jaala, indicating Viking contact, and there are traces of human settlement from 6000 years ago. Swedes built a fortress here in the 18th century, but the whole village was destroyed in 1790 during the Gustavian Wars with Russia. Today it's a quiet little place with 2000 inhabitants. The *harju* (ridge) offers the best views; look for remains of Retuutti, the old 18th century Swedish fortress. The church was built in 1878.

On a headland south of Jaala, **Hiidenvuori** is a prehistoric fortress site that offers a scenic view across Lake Pyhäjärvi. The hill is within the municipal borders of Iitti, and the turn-off to the narrow gravel road that leads to the hill is half-way between Iitti and Jaala.

Verla
This old cardboard factory is in a beautiful location by the river that borders Jaala and Valkeala municipalities. The brick houses were built in the late 19th century, and they house a factory museum. The finest building is the wooden Patruunan pytinki, the stately home of the factory owner, built in 1898. The museum is open from mid-May to 30 August Tuesday to Sunday from 11 am to 5 pm. Guided tours cost 15 mk. To get there, take road No 60 between Kuusankoski (or Kouvola) and Jaala, then turn east on road No 369 and follow the signs to Verla. There are also prehistoric paintings on rocks across the river.

Places to Stay & Eat

Most accommodation possibilities are scattered around the countryside but you can enquire about rooms and cottages at *Herttareeti* (☎ 384 462) on road No 60, near the Jaala village.

Kelopirtti is an attractive log roadhouse along the main road No 60, with simple meals on the menu. There is also tourist information available.

South Karelia

If you study the map, you may come to the conclusion that just a tiny fraction of South Karelia is Finnish territory. There is barely 10 km between Lake Saimaa and the Russian border at the narrowest point, near Imatra. The once busy South Karelian trade town Vyborg (Finnish: Viipuri) and the Karelian isthmus reaching to St Petersburg are now part of Russia, and not as part of the autonomous Karelian republic.

The pulp factory just across the border at Svetogorsk (Finnish: Enso) emits a nasty thick smoke. There are also pulp factories on the Finnish side of South Karelia (one small place is even called Pulp), and many more along the Kymi River Valley. The complex post-war arguments on Karelia and its (still theoretical) return to Finland include a notion that Finns wouldn't have caused the horrendous environmental damage inflicted on Russian Karelia, including the moonscape near Murmansk, where thousands of sq km of forest is dying of sulphur poisoning from nickel smelters. The opposing argument maintains that the efficient Finnish forest administration would not have left any (Russian) Karelian forests intact, as they still are today.

Wars have been a feature in this troublesome region, and there are Russian fortifications and kms of WWII trenches to be seen in South Karelia.

LAPPEENRANTA

Lappeenranta (Swedish: Villmanstrand) is the capital of South Karelia. It is an old spa and garrison town at the southern end of Lake Saimaa, near the Russian border (see the Eastern Finland map in the Savo chapter). Thanks to its interesting sights, beautiful location and friendly people, Lappeenranta is one of the most frequently visited cities in Finland.

History

The early Lappeenranta area on the shores of Lake Saimaa was a busy Karelian trade centre. It was officially established as a town by Count Per Brahe in 1649. Queen Kristina of Sweden accepted the coat of arms, which depicts a rather primitive man, after whom the Swedish Villmanstrand was unflatteringly named (Villmanstrand means 'Wild Man's Shore' in Swedish). Apparently jealous Vyborg businesses lobbied against their emerging rival, and Lappeenranta lost its town status in 1683.

Following a Russian victory on 23 August 1741 and the town's complete destruction, Lappeenranta was ceded to Russia in 1743, and it remained part of tsarist Russia until independence in 1917. Fortified during the 1780s Lappeenranta remained a small village, numbering only 210 people in 1812. A spa was founded in 1824, but it was only after railways and industries were developed that Lappeenranta started its growth. In 1967, the size of the administrative area grew 30-fold after adjoining municipalities were incorporated into Lappeenranta. Today the beautiful lakeside setting is shadowed by oversized industries that provide work and wealth to many of Lappeenranta's 56,500 inhabitants.

Orientation

Kauppakatu and Valtakatu are the main streets. The railway station is approximately one km south of their intersection. The university area and cheapest places to stay are in the western part of town.

Information

Tourist Office The tourist office (☎ 415 6860) at the bus station is open in summer

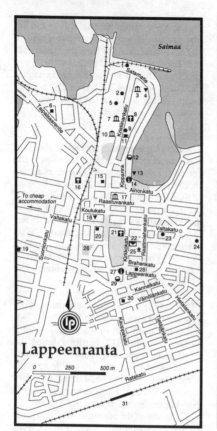

PLACES TO STAY

6	Hotelli Pallo
15	A & P Hotelli Patria
19	Kesä-LOAS
20	Cumulus
28	Sokos Hotel Lappee
30	Matkahovi

PLACES TO EAT

4	Majakka
11	Majurska
12	Rantacafé
13	Ship Restaurants
14	Martat & Other Stalls
18	Wing Wah & Emigrants & Café Sara

OTHER

1	Ceramics Studio
2	Art Exhibition
3	South Karelia Museum
5	Workshops
7	Art Museum
8	Orthodox Church
9	Handicraft Shops
10	Cavalry Museum
12	Passenger Quay
14	Tourist Information
16	Lappeenranta Church
17	Wolkoff Talomuseo
21	Lappee Church
22	Post Office
23	Library
24	Water Tower
25	Police
26	Market Square & Indoor Market
27	Tourist Office
29	Bus Station
31	Railway Station

Monday to Friday from 8 am to 6 pm. The information booth at the harbour is open in summer daily until 9 pm. The town also runs an information booth at a parking area on road No 6, open in summer (until 31 July) daily until 7 pm.

Post & Telephone The main post office (53100 Lappeenranta) is on the corner of Kirkkokatu and Pormestarinkatu.

Travel Agencies Trips to Russia should be arranged two weeks prior to departure, although tours to Vyborg conducted by the tourist office can be booked five days before departure. Tourcenter Sojuz (☎ 453 0024, fax 453 0027) at Kauppakatu 53 is run by Russians, and will arrange tours to anywhere across the border.

Library The public library at Valtakatu 47 is open Monday to Friday from 10 am to 6 pm and Saturday from 10 am to 3 pm.

Books & Maps Akateeminen Kirjakauppa has books in English. Imported magazines can be bought at R-kioski on the corner of Kauppakatu and Valtakatu.

Left Luggage There are lockers at the railway station.

Emergency Services In a general emergency, ring ☎ 112. For a doctor, call ☎ 10023. There are pharmacies on Valtakatu at Nos 34, 37 and 54.

Fortress

The old town of Lappeenranta (the Fortress) was built when Finland was part of tsarist Russia. Many museums and handicraft workshops can be found in this fascinating part of town. One ticket is valid for all three museums and costs 15 mk. All three museums are open Monday to Friday from 10 am to 6 pm and on weekends from 11 am to 5 pm.

The Fortress has many cosy workshops and boutiques selling ceramics, art and hand-knitted garments. Shops are also open on Sunday.

Cavalry Museum The cavalry tradition is cherished in Lappeenranta. The town's oldest building, a former guardhouse in the Fortress area, houses the Cavalry Museum, which exhibits uniforms, saddles and guns. The red trousers and skeleton jackets of the cavalry, which could be seen on the streets from the 1920s to the 1940s, reappear every summer: from 1 June to mid-August, cavalrymen ride around the harbour and the Fortress area for three hours every day (except Sunday and Monday).

South Karelia Museum The historical museum at the northern end of the fortress is the provincial museum of South Karelia. Exhibits include Karelian national costumes. The most interesting part of the museum is the Vyborg section. Before WWII, Vyborg was the capital of Karelia and the second biggest town in Finland. A detailed model of the old Vyborg has been constructed in the museum. Admission is 10 mk; 5 mk for students. The same ticket is also valid for the South Karelia Art Museum and the Cavalry Museum.

South Karelia Art Museum This museum has a permanent collection of paintings, as well as temporary exhibitions.

Churches

The oldest **Orthodox church** in Finland, built in 1785 by Russian soldiers, can be found in the Fortress. The church is open from 1 June to 15 August daily (except Monday) from noon to 4.30 pm. The **Lappee Church** in the middle of town was built in 1794. It's open to the public from 1 June to 15 August daily between 9 am and 7 pm. The large red brick **Lappeenranta Church** was originally built as an Orthodox church in 1924. It is open daily from 10 am to 5 pm.

Laura Korpikaivo-Tamminen Museum

This museum at Kantokatu 1 exhibits textile handicrafts, including a permanent collection of over 2000 handmade pieces. It's open in June, July and August Monday to Friday from 10 am to 6 pm and on weekends from 11 am to 5 pm. In winter, it is open daily (except Monday) from 11 am to 5 pm. Admission is 10 mk.

Wolkoff Talomuseo

The Russian family who occupied this house left in 1983; 10 rooms have been maintained as they were. There are all kinds of furniture and household items around the building. The house can only be viewed on a guided tour. These start 15 minutes past the hour from 10.15 am to 4.15 pm and are the reason for the steep 20 mk admission.

Observation Tower

This water tower, near the intersection of Valtakatu and Myllykatu, has a collection of old radios and also holds art exhibitions. It's open daily, from 10 am to 8 pm in June and July and 11 am to 6 pm in August. Admission is 5 mk.

Organised Tours

Sightseeing tours on a special bus (it has flowers on the windows) depart from the harbour in summertime three times a day, at

11 am, noon and 1 pm. The tour takes one hour and costs 15 mk.

Cruises on Lake Saimaa are numerous, and can be taken from late May until late August. Saimaa Canal, a 43 km waterway with eight locks from Lake Saimaa to the Gulf of Finland, is a local sight in its own right. Discounts are available for children and elderly people.

The MS *Camilla* is a modern boat that sails from noon on the Saimaa Canal for 60 mk per person. There are island cruises in the evenings, daily except Monday. Tickets cost 70 mk.

The MS *Carelia* sails to Vyborg on day tours, which cost from 100 to 140 mk. Enquire at the tourist office well beforehand.

The MS *El Faro* sails island cruises during the day, and a canal cruise in the afternoon. Tickets for each tour cost 50 mk.

The MS *Katrilli* is a modern boat that usually does canal tours for 50 mk.

The SS *Taimi* sails at weekends. Tickets cost 50 mk.

Places to Stay – bottom end

The most inexpensive youth hostel in Lappeenranta is *Huhtiniemi* (☎ 451 5555) at Kuusimäenkatu 18, in front of the camping ground. Accommodation in small dormitories costs 55 mk, but there are only 24 beds. There are 20 rooms in *Finnhostel Lappeenranta* in the same place, but singles/doubles are more expensive, at 120/240 mk. The youth hostel is only open from 1 June to 31 August. Huhtiniemi also has a well-kept *camping ground*. Camping costs 58 mk per family or 30 mk per person. Two/four-bed cottages cost 170/190 mk. A more exotic alternative is staying in a cottage on the island of Nuottasaari. Four/six-bed cottages cost 200/220 mk, and prices include the use of a rowing boat and a sauna. The cottages have cooking facilities.

Karelia-Park (☎ 453 0405) at Korpraalinkuja 1 is a comfortable youth hostel, open from 1 June to 31 August. There are 20 rooms, with beds at 70 mk. The hotel option charges 180/230 mk but doesn't include breakfast.

Places to Stay – middle

Near the railway station, *Matkahovi* (☎ 415 6705) at Kauppakatu 52 has singles/doubles from 180/260 mk, including breakfast. Behind the fortress area, *Hotelli Pallo* (☎ 411 8456) is a small guesthouse with rooms from 160/250 mk, including breakfast. From 1 June to 31 August, *Kesä-LOAS* (☎ 453 0900) at Leirikatu 2F offers accommodation for travellers. Singles/doubles are 190/240 mk.

There are student apartments in several locations. Another option is long-term rental.

Places to Stay – top end

In the upper price bracket, *A&P Hotelli Patria* (☎ 5751) at Kauppakatu 21 is the best hotel in Lappeenranta. There are 135 rooms, three restaurants and two saunas. In summer, all rooms cost 410 mk, but the regular rate is 455/530 mk.

Cumulus (☎ 677 811), at Valtakatu 31, has 95 rooms, two restaurants, two saunas and a swimming pool. In summer, all rooms are 365 mk, at other times higher.

Sokos Hotel Lappee (☎ 67861) at Brahenkatu 1 is the largest hotel in town, with summer rooms for 425 mk, at other times for 475/560 mk.

Hotel Saimaa (☎ 415 2800) is at the lakefront at Marssitie 5, one km west of the centre. Rooms cost 250/340 mk, including breakfast.

Marjola (☎ 452 4160) has an isolated location north of the huge pulp factory on Mikonsaarentie. Rooms cost 240/330 mk.

Places to Eat

Lappeenranta has relatively few good places to eat, all of them near the harbour. The market square boasts an unusually large number of snack stalls, selling local specialities such as vety and atomi meat pies. At the harbour, try sweet or savoury waffles filled with jam, whipped cream, cheese or ham. *Martat* has the tastiest ones – ask for hillovohveli.

One of the best cafés in Finland, *Majurska* at Kristiinankatu 1, in the Fortress, should be visited for its atmosphere alone. Majurska serves coffee and tea with home-baked buns and cakes. Apple pie is a speciality, and you can drink either Majurska's own drinks, or alcohol. It is open daily from 10 am to 6 pm. A nice little restaurant with hints of maritime atmosphere, *Majakka* at Satamatie 4, is just north of the harbour. *Rantacafé* is a clean place in the customs building at the harbour.

The novelty restaurant is *Prinsessa Armaada*, a ship at the head of the harbour. The SS *Suvi-Saimaa* is an old steamship offering beer.

There are restaurants in the town centre that make you believe you're in another country. The Kauppakanava shopping centre between Kauppakatu and Valtakatu includes the Chinese *Wing Wah* and the popular *Emigrants* and *Café Sara*.

Things to Buy

Although there are modern shopping areas on Valtakatu and behind the bus station, the Fortress area has more interest if you're looking for local handicrafts. The Majurska building includes several sales exhibitions. There are also sales exhibitions at Kristina Workshop.

Getting There & Away

Air Some of the smaller airlines operate several flights between Helsinki and Lappeenranta each weekday.

Bus All buses along the eastern route, between Helsinki and Joensuu, stop in Lappeenranta. Buses run hourly from Lappeenranta to Imatra, 37 km north-east. There are handy connections to smaller places in South Karelia, although some buses only run once a day, Monday to Friday.

Train Seven to eight trains a day between Helsinki and Joensuu will take you to Lappeenranta. The trip from Helsinki takes a bit more than 2½ hours.

Ferry From late June to mid-August, the SS *Kallavesi* sails three times a week from Savonlinna. A one-way ticket costs 240 mk, and you can sleep in the cabin in Savonlinna before departure at a reasonable rate – about 100 mk.

Getting Around

There is an extensive bus network, and you can catch a local bus at the railway station. Bicycles can be hired at Pyörä-Expert (☎ 411 8710), Valtakatu 64, for 30 mk per day.

LUUMÄKI

Luumäki, also known as Taavetti, is midway between Lappeenranta to the east and Kouvola to the west. The large fortress on Linnalantie, one km from the railway station but near main road No 6, was built in the 17th century. The **Svinhufvud & District Museum** nearby at Linnalantie 35 has exhibits that relate to Mr PE Svinhufvud, Finland's president from 1931 to 1937. The museum is open Monday to Saturday from noon to 3 pm. Admission is 8 mk.

YLÄMAA

Ylämaa, to the south of Lappeenranta is a rural municipality of 1650 inhabitants, best known for the gemstone spectrolite, a special kind of labradorite found only here. Spectrolite is a dark stone which glitters in all the colours of the spectrum.

The **Ylämaa Church**, in the municipal centre, was built in 1931. Its façade is made of spectrolite. The church is open in June, July and August daily from 9 am to 4 pm.

The **Jewel Village**, on the No 387 Lappeenranta to Vaalimaa road, is Ylämaa's main attraction. The village consists of two stone grinderies, a goldsmith's workshop and a gem museum. A cafeteria and a tourist information desk are connected to the museum. The gem museum has a collection of spectrolites and other precious stones. Admission is a hefty 15 mk. The museum and the shops are open from 1 June to 31 August daily from 10 am to 6 pm.

Places to Eat

Ylämaa has nowhere to stay. It does, however, have a couple of eateries, both down-to-earth bars. *Korupirtti kahvila* is a café which serves meals, while *Rosita Baari* offers beer and meals.

SOUTH-EAST

Getting There & Away

Saimaan Liikenne runs regular afternoon school buses from Lappeenranta, 21 km north. In summer, catch the afternoon bus from Lappeenranta, which runs Monday to Friday only. There are more buses when schools are open.

LEMI

This small place west of Lappeenranta is known for its Lemin särä – mutton roasted in a wooden trough in an oven. It is served at the lakeside *Säräravintola Kippurasarvi* (☎ 414 6470) in the very northern corner of the centre at Rantatie 1. Another place to try särä is at the local museum (☎ 414 6370) on Vainikkalantie – turn right at the church. The dish has to be ordered two days prior to the dinner.

The church, built in 1786, features a unique ceiling. It is open from 8 am to 4 pm Monday to Friday. The local museum is open in the afternoons daily except Monday and Thursday.

Getting There & Away

Lemi is 25 km west of Lappeenranta. There are half a dozen buses Monday to Friday, as well as one on Saturday.

IMATRA

North-east of Lappeenranta is Imatra, probably the strangest place in Finland, bearing a legacy of wars, industrial pollution and human greed possibly greater than that of any other Finnish town.

Among Imatra's four centres, scattered across a large area, are attractions marred by embarrassments of the first degree. Take the waterfall, for example – once the prime 19th century tourist attraction in Finland. In 1929, its raging waters were harnessed to produce hydroelectricity. Now all that remains is the ugly moonscape of the deep gorge.

The famous Alvar Aalto Church is fine from inside, but outside you have to put up with the smell from the nearby pulp factory – incidentally also designed by Aalto and for a long time hailed for its 'beauty'.

Having said this (and probably thereby having made 32,000 new enemies), I must concede that Imatra does deserve to be visited, if only for the pleasant walk along the river, from the railway station to Imatrankoski.

Orientation

There are four centres. Imatrankoski at the rapids (or the power station) is where people want to spend their time shopping and dining. Lappeentie is the main street. Mansikkala is the administrative centre, with architecture not dissimilar to the Soviet ideal. That's where you'll find the elevated railway station and the isolated shopping centre, which houses the tourist office. Vuoksenniska is an industrial area (surrounded by two gigantic pulp factories) and a former independent municipality. Tainionkoski is a smaller centre.

Information

Tourist Office The tourist office (☎ 681 2500) operates from the monster shopping centre Mansikkapaikka in Mansikkala, not far from the central station. It's open in summer on weekdays from 9 am to 7 pm and at other times from 8 am to 4 pm.

Post & Telephone There's a post office in Imatrankoski at Tainionkoskentie 1, 55100 Imatra. Another is in Mansikkala, at Koskikatu 1, 55120 Imatra.

Travel Agencies The tourist office in Mansikkala will assist you with regional travel arrangements.

Library There's one on Olavinkatu in Imatrankoski, but the one in Mansikkala, in the town hall building, is more interesting. There are regional maps in a scale of 1:20,000, and plenty of newspapers and magazines in various languages.

Books & Maps Suomalainen Kirjakauppa at Lappeentie 8 sells books and magazines, or check R-kioski on Tainionkoskentie.

Left Luggage There are 10 mk lockers at the

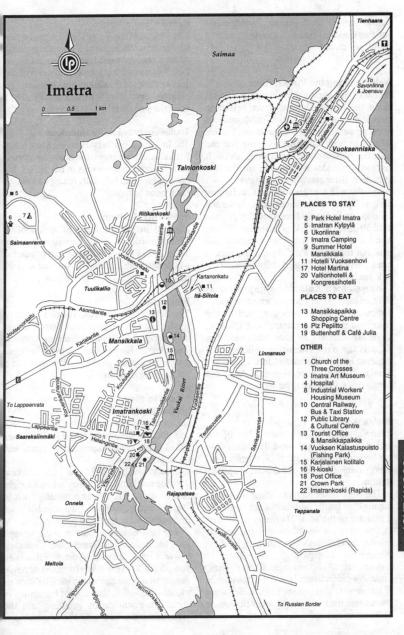

Imatra

0   0.5   1 km

Saimaa

Tienhaara

To
Savonlinna
& Joensuu

Vuoksenniska

Tainionkoski

Ritikankoski

Saimaanranta

Tuulikallio

Kartanonkatu

Itä-Siitola

Asomäentie

Mansikkala

Karjalantie

Linnansuo

To Lappeenrata

Imatrankoski

Saareksiinmäki

Helsingintie

Onnela

Rajapatsas

Vuoksi River

Teppanala

Meltola

To Russian Border

PLACES TO STAY

2   Park Hotel Imatra
5   Imatran Kylpylä
6   Ukonlinna
7   Imatra Camping
9   Summer Hotel
    Mansikkala
11 Hotelli Vuoksenhovi
17 Hotel Martina
20 Valtionhotelli &
    Kongressihotelli

PLACES TO EAT

13 Mansikkapaikka
    Shopping Centre
16 Piz Pepiitto
19 Buttenhoff & Café Julia

OTHER

1   Church of the
    Three Crosses
3   Imatra Art Museum
4   Hospital
8   Industrial Workers'
    Housing Museum
10 Central Railway,
    Bus & Taxi Station
12 Public Library
    & Cultural Centre
13 Tourist Office
    & Mansikkapaikka
14 Vuoksen Kalastuspuisto
    (Fishing Park)
15 Karjalainen kotitalo
16 R-kioski
18 Post Office
21 Crown Park
22 Imatrankoski (Rapids)

SOUTH-EAST

central station. Matkahuolto, the organisation that runs the Finnish bus system, charges 12 mk per piece.

Walking along the Vuoksi River

Probably the highlight in Imatra is a stroll along the mighty Vuoksi River, spanning three km from central station in Mansikkala to the power station in Imatrankoski. On this refreshing walk along the riverside you can visit the museum and the fishing park – it certainly provides a substitute for the less attractive vistas elsewhere in Imatra.

Vuoksen Kalastuspuisto is a fishing park on Varpasaari in Mansikkala. Spike and salmon can be caught here. One-day permits cost 30 mk; one-week permits are 50 mk. You can also catch fish from the netted fish tank but these fish ain't cheap. The park is open 1 May to 31 August daily from 10 am to 9 pm.

Karjalainen kotitalo, signposted as 'Ulkomuseo', is an open-air museum with a dozen Karelian houses gathered at the riverfront. Featuring a traditional lifestyle, there are exhibits in *aitta* buildings. The Tupa is the most interesting building. The museum is open in June and July Tuesday to Sunday from noon to 6 pm. In May and August, you get in only on weekends.

Imatrankoski

Imatra's rapids were formerly one of the highest waterfalls in Finland. The water flow has been restricted since 1929, when a local energy company built a hydroelectric power station.

The impressive summer show is another highlight in Imatra and should not be missed if you are in the area. The water is allowed to flow free on weekdays at 7 pm and on Sunday and holidays at 3 pm. Imagine how things were in the past!

Another attraction, the Crown Park, Finland's oldest natural park, is in the middle of the rapids. You can see holes which were carved into the rocks by the water flow some 4500 years ago.

Kolmen Ristin Kirkko

The Church of the Three Crosses on Ruokolahdentie in Vuoksenniska was designed by Alvar Aalto, the most famous Finnish architect. As an interesting detail, only two of the 103 windows of the church are identical. The church is open from 9 am to 8 pm. Bus No 1 will take you there.

Teollisuustyöväen Asuntomuseo

The Industrial Workers' Housing Museum in Ritikankoski portrays the housing conditions of industrial workers in the 1890s. It's open in June and July daily (except Monday) from noon to 6 pm.

Imatra Art Museum

Located in the premises of a school in Vuoksenniska, this art museum is open Tuesday to Friday from noon to 6 pm and at weekends from 2 to 6 pm. Admission is 10 mk.

Rajamuseo

The Border Museum at Kivikatu 1, north of Imatra and two km from road No 6, exhibits the tragedy of Finland's changing borders. The museum is open Tuesday to Friday from 3 to 6 pm and on weekends from noon to 6 pm. Admission is free.

Places to Stay

Imatrankoski *Hotel Martina* (☎ 476 3555) at Lappeentie 3 has singles for 200 to 300 mk and doubles for 300 to 400 mk. The lower prices apply on weekends, in summer, and for older rooms.

Valtionhotelli (☎ 68881) at Torkkelinkatu 2 is the most famous building in Imatra, right next to the rapids. It was originally built in 1902 to replace a burnt-down wooden hotel that had stood in the same place.

The new hotel was built in Art Nouveau style and called 'The Grand Hotel Cascade'. It was a favourite spot of the St Petersburg aristocracy – every day, 14 trains brought people to admire the waterfall. The flow of tourists, as well as the habit of romantically committing suicide by jumping into the waterfall, continued until the beginning of

WWI. Singles/doubles in the castle hotel cost 495/710 mk. On the new side, rooms at *Kongressihotelli* cost 495/600 mk. If there are any discounts on these prices in summer, they are likely to be in the less romantic Congress Hotel. There are 54 rooms in the castle, and 38 in the modern Kongressi-hotelli.

North of Imatrankoski, *Vuoksen kalastus-puisto* (☎ 432 2123), the fishing park, has doubles for 220 mk in a cottage. Camping costs 58 mk per tent.

Elsewhere *Imatra Camping* at Leiritie 1, in the Imatra Leisure Centre, is open from 1 June to 11 August. Camping is still possible after that – showers are open but there is no service and no-one to collect camping fees. The cheapest beds in town are at *Ukonlinna* (☎ 432 1270), also in the leisure centre. It is a recently renovated youth hostel with tiny rooms. The setting is fantastic but may be deserted outside the high season. Bus No 3 takes you there every hour or so from central station. Accommodation costs 30 to 35 mk.

Imatran Kylpylä (☎ 68251), also in the leisure centre, has 95 rooms, swimming pools and a host of activities. Rooms cost 400/550 mk.

In Itä-Siitola, *Hotelli Vuoksenhovi* (☎ 472 0011) at Siitolankatu 2 has 94 rooms, priced at 380/400 mk on weekdays (less on week-ends). *Summer Hotel Mansikkala* (☎ 2091) at Rastaankatu 3 is open from 1 June to 11 August. It is close to the train station.

In Vuoksenniska, *Park Hotel Imatra* (☎ 473 4300) at Torikatu 4 charges 220/320 mk for rooms. There are 20 rooms, a sauna and a restaurant.

In the village of Rauha on road No 6, west of Imatra, *Karjalan Portti* (☎ 432 8880) is a Karelian-style house with doubles from 200 mk. There's a vehicle museum, an antique shop and a restaurant.

Places to Eat
The best place to sample rare cuisine is *Buttenhoff* on Lappeentie near the rapids. It is the most legendary restaurant in Imatra, with a 100 year history. Downstairs at *Café*

Julia, you can finish by having a cup of coffee and one of the tempting cakes.

A number of places offer good lunch prices. *Piz Pepiitto* at Tainionkoskentie 10 has a pseudo-Italian decor and serves pizza, pasta, steaks and hamburgers. *Smuggler*, at Helsingintie 1, not far from the rapids, serves steaks, salads and pizzas, and has a good lunch offer. *Valtionhotelli* at Torkkelinkatu 2 serves à la carte meals (breakfast, lunch and dinner). It's not cheap but it is licensed.

For something a little different, try *Kankaan Kievari* at Kaukopäänkatu 8, in the suburb of Kaukopää. Near main road No 6, it's built of pine in the Lappish style. An inexpensive buffet is available from 11 am to 7 pm daily. There are also a number of other places in the Vuoksenniska area.

At Mansikkala, the shopping centre has the widest variety, including *Caroline*, a café, salad and hamburger restaurant, *Kaffe*, a nicer café, and *Pupi Olteri*, which also serves meals. There's another café at the library.

Getting There & Away
Imatra is well served by all eastbound trains and buses from Helsinki, and by hourly buses from Lappeenranta. There are seven trains a day from Helsinki to Imatra. The central station at Mansikkala has four bus platforms for various destinations, and a number of travel-related services.

Getting Around
Imatra is a large place. Bus No 1 runs to Vuoksenniska; bus No 3 will take you to Ukonlinna hostel.

RUOKOLAHTI
Ruokolahti, just north of Imatra, has an unusual bell tower from 1752. The nearby church and a local museum complete the attractions. The commercial centre is one km north.

Ruokolahti, at 1192 sq km, is the largest municipality in the south-east. Small villages, plenty of small lakes and dense forests are characteristic of the area.

SOUTH-EAST

PARIKKALA

When travelling through the municipality of Parikkala (population 5000), the train almost reaches the Finnish-Russian border. This is the jumping-off point for trains to Savonlinna, 60 km north-west. There are a number of attractions around Parikkala.

Things to See

Southern Parikkala is more scenic than the commercial centre, and includes several minor attractions. Beyond a fine lakeside road is the large **church**, which was finished in 1840. It's open daily until 8 pm (Saturday to 6 pm) but offers little of interest apart from its size. The yellow house behind the church is **Käsityökeskus**, a handicrafts centre and a summer tourist information office.

Follow Tiviäntie between the village and road No 6. At the east end of the road, a new **Orthodox tsasouna** gives you an excuse to take some exercise by walking up the staircase. The small chapel is usually closed (and not especially interesting) but the view is fine.

Walks

From the small war memorial opposite the church, the two km gravel road towards Kasuri is another fine route, and takes you to the youth hostel. From the main road here, you can start the three km trail around Lake Likolampi (marked with blue ribbons), or you can go to Kägöne. From there, you can also do the 3.5 km Harjureitti (red ribbons), a fine walk around Lake Pitkälampi and farther, via Pikku Punkaharju (a smaller version of the more famous Punkaharju ridge), to Lake Tiviänlampi.

Places to Stay & Eat

Karjalan Lomahovi (☎ 430 851), four km south of the railway station, is the cheapest place to stay in the region. There are dormitory beds for HI members from 40 mk, and smaller rooms where beds cost 45 to 55 mk. The youth hostel is a dilapidated ex-school building but you'll sleep well. The good news is that the only shower is in the reception building which doubles as a sauna, and

this includes the pool. Breakfast is 25 mk extra. The place is better known as a spa and a proper hotel but many guests come for three to five days, and the package includes half board and physiological treatment. Doubles start from 300 mk.

Kägöne (☎ 470 371) is another fine place to stay, a creation of sheer fantasy that looks very Karelian. No cost was spared when it was initially built in 1986, but after a number of lessons in truth, prices are reasonable for the luxury. It has five rooms at 190/310 mk, and the fine sauna experience includes an unforgettable descent down to the clear waters of Lake Pitkälampi. A daily buffet is 55 mk, until 4 pm, and there are meals from 35 mk. The shop upstairs sells some rare nature products that are worth a look.

In Parikkala village there are a number of places to eat. *Kaakonranta* serves a buffet at 45 mk (50 mk on Sundays) in what is actually a local bus terminal, and *Parikkalan Piika* in the same building provides you with a slightly British atmosphere for drinking beer. *Kahvio Myllytupa* is a local mill that sells flour, and there's fresh bread and such with coffee and soft drinks. The place offers the best lake view from its terrace. *Grilli kioski* at the south end of the village remains open until 10 pm.

Getting There & Away

There are regular trains from Helsinki and Joensuu, and trains and buses from Savonlinna. Buses to Savonlinna wait at the railway station, displaying the VR logo, and train passes are valid on these buses. For other destinations, cross the road to the taxi station. That building doubles as a bus station.

AROUND PARIKKALA

Särkisalmi

Several km north of Parikkala, in the village of Särkisalmi (where the road turns west to Savonlinna), you'll find a dairy museum, and *Lohikontti* (☎ 483 201), a restaurant and a hotel with rooms from 160/260 mk.

Siikalahti

Among the freshwater birdwatching lakes in Finland, Siikalahti is probably second to none. Some 40 species nest in the area just south of Parikkala village. In the 1960s, the bay was threatened by local efforts to transform it into farmland, but environmentalists have been able to save it as a protected area. The World Wide Fund for Nature has also contributed. The best time to visit the area is from May to June. The information centre is three km from the village. A nature trail of 500 metres leads you to the island of Ripekesaaret, where you can scan the bay from a birdwatching tower.

Getting There & Away From behind the Parikkala railway station and across main road No 6, a crossing marks the road that takes you directly to the parking area (three km away) from where you will find the small islet with an observation tower. By another access road, No 4011 (which starts 1.5 km farther south in the direction of Kannas), it is approximately seven km to the parking area. This loop is recommended for those travelling by either bicycle or car.

Russian Border Lookout

South of Parikkala, Russians have an observation tower across the lake. Approximately 10 km south of the railway station, the train passes along a bridge from where Russian territory is visible.

Rönkkönen Statue Park

Approximately 15 km south of Parikkala on the eastern side of road No 6, a weird collection of statues can be seen at any time. This is a personal achievement of a local eccentric who has also planted a number of trees and plants in the park. Admission is free. The only place where you can spend money here is a kiosk that sells snacks and drinks.

Not far from here, **Koitsanlahden hovi** is a tragic manor house that was the regional centre of serfdom until 1858. From the 17th century, local farmers were subject to the whims of Koitsanlahti's masters. The museum is administered by the National Board of Antiquities, but it has been neglected recently and may be closed when you get there.

UUKUNIEMI

Uukuniemi, north-east of Parikkala, is the

Siikalahti Bay is the best place for birdwatching in Finland.

smallest municipality on the Finnish mainland. With a population of 620, which decreases by over 2% annually, it is not the most vibrant place on Earth. In fact, it has the second highest percentage of retired people in the country – over 39% of the population.

Uukuniemi is on a headland just at the Russian border. You can watch the daily life of Russian wilderness across Lake Pyhäjärvi. Before WWII Uukuniemi was a proud community, but the war cut it into two pieces, and four-fifths of it landed on the Russian side. Apparently feeling a strong sense of Uukuniemi spirit, the small community has remained an independent entity.

In 1995 archaeological excavations started in the Papinniemi area. A wealthy site with remains of a church and an associated village from the 17th century will be carefully researched during the next 10 years or so. There will be public access to the site. The significance of the Papinniemi discovery relates to the frontier status of Uukuniemi. Lutheran and Orthodox cultures meet here

Places to Stay & Eat
Papinniemen leirintäalue (☎ 484 542) is a camping ground, open in summer only. It's a well equipped area, with half a dozen cottages for rent. A small number of private cottages are also for rent through Lomarengas (see Facts for the Visitor).

There are no restaurants in Uukuniemi.

Getting There & Away
There's one bus Monday to Friday that leaves in the afternoon from Parikkala, and stops at Saari and Niukkala. The bus returns next morning.

Häme

The historic area of Häme (Swedish: Tavastland) is a place of contrast: from the busy towns of Hämeenlinna and Tampere to the old villages of Hattula and Kangasala; from the wilderness of North Häme to the flat farmland of the south.

In addition to a wealth of historic places and interesting towns and villages, Häme offers many opportunities for trekking, canoeing and lake travel.

Part of Häme spans further east into the region of Lake Päijänne which we cover in the Central Finland chapter.

HISTORY

The first evidence of human settlement in Häme dates from 6000 years ago and includes discoveries in Janakkala, Tammela and Kangasala. The first settlements were established in hills along the Kokemäenjoki River and the Vanajavesi lake system.

The emerging society built a chain of fortresses and reached its peak approximately 1000 years ago, right before the region was conquered by Catholic Sweden. Prehistoric Häme covered most of southern Finland and was constantly at war with the Karelians.

In 1249 Earl Birger, on a Catholic crusade, arrived in Häme via the Ox Road. He attacked the fortress at Hakoinen and founded the Swedish stronghold of Tavastehus (Hämeenlinna in Finnish) opposite the old trading post. Swedish settlers then established large estates causing irritation among locals who had traditionally been hunters and fishers. During the 19th century, industries developed in places like Forssa and Tampere giving rise to socialist ideas among workers and a workers' movement, which consequently spread to other provinces. Since then, Häme has been a pioneer in modern culture and this, along with its natural attractions, make the region an interesting place to visit.

Highlights
- The Pyynikki sand ridge area in Tampere.
- The Särkänniemi theme park area in Tampere.
- Tampere Cathedral, a masterpiece of National Romantic and Art Nouveau architecture, with controversial semi-religious art.
- The castle and museums of Hämeenlinna.
- Natural and historical attractions along Route 66.
- The 'Tradition Village' Perinnekylä near Virrat.
- Hattula, the oldest church in Häme, with very fine paintings.
- Hakoinen, the first fort in Häme.

Hämeenlinna

Hämeenlinna (Swedish: Tavastehus), is the capital of the Province of Häme and one of the oldest towns in Finland. There was already a trading settlement at Lake

255

Vanajavesi in the 9th century. Häme Castle was built in the 13th century by Swedes on a crusade to Finland. Later, Hämeenlinna developed into an administrative, educational and garrison town.

These days Hämeenlinna's many attractions and its proximity to Helsinki make it a popular place to visit. The population is 44,500.

Orientation

Hämeenlinna lies on both sides of Lake Vanajavesi. The town centre is a compact area between the lake in the south and east, the main Helsinki to Tampere road in the west and Häme Castle in the north. Raatihuoneenkatu is the main street and part of it is only open to pedestrians.

Information

Tourist Office The tourist office at Sibeliuksenkatu 5A (☎ 621 2388) is open Monday to Friday from 9 am to 5 pm, and in summer Saturday also from 9 am to 2 pm.

Post & Telephone The post office is at Palokunnankatu 13-15. Häme's post code is 13100.

Library The public library at Lukiokatu 2 is open from 10 am to 7 pm Monday to Friday and has a café.

Books & Maps Suomalainen Kirjakauppa and Info compete almost face-to-face on Raatihuoneenkatu.

Travel Agencies The tourist office doubles as a regional agency for tours and cottage rental.

Left Luggage All lockers at both railway and bus stations are of the 10 mk variety.

Emergency Services In a general emergency call ☎ 112; for a doctor, ☎ 10023. There are pharmacies on Sibeliuksenkatu at Nos 3 and 11.

Häme Castle

The castle is a must for everyone visiting Hämeenlinna. Its construction was started during the 1260s by Swedes, who wanted to establish a military base in Häme. A major change took place in 1837 when the castle was turned into a jail. The last prisoners were moved out in the 1980s and renovation of the castle was finally completed in 1991. Today the castle is an extensive museum and also a venue for local events.

The castle is open daily from May to August from 10 am to 6 pm; from September to April it's open from 10 am to 4 pm. Admission is 14 mk. The Varikonniemi area, across a narrow channel opposite the castle, has been a trading settlement since the 7th century. Near the castle, the old prison has been converted into a museum. It's open in summer daily from 11 am to 5 pm. Admission is 5 mk.

Museums

Hämeenlinna has several interesting museums that have a joint ticketing system. A 10 mark ticket purchased from one museum is valid in the other two.

Sibelius Museum Jean Sibelius, the most famous Finnish composer, was born in Hämeenlinna and went to school here. His first home, at Hallituskatu 11, has been converted into a small museum. You can see Sibelius' piano and you may hear recordings of his music on request. It is open from May to August daily from 10 am to 4 pm, and from 1 September to 30 April from noon to 4 pm.

Historiallinen Museo The Historical Museum at Lukiokatu 6 has temporary exhibitions and a permanent collection of interesting items such as old money, weapons and medieval sculpture. There's an English guidebook available. It is open in summer Monday to Saturday from 10 am to 4 pm and on Sunday from noon to 6 pm. At other times, doors open at noon.

Palanderin talo, the old house across the street at Lukiotie 4, is a recently opened annex to the Historical Museum, and opens at noon, 1 and 2 pm. The house, built in 1861, now features a well renovated interior, Art Nouveau furniture and copper utensils. The entrance fee of 15 mk includes the Historical Museum but not the other museums in Hämeenlinna.

Hämeenlinna Art Museum This museum, at Viipurintie 2, has an interesting collection of Finnish art from the 19th and 20th centuries, including some well-known works. There are also frescoes by Akseli Gallen-Kallela on the ceiling. The museum is open from noon to 6 pm Tuesday to Sunday until 8 pm on Thursday.

Places to Stay

See Aulanko for the cheapest place to stay near Hämeenlinna. *Matkustajakoti Vanaja* (☎ 682 2138) is 100 metres south-west of the railway station at Hämeentie 9. There are 17 rooms, priced at 120/190 mk.

Hotel Emilia (☎ 612 2106) at Raatihuoneenkatu 23 is in the very heart of town. Singles/doubles cost 300/400 mk from Monday to Friday; 280/350 mk on weekends and in summer.

Cumulus (☎ 64881) is a central hotel at Raatihuoneenkatu 16-18. There are 100 rooms, two saunas and other facilities.

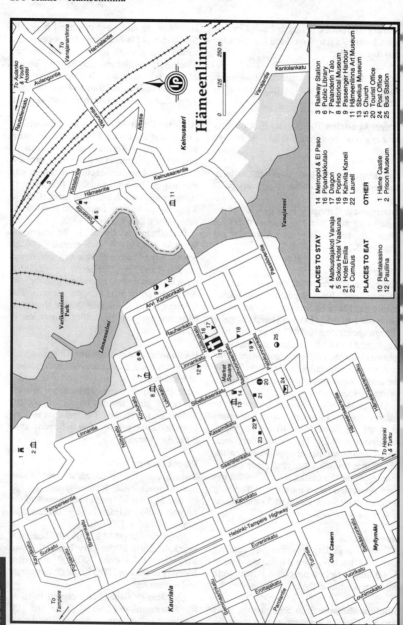

Hämeenlinna

PLACES TO STAY

4 Matkustajakoti Vanaja
5 Sokos Hotel Vaakuna
21 Hotel Emilia
23 Cumulus

PLACES TO EAT

10 Rantakasino
12 Pauliina
14 Metropol & El Paso
16 Piparkakkutalo
17 Dragon
18 Popino
19 Kahvila Kaneli
22 Laurell

OTHER

1 Häme Castle
2 Prison Museum
3 Railway Station
6 Public Library
7 Palanderin Talo
8 Historical Museum
9 Passenger Harbour
11 Hämeenlinna Art Museum
13 Sibelius Museum
15 Church
20 Tourist Office
24 Post Office
25 Bus Station

Singles/doubles cost 420/475 mk; in summer all rooms are 345 mk.

Sokos Hotel Vaakuna (☎ 65831), at Possentie 7 not far from the railway station, is an attempt to build a hotel which resembles Häme Castle. There are 121 rooms, three saunas and all imaginable mod cons. Singles/doubles are 475/560 mk except in summer when all rooms cost 390 mk.

Places to Eat

Pauliina at Linnankatu 3 is such a popular place that you can hardly fit in at lunch time; it's open until 5 pm. The food is good and you can eat lunch for 35 to 80 mk.

Piparkakkutalo, at Kirkkorinne 2 one block east of the church, has old-fashioned decor. The food is good but expensive at 60 to 100 mk per portion. *Popino*, on Linnankatu between the church and the bus station, is one of the most popular pizza and pasta restaurants. It's especially good value during lunch hours.

Metropol is a bar, in the market square on Sibeliuksenkatu, and *El Paso* upstairs serves reasonably priced lunches. *Dragon* on Raatihuoneenkatu is a Chinese restaurant in a cellar and also has quite reasonable prices.

Kahvila Kaneli at Palokunnankatu 16 serves coffee and tasty pastries. *Laurell*, another traditional café, is at Raatihuoneenkatu 11 and Palokunnankatu 11.

In summer, *Rantakasino* at the harbour serves very good lunch packages with salad and other extras.

Getting There & Away

Bus The bus terminal is right in the town centre at Palokunnankatu 25. There are hourly buses between Helsinki and Tampere and they all stop in Hämeenlinna. From Turku, there are eight buses a day. There are also regional buses. Beware of the expensive toilet charge at the station.

Train The railway station is one km north-east of the town centre. All trains between Helsinki and Tampere stop at Hämeenlinna – there are hourly trains. From Turku, you will have to change trains in Toijala.

AROUND HÄMEENLINNA
Aulanko

This beautiful park, north-east of Hämeenlinna, was founded early in the 20th century by Mr Hugo Standertskjöld, who dreamt of a Central European-style park with small ponds and pavilions. He spent a fortune to achieve his goal and the result was Aulanko with its exotic trees, swannery, observation tower and little pavilions. In 1930, it was declared a nature conservation area and today is one of the most varied parks in Finland. Although the best way to move around it is on foot, the one-way sealed road (loop) is accessible by private car. The observation tower is open in summer, daily from 11 am to 7 pm (in May closing at 5 pm). Joutsenlampi (Swan Pond) is surrounded by exotic trees that can be viewed from a marked trail. You can also play golf and ride horses in Aulanko.

Ateljee Juhani Palmu Next to Rantasipi Aulanko (see Places to Stay below), this fine old building exhibits the art of a fairly well-known Finnish painter, Mr Juhani Palmu. It is open in summer on weekdays from 11 am to 7 pm and on weekends from noon to 4 pm.

Activities The Aulangon Satuteatteri (Aulanko fairytale theatre) performs familiar fairy tales every summer. All the actors are children, some of them quite young. The open-air theatre is by the artificial castle close to the Hotel Aulanko. Performances are in Finnish. Tickets cost 25 mk.

Places to Stay Coming from Hämeenlinna, there's a *camping ground* just after the Rantasipi Hotel (☎ 682 8560) with 42 five-bed cottages, from 200 mk per night. Camping is 70 mk. There are two saunas and a canteen here. The cheapest place to stay is *Kuusisto* (☎ 628 8560), the youth hostel, a nondescript white building opposite the camping ground (for which it also serves as reception). Open from mid-May to 31 July, it offers accommodation for HI members in doubles and triples at 60 mk per person, sheets included.

Aulangon Heikkilä (☎ 675 9772) near the park, some two km from the main road, has simple cottages at a nice lakeside location. The cheapest rooms start from 150 mk and two bed cottages are 200 mk.

Rantasipi Aulanko (☎ 658 801) has a long tradition and is considered one of the finest hotels in the region. Its lakeside location could not be better. There are 245 rooms, five saunas and other facilities. Singles/doubles are 540/660 mk; in summer all rooms are far cheaper at 380 mk.

Places to Eat In addition to restaurants in the Rantasipi Aulanko, there's *Katajisto* – a fine old wooden building associated with the camping ground. It's open in summer from 11 am to 10 pm.

Getting There & Away Bus Nos 2, 13 or 17 will take you to Aulanko. Bicycles can be rented at Sokos Hotel Vaakuna for 40 mk per day and at the camping ground in Aulanko for 10 mk per hour.

Vanajanlinna

The hunting mansion of Vanajanlinna, 10 km from Harviala towards Lahti, was built between 1919 and 1924 by the wealthy Rosenlew family. Many of the rooms are richly decorated. Vanajanlinna was long used as the school of the Finnish Communist Party. It can be visited in summer on weekdays from 8 am to 3 am and in winter from 8 am to 4 pm.

Places to Stay *Vanajanlinna* (☎ 619 6565) is also a fascinating place to stay. Rooms do not have facilities but the setting is superb. Singles/doubles are 265/350 mk.

Getting There & Away Hourly buses from Hämeenlinna to Turenki stop at Harviala.

Hattula Church

Pyhän Ristin kirkko (Church of the Holy Cross) in Hattula was built in the 14th century. It is one of the oldest churches in mainland Finland and has beautiful paintings on the walls and a number of old statues. The

church is on road No 62, just five km north of Hämeenlinna. It is open from 15 May to 15 August daily from 11 am to 5 pm. Unfortunately, there's an admission fee of 15 mk, which is very rare for Finnish churches. The old grain store built in 1840, close to the old church, houses the tourist office and sells handicrafts.

Getting There & Away Take bus No 5 or 6 from Hämeenlinna and get off close to the church.

Panssarimuseo

The garrison area of Parola, north-west of Hämeenlinna, includes the fine Panssarimuseo (Tank Museum), which displays military equipment in the open air and inside a large hall. The museum is outside the military precinct. It is open May to September all day. Entry is 20 mk.

Getting There & Away Take local bus No 5 or 6 from Hämeenlinna; both run twice every hour. The museum is well signposted on road No 3051 south of Parola village. Road 3051 can be accessed either from Hattula or from the Hämeenlinna to Tampere road (No 3).

Hauho

This small village has a finely preserved wooden township called **Vanha Raitti**. It includes a small museum and a medieval stone church built in the 15th century. There are several old wooden statues inside.

A bit isolated from the daily life of Hauho, **Hauho-seuran kotimuseoalue** is a local museum area with several old houses and a windmill. The museums are open in summer, daily from 10 am to 4 pm. Call ☎ 631 1201 for tourist information.

Getting There & Away Hauho is 32 km north-east of Hämeenlinna; there are direct buses almost hourly. Also, the buses that run almost hourly between Tampere and Lahti stop at Hauho.

South Häme

This section covers all of South Häme except for attractions on and around the Ox Road, which are in the following Ox Road section.

IITTALA

Iittala is a village 23 km north-west of Hämeenlinna along the main Helsinki to Tampere road. It is best known for its glass factory, which also markets its products under the brand 'Iittala'.

Glass Centre

You will find the Glass Centre directly opposite the bus terminal. From May to August, it is open daily from 10 am to 8 pm, and at other times it is open from 9 am to 5 pm. The interesting glass museum exhibits objects designed and manufactured locally. It also gives an insight into the history of Finnish design. Admission is 7 mk. There is an art exhibition from mid-June to mid-August. Tickets are 25 mk. In the back room of the restaurant, you can watch craftspeople blowing glassware.

Things to Buy

A little chocolate factory also sells its products. There are several shops in the area, the most interesting of which is the glass shop where you can buy second grade products at 35% below normal price.

Getting There & Away

Iittala is 23 km north of Hämeenlinna near road No 3; buses from Hämeenlinna run every two hours or so.

JANAKKALA

Well visible from the Helsinki to Hämeenlinna motorway, Linnatuuli petrol station serves as a central landmark for the area. Although most attractions are in the old village of Janakkala, there are three other centres: the administrative centre of Turenki, and the villages of Tervakoski (with its paper

mill) and Leppäkoski. The population of the entire municipality is 15,500.

Information

Linnatuuli petrol station on road No 3 (E12) is also home to the friendly tourist office and a restaurant (☎ 754 272). It's open in summer Monday to Saturday until 9 pm and on Sunday until 6 pm. The map on the wall of the tourist office is a terrific locator for prehistoric sites in the area.

Tervakoski

This small town, south of Janakkala, is known for its paper industries, as well as for **Puuhamaa** (Action World), which offers a host of activities for children, including water slides, bowling, minigolf, video games, bicycles and minicars. Puuhamaa attracts lots of Finnish children and is open from late May to mid-August daily until 7 pm. Tickets cost 75 mk per person. Puuhamaa is signposted on all roads.

Janakkala Village

One of the richest historical treasure troves in Häme is to be found in Janakkala although you must be at least an amateur archaeologist to agree with this. There are traces from various eras in Finland's history.

Hakoinen Close to the Linnatuuli petrol station, **Linnavuori**, the old fortress site of Hakoinen, is one of the most interesting in Finland. Located near a privately owned manor house, it has a small parking area at its foot and a clear location map. The fort was used at the beginning of the 1200s but defeated by the Swedes and later replaced by the new castle in Hämeenlinna. Rare plants can be found on the hill. Follow the sign that says 'Hakoisten kartano' on road No 130 and climb the path from the sign that says 'Linnavuorelle'.

Laurinmäen Museo The Laurinmäki Museum has a number of old buildings and a windmill. The furniture reflects 19th century traditions. It is open in summer on Wednesday from 2 to 6 pm, and on weekends from noon to 6 pm; entry is 6 mk. Starting from the museum, **Laurinmäen kulttuuri ja luontopolku** is a nature trail that takes you to the Määkynmäki Hill and a number of sites in the forest and along Veittostentie. The guidebook, which can be borrowed at the beginning of the trail, is written in Finnish but has clear maps. Also in this area, **Laurin lähde** is a small, natural spring with crystal clear water. It's conveniently located near the museum on the road leading there.

Janakkala Church The old village of Janakkala features a medieval church. It was probably the last of the 70 (remaining) stone churches built during medieval times. The small wooden statue to the right of the altar is the oldest item in the church. The paintings of the pulpit were discovered in the early 1990s. The church is open Monday to Thursday from 1 to 7 pm, Friday from 1 to 6 pm and Sunday from 11 am to 6 pm.

Getting There & Away

Linnatuuli is practically the only petrol station along the main Helsinki to Hämeenlinna road (No 3). Most buses between Helsinki and Hämeenlinna stop at Tervakoski. To get to the village of Janakkala or Hakoinen, take a bus from Hämeenlinna towards Loppi. From Linnatuuli, find your way to road No 3, which runs parallel with road No 130.

LOPPI

The wooden church of Loppi, just one km south of the large new one in the village centre, is one of the oldest in Finland. The church is at least 330 years old and retains much of its original simplicity.

There is another attraction some distance from the main village of Loppi. That's **Marskin maja**, the summer hide-out of the former president CG Mannerheim. The colloquial name here translates as 'hut of the marshal'. To get there, drive west along road No 54, turn left onto road No 2832 and follow the signs. The house is open in summer daily from 11 am to 5 pm and has a café. Admission is 10 mk.

Getting There & Away

There are regular buses from Riihimäki, Karkkila and Hämeenlinna.

RIIHIMÄKI

The town of Riihimäki (population 25,700) has grown around a major railway junction. Located in the very south of the Province of Häme, it offers little in terms of attractions.

Most of Riihimäki's interesting sights are out of the town centre, along the main Helsinki to Hämeenlinna road. The centre is located to the west of the railway station. Hämeenkatu and Keskuskatu are the main streets.

Information

The tourist office (☎ 741 225) at Temppeli-katu 8 is in the art museum.

Things to See

There are several attractions on the old main road. It was recently dwarfed by the motor-way and visitor figures consequently dropped significantly, but the area is still worth a visit. The **Finnish Glass Museum**, in the former Riihimäki Glass Factory at Tehtaankatu 23, has an exhibition of Finnish glassware dating as far back as the 17th century. The museum is open from April to September daily from 10 am to 6 pm. From October to March, it's open from Tuesday to Sunday. Next to the Glass Museum, the **Hunting Museum** has the same opening times as the Glass Museum. **Hyttikortteli** used to be the accommodation area for workers in the glass factory. Now restored, it houses artists and artisans and a shop museum. You can get to this area from the Riihimäki railway station every hour by local bus.

Riihimäen taidemuseo, the Art Museum of Riihimäki at Temppelikatu 8 has a collection of paintings from the early 20th century. It's open daily (except Monday from September to April) from 10 am to 6 pm. The **Riihimäki Town Museum** is in an old house on a hill close to the railway station at Öllerinkatu 3. It has historical objects from the area and from the community of Antrea in Karelia (now in Russia). The museum is open on Wednesday and Sunday from noon to 6 pm.

Places to Stay

Riihimäki youth hostel (☎ 741 471) at Merkuriuksenkatu 7 is outside the town centre some 300 metres from the railway station. It is open from mid-May to 31 August. Dormitory beds begin at 40 mk and singles/doubles are 130/170 mk for HI members.

Sokos Hotel Riihimäki (☎ 7721) at Hämeenaukio 1 has singles/doubles for 400/480 mk. In summer all rooms are 365 mk. For cheaper youth-hostel beds, go to the reception of Sokos Hotel and ask about *Riihimäen Seurahuone* at Hämeenkatu, right in the centre of town. Beds here cost 100 mk per person.

Getting There & Away

Bus Most buses between Helsinki and Hämeenlinna stop in Riihimäki. There are three or four buses a day from Turku.

Train Riihimäki must be the easiest place in Finland to reach by train. Practically all northbound and eastbound trains from Helsinki stop here. It is also the last stop for some local trains from Helsinki.

SÄÄKSMÄKI

This historical and scenic area several km south of Valkeakoski along the main road is one of the highlights of Häme.

Rapolan Linnavuori

The ancient fortification on the Rapola Hill is the largest prehistoric fortress in Finland. There are fine views and you can follow a marked trail that will take you to 100 burial mounds on the western side of the hill. Fortifications can be vaguely seen. The information table at the foot of the fortress is unusually informative. It displays a map of the Sääksmäki area which shows a great number of sites from 500 BC to 1000 AD, including Sami mounds (Lapinraunio). You can get to Rapola either by following the

signs from the main road, or by taking the narrow road, Rapolankuja, that passes by the privately owned Rapola estate. Another manor house, next to the hill's access road and car park, occasionally has summer exhibitions.

Sääksmäki Church

This fine stone church was built at the end of the 15th century and reconstructed in 1933. In addition to the interesting paintings inside, there is a small church museum.

Visavuori

Once the studio of Emil Wickström, a sculptor from the National Romantic era, this is the best-known sight in the region. Visavuori consists of three houses, the oldest of which is the **home of Emil Wickström**, built in 1902 in Karelian and Art Nouveau styles. There is fantastic Art Nouveau furniture. The beautiful **studio** with hundreds of sculptures was built in 1903 and later expanded.

The astronomical observatory also gives a glimpse of the attractive lake scenery. Finally, **Kari Paviljonki** is dedicated to Kari Suomalainen, Emil Wickström's grandson. He can still be considered the most famous political cartoonist in Finland; in the early 1960s, he received an award from the US National Cartoonist Society for his daring cartoons on communism. The museum is open from 1 May to 30 September daily from 11 am to 7 pm, closing at 5 pm on Monday. From 1 October to 30 April, it's open daily (except Monday) from 1 to 5 pm. Admission costs 30 mk and 20 mk for students.

Visavuori is one km from the main Helsinki to Tampere road. There are also ferries from Tampere, Hämeenlinna and Valkeakoski in summer. The daily Silverline ferry between Tampere and Hämeenlinna will give you almost one hour to explore the area. The fare is approximately 145 mk from Hämeenlinna (200 mk return) and 60 mk from Valkeakoski.

Places to Stay & Eat

Ilola (☎ 588 9027) offers the best value for money. You can stay there for 140 mk in summer, 120 mk in winter and breakfast is included in the price. Accommodation is in old farm buildings, which have been fully renovated. The family speaks English. The farm is in Metsäkansa, seven km from road No 3 along the road to Toijala. Buses travelling between Toijala and Valkeakoski stop about 400 metres from the Ilola house.

Two restaurants compete at both ends of the beautiful Sääksmäki bridge on road No 3. Whether *Silta* is better than *Viidennumero* (literally 'number five') is a matter of speculation, but they both offer cheap food and fine scenery.

Getting There & Away

Sääksmäki can be reached via national road No 3. See Visavuori for a pleasant ferry connection.

VALKEAKOSKI

Valkeakoski, an industrial town between Hämeenlinna and Tampere further north, is probably best known for its bad smell, which is caused by its pulp and paper industries. Over 21,000 people live here.

Orientation

Valkeakoski is divided into two parts by a canal connecting lakes Mallasvesi and Vanajavesi. The town centre is in the northern part of town. There are two bridges over the canal and you can take nice walks along the canal banks.

Information

The tourist information office (☎ 584 6997) is at Kauppatori 9, the main street.

Things to See

Kauppilanmäen museo is an open-air museum on Kauppilankatu featuring old buildings. It's open from 2 June to 15 August daily (except Monday) from noon to 5 pm. Admission is 5 mk. **Myllysaaren museo** next to the main bridge traces Valkeakoski's development from a village to an industrial town. It's open Monday to Thursday from 11 am to 6 pm and on Sunday from noon to 4 pm. Admission is 5 mk.

Places to Stay & Eat

Apianlahti Camping (☎ 584 2441) on Apiankatu, approximately one km from the bus terminal, has four bed cottages for 130 to 200 mk. It costs 65 mk to pitch a tent. The cheapest place to stay is the *youth hostel* (☎ 576 6405) at Apiankatu 43, open from 1 June to 15 August. Basic dormitory beds cost 65 mk and singles/doubles are 120/165 mk for HI members. *Rantahotelli Waltikka* (☎ 57711) is a top-end hotel at Hakalantie 6, with doubles in summer for 300 mk (360 mk) at other times.

Prikka is a café at the bus station. All other restaurants are in the commercial centre across the river, including *Rosso* for standard meals and *Ravintola Parila* nearby.

Getting There & Away

The town is around three km from main road No 3; the turn-off is north of the Sääksmäki bridge. You can get to Valkeakoski by bus from Hämeenlinna and Tampere.

URJALA

Urjala, north-west of Hämeenlinna, is a historic town on the Turku to Tampere road. It has a number of places worth seeing. **Kivisakasti** is a medieval stone building dating from 1450. **Urjalan museo**, a local museum, is nearby. The village also has a church that was built in 1806. Urjala can be reached by bus from Turku or Tampere.

Places to Stay & Eat

Motelli Pentinkulma (☎ 60980) is a large roadhouse made of grey logs felled in Russia. You can eat here or stay overnight in an annex.

NUUTAJÄRVI

The famous glass manufacturer, also called Nuutajärvi, is based in this small village four km west of the main Turku to Tampere road (No 9). **Glass blowing** can be seen and there is a large red building which contains an enormous factory sales point with inexpensive second quality glassware. The 'Museo' sign leads you to the **Prykäri Glass Museum**, which exhibits old glassware and tools. The museum is open daily from 10 am to 6 pm. Entry costs 6 mk. You can also eat in Nuutajärvi, although meals are a bit costly.

Ox Road

One of the oldest roads in Finland and still partly unpaved, the Ox Road (Härkätie) is a pleasant drive through rural landscape; it has several fine attractions scattered nearby.

Lounais-Häme (South-West Häme) has a long and turbulent history and its people have a distinctive dialect and traditions of their own. Nature is also attractive here: there are several lakes and large areas of marshland.

RENKO
Renko, 15 km south-west of Hämeenlinna, is the first stop along the Ox Road. **Härkätien museo** is the local museum, devoted to the Ox Road and its history.

Getting There & Away
Renko is 15 km from Hämeenlinna and there are regular buses. A more direct route is to drive 10 km on road No 10 from Vanaja. The alternative is the original Härkätie from Hämeenlinna.

LIESJÄRVI NATIONAL PARK
This small national park protects a narrow ridge that runs between lakes, adjoining areas of forest and meadows. **Korteniemen museotila** is a farm estate, still inhabited, that has been allowed to coexist within the park boundaries. You can eat here.

Getting There & Away
The easiest way to get to the park is by the Helsinki to Pori road (No 2). The national park sign will take you to Korteniemen museotila, but there's another access road further north, with a sign that says 'Liesjärvi'. Follow this road for 2 km to Pirttilahti, which gives access to the long ridge that will take you to Kopinlahti.

TAMMELA
Tammela, on the shores of Lake Pyhäjärvi, is a historic municipality in south-west Häme. Estates were established here in medieval times. North of Tammela village, the impressive **Mustiala Manor** was originally owned in the 16th century by the Swede, Marshal Klaus Horn. Now the estate houses an agricultural school and there is a small museum devoted to farming tools, which is open on Sunday only. Tammela provided the expansionist King Gustav II Adolf of Sweden with 24 soldiers during the Thirty Years' War in 1630 (the largest number of such soldiers from anywhere in Finland) and the 'Hakkapeliitat' are now honoured by a statue near the church and an annual event in August.

Tammela Church
The old church in the village of Tammela dates from the early 1500s. It was extended in 1785 to become an unusually long church and artefacts have been added, which make it like a museum. There are medieval sculptures, old coats of arms and stocks (jalkapuut). The church is open daily May to August from 9 am to 4 pm except Sunday when it's open until 6 pm.

Places to Stay & Eat
Tammelan Krouvi (☎ 436 0647) has just two rooms at 190/250 mk, including breakfast. The place serves meals and alcohol including tasty but rare lager from the nearby Mustiala Manor, which brews its own dark beer under the name Pehtoori.

The small centre offers a variety of places to eat. *Grilli* stays open late. In the municipal complex, *Café Tammela* serves lunch until 3 pm on weekdays.

Getting There & Away
Tammela is a short way from the Ox Road and eight km from Forssa. Regular buses run from Forssa and charge 10 mk for the 10 minute ride.

SAARI PARK
The scenery in Saari Park, south of Tammela,

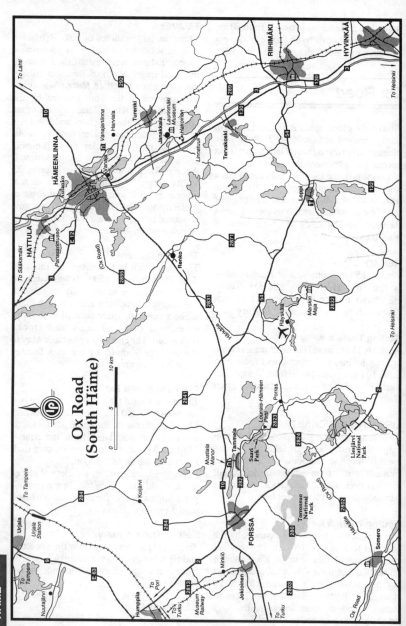

Ox Road
(South Häme)

0   5   10 km

To Tampere

To Lahti

10

HÄMEENLINNA

HATTULA

To Sääksmäki

E 12

3

Panssarimuseo
(Ox Road)

2855

Renko
2871

To Tampere

Urjala

Urjala
Station

To Tampere
9

Nuutajärvi

E 63

Humppila

284

Koijärvi

284

Minkiö

2
To Pori

2813

Museum
Railway
To Turku

Jokioinen

2

FORSSA

283

Tammela

10

Mustiala
Manor

Saari
Park

Lounais-Hämeen
Pirtti

2823

2824

Liesjärvi
National
Park

Torronsuo
National
Park

2803

Somero

2802

Ox Road

Häntälä

To Turku

Ox Road

2841

2831

Hämeenkoski

Porras

2

To Helsinki

Räyskälä

Marskin
Maja

2632

54

Loppi

132

2692

130

Tervakoski

Linnatuuli

54

Janakkala

Laurinmäki
Museum
Häkoihän

Harviala

Turenki

Vanaja

Vanajanlinna

292

RIIHIMÄKI

HYVINKÄÄ

130

3

To Helsinki

HÄME

inspired many painters during the National Romantic era. The attractive sand ridge is part of the estate of Saari, which includes a private manor nearby. The park allows public access to anyone, any time. For the best view, climb the 20 metre **observation tower**. You can get the keys from the restaurant Lounais-Hämeen Pirtti, which is on the eastern side of the park.

Lounais-Hämeen Pirtti was built by local municipalities who needed a building to nurture their traditions. The building is a cultural heritage site, with snacks and meals available. There is also information available on walks in the surrounding forests.

The village of Porras, south of the Saari Park, serves as a deviation point from the Ox Road. It's a nice old area.

TORRONSUO NATIONAL PARK

The largest marshland in south Finland, Torronsuo, is now protected. There is little in terms of public facilities, so you need waterproof boots and plenty of initiative to see anything. The best access road is No 280, which leads to Somero from road No 2. The crossing is south of Forssa.

SOMERO

The Ox Road town of Somero has been a municipality since the 15th century. The **kivisakasti**, a stone building at the northern end of the graveyard in the grounds of the old church, dates from that time. The church dates from 1859. It's open in summer daily from noon to 3 pm and there are several old houses nearby. **Someron torpparimuseo**, the local museum, includes a windmill and some very old peasants' houses. The museum, on the Ox Road north of the centre, is open in summer on weekends and also from Tuesday to Friday in July and on Wednesday in June.

Ateljee Hiidenlinna is the isolated home of Reino Koivuniemi, a local artist, who built this castle-like studio to exhibit his sculpture. To get there, take your wheels first to the village of Somerniemi and follow signs from there. It's open from June to August on week-

days between 10 am ar tember on weekends fro

FORSSA

Forssa is the largest tov Häme with almost 20,000 rapids (Swedish: fors), fi ...icn this industrial town takes its name, are the source of hydroelectric power used by local industries. There are several fine museums, although Forssa is not an attractive town to spend much time in.

Forssa Church

The large brick church dating from 1918 was designed by Josef Stenbäck. It is one of the most beautiful churches that's been built in the 20th century, and features colourful stained-glass windows.

Tehtaalaisen Kotimuseo

Behind the church, Ronttismäki is an old workers' precinct, with a house museum on II Linja showing how three local families used to live. Their simple lifestyle was complemented by domestic manufacturing. The museum is open in summer on Wednesday from 5 to 6.30 pm and on Sunday from noon to 3 pm. For entry, pay as you wish.

Riverside Museum Area

More established is the area near the river. Upstairs in the nice library building, **Luonnonhistoriallinen museo** has an extensive collection of stuffed animals, including a number of mutants. The museum is open in June and July Tuesday to Sunday from 11 am to 5 pm and during other months on Wednesday, Friday and Sunday from 1 to 5 pm. Entry is free, or pay as you wish. The library is open from 2 to 7 pm on Monday and Wednesday and from 11 am to 4 pm on other weekdays.

The nearby **Lounais-Hämeen museo**, the regional museum of South-West Häme, is located in the oldest building in Forssa (built in 1849). The two upper floors have everything from prehistoric tools to bank notes and the bottom floor is devoted to temporary exhibitions. Ask for the leaflet in

. The museum is open daily 9 am to 1 (noon to 4 pm on weekends). Entry is 5 mk.

Places to Stay & Eat

Hotel Axel (☎ 41531) at Hämeentie 7 is a modern hotel on the second floor of the Torikeskus shopping centre. The hotel has 72 rooms, two restaurants and two saunas. In summer all rooms cost 360 mk. The hotel is located opposite the bus station behind the small park.

Rantasipi Forssa (☎ 41941), outside the town centre at Saarelantie 12, has 102 rooms.

At the crossing of the noisy main road Nos 2 and 10, is motel *Autokeidas* (☎ 41991). You can eat here at the *Hesburger* drive-in.

Central Forssa has a large selection of down-to-earth eateries, including a café and a kebab restaurant at the bus station. *Sinivuokko* in the Forssamarket supermarket and *Rosso* near Hotel Alex have decent meals.

Getting There & Away

There are hourly buses from Helsinki and bus services from Pori, Turku and Tampere every two hours or so.

JOKIOINEN

Jokioinen (population 5600), south-west of Forssa, has a unique history and several attractions. In the 16th century, King Erik XIV of Sweden (who later went insane) gave exclusive rights to the Swedish war hero Klaus Horn to establish an estate in the Jokioinen region. At the time of independence, in 1917, it had grown to be the largest such estate in Finland. The main estate, in the town centre, now houses an agricultural research institute. There is also an odd-looking red granary, with three floors and a clock tower. The granary was stolen from the nearby Humppila in the 18th century. Today it's open in summer as a gallery.

The little **church** of Jokioinen (1631), almost one km past the granary, is the second oldest wooden church in Finland, but I found it uninteresting as all the renovations they've done hide the original architecture. The church is open in summer from 7 am to 3 pm Monday to Friday and from 1 to 5 pm on weekends. The large bell tower, however, is original and unique in style.

For train buffs there's a real gem here. A private **museum railway** runs from Jokioinen to Humppila. In the village of Minkiö there is a small station where toy-train carriages and locomotives are being renovated. The 14 km trip via Minkiö takes one hour and runs from June to August on Sunday. Only four or five trips are made, so get there early.

There's also a **vicarage museum**, which looks like a haunted house, near the Jokioinen centre. The museum is open in summer from noon to 5 pm.

Getting There & Away

Jokioinen is some 10 km west from Forssa not far from road No 10. There are buses from Helsinki to Jokioinen. It's easier to visit Forssa first and then catch another bus from there.

Tampere

Tampere, a proud city of self-assured people, is the second-largest city in Finland, with 180,000 inhabitants. Long known for its textile industries, it has often been called 'the Manchester of Finland'.

Tampere is one of the most visited cities in Finland due to good transport connections and plenty of attractions. There are several world-class sights, including the awkward Lenin Museum, one of the museums most frequented by foreign visitors to Tampere. Pyynikki Hill and the adjacent Pispala suburb have excellent examples of the sand ridges that are found around Finland. There are good views from the ridges and the whole area is pleasant for short or long walks. Särkänniemi, with its numerous theme parks, is one of Finland's top tourist traps and is especially popular with children.

History

In the Middle Ages, the area around Tampere was inhabited by the notorious Pirkka tribe who collected taxes as far north as Lapland. The 15th century Messukylä Church was built near an old market place. A number of Swedish-run estates were established around the forests and the two lakes that surround Tampere. Modern Tampere was founded in 1779 during the reign of Gustav III of Sweden. The Tampere Rapids (Swedish: Tammerfors), or Tammerkoski Rapids, which today supply abundant hydroelectric power, were a magnet for textile industries in the 19th century. Tax concessions brought a large number of Finnish and foreign companies to this busy town, and the Scottish industrialist James Finlayson arrived here in 1820.

The Russian Revolution in 1917 increased interest in socialism amongst Tampere's large working-class population. It became the capital of the 'Reds' during the Civil War that followed Finnish independence.

Tampere is the largest Nordic city without access to the sea. It has two universities, a national television station (TV2) and some superb architecture. The large municipality of Teisko was joined with Tampere in 1973.

Orientation

Tampere has a beautiful setting between Lake Pyhäjärvi and Lake Näsijärvi. The Tammerkoski Rapids connect the two lakes. Hämeenkatu, the main street, runs from the railway station to the Aleksanteri Church. The commercial centre sprawls on both sides of Tammerkoski and the railway station.

Information

Tourist Office The efficient tourist information office (☎ 212 6775, fax 212 6463) and the provincial tourist organisation Pirkanmaan Matkailu share an office at Verkatehtaankatu 2, around the corner from Sokos Hotel Ilves. The offices have a variety of leaflets.

Pirkanmaan Matkailu sells trekking maps of North Häme and arranges contacts with private tour operators based elsewhere. In June, July and August, the tourist office is open from 8.30 am to 8 pm Monday to Friday, 8.30 am to 6 pm on Saturday and 11.30 am to 6 pm on Sunday. At other times of the year it's open Monday to Friday from 8.30 am to 5 pm.

Vuoltsu at Vuolteenkatu 13 offers a number of facilities for travellers, including left-luggage services, bicycle hire and coffee. It is open from late June to 31 August from 4 to 10 pm.

Money Forex at Hämeenkatu 1 has the best rates. It's open Monday to Saturday 9 am to 6 pm.

Post & Telephone The main post office at Rautatienkatu 21, 33100 Tampere, between the railway station and the cathedral, is open Monday to Friday from 8 am to 8 pm, on Saturday from 10 am to 3 pm and on Sunday from 2 to 8 pm. The telegraph service is also open every day.

Library Don't miss the Tampere City Library at Pirkankatu 2, opposite the Aleksanteri Church. Locals call it 'Metso' (Wood Grouse) because its unusual architecture resembles a bird. It is the work of Reima and Raili Pietiläand and was built in 1985. The *käsikirjasto* section has English magazines, 1:20,000 maps of all of Häme, town and trekking maps and guidebooks. There are also two museums here. The newspaper reading room at Puutarhankatu, by the river, has magazines in English. It's open daily.

Books & Maps Akateeminen Kirjakauppa, at Tuomiokirkonkatu 28 near the railway station, has the widest choice of books in English. A large variety of imported newspapers is available at the railway station.

Travel Agencies Kilroy Travels, the student travel agency on Tuomiokirkonkatu, is open Monday to Friday from 9 am to 5 pm.

Consulates The British consulate (☎ 249 4111) is in the Finlayson area.

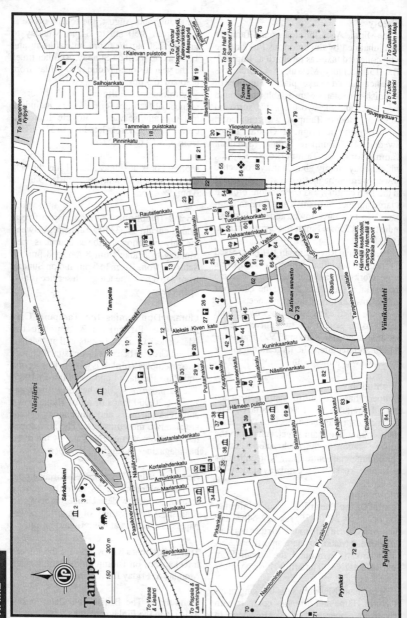

Tampere

HÄME

PLACES TO STAY

13 Sokos Hotel Tammer
14 Pinja
15 NNKY:n retkeilymaja
17 Kauppi
21 Victoria
25 Cumulus Koskikatu
35 Uimahallin Maja
51 Arctia Hotelli Tampere
53 Iltatähti
57 Rantasipi
58 Sokos Hotel Villa
63 Sokos Hotel Ilves
71 Arctia Hotel Rosendahl
82 Cumulus Hämeenpuisto

PLACES TO EAT

10 Finlaysonin Huvila
12 Plevna
19 Salhojankadun pubi
20 Attila House
29 Anttila
30 Ohranjyvä
40 Maali pub
42 Hesburger
43 Kauppahalli Market
44 McDonalds
48 Vanha Posti
49 Anatolia
50 Linkosuo
51 Pub Leena & Pekka
54 Bunkkeri
59 Salud
64 Silakka
67 Laukontori Market

76 Nääs Burger
78 Causicca
79 Tampere University
83 Klingendahl

OTHER

1 Amusement Park
2 Sara Hildén Art Museum
3 Aquarium & Planetarium
4 Näsinneula (Observation Tower)
5 Children's Zoo
6 Delfinaario
7 Passenger Wharf
8 Näsilinna
9 Finlayson Church
11 British Consulate
16 Tampere Cathedral
18 Tammelantori Market
22 Railway Station
23 Main Post Office
24 Akateeminen Kirjakauppa (Bookshop)
25 Finnair
26 Newspaper Reading Room
27 Old Church
28 Viking Line
31 Swimming Pool
32 Catholic Church
33 Workers' Museum of Amuri
34 Tampere Art Museum

36 Hiekka Art Gallery
37 Tampere City Library
38 Moominvalley Museum
39 Aleksanteri Church
41 Student House
45 TKL (Transport Office)
46 Keskustori Square & Local Buses & Silja Line
47 Tampere Theatre
51 Forex
52 Hertell
55 Tullikamari
56 Tullintori (Shopping Centre)
60 Kilroy Travels
61 Tourist Office
62 Verkaranta
65 Koskikeskus (Shopping Centre)
66 Kehräsaari
67 Laukontori Market
68 Lenin Museum
69 Workers' Theatre
70 Pyynikki Tower
72 Pyynikki Summer Theatre
73 Passenger Wharf for Lake Pyhäjärvi
74 Vuoltsu
75 Orthodox Church
77 Tampere-talo (Concert Hall)
79 Tampere University
80 Police
81 Bus Station
84 Speedway

Left Luggage The railway station has a number of lockers as well as a proper left-luggage facility. There are lockers at the bus station, or at Vuoltsu (see Tourist Offices above).

Emergency Services In a general emergency call ☎ 112; for a doctor, ☎ 10023. The Central Hospital (☎ 247 5111), two km east of the railway station, deals with medical emergencies. There are pharmacies on Hämeenkatu at Nos 14, 16 and 31, and there are two on Keskustori.

Churches

The Catholic church (☎ 127 280) at Amurinkatu 21 has one or two services every day. Lutheran churches have services on Sunday at 10 am. An English service is given downstairs in the cathedral on the first Sunday of each month.

Tampere Cathedral The Tampere Cathedral on Tuomiokirkonkatu is one of the most notable examples of National Romantic architecture in Finland and should not be missed. It was designed by Lars Sonck and was finished in 1907. The church is the largest in Häme, seating 2250 people, and there are regular concerts here. There are also controversial paintings by Hugo Simberg and Magnus Enckell (there are plenty of naked boys). The church is a magnificent landmark and should be appreciated from all sides. It is open in summer daily from 10 am to 6 pm and in winter from 11 am to 3 pm.

HÄME

Orthodox Church This conspicuous church near the railway station is open from 1 May to 31 August Monday to Friday from 10 am to 3.30 pm and at other times on request. There are services on Saturday at 6 pm and on Sunday at 10 am.

Messukylä Old Church This stone church in the eastern suburb of Messukylä is the oldest in Tampere, probably dating from the 15th century. It is seldom used, but is worth a visit. It is open from 1 May to 31 August daily from 9 am to 5 pm.

Kaleva Church Many locals consider this modern concrete church ugly, but it is quite impressive once you get inside. The famous Pietilä couple was responsible for its design. It is open in summer from 10 am to 6 pm and in winter from 11 am to 3 pm.

Aleksanteri Church There is nice woodwork in this landmark at the western end of the main street. It is open in summer from 10 am to 6 pm and in winter from 11 am to 3 pm.

Old Church Another landmark, the old wooden church north of the central Keskustori Square, sometimes has gospel concerts on Saturday evenings. It is a simple church, open in summer daily from 10 am to 3 pm and in winter from 11 am to 1 pm.

Museums

Workers' Museum of Amuri The Amurin työläismuseokortteli, an entire block of wooden Amuri workers' quarters, has been preserved while other houses have been demolished to make way for new apartments. This large museum complex is the most realistic home museum in Finland – many homes look as if the tenant had just left to go shopping. Ask if you can borrow or buy (for 10 mk) an English booklet at the ticket booth. The museum is open from mid-May to mid-September daily (except Monday) from 10 am to 6 pm. Admission is 15 mk.

Tampere Art Museum Just next door at Puutarhakatu 34 is the Taidemuseo, which displays contemporary art. The admission charge is 10 mk, 3 mk for students.

Lenin Museum Apparently one of the few surviving Lenin museums in the world, this place at Hämeenpuisto 28 attracts a surprising number of visitors, most of them foreign. Few Russians come here, unlike the old days. Ask for an English leaflet for explanations. The museum is open weekdays 9 am to 5 pm and weekends from 11 am to 4 pm. Admission is 10 mk.

Muumilaakso Tove Jansson, the Finnish artist and writer, created her Moomin figures decades ago, but the Japanese TV cartoon has created a new 1990s Moomin boom judging by the popularity of this small exhibition in the basement of the Tampere City Library. Nearly all the original drawings by Ms Jansson are now displayed here.

The museum is open on weekdays 9 am to 5 pm and on weekends from 10 am to 6 pm. Admission is 15 mk. The **Kivimuseo** – a museum devoted to rare stones – is also here, and has similar opening hours to the Muumilaakso.

Hiekka Art Gallery There are paintings and gold and silver items in this impressive building at Pirkankatu 6. It's open on Wednesday and Sunday from noon to 3 pm. Admission is 10 mk.

Verkaranta This former factory building, by the river near the tourist office, exhibits and sells handicrafts. For a small fee, you can use the loom upstairs to create something.

Finlayson Factory Area

This old factory area includes the **factory church** and Finlaysonin palatsi, a fine restaurant in the former palace of the factory owner. **Pelikaani**, a sports hall, once contained 1200 spinning machines; now you can play badminton here. **Työväen Keskusmuseo** is dedicated to revolutionary aspects of the workers' movement. It is open Tuesday to Sunday from 11 am to 6 pm.

Finlayson Galleria next door has art exhibitions. The Finlayson factory area was opened to the public in 1993.

Hatanpää

This old estate now houses the **Haihara Dolls Museum**, with over 3000 dolls presented in changing exhibitions. The old manor house previously housed the City Museum and is surrounded by a large park. The place is open in summer daily (except Monday) from 10 am to 5 pm. From October to March it is open Wednesday to Sunday from noon to 5 pm. Admission is 15 mk. Outside the museum, Arboretum Park has about 350 species of flora. The park is always open. Bus No 21 runs to Hatanpää every 15 to 30 minutes.

Näsilinna

The 'Castle of Näsi' houses **Hämeen museo**, the museum of Häme. The fine display upstairs highlights regional history from rare prehistoric discoveries up to the urban growth of the industrial revolution. The old *savupirtti* house from Kylmäkoski (south of Tampere) was transferred here during the 1910s and is a good example of how people used to live before modern novelties, such as chimneys, were discovered. The museum is open Tuesday to Sunday from 10 am to 6 pm. Admission is 10 mk.

Haihara

This old estate, east of Tampere, previously housed the popular Dolls Museum. It is now owned by the cultural department of Tampere and is set to become an arts and culture centre. To get there, take eastbound bus No 15 all the way to its terminus.

Särkänniemi

In 1995, the 30 millionth visitor spent a pleasant day in Särkänniemi, an area north of the centre which is home to a number of different theme parks. The area was established in 1969 and is one of the top attractions in Finland. You can walk to Särkänniemi via the small Näsinpuisto Park, or catch bus No 4 from the railway station.

From mid-May to mid-August, it departs every 20 minutes between 11.30 am and 8.15 pm. For 120 mk you can visit anything, anywhere during one single day, and there are discounts for children and elderly people. Each attraction has an individual gate, so you can walk around the area without spending a single markka. A stamp on your arm allows you to re-enter a specific attraction on the same day.

Amusement Park Over 20 hair-raising experiences await in this top-class park. Additionally, there are several attractions for very young children at the Ipanaario section of the park. The park is open in summer, generally from 11 am to 8 pm. There's a 10 mk admission fee and a 'wristband' for admission to all attractions costs 70 mk per day.

Akvaario The aquarium consists of two floors of colourful fish from many continents and an open-air pool for seals. The aquarium opens at 10 am and closes around 6 pm in summer and a bit earlier in winter. Admission is 25 mk.

Lasten Eläintarha This children's zoo is small and almost devoid of interest to an adult, who has to pay 25 mk for admission. Children under four years of age get in free and can see domestic animals or enjoy the playgrounds. The zoo is open from 9 May to 30 August from 10 am to 6 or 7 pm daily.

Delfinaario There are one to five dolphin shows daily from 17 April to 27 September and an entertaining dolphin training show (in Finnish) daily at other times. Admission is 30 mk.

Näsinneula This is the highest observation tower in Finland (168 metres) and the view is excellent. There is a restaurant and a café. It's open daily from 10 am, all year round. Admission is 12 mk.

Planetaario This is a fine planetarium. Ask for headphones for a (slightly monotonous) simultaneous translation in English or Swedish. There are hourly shows daily all year round. Admission is 25 mk.

Sara Hildén Art Museum

This modern building on the shore of Lake Näsijärvi displays contemporary art. Ms Sara Hildén was a local business person and art collector who donated her vast collection of Finnish and international modern art to the organisation that runs the museum. The concrete building was designed by Pekka Ilveskoski and was opened in 1979. There are good views from the café, which has Alvar Aalto furniture. The museum is open daily from 11 am to 6 pm and admission is 15 mk. In winter the museum is closed on Monday.

Villa Urpo

This fine private mansion, located at an isolated lakeside spot, is the home of the Lahtinen family.

Urpo Lahtinen was a famous publishing magnate who spent some of his fortune on art purchases. His collection includes modern Finnish and Spanish works of art. The only problem is that you probably won't be able to visit this lavishly designed private palace on your own. Form a group and contact the tourist office; alternatively, they might be able to include you in an existing group.

Activities

Saunas & Swimming The newer indoor *uimahalli* (swimming pool) at Joukahaisenkatu 7, behind the Kaleva Church, is open 6 am to 7.45 pm weekdays and 10 am to 4.45 pm on weekends. It is closed on Tuesday mornings.

The older swimming pool, adjacent to the youth hostel building, is closed in summer and on Wednesday and Sunday. Both places have good public saunas and facilities.

Fishing To fish in the Tammerkoski Rapids in the town centre, you will need a daily or weekly permit, available from the tourist office.

Walking The first place you visit on foot should be Pyynikki Ridge, which offers spectacular views of both lakes. The old observation tower is open daily from 9 am to 8 pm. The protected pine forests stretch to the suburb of Pispala. You can also take westbound bus No 15 to its terminus and walk back from there along the ridge.

Lake Cruises Tampere has two beautiful lakes on which to go cruising in summer. If you can, do both; if you are short of time, Lake Pyhäjärvi is probably your best bet, but if you have time for just one long trip, you should sail on Lake Näsijärvi.

Finnish Silverline and The Poet's Way (☎ 212 4804) are both located in the tourist information office at Verkatehtaankatu 2. The office is open from 9 am to 4 pm Monday to Friday. From 4 June to 16 August, it's open Monday to Friday from 8.30 am to 5 pm and on Saturday from 8.30 to 1 pm.

Lake Pyhäjä Finnish Silverline operates the MS *Silver Star*, the MS *Tampere* and a new paddle-wheel ferry on routes between Tampere and Hämeenlinna. There are daily departures from early June to mid-August. If you want to return to Tampere the same day, you can go as far as Visavuori (212 mk return).

The MS *Teemu* and the MS *Ratina* have regular services to Sotkanvirta on Wednesday and Saturday, to Nokia on Thursday and to Vesilahti (as well as to the island of Viikinsaari) hourly from 10 am to midnight. If the weather is fine, Viikinsaari is a pleasant place for a picnic.

Lake Näsijärvi The Poet's Way, from Tampere to Virrat, is one of the finest routes in Finland. The SS *Tarjanne* sails smoothly in both directions three times a week. For about 100 mk per person, you can sleep in this old boat before or after your trip. A one-way ticket costs approximately 225 mk to Virrat, 165 mk to Ruovesi. The boat transports bicycles for about 30 mk. From 1 June to 18 August, the unusual paddle-wheel ferry MS *Finlandia Queen* has cruises from

Särkänniemi every two hours from noon to 6 pm Tuesday to Sunday. The fare is 50 mk.

Festivals

There are three notable annual festivals in Tampere. Usually held in winter, the Tampere Film Festival concentrates on short films. The Pispalan Sottiisi, an international folk-dance festival, takes place in early June. The Tampere Theatre Summer is a six-day theatre event held during the second or third week of August.

Places to Stay – bottom end

Camping Camping Härmälä (☎ 265 1355) in the suburb of Härmälä, five km south from the town centre, has three-bed cottages from 120 mk and camping at 70 mk per tent. It is open from mid-May to late August. You can get there on bus No 1.

Hostels Uimahallin maja (☎ 222 9460) at Pirkankatu 10-12 is the oldest of them all. Dormitory beds cost 75 mk and singles/doubles start at 125/210. Much more pleasant is NNKY:n retkeilymaja (☎ 222 5446) at Tuomiokirkonkatu 12A, a YWCA youth hostel close to the railway station. Beds in five-bed rooms are 45 mk and singles/doubles start at 105/150 mk. It's open from 1 June to 25 August.

Domus Summer Hotel ☎ 255 0000) at Pellervonkatu 9 is open from June to August. Prices range from 60 to 160/220 mk, depending on whether you stay at the hostel or the Summer Hotel.

Places to Stay – middle

A good deal nearer the railway station is Iltatähti (☎ 222 0092) at Rautatiekatu 18. With your own sheets, singles/doubles will cost 150/215 mk. Sheets are extra. There are also cheap dormitories and monthly room rates are available from 1400 mk per month.

Gasthaus Abrahamin maja, south-west of the centre (☎ 223 5317 at Viinikankatu 22, is a non-smoking, non-drinking guesthouse with beds at 100 mk, or singles/doubles at 130/220 mk. These rates include breakfast but not sheets.

There are also a few places in the western suburbs. Singles/doubles at Sportmotelli (☎ 344 4281) at Vuorentaustantie 5 in the suburb of Lamminpää, start at 130/250 mk without breakfast (that's 25 mk extra). On weekends the rate is 110 mk per person. Sportkievari (☎ 344 5500) nearby at Oksatie 1 has singles/doubles at 125/250 mk, but doubles get a 50 mk discount on weekends. Haapalinna (☎ 345 3335) at Rahtimiehenkatu 3, to the west of the suburb of Pispala, has singles/doubles for 200/300 mk.

Härmälän Kesähotelli (☎ 265 1355) at Nuolialantie 48, very close to the camping ground, is a summer hotel open from early June to late August. It has singles/doubles at 145/215 mk.

There are also several places to the east. Jäähovi (☎ 255 9900) at Sammon valtatie 2 is an ice-hockey-related motel with singles/doubles at 220/330 mk, or a little less on weekends. Rustholli (☎ 362 2331) at Rusthollinkatu 18 is a traditional and popular holiday resort with a rustic restaurant and cottages from 350 mk, excluding taxes.

Places to Stay – top end

Most hotels in Tampere have lower rates in summer (from Midsummer to early August) and on weekends. At other times, expect prices to rise by up to 200 mk. Most hotel prices include breakfast.

Cumulus Hämeenpuisto (☎ 242 4242) at Hämeenpuisto 47 has 181 rooms with singles/ doubles at 430/475 mk (345 mk in summer).

Cumulus Koskikatu (☎ 242 4111) is at Koskikatu 5. This hotel at the Finnair bus terminal has 227 rooms and a number of facilities, including two restaurants and two saunas. Singles/doubles are 470/550 mk (365 mk in summer).

Sokos Hotel Ilves (☎ 212 1212) is at Hatanpään valtatie 1. Reputedly the best hotel in Tampere, it charges 465 mk for all its rooms in summer. At other times singles/doubles cost 585/710 mk.

Kauppi (☎ 253 5353) at Kalevan puistotie 2 has singles/doubles at 220/340 mk (200/280 mk in summer).

Tampereen kylpylä (☎ 259 7111) is at Lapinniemenranta 12. Singles/doubles at this fine spa hotel cost 400/490 mk and prices include breakfast and access to the pools. In winter, prices are 580/720 mk.

HÄME

Pinja (☎ 241 5111) is at Satakunnankatu 10. This attractive town hotel near the cathedral has singles/doubles for 280/380 mk. In winter prices are 350/450 mk.

Rantasipi (☎ 245 5111) is at Yliopistonkatu 44. This hotel, between the railway station and the Tampere-Talo Hall, has 138 rooms and excellent facilities, including a fine sauna section. Singles/doubles for 450/520 mk, except in summer and on weekends when all rooms are 380 mk.

Arctia Hotel Rosendahl (☎ 244 1111) is at Pyynikintie 13. This impressive, modern hotel below Pyynikki Ridge has 213 rooms, three restaurants and five saunas. Singles/doubles go for 380/380 mk in July and on weekends and 450/520 mk at other times.

Sokos Hotel Tammer (☎ 222 8111) is at Satakunnankatu 13. One of the oldest hotels in Tampere, it charges 370 mk for all rooms on weekends and 400/515 mk at other times.

Arctia Hotelli Tampere (☎ 244 6111) is at Hämeenkatu 1. This hotel opposite the railway station has 127 rooms with singles/doubles at 330/390 mk in summer and on weekends, and 450/480 mk at other times.

Victoria (☎ 242 5111) at Itsenäisyydenkatu 1 is also near the railway station and has singles/doubles for 290/340 mk in summer and on weekends, and 330/380 mk at other times.

Sokos Hotel Villa (☎ 222 9111) is at Sumeliuksenkatu 14. Rooms at this pleasant hotel adjacent to the Tullintori shopping centre are all 370 mk on weekends and 400/515 mk at other times.

Places to Eat

Lunch Eateries Most restaurants in Tampere have special lunch prices. Even department stores such as Anttila serve meals at reasonable prices, starting well below 30 mk. These meals include salad and other extras.

Linkosuo at Hämeenkatu 9 is a traditional bakery with lunch packages. *Ohranjyvä* at Näsilinnankatu 15 is frequented by local journalists. A home-made lunch costs 35 mk on weekdays, but this is really a beer-drinking place.

Plevna on Satakunnankatu, within the Finlayson precinct, is a Central European restaurant that serves sausages and other heavy stuff. *Silakka* in the Koskikeskus shopping complex has an attractive daily fish buffet, including salads and a fish soup, for approximately 50 mk.

Restaurants with a View *Näsinneula*, the highest tower in Tampere, has a revolving restaurant. *Kahvila Pyynikin Näkötorni*, a café in a lower tower in Pyynikki, has coffee and snacks.

International Restaurants *Salud* at Otavalankatu 10 is a local favourite for gourmet food, including dishes with kangaroo or alligator meat. The salad buffet is also great. Call ☎ 223 5996 to reserve a table.

Anatolia at Verkatehtaankatu 5 serves good Turkish food at inflated prices. *Coussicca* at Nyyrikintie 2 is a Russian restaurant which is popular among locals but also a bit steeply priced.

Klingendahl at Hämeen puisto 44, at the east end of the centre, is an interesting place in a renovated industrial property.

University Restaurants The two most recommended places to eat and meet up with local students are the *Tampere University main building* and *Attila House*, where substantial meals can be had for less than 20 mk. Coffee and snacks are also inexpensive.

Fast Food The main street, Hämeenkatu, has many pubs and fast food outlets. The local speciality, mustamakkara, or black sausage, may look disgusting, but it is nutritious and delicious. Locals prefer the original Tapola brand, perfect with milk and cranberry jam.

Mustamakkara can be had at *Laukontori market*, or the *Kauppahalli indoor market*. Probably the only mustamakkara fast-food restaurant in the world can be found in the western suburb of Lielahti. To get there, take bus No 11.

Hesburger, the booming Turku chain with tasty burgers, now has an outlet on Hämeenkatu opposite the Kauppahalli. The strategic location brings a rival to the nearby double arches of *McDonald's* on the corner of Kauppatori and Hämeenkatu, the best location in Tampere. This may be the reason why McDonald's opened its first Finnish restaurant here in 1984.

Before hamburgers arrived in a big way,

kebabs had already left a lasting impact on Tampere. *Abu Fuad* was for a long time the leading chain, but now faces stiff competition from several others.

A number of small restaurants offer the cheapest prices around Tampere. One of them, *Nääs Burger* at Kalevantie 5 opposite the university, has meals from 25 mk but the food is not that tasty.

Self-Catering The cheapest food stores in Tampere are the numerous *Vikkula* shops, which have a special *tarjous* price on almost everything. There are also other discount chains, such as *Rabatti* and *Alepa*. Visit the *Kauppahalli market* (on Hämeenkatu) and the marketplaces for fresh vegetables and other food.

Entertainment

Music Tampere is a centre for the performing arts – check the current programme at the tourist office.

The Tampere-talo Concert Hall (☎ 243 4500) has classical concerts on Friday, except in summer; tickets are available on the spot. There are popular nightly rock concerts in the Tullikamari next to the Tullintori shopping centre not far from the railway station (an admission fee is charged), and rock or blues concerts are frequently held in the Student House at Kauppakatu 10.

Theatre Tampere is known for its several theatres, but performances are generally in Finnish. Popular plays are presented from 15 June to 16 August in an unusual revolving summer theatre behind Pyynikki Ridge, at the Lake Pyhäjärvi waterfront. Even if the play is in Finnish, the experience, on a warm summer evening, may well be worth the 100 mk you'll pay for a ticket. Catch bus No 12.

Bars *Salhojankadun pubi* on Salhojankatu is the most traditional pub in Tampere and is well known among travellers. There are several other interesting bars on Hämeenkatu, the main street.

Pub Leena & Pekka in the Arctia Hotelli Tampere is quite popular, but you have to be over 22 years of age to get in. *Vanha Posti* serves beer from the local PUP brewery. *Bunkkeri* at the railway-station building revives old war-time memories and serves beer. *Maali pub* at Hämeenkatu 31 is an ice hockey pub, founded by some local players, which shows ice hockey on a large screen. This place is good for enthusiasts.

Spectator Sport Tampere has two ice-hockey teams in the national league. The Hakametsä Ice Hall is the venue for matches on Thursday and Sunday from September to March. Take eastbound bus No 25 to its terminus and see for yourself. You'll also find Europe's only ice hockey museum (☎ 124 200) on the premises. It's open during matches, or at other times on request.

Football (soccer) is played in summer at the Ratina stadium.

Things to Buy

Tampere is probably the most interesting Finnish town in which to go shopping: it has a large variety of shops and lacks the unnecessary sophistication that makes Helsinki more expensive.

Discount shops such as Rihkama-Pörssi, Super-Myynti, Vapaa-Valinta and a few others sell glassware at reasonable prices, and there is an unusually large number of second hand shops for goods or books.

Probably the cheapest film in Finland, if purchased in bulk, can be found at Hertell on Tuomiokirkonkatu. There are two shopping centres, Koskikeskus and Tullintori, on either side of the railway station. Interesting handicrafts can be found at Kehräsaari, a factory converted into a shop-cum-office centre, or at Verkaranta, across the Tammerkoski River.

Markets There are several market squares in Tampere. Keskustori, the central market, is busy only on the first Monday of each month, but in summer, there is a weekday evening market. There is a weekday vegetable market at Laukontori, also called *alaranta* ('lower lakeside'), where Lake Pyhäjärvi boats depart. It's open from 6 am to 2 pm. There's

HÄME

also a Saturday market here, open till 1 pm, and one at Tammelantori. The traditional Market Hall at Hämeenkatu 19 is open from 8 am to 5 pm Monday to Friday and from 8 am to 2 pm on Saturday.

Getting There & Away
Air You can fly to Tampere direct from Stockholm and Tallinn: all other flights come from Helsinki. There are approximately five flights every weekday from Helsinki to Tampere and a few flights on weekends.

Considering the time wasted on airport transport at both ends, it doesn't make much sense to fly unless you have a connecting flight. There are also flights between Tampere and Oulu. Finnair (☎ 222 1200) is at Kyttälänkatu 2.

Bus The bus terminal, 300 metres south of Koskikeskus, serves the entire Province of Häme. Regional buses for Nokia, Lempäälä, Kangasala and beyond, run most notably by the Paunu company, are most conveniently caught from Keskustori (central square).

Train The railway station is right in the city centre. There are hourly trains from Helsinki during the day and several trains a day from Turku, Jyväskylä, Pori and Oulu.

Hitching If you're heading for Helsinki or Turku, try hitchhiking at the Viinikka round-about not far from the university. For Jyväskylä or Lahti, walk east beyond the Kaleva Church to the large hospital two km from the railway station. For Vaasa, you'll have to catch westbound bus No 11 and then walk a little further.

Getting Around
To/From the Airport The Finnair bus terminal is in the Cumulus Hotel at Koskikatu 5. Each arriving flight is met by a bus to Tampere.

Bus The local bus company TKL offers a 24-hour pass for local buses. It costs 25 mk and can be purchased at the tourist office or from the TKL office at Aleksis Kiven katu

11. Individual tickets cost 9 mk and include a transfer within an hour. A useful route map is available at the TKL office for a few markkaa.

Bicycle You can hire bicycles at Urheilu-10 (☎ 255 2600), at Sammonkatu 13 and from Keskuspyörä (☎ 212 4074) at Lapintie 6.

Pirkanmaa

The area around Tampere is called 'Land of Pirkka' and refers to the historical tribe that used to collect taxes for the Swedish king here and as far north as Lapland. Pirkkala is the small municipality that still carries the name, but it has lost most of its territory and all of its power. Tampere airport is located in Pirkkala.

ERÄJÄRVI
Now a part of the municipality of Orivesi, Eräjärvi, east of Tampere, may have some of the oldest traces of human settlement in the region. Locals maintain that Eräpyhä Hill (159 metres), which offers fine views to Lake Längelmävesi, may have been a holy place for prehistoric hunters and fishers.

The Nunnankirkko ('Nun's Church') stone area down at the lakeside, some 10 km from the village of Eräjärvi, has historical significance. In the main village, the Kivimuseo (Stone Museum) has local rarities on display. It is open from noon to 6 pm daily in July; in June and August, it's open on weekends only. Several km due west from the village, the abandoned Uiherla mine has fine 'pools' for swimming if the weather is fine.

Getting There & Away
There are buses from Orivesi to Eräjärvi but you will need to walk to the attractions.

HÄMEENKYRÖ
Hämeenkyrö (population 9600), north-west of Tampere, is a wealthy rural municipality that is best known as the birthplace of FE

Sillanpää, winner of the Nobel prize for literature in 1939. It has a number of other attractions scattered around the beautiful countryside. The village of Hämeenkyrö has banks, restaurants, cafés and supermarkets.

Things to See & Do

Myllykolu This small house is the birthplace of Mr Sillanpää. The setting is very picturesque. Follow the Maisematie road south of the village of Hämeenkyrö and turn towards Heinijärvi, then Kierikkala. In summer there are theatre plays by or about Sillanpää. The house is open from 1 June to 16 August from 1 to 6 pm Tuesday to Sunday. Follow the Taatan taival track that takes you to the Maisemakahvila café, a beige manor with superb views of the lake below. It is open from 15 June to 15 August from noon to 8 pm daily.

Töllinmäki This simple museum in the village of Heinijärvi is the house where Mr Sillanpää lived as a boy. It is open at the same times as Myllykolu. If you have little time, skip this one.

Other Attractions There is a **local museum** in the old red brick building beside the village church. It's open from 1 June to 16 August from 11 am to 6 pm daily. The church has similar opening hours.

The **Frantsilan yrttitarha** by the river is a herb garden, and the Kehäkukka café serves home-made herb tea. Down at the pier, the MS *Purimo* offers cruises for groups. Five km north of Hämeenkyrö is the spectacular **Kyröskoski Waterfall**, which can only be seen at full flow during the spring floods.

Places to Stay & Eat

There is no accommodation in the village of Hämeenkyrö. *Pinsiön majat* (☎ 406 074), open all year round, is five km from the Tampere to Vaasa road along the parallel old road. Follow the 'Pinsiö' sign. Dormitory beds cost 70 mk for HI members and there are boats and bicycles for hire.

Hämeenholvi, near the church, serves lunch, but all other places are across the main road, including *Kahvila Katariina* at the bus station and *Katukeittiö Kotipiha*, which serves hamburgers.

Getting There & Away

Hourly buses make the 30 minute, 36-km trip between Tampere and Hämeenkyrö.

IKAALINEN

Further north-west of Tampere, this small town, surrounded by Lake Kyrösjärvi, is on a peninsula off the main Tampere to Vaasa road. The main street has a number of banks, supermarkets and other businesses that serve a little over 8000 inhabitants. A huge spa is the pride of Ikaalinen.

Information

The tourist office (☎ 450 1221) at Valtakatu 7 is easy to spot. You can hire canoes here. It's open in summer from 8 am to 4 pm Monday to Friday and from 10 am to 2 pm on Saturday; in winter, it's open on weekdays only.

Every year in early June, Ikaalinen celebrates accordion music during the Sata-Häme Soi Festival. For further information, contact the local cultural office (☎ 450 1249).

Things to See

Vanha Kauppala, the 'old township' quarters, has few remaining wooden houses, but this is still a nice area to walk around. You can get a map of the area from the tourist office free of charge. The small museum opposite the tourist office on Valtakatu displays old musical instruments. It is open in June and July.

There is a small **Pesäpallo (Baseball) Museum** in a school area on Koulupolku. The beautiful cross-shaped **church**, built in 1801, is open in summer from 9 am to 6 pm daily. Right beside the church is a small **local museum**, which is open in summer from 10 am to 1 pm on Wednesday and from noon to 2 pm on Sunday.

The largest spa in Scandinavia, **Ikaalisten Kylpylä** (☎ 4511), is about 10 km north of the town of Ikaalinen. In winter there is a

HÄME

road across the frozen Lake Kyrösjärvi, which cuts the distance to a third.

Places to Stay

The cheapest accommodation option is *Toivolansaari Camping* (☎ 458 6462), on the small island that is linked to the town by a bridge. Rooms cost 130 to 220 mk. The place is open from early June to mid-August. *Ikaalisten kesähotelli* (☎ 450 1221), not far from the water tower in the eastern part of town at Myllymäenkatu 6, has doubles for 220 mk, but is only open from early June to early August. *Ikaalisten Hotelli* (☎ 458 6325) at Keturinkatu 1, in the town centre, has singles/doubles for 200/300 mk in summer; winter prices are higher.

There are five large hotels in the spa area. The centre of activity is the Maininki building, with its Tropiikki spa, restaurants and sports facilities. Admission to the pool and sauna section costs 50 to 60 mk. Accommodation is available in singles/doubles from 355/490 mk, with discounts available for prebooked rooms.

Places to Eat

At Ikaalisten kesähotelli in the centre, you can eat at *Arina* or drink coffee at *Kahvio Vanha Kauppala*. Down the road from the hotel, *Pizzeria Jokeri* has pizzas. Discount supermarkets include *Siwa* and *Sale*, in the town centre. You can buy fresh bread from *Kotileipomo* in the village near the main road and from *Myllyn leipä* along the road.

Getting There & Away

Several buses a day make the one hour trip from Tampere to Ikaalinen and the Kylpylä.

KANGASALA

Geographically, the municipality of Kangasala, to the east of Tampere, is a continuation of the same formation as Pyynikki Ridge. Consequently, Kangasala offers a lot of scenic value for visitors who stop at any of the three ridges that cross Kangasala. Mr Topelius's popular song *Summerday in Kangasala* was written in praise of the scenery. Over 21,000 people live in the area.

Things to See

The **old church**, built in 1765, has been carefully renovated. It's open daily in summer. The **local museum** is open daily in summer from 11 am to 5 pm. Several km to the east in Vehoniemi, an **automobile exhibition** includes displays relating to road history. It's open from 1 May to 31 August from 10 am to 7 pm daily and on weekends in winter from noon to 6 pm. Admission is 20 mk. You can also climb an observation tower at this place.

Getting There & Away

Regular Paunu buses will take you to Kangasala from Tampere.

LEMPÄÄLÄ

This rural municipality 23 km south of Tampere has an old **stone church**, which is open to the public in summer from 9 am to 6 pm Monday to Friday. The beautiful bell tower has a small museum, which is open in summer on Sunday around noon. It is a short walk to the church from the railway station. Finnish Silverline ferries call at the Lempäälä canal jetty daily during the summer season. Paunu buses for Lempäälä depart from Tampere every 30 minutes. Only local trains between Helsinki and Tampere stop at Lempäälä.

Places to Stay

Hiidenvuolle (☎ 375 0489) at Lipontie 144 has accommodation from 45 to 90 mk per person. Cross the bridge on Valkeakoskentie to the east and turn right to Lipontie. *Hotelli Kanava* (☎ 375 3700) at Latotie 1 near the canal, is the top-end establishment here, with rooms from 230 mk.

NOKIA

Nokia, Tampere's western neighbour, is the home of Finland's most internationally known company (named after the town). Nokia was part of the large Pirkkala municipality, which controlled an area from Viiala to Ähtäri from the late 13th century. Industries grew on the shores of the Nokia River but the famous Nokia mobile phones are not

Finland Calling

When Orthodox priest Mr Pietarinen consecrated a Global System Mobile (GSM) link tower in Ilomantsi, at the Russian border, for Finland's mobile phone network, he dialled the head of the Orthodox Church in Greece and enquired about recent news in Greece. CNN was there and broadcast the event around the world.

Mobile phones have an eager market in Finland. According to recent surveys, Finns share first place with Swedes as the highest per capita users of mobile phones. Nokia, Finland's most successful company, is one of the leading manufacturers of cellular phones. Benefon, in Finland's silicon valley, Salo, provides Nokia with a rival.

The first GSM network in the world was inaugurated in Finland in 1991 and local operators offer more services than operators in most countries, from fax and e-mail facilities to message services and displays showing the caller's phone number.

It's a great surprise to find wilderness guides operating white-water rafting or snowmobile safaris carrying a slim mobile phone.

Oulu, another 'silicon valley' in Finland, is the world leader in sensor-based bus tickets that work similarly to phone cards. The ticket machine will automatically charge the ticket price from the smart card.

Finnish students are among the most enthusiastic Internet users and many magazines run regular Internet pages. Computers, desk-top publishing, telefaxes and other modern gadgets are common in even the smallest companies.

Finns can conduct most of their banking transactions using an ATM, found at every corner in central Helsinki, and even in the smallest villages. Bills are paid, travel insurance is purchased and future transactions can all be negotiated using an ATM.

Finns have never shown any objection to modern technology, although old traditions are also appreciated. But how would the country cope with an electrical blackout? ■

---

manufactured here. Nokia is a possible day trip from Tampere, although this is not a beautiful town. With over 26,000 inhabitants, it's large enough to have an extensive range of services.

Information

The tourist information office (☎ 423 255) is at Välikatu 18. It is open from 8 am to 4 pm Monday to Friday. The Museokrouvi café, in the Hinttala museum, also provides tourists with information.

Things to See & Do

The **wooden church** was designed by Mr Engel and was completed in 1838. It is open from 1 June to 15 August from noon to 6 pm.

Opposite the church on Nokianvaltatie, **Hinttala** is a local museum with several buildings and items relating to peasants' lifestyle. The museum is open from 1 June to 31 August from noon to 8 pm.

The modern indoor pool, not far from Hotelli Iisoppi on Välikatu, is not a bad place to swim. For more luxury, try the Eden spa on the western Tampere to Turku road. Expect to pay 60 mk for two hours of swimming and bathing.

Places to Stay & Eat

Viinikanniemi Camping (☎ 413 384) has cottages from 165 mk. It is open from 8 May to 13 September. *Hotelli Iisoppi* (☎ 341 3444) at Välikatu 20 is a central hotel with a restaurant that serves as a night spot for locals. There are 18 rooms for 265/350 mk but you can bargain.

There are few gourmet restaurants in Nokia. Opposite Iisoppi, *Ossburger* serves inexpensive snacks and *Kahvila Kataja* coffee. *Hesburger* has a drive-in restaurant on Nokianvaltatie.

Getting There & Away

There is a Paunu bus from Tampere to Nokia every 10 to 30 minutes; the fare is 12 mk.

HÄME

VESILAHTI

Once an important settlement for Lapps, Vesilahti is now a sleepy but fairly scenic municipality south of Lake Pyhäjärvi. An established 'tourist' route, the Klaus Kurjen Tie (named after a historical character who lived in Laukko Manor, now one of the attractions along this route) is a nice road for cycling if the weather is fine.

According to the *Kanteletar* epic, Klaus Kurki killed the young girl Elina here. The 'Murder of Elina' is one of the oldest legends in Finland and in 1992, a new opera based on it was presented by the National Opera of Finland.

The village of Vesilahti has a number of services, including a tourist information office. The very old village of Narva is worth a stop; the village restaurant, Voisilmä, has inexpensive snacks. There is also a tiny museum not far from Narva.

Places to Stay

Contact the Tampere tourist office in advance for more information on farm holiday possibilities along the Klaus Kurjen Tie route.

Getting There & Away

Lempäälä is the gateway to Vesilahti, and road No 313 starts a few km south of the Lempäälä railway station. Buses run on this route. In summer, there are also ferries from Tampere to the starting point of the route.

KURU

In the tiny village of Kuru, north of Tampere, you can visit an old church and a small local museum. Several buses a day run from Tampere to Kuru. One of the national parks in Häme, Seitseminen, is inside the municipal area of Kuru.

Seitseminen National Park

Protected mainly for its virgin forests, Seitseminen is west of the village of Kuru, some 80 km from Tampere. The excellent information centre (☎ 447 240) one km south of the Kuru to Parkano road is open daily from 1 April to 30 September from 10

am to 6 pm; in winter, it's open on weekends only. A café sells drinks, sandwiches and sweets. Free maps of the park are available at the centre, which also features interesting exhibitions.

There are a few attractions that can be reached in a vehicle or by following walking tracks. Kovero House, seven km south of the information centre, has been converted into a museum, which is open in summer daily from 10 am to 6 pm. The Multijärvi trail, a two km loop around a forested hill, can be congested on weekends.

Places to Stay You can pitch your tent at any of the several camp sites inside the park. Three old houses within the park area can be booked for groups. Call Metsähallitus (☎ 448 1821) in Parkano.

Getting There & Away Several unsealed roads lead to the park, but the normal entry point is the tiny village of Länsi-Aure, on the Kuru to Parkano road. There are buses from Tampere via Kuru. Hitchhiking is possible but not very easy.

Route 66

You guessed it. When the famous song – the chorus of which goes *Get your kicks on Route 66* etc – was translated into Finnish, the popular rock star Jussi Raittinen adapted the lyrics to this national highway. What he didn't have to do was to establish the historical significance or reputation of this very old road. The road was already something of a legend.

Road No 66, which starts north-east of Tampere and winds north, is one of the oldest roads in Finland. Not that there is much left of the original path, it was all asphalted and widened ages ago. But it has attractions which are more than 200 years old and many places with associated legends.

ORIVESI

Road No 66 begins in Orivesi. There's

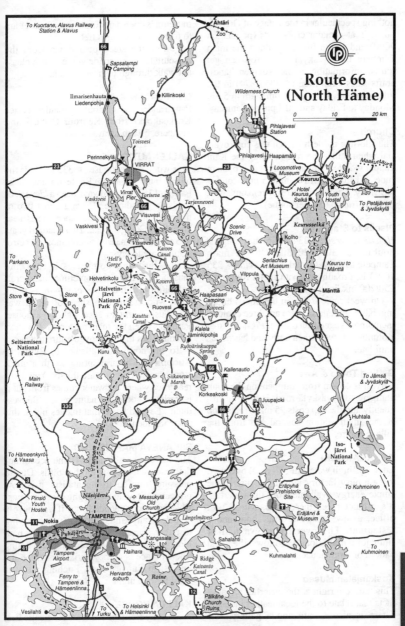

Route 66 (North Häme)

0   10   20 km

nothing spectacular in the village of Orivesi, but it is at a major crossroads (population 9000) and is the first stop along the main Tampere to Jyväskylä road. You can get tourist information at the Auvinen handicrafts sales exhibition (☎ 335 2874) in the village centre. It is open from 9 am to 5 pm Monday to Friday and till 1 pm on Saturday.

Church
The silo-like modern church was controversial when built, one reason being the Kain Tapper woodcarving in the altar. It is open in June and July from 10 am to 5 pm Monday to Friday. The old bell tower remains, with its *vaivaisukko* (pauper statue).

Places to Stay & Eat
Hotelli Orivesi (☎ 334 0666) has singles/doubles at 300/320 mk. On the main Tampere to Orivesi road, *Orimotelli* (☎ 335 7001) is a roadhouse with motel rooms for 150/200 mk, including breakfast.

On weekdays, *Bella*, in the Sokos building, has a set lunch. There are three choices, including a vegetarian option. *Pikku-Jussi* at Koluntie 4 serves lunch daily and has meals until late.

Getting There & Away
Orivesi is 43 km from Tampere on the main Tampere to Jyväskylä road. Buses run frequently and the trip costs 25 mk. Trains stop at the small station several km from the village centre.

KORKEAKOSKI
Literally 'high waterfall', Korkeakoski used to be a busy factory village because of the ample energy available from the waterfall. It's a quiet place these days, with a post office, a few banks, several shops and a restaurant. The oversized town hall of Juupajoki municipality follows the local pattern of large houses.

Koskenjalan Museo
This museum right at the waterfall has artefacts that relate to the local leather industry. There is also a café and a gallery. The museum is open daily in summer from 11 am to 6 pm. Admission is free.

Follow the steep path down from the museum to the riverside gorge. It is a pleasant walk through lush vegetation.

Getting There & Away
Paunu and a few other bus companies service Korkeakoski from Keuruu, Orivesi and Tampere, 59 km away.

KALLENAUTIO
This wooden roadhouse (☎ 335 8915) is the oldest building along Route 66 and dates back to 1757. It has always been a *kievari*, or roadside guesthouse. There are just two of them left in Finland; the other one is near Halikko on King's Road. Two hundred years ago they were nearly as common as petrol stations are today.

The building comprises a café and museum and there are sometimes handicraft exhibitions. You can see how *päre* is made from wood. This thin sheet of wood was previously burnt to shed light in a house. Päre was often the main reason for the devastating fires that destroyed entire towns.

To the north of Kallenautio, **Ryövärin Kuoppa** is a natural spring worth a quick stop, especially if you are thirsty. You don't really see where the water comes from but it is fresh and good. The name means 'thieves' ditch'. Legend has it that thieves hid in this place in olden days.

SIIKANEVA MARSHLAND
The largest marshland in Häme accommodates unusual owls and other birds. Due to pressure from environmentalists, it is now protected. Staying overnight is neither possible nor recommended, but if you have a vehicle of any kind, it may be worth driving to either starting point of the six km path loop, which can be walked in a few hours. The entrance is at the 'Varikko' sign on the Orivesi to Ruovesi road. Pitching a tent is legal for one night.

KALELA HOUSE
A celebrity from the National Romantic Era,

Mr Gallén-Kallela stayed a long time in this studio set in the wilderness and in fact painted most of his famous *Kalevala* works here. There are exhibitions every summer. To get here, follow main road No 66 five km south from the village of Ruovesi, then turn east. It's three km to Kalela along a gravel road. The place is definitely worth the effort of getting to. Kalela is open from late June to early August till 5 pm daily. Admission is 30 mk. The SS *Tarjanne* also stops here on request.

RUOVESI

Once voted the most beautiful village in Finland, Ruovesi retains much of its past charm. There is not much to see or do in the village, but the journey through the wilderness of northern Häme has a lot of scenic appeal for visitors. The population of Ruovesi is almost 6000.

Information

Ruoveden Matkailu, the local tourist information office (☎ 486 1388), is on the island of Haapasaari. Because of the camping ground here, the office is open daily, from 8 am to 10 pm in summer and from 8 am to 4 pm in winter.

Things to See

Local Museum This museum features a North Häme house dating from the 18th century. It is open from 14 June to 9 August from noon to 6 pm. Entry is 5 mk.

Runebergin Lähde The 'Runeberg Spring' does not necessarily have anything to do with the national poet, though it is believed that one of his poems was inspired by this pleasant spring. Located a little to the north of the village centre, it is worth a visit for its unusual vegetation. Bring your water bottle and fill it with fresh pure water.

Places to Stay

The cheapest place to sleep is *Haapasaaren lomakylä* (☎ 486 1388), on the small islet north of the village. It's open from 1 May to 30 September. Rooms start at 95 mk and you

can also camp here. Of the two small hotels in the village, *Hotelli Ruovesi* (☎ 476 2273) has a greater capacity and cheaper rooms (singles/doubles for 190/270 mk) than *Hotelli Liera* (☎ 476 2180).

Getting There & Away

Ruovesi is on the famous Route 66 and several buses a day connect the village with Tampere and other places in the region. There are also direct buses from Helsinki. Ruovesi is off the main road, so take that into account if you hitchhike.

HELVETINJÄRVI NATIONAL PARK

The main attraction of this national park, often called 'the Hell' for short, is a narrow gorge, probably created as the ice moved the huge rocks apart some 10,000 years ago. The scene inspired the design of the Finnish pavilion at the Seville World Exhibition in 1992. There are paths to follow and you can even stay overnight.

TORISEVA

One of the most spectacular gorges in the region surrounds three lakes, which together constitute a nice five km walking loop. Start from the small café on the top of the hill, near the parking area, some five km south of the town of Virrat. The café has a map that shows the track.

VIRRAT

The town of Virrat is the end point for ferry trips from Tampere. It is useful to have a bicycle with you, as you may have to travel long distances here. The businesses here serve some 9000 inhabitants.

The first church of Virrat was built in 1651, and the present-day red-coloured wooden church dates from 1774. Its simple interior reflects the original plan.

Information

The tourist information office (☎ 485 1276) is in the town hall, in the centre of Virrat.

Places to Stay

Located quite near the harbour and the

church, *Summer Hotel Domus* (☎ 475 4570) at Rantatie 11, open from 1 June to 15 August, has singles/doubles for 105/190 mk for HI members. The best hotel is *Hotelli Eetvartti* (☎ 475 5454) opposite the market at Virtaintie 35. It has singles/doubles for 190/240 mk. *Matkustajakoti* (☎ 475 5365) across the street has a somewhat eccentric manager but the rates (100/200 mk including breakfast) are good value for accommodation in this small house right in the centre of town.

There are two camping grounds outside the town centre. *Lakarin leirintäalue* (☎ 475 8639) has bungalows from 100 mk and *Suvi-Nuuttila* (☎ 475 8634) is not much dearer.

Places to Eat

There's the standard *grilli* at the market but Virrat also has restaurants. *Pub Kahvila 66* is named after the famous road and includes a grilli section for hamburgers. On the crossing of Virtaintie and the road that leads to the harbour, *Martinkarhu* serves pizza and has a beer terrace in summer. Keskustie has a few places, such as *Toriseva* and *Konditoria* just across the street. *Rantaterassi* at the harbour serves snacks.

Getting There & Away

See the Häme and Tampere sections for details of ferry transport to and from Virrat. Several buses a day connect Virrat to Tampere and other towns in the region.

PERINNEKYLÄ

The 'Tradition Village' features four museums, handicraft sales and a restaurant with a 45 mk buffet lunch (60 mk on weekends). The area is six km north-west of Virrat, at the Herraskoski Canal, itself an interesting place to visit. There is also a Finnish canal museum here. Set aside half a day for this area and bring some food if the weather is fine. There's a camping ground across the road.

Things to See & Do

The museums, shops and most attractions are open from late May to 31 August daily from 11 am to 6 pm, although some places are closed on Monday in the low season. The main building of the **Talomuseo** has furniture, traditional Sunday decorations from the 1840s and a smoke sauna. There are also a few other houses.

The **Metsäkämppä-museo** features a large house and two small huts once used by loggers. The houses have tools used by forest workers. The **Sotaveteraanien museo-huone**, or War Veteran Museum Room, has guns and other things that were used during WWII. The handicraft shop next door is open daily. The **Kanavamuseo** has an exhibition relating to the canal and is open daily from 9 am to 8 pm.

Tuulimylly, a windmill dating from 1828, has been renovated and is in working condition. The nature trail or the gravel road (old road No 66) will take you to **Herrasen Lintutorni**, a birdwatching tower that provides a good view of birdlife on Lake Toisvesi bay. **Kenttälinnoitusalue**, the area between the Herraskoski rapids and the canal, was used by Russian troops as a depot during the war in 1808. When Finland was part of tsarist Russia, a ditch system was dug in 1915 as a large strategic defence system against expansionist Germany. Today the area has renovated ditches and a bunker. A French 19th century cannon completes the attraction. Walk west towards the rapids.

Herraskoski The actual rapids are to be found along the gravel road that is the old road No 66, a bit west from Perinnekylä. Many locals fish here. Driving along the old road is a short cut to the present-day road No 66 that continues north from here.

LIEDENPOHJA

This small village at the north-west corner of Lake Toisvesi has several landmarks. The first to strike you is the Russian helicopter that was brought here in 1995. You will have to pay 10 mk for entry to see the monster, which is open daily from 10 am to 9 pm. The small kiosk sells snacks.

A section of the old road (No 66) runs

through the village, which has a local museum and a church dating from 1961. Teuvon Tupa is the local pub.

Just north of Liedenpohja, **Ilmarisen Hauta** is a deep gorge that runs a few hundred metres parallel to road No 66. Look for the parking area as the sign is difficult to spot.

From here, Route 66 continues to the regions of Vaasa and Pohjanmaa. See Alavus and Kuortane for attractions and services further north.

Central Finland

Central Finland lacks a clear character to set it apart from other regions. It is not the flat farmland of Pohjanmaa or the rich and busy south. Nor is it true lakeland like much of Savo or hilly like Lapland. Instead, it's a little bit of everything: forests and farmlands, lonely lakes and low hills, farmhouses and villages, and gravel roads that cross the sparsely populated countryside.

Historically, the area between Häme, Savo and Pohjanmaa was just wilderness. The present Province of Central Finland was founded as recently as 1960, carving areas out of all three regions. Lake Päijänne has long been a cultural frontier between Häme and Savo, and so is included in this chapter.

This is typical Finnish landscape. Here, people struggle to survive amidst the might of nature – in summer the *halla* (night frost) can sometimes destroy much of the crop. But for those visitors willing to try canoeing along scenic rivers, walking through forests or just cruising on Lake Päijänne, Central Finland will display its subtle beauty, and may provide the most lasting memories of Finland.

Jyväskylä

Jyväskylä (population 73,000) was founded in 1837 and is the capital of the Province of Central Finland. Its reputation as a national-istic town goes back to the earliest days – it has fostered Finnish education and literature, and the first Finnish-language schools were established here.

Before WWII the population was 10,000, but by the time the Province of Central Finland was carved out from neighbouring provinces in 1960, it had grown to 40,000. Today, Jyväskylä is a busy town with a large population of young people.

In 1966 the University of Jyväskylä was inaugurated; it was to become renowned for

Highlights

- Alvar Aalto Museum and Aalto-designed buildings in and around Jyväskylä.
- Boat trips and natural attractions of Lake Päijänne.
- Historical attractions around Hollola.
- Bicycle tours from Lahti.
- Petäjävesi Church, the finest example of peasant architecture.
- Ski jumping in Lahti and Jyväskylä.

its architecture. Indeed, the whole town is well known for its architecture, many of its buildings having been designed by Alvar Aalto. This reputation might come as a sur-prise to the traveller, whose first impression might well be that the town consists of a cluster of box-like supermarkets!

The Jyväskylä Arts Festival in early June features concerts, exhibitions, theatre and dance.

Orientation

The town centre lies between the railway and bus stations, with a lush university campus and most museums to the west. Kauppakatu,

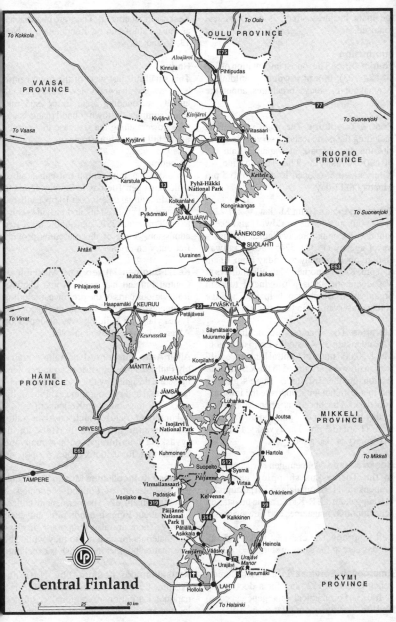

Central Finland

CENTRAL FINLAND

the main business street, is partly pedestrianised.

Information

Tourist Office The tourist information office (☎ 624 903), in a nice wooden building at Asemakatu 6, stocks brochures about the region.

Post & Telephone The main post office, including the poste restante service, is opposite the church park at Vapaudenkatu 60, 40100 Jyväskylä. The Tele office, at Kilpisenkatu 5, is open from 9 am to 5 pm Monday to Friday.

Travel Agencies Helin Matkat (☎ 211 222) at Väinönkatu 34 sells worldwide air tickets. Student discounts are available. VR has a travel agency (☎ 331 3245) at the railway station, open Monday to Friday from 10 am to 6 pm. Keski-Suomen Matkailuyhdistys at Vapaudenkatu 38 is a provincial tourism organisation which can help you arrange cottage reservations in the region.

Libraries The spacious public library at Vapaudenkatu 39-41 stocks English fiction. The 1:20,000 maps of Central Finland, easily seen in drawers, are stored in the *käsikirjasto* section on the 3rd floor. There's also an Internet terminal – it's opposite the information desk. The library is open Monday to Friday from 11 am to 7 pm, and on Saturday from 11 am to 3 pm. The Jyväskylä University library is also good.

Books & Maps Akateeminen Kirjakauppa is in the Torikeskus shopping centre at Väinönkatu 11. Suomalainen Kirjakauppa is at Kauppakatu 33. R-Kioski at the bus station sells imported magazines and newspapers.

Left Luggage The cheapest lockers (5 mk per day) are at the railway station.

Emergency Services In a general emergency phone ☎ 112, and for a doctor ring ☎ 10023. For medical emergencies go to Kyllön terveysasema (☎ 626 400) at Keskussairaalantie 20. There are pharmacies at Puistokatu 4 and on Kauppakatu at Nos 13, 35 and 39.

Harju

This small hill just west of the town centre has a tower with a good view over Jyväskylä and its surrounding area. Entry is 5 mk. Every summer, the town council plants beautiful flowers along the staircase that climbs up the hill from Yliopistonkatu.

Museums

Jyväskylä has four central museums, all of which are open Tuesday to Sunday 11 am to 6 pm. Individual tickets cost 10 mk each, but a joint ticket costs 20 mk and provides entry to each museum. ISIC card-holders get free admission. Some of the museums provide free entry on Friday.

Keski-Suomen Museo The Museum of Central Finland has artefacts and displays from various parts of the province, including an interesting exhibition on the history of Jyväskylä. The building was designed by Alvar Aalto and finished in 1961.

Alvar Aalto Museum Alvar Aalto is arguably Finland's most illustrious architect. This museum, designed by the man himself, contains actual and photographic exhibits of his work. The museum is on Keljonkatu.

For further 'field research' on Alvar Aalto, the museum provides leaflets about Jyväskylä's buildings, with a map and English text, for 0.50 mk each.

Suomen Kotiteollisuus Museo The Handicrafts Museum of Finland is located at Seminaarinkatu 32. The permanent collection is about Finnish handicrafts and their history. There are also temporary displays and materials for children to play with. The information booklet in English is excellent.

Kansallispuku Keskus The National Costume Centre at Gummeruksenkatu 3 is a national exhibition of regional costumes, located in the basement of a townhouse.

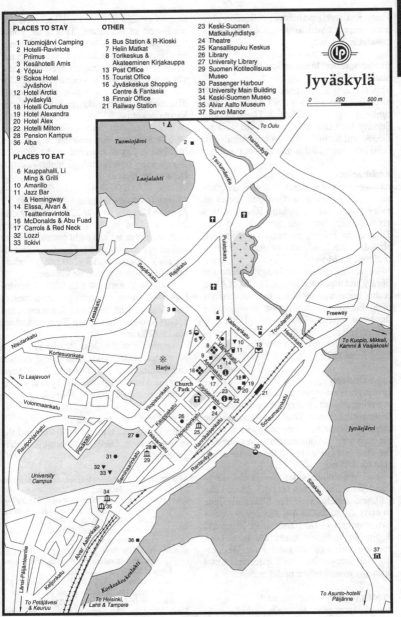

PLACES TO STAY

1 Tuomiojärvi Camping
2 Hotelli-Ravintola Priimus
3 Kesähotelli Amis
4 Yöpuu
9 Sokos Hotel Jyväshovi
17 Hotel Arctia Jyväskylä
18 Hotelli Cumulus
19 Hotel Alexandra
20 Hotel Alex
22 Hotelli Milton
28 Pension Kampus
36 Alba

PLACES TO EAT

6 Kauppahalli, Li Ming & Grilli
10 Amarillo
11 Jazz Bar & Hemingway
14 Elissa, Alvari & Teatteriravintola
16 McDonalds & Abu Fuad
17 Carrols & Red Neck
32 Lozzi
33 Ilokivi

OTHER

5 Bus Station & R-Kioski
7 Helin Matkat
8 Torikeskus & Akateeminen Kirjakauppa
13 Post Office
15 Tourist Office
16 Jyväskeskus Shopping Centre & Fantasia
18 Finnair Office
21 Railway Station

23 Keski-Suomen Matkailuyhdistys
24 Theatre
25 Kansallispuku Keskus
26 Library
27 University Library
29 Suomen Kotiteollisuus Museo
30 Passenger Harbour
31 University Main Building
34 Keski-Suomen Museo
35 Alvar Aalto Museum
37 Survo Manor

Jyväskylä

0   250   500 m

Tuomiojärvi

Laajalahti

To Oulu

Rantaväylä

Taulumäentie

Puistokatu

Seppänkatu

Rajakatu

Keskikatu

Nisulankatu

Kortesuonkatu

Kalevankatu

Freeway

Tourulantie

Heikinkatu

To Kuopio, Mikkeli, Kammi & Vaajakoski

To Laajavuori

Voionmaankatu

☀ *Harju*

Church Park

Yliopistonkatu

Kauppakatu

Asemakatu

Vapaudenkatu

Kilpisenkatu

Schaumankatu

Jyväsjärvi

Rautpohjankatu

Pitkäkatu

Vaasankatu

Seminaarinkatu

Hannikaisenkatu

Rantaväylä

University Campus

To Laajavuori

Länsi-Päijänteentie

Keljonkatu

Alvar Aallonkatu

Korkeakoskenlahti

To Petäjävesi & Keuruu

To Helsinki, Lahti & Tampere

Satakatu

To Asunto-hotelli Päijänne

There is a small permanent collection plus temporary exhibitions. Look out for a booklet in English.

Environmental Information Centre Kammi

This is based across Lake Jyrasjarvi. Catch local bus No 15 to Kuokkalantie 4. The centre is open Tuesday to Thursday and Sunday between noon and 6 pm, and on Friday and Saturday until 4 pm. Admission is 30 mk, and all information is in Finnish.

Architecture

At times the town is crawling with architecture buffs pointing wide-angled lenses at every Alvar Aalto building. If you're into architecture, the best time to arrive is Tuesday to Friday, as many buildings are closed on weekends and the Aalto Museum is closed on Monday.

Interesting public buildings include the library and the tourist office. The list of Alvar Aalto buildings includes the university's main building – don't miss it – and the theatre at Vapaudenkatu 36, from 1982. Restaurant Elissa at Väinönkatu 7 is located in an Alvar Aalto-designed workers' club that dates from 1925.

Lake Cruises

Jyväskylä is emerging as a new cruise centre in summer due to the recently opened Keitele route north of town. This runs through some impressive canals constructed by Russians in the early 1990s. You can return the same day, but a one-way ticket to Suolahti is also available for 145 mk.

You should consider the Jyväskylä to Lahti route. Shorter cruises on northern Lake Päijänne are also available from early June to early August. The *MS Kymppi* has daily two-hour cruises for 50 mk, at 11.30 am and 3 pm. In addition, there are three-hour evening cruises (65 mk) at 7 pm on Wednesday and weekends. Check dates and times with any tourist office in the region.

Places to Stay – bottom end

The cheapest place to stay is *Retkeilyhotelli*

Laajari (☎ 253 355) at Laajavuorentie 15, north-west of the centre. This is the youth hostel part of a large hotel complex. Dormitory beds cost 30 mk for HI members; 55 mk if you want sheets and an evening sauna. There are also singles/doubles at 160/200 mk, with showers and a shared kitchen. HI discounts apply. Take bus No 2 from Vapaudenkatu.

The pleasant *Tuomiojärvi Camping* (☎ 624 895) on Taulumäentie has several four-bed cottages scattered in the lakeside woods. They cost 180 mk per night. Take bus No 8 to get there.

Places to Stay – middle

Pension Kampus (☎ 607 223) at Vaasankatu 29 is a clean hostel near the university campus. There are just eight rooms, all clean and equipped with modern facilities, including a TV. Rooms are 180/260 mk, including breakfast. You may use the kitchen.

Kesähotelli Amis (☎ 612 920) at Sepänkatu 3 is a summer hotel, open from June to mid-August, with 99 rooms. Each room has a toilet, shower and kitchen. Singles/doubles are 190/280 mk.

Asuntohotelli Päijänne (☎ 656 311 office hours) has small rooms with shared kitchen and bathroom at 100/140 mk. It's located several km south-east of Jyväskylä at Salmirannantie 5. Take bus No 19.

Places to Stay – top end

There are a few top-end hotels around the railway station. Generally, Jyväskylä offers good value.

Alba (☎ 636 311) is located lakeside at Ahlmaninkatu 4. Singles/doubles cost from 310/380 mk.

Sokos Hotel Alexandra and Alex (☎ 651 211) are two hotels sharing a reception at Hannikaisenkatu 35. Singles/doubles cost from 420/500 mk; in summer all rooms are from 350 mk. Alexandra is better and more expensive.

Hotel Arctia Jyväskylä (☎ 330 3000) at Vapaudenkatu 73 is a very modern hotel with 150 rooms. Singles/doubles are 550/650 mk.

Hotelli Cumulus (☎ 653 211) at Väinönkatu 3 has over 200 rooms, three restaurants and other facilities. Singles/doubles cost 450/520 mk.

Sokos Hotel Jyväshovi (☎ 630 211) is the town's

oldest and most central hotel. It's at Kauppakatu 35 and was renovated in 1995. Singles/doubles cost 450/530 mk.

Hotelli Milton (☎ 213 411), opposite the railway station, is a family hotel at Hannikaisenkatu 29. Singles/doubles are 290/390 mk, with a discount of 100 mk on weekends and from 20 June to 31 July.

Hotelli-Ravintola Priimus (☎ 609 111) is at Taulumäentie 45. This training college for future hotel workers has singles/doubles for 380/480 mk.

Rantasipi Laajavuori (☎ 628 211) in the Laajavuori area, north-west of the centre, has sports facilities in and around the hotel. There are 196 rooms, with singles/doubles at 450/520 mk.

Yöpuu (☎ 620 811) at Yliopistonkatu 23 is an old-fashioned hotel with plenty of charm and style. With only 26 rooms, the place is often full. There are two beautifully decorated restaurants, *Ranskalaiset Korot* on Yliopistonkatu, and *Pöllöwaari* around the corner on Kansakoulunkatu. Singles/doubles are 350/400 mk.

Places to Eat

The cheapest meals in town are available at university restaurants. *Lozzi* is an interesting restaurant that was designed by Alvar Aalto. Meals, available in summer, are excellent value. *Ilokivi* in the Student Union building is an ordinary restaurant, with meals a little over 20 mk. On the 2nd floor of the university library, you can get cheap soups and snacks.

Most restaurants serve discounted lunches. One of the best deals is *Pikantti* in the Citymarket building. There are four lunch options for 25 to 40 mk, and they include salad, malt drink, bread and dessert. Less attractive but slightly cheaper is *Reimari*, opposite the tourist office, where lunch is available on weekdays only.

Excellent for both beer and food is the delightful rural *Red Neck* at Asemakatu 7, not far from the railway station. It has Finnish music, old farm tools on the walls and tractor seats as chairs. Although you won't understand the jokes on the menu, this place is a must. For a late-night snack, head for Kauppakatu 41, where *Troija Kebab* does inexpensive kebabs till the early hours.

Another Alvar Aalto-designed restaurant is *Elissa* at Väinönkatu 7. Bulky air-con units have scarred the ceiling of this sacred building – but the food is not bad and Pesiaali lager has been brewed on the premises since 1994. There are inexpensive lunch options.

Entertainment

Ilokivi hosts rock concerts on Wednesday and Thursday evenings. Sample traditional entertainment at *Red Neck* or go bar-hopping along Kauppakatu, the pedestrian section of the main street. This has several places worth trying, such as *Jazz Bar* at No 32, with quiet but good jazz, and *Hemingway*, dedicated to the great American writer.

Downstairs at Väinönkatu 7 is *Alvari*, a pub worth a visit. Next door to it is *Teatteriravintola*, a nightclub that keeps its doors open until the early hours of the morning.

A six-screen movie complex, *Fantasia*, is in the Jyväskeskus shopping centre.

Things to Buy

Jyväskylä is quite a good place for shopping. The market square is busy until 2 pm, and there are handicrafts for sale. *Aivia* at Kauppakatu 25 is a large shop selling Finnish handicraft. Opposite the bus terminal, *Torikeskus* has over 50 shops to explore.

Another large shopping centre is Jyväskeskus on the corner of Kauppakatu and Asemakatu.

Getting There & Away

Air There are several flights from Helsinki to Jyväskylä each weekday and fewer on weekends.

Bus The bus terminal near the hill serves the entire southern half of Finland, with several daily express buses connecting Jyväskylä to the big cities.

Train The railway station is between the town and the harbour. There are direct trains from Helsinki, Turku, Joensuu and Vaasa.

Boat Lake Päijänne steamers depart from Jyväskylä and Lahti at 10 am Tuesday to

Saturday (except Thursday), arriving at either end at 8 pm the same day. Try to catch the SS *Suomi*, one of the oldest steamers still plying the Finnish lakes. A one-way ticket costs 210 mk.

Getting Around

To/From the Airport Finnair buses meet each arriving aeroplane.

Bus The most convenient place to catch local buses is at the church park. Timetables are available. Tickets cost 9 mk, or use your 10-km Coach Holiday Pass coupons for individual journeys.

Bicycle Bicycles can be rented at the tourist office and at Retki & Pyöräily. Both places charge 35 mk per day, with weekly rates available at the tourist office.

AROUND JYVÄSKYLÄ

Säynätsalo

The large Säynätsalo Civic Centre south-east of Jyväskylä is one of Alvar Aalto's most famous works, the architect winning an international competition in 1949 to design it . The building was completed in 1952. The library is open every afternoon from Monday to Friday; the municipal office opens during office hours. On the small island of Juurikkasaari, just off Säynätsalo, Alvar Aalto's boat (his own design) features a humble note 'Nemo Propheta in Patria' (No-one is a prophet in one's own land). Follow the sign that says 'Aallon vene'.

On the island of Muuratsalo, accessible via Lehtisaari, Aalto's Villa was a test building, on which the architect tried out various brick materials. For opening times, contact the Alvar Aalto Museum. Admission is 30 mk.

Getting There & Away Bus Nos 16, 17M and 21 run regularly from Jyväskylä to Säynätsalo.

Muurame

If you are driving along the main Tampere to Jyväskylä road, you might want to stop in

Muurame – 13 km south of Jyväskylä – to have a look at the Saunakylä (Sauna Village). This open-air museum, open daily in summer from 10 am to 6 pm, has a variety of old saunas. Entry is 10 mk.

Visible from Saunakylä is Muurame's multi-purpose leisure centre, an architectural 'legacy' from the 1980s. It serves Muurame's 7000 people. A white church designed by Alvar Aalto during the 1920s is open in summer from 10 am to 6 pm.

Riihivuori Hill is a local downhill skiing centre some 5 km from the main Tampere to Jyväskylä road, just south of Muurame.

Places to Stay *Hotelli Kultakenkä* (☎ 631 294) on Mäkijärventie is a resort hotel, with rates from 100 mk per person. Serious skiers should try *Riihivuoren Lomakylä* (☎ 311 0911) on the top of Riihivuori Hill. Beds start from 80 mk. *Niemelän Lomamökit*, a small cottage business right at the bottom of Riihivuori Hill, rents out large cottages for 250 mk.

Laukaa

Laukaa (population 16,000) is a wealthy municipality to the north of Jyväskylä. The oldest established municipality in the region, it dates back to 1593. The main village has a small museum, a library and a number of shops and places to eat. The large church is open in summer from Wednesday to Sunday between 1 and 7 pm.

Places to Stay & Eat *Hotelli Peurunka* (☎ 839 601) is a huge spa complex 5 km from the main village, to the north-west of the railway line. It is particularly popular with war veterans and is therefore geared towards them. It's good for swimming, has some restaurants and may even interest those who want to look at modern architecture. Rooms are 300/400 mk, and treatment packages are available from two to 13 days. The nearby golf course is run by the same company.

There are several restaurants in the main village, such as *Ruokahelmi* opposite the bus station. There's a café at the bus station, and

Herkkuvakka Grilli is nearby. In the village itself, *Sudentassu* is a popular place to drink beer.

Tikkakoski

This small village west of Laukaa is an airforce base, but there are several attractions. To get there, go along the narrow road No 6301 towards Uurainen (it runs parallel to road No 4). The scenic route is great for cycling.

Tikkamannila Once a cow shelter, this building now houses a flax museum. It also has a fine display of Finnish guns, many made locally. There is also a rare stone exhibition plus handicrafts and flax products on sale. Admission is 15 mk. You can buy fresh pies from the café until 8 pm.

Outside the house is a tiny war museum, featuring a mock-WWII underground shelter, built in 1994.

Tikkamannila is 500 metres from the Jyväskylä to Oulu road (No 4).

Keski-Suomen Ilmailumuseo The Aviation Museum of Central Finland is the highlight of Tikkakoski. Despite its name it's more of a military museum and will be of interest to students of WWII. Rare aeroplanes include a fighter from the 1920s; a Russian Polikarpov U2 that was shot down with a single shot in December 1939; and a self-made aeroplane belonging to Raimo Päätalo, who was punished for the 'unforgivable crime' of flying it without a proper licence.

A Japanese 'Finlandia Family Club' has donated 21 meticulously created dioramas depicting action from WWII. The aviation museum is open daily in summer from 10 am to 8 pm, and at other times daily from 11 am to 5 pm. Admission is 30 mk but a joint ticket with Tikkamannila's gun museum costs 40 mk.

Places to Stay & Eat The only place anywhere near Tikkakoski is *Ränssi-Kievari* (☎ 311 0086), at a beautiful lakeside location near the village of Kuikka, some five km

west of Tikkamannila. The large yellow house dates from 1820 and has been a guesthouse for more than 100 years. These days, beds cost 130 mk per person, including meals. A smoke sauna can be heated for 800 mk, but if you're lucky you can bathe for free late at night when it's still warm and the richer people have finished with it.

Western Central

This section includes the towns of Mänttä and Ähtäri, which are actually outside the Province of Central Finland, but conveniently located along travel routes.

PETÄJÄVESI

This rural municipality lies 35 km west of Jyväskylä. Its highlight is a cross-shaped wooden church, which was the third Finnish attraction to be placed on the UNESCO World Heritage List. Petäjävesi is also the starting point for the Wanhan witosen paddling route along the waterways to Rasua Camping, near Jämsänkoski.

Petäjävesi Church

Built in 1764, this church is probably the most notable example of 18th century peasant architecture in Finland. Prior to its construction, there had been some debate about whether this village should get a church at all. While a reply to applications (sent to Stockholm for approval) was delayed, one Jaakko Leppänen started the job minus permission and properly drawn instructions. The result was a local variation on a combination of Renaissance and Byzantine architecture. It's a marvellous, though rather awkward, wooden building with a great deal of fine detail. The church has not been used since 1879, when the new church was opened.

The old church, near road No 23 between Keuruu and Jyväskylä, is open from 9 am to 6 pm in June and August, and from 9 am to 9 pm in July. Entry costs 10 mk (and is worth it). At other times of the year, enquire at the

Jyväskylä tourist office. They will be able to arrange for someone to open the door, for a fee.

Places to Stay & Eat
Petäjäveden kesähotelli (☎ 854 099 or 855 459) is a summer hotel, open from June to August.

You can eat at *Kyläseppä*, which is also an Esso petrol station, or at *Lipetti* beyond the village centre.

Getting There & Away
Unless you trek along the Maakuntaura, you will need to catch an express bus between Tampere and Jyväskylä via Keuruu. Alternatively, the Töysän Linja bus runs almost hourly between Jyväskylä and Petäjävesi. It is a 35-km trip.

HIMOS
One of the most popular downhill-skiing areas, the Himos is near the town of Jämsä on the main Tampere to Jyväskylä road. The slopes have neither length nor height to boast about but nevertheless attract people from big cities in south Finland. Cottages for daily or weekly rent are dotted around the slopes and in Jämsä village.

KEURUU
The little town of Keuruu is on the northern shore of Lake Keurusselkä and boasts one of the most interesting wooden churches in Finland. The population of 12,000 includes people from surrounding villages.

Information
The tourist information office (☎ 751 7144), in the town hall at Multiantie 5, is open in June, July and August from Monday to Friday between 9 am and 3 pm.

Things to See & Do
Keuruu's fascinating old **wooden church**, built in 1758, has superb portraits of Bible characters, and there are old artefacts on display in the back room. Don't miss the photos of mummified corpses, which were found below the chancel. The church is open

15 May to 31 August from 10 am to 5 pm daily. Admission is 5 mk.

Ulkomuseo, a local open-air museum behind the new church, contains several old buildings, complete with local tools and paraphernalia. The museum is open in June, July and August from Tuesday to Sunday between 11 am and 5 pm. Entry is 5 mk.

There are **lake cruises** from early June to mid-August. The MS *Elias Lönnrot* sails daily from Keuruu to the Hotel Keurusselkä and back. Departure times are noon and 2 pm (in July also at 4 pm). A ticket costs 35 mk one-way, 60 mk return. The trip at 2 pm on Saturday continues on to Mänttä.

An information map near the church points out the town's other attractions, which include a new church and some local art exhibitions.

Places to Stay & Eat
An economical option, *Camping Nyyssänniemi* (☎ 720 480), is open from 5 June to 9 August. Cottages cost 120 to 250 mk. The top-end *Hotelli Keurusselkä* (☎ 80800), 10 km from the town centre, has singles/doubles for 330/440 mk, but also offers package deals.

Keuruu has several eating and drinking establishments. A café, *Katariinan kamari*, is located in a log house almost opposite the church. Try *City-Grilli* for hamburgers. *Mestarikokit* is a lunch-time restaurant along road No 23, not far from the village centre.

Getting There & Away
Buses to Keuruu can be caught from Jyväskylä or Tampere. There are several trains a day from Jyväskylä and Haapamäki.

HAAPAMÄKI
Haapamäki used to be a busy railway junction, but when a track through Parkano opened, Haapamäki virtually ceased to exist. It is now – administratively – a 'suburb' of the town of Keuruu. But a few trains still pass by and train buffs will enjoy the **Höyryveturipuisto** (Steam Locomotive Museum). In summer, there are activities for children. The museum is officially open June

to mid-August from 10 am to 8 pm, but locomotives are located outside so can be seen all year round.

Places to Stay & Eat

Junamotelli Niklas (☎ 733 160), a motel built in old railway carriages, has bunks for 100 mk per person. Breakfast in the nearby *Ravintola Niklas* costs 25 mk.

Getting There & Away

There are several buses a day from Keuruu, 16 km to the east. Trains from Seinäjoki, Jyväskylä and Orivesi stop here several times daily.

PIHLAJAVESI

The sleepy little village of Pihlajavesi is west of Keuruu. Its shops, banks, post office and public library are all near the railway station.

Things to See

Pihlajavesi's old wilderness **church**, built in 1780, is fairly similar to the one in Inari in Lapland. It's two km by gravel road from the station area; follow the 'Vanha kirkko' signs. A guide will take you in on summer weekends from noon to 7 pm; at other times use the old key which hangs above the door. The 'new' church, built in 1870, is a few km west of the railway station. There is a small local museum nearby.

Getting There & Away

Three trains a day run between Seinäjoki and Haapamäki; many of them stop at Pihlajavesi on request.

MÄNTTÄ

The main reason for visiting the industrial town of Mänttä (population 7200) is to see the Serlachius Art Museum, one of the best art collections in Finland. There are also good places to stay. The tourist information booth at the Makos hamburger restaurant on Ratakatu is open daily until 11 pm.

Things to See

Mänttä is dominated by the huge Serlachius paper factory. The Art-Nouveau 1928 church was financed by the factory, and has unique wood carvings on the altar and pulpit. It is open daily from 10 am to 6 pm (Sunday until 7 pm).

Joenniemi Manor, the private home of the late industrialist Gösta Serlachius, now houses the **Gösta Serlachiuksen Taidemuseo**. Its large collection features art from various European countries but the highlight is the Finnish section, which includes all the major names from the 'Golden Age' of Finnish art. The museum is open daily (except Monday) June to August from 11 am to 6 pm; the rest of the year on weekends only, from noon to 5 pm. Opposite the museum is a restaurant.

Honkahovi is another mansion belonging to the Serlachius family. It's a 1938 Art-Deco structure containing temporary art exhibitions and open year round. You can walk between Honkahovi and the Joenniemi Manor along the Lemmenpolku track on the shore of Lake Melasjärvi.

Places to Stay & Eat

The *youth hostel* (☎ 488 8641) is in the modern dormitory building of a school, at Koulukatu 6, not far from the centre. There are beds from 55 mk. It is open from June to mid-August.

There are two hotels right in the centre of Mänttä. *Casa Mia* (☎ 474 6041), at Kauppaneuvoksenkatu 2, has 14 rooms, priced at 260/330 mk. There's also a restaurant. *Hotelli Alexander* (☎ 474 9231), at Kauppakatu 23, has rooms from 150/290 mk, including one meal. Its restaurant, *Old Alexander*, serves a daily lunch for about 50 mk, and dinner until late.

Kotipizza is near Hotelli Alexander. There are a few grillis around the central square, such as *Makos Burger* and *Pysäkki*. Pubs include *Kestikeidas*.

Getting There & Away

In summer, you can catch the Saturday steamer from Keuruu. Otherwise, there are several buses a day to Mänttä from Tampere, Keuruu and Orivesi. The bus station is 700 metres west of the centre.

ÄHTÄRI

Ähtäri is a success story in attracting families through commercial tourism. It features a zoo, the 'Mini-Finland' park and a Western Village, as well as hotels and restaurants. Admission charges are high, but this is not a bad place if you have 100 mk or so to spend! Much more interesting is the Vehicle Museum between the village and the zoo. It houses a good collection of vintage cars, old radios and other paraphernalia.

Information

Ähtärin Matkailu (☎ 533 1754), at Ostolantie 4, is open June to early August on weekdays between 8 am and 6 pm and on Saturday from 10 am to 4 pm. The rest of the year, it's open Monday to Friday from 8 am to 4 pm.

Places to Stay

The cheapest place to stay in Ähtäri is *Ähtärin retkeilymaja* (☎ 533 7482) at Koulutie 16. This is a youth hostel in a school building, open year round. There are bicycles for hire. *Gasthaus Hankola* (☎ 533 0198) at Hankolantie 17 has singles/doubles for 100/200 mk.

The zoo area has no bottom-end places. *Eläinpuiston mökkikylä* (☎ 393 613) has a camping ground and over 50 cottages, ranging from 170 to 290 mk. Prices inflate in July. *Arctia Kylpylähotelli Mesikämmen* (☎ 391 111) is a wilderness hotel, beautifully landscaped in bedrock. It has over 100 rooms, a spa area with three saunas, and two restaurants. The cost is 300/390 mk for singles/doubles; slightly less in winter.

Across the lake, five km from the village, *Hyvölän Talo* (☎ 533 0071) has beds from 80 mk, breakfast included. Nine km from the zoo at Nousulahti, *Leppälän mökkimajoitus* (☎ 533 6244) is a farm estate with cottages at 70 to 100 mk per person, including breakfast.

Getting There & Away

Trains heading east from Seinäjoki stop at Ähtäri and at the Zoo station (on request). There are three or four trains a day. Bus connections from around the region are also excellent.

Northern Central

This region comprises dense woods, enormous lakes, small villages and narrow roads. It's not exactly Siberia (some of the places are more accessible) but there is still a hint of adventure.

SUOLAHTI

There are few attractions in this small, industrial town. You can come by boat from Jyväskylä or drive there along the scenic road No 642 from Laukaa. The harbour has an old locomotive, a kiosk for provisions and information. North of Suolahti is Paatela with its Keitele canal lock, and a café.

Hotelli Keitele (☎ 541 061) has rooms at the road crossing not far from Suolahti. Cheaper is *Suolahden Matkustajakoti* (☎ 542 500) at Kellosepänkatu 17 in the centre, with rooms from 100/150 mk.

ÄÄNEKOSKI

Much larger and relatively more pleasant, this town is dominated by an even bigger factory. Unfortunately, this one is of the pulp variety so occasional stench is not rare. Coming from Suolahti, you will bump into the local museum, which also serves as an information office. Nearby, the large town centre has all services you might need.

Places to Stay & Eat

Hotelli Hirvi (☎ 520 121) is the top-end hotel near the town centre. There are 54 rooms, two restaurants, two saunas and a pool.

Among the many places to eat, *Café Panorama* is in the imposing supermarket in the centre and there's *Kotipizza* at the market.

SAARIJÄRVI

The small town of Saarijärvi, home to 10,800 people, is surrounded by water on almost all sides. This is where the Karstula to Saarijärvi canoeing route ends. In the main village, there's a museum at Lake Herajärvi and an impressive church from 1849.

Kolkanlahti

Most of Saarijärvi's attractions are along the main road No 13, spanning over 15 km. Six km north of Kolkanlahti, **Säätyläismuseo**, or Upper Class Residence, is the former home of Finland's national poet, JL Runeberg, showing where he worked in the 1820s. Now a museum, it's open daily from noon to 7 pm in summer.

Vesieläinpuisto is a small zoo with aquatic animals. Farther north, **Julmat Lammit** is a nature conservation area, with deep lakes of crystal-clear water.

Summassaari

On this island, south-east of Saarijärvi, there's a Stone Age Village – a reconstruction of a settlement which was here approximately 5000 years ago. The village is open in summer from Tuesday to Sunday between noon and 7 pm, and information is available on the prehistoric discoveries.

Places to Stay & Eat

In Kolkanlahti, *Ahvenlahti Camping* (☎ 429 1300) has many cottages for rent, and is open from 1 June to late August. Nearby, *Hotelli Menninkäinen* (☎ 439 711) has rooms from 360 mk, and there are canoes for rent.

In Saarijärvi you'll find *Seurahuone* (☎ 421 951), at Ilolantie 14, with singles from 250 mk.

At Summassaari there's a *spa* (☎ 421 311) with singles/doubles for 300/470 mk in summer. There are discounts in autumn and spring.

There are restaurants and cafés in hotels. Check out *Ravintola Lyhty*, a restaurant-cum-pub at Nahkurintie 2, or *Paavon Pub* for beer.

Getting There & Away

Many of the westbound buses from Jyväskylä will take you to Saarijärvi.

PYHÄ-HÄKKI NATIONAL PARK

The virgin forest of Pyhä-Häkki, protected since 1912, became a national park in 1956. Much of the park is marshland. Old trees remain the main attraction, especially *iso puu*, which is over 500 years old. Little wildlife can be seen, though with a bit of luck you might spot hole-nesting birds, owls or even a few elk.

Getting There & Away

The narrow, north-easterly road between Saarijärvi and Viitasaari runs through Pyhä-Häkki. It is worth driving through the park, even if you don't have time to stop.

KARSTULA

The remote village of Karstula, whose population of 5500 includes inhabitants of the outlying areas, is in a beautiful setting, surrounded by lakes. It is here that one of the most exciting canoeing routes starts. You can rent canoes in Karstula or at the other end, in Saarijärvi.

Places to Stay

Vanhan Tussarin Majatalo (☎ 461 402) on Koulutie has singles/doubles for 230/330 mk. Its rates are slightly lower than those of *Harkko* (☎ 461 311) at Keskustie 7, which has rooms from 300 mk.

Getting There & Away

Karstula is a few km west of the main Jyväskylä to Kokkola road. There are express buses that cover the 100 km from Jyväskylä.

VIITASAARI

Midway between Oulu and Tampere is Viitasaari. The setting is scenic, but there's not much to see in the village itself. It's a quiet little place with over 8000 inhabitants. Viitasaari is known for its taste in 'different' art and music.

There is an exhibition of modern art in two school buildings off the main road. It's open daily in summer till 8 pm. Entry is 30 mk, 20 mk for students.

Viitasaari is known for the 'Time of

Music' Summer Festival – its modern, experimental music definitely outside the mainstream. Further information is available from Time of Music (☎ 573 195, fax 579 3515), 44500 Viitasaari.

Places to Stay

Viitasaari has just one hotel. Singles/doubles at *Hotel Pihkuri* (☎ 571 440) at Kappelintie 5 are expensive, at 360/470 mk. It's at the far end of the village. There are 24 rooms in a motel-style setting, and two saunas.

Everything else is quite far away. *Hännilänsalmen leirintäalue* (☎ 572 550) is a camping ground in a beautiful lakeside location some four km south of Viitasaari. Cottages start at 150 mk.

Hotelli Ruuponsaari (☎ 571 480) is 15 km west of Viitasaari. There are cottages from 145 mk.

Wiikin kartano (☎ 530 242) is an old estate mansion, but its stone-walled hotel rooms are in a magnificently renovated cowshed! Singles/doubles are 200/270 mk. There are also small bungalows from 150 mk. The set lunch, served 11 am to 7 pm, starts at 40 mk and includes salad, bread and dessert. The place is close to the main Jyväskylä to Oulu road, some 14 km north of Viitasaari village.

Places to Eat

Liisan Kievari is a decent lunch-time restaurant, but *Henrik* is more popular with the locals. There are huge supermarkets in Viitasaari.

Getting There & Away

Viitasaari is well connected by express and normal bus routes to all major towns in Central Finland. If you drive, take road No 4 or No 77 (the Vaasa and Kuopio road).

KONGINKANGAS

You can observe a genuine rural lifestyle here – with hints of modernity – and there's a beautiful white church. The small museum is open in July only from Wednesday to Sunday between noon and 5 pm. *Killinki* is the local restaurant.

Lake Päijänne Region

One of the largest lakes in Finland, Päijänne provides Helsinki with drinkable tap water and everyone else with scenic waterways. There are both narrow and wide roads on both sides of Lake Päijänne, which draws together three provinces – Central Finland, Mikkeli and Häme.

LAHTI

With 95,000 inhabitants, Lahti is the fifth largest urban centre in Finland. Although it has a reputation as a winter sports centre, it's not very interesting in other respects. Lahti was founded in 1905 and lacks anything that could be called 'old town'. Its growth record is impressive and the 10,000 Karelian refugees who arrived here after WWII have contributed their entrepreneurial spirit to what the locals call the 'Business City'. In the 1950s and 1960s, labour-intensive industries increased the population further, but also led to sad unemployment figures in the 1990s.

Yes, there's cultural life here – the ubiquitous Alvar Aalto and Eliel Saarinen buildings, plus museums and sports facilities. And Lahti makes an excellent base for visiting nearby attractions – bicycle routes have been established, along with designated places to stay. Lahti's location by Lake Vesijärvi – which is connected to Lake Päijänne – makes it a good place to start a ferry trip to Jyväskylä.

A major venue for winter sports in Finland, Lahti has hosted five world championships in Nordic skiing. In summer, writers gather at a convention in Mukkula.

Orientation

The compact town centre is situated around the main street, Aleksanterinkatu. The famous Sports Centre is just to the west of the town centre. Mukkula, the recreational area by Lake Vesijärvi, is four km to the north.

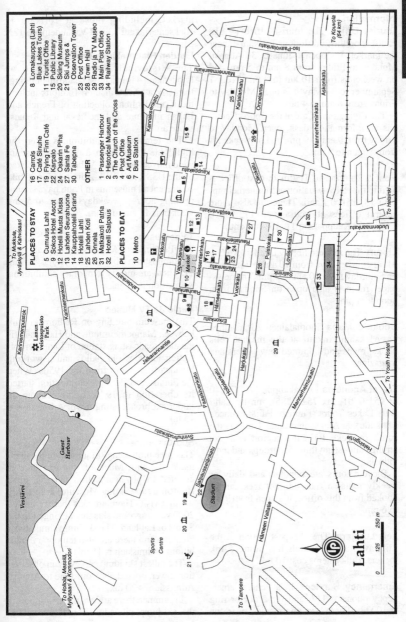

PLACES TO STAY

5 Cumulus Lahti
9 Sokos Hotel Ascot
12 Hotelli Musta Kissa
13 Lahden Seurahuone
14 Kauppahotelli Grand
18 Hotelli Lahti
25 Lahden Koti
26 Onnela
31 Matkakoti Patria
32 Hotelli Salpaus

PLACES TO EAT

10 Metro
16 Carrols
17 Café Sinuhe
19 Flying Finn Café
22 Karpalo
24 Oskarin Piha
27 Santa Fe
30 Tabepna

OTHER

1 Passenger Harbour
2 Historical Museum
3 The Church of the Cross
4 Post Office
6 Art Museum
7 Bus Station
8 Lomakauppa (Lahti
  Blue Lakes Tours)
11 Tourist Office
15 Public Library
20 Skiing Museum
21 Ski Jumps &
  Observation Tower
23 Post Office
28 Town Hall
29 Radio ja TV Museo
33 Main Post Office
34 Railway Station

Lahti

Information

Tourist Office The tourist office (☎ 818 2580) is on the 2nd floor at Torikatu 3, near the market. It's open 1 June to 31 August, Monday to Friday from 8 am to 5 pm, and on weekends from 10 am to 2 pm. From 1 September to 31 May it is open Monday to Friday from 8 am to 4 pm.

The Flying Finn Café at the Sports Centre has an information desk, open Monday to Friday from 9 am to 9 pm, and on weekends from 10 am to 3 pm.

Post & Telephone The main post office is next to the railway station at Mannerheimin-katu 13, 15100 Lahti. There are also more central offices at Mariankatu 17, 15110 Lahti, and Kauppakatu 11, 15140 Lahti.

Library The modern library is at Kirkkokatu 31, open weekdays from 10 am to 7 pm, and on Saturday from 10 am to 3 pm. The news-paper room is also open on Sunday from noon to 4 pm.

Books & Maps Suomalainen Kirjakauppa on Aleksanterinkatu at the market sells books, maps and imported newspapers and magazines.

Travel Agencies Lomakauppa (☎ 783 440 or 751 0701, fax 752 3385), run by Lahti Blue Lakes Tours (Finnish: Päijät-Hämeen Matkailu), at Aleksanterinkatu 4, covers the southern Lake Päijänne region and can arrange almost anything for groups and indi-viduals.

Bicycle tours are popular, and daily or weekly rental of lakeside cottages can be booked from this office. It's open from 9 am to 6 pm.

Left Luggage The cheapest option is the railway station, which has some 5-mk lockers. Bulky items cost 10 mk.

Emergency Services In a general emer-gency phone ☎ 112, and for a doctor ring ☎ 10023. There are pharmacies near the market, including those at Torikatu 1, Aleksanterinkatu 13 and Vapaudenkatu 12.

Lahden Historiallinen Museo

The Historical Museum of Lahti at Lahdenkatu 4 is in a most beautiful building, formerly a private manor. Exhibits include the Klaus Holma collection of French and Italian furniture and medieval and Renais-sance art.

The temporary exhibition is often the highlight. Items from a Vyborg museum were moved here after Vyborg was annexed by the USSR in WWII. Admission is 20 mk. At present all museums in Lahti have similar opening hours – weekdays 10 am to 5 pm; weekends 11 am to 5 pm.

Taidemuseo

The Taidemuseo (Art Museum) of Lahti is in an administrative building at Vesijärvenkatu 11. There are mostly temporary exhibitions. Admission is 20 mk.

Radio Ja TV Museo

This museum building on Radiomäki Hill, between Mannerheimintie and Harjukatu, is the old broadcasting station of Lahti. Its col-lection includes old radios and a working broadcasting studio from the 1950s. When the Finnish broadcasting corporation started its operation in 1926, Lahti became an important broadcasting town. Admission is 15 mk.

Sports Centre

The three protruding ski jumps are the land-mark of Lahti. Much of the area here is devoted to physical action but the small **Hiihtomuseo** (Skiing Museum) is certainly worth a visit. There are skis that were used 2000 years ago and skis that belonged to the Samis of Lapland. The ski jump simulator is great fun and there are also temporary exhi-bitions. Admission is 15 mk.

The tallest ski jump serves as an observa-tion tower, open daily from June to August. Admission is 20 mk.

In summer, there are two open-air pools in the ski-jump pit; admission is 15 mk. In winter, there is a total of 145 km of ski tracks, 35 km of which are illuminated. Skiing gear can be rented in the main building.

Architecture

The **Ristinkirkko** (The Church of the Cross) was designed by Alvar Aalto and finished in 1978. Although the exterior is made of brown brick, the interior is typically Aalto: wooden benches, white walls and, on the ceiling, four concrete structures which look like rays emanating from the cross. The church, at Kirkkokatu 4, is open daily from 10 am to 3 pm.

Visible from the church, **Kaupungintalo** (town hall) was designed by another famous Finnish architect, Eliel Saarinen. At Harjukatu 31, the building is open to the public on Friday. There are guided tours from 2 to 3 pm.

Other Attractions

Along Kaarikatu on the southern side of Lahti, **Launeen perhepuisto** (Laune Children's Park) is open year round and is certainly one of the largest and best-planned children's parks in Finland.

Lanun veistospuisto is an exhibition of 12 sculptures by Olavi Lanu in the park at Kariniemi, north of the town centre.

Kahvisaari is an island between Kariniemi and Mukkula, connected by a bridge. You can rent canoes there for 50 mk per day.

Myllysaari is another island connected by a bridge. Follow the 'Kommodori' sign on Jalkarannantie (the Lahti to Hollola road that follows Lake Vesijärvi). There's a summer restaurant and a smoke sauna that can be rented by appointment. Contact the Lahti tourist office.

At the garrison of Hennala, south of Lahti, **Sotilaslääketieteen museo** (Museum of Military Medicine) is open from Tuesday to Saturday. Enquire at the tourist office for admission.

Places to Stay – bottom end

Onnela (☎ 883 3300) at Onnelantie 10 to the east of the centre is among the most innovative of Finnish hostels – you can even sleep in a nuclear shelter designed by the eccentric owner! There's a sauna, kitchen and TV, plus bicycles for hire. You pay only 50 mk per night.

In 1995, however, Onnela was advised to withdraw from the Finnish YHA, and it now functions as an independent hostel. Check it out, as it's the best in town in this price bracket.

Another place within walking distance of the railway station is Lahti's youth hostel, *Lahden kaupungin retkeilymaja* (☎ 782 6324), at Kivikatu 1. Follow the main Lahti to Helsinki road from the station, turn into Kaarikatu, and walk through the open field and past the Laune Children's Park. The hostel lies among tall apartment blocks and has barrack-type buildings, some of which are used by homeless men. For 50 mk, HI members can use the kitchen in their building and the facilities in the common building, No 5. Reception is in building No 19.

In Mukkula, the *Mukkulan leirintäalue* camping ground (☎ 306 554) has cottages for 195 to 350 mk. Camping costs 65 mk per family, or 30 to 35 mk per person. The area is very scenic, but it's 5 km north of Lahti; take bus No 30.

Places to Stay – middle

Matkakoti Patria (☎ 782 3783) at Vesijärvenkatu 3 close to the railway station has singles/doubles for 100/160 mk.

Lahden Koti (☎ 752 2173) at Karjalankatu 6 is a renovated apartment building which has been converted into a hotel. All apartments are tastefully decorated and come with a well-equipped kitchen and a bathroom. Studios cost 250/310 mk; two-room apartments from 380 mk. In summer prices are lower.

Hotelli Musta Kissa (☎ 85122), at Rautatienkatu 21, has singles/doubles from 180/280 mk.

Mukkulan Kartanohotelli (☎ 306 554) in Mukkula, four km north of Lahti, has singles/doubles from 200/240 mk. The lakeside location is superb and the old mansion is a romantic place to stay.

Less romantic is the concrete block *Mukkula Summer Hotel* (306 251) at Ritaniemenkatu 10, with singles/doubles at 170/240 mk; 15 mk less for HI members.

Places to Stay – top end

Lahti has many good hotels, which are also responsible for much of the town's nightlife.

Sokos Hotel Ascot (☎ 89711), at Rauhankatu 14, has singles/doubles for 425/510 mk.

Lahden Seurahuone (☎ 85111) at Aleksanterinkatu 14, right in the town centre, is reputedly the best hotel in Lahti. Singles/doubles are 330/420 mk; less on weekends. There are special prices in summer.

Hotelli Lahti, at Hämeenkatu 4, has singles/doubles for 235/310 mk.

Cumulus Lahti (☎ 813 711), at Vapaudenkatu 24, has 174 rooms, two restaurants and two saunas. Singles/doubles cost 395/450 mk; 325 mk in summer.

Kauppahotelli Grand (☎ 752 5146), at Vapaudenkatu 23, has rooms in summer and on weekends for 320 mk; at other times the cost is 330/420 mk.

Hotelli Salpaus (☎ 813 411), at Vesijärvenkatu 1, is the top-end hotel closest to the railway station, with singles/doubles at 380/420 mk. There are 145 rooms, a restaurant and two saunas.

Places to Eat

Lahti has a number of good eating and drinking places, including *Carrols* and *Pizza Hut* on Aleksanterinkatu near the market. The market itself, and the nearby indoor market, Kauppahalli, are also worth a browse.

There are no places to eat near the youth hostel. *Zanzibar kioski* at the Laune park is closest; it's open until 7 pm, but serves only coffee and snacks.

Visible from Laune park, the enormous supermarket area on the Lahti to Helsinki road includes a drive-in *McDonald's*; its rival, *Burger Café*, is in the Kesoil petrol station across the road. Citymarket on the same road has its *Pikantti* for lunch packages.

At the sports complex, the *Flying Finn Café* devotes most of its space to souvenirs and tourist information, but coffee and snacks are available. *Karpalo* in the stadium building is open all day and serves inexpensive lunches.

More central is *Café Sinuhe* at Mariankatu 21. It is a pleasant, street-style café in the centre of town. The pastries are fantastic. *Oskarin Piha* is a popular café in the backyard of Hämeenkatu 17. *Santa Fe* at Vuorikatu 35 serves Tex-Mex food. *Tabepna* is a Greek restaurant near the railway station. If you'd like to eat in an unusual restaurant, check out *Metro* at the market.

Getting There & Away

Bus Each day, there are more than 35 buses from Helsinki (102 km south), at least 10 buses from Tampere (128 km) and about 10 from both Jyväskylä (171 km) or Turku (214 km).

Train There are at least 15 direct trains a day from Helsinki and Riihimäki. Travellers from Tampere change trains at Riihimäki.

Boat Lake Päijänne ferries depart from Lahti and Jyväskylä Tuesday to Saturday (except Thursday) at 10 am, arriving at either end at 8 pm the same day. Try to catch the SS *Suomi*, one of the oldest steamers still plying the Finnish lakes. A one-way ticket costs 210 mk. Bicycles cost an additional 30 mk.

There are shorter launches to Heinola, departing from Lahti Wednesday to Sunday at 10 am, and from Heinola at 3.30 pm. A one-way ticket to Heinola costs 90 mk.

HOLLOLA

Hollola, west of Lahti, is the most historical place in this area, and close enough to Lahti and Messilä for a leisurely bicycle tour. To get there, take the narrow road around Lake Vesijärvi.

Messilä

Even if you want to give downhill skiing a miss, don't be put off visiting Messilä, just east of Hollola.

It's another old estate, with several places to sleep, eat and shop. The wooden manor house serves food, too. Messilän Pajat is a separate building featuring local craft (and a bakery). Take a look at the modern hotel building out the back – you might conclude that a box-shaped glass structure with a flat roof probably wasn't such a good idea! Messilä also has a golf course and a guest harbour.

Pirunpesä (Devil's Nest) is a steep rock cliff near Messilä. A marked trail takes you there, or you can walk the entire seven-km *luontopolku* (nature trail) which goes via a series of hills and some good views. One of these hills, **Tiirismaa**, is a downhill-skiing resort in winter.

Between Pirunpesä and the other attractions in Hollola lies **Lake Kutajärvi**, a shallow resting place for migratory birds. In May, plenty of local people gather to scan the lake for rare species.

Pyhäniemen Kartano

There are several manor houses in Finland, but the one in Pyhäniemi certainly deserves a visit.

This wooden mansion, dubbed the 'Hollywood of Hollola' in the 1930s, when many films were staged here, has had quite a colourful history. It was established in the 15th century. Swedish king Gustav III granted the estate to the Schmiedefelt family in 1780 and even visited it himself in 1783.

The estate grew to enormous proportions; its industries included a sawmill, a wheel factory, a Swiss-run dairy that exported its products to St Petersburg, and a Savings Bank.

The wealth of this empire was lost by gambling in Monte Carlo in 1912, and during the Civil War it remained neutral property as a consulate under the Dutch flag.

Finns are today attracted by its interesting art exhibitions in summer. It is open daily June to August from 11 am to 6 pm. Admission is 40 mk, including coffee and snacks.

Hollola Church

This large church dates from 1480 and has much of interest inside. The armoury serves as the entrance and the enormous door to the main hall deserves a close look. It's shown on the current 8-mk postage stamp.

In the main hall, you will see 10 sculptures from the 15th century, and coats of arms from a von Essen family funeral. The conspicuous bell tower from 1831 was designed by CL Engel.

The church is not far north of Pyhäniemi. It's marked 'Hollola kk' on signs and bus timetables. The church is open to visitors from 1 June to mid-August between 11 am and 6 pm.

Opposite the church you will find the Marian Portti gallery, which opens daily in summer. Nearby is a food store and, up a short alley, Astra Pulkinnen's handicrafts shop. The alley and gardens here are well preserved.

Hollolan Kotiseutumuseo

The local museum of Hollola actually consists of two museums. Esinemuseo, the large red building not far from the church, contains a collection of local paraphernalia, including a Stone Age axe. Hentilä museum features old buildings which have been transferred from nearby locations. The actual Hentilä house was built from 1837 onwards.

The museum is open Tuesday to Sunday from noon to 6 pm. Entry costs 10 mk. Not far from both museums, Linnamäki is a hill with a tower which is always open and offers fine views of the surrounding area.

A map is available of a three-km *luontopolku* (Nature Trail) around the area.

Rälssipiha

This private farm estate is one of Hollola's major horse-breeding centres. It's one km from the church (follow the signs behind the museum).

Formerly an old Swedish *frälse*, or tax-free estate, it now has a summer café, sales of local handicraft, and horse and carriage rides from 20 mk per person. The estate is closed on Monday. Children might enjoy it.

Places to Stay & Eat

Messilä (☎ 86011) has plenty of choices. There are modern rooms for 300/370 mk, cheaper but very clean rooms in nicer old buildings, plus a holiday village with well-equipped cottages.

The better restaurants in Messilä include

Kartanoravintola for gourmet food, *Talli-ravintola* for beer and *Markkinaravintola* for dancing and events.

Opposite the church, *Kunnantupa*, located in a red wooden house dating from 1902, has a Häme-type smorgasbord at lunch time and you can get coffee and snacks whenever it's open. Rälssipiha also has a summer café.

Getting There & Away

The main attractions of Hollola are 15 to 18 km west of Lahti. Pekolan Liikenne Oy runs regular buses from Lahti which complete a circle via all the major attractions and the commercial centre, Salpakangas. Buses run either way, so any local bus in Hollola will take you back to Lahti eventually.

ASIKKALA

On the south-western shore of Lake Päijänne, the celebrated municipality of Asikkala certainly has plenty of natural beauty. Some of its islands now constitute the Päijänne National Park, and views from Pulkkilanharju ridge along road No 314 offer typical lakeland scenery. There are two centres, the busy Vääksy Canal and the Asikkala church area.

Asikkala Church & Museum

This large 1880 church is open in summer. The nearby kotiseutumuseo is a local museum, housed in several buildings and featuring old carriages, prehistoric discoveries and farming tools. It may not be the best-kept museum in Finland but it's still worth a look. It's open from 1 June to 13 August, Tuesday to Saturday, from noon to 5 pm. Entry is 5 mk.

Urajärven Kartano

The property of the von Heideman family, this estate is one of the finest in Finland. It has a museum, a café and an attractive garden. Valhalla, a lookout, can be reached by walking along a scenic track. Urajärvi manor (☎ 667 191) is worth a look if you have a vehicle. To get there, take road No 313 east of Vääksy. It is open daily June to August from 11 am to 5 pm. Entry is 10 mk.

Päijänne National Park

This national park was founded in 1994 to protect some of the impressive nature in the southern part of Lake Päijänne. The narrow Pulkkilanharju ridge, part of the Asikkala to Sysmä road, is now part of the national park.

The main feature of the national park is Kelvenne Island, an unusually long ridge in the middle of southern Lake Päijänne. The pine forest is beautiful and quiet, apart from when it's invaded by a fleet of local boats during the high season! In the 1970s, a huge international holiday village was planned for this fragile island, comprising an airport, casino and cable-car system! Fortunately it didn't happen.

There are designated camping grounds. Walking from one end of the island to the other – approximately 10 km or so – is *the* thing to do. En route, there's a large lake, a few lagoon beaches and varied landscapes. Look for park information at Padasjoki, Asikkala, Sysmä and Pulkkilanharju ridge.

There's a regular summer boat service to the island from the pier at Kullasvuori near Padasjoki town. Check the information booth at Pulkkilanharju ridge for information on other regular boats.

Places to Stay

This listing includes accommodation in the municipality of Asikkala. Among the possibilities are private lakeside cottages, well worth the price if you want to spend a week in a beautiful setting. Enquire at Lomakauppa (Päijät-Hämeen Matkailu) in Lahti for reservations.

Hoimela (☎ 766 6394) is a small manor house behind the birch tree-lined alley along road No 314. It has some fine rooms starting at 170/280 mk, including breakfast. A good place to get away from it all is Hoimela's *Villa Taiga*, where weekly rates apply. It's a superb two-storey house in the middle of the woods, complete with all the mod cons.

Lehmonkärki is a strictly bookings-only place with very fine cottages, each with an individual stretch of beach overlooking Lake Päijänne. Snowmobile safaris and paragliding over the ice in winter, and fishing, lake cruises and survival games in summer, are among activities that can be arranged. Snowmobile safaris include 120 km of travel, instruction, all meals and other services for 1000 mk per day – less than you'll pay in Lapland.

Pätiälän lomamökit are isolated cottages associated with the Pätiälä manor; they include rustic but very clean log cabins around the lakeside. Meals are available in the manor house by appointment only – the owners speak excellent English. Otherwise, bring your own food and come for several days. There are 17 cottages, many with a private sauna, kitchen and toilet.

VÄÄKSY

The de facto centre of Asikkala is mostly known for Vääksy Canal, the busiest canal in Finland – over 15,000 vessels pass through it every summer. The new **Vääksyn Vesimyllymuseo** is a small water-mill museum open on weekends in summer from noon to 4 pm and in July from Tuesday to Sunday from noon to 4 pm. Entry is free.

There's a museum in the **Danielson-Kalmarin huvila**, a very fine wooden building that is over 100 years old. It's open in summer between noon and 7 pm, and the 15-mk entrance fee includes a cup of coffee.

Automuseo near Hotel Tallukka has an exhibition of vintage cars and motorbikes. It's open May to August daily from 10 am to 6 pm, entry is 20 mk. Ask for discounts. In the hotel itself, **Päijänne Luontokeskus** is an exhibition on Lake Päijänne nature and is open year round daily except Monday from noon to 6 pm (closing 4 pm on Saturday). Entry is 10 mk.

Places to Stay

One km east of the bus station, *Tallukka* (☎ 68611) at Tallukantie 1 is a large top-end hotel which plays a role in the local nightlife. There are 129 rooms at 255/340 mk.

Places to Eat

In the bus station area, there's a café called *Sinilintu*, a grilli, and a Siwa supermarket for self-catering. Across the street is the *Impivaara*, a restaurant near the library and *Jossun pizza*. At the canal, *Kanavan kahvila* is a 1950s-style restaurant serving homemade food. Right at the waterfront, *Sulkuportti* is a summer-only restaurant – it has to be since everybody eats outside. The new commercial centre of Vääksy has at least four large supermarkets, *Kahvila Kulkurintytär*, which sells coffee and snacks, and a restaurant, *Bella*.

Getting There & Away

Vääksy is busy in summer; there will be plenty of buses and private cars moving in its direction. At the canal, you can catch one of the boats which sail between Lahti and Heinola in summer. It's 30 mk to Lahti and 45 mk to Heinola on the MS *Tehi*.

HEINOLA

Heinola (population 16,000) is today overshadowed by Lahti to the south but is a much older town. It has a scenic waterfront setting, with the Jyrängönvirta River flowing through it. In addition to summer cultural attractions, Heinola serves as a starting point for scenic summer lake cruises.

Apparently, local business life has suffered from the opening in 1993 of a bypass highway across the new bridge, which deviates practically all long-distance traffic from the centre of Heinola. The bridge is currently Finland's longest, at 942 metres, though a longer one – 1040 metres – will open at Replot in 1997.

Information

The tourist office (☎ 715 8444) is at Torikatu 8.

Forskullan Kartano

This manor on the banks of the Jyrängönvirta River has a good reputation for culture, with an art gallery, museum and antique furniture. There's a pleasant park and a summer café. The manor was recently closed, apparently due to a scandal involving not-so-authentic art that was for sale. Enquire at the tourist office.

Heinolan Harju

The ridge of Heinola has several attractions. The 1900 **Harjupaviljonki** pavilion is a distant imitation of a Japanese temple. In summer there is an art exhibition, open daily from 11 am to 8 pm. Nearby, the **tower** is also open daily in summer and offers good views. **Heinolan lintutarha** is a bird park with over 100 species caged in several buildings around Lake Kirkkolampi. The park is open daily and has free admission.

Museums

Heinola has three museums on Kauppakatu. **Heinolan kaupunginmuseo**, at Kauppakatu 14, is in an 1830s Empire-style building and contains antique furniture and temporary exhibitions. Entry is 8 mk.

Taidemuseo at Kauppakatu 4 is the local art museum and includes a permanent collection. During special exhibitions, admission is 20 mk; at other times free.

Aschanin talo at Kauppakatu 3 is the oldest house in town, dating from the late 18th century. Entry is 8 mk. The museums are open Tuesday to Sunday noon to 4 pm, with hours extended on Wednesday till 8 pm.

Churches

The Lutheran church on Siltakatu was built in 1811 and is open daily except Monday, usually until 5 pm. Heinola also has an Orthodox Church which contains icons from the Valamo Monastery.

Places to Stay

The camping ground, *Heinäsaaren leirintäalue* (☎ 153 083), is on the island of Heinäsaari, 1.5 km from the town centre, with cottages from 150 mk. The new bridge overshadows the otherwise scenic location.

Finnhostel Heinola (☎ 141 655), at Opintie 3, is open in June and July only. All accommodation is two-bed rooms, the cost 55 mk per bed for members.

Matkakoti Puistola (☎ 143 585), at Maaherrankatu 5, has singles/doubles for 140/200 mk. A bit more pricey is *Heinolan Seurahuone* (☎ 197 611) at Lampikatu 16.

Hotelli Kumpeli (☎ 158 214), at Muona-miehenkatu 3, is the top establishment in Heinola. There are 120 rooms at 415/520 mk, with summer and weekend discounts available, plus a restaurant and four saunas.

Places to Eat

Harjupaviljonki on the hill is a most attractive place to enjoy a cup of coffee in summer. There are several places on Kauppakatu, the main road, including *Kettu ja Kana* at No 5, *Heinolan Heili* at No 6 and *Hannamuori* at No 17. Siltakatu, another street worth a look, has *Rosso* and the cheap *Kestitupa*.

Tähtihovi is a petrol station and roadhouse along the new bypass road at the bridge. It offers all kinds of services, including food.

Getting There & Away

Bus There are buses roughly every half-hour from Lahti. Heinola is 136 km north of Helsinki.

Boat PRH ferries from Lahti sail to Heinola in summer. See Lahti for details.

HARTOLA

This sleepy village to the north of Heinola has proclaimed itself a kingdom – not as part of a secessionist movement but a promotional stunt to attract visitors! The reason for this is the special rights granted by King Gustav III during the Swedish era.

Hartola has a tourist information office (☎ 161 311) on the main road. The 1913 **church** was designed by Josef Stenbäck, architect of National Romantic churches. This one seems 'heavier' than others by him, but its grey stone looks quite nice.

Itä-Hämeen Museo

The regional museum of seven East Häme municipalities is located in the 19th century Koskipää Manor, and covers history dating back to the 16th century.

There are several exhibitions and a cluster of old buildings. The museum was founded in 1928 by writer Maila Talvio, now honoured by a memorial room. The museum is open daily year round, in summer from 11 am to 6 pm and at other times of the year from noon to 4 pm. Admission is 10 mk. There's a café open in summer. The suspension bridge over the Tainionkoski rapids was built in the 1930s.

Places to Stay & Eat

Gasthaus Koskenniemi (☎ 161 135) is the best place to stay in the area. The smallest cabins start from 100 mk and house two people. There are very fine cottages for 370 mk and 12 rooms in the main building. Facilities include a restaurant with excellent home-made food, showers, a camping ground and fishing in the Tainionvirta rapids – the licence is 80 mk.

Linna (☎ 162 250) at Kaikulantie 86 is the top-end hotel, with singles/doubles at 170/340 mk. There are 25 rooms, all with TV and shower.

Probably the easiest way to find food is to visit the petrol station at the southern Hartola crossing on road No 59; *Kuninkaan Portti* is the large restaurant at the Shell petrol station. *Pizzeria Jokari* nearby is a more down-to-earth eatery.

Getting There & Away

Hartola is on the eastern Lahti to Jyväskylä road No 59. There are several express buses running daily between Lahti and Jyväskylä. Hitchhiking is a possibility on this rather busy road.

SYSMÄ

Sysmä (population 5400) occupies a large area on the eastern shore of Lake Päijänne and has a number of interesting places to visit. A series of classical concerts, *Sysmän suvisoitto*, take place in various locations on both sides of Lake Päijänne in early July every year.

Sysmä Centre

The highlight of the village of Sysmä will be **Vanha Kerttu** as long as 'old' Kerttu Tapiola keeps entertaining visitors in her large art gallery. She's very funny and friendly. In the same building, **Suomen Harmonikka-museo** houses a large collection of that most horrendous of musical instruments, the

accordion. This private collection is open year round, Monday to Friday from 10 am to 6 pm, and on Saturday from 10 am to 2 pm. Entry is 25 mk. There's also a bookshop with some material in English and a health-food shop with coffee and snacks.

The 15th century stone **church** is open daily from 1 June to 31 August on weekdays from 8 am to 3 pm, weekends from 9 am to 6 pm. The **local museum** is open on Sunday only, from 11 am to 2 pm.

Virtaa

The estate in this small village dates back to the 16th century. Today, **Virtaan kartano** (☎ 178 162) is a run-down yet impressive manor house which operates as a guesthouse in summer, with beds from 135 mk per person, including breakfast.

There are two saunas at the rapids of Tainionvirta and you can get to Virtaa by canoe from Hartola. Virtaa is seven km south of Sysmä.

Onkiniemi

This small village is on the Hartola to Heinola road No 59. The **balancing rock** near the main road is its landmark.

Nukketalot, or Puppet Houses (☎ 186 959), are extremely popular with Finnish kids. A very eccentric couple and their talented son have created more than 350 hand puppets – some appearing regularly on TV – and give daily performances. Arrive any day between noon and 4 pm and see what happens.

Entry costs 30 mk, but enquire first in case the performance is sold out. Most people fall in love with the place, the people and the puppets, so you probably won't be disappointed. Some items are for sale, and the Tikkutollo building is a self-service café.

Places to Stay & Eat

Sysmä Camping (☎ 171 386) is good value, with two-bed cottages from 60 mk per night. It's very close to the shops and services of Sysmä and has boats and canoes for rent. Camping is 55 mk and there's every facility, including a sauna and a café. It's open from

1 June to 31 August. *Hotelli Uoti* (☎ 172 766) at Keskustie 1 has singles/doubles for 200/260 mk; less if you ask for a discount.

Finding a place to eat is no problem in Sysmä, especially in summer. Hamburgers are available in *grillikioskis*, and there are cafés and a few beer-drinking *baaris*, on Sysmäntie and Uotintie.

Getting There & Away

Sysmä is well connected to Helsinki by express buses. The car ferry *Linta* from Kuhmoinen, across Lake Päijänne, arrives at Suopelto, seven km west of the village. There are up to three launches daily from June to 13 August. One-way costs 60 mk per adult; 45 mk for a car. Bicycles are free, motorcycles are 25 mk.

LUHANKA

Only 1000 people live here, 40% of them retired. Luhanka is surrounded by Lake Päijänne on most sides, and the isolation adds to the beauty of the scenery. You will drive through Luhanka if you follow road No 612 north from Sysmä. Considering Luhanka's present population, the 1893 church is oversized. It was designed by Josef Stenbäck, who was later inspired by National Romantic ideals.

Places to Stay

Luhangan Lomakeidas (☎ 66136), a holiday village just south of the main village, has 15 cottages, from 100 mk. *Ruohtulan Tila* (☎ 63173), a farmhouse near the village of Tammijärvi, has B&B for 120 mk per person in summer.

JOUTSA

Joutsa is one of the small villages east of Lake Päijänne. There are few sights (the church dates from 1820 and there's a small museum two km north of the church), but there are a few places to stay overnight. The annual Joutsa Folk Festival takes place in early July at the museum.

Places to Stay

The cheapest place is *Vaihelan tila* (☎ 889 107) near the village of Pappinen, halfway between Luhanka and Joutsa. It is one of the several pleasant youth hostels that have been established at farm estates. Beds start at 35 mk per HI member.

In the village itself, *Gasthaus Vanhatalo* (☎ 882 718) at Jousitie 39 has rooms for 100/180 mk.

Rantasipi Joutsenlampi (☎ 880 301), an isolated wilderness congress hotel in the middle of nowhere, has 42 rooms and all kinds of sports and business facilities. In summer all rooms cost 355 mk.

PADASJOKI

Padasjoki, on the western shore of Lake Päijänne, is one of the busiest summer destinations for Helsinkites. Padasjoki is also one of the municipalities that has adopted ecologically sound methods in local administration; if you're interested, ask a local to tell you about them.

There is not much to do here, but there are occasional boat launches from the pier to Kelvenne Island in the Päijänne National Park. **Taidekahvila Patamuori**, at Keskustie 16, has art exhibitions year round. It's open daily and entry is free.

Palsan vesimylly is a water-mill museum at Vesijako. The mill dates from the 18th century and is still used (for fun only) on summer Sundays from noon to 4 pm, when you can also buy porridge made from the mill flour. The museum is open daily from 21 June to 30 July, from 10 am to 8 pm. It has a café, art exhibitions and a shop. Entry is 15 mk. To get there, drive some 10 km to Auttoinen on road No 319, and turn right to road No 320.

KUHMOINEN

Kuhmoinen is quite a popular summer retreat for city-dwellers, but it offers surprisingly few services for travellers. The village is a base for visits to Isojärvi National Park farther north, a pleasant trekking region with rocky hills, beautiful forest lakes and some interesting wildlife.

Kuhmoinen village has hardly anything of interest, other than an old village road and the Päijänne lakefront. The main street, Toritie, has a few banks, a post office and some shops, which serve the population of 3200 – many more in summer. There are also a few restaurants along Toritie. The café at the bus terminal serves simple meals from 25 mk.

Getting There & Away

Catch a Jyväskylä-bound *pikavuoro* (express) bus from Helsinki or Lahti, or one of the several daily buses from Tampere. The car ferry *Linta* from Suopelto (in Sysmä), across Lake Päijänne, arrives at Kuhmoinen pier in the village. There are two to three launches daily from 1 June to mid-August. One-way costs 60 mk per adult; 45 mk for a car. Bicycles are free, motorbikes are 25 mk.

ISOJÄRVI NATIONAL PARK

Isojärvi gets few visitors, other than vacationing Finns, but it is well worth the effort if you want to spend a day or two in a quiet, picturesque forest and see what used to be a focal point of Finland's traditional logging culture. The park was established in 1982 and facilities are provided. Come in the middle of the week, when you may have most of the park to yourself.

Information

Heretty House, on the main gravel road, serves as an information centre in summer. You can pick up a free map and guide at any time from the *opastuskatos* (shelter) behind the main building.

Things to See & Do

There are a number of walking routes in the Isojärvi area, with good paths – marked in blue – and sufficient route information along the way. Close to Heretty, the *annuslahti* recreational area has cooking facilities and a campfire site. Most people head first for Lake Lortikka, which has a sauna, a camp site and two houses providing accommodation. Take the red-marked nature trail to Lortikka Hill, near the southern end of Lake

Lortikka. There are other trails in Latokuusikko and near Heretty.

Huhtala Huhtala House is an open-air museum consisting of several 18th century farmhouses. The main building is open June to mid-August on weekends from 11 am to 5 pm. Some 1.5 km from Huhtala is a parking area and a quick one-km hike to your left brings you to Kalalahti at the shore of Lake Isojärvi. There are two boats you can use but they are chained and locked – get the key from Heretty House.

Places to Stay

There are camp sites in Kuorejärvi, Lortikka, Kalalahti and on one of the islands. Lortikka also has a cabin with 15 beds (☎ Jyväskylä 211 455), which you'll have to reserve in advance; the key is available at Heretty House. Avoid weekends, which tend to be busy. There are also old storage buildings where trekkers can stay overnight for free. Four km from Heretty along the main road, a local family rents out a house; enquire about this at Heretty.

Getting There & Away

There is no bus service. By car, Isojärvi is most easily reached from the main Tampere to Jyväskylä road. Turn south at Länkipohja and take the gravel road to your left two km farther up. This is an unpaved road (No 329). If you want to see Huhtala House first, follow the sign a few km farther along. If you take a taxi from Länkipohja to Huhtala, it would be advisable to trek from there to Lortikka. From the Huhtala fork, it is another seven km to Heretty.

It is 18 km from Kuhmoinen to Heretty. Cross over the main road from the Kuhmoinen bus terminal, drive two km and turn left to road No 329.

There's a road barrier on the narrow road to Lortikka (as signposted), but you can reach Lortikka by mountain bike.

KORPILAHTI

This scenic region can be accessed by ferry

across Lake Päijänne from Kärkistensalmi. By 1997, this ferry will have been replaced by road access via a 787-metre bridge. At the southern end of the strait, *Kärkisten Motelli*

(☎ 824 101) is a hotel and restaurant, with rooms from 200 mk. In the main village, there's a camping ground on Rantatie behind the old *pappila* (vicarage) building.

Savo

If asked to nominate one region of Finland as their favourite, few travellers would hesitate in choosing Savo, also known as the Lakeland. Savo officially comprises the provinces of Mikkeli and Kuopio (though, in this book, the western area of Mikkeli, which lies around Lake Päijänne, is covered in Central Finland).

Savo epitomises the isolation of Finns – this is where you'll find numerous lakes, islands, narrow straits, canals and unspoilt beaches. Here, too, are the most popular steamer routes. No pulp factories pollute the pristine landscape in the southern part of Savo (Province of Mikkeli), and northern Savo is left equally untouched. Only Varkaus manages to spoil it.

But this watery area would not be what it is without its people, the *savolaiset*. No other group in Finland seems to make so much fuss about themselves, but with good reason: these are witty, open-hearted and easy-going people. Outsiders joke about the Savo dialect, but perhaps they just envy the locals their beautiful country.

HISTORY

Only recently has the Savo region been subject to archaeological research. Prehistoric paintings on rocks, hilltop fortresses and other signs of human habitation have been discovered.

Despite these findings, it is likely that Savo was virtually uninhabited 1000 years ago when cultures in Häme and Karelia flourished.

The earliest medieval inhabitation in Savo emerged in the Mikkeli and Juva regions, and in 1475 a castle was founded at today's Savonlinna. However, it was not until the 1500s that Finnish immigration reached the large Savo region, encouraged by the king of Sweden. There were a few Swedish-run estates in the region, mostly around Mikkeli, but not as many as in south-western Finland.

Russian attacks in the 1700s cut south-east

Highlights
- The most typical Finnish lake scenery, with the country's largest lake, Saimaa.
- The scenic Kolovesi National Park and Punkaharju.
- The medieval castle at Savonlinna, the most dramatically positioned of all Finland's castles.
- The Orthodox Church Museum in Kuopio, with the best collection of Eastern treasures.
- Cruises from Savonlinna and Kuopio.
- Colourful markets in Mikkeli, Savonlinna and Kuopio.
- The Valamo Monastery in Heinävesi.
- The largest wooden church in the world, at Kerimäki.
- The Infantry Museum in Mikkeli.

Savo into two parts. Consequently Russian influence became evident – increasingly so after 1809, when all Finland came under the suzerainty of the tsar.

Lake traffic has long been a typical feature of this area. Modern development has been slow, so Savo remains an idyllic region with little to disturb the tourist.

313

Eastern Finland

Savonlinna

Savonlinna (population nearly 28,700) would be your first choice if you wanted to see just one place outside Helsinki. It has some of the best lake scenery in Savo, the most dramatic medieval castle in Finland and a number of other superlative attractions in the vicinity. Consequently, Savonlinna is extremely busy in summer, especially during the July Opera Festival. Prices vary considerably with the season, and rise sky-high during the month-long Opera Festival.

Savonlinna is one of Finland's most beautifully situated towns. Lake Haapavesi and Lake Pihlajavesi surround the town on both sides, and the town centre is on two islands.

History

The slow growth of Savonlinna began in 1475 with the building of Olavinlinna Castle on an island between two large lakes. In 1639, Savonlinna received a municipal charter at the instigation of Count Per Brahe, founder of quite a number of towns around Finland. In 1743, this small market town was joined to Russia; it was returned to the Finnish grand duchy in 1812. By the 1920s, Savonlinna was important as the major hub for steamboat traffic in the Lakeland, and has retained this important role to the present day.

Information

Tourist Office The tourist office (☎ 273 492, fax 514 449), at Puistokatu 1 near the market, provides information about most places in the region, sells tickets, reserves accommodation and organises tours. The office is open daily from 8 am to 6 pm, except in July, when hours are 8 am to 10 pm. In winter, it is open Monday to Friday from 9 am to 4 pm.

Post & Telephone The main post office is next to the bus terminal, at Olavinkatu 61, 57100 Savonlinna, and is open Monday to Friday from 9 am to 5 pm. Telephones are in the bus terminal building across the street.

Another post office, at Koulukatu 10, 57130 Savonlinna, has similar opening hours.

Libraries The town library is on a small hill on Tottinkatu. It's open Monday to Friday from 11 am to 7 pm. There is a music branch library at Kirkkokatu 12, open on Friday from 10 am to 4 pm and the rest of the week from 1 to 7 pm. It has a good selection of CDs, including operas.

Bookshops Suomalainen Kirjakauppa at the Kauppalinna shopping centre sells English magazines and paperbacks, but you can also try the R-kioski at the market railway halt, or at Olavinkatu 19.

Travel Agencies The tourist office arranges everything regionally.

Left Luggage You can leave your gear at the tourist office for free, but at your own risk.

Emergency Services In a general emergency phone ☎ 112, and for a doctor ring ☎ 10023. Pharmacies are on Olavinkatu at Nos 40, 41 and 56.

Olavinlinna

Olavinlinna Castle is the principal sight of Savonlinna, and probably of eastern Finland. Founded in 1475 by Erik Axelsson Tott, governor of Vyborg and the Eastern Provinces, Olavinlinna was meant to protect the eastern border of the Swedish empire. It got its name from Olof, a 10th century Norwegian Catholic saint. Russians occupied the castle from 1714 to 1721, and took control of it again in 1743, this time for almost 200 years, adding the red towers and a yellow house inside its walls. Two small museums in the castle have exhibits on its history plus displays of Orthodox treasures. You are not allowed to visit the castle without a guide, but there are hourly guided tours every day of the year, from 10 am to 5 pm between June and mid-August and from 10 am to 3 pm at other times of the year. Guides speak English, Swedish, French, German and Italian as well as Finnish. Entry is 20 mk; 10

SAVO

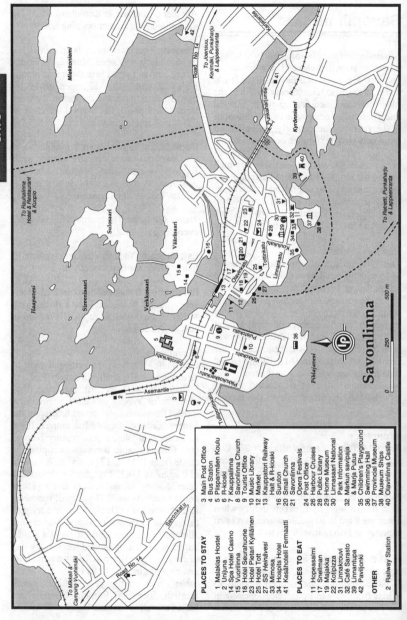

Savonlinna

PLACES TO STAY

1 Malakias Hostel
2 Unijuna
14 Spa Hotel Casino
18 Vuorilinna
23 Hotel Seurahuone
25 Hotel Pietari Kyläläinen
27 Hotel Tott
33 SS Heinävesi
34 Hospits Hotel
41 Kesähotelli Fermaatti

PLACES TO EAT

11 Hopeasalmi
17 Snellman
19 Majakka
22 Kolipizza
31 Linnakrouvi
32 Café Sarasto
39 Linnantupa
42 Paviljonki

OTHER

2 Railway Station
3 Main Post Office
4 Bus Station
5 Piispanmäen Koulu
6 R-kioski
7 Kauppalinna
8 Savonlinna Church
9 Tourist Office
10 Music Library
12 Market
13 Kauppatori Railway
   Halt & R-kioski
16 Station
20 Small Church
21 Savonlinna
   Opera Festivals
24 Post Office
26 Harbour Cruises
28 Public Library
29 Home Museum
30 Linnasaari National
   Park Information
32 Markun savipaja
   & Marja Putus
35 Children's Playground
36 Swimming Hall
37 Provincial Museum
38 Museum Ships
40 Olavinlinna Castle

mk for children. A motorised floating bridge to the castle is removed when ships pass.

Savonlinnan Maakuntamuseo

The provincial museum is in an old Russian warehouse near the castle, and has a well-displayed collection highlighting traditional Savo life and local artefacts and tools. There are free English-language leaflets available. Don't miss the old boats behind the main building; the ships *Salama*, *Mikko* and *Savonlinna* all house exhibitions. The museum is open daily in July from 10 am to 8 pm daily; during the rest of the year, it's open Tuesday to Sunday from 11 am to 5 pm. Admission is 15 mk.

Suruton

This old villa, its name meaning literally 'one without sorrow', was originally built to accommodate guests of the nearby spa. The permanent doll museum is open daily in summer from 11 am to 5 pm; in winter it's closed on Monday. Entry is 10 mk; 5 mk for students and children.

Rauhalinna

This romantic Moorish-style wooden villa was built in 1900 by Nils Weckman, an officer in the tsar's army, as a wedding anniversary present for his wife. Rauhalinna is open from early June to early August. For a real treat, try the excellent *herkkupöytä* buffet. There is also a café. Upstairs, the Hotelli Rauhalinna (☎ 523 119) has fine rooms for rent. Singles/doubles cost 290/380 mk and suites are 900 mk. To get there, take a motor boat from Savonlinna harbour. From Monday to Saturday, there are also a few buses from the Savonlinna bus terminal to a school near Rauhalinna. It is a half-km walk from there. Drivers should follow road No 468 towards Rauhalinna. This road also leads to **Putkinotko**, the summer home of Joel Lehtonen, a Finnish author who died in 1934. Putkinotko is open in June and July daily except Monday from 11 am to 5 pm. Admission is 5 mk.

Other Attractions

The imposing 1878 **church** is open daily in summer from 10 am to 6 pm. The **Pikkukirkko**, the small 1845 Orthodox Church, is on Olavinkatu and only opens for church events.

The Piispanmäen koulu (school), 300 metres north of the tourist office, houses the summer art exhibition **Pyrri**, which has a notoriously expensive admission fee. The tourist office has more details.

One of the old houses on Linnankatu, No 13, is open in July as a **home museum** with memorabilia from the 1920s. Hours are from 11 am to 5 pm daily; admission is 5 mk.

Harbour Cruises

In summer, Savonlinna's dock is one of the busiest in Finland. In addition to scheduled passenger ferries to/from Kuopio and Lappeenranta, a number of local boat services are available. These may come in handy if you want to combine some lake scenery with bicycle touring, or if you want to see Olavinlinna Castle from a different angle. This is a list of regular boat trips around Savonlinna:

The SS *Heinävesi* sails daily at 11 am (6 June to 19 August) to Retretti in Punkaharju. A ticket costs 85 mk one-way, 130 mk return.

The MS *Saimatar* sails a mirror-image service between Punkaharju and Savonlinna, leaving Savonlinna at 3 pm. A one-way ticket is 70 mk, a return 100 mk.

The MS *Princess of Saimaa* has daily cruises (6 June to 23 August) at 11 am and 1, 3 and 5 pm. In July, there's an extra departure in the evenings. The one-hour cruise costs 30 mk.

The MS *Salmetar* sails to Rauhalinna and back at 10.30 am and 12.30 and 2.30 pm from 1 June to 20 August; in July, there are also departures at 4.30 and 6.30 pm. The fare is 30 mk.

The SS *Figaro* departs for 75-minute cruises at 10 am, noon and 2 and 4 pm daily (17 June to 16 August); on weekends, there are also 6 and 8 pm cruises. The fare is 40 mk.

The MS *Faust* has four one-hour cruises every two hours between 11.30 am and 5.30 pm, every day. Tickets are 30 mk per person.

The *Timppa* and the *Timppa II* have nine cruises a day from 1 June to 31 August, at 30 mk per person.

SAVO

SAVO

Festivals

The Savonlinna Opera Festival is probably the most famous and popular of all of Finland's summer festivals. It offers four weeks of high-class opera performances in the most dramatic location in Finland: Olavinlinna Castle. The Opera Festival usually takes place in July and early August. Generally, there is one opera or ballet performance in the castle every evening, and some concerts at various locations around Savonlinna.

For details of exact dates and programs, contact Savonlinna Opera Festivals (☎ 576 750, fax 21866), Olavinkatu 27, 57130 Savonlinna. The box office is open Monday to Friday from 9 am to 4 pm. Tickets for same-night performances are sold after 6 pm from the booth near the bridge. No last-minute discounts are available. The Savonlinna Tourist Office also sells tickets, as does Lippupalvelu in Helsinki. Ticket prices cost between 270 and 590 mk, and there are approximately 50 back-row tickets for 150 mk. Bring warm clothes and some food, and be prepared for hard seats.

Places to Stay – bottom end

Savonlinna is notoriously expensive even at the bottom-end category. The cheapest option is actually the SS *Heinävesi* which has cabins for 65 to 80 mk during the summer sailing season. Enquire at the harbour in the evenings, after the last sailing. The ship has 30 beds and is seldom full. The experience is worthwhile, but facilities are basic and the traffic around the harbour is a bit noisy. Check the *Puijo* and the *Kuopio*, too, and expect to pay from 100 to 200 mk per cabin.

At the railway station, *Unijuna* rents out five rooms during the Opera Festival, costing 180/260 mk. *Mimosa* (☎ 940-503 6076) at Linnankatu 12 near the castle has four rooms from 120 to 150 mk, but God only knows how one can get to stay at this price this close to the castle – it always seems to be full.

Close to the market on Casino Island at Kylpylaitoksentie, *Vuorilinna* (☎ 739 5495) functions as a youth hostel from June to August, but cheap it ain't (unless you consider 120 mk inexpensive). Outside the Opera Festival season, HI members pay 9? mk. However, the staff might recommend that you stay in their student accommodation, which costs 200/270 mk (high-season rates are 310/390 mk). For this you get either your own kitchen, or one that's shared with the occupants of just one other room.

In July you can find refuge at *Malakia* (☎ 23283) at Pihlajavedenkuja 6, two km west of the town centre. Each room has cooking facilities and two beds. HI members pay 120 mk per night. If you feel like staying in a hotel, you can pay 200/310 mk for the luxury of sheets.

Places to Stay – middle

Hospits Hotel (☎ 515 661) at Linnankatu 2? is the best-value accommodation in this price bracket. There is a pleasant garden, with access to the beach, and its proximity to the castle is a bonus. You can use the sauna downstairs. Singles/doubles start at 150/30? mk.

Seven km outside Savonlinna, *Camping Vuohimäki* (☎ 537 353) has cottages from 410 mk in the high season and from 295 mk during the rest of the summer. Basic quadruples start at 235 mk. Turn left after the rapids at Laitaatsilta.

Kesähotelli Fermaatti (☎ 521 116) three km from the centre at Kyrönniemenkuja 1 is a summer hotel with 28 doubles for 320 mk each.

Places to Stay – top end

Hotels in Savonlinna are especially expensive during the Opera Festival. *Spa Hotel Casino* (☎ 73950) on Casino Island, near the Kauppatori railway halt, is not a bad place to stay. Guests have unlimited access to the pool, sauna and Turkish bath. Singles/doubles are 430/590 mk (510/710 mk in July). *Hotel Seurahuone* (☎ 5731), opposite the harbour at Kauppatori 4-6, has singles/doubles which cost 430/580 mk and rise to 530/680 mk during the Opera Festival. Apartments at *Hotel Tott* (☎ 514 500) at Satamakatu 1, near the harbour, cost 390/51? mk, or 530/680 mk during the Opera Festival.

eason. Ordinary rooms cost 420/580 mk
580/790 mk in July) and include breakfast
and morning sauna. *Hotel Pietari Kylliäinen*
☎ 739 5500) is a nondescript town hotel at
Olavinkatu 15. Singles/doubles cost 310/360
nk (395/480 mk in July).

Places to Eat

The best place to have a lörtsy and coffee is
he colourful market at the harbour. The boat
Hopeasalmi is moored at the market square
and serves mid-priced meals and salads.

There are several grilli or kahvila (cafés)
n the town centre serving fast food or simple
meals. The restaurant on the 2nd floor of the
Hotel Tott does lunch for 38 mk. A popular
evening pub is *Majakka*, opposite the
harbour. It also serves lunch from 32 mk; ask
for the kotiruoka (home-made food). *Snell-
nan* on Olavinkatu is the town's top-end
restaurant. For the best value, cross the long
oridge east from Savonlinna and stop at
Paviljonki on your left, just over the bridge.
This is a catering college, and the meals are
every bit as good as they *ought* to be!

The most pleasant places are near the
castle. *Café Sarasto* at Linnankatu 10 has
pastries and a pleasant garden. *Linnakrouvi*
looks a bit tacky with its beer terrace but the
house is old and has heaps of style, and meals
are available. Inside the castle, *Linnantupa*
serves traditional Finnish food for 50 mk, or
soup for around 30 mk, until 3 pm.

Things to Buy

Savonlinna has a modern commercial centre

to the west of the market. The market is open
daily in July, and from Monday to Saturday
during the rest of the year, with handicrafts
and souvenirs on sale. On Linnankatu, near
the castle, there are several renovated old
wooden houses. At No 10, Markun savipaja
sells local pottery and Marja Putus has fine
clothes made of wool, linen and silk. The
Käsityöläismyymälä (handicrafts shop) in
the building opposite has more variety but
perhaps less of interest.

Getting There & Away

Air There are two to three flights a day from
Helsinki to Savonlinna. The cheapest return
ticket from Helsinki currently costs around
370 mk.

Bus Savonlinna is the major travel hub for
the south-eastern Savo bus network. There
are three express buses a day from Helsinki
to Savonlinna, and buses run almost hourly
from Mikkeli.

Train Savonlinna is off the main railway
network, so you'll need to get off in
Parikkala and catch either another train or a
bus to Savonlinna, 59 km away. Train tickets
and passes are valid on certain buses. There
is also a bus service from the Pieksämäki
railway station, but the journey is twice as
long. The main Savonlinna railway station is
a bit far from the town centre, but trains also
stop at the small Kauppatori railway halt.

Boat You can reach Savonlinna from as far

Olavinlinna Castle in Savonlinna.

away as Kuopio in the north or Lappeenranta in the south. See the sections on Kuopio and Lappeenranta for details. There are also several boats a day to/from Punkaharju.

Getting Around

Using the city bus service costs 9 mk per ride within the Savonlinna area. Taxis depart from opposite the tourist office but are expensive. Kesport, above the harbour at Olavinkatu 44, has the best selection of rental bikes. You may find scooters for rent at the market from 150 mk per four hours. Boats of almost any kind can be rented at Vuokravenho; enquire at the tourist office.

Around Savonlinna

The area around Savonlinna, with its scenic islands, peninsulas, bays and straits, is the most beautiful part of Lakeland.

PUNKAHARJU

One of Finland's natural wonders, Punkaharju is among the 'must-see' places in Savo. The village of Punkaharju (population 4500) makes a convenient base, but you'll also find accommodation in several other places. The village has a tourist office, post office, bus and railway stations, and several shops.

Punkaharju Ridge

The long sand-ridge formation is one of the remaining signs of the Ice Age, which produced similar ridges all over the country. Because the ridge crosses a large lake, it has always been an important travelling route. There is less traffic on the scenic old road, the Harjualue, but unfortunately the new highway and the railway tracks don't offer good views. Near the railway station in the village, however, the tower offers fine views of the area. Entry is free, and it's open in summer until 8 pm.

The best way to cross the ridge is to walk or cycle. There are several side trips on the headlands, and even on the main ridge. Just

a few hundred metres of the original unsealed road remain.

Those arriving by train should alight at the Retretti railway station, walk towards Punkaharju village and turn right. The best views are along the first couple of km after the Finlandia crossing. For superb views take one of the paths up to the ridge top. The train travels through the less picturesque half of the ridge, but buses cross the entire Harjualue and even make a visit to the island of Vaahersalo.

Retretti

An unusual but popular tourist attraction, Retretti is an art exhibition inside an artificial cave. Inside the cave are waterfalls, a concert hall and special effects, including lights, sounds and shadows. The annual exhibition is held in one of the ground-level buildings. Regional tourist offices can provide further information. Entry to Retretti is a hefty 65 mk (10 mk less for students), but this is good value if you spend half a day there. Retretti is open daily from 23 May to 30 August from 10 am to 6 pm (until 7 pm in the high season). You can get there by bus, train (get off at Retretti station) or on the daily steamer from Savonlinna. The Retretti area also has the popular Kesämaa, a large fun and water park. Entry is 50 to 55 mk.

Lusto

Finland now has a museum devoted to that most Finnish of industries, forestry. The building is partly made from concrete to meet the not-so wood-friendly regulations. Wood, timber and forestry-related technology are on display. The museum is complemented by a large research park (with tracks and all kinds of trees). In summer, the museum is open daily from 10 am to 6 pm and the park can be visited 24 hours a day because of the white nights. From November till April, the museum closes at 5 pm and opens daily except Monday. The park is always open. Admission to the museum is 35 mk, though there are some discounts. Nearby, the former railway station now houses the Punkaharju Information Centre.

Top: Rowing boat on Lake Sarkavesi, south of Mäntyharju
Middle: Kuopio Market Square in summer
Bottom: Old slash-and-burn technique using traditional tools and clothing, Savo

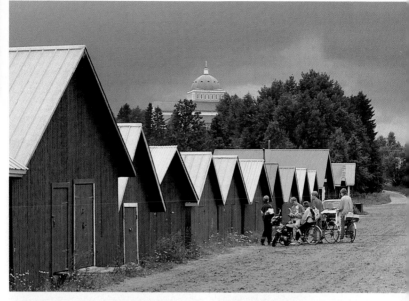

Top: Kerimäki Village
Left: Pauper Statue outside Larsmo Church
Right: A chapel of the Valamo Monastery, Heinävesi

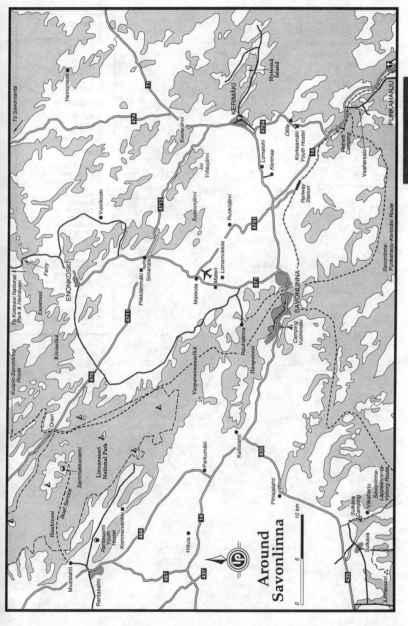

Around
Savonlinna

SAVO

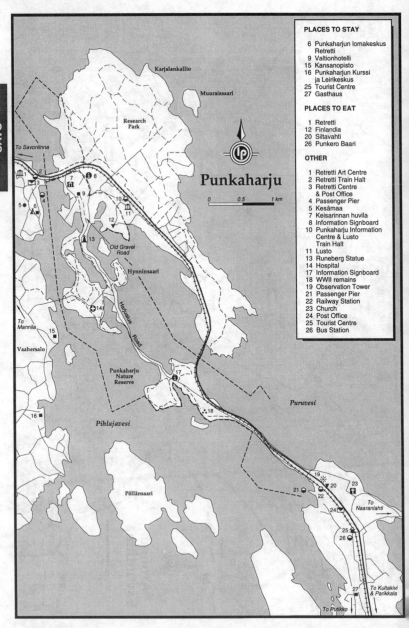

Punkaharju

0   0.5   1 km

PLACES TO STAY

6 Punkaharjun lomakeskus
   Retretti
9 Valtionhotelli
15 Kansanopisto
16 Punkaharjun Kurssi
   ja Leirikeskus
25 Tourist Centre
27 Gasthaus

PLACES TO EAT

1 Retretti
12 Finlandia
20 Siltavahti
26 Punkero Baari

OTHER

1 Retretti Art Centre
2 Retretti Train Halt
3 Retretti Centre
   & Post Office
4 Passenger Pier
5 Kesämaa
7 Keisarinnan huvila
8 Information Signboard
10 Punkaharju Information
   Centre & Lusto
   Train Halt
11 Lusto
13 Runeberg Statue
14 Hospital
17 Information Signboard
18 WWII remains
19 Observation Tower
21 Passenger Pier
22 Railway Station
23 Church
24 Post Office
25 Tourist Centre
26 Bus Station

which is open daily from May to August between 9 am and 5 pm.

Putikko

This pretty little village south of Punkaharju has local artists' studios, including Sininen Ikkuna, and the Galleria at the railway station. Putikon kartano is a manor house, just outside the village on Vanhatie.

Cruises

For something special, the SS *Heinävesi* sails daily in summer from Savonlinna to Retretti and Valtionhotelli, departing at 11 am and returning at 3.40 pm. The MS *Princess* has daily cruises around the Punkaharju area every two hours from noon to 8 pm.

Places to Stay

The best value is the *Tourist Centre* (☎ 441 771) youth hostel next to the *apteekki* (pharmacy) opposite the bus station. There are dormitory beds for 100 mk, and the place rents out bicycles for 40 mk, and canoes for 100 mk per day – a terrific way to explore Punkaharju. There's also tourist information and a café.

Gasthaus (☎ 441 371) at Palomäentie 18 is a clean guesthouse some two km from the railway station – buses will drop you off at the door if you ask. Doubles are 300 mk and the sauna and swimming pool cost 30 mk per person. The owners also run a quiet farm estate with 12 well-equipped rooms, which cost 230/300 mk. This is a place where you can relax, and take part in rural activities, including canoeing, fishing or gathering berries in the woods. Transport is provided from the guesthouse or youth hostel in Punkaharju, 16 km away.

Punkaharjun Lomakeskus Retretti (☎ 739 611) is one of the largest camping grounds in Finland, and contains 160 cottages. The location is fine but the place is often crowded. The cheapest huts at the back sleep two people and cost 210 mk in the high season, and 170 mk in early June and in August. Four-bed cottages are 310 to 550 mk, or 270 to 450 mk in quiet times. Pitching

a tent is expensive at 75 mk, or 38 mk for an individual.

Just across the Tuunaansalmi strait, *Valtionhotelli* (☎ 739 611) is a romantic hotel, the oldest in Finland. Singles/doubles start at 285/400 mk (420/550 mk in the high season). There are also two-bed cottages for 210 mk in July (170 mk in June and August).

A cheap place to stay is *Punkaharjun Kurssi ja Leirikeskus* (☎ 644 189), across the Potkusalmi bridge on the island of Vaahersalo. Dormitory beds cost 105 mk in summer, but it is often full. Also on the island, a short walk from where the bus turns back, *Kansanopisto* (☎ 311 471) has singles/doubles from 235/260 mk. *Mannila* (☎ 644 265) is 1.3 km from the bus stop, and has B&B for 110 mk per person.

The train will stop on request at *Kultakivi* (☎ 645 151), nine km south of Punkaharju village. This holiday village has a huge reception building, well visible from the road and train, and offers 135 cottages from 215 to 320 mk, or less during the low season. This place boasts the first nudist beach in Finland.

Places to Eat

In the main village, go to *Siltavahti*, next to the railway station. Meals from 35 mk are available. The staff here are responsible for the tower; if it's closed, ask them for the keys. The *Tourist Centre* does sandwiches with local fish; try the drink made from blackcurrant leaves. At the bus station is *Punkero Baari*, which serves snacks.

For a splurge, a good buffet is available daily at *Finlandia*, a beautiful house built in 1914, one km from the ridge road. The home-made lunch is served daily from noon to 4 pm for 65 mk (45 mk in winter). There is also a good buffet lunch (70 mk) at *Valtionhotelli*.

Retretti has a café, and a restaurant with meals for 55 mk.

Getting There & Away

All trains between Parikkala and Savonlinna stop in the village of Punkaharju and at Retretti. There are buses from Savonlinna and Parikkala, too. If you're driving from

SAVO

SAVO

Kerimäki, road No 4794 is sealed and is highly recommended.

RANTASALMI

Rantasalmi is the place to go to catch boats to Linnansaari National Park, which is situated on the Lake Haukivesi islands. Almost 5000 people live inside the Rantasalmi municipal area. The tourist information office (☎ 737 1410) is in the village centre at the Geotalo building. The large church is open daily in summer from 10 am to 6 pm.

Järviluonnonkeskus

The Lakeland Centre is devoted to natural aspects of the Finnish Lakeland. The building also serves as an information centre for Linnansaari National Park. The centre is open daily in summer from 10 am to 6 pm, and at other times of the year from Monday to Friday between 10 am and 4 pm. Admission is free. Next door, Geotalo is a stone exhibition; admission is 15 mk. The local museum is nearby and is open daily in summer from 10 am to 6 pm. Admission is 10 mk.

Places to Stay

The cheapest place to stay in Rantasalmi is the HI hostel, *Rantapyyvilä* (☎ 440 124), which gets mixed reports. Its lakeside location is some four km from the village of Rantasalmi, but not close to the national park. The hostel is open year round, with dormitory beds from 55 mk. In the village itself, *Hotel Rinssieversti* (☎ 440 761) has singles/doubles for 290/380 mk.

Kommervenkki (☎ 448 188), in a rural setting eight km from Rantasalmi, provides opportunities for several activities. The cheapest singles/doubles start from 150/225 mk. The nearby *Rantasalmi Center* (☎ 448 200) is a spa. Rooms cost 450/580 mk, including breakfast. There are all kinds of treatment programs, including a traditional smoke sauna.

Places to Eat

Up the street from the tourist office and near the bus station is *Marjuska*, a lunchtime res-taurant. There's also *Kalle Kustaa*, which opens until late.

Getting There & Away

Regular buses between Savonlinna and Pieksämäki travel via Rantasalmi. Train passes are valid on some buses. In July, there's a train service from Punkaharju via Savonlinna.

LINNANSAARI NATIONAL PARK

One of the main attractions of the Savonlinna region, Linnansaari National Park is located entirely on uninhabited islands. The rare Saimaa marble seal is known to live there, though few visitors have actually seen it. Several rare birds, including osprey, can be seen and heard. The park centres around Sammakkoniemi harbour on Linnansaari Island, which derives its name from the Linnavuori (Fortress Hill). The view from the hill is spectacular.

Once in **Sammakkoniemi**, you will find a canteen for provisions and a small museum. A few marked trails deviate from here revealing varied island vegetation and fabulous cliff-top scenery.

Information

The main park information centre is in the Järviluonnonkeskus (Lakeland Centre) at Rantasalmi. Take a copy of the free map which is available in information offices. There is usually a biologist working at Sammakkoniemi, who will provide suggestions on how you might spend your time.

Places to Stay

You can stay at the established camping grounds for free, or reserve a bed in a cottage by ringing ☎ 949-659 475 (a mobile phone). Beds in these comfortable cottages in Sammakkoniemi cost 62 mk, or it's 200 mk for the entire cottage. You can use the sauna for 25 mk and rent a boat for 70 mk per day. The Lakeland Centre will help you to find accommodation.

Getting There & Away

There are buses to Rantasalmi from

Savonlinna and Pieksämäki (train passes are valid on most of these). From Rantasalmi, it's an extra three km to reach the Mustalahti quay. The Lakeland Centre has information on taxis, or you could walk. MS *Linnansaari* has two daily launches from Mustalahti to Sammakkoniemi; return tickets cost 75 mk.

ENONKOSKI

The large municipality of Enonkoski (population 2140) does not attract masses of tourists, so this is one good reason not to leave it out of your itinerary. Kolovesi National Park, one of Savo's natural wonders, can easily be visited from here. There are some terrific places to stay along the route, and a bicycle tour is highly recommended. You can either rent a bicycle in Savonlinna, or transit between Savonlinna and Heinävesi via Enonkoski.

Information

The tourist office in Savonlinna also functions as a sales agent, so you won't be left short of local information. In Enonkoski village, Enohovi has information leaflets, or you can try Koloveden Opastuskeskus (☎ 479 040), Kolovesi National Park's information centre. It's open weekdays 10 am to 6 pm (closed on Monday in June and August), and on weekends until 3 pm. The modern library has one regional map in a scale of 1:20,000, and they have books about the area. It's open on weekdays in the afternoon.

Things to See

The **national park centre** is in an old red house, along with a café and an exhibition of local handicraft. The small single-arch stone bridge next to the house is thought to have been built in 1904, and is now protected. The 1886 **church** is open daily in summer from 9 am to 8 pm. The museum behind it is worth a visit for its displays on local history.

Places to Stay & Eat

This list follows geographical order northwards from Savonlinna.

Materi (☎ 523 423) is a very fine manor house near the airport, some 10 km north of Savonlinna. There are 20 beds in various buildings, and the rate of 120 mk per person includes sheets, a sauna bath and breakfast. The excellent buffet is 50 mk on weekdays, and includes salmon and mushroom salad. The separate *Tuulipyörä* is a pub built in an old cow house, and displays extremely innovative style. Don't miss it.

The small road opposite Materi takes you to *Lomamokkila* (☎ 523 117) at Mikonkiventie 209 which has accommodation from 110 mk, including breakfast, in rooms and cottages.

Two km west from Simanala on Muholantie, *Piikkilänmäki* (☎ 674 179) has very clean rooms for 140 mk per person, including breakfast. The place is very quiet.

Enonhovi (☎ 479 431) gives the best value for money, especially if you produce a valid HI card. The rooms are clean and fishing tours and bicycle rental are possible if you speak nicely to the owners. This place is right in the middle of the village, and can serve as a base for further exploration. HI members pay from 65 mk, while non-members pay 140/180 mk for singles/doubles. Lunch starts from 28 mk.

There's also *Koski-Torppa* at the rapids, serving inexpensive hamburgers and pizza, and there are a few discount food stores in the nearby village centre.

Getting There & Away

In summer, there's an afternoon bus departing from Savonlinna Monday to Friday at 2.15 pm. During school term time there are several afternoon buses, but there's nothing on weekends. There's a direct bus between Kuopio and Lappeenranta, via Enonkoski, on Friday and Sunday.

AROUND ENONKOSKI
Vuorikoski

Here you can visit the old 19th century **mill** which is still in use, and buy flour which has been made there. Vuorikoskentie, the gravel road around Lake Ylä-Enonvesi, will take you to Vuorikoski.

SAVO

SAVO

Simanala

In this small village, **Tuunala Hunajapuoti** produces and sells honey. In summer, you can visit this place from 10 am to 8 pm.

Canoeing the Ulpukka Route

There are lakes, rivers and several easy rapids along this route, which starts from Lake Kuhajärvi, and runs on rivers via Lake Tänkky, and through another river system at Kärenkoski rapids. The trip costs a minimum of 250 mk, including gear and insurance as well as the services of a tour leader. There's another tour which takes eight to 12 hours, and costs 490 mk, including meals. Enquire at Simanalan Jokimelojat (☎ 479 222) in Simanala.

Sirpa's Farm

A charming lady runs this sheep farm (☎ 446 600) where you can purchase woollen products. The farm is on road No 471, about 15 km north of Enonkoski past the (free) ferry across the Hanhivirta strait.

Kolovesi National Park

This fine national park was founded in 1990, and covers several islands which feature unusually well preserved pine forests. There are high hills, rocky cliffs and caves, and even prehistoric paintings on rocks. Saimaa marble seals are known to live in the area. You can get further information in Enonkoski or Rantasalmi, or at regional tourist offices.

All motor-powered boats are prohibited in the park. A rowing boat is practically the only way to see the fantastic scenery, and groups get to travel in an old 'church longboat' with up to 10 pairs of oars. A guide is an unavoidable expense if you want to find the best places.

Rowing & Canoeing You can rent or borrow a rowing boat or canoe at Pohjataipale or Säynämö. In Enonkoski, contact Norppa-Veneet (☎ 479 076) for boat rentals. North of Enonkoski, near Savonranta – 52 km north of Savonlinna – Kolovesi Retkeily Ky (☎ 673 628) has rowing boats and canoes. To

get there, drive north from Enonkoski towards Heinävesi and look out for the sign 'Kolovesi Retkeily' on road No 471 after a steep ascent. The cheapest boat-rental option is 80 mk, but if you pay 120 mk, maps and guides are included. If you are looking for maps at the scale of 1:20,000, the code is 4212, and sheet Nos 05, 06 and 08 cover the area. From road No 471, follow the sign that says 'Selkälahti' and 'Koloveden kansallispuisto'.

Places to Stay The national park area includes just two camping grounds, one at Lohilahti near the southern access road No 471, and the other on the island of Pitkäsaari. *Kolovesi Retkeily* (☎ 673 628) is the main tour operator for the park, and rents cottages in the park area for 300 mk. Alternatively, you can camp in their private camp site, or negotiate other arrangements.

KERIMÄKI

The first thing that strikes you in Kerimäki is the huge church. Kerimäki is a small place (population 6500), yet it has the largest wooden church in the world. The small tourist information booth, open daily, does not give out much information but sells souvenirs instead.

Kerimäki Church

Dominating the entire village, this wooden church was built in 1847 to seat 3300 people. The church's size was not a mistake (one version says 'feet' on the plan were read as 'metres') but was quite deliberately inflated from original plans when built by megalomaniac locals. Worshippers would come to the church from across the lake in their *kirkkovene* longboats. For 5 mk, you can climb the *tapuli* (bell tower), but you need a 24-mm lens to capture the entire church on film. The church is open daily from June to mid-August until 8 pm.

Museums

The **Järvikalastusmuseo** has exhibitions on local fishing. It is near the church and is open from 1 June to 31 August from noon to

3 pm; in the high season, the opening hours are 11 am to 6 pm. Admission is 5 mk. Cross the back yard to an **open-air museum** featuring old grey buildings and a windmill. Behind this area, visible from the main road, is a row of wooden **boat shelters**. They make a good photo.

At Hotelli Herttua, there's a **war exhibition** which includes a collection of old guns. Behind the hotel is a renovated bunker and a stretch of WWII trench line – even though no battle was fought here! Inside the hotel you can see the exhibition on war history for 15 mk. This small *sotahistoriallinen näyttely* has no English text.

Hytermä

This protected island celebrates one of the weirdest of human achievements: it has a monument to Romu-Heikki ('Junk Heikki'), a man who built large structures with millstones. The island is also quite beautiful, so you should try to visit it, perhaps by hiring a rowing boat at Hotelli Herttua.

Places to Stay

Worth checking out is *Lomalohi* (☎ 541 771), seven km from Kerimäki going towards Savonlinna. This popular, down-to-earth camping ground also has a few cottages from 150 mk. There are several discount options to ask for. Nearby, *Kerimaa* (☎ 57511) has more than 50 attractive cottages from 450 mk in the high season.

In the village of Kerimäki, *Kerihovi* (☎ 541 225) is an attractive old wooden house with singles/doubles for 180/300 mk in summer, or 150/250 mk at other times. There are meals for about 40 mk. A top-end alternative, 1.5 km from the village, is *Hotelli Herttua* (☎ 575 501) but it's expensive at 490/640 mk.

The best value in the municipality of Kerimäki is *Korkeamäki Hostel* (☎ 442 186), eight km south of Kerimäki village on Kerimäki to Punkaharju road No 4794. This quiet farmhouse, run by a friendly Savonian couple, provides accommodation from 1 June to 31 August in three old houses. Youth-hostel prices apply, and start at 45 mk.

If Korkeamäki is full, try *Ollila*, just next door by rural standards. It is slightly more expensive, with huts from 140 mk; the price includes breakfast.

Getting There & Away

There are buses between Savonlinna and Kerimäki every hour or so. Enough traffic uses the road to make hitchhiking viable; walk one km from Kerimäki to reach the main road. Note that the 'Kerimäki' railway station is not close to anything, so it's not worth getting off the train there!

SULKAVA

Scenic Sulkava (population nearly 3800) is known for its rowing-boat competitions – it's water sports that count here. The village of Sulkava is a sleepy little place, with many attractive wooden houses around the small commercial centre near the bridge. See the section on Juva for canoeing route information.

Information

The small commercial centre is handy, with both tourist information (☎ 739 1236) and the post office in the same building, and a bus station outside. You can rent a bicycle at the TV & Kodinkone shop if you can speak Finnish or can negotiate in international sign language. The harbour has a host of services, including showers, toilets and a coin-operated laundry machine.

Church

The church was built in 1822 and has an attractive interior. It is open daily in summer from 10 am to 6 pm. The bell tower dates from 1770.

Vilkaharju

This protected ridge along road No 438 has two *luontopolku* trails, 3 km and 3.6 km long, and marked by yellow ribbons. On Lake Pöllälampi you can rent boats and purchase a 50-mk four-hour fishing permit; two salmon are included in the price. Enquire about the permit at Sulkava Camping.

SAVO

Farther south is the museum area of Rauhaniemi, but this may be closed.

Linnavuori

This prehistoric fortress is probably the most interesting sight in the Sulkava area. It's well signposted. The view from the top is of ideal lakeland scenery and old fortifications. At the bottom, there's a covered BBQ area. Occasionally, you can get there on a boat cruise from Sulkava.

Places to Stay

Next to the bus terminal, *Motelli Muikkukukko* (☎ 471 651) has 10 rooms for 180/320 mk. The reception is in the restaurant; a 32-mk lunch is served until 2 pm, and evening meals can be purchased until late.

Seven km from the main village, in the Vilkaharju area, *Sulkava Camping* (☎ 471 223) – also known as Vilkaharju Camping – is located on a scenic headland across a pedestrian bridge (road access is possible). There are also almost 20 cottages for four/six people for 110/180 mk, or 165/260 mk in the high season.

Owned by the same company, *Sulkavan Lomakeskus* is seemingly popular among Finnish families, but it's not even attractive.

There are other places around the municipality. The best choice is on the island of Partalansaari, south of Sulkava.

Partalansaaren Lomakoti (☎ 478 850) at Hirviniementie 5 is a youth hostel not far from the cannon at the Sarsuinmäki WWII battery site. Dormitory beds cost just 50 mk for HI members, but there are also cottages from 300 mk. Facilities include a sauna, food, and bicycles and boats for hire. Another option, *Mehtäläisen maja* (☎ 648 622), on Syväjärventie eight km from Sulkava, is a farmhouse which provides accommodation and has domestic animals and art for sale.

Places to Eat

Right at the bus terminal, *Matkahuollon baari* is cheap but nothing special. *Mäkitupa Baari* nearby is equally inexpensive and a bit better. *Muikkukukko* is even better. Probably the best value is *Ravintola Alanne* at the harbour, 500 metres from the bus terminal. A lunch pack is 30 mk (more on weekends, when a tasty cake is included), and dinner is 45 mk, including a piece of cake. *Eväsgrilli*, opposite the bus terminal, has junk food. There are also supermarkets near the bus terminal.

Getting There & Away

There are regular buses to Sulkava from Savonlinna, 39 km away.

Mikkeli

Mikkeli (population 32,500) is the capital of the Province of Mikkeli (which comprises South Savo and part of what is generally called East Häme). It is an under-visited town, despite offering attractions which include several museums, cruises and long street names.

History

There is enough prehistoric evidence to suggest that Mikkeli was one of the earliest inhabited regions in Savo. But it was not until 1838, when it became part of the Province of Mikkeli, that the one-time market town became an administrative and military centre. During WWII, it was used as the Finnish army's headquarters, mainly because there were no conspicuous high-rise houses. Marshal C G Mannerheim resided in Mikkeli during WWII; today, local memories of his residence are preserved in various museums.

Information

Tourist Office Tourist information is provided by Mikkelin Matkailu Oy (☎ 151 444) at Hallituskatu 3A, near the market. There are some excellent pamphlets. The office is open from 1 June to 15 August, Monday to Friday from 9 am to 5.30 pm and Saturday from 10 am to 3 pm. During the rest of the year, it's open Monday to Friday from 9 am to 4.30 pm.

Post & Telephone The main post office and the Tele office are at Hallituskatu 4, 50100 Mikkeli.

Library For 1:20,000 maps of the entire Province of Mikkeli, go to the public library off the market square, at Raatihuoneenkatu 6. Upstairs in the *opintolukusali* (study hall), the warden will open the locked drawers in the *maakuntakokoelma* (provincial collection), where the maps are kept. The library is open Monday to Friday from 10 am to 7 pm, but the newspaper room opens on Saturday as well, until 2 pm.

Books & Maps Suomalainen Kirjakauppa is next to the tourist office at the market.

Left Luggage The railway station has lockers for 10 mk per day.

Emergency Services In a general emergency phone ☎ 112, and for a doctor ring ☎ 10023. There are pharmacies near the market at Porrassalmenkatu 21, Maaherrankatu 28 and Savilahdenkatu 5.

Jalkaväkimuseo
Probably the best museum in Mikkeli, with

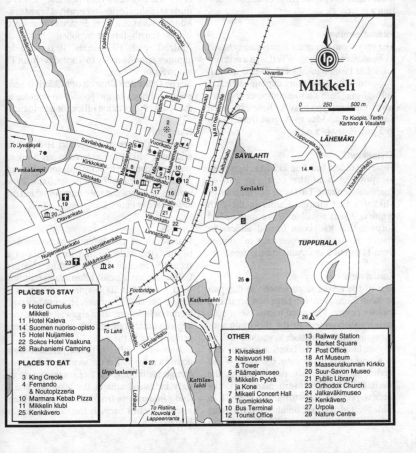

PLACES TO STAY
9   Hotel Cumulus Mikkeli
11   Hotel Kaleva
14   Suomen nuoriso-opisto
22   Sokos Hotel Vaakuna
26   Rauhaniemi Camping

PLACES TO EAT
3   King Creole
4   Fernando & Noutopizzeria
10   Marmara Kebab Pizza
11   Mikkelin klubi
25   Kenkävero

OTHER
1   Kivisakasti
2   Naisvuori Hill & Tower
5   Päämajamuseo
6   Mikkelin Pyörä ja Kone
7   Mikaeli Concert Hall
8   Tuomiokirkko
10   Bus Terminal
12   Tourist Office

13   Railway Station
16   Market Square
17   Post Office
18   Art Museum
19   Maaseurakunnan Kirkko
20   Suur-Savon Museo
21   Public Library
23   Orthodox Church
24   Jalkaväkimuseo
25   Kenkävero
27   Urpola
28   Nature Centre

its extensive weaponry and WWII exhibitions, the Infantry Museum is located inside old barracks near the town centre. The display is top class. It's open daily in summer from 10 am to 5 pm; at other times of the year, it's usually open on Wednesday and weekends only. Entry costs 10 mk.

Suur-Savon Museo

Another good museum, the provincial museum of Greater Savo, is in an attractive building. It features several mysterious artefacts, and items tracing Mikkeli's history. The museum is open daily (except Monday) from April to August from 11 am to 3 pm. Entry is free.

Päämajamuseo

The very room where the Finnish army based its headquarters during WWII is in a primary school at Päämajankatu 1-3. This is a small museum, with everything explained clearly in English. There's also a computer program which can keep you busy for hours. It's open daily from mid-May to August from 10 am to 5 pm. Entry is 5 mk.

Kivisakasti

This, the oldest building in Mikkeli, is easy to spot – it's at the northern end of Porrassalmenkatu. This is all that remains of Mikkeli's first church. Earlier in the 20th century, it was possible to see mummified corpses that had been buried under the church. Kivisakasti is open daily in summer from 11 am to 5 pm. Admission is free.

Kenkävero

One of the favourite attractions in this part of Savo, Kenkävero is a large handicraft and activity centre. The word means 'shoe tax', and probably refers to the old custom of changing into better shoes as you stepped out of your longboat at the lakeside on your way to attend the Sunday church service – and having to immediately pay a tax for the privilege! The Kenkävero mansion is the largest *pappila* ('pastor's residence') in Finland, and was left uninhabited for years before being reopened in 1990 after a careful

restoration. Visitors can make their own handicrafts here – you can use a loom, paint on silk or work with wood. Admission costs 10 mk. You pay extra for the materials you use, but the instruction is given for free.

Churches

Mikkeli boasts two enormous Lutheran churches; one is used by city people and the other by rural folk. **Tuomiokirkko** is the cathedral in the town centre. At 2734 sq metres it is the largest church in Finland but has barely 1000 seats. It is open in summer only, every day from 10 am to 6 pm. It has a crypt and a notable altar painting, and is a majestic building overall. **Maaseurakunnan Kirkko**, a short distance to the west, is the fourth largest wooden church in Finland, with 1900 seats. It is open in summer only, Monday to Thursday, from 11 am to 5 pm.

The **Orthodox Church** of Mikkeli is generally not open to the public, so enquire at the tourist information office for admittance.

Naisvuori

There is a tower on Naisvuori Hill, in the middle of Mikkeli. You have to pay 5 mk to walk up it, but the tower is still something of a must. It's open only in summer. Sample the waffles with jam and ice cream for which the tower café is famous.

Urpola

Just south of the Infantry Museum and beyond the railway line in Urpola is a recently opened Luontokeskus (Nature Centre). It has a small information building with maps, but its major attraction is a jungle-like (in late summer) river valley with an old mill. Information signs along the trail depict a number of animals, but few of them actually live in the valley.

East of Urpola, there's a pleasant walk across a ridge and, if the weather is fine, you can go swimming. Farther south-east, in an ugly industrial area at the lakeside, you'll find a *hiidenkirnu* (rock-drilled well) which, at eight metres deep, is the third largest in Finland.

Visulahti

Visulahti, six km from Mikkeli, comprises the following expensive tourist attractions: Mini-Finland, the Dinosauria Park, the Wax Museum and the Vintage Car Museum. The dinosaurs were here well before Steven Spielberg decided to make billions on them. Visulahti is open daily in summer.

Places to Stay – bottom end

Rauhaniemi Camping (☎ 211 416), open from 1 June to mid-August, has cottages for rent 2.5 km from the centre.

Places to Stay – middle

Suomen nuoriso-opisto (☎ 414 800) at Paukkulantie 22 along the Mikkeli to Kuopio road No 5 – some 1.5 km from the centre – is a summer hotel with inexpensive accommodation.

Ritvalan Matkakoti (☎ 335 820) at Porrassalmentie 16A has seven rooms for 120/220 mk.

Visulahti (☎ 18281), some five km from the centre towards Kuopio along road No 5, is a large tourist centre with almost 30 cottages for rent. The camping ground is open from late May to 31 August.

Tertin kartano (☎ 176 012) at Kuopiontie 68 in Norola – seven km from Mikkeli along road No 5 and two km from Visulahti – has B&B in pleasant rooms for 360 mk.

Places to Stay – top end

Mikkeli has a few good hotels.

Hotel Cumulus Mikkeli (☎ 20511) at Mikonkatu 9 is rivalled only by the Vaakuna in quality. It has 140 rooms, three restaurants and three saunas. Singles/doubles cost 450/520 mk; in summer all rooms are 355 mk.

Hotel Kaleva (☎ 206 1500) is by the market at Hallituskatu 5. All rooms cost 350 mk.

Hotel Nuijamies (☎ 363 111) is more like a sleazy nightclub for Savonites in their 50s who enjoy dancing to Finnish tango stars, than a hotel. It's near the market at Porrassalmenkatu 21. Singles/doubles start at 300/350 mk.

Sokos Hotel Vaakuna (☎ 202 0422) at Porrassalmenkatu 9 was previously known as Hotel Alexandra. It is the best hotel in Mikkeli, with a fine restaurant in the central courtyard and superbly equipped rooms. There are three saunas and two whirlpools. Singles/doubles are 450/530; ask for discounts on weekends.

Varsavuori (☎ 367 032) at Kirkonvarkaus has 98 double rooms from 270 to 440 mk. Drive two km south of Mikkeli, turn left and proceed one km.

Places to Eat

Mikkeli's *tori* (market) is probably the best in Finland, and should not be missed. It's busy till 2 pm, there's heaps of atmosphere and there are always good snacks and vegetables available. *Marjatan torikahvila* is a famous and enjoyable café in the market. A recently introduced snack called friteerattu kuore is a small (undervalued) fish, fried in batter, and may only be available occasionally. Ask around. Viipurin rinkilä is a Vyborg speciality. The Kauppahalli is also good for fresh bread, vegetables and fruit.

Near the market, the bus station has a café, as well as the Turkish *Marmara Kebab Pizza* that has meals from 30 mk. *King Creole* at Vuorikatu 11 hails Anglo-American culture, though the décor could be better. There are meals, coffee and beer.

Kenkävero is famous for its herkkupöytä buffet. It is not very cheap but good for a splurge.

For lunch specials, enquire at restaurants on Maaherrankatu (or other streets near the market) – *Fernando* at No 17 is not a bad place to start, but *Noutopizzeria* nearby is much cheaper. This place caters almost exclusively for families with children.

Mikkelin klubi is a private club at Maaherrankatu 13. It is generally not open to the public, but is famous for its WWII Marskin ryyppy, an ice-cold vodka drink in a full glass. Enquire at the tourist office.

For a mega splurge, the buffet at *Tertin kartano* (☎ 176 012) is worth every markka (and it will take lots of them). You can dine on game, and try specialities made from local herbs, berries and mushrooms. It's located in an old estate mansion, which has witnessed colourful history and has been meticulously renovated. It's seven km from Mikkeli heading towards Kuopio; the tourist office can provide directions and other information.

SAVO

Getting There & Away

Air There are two to three flights from Helsinki to Mikkeli each weekday.

Bus The bus terminal is right in the centre of town. Plenty of express buses stop here on their way from Helsinki to towns farther north.

Train The railway station is also in the town centre. Mikkeli is the main station between Kouvola and Pieksämäki, or along the Helsinki to Kajaani route.

Getting Around

Local buses can come in handy if you want to visit Visulahti or other places farther afield. It is not possible to rent bicycles in Mikkeli, but for repairs and spare parts enquire at Mikkelin Pyörä ja Kone at Mikonkatu 14, just below Naisvuori Hill.

Around Mikkeli

MÄNTYHARJU

Mäntyharju epitomises the beautiful Savo landscape. But, typically for Finland, the commercial centre near the railway station is extremely modern, to the point of being ugly.

The major sights are several km west of the centre. Because of frequent train connections, you can break your journey for approximately three or six hours, and visit the main attractions on foot.

Most of the accommodation is scattered around the large municipality. Mäntyharju's Lutheran Church was founded in 1595.

Information

There's an informal tourist information facility (☎ 684 038) at the bus station, and free material is available in several places around the town. The post office is in the commercial centre. There's no left-luggage facility at the railway station but you can negotiate with the ticket vendor.

Mäntyharju Church Area

The old centre of Mäntyharju has an extremely idyllic location between two lakes. There are several attractions.

Iso-Pappila was previously owned by the Lutheran Church. The large yellow building, built in 1812, now houses an annexe to Salmela, the main gallery.

In the same area, the **local museum** consists of several buildings. The red building houses the main exhibition on local history. The information is in Finnish only, but there's plenty to see. Riihi is a two-storey building in the woods with a display of farming tools. At the back, the stone-walled house has carriages and other large vehicles, and a dugout canoe that was found at the bottom of Lake Kanajärvi.

The museum is open daily noon to 6 pm, and admission costs 10 mk. Nearby, east of Iso-Pappila, a small hill near the main road has an artificial WWII-style battle site that was finished in 1995. No fighting ever took place here.

Farther west, **Taidekeskus Salmela** is the main art gallery; in summer there's a special exhibition. The admission is a hefty 40 mk, but the same ticket is also valid for Iso-Pappila. There's a café at Salmela.

The unique 1822 church houses 2000 people and is made from enormous logs. It's open in summer from 9 am to 6 pm. Behind the church, go along Kirkkotie to see a well-preserved old village road.

Uittotupa

At Uittotupa, not far from the main road No 5, is **Uittomuseo** which has displays of floating logs (a tradition). Pilkkumi is a pottery studio. Miekankoski rapids are good for fishing, but you need a local permit.

Places to Stay & Eat

The only place to stay in central Mäntyharju is *Ravintola Punahilkka* (☎ 464 900), close to the railway station at Asematie 1. There are five rooms, from 150/250 mk.

The best room has a bathroom and kitchen, and costs 200/300 mk. Meals are served throughout the day and cost from 30 mk.

Uittotupa (☎ 685 170), not far from the main road No 5, has inexpensive lodging.

Near road No 5, there are two more possibilities. *Mäntymotelli* (☎ 685 101) has 46 rooms, several cottages and offers a number of activities. *Vihantasalmi* (☎ 685 241) is a camping ground 16 km from Mäntyharju. There are over 30 cottages and a sauna. The place rents out canoes and boats.

There are several places to eat in the centre. The best is *Rosmarin* behind the bus station. It serves a daily special for between 27 and 54 mk. Coffee, pastries and bakery products are available at *Leipurin puoti*. *Koivugrilli* is the place for junk food. There's also a café in the railway station.

Getting There & Away

Mäntyharju is pampered by the railways – practically every train stops at its small station. The bus station is within walking distance of the railway station and there are buses to various destinations in the region.

MOUHU

Just two km north of Mouhu and on the shore of Lake Sarkavesi, *Lankkumyllyn kiewari* (☎ 462 770) is a good place to stay to enjoy the white nights of summer. There are seven cottages, from 160 mk, which house two to four people. There are also two lakeside saunas, a unique bar which has a table constructed above rapids, and a quiet island that has been turned into Inkkarialue (an 'Indian Land', referring to North America rather than the Subcontinent). Lake Sarkavesi itself

is a scenic narrow lake that connects two larger lakes. You can hire a rowing boat to explore this very fine waterscape.

Getting There & Away

Mouhu itself can be reached by a local train that will stop on request. There are two trains a day between Kouvola and Mikkeli. Better yet, there's a direct bus service to Lankkumyllyn kiewari between Kouvola (departs at 10.10 am) and Mäntyharju (departs at 12.10 pm). If you drive, proceed six km from Mäntyharju on road No 416, turn left towards Mouhu and continue 10.2 km along the gravel road. Kouvola is 60 km away.

RISTIINA

Ristiina (population 5200), one of Savo's historic villages, was founded by Count Per Brahe in 1649 and named after Kristina, his wife (and after the queen of Sweden). Little remains of the village's glorious past, though there are several places that reflect Per's aspirations.

The main attractions of Ristiina municipality lie 20 km from the village, and can also be reached by lake cruises from Mikkeli. The tourist office will provide a map, and you can rent bicycles from the Brahe hotel.

History

In 1649 Count Per Brahe was granted the rural area now known as Ristiina. A wooden church was built, and work began on the small castle which overlooks the Savonian landscape.

The locals claim that Ristiina's current

Prehistoric rock paintings at Astuvansalmi near Ristiina.

fate was sealed by the whim of a bureaucrat during the 1830s. Ristiina was chosen to be capital of the newly established province of Mikkeli, but a government officer got tired on his way there, and paused to rest in the town of Mikkeli – and decided that the capital should be in Mikkeli. So Ristiina's gloriously promising future was lost and it became something of a backwater.

Ristiina Village

There's quite a distance between the main road and Ristiina's principal attraction, the castle ruins, but most shops and places to stay and eat are situated along the main street, Brahentie. Information is provided by the Klemmari shop at Brahentie 16, some 500 metres from the main road.

Brahelinna is the castle that was built by Per Brahe; its ruin is on a hill over two km from the main road. The castle's high walls and the surrounding forest make the walk up there worthwhile.

A sign saying 'Dunckerin kivi' points to a stone that was erected to honour a local, Mr Duncker, who fought and died during the 1809 battles against Russia. The view from the memorial is excellent. Take a look too at the foot of the hill – the sadly abandoned restaurant Brahelinna went bust in the early 1990s. **Gränna talo**, which was transferred here from Mikkeli, has art exhibitions in summer, normally from late June to July only. There's also an open-air summer theatre and a windmill in the area.

Working back towards the main road, the 1775 **church** is unique in terms of interior decoration as no other church in Savo exhibits so many paintings from the heyday of the Swedish empire. The count and his wife Kristina are more prominently displayed than Jesus Christ himself. The church distributes a leaflet in English, and is open daily from 11 am to 5 pm.

Only 500 metres from the church, **Käsityökeskus** is a handicraft centre which makes mats and other goods using traditional methods. There's a shop if you'd like to buy souvenirs.

Astuvansalmen Kalliomaalaukset

The Rock Paintings of Astuvansalmi are some of the finest prehistoric rock paintings in Finland. They are on a steep rock cliff, more than 20 km east of Ristiina village. Their age is estimated to be 3000 to 4000 years, and the paintings as a whole span 60 metres. There's a walking track from the road, and cruises from Mikkeli harbour in summer.

Pien-Toijolan Talomuseo

A visit to this open-air museum should be combined with a look at the rock paintings; there is a marked trail from here. The estate dates from 1672, and consists of over 20 old houses, some of them from the 18th century. The museum is open daily in summer.

Places to Stay & Eat

Brahe (☎ 661 078) is the only place to stay in Ristiina itself. It's along the main street, at Brahentie 54. A single room is 150 mk but a youth-hostel dorm bed is just 35 mk for members – you may have to haggle to get this low price. Brahe also has a decent restaurant and provides some local nightlife. The rooms are in a separate building, previously used as a school dormitory. There are bicycles (50 mk), boats and canoes (70 mk) to rent.

Löydön kartano (☎ 664 101), five km north of Ristiina near the village of Löytö, is a pleasant hostel in an old manor house. Dormitory beds cost from 45 mk for HI members. If you are lucky, you might get a large room. A pleasant walk past fields will take you to an old lakeside sauna which you can use if you ask (sadly, it's heated by electricity). A substantial breakfast is 25 mk. Look for the sign on the main Mikkeli to Ristiina road. There's a bus stop at Kartanontie, the gravel road that takes you to the hostel. If you take a bus, write down the name and show it to the driver – it's easier than trying to pronounce it!

As long as *Brahelinna* remains closed, the only restaurants are on the northern side of Ristiina, near the main road. At the crossing, Shell and SEO petrol stations serve meals, and *Pökkälä* has beer. *Sataman valot* is another bar; it's near the information office. *Baari Vossikka* at the bus station sells coffee and beer, as well as meals from 30 to 50 mk. *Martan baari* is nicer, selling proper meals for around 40 mk as well as baked goods. It's open until 9 pm. There are a few large supermarkets.

If you make it to Pien-Toijola and the rock paintings, the nearby *Kallioniemen kesäkahvila* in a large 1897 villa is a summer café and restaurant. It's protected and worth a look even as a minor tourist attraction.

Getting There & Away

There are regular buses from Mikkeli to Ristiina. Express buses stop at the crossing only. Usually the train from the south that arrives after 9 pm in Mikkeli will be too late to catch the last bus to Ristiina. For cruises, enquire at the Mikkeli tourist office.

JUVA

The village of Juva, midway between Mikkeli and Varkaus at Lake Jukajärvi, spans several km from the main road No 5 in the west to the Partala area in the east. The village centre is along the main street, Juvantie. You can get travel information at the town hall (☎ 755 5224) at Juvantie 13, or at the sculpture exhibition (☎ 651 647) near the main road.

History

Juva was one of Savo's first inhabited areas during the 14th century. The centre of a large administrative area, it had a wooden Catholic church and large estates gradually emerged – some manor houses still remain. Unfavourable border changes during the 18th century meant a blow for Juva's trade contacts with the east, and the area declined. Population is decreasing and is currently only 8200 – more than 3000 fewer than 100 years ago, in an area twice as large as Singapore.

Things to See & Do

Just at the crossing on road No 5, **Puutaitonäyttely** has a collection of 500 wooden sculptures made by 40 artists. It is

open daily June to September from 10 am to 7 pm, and admission is 30 mk. East from here, the **water tower** is open daily in summer, and serves coffee and snacks.

Central Juva is a mainly commercial area, but the imposing 1863 church is made of stone, and is open on weekdays from 10 am to 6 pm and on weekends from 9 am to 2 pm. Nearly opposite the church, **Käsityökeskus** sells and exhibits local handicraft.

All the museums are at the east end of Juva. **Suomen Mehiläismuseo** is a national museum devoted to bee-keeping. There are 500 exhibits and on sale you'll find honey and other bee-keeping-related items. The museum is open from 1 June to 31 August daily from 11 am to 6 pm. **Vihertietokeskus** is an information centre which promotes 'green' ideas in farming and gardening.

The imposing Partala manor area houses two museums. **Juvan museo** is a local museum in the main building. **Karjalaisten museo** displays items from Soviet-occupied Karelia. These museums are open in June, July and August from 11 am to 5 pm daily except Monday. **Pikko-Pirtti** is a handicraft shop and café in a converted stable – it's closed on Sunday.

Canoeing the Vesiluontopolku Route

Previously known as Oravareitti, the Juva to Sulkava canoeing route has been renamed the 'Aquatic Nature Trail'. It's a 52-km scenic route that travels via lakes, rivers and rapids. Only one section is unpassable – at Kuhakoski rapids, where canoes must be carried 50 metres past a broken dam. Otherwise the rapids are relatively simple, though the water level drops 25 metres between Juva and Sulkava. A waterproof map in English and German is available for 25 mk, and includes all essential information. Contact Juva Camping for canoe rentals.

Places to Stay

Juva Camping (☎ 451 930) has cottages starting at 170 mk, not far from the main road No 5. You can also rent rowing boats and canoes here. *Toivio Youth Hostel* (☎ 459 622) is approximately 10 km from the village, on the Sulkava road. Dormitory beds start at 35 mk. It's open from 1 May to 30 September. Near the main road No 5, *Hotelli Juva* (☎ 651 650) has doubles for 340 mk, which includes breakfast. The place also arranges cheaper accommodation at *Kesähotelli Juva* in the village centre, at 240 mk for doubles, including breakfast in the actual hotel.

Places to Eat
Ravintola Tavast, at the tourist office in the village centre, provides inexpensive meals throughout the day. Around the corner on Kiiverintie, *Siljankka* serves coffee and cheap meals, including vegetarian dishes. There are also several pubs, grillis and cafés in Juva, including a café at the bus station.

Getting There & Away
Juva is most conveniently reached by regular northbound express bus from Mikkeli. The village itself is three km from the main road, so hitchhikers will probably end up walking all the way.

Central Savo

PIEKSÄMÄKI
Pieksämäki was recently blacklisted as the least attractive place to live in Finland. But over 13,600 people still choose to live there, and local pride is fierce. The railway junction is the reason for the town's existence – the railways employ over 1000 people in Pieksämäki.

Information
The post office is next to the railway station. The library in the Poleeni building is at the lakeside, and has a good supply of books, newspapers and magazines as well as tourist information material. It's open Monday to Friday from 9 am to 7 pm, and has a café.

Things to See & Do
The main attraction in town is the incredibly bad planning. The access route between the

railway station and the town centre is ugly to the point of being entertaining. The highlight of this town is understandably the beautiful **Lake Pieksäjärvi**, which is surrounded by lovely parks. In summer, you can swim in the lake.

The **Poleeni** cultural centre at Savontie 13 is quite impressive, and the railway station has done a great job of preserving some old locomotives. **Savon Radan museo** is located in the original railway station, built in 1889 when the railroad was opened; access is from platform No 6. The museum explains about the Savo railroad system, and is open Tuesday to Saturday from 11 am to 6 pm from the first Tuesday in June. Admission is 10 mk, and there are discounts.

Places to Stay & Eat
The cheapest place to stay in the town itself is *Gasthaus Ranta* (☎ 615 755) at Torikatu 12. It's a smallish town house on a quiet street, with singles/doubles at 170/250 mk; the price includes breakfast.

Lomapirtti (☎ 424 586) at Uistinkuja 6 is located on Lake Vangasjärvi, almost five km west from the railway station. There are 12 rooms from 150/180 mk, a restaurant and a sauna. Activities include boat and bicycle rentals.

Hotelli Savonsolmu (☎ 614 022) is an enormous establishment close to the railway station and on a headland at Toikantie 9. There are 100 rooms, from 280/360 mk, and all kinds of activities are available.

Pieksämäki has a great variety of places to eat. *JR Grillikioski* is an attractive log house close to the railway station, and serves junk food at reasonable rates. *Cantina Pedro* is a bit difficult to find on Torikatu at the market, but it's a lively Tex-Mex restaurant with beer, live music and games. Just across the corner at Keskuskatu 16, *Päärynäpuu* is a more traditional restaurant, with decent meals.

Getting There & Away
Pieksämäki is one of the busiest railway junctions, and trains arrive from four directions. Buses travel to and from Savonlinna.

Train passes are valid on most buses heading that way. Railway and bus stations are at the same spot, so changing from one to the other is usually no problem. When trains are delayed, the whole system breaks down, but all trains wait for the late services to arrive.

HEINÄVESI

The most beautiful lake route in Finland passes by the large municipality of Heinävesi (population 5100). Canals provide a means of local transport. Several attractions around Heinävesi help to make it one of the most rewarding areas to explore in Finland.

The main village lies amid hilly country. Few travellers actually stay in Heinävesi village, but its shops and tourist office make a visit worthwhile.

Information

The tourist office (☎ 578 1273) on the main street, Kermanrannantie 7, is open daily in summer from early morning to 5 pm; after 1 August, it's open on weekdays from 9 am to 4 pm.

Library Heinävesi has an excellent library where you can look at regional maps with a scale of 1:20,000, as well as imported magazines. It's open Monday to Thursday from 11 am to 7 pm, and on Friday until 5 pm.

Things to See & Do

Climb up to the **church** for views over Lake Kermajärvi. The church, built in 1892, seats 2000 people and is open daily from 15 May to 15 August from 10 am to 4 pm.

Down the hill from the church, the **local museum** has a large collection of old tools and somewhat worn-out furniture. It's open on weekends from noon to 4 pm and closes an hour earlier on weekends. Entry is 5 mk.

There is a **handicrafts centre** opposite the museum. If you don't want to buy anything, you can have a go at making your own rug. Renting a loom costs 10 mk per day, and materials a bit more, but instruction is provided free of charge. It's open Monday to Friday from 8 am to 4 pm.

Places to Stay & Eat

There is just one place to stay in the village itself. *Gasthaus* (☎ 562 411) opposite the bus terminal has singles/doubles from 290/390 mk. The rooms are very clean and comfortable, and there's a TV and mini-bar in each room. The hotel serves an excellent breakfast, which is included in the price, and the bar is the focus of local nightlife, but it won't interfere with your sleep.

There are several places to eat in Heinävesi. *Kukkopilli*, a little way up the road, is a pub and a restaurant which serves pizza and meals, and has lower rates during lunch hours. Across the street behind the post office, *Brunssi* is a simple eatery, but meals are cheap. It's open Monday to Friday from 9 am to 4 pm. Also in the centre, the Shell and Kesoil petrol stations serve snacks and meals.

Things to Buy

Most artisans hold sales exhibitions in small villages around Heinävesi. Several km south of the village, the Kerman Savi is a ceramics factory which sells a good variety of local pottery.

Getting There & Away

The bus terminal is conveniently located in the village centre; local buses travel around the lake. The railway station is five km to the south. There's a coin-operated public telephone at the station, but the old station building is now a private home, so you have to buy your ticket in the train.

From mid-June to mid-August, passenger ferries from Kuopio or Savonlinna call at the Heinävesi jetty, just below the village. The trip costs 145 mk from Kuopio, 175 mk from Savonlinna. For about 50 mk, you can cross Lake Kerma to Karvio.

AROUND HEINÄVESI

Karvio

Karvio is one of Heinävesi's main tourist centres. Attractive rapids are its highlight, and the canal serves as a jetty for ships. The rapids are good for fishing (a permit is required) and there are three choices of

SAVO

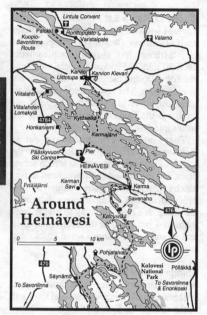

Around Heinävesi

accommodation. The Neste petrol station doubles as the Matkahuolto bus station, and tourist information and pottery are also available there. Printed T-shirts and self-made paper can be bought at Tekstiilityöpaja near Neste, which is open daily in summer until 7 pm.

Places to Stay & Eat Karvio is central enough to serve as a base for covering the northern side of Heinävesi. You can rent bicycles and rowing boats in several places, and visit Valamo and other places from here; you can also obtain fishing permits. *Karvio Camping* (☎ 563 603) is a clean place, open from 30 April to 10 September, with good four-bed cottages at 180 to 300 mk; after school holidays prices start from 90 mk. Across the road is *Uittotupa* (☎ 563 519), which has small bungalows (doubles) for 100 mk and large cottages for 300 mk. Uittotupa is renowned for its homemade bread, which can be sampled at lunch (35

mk, including salad and a drink) or purchased by the loaf. Across the bridge is *Karvion Kievari* (☎ 563 504), a pleasant old manor house with a few singles/doubles for 100/200 mk. Room No 8 has a good view of the rapids. For a splurge, try the excellent buffet lunch for 55 mk.

Getting There & Away You can get to Karvio by bus or ferry, and there is plenty of traffic for hitchhikers. There are two direct buses daily from Varkaus, with departures at 1.45 and 7.40 pm.

Kerma
You can use the Kerma canal as a jumping-off point from the ferry or bus, and proceed from here to Savenaho, also called *Wirran Wietävä* (☎ 566 251), which rents rooms from 100 mk per person. This place has a private jetty, so you can get on/off the boat right here. The smoke sauna is gone; it burned down three times until they decided not to rebuild it anymore!

Palokki
Palokki used to have a busy sawmill, but when a power station was built upriver, the river almost ran out of water and the population, deprived of its industry, dwindled. Palokki has a couple of attractions, including the convent of Lintula. **Ronttopuisto** (Brontosaur Park) features ugly iron creatures, which are popular with children, plus several small private museums. In an exhibition downstairs in the main building, you can see the work of five generations of smiths. It's open all day in summer. Behind the garden are two houses – the Paja has ironsmith's tools and the Perinneaitta displays other old objects.

Places to Stay & Eat *Ronttopuisto* (☎ 563 188) has a few pleasant cottages. Small bungalows cost 150 mk and sleep three people. The smoke sauna has a minimum charge of 150 mk. You can use the rowing boat for free. Fresh bread is baked daily, and meals are available, but you can also bring your own food and prepare it in a sheltered cooking area at the riverside.

Getting There & Away To get to Palokki, get off at the ferry dock of the same name. From Karvio, turn to road No 542 towards Tuusniemi.

Lintula

The only Orthodox convent in Finland, Lintula is much quieter than the popular Valamo monastery, described later in this chapter. Lintula was founded in Karelia in 1895 and transferred during WWII to Savo and then Häme. The nuns found the present location in 1946. You can visit from 1 May to 31 August from 9 am to 6 pm daily. The shop sells wool and candles which are manufactured at the convent. Places you can visit at Lintula include the new church, and a nice café. To get there, follow the 'Lintulan luostari' signs north from Palokki.

Places to Stay *Lintulan vierasmaja* (☎ 563 106) is a small red house at the back of the convent. There are simple but clean rooms, with separate bathroom. Both sexes may stay here, at 100/160 mk.

Pohjataipale

The best place to stay around Heinävesi is *Pohjataipaleen kartano* (☎ 566 419), the youth hostel some 13 km south of the railway station and 18 km from the village of Heinävesi. The old sauna and the rowing boat can often be used free of charge. There are only 24 beds available, at 45 to 65 mk, but the place is not always full. It's been dubbed as a paradise, and some people come back every summer. The excellent homemade food is another highlight of this fantastic place.

Getting There & Away The gravel road from Heinävesi twists and turns so ask at the tourist office about the exact route. If you call the hostel beforehand, you will be picked up from the train or bus by the friendly owners. Catching a local taxi may end up being a rip-off, so avoid it. The hostel also has a jetty,

where boats on the Heinävesi route will drop you off on request. You can also depart from Pohjataipale by boat if you lift the flagpole at the jetty. There's a schedule at the jetty.

Suuraho

In Suuraho, to the east of Valamo near road No 23, Heinäveden Yrttipaja prepares and sells herbs and other natural products. It's a good place to visit if you want to learn about mushrooms, berries or edible plants, and how to use them.

Säynämö

The last ferry dock inside the municipality of Heinävesi, *Säynämö* (☎ 567 435) is run by the Kansan Raamattuseura, a Lutheran mission. It offers beds from 85 mk per day in rooms, or cottages from 130 mk. Canoes and rowing boats are available for rent and fishing permits are sold.

Valamo Monastery

The Orthodox monastery of Uusi-Valamo (new Valamo) – the only one in Finland – is one of Savo's most popular attractions. Its history goes back 800 years to the island of Valamo on Lake Lagoda.

The original Valamo monastery was annexed by the Red Army during WWII. Most of its treasures were brought to Finland, and some of them remain here (others are in Kuopio).

New Valamo has grown considerably over the last couple of decades, partly because of increased tourism, which is the monastery's only source of income. Tuohus sells large supplies of religious souvenirs and other items in the information building. Laffka is a summer shop. Valamo is often crowded; you'll get more peace and quiet if you visit in spring or autumn.

Taking photos in the churches, or of the monks, is forbidden unless you get permission at the gate.

The two churches contain a number of priceless icons; these can be seen during monastery tours, conducted regularly in English for 20 mk per person. The new church was finished in 1977, while the old

SAVO

one was built in 1940. There are up to five services daily. Down at the riverside, the small *tsasouna*, chapel of St Nicolas, is also worth a look. The grounds around the monastery make Valamo an attractive place to relax; take a picnic. The cemetery is one km from the monastery.

Work Valamo is one of the few places in Finland to offer 'working holidays' for travellers. The work is defined as *talkoo*, which translates roughly as voluntary work. You will be provided with food and lodging only, and most people volunteer for the experience rather than for quick money. You will have to write beforehand to Valamo Monastery (☎ 570 111, fax 570 1510), Valamontie 42, FIN-79850 Uusi-Valamo, for information and application forms. The form includes questions such as 'church affiliation', and 'Why do you want to come to Valamo Monastery?' Men can work for a minimum of two weeks, while two weeks is the maximum amount of time a woman can spend there.

Places to Stay & Eat The cheapest place to stay in the monastery is in either of the two houses of *Valamon luostarin vierasmaja* (☎ 570 1504), where beds start at 100 mk, including linen. Red Guesthouse is cleaner, White Guesthouse is quainter. *Luostarihotelli* is the hotel – it has 29 rooms in two buildings, with singles/doubles costing 175/290 to 250/400 mk. The monastery suite is 600 mk. All accommodation prices include breakfast.

Trapesa has a tempting buffet for 55 mk until 9 pm, and a Russian-style 'high tea' in the evenings for 38 mk. *Papinniemen kauppa* is a local shop between Valamo and the main road, for self-catering items.

Getting There & Away You can reach Valamo from Kuopio on a Monastery Cruise. The service is available three times a week in summer and costs 240 mk return. There are also cruises from Valamo for 65 to 75 mk, including the interesting Lintula cruise (to visit the Lintula Convent). Regular buses, from Heinävesi, Joensuu, Mikkeli and even

Helsinki, will take you to the monastery, or at least drop you off at the Valamo crossing some four km from it. From Varkaus, there are two direct buses, with current departures at 1.45 and 7.40 pm.

Varistaipale

At 14.5 metres, the canal system in Varistaipale (also known as Varistaival) is the highest in Finland. It takes 45 minutes for boats to pass through the canal, going upriver.

Kanavamuseo is a canal museum, with photos and maps of several canals in Finland, as well as of old machines and tools. There is a free English-language leaflet available. The museum is open daily 10 am to 6 pm, and admission is free.

Just next to the canal, Kanavapaja sells pottery, and Korintti manufactures and sells wooden items. Shops are open daily in summer from 10 am to 8 pm.

Getting There & Away From Karvio, take road No 542 towards Tuusniemi. Cruises from Valamo will take you to Varistaipale.

Viitalahti

You can easily miss this cluster of houses on the No 4784 Heinävesi to Karvio road, but there are three places to stay. *Honkaniemi* (☎ 568 761) is a recreational facility for old people, which will accommodate individual travellers. Follow the sign that says 'Honkaniementie', and continue on for 1.7 km. Rates start from 100 mk per person. *Vänttinen* (☎ 568 723) offers rooms from 100 mk per night. Another reasonably priced place is the lakeside *Viitalahden lomakylä* (☎ 568 707) with cottages from 100 to 160 mk. The large Lipokasverstas House sells locally made honey.

LEPPÄVIRTA

Soisalo, the largest island in Finland, is surrounded by lakes, canals and rivers. Leppävirta is one of the canal towns that make the trip around Soisalo possible.

Things to See & Do

Stop at both churches along the main street, and check out the museum at the larger church, which opens daily except Monday in summer. There is also the tourist centre, Unnukka, just off the main road. This is the place to buy discounted factory products. The historic Konnus Canal, six km from the village, has an exhibition and offers fishing opportunities.

Places to Stay

Mansikkaharju Camping (☎ 554 1383), 500 metres south of Unnukka House, has cottages for 100 to 200 mk. There is a *youth hostel* (☎ 553 3032) at Tuikkalantie 6, near the bus terminal, open from mid-June to early August. There are 70 beds, all in double rooms, for 60 mk. Much more expensive is *Linnunlaulu* (☎ 553 1511), where singles/doubles cost 310/420 mk; the price includes breakfast, sauna and swimming.

Getting There & Away

Buses between Varkaus and Kuopio call at the Leppävirta bus terminal; there are several buses daily. Hitchhiking along the highway is no problem.

SUONENJOKI

Strawberry Town, home to 8600 people, attracts crowds of strawberry pickers every summer, and travellers should be able to earn some extra cash if there is a labour shortage. There is a local museum and a church near the railway station.

Information

Suonenjoki has all the essential services, located around the railway station. Tourist information is available at Herralantie 6, opposite the bus terminal.

Work

Suonenjoki is known for its strawberries and for employment opportunities in the strawberry fields. The local employment office (☎ 512 698) at Ainonkatu 2 would be your best bet, but paperwork should be arranged

in advance. (See Work in the Facts for the Visitor chapter.)

Places to Stay

The youth hostel at Koulukatu 23 was closed recently but may reopen. *Matkustajakoti Aula* (☎ 510 127) at Asemakatu 5 has a few inexpensive rooms. *Mansikkapaikka*, or 'Strawberry Place' (☎ 511 761), at Koulukatu 2 has singles/doubles for 250/350 mk.

Getting There & Away

There are several Kuopio-bound trains that stop at Suonenjoki. Catching a bus from Mikkeli, Kuopio or Pieksämäki is not a problem either.

VARKAUS

The town of Varkaus has a superb location, surrounded by water, but its centre is rather depressing, due to several huge factories that dominate the view. Over 24,000 people have made their home in Varkaus, many of them working for local paper and pulp industries. Although *varkaus* means 'stealth', Varkaus is not a dangerous place to visit! In fact, there are several reasons to come here, most notably the good museums. In summer, there is an evening market in the square – it's held on Tuesday from 4 to 8 pm.

Orientation

Varkaus has grown over several islands and headlands, and is surrounded by water. The main commercial centre is close to the central station, and is located on one street, Keskuskatu. Another centre is at the foot of the enormous pulp factory, on Ahlströminkatu. Attractions are scattered around the area. Taipale and its canal are two km east.

Information

Tourist Office The tourist information office (☎ 552 7311) is along the main street near the factories, at Kauppatori 6. In summer it's open Monday to Friday from 9 am to 6 pm and on Saturday till 2 pm. In winter it's open only during office hours.

Post & Telephone There are post offices

near the railway station, and near the tourist office at Ahlströminkatu 18.

Left Luggage Matkahuolto at the central station keeps your luggage until 6 pm for 12 mk. There are also 10-mk lockers which are accessible until the last train has departed.

Mekaanisen Musiikin Museo

If you have a vehicle, it is well worth driving the two km from the town centre to the Museum of Mechanical Music (☎ 558 0643) at Pelimanninkatu 8. A Finnish-German couple runs this delightful collection of 250 unusual musical instruments. It has been voted the best museum in Finland, but I would rather call it the funniest show. The two floors of old, carefully renovated mechanical instruments from the USA and Europe are presented in a hilarious way. There are guided tours every half-hour, if there is demand, and admission is 40 mk. The museum is open from early March to mid-December, Tuesday to Sunday from 11 am to 7 pm; in July, opening hours are 10 am to 8 pm.

Taipale

Two km east of the town centre is a canal area. The new canal was built by Russians, and the old canal area includes **Keskuskanavamuseo**, a canal museum with information on the history and use of Finnish canals. There's information in English. Even the new canal is worth a look, especially when logs are floated through it. The museum is open from 11 am to 6 pm daily. Admission is 5 mk. Cruises on the SS *Paul Wahl* leave from the northern jetty at the canal on Saturday and Sunday at 2 pm.

Other Museums

Varkaus has seen a boom in museum building, and there are currently six or seven museums here. **Varkauden museo** is the local museum at Wredenkatu 5, in the town centre. There are displays relating to local history, from archaeological finds to items from more recent phases of industrial devel-

opment. There are also temporary exhibitions upstairs. Admission is free.

Taidemuseo is the new art museum at Ahlströminkatu 15. There are temporary exhibitions.

Esa Pakarisen museo at Savontie 7, beyond the factory, is devoted to the Finnish entertainer who died in 1989. At the same address, **Työläisasuntomuseo** is a home museum of a factory worker. These museums are open on Wednesday from 3 to 7 pm, and on Thursday, Friday and Sunday from 11 am to 3 pm. There's an admission fee.

At Varkauden portti factory sales centre on road No 5, there's a private vehicle museum.

Places to Stay

As the youth hostel is now closed, there is no cheap accommodation available, unless you go to *Camping Taipale* (☎ 552 6644) and rent a cottage for three to four people, from 200 mk.

Gasthaus Joutsenkulma (☎ 556 4688) at Käärmeniementie 20 is approximately one km south of the railway station, away from the town centre. In summer, singles/doubles cost 160/250 mk; in winter, prices are a bit higher.

There have been major recent changes in the hotel scene. At one point, two of the three hotels went bankrupt. Keskus-Hotelli gained ownership of the other two, and the reception for all three is now at *Hotel Oscar* (☎ 579 011) at Kauppatori 4. Rooms there are 465/580 mk, but summer discounts are considerable. *Keskus-Hotelli*, at Ahlströminkatu 18, is a bit cheaper, with summer prices as low as 210/320 mk.

Lomakeskus Kuntoranta (☎ 552 8751) is located seven km north of Varkaus at Pussilanjoki. It's a resort with a small spa, and 101 rooms and 10 cottages. Rates are 250/340 mk.

Places to Eat

You will find snacks at the central station. Kauppakatu near the station is also good for eateries. *Herkkupizza* at Kauppakatu 18 has pizzas at 30 mk. *Kahvila Aaretti* at Kauppakatu 32 has cheap daily specials, and is open until 6 pm. Farther west at Kauppakatu 41, *Kotipizza* has you-know-what, and *Le Pont de Paris* has coffee in what is supposed to resemble a French café.

On the other side of town, Keskustori is the main place for food, including a grilli, a supermarket, *Next Step* for beer, and several restaurants in the two hotels.

For more style and class, Varkauden kotiseutukeskus runs *Ravintola Tyyskänhovi* at the southern end of Ahlströminkatu. It's open Monday to Friday until 5 pm, and on weekends until 3 pm.

If you venture into the church area, you'll find *Niittylän hovi* at Savontie 5. It's a nice old house which serves a buffet lunch from Monday to Friday, and à la carte meals at weekends.

Getting There & Away

There are several flights a day from Helsinki to Varkaus. Keskusliikenneasema is the central station, which includes railway and bus stations, and a taxi office. Transport to the airport goes from here, but has to be pre-booked. Note that the train and bus offices close quite early in the afternoon so get there early if you need any special tickets. Trains between Joensuu and Turku stop in Varkaus five times daily in each direction.

Kuopio

Kuopio is the undisputed centre of North Savo, and one of the major lake shipping centres in Finland. Views from Puijo Hill are as unforgettable as the bustling Kuopio Market or the treasures of the Orthodox Church Museum. With a population of 84,000, the town is large enough to have a culture of its own and plenty of attractions. Accommodation is available in all price categories, so you could spend several days in Kuopio.

History

The earliest discoveries indicate that there has been habitation in the Kuopio region for at least 1000 years. The first Savonian people entered the area at the end of the 15th century. In 1552 the first church was built on the peninsula, which probably got its present name from the Skopa family, who were local priests. In 1652 the ambitious Count Per Brahe founded the 'church village' of Kuopio, which had little significance until 1775, when Gustav III of Sweden incorporated Kuopio as a provincial capital. Several important figures of the National Romantic era lived here from the 1850s, but the main growth of Kuopio has occurred during the 20th century.

Orientation

Kuopio spans an extensive area around Puijo Hill. Bus and railway stations are at the northern edge of the town centre, within walking distance of most places. The market square is the lifeblood of Kuopio.

Information

Tourist Office The tourist information office (☎ 182 584) at Haapaniemenkatu 17 is easy to find, next to the town hall. In summer it's open Monday to Friday from 8 am to 5 pm and on Saturday from 9 am to 1 pm. In winter, it's open weekdays from 8.30 am to 4 pm.

Nuorisokeskus at Kauppakatu 44 is an 'International Meeting Place' which provides information, showers, laundry facilities and free left-luggage storage. It's open from early July to mid-August, Monday to Friday.

Post & Telephone The main post office is at Kuninkaankatu 19, 70100 Kuopio. The market post office is open Monday to Friday from 9 am to 6 pm. It has public telephones.

Library The public library at Maaherrankatu 12 has a large collection of records to listen to, and plenty of travel books upstairs. For 1:20,000 maps of the region, enquire at the *neuvonta* desk in the Opintolukusali room.

SAVO

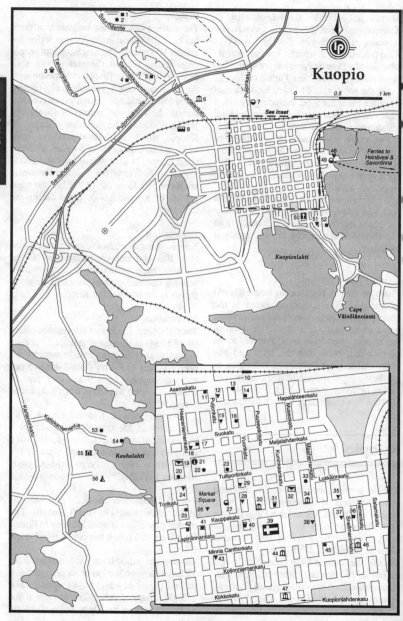

Kuopio

0   0.5   1 km

See Inset

Ferries to
Heinävesi &
Savonlinna

Kuopionlahti

Cape
Väinölänniemi

Rauhalahti

Inset:

Asemakatu
Hapelähteenkatu
Haapaniemenkatu
Puijonkatu
Suokatu
Vuorikatu
Puistokatu
Maljalahdenkatu
Museokatu
Maaherrankatu
Kuninkaankatu
Tulliportinkatu
Lukkarinkatu
Satamakatu
Niemenkatu
Snellmaninkatu
Torikatu
Market
Square
Kauppakatu
Lapinlinnankatu
Minna Canthinkatu
Koljonniemenkatu
Kirkkokatu
Kuopionlahdenkatu

Suurtorintie
Sammakkolammentie
Taivaanmartontie
Karjalankatu
Puijonlaaksontie
Puijonkatu
Sivenähdentie
Kallaniemientie
Karlanonkatu

PLACES TO STAY		24	Trube & Carrols	8	Swimming Hall
		26	Kauppahalli	10	Railway Station
1	Hotelli Puijo	28	Amarillo	13	Finnair
3	Tekma	29	Burger Park	19	Market Post Office
4	Savonia	31	Vanha Trokari &	20	Suomalainen
5	Kievari Matias		Kuopion Uusi		Kirjakauppa
11	Cumulus		Panimo	21	Tourist Office
14	Puijo-Hovi	35	Vapaasatama Sampo	22	Town Hall
16	Matkakoti Souvari	37	Pikku Haapis	23	R-kioski
17	Hospitsi		Hirvenpää Bub	27	Finnair Buses
25	Hotelli Atlas	38	Snellu-Grilli	30	Kuopion Taidemuseo
36	Hotelli Jahti	40	Henry's Pub & Pasta	32	Post Office
42	Hotelli Kuopionhovi		Factory	33	Public Library
45	Sokos Hotel Puijonsarvi	41	Burts Cafee	34	Kuopion Museo
52	Arctia Hotel Kuopio	43	Kummisetä	39	Lutheran Church
53	Rauhalahti	48	Wanha Satama	44	Valokuvakeskus
56	Rauhalahti Camping	51	Musta Lammas	46	Snellmanin kotimuseo
				47	Korttelimuseo
PLACES TO EAT		OTHER		49	Passenger Harbour
				50	Orthodox Church
9	University Restaurant	2	Puijo	54	Smoke Sauna
12	Kotipizza	6	Orthodox Church	55	Rauhalahti Manor
15	Zorbas		Museum		
18	Tramps	7	Bus Station		

The library is open Monday to Friday from 9 am to 7 pm and on Saturday till 3 pm.

Bookshops Suomalainen Kirjakauppa on Tulliportinkatu near the market sells books. Imported newspapers and magazines are available at R-kioski near the market at Tulliportinkatu 29, and at the bus station.

Travel Agencies The VR travel agency is located at the railway station. Finnair has an office opposite the railway station.

Left Luggage The railway station has 10-mk lockers, but Nuorisokeskus keeps your gear for free.

Emergency Services In a general emergency phone ☎ 112, and for a doctor ring ☎ 10023. There's a pharmacy at Puijonkatu 23. There are clinics at Niuvantie 4 and Tulliportinkatu 17 C.

Puijo

The symbol and pride of Kuopio, Puijo Hill and its observation tower should not be missed. The lift up to the top costs 15 mk and can be taken until midnight in June and July

and until 10 pm in August. There are excellent views of Lake Kallavesi and beyond. The Puijo area has one of the best-preserved spruce forests in the region. The whole area has been divided into several areas of activity to keep everyone happy. There are several walks, including a marked nature trail, facilities for winter sports, and even a golf course. To get there, follow the road past the bus terminal. If you're fit you could walk or cycle there; if not, take taxi bus No 6.

Orthodox Church Museum

This is one of the most interesting museums in Finland. Its collections were brought to the present territory of Finland from monasteries, churches and *tsasouni* (chapels) in USSR-occupied Karelia. With artefacts dating from the 10th century, this is the most notable collection of Eastern Orthodox icons, textiles and religious objects outside Russia. The museum is one km west from the railway station, at Karjalankatu 1. It's open daily (except Monday) from May to August from 10 am to 4 pm; in winter, it's open from Monday to Friday between noon and 3 pm and at weekends from noon to 5 pm. Entry is 15 mk, 10 mk for students. Take bus No 7.

Kuopion Museo

At Kauppakatu 23 is a beautiful Art-Nouveau building which houses the Kuopio Museum. It is recommended for its archaeological and cultural displays. The 2nd floor has an extensive collection of stuffed animals. It's open on Wednesday from 9 am to 8 pm, on Sunday from 11 am to 6 pm, and on other days from 9 am to 4 pm. Entry is 15 mk. There's an English-language guidebook available.

Nearby, **Kuopion Taidemuseo** at Kauppakatu 35 is the Art Museum of Kuopio, featuring mostly modern art in temporary exhibitions. It is open daily. Admission is 15 mk.

Yet another branch of Kuopio Museum, **Snellmanin kotimuseo**, is in an old house at Snellmaninkatu 19, where Mr JV Snellman, an important cultural figure during the National Romantic era of the 19th century, used to live. The museum is similar to Korttelimuseo, but less interesting. It's open daily from mid-May to August from 10 am to 5 pm. Admission is 10 mk.

Korttelimuseo

The block of old town houses (entrance at Kirkkokatu 22) is another of Kuopio's delightful museums. It consists of several homes – all with period furniture and décor – seven of which are open at present. Apteekkimuseo in building No 11 could easily be a museum in its own right, since it contains old pharmacy paraphernalia – with luck you'll hear stories about them. There is also a nice museum café, where you can have coffee and taste the delicious *rahkapiirakka*. The museum is open from 15 May to 15 September daily from 10 am to 5 pm, with hours extended on Wednesday till 7 pm. In winter, it's open daily (except Monday) from 10 am to 3 pm.

Valokuvakeskus

The photographic centre at Kuninkaankatu 14-16 is devoted to Victor Barsokevitsch, who was a local portrait photographer. His studio is now a photo gallery, but there are enough old cameras and photos to call this a museum. In the garden, you can enjoy a cup of coffee in summer, and be astounded by the camera obscura, a scientific phenomenon in which the surrounding scenery is reflected through a hole in a darkened room. The place is open daily in summer, and is kept open year round.

Rauhalahti

The accommodation centre has grown around the Rauhalahti manor, which has been converted to a children's park called Uppo-Nalle, after the bear in Elina Karjalainen's fairy tales. Even if you've never heard of this bear and its wonderful adventures, the whole area is full of activities for bored children. Uppo-Nallen koti is a fantasyland created inside an old red house, and there's a café with a playroom, and handicraft for sale. The area is open in summer from noon to 8 pm, and a 10-mk admission fee applies.

Lake Cruises

Roll Cruises dominate the daily cruises from June to late August on Lake Kallavesi. The MS *Ukko* sails three times a day, and the SS *Lokki* has three cruises from Tuesday to Sunday. These cruises cost approximately 60 mk, and last two to three hours. There are also winery cruises which include wine tasting. Tickets for all cruises are available at the harbour.

The SS *Leppävirta* does three two-hour cruises daily. The best deal would be the smoke-sauna cruise on Tuesday, which costs 75 mk for the cruise, sauna and towel rent. Departure is at 6 pm.

Festivals

There are several events in Kuopio, but the 'Kuopio tanssii ja soi' Dance Festival in late June and early July is the most international and the most interesting. For information, contact Kuopio Tanssii ja Soi (☎ 282 1541, fax 261 1990), Torikatu 18, 70110 Kuopio.

Places to Stay – bottom end

You can find cheap accommodation in cottages at *Rauhalahti Camping* (☎ 361 2244);

the cost is from 130 mk for two people. Four people can stay in cottages that cost 210 mk per night. There are 90 cottages, and a large reduction is available for subsequent nights. The camping ground has a smoke sauna where you can bathe at 50 mk per person – though sometimes a minimum person rule applies here. Tent charges start from 35 mk per person. There are bicycles and many kinds of boats for rent. The youth hostel of the same name is in the middle category.

Tekma (☎ 222 925) at Taivaanpankontie 14B, on a hill above the university area, is the youth hostel nearest to town. It was closed in 1995, but it's worth getting into if it reopens.

Places to Stay – middle

There are three matkakoti hostels near the railway station. The nearest is *Puijo-Hovi* (☎ 261 4943) at Vuorikatu 35, where singles/doubles cost 120/180 mk. Try bargaining on weekends. Another option is *Matkakoti Souvari* (☎ 262 2144) at Vuorikatu 42, almost across the street. Singles/doubles are 150/200 mk, and lower prices apply when things are quiet. The best value is *Hospitsi* (☎ 261 4501) at Myllykatu 4, a bit closer to the market square. It is an old house with a certain character, and singles/doubles start at 90/180 mk.

To the south of Kuopio, *Rauhalahti* (☎ 361 1700) at Katiskaniementie 8 is a superb hotel and spa that has accommodation for HI members. The Finnhostel, open year round, has beds for 135 mk. This may sound like a lot but you get your own room with a well-equipped kitchen, an enormous breakfast (all-you-can-eat, including salmon, sausages and fruit) and a morning sauna (in the spa). The reception may not be the friendliest you have seen, and finding your room may be a problem, but everything's very clean and efficient, and the location is quiet. You can also stay in the hotel (from 310/410 mk in summer), or try the large smoke sauna that has public bathing on Tuesday. To get to Rauhalahti, take bus No 6 all the way to the hotel (runs only for two months in summer), or bus No 19 which

stops close by, or No 16, 20 or 21 to the Kartanontie crossing with a walk of almost one km. Some long-distance buses from the south will drop you off at this bus stop.

Kievari Matias (☎ 282 8333), outside the town centre at Hiihtäjäntie 11, has modern, clean singles/doubles for 180/260 mk, breakfast and morning sauna included.

The SS *Leppävirta* at the harbour rents cabins at 100 mk per person in summer. Ask around for other boats, too.

Places to Stay – top end

Despite a number of bankruptcies, there are still several good hotels in Kuopio.

Arctia Hotel Kuopio (☎ 195 111) at Satamakatu 1 is a large building on the shores of Kallavesi. There are 137 rooms, several restaurants and saunas, and a pool. Rooms are from 430 mk, including breakfast.

Hotelli Atlas (☎ 261 7133) is a renovated hotel at Haapaniemenkatu 22 right at the market. Singles/doubles cost 260/340 mk, including breakfast and sauna.

Cumulus (☎ 154 111) is close to the railway station at Puijonkatu 32. There are 143 rooms, two restaurants, three saunas and a swimming pool. Singles/doubles in this large hotel are 420/475 mk, or 345 mk in summer and on weekends.

Hotelli Jahti (☎ 263 2822) at Snellmaninkatu 23 is a smallish but very clean hotel not far from the harbour. There is a restaurant and a sauna. Singles/doubles cost 290/350 but there are discounts in summer and on weekends.

Hotelli Kuopionhovi (☎ 261 8800) at Haapaniemenkatu 20 is another very central hotel. The place has several popular eateries. Rooms are 250/320 mk, or less on weekends.

Hotelli Puijo (☎ 261 4841). This hotel on top of Puijo Hill was originally built in the 1920s. Singles/doubles are 270/330 mk, including breakfast, sauna and free entry to the tower.

Savonia (☎ 225 333) is a hotelier's training college and is located on the western side of the motorway (freeway) at Sammakkolammentie 2. Rooms cost 280/340 mk.

Sokos Hotel Puijonsarvi (☎ 170 111) is centrally located at Minna Canthinkatu 16. It has innovative architecture, and there are restaurants across the street which are part of the hotel. There are 230 rooms, 26 saunas (four of them are public, the rest are in individual hotel rooms) and a host of other features. There are rooms in the older section from 370 mk in summer, and in the new section from 415 mk.

Places to Eat

There are indoor and outdoor markets in the main square where you can try kalakukko, a local fish inside a rye loaf (eaten cold or hot), or buy fresh fruit, coffee and snacks. The nearby *Trube* at the Sokos building near the market has the best pastries and cakes. *Carrols* hamburger restaurant has a good location next door. Behind the Kauppahalli building, *Burts Cafee* rivals Trube.

For lunch specials, hunt for places where locals eat. On the narrow alley of Käsityönkatu, you'll find *Henry's Pub* and *Pasta Factory*, as well as *Amarillo* and *Burger Park*. These places offer a great variety of food that should suit almost everyone. *Zorbas* at Puijonkatu 37 could be described as a Savonian-Greek restaurant. It offers weekday lunch specials at 34 mk – salad, bread and coffee included.

If you want to try something local, go to *Vapaasatama Sampo* at Kauppakatu 13, the oldest restaurant in Kuopio (over 65 years old, in fact). It is a smoky place, and not the friendliest one I have visited, but it serves muikku (whitefish) in various forms and charges 42 to 55 mk for a meal.

By far the most attractive gourmet restaurant is the vaulted *Musta Lammas* at Satamakatu 4, where some dishes are under 100 mk. It's open Monday to Saturday from 5 pm to midnight only.

Snellu-Grilli in the church park on Maaherrankatu has tasty junk food at reasonable rates. Nearby, *Vanha Trokari* on Kauppakatu is a stylish pub associated with *Kuopion Uusi Panimo*, the new local brewery.

Opposite Hotelli Jahti on Snellmaninkatu, *Pikku Haapis Hirvenpää Bub* is nothing special but the lunch is quite inexpensive. You'll spot it by the stuffed elk's head above the entrance.

For beer, *Wanha Satama* at the harbour is a lively pub. Check out *Tramps*, a pub-cum-restaurant at Maljalahdenkatu 35, behind the town hall. Previously known as Foggy's, this place is no longer very popular. Very popular is *Kummisetä*, another pub-cum-restaurant, at Minna Canthinkatu 44. It is more expensive, but on sunny summer days its terrace is really packed.

Getting There & Away

Air There are half a dozen direct flights from Helsinki to Kuopio every day.

Bus The busy bus terminal just next to the railway station serves the entire southern half of Finland, with regular departures to all major towns and villages in the vicinity. Each destination has its own platform.

Train Five trains a day run to Kuopio from Helsinki, 465 km away. The fastest connection takes just 4½ hours. Kouvola, Pieksämäki, Iisalmi and Kajaani also have direct trains to Kuopio.

Boat Passenger and cruise ferries depart from the passenger harbour, 500 metres east of the cathedral. Roll Cruises operates several cruises and a few routes. From mid-June to mid-August, Tuesday to Sunday, ferries depart at 9.30 am for Savonlinna, with stops along the way. This trip, 12 hours in total, goes through practically virgin countryside, traversing narrow straits and several canals. For 18 mk, you can take your bicycle. The trip costs 135 mk to Karvio (for Valamo Monastery) and 280 mk to Savonlinna. It is also possible to stay overnight before or after the journey. Cabin bunks start at 100 mk per person. Lunch and dinner are available, but meals are expensive, and the food is not good either, so bring your own. A bar is open throughout the journey.

Another possibility is a Monastery Cruise with Roll Cruises. You travel on two ferries, with bus transport to/from Valamo and Lintula monasteries. This cruise operates from early June to early August and leaves from Tuesday to Sunday at 10 am, returning at 9.30 pm. The price is 270 mk per person.

Getting Around

To/From the Airport Finnair runs airport buses which depart from the airport after each aeroplane arrival. From Kuopio, buses leave from the market at the Anttila building 65 minutes before each departure.

Bus The extensive local bus network comes in handy for excursions in and around Kuopio. There are timetables available for 5 mk. A single ticket currently costs 9 mk but price hikes are frequent. On Sunday, an elevated rate of 13 mk applies. Some of the buses travel beyond Kuopio City limits, and rates are higher.

North Savo

SIILINJÄRVI
Almost 20,000 people live in Siilinjärvi, but that doesn't make it a very special place to visit. It probably has one of the ugliest commercial centres in Finland – built on a low hill and surrounded by extensive road systems, the buildings reflect the lavish construction style of the 1980s. Most people live as far from the centre as possible.

Having said that, I discovered a youth hostel and a café in Siilinjärvi that are among the best in Finland. A beautiful 1923 church is opposite the bus station (open from 9 am to 3.30 pm), and there's a modern library nearby.

Fontanella (☎ 462 1200) is the only real attraction in the centre of Siilinjärvi. It's a new spa with fantastic architecture. Admission costs from 30 to 58 mk and you get three hours in there.

South of Siilinjärvi, **Kasurila** (☎ 461 6100) is a local downhill skiing centre, although it doesn't exactly rival Alpine standards. The Shell petrol station has meals, and serves as a landmark along the secondary road No 559.

Places to Stay & Eat
From the commercial centre, walk across the bridge from behind the Esso petrol station to Tarinaharju, go past an old hospital and follow the signs to *Pikku-Tarina* (☎ 462 3022). One of the finest youth hostels in Finland, it opened in 1995 and doubles as a

conference hotel. Always request hostel accommodation, which is 45 mk for members (though beds in good doubles are more expensive). Spotlessly clean and friendly, it is in a manor-like old hospital building, surrounded by pine trees and a golf course. There are proper meals and alcohol available, and the breakfast is generous. The sauna is electric. From the railway station, turn south (left) and then right to Tarinantie.

Hotelli Sandels (☎ 462 1422) is right in the centre of town between the bus and railway stations at Toritie 1. At first glance it looks sleazy, but it's clean and comfortable. There are two restaurants in the building and 19 rooms, with singles/doubles from 220/320 mk. Some rooms are larger than others.

Kotikahvila Käskassara at Asematie 6, not far from the railway station (turn right), is definitely the best place to have a cup of coffee and enjoy some home-made confectionery. There's also a special playroom for children. Unfortunately, the café is closed on Monday.

Matkasiili is a restaurant at the bus terminal. There are quite a few eateries in the commercial centre, such as *Rosso*, *Kotipizza*, *Vanha Kettu* and a few others. The best is *Fontis* in the Fontanella spa, although it's not the cheapest.

Getting There & Away
Siilinjärvi is 20 km north of Kuopio, and bus No 33 (from behind the Kuopio town hall) will take you to the commercial centre. Catch bus No 34 on Sunday. All trains stop at Siilinjärvi, and the station is well within walking distance to everything in town (except Kasurila).

LAPINLAHTI
Lapinlahti enjoys a scenic location surrounded by Savonian waters. Over 8000 people live here. The church is open daily in summer from noon to 5 pm.

Eemil Halosen Museo
The Halonen family lived in Lapinlahti, and several members became known nationally

some 100 years ago. Pekka Halonen was the most famous of them, and this museum displays sculptures by Pekka's cousin Eemil Halonen, who was one of the most notable Finnish sculptors of the early 20th century. The museum is on Eemil Halosentie, not far from the village centre. An enormous number of sculptures are on display in an old cow shed, and it's well worth a visit.

The museum is open daily 10 am to 6 pm (in July until 8 pm). On Saturday the museum closes at 4 pm. Admission is 15 mk, and there is a 50% discount for students. The nearby **Taidemuseo** (art museum) on Suistamontie arranges temporary exhibitions and has similar opening hours and an admission fee of 10 mk, more during special exhibitions.

Käsityöläisaukio

The 'artisan centre' across the tunnel from the centre, at Juhani Ahontie 5, has a number of interesting studios and handicraft sales points to visit. Käsityökeskus is the central sales exhibition, and across the pedestrian street you will find such gems as the TBK gemstone studio with its superb expertise on geology and precious stones.

Places to Stay & Eat

Nerkkoon retkeilymaja (☎ 35281), some eight km north of Lapinlahti on road No 5, started in 1994 in a brand-new school building. The youth hostel is open from early June to early August, daily until 11 pm, and there are beds from 35 mk for HI members. There's a café and art exhibitions. The better house includes a well-equipped kitchen.

In the very south end of Lapinlahti at the Neste petrol station, *Matin ja Liisan Asema* (☎ 732411) includes an old locomotive, and the *Viskuri* shop sells food items. There are just five rooms at 190/290 mk. Each room has a TV and shower. The restaurant serves all-day lunches from 28 to 45 mk.

Some two km south-west from the railway station, *Portaanpään retkeilyhotelli* (☎ 731 441) is an old manor-like building with singles/doubles at 130/160 mk if you bring your own sheets. There are meals available.

The place is open from 1 June to 15 August daily until 9 pm.

Restaurants in the centre include *Iloinen Viiri*, *Resiina* and *Bella*.

Getting There & Away

All trains stop at the railway station in Lapinlahti. The most scenic route is from Pielavesi (road No 77) via Martikkala, and then by (free) ferry across the Akkalansalmi strait.

IISALMI

Iisalmi (population 24,000), 85 km north of Kuopio, is the regional centre for Upper Savo. It is known for its Olvi Brewery and annual beer festival, but there are also several historic places around the town. During the 18th century, the area became known for the Runni 'health springs', and in 1808 one of the successful (for Finland, that is) battles against the Russians was fought in Koljonvirta, near Iisalmi.

Orientation

Savonkatu, directly opposite the railway station, is the main street and in summer is partly pedestrianised. The lakeside area near the brewery is home to several restaurants and is easily the nicest area in Iisalmi. Koljonvirta, five km north of Iisalmi, is another tourist centre.

Information

Tourist Office The tourist office at Kauppakatu 22 (☎ 150 1223) is open in summer from Monday to Friday from 8 am to 6 pm and on Saturday from 10 am to 2 pm. In winter it's open until 3.30 pm.

Post & Telephone The post office is at the market at Riistakatu 5, 74100 Iisalmi.

Library There's a good public library at Kirkkopuistonkatu 9.

Books & Maps Suomalainen Kirjakauppa at Savonkatu 19 sells books, maps, and imported newspapers and magazines.

Left Luggage You can store your bag in a locker at the railway station for 10 mk.

Emergency Services In a general emergency phone ☎ 112, and for a doctor ring ☎ 10023. There's a pharmacy at Savonkatu 15.

Evakkokeskus

This exhibition at Kirkkopuistonkatu 28 displays icons and miniature models of Orthodox churches and tsasounas from (Russian) Karelia. The name translates roughly as 'Refugee Centre', and the place concentrates on the Orthodox heritage of the Karelian areas. Some of the icons had lain forgotten in attics and barns, and were later discovered to be valuable. The restaurant is decorated with frescoes by a Greek painter. It's open daily (except Monday) year round; hours in summer are noon to 6 pm. Admission is 15 mk.

The church has beautiful illustrations which were painted in 1995 by a Russian. The church is open in summer daily from 10.30 am to 4.30 pm. At other times, ask at the Artos hotel.

Local Museum

This small museum not far from the town centre is open from noon to 8 pm daily.

Brewery Museum

This museum at the harbour was the first brewery museum in the Nordic countries. It's open daily from 1 May to 30 September, from 10 am to 9 pm. Entry is free.

Places to Stay

The cheapest place to stay in Iisalmi, and one of the cleanest, is *NNKY retkeilymaja*, or YWCA youth hostel (☎ 13586), at Sarvikatu 4C, open from 1 June to 8 August. Accommodation costs 55 mk per person in doubles, and you can use the sauna for 30 mk. There is a shared kitchen and bathroom for every three rooms.

The cheapest hotel is *Artos* (☎ 12244) at Kyllikinkatu 8, with singles/doubles from 195/290 mk on weekends (290/360 mk at

other times). The 'backpacker package' includes dinner and breakfast, and is available for 290/420 mk. The hotel is run by the Orthodox Church, and has loads of atmosphere.

Koljonvirta (☎ 23511) at Savonkatu 18 costs 350 mk per room. This is a modern Sokos hotel with excellent rooms.

Seurahuone (☎ 15501) at Savonkatu 24 has singles/doubles for 250/350 mk in summer. This is the traditional 'society house' hotel that every old town seems to have. Rooms are OK now, although the lobby and the restaurant are a bit worn.

Places to Eat

Iisalmi offers good value for money. The cheapest meals are available at the railway station; for 28 mk you get a decent meal, including extras.

Savonkatu has several places, including *Rosso* and *Blue Moon* at Savonkatu 17, which do lunch for 30 mk, including all extras. Game and smoked food are the specialities.

Good cafés include *Café Emilia* at Savonkatu 22, which serves kulibiakka (salmon pie), inexpensive lunch and a variety of imported beer. *Iisoppi* is another popular café.

Olutmestari at the harbour is not very cheap, but its terrace seats 300 people and the brewery museum is upstairs. The nearby *Korkki* is the smallest restaurant in the world, with a wide variety of drinks available. Across the strait at the brewery, *Oluthalli* is a grandiose project with a large beer hall and a fine dining restaurant, plus a section of the brewery museum in the premises.

Timosaurus at Kilpivirrantie 1, one km north of the town centre, is an Esso petrol station open 24 hours a day. It serves meals for about 30 mk, including salad, coffee and bread.

Getting There & Away

Bus Iisalmi is the hub for bus traffic in Upper Savo, and a link between West Coast and North Karelia, so you can catch buses from

Joensuu in the east or from Kokkola, Raahe or Oulu in the west.

Train There are five trains a day from Helsinki to Iisalmi, via Lahti, Mikkeli and Kuopio. Coming from the north, you can reach Iisalmi from Oulu, Kajaani or even Ylivieska in the west.

AROUND IISALMI
Koljonvirta
The riverside village of Koljonvirta was the scene of a battle between Finland and Russia on 27 October 1808. Here the Finns defeated the Russians for once, killing or injuring almost 1000 Russians and losing just 33 men. There are several war memorials in the area. Koljonvirta has a camping ground, and you can walk the 2.5-km Mansikkaniemi track.

Juhani Aho Museum This museum honours a local author, who was born in 1861 and lived here as a child. There are old houses and 500 items on display. The museum is open from 1 May to 31 August from 9 am to 1 pm and 2 to 6 pm daily. Admission is 10 mk.

Church The old church, a 1.5-km walk from Koljonvirta, was built in 1779 and features 20 paintings by Mikael Toppelius. The bell tower dates from the 1650s. The church is open daily in summer from 11 am to 6 pm.

Places to Stay *Koljonvirran Camping* (☎ 49161) has two-bed huts for 135 mk and four-bed ones from 180 mk. It's an idyllic spot and well worth staying at for a night or two. Adjacent to the precinct, there is an exhibition of wooden sculptures from previous sculpture festivals.

Runni
This village, 23 km west of Iisalmi, has a spa, and a 1.3-km walking track which will take you to the Kiurujoki River and the spring from which the place derives its name (*brunn* is Swedish for a natural spring). The MS *Pepsi* will take you to Runni and back on Wednesday, Friday and Sunday for 50 mk, and there are cruises on Lake Iisjärvi on Tuesday and Thursday for 45 mk.

Places to Stay The traditional *Runnin terveyskylpylä* (☎ 768 751) has various spa-treatment possibilities, including pools and spring water with high iron content. The hotel has rooms for 385/550 mk, but walk-in prices may be as low as 180 mk.

SONKAJÄRVI
This isolated place is becoming known for its most unusual summer event, the national wife-carrying championships. The place is worth a visit as a side-trip between Iisalmi and Kajaani (an extra 15 km of driving), and there are several attractions. The population is 5800.

The first thing that strikes you is the huge library, designed by Ms Saara Juola and finished in 1994. It's open daily except Sunday from noon to 7 pm (closing at 5 pm on Friday and 3 pm on Saturday), and stocks *Newsweek*.

The parking area opposite the Art-Nouveau church (open Monday to Friday until 3.30 pm) denotes the crossing for **Pullomuseo**, an international bottle museum. There are hundreds of bottles from many countries, and the display is well set out. The museum is open from 1 June to 31 August daily (except Monday) from 10 am to 6 pm. Admission is 10 mk. The 18th century building nearby houses the local museum which displays old cameras and traditional tools. Admission is free.

Places to Stay & Eat
There is nothing in Sonkajärvi, but farther north *Hirvijärvi* (☎ 82126) has cottages, and at Sukeva *Motelli Yökyöpeli* (☎ 81151) is a roadhouse with five rooms for 150/250 mk. Also in Sukeva, *Lohiranta* (☎ 82125) has cottages.

Restaurant *Hollivoot* is Savonian spelling of Hollywood, and commemorates some Finnish movies that were filmed in Sonkajärvi. *Justiina* and *Raileri* are normal hamburger joints.

Top: Steamship dock, Kuopio
Left: Taipale Canal and logs being floated, Varkaus
ight: Late evening in the Ruunaa area, Lieksa

Top: Vuonislahti Youth Hostel, southern Lieksa
Left: Coffee brewing, Ruunaa area, Lieksa
Right: Logs waiting to be transported downriver, Lieksa

AMERIIKKA

When 'everybody' was departing from Finland to the distant and promising new land, America, a strange restlessness attacked a poor peasant in the northern wilderness of Vieremä in Upper Savo. One morning, the uneducated farmer took his horse and left for America. Late in the evening when the sun was shining just above the horizon, he grew tired and decided that this must be America. He settled down, and lived there until his death. Since then, the place has been called Ameriikka ('AH-meh-reek-kah').

Today, Ameriikka, 10 km west of Vieremä on road No 5951, boasts a **Horse-Carriage Museum**, open from mid-May to 31 August daily from 10 am to 6 pm.

North Karelia

There is no area in Finland like North Karelia, or Karjala as it is called in Finnish. When Finland lost the Karelian Isthmus and the Salla region after WWII, this province was the only part of Karelia to remain Finnish territory. Some 500,000 Karelian refugees had to be settled in Finland after WWII.

Under the shadow of the Soviet Union, Karjala was a taboo subject. Starting a discussion about how and when Karelia should be returned to Finland was a definite end to any political career.

All nations have their symbols and their nationalistic dawn. For Finns, Karelia provided both. The wild Karelian 'outback' inspired artists during the National Romantic era, from Sibelius, the composer, to Gallén-Kallela, the painter. This sparsely populated frontier region (just 175,000 people live in the province these days) does its best to live up to all Karelian legends.

For the traveller, it is a unique region where you can meet friendly people, visit beautiful Orthodox churches and take advantage of the good facilities provided along trekking paths.

HISTORY

The first known people in North Karelia were Sami people, who travelled through the area about 5000 years ago. The first permanent settlers arrived from the relatively densely populated area around Lake Lagoda about 1000 years ago.

In 1227, a crusade from Novgorod (in present-day Russia) forcibly baptised Karelians to the Orthodox faith, sparking skirmishes that did not end until the Treaty of Nöteborg in 1323 established Novgorod's suzerainty over the region.

Karelians have survived constant war with both Sweden and Russia. In 1617 Swedes annexed much of Karelia. North Karelia was constantly attacked by Russia and religious

Highlights

- Extensive trekking routes in unspoiled wilderness.
- Canoeing routes along the Pankasaari and Jongunjoki Rivers.
- Pielisen Museum in Lieksa, probably the best open-air museum in Finland.
- Views of Lake Pielinen and surrounds from Koli hill.
- Old Karelian traditions in and around Ilomantsi.
- The now-accessible frontier land of far east Finland.

intolerance forced Orthodox believers across the border into Russia. The Treaty of Uusikaupunki in 1721 saw North Karelia remain Swedish territory and South Karelia fall to Russian feudalism.

Much of the *Kalevala* is based on Karelian folklore and poetry: its author, Elias Lönnrot, found excellent oral traditions around Ilomantsi.

Modern development has been late to North Karelia; old traditions still survive beneath the surface.

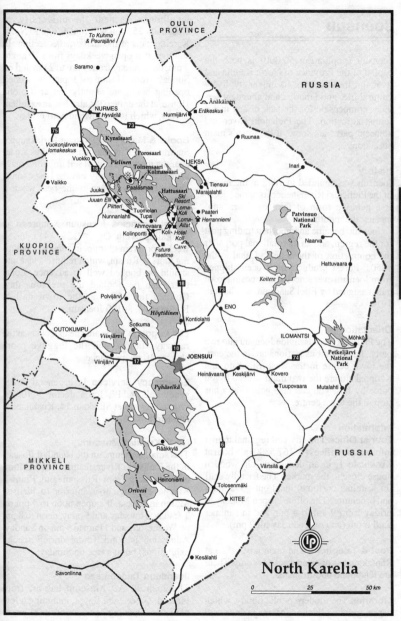

North Karelia

Joensuu

Joensuu (population 50,000) is both the capital of the Province of North Karelia and its major travel centre. Its university, lively cultural life, good market and abundant services compensate for the lack of any major tourist attraction. The Pielisjoki River and adjacent parks are some of the town's main attractions.

History

Joensuu was founded in 1848 at the mouth of the Pielisjoki River, hence its name ('joen' is a genitive form of joki, or river; 'suu' means 'the mouth').

Joensuu became an important trading post for the region, and an international port after the completion of the Saimaa Canal in the 1850s. Forest products have been shipped from Joensuu ever since. The imposing town hall, designed by Eliel Saarinen, was built in 1914.

Orientation

The Pielisjoki rapids divide Joensuu into two parts. Train and bus stations are in the east, the town centre in the west. Siltakatu and Kauppakatu are the two main streets. If you come by bus, you can also get off at a bus stop in the town centre.

Information

Tourist Office The city and regional tourist information offices (☎ 167 5300) are both at Koskikatu 1, in an decorative old wooden house close to the market. The friendly staff (in Karelian costume) hand out good maps and brochures. The office is open Monday to Friday from 9 am to 4 pm, and in summer until 6 pm (and on Saturday till 2 pm).

Post & Telephone The main post office at Rantakatu 6 is open on weekdays only. There are telephone booths inside.

Libraries The modern public library, which has a good collection of magazines and handbooks, is near the university, at Koskikatu 25. You will find 1:20,000 North Karelia maps at the käsikirjasto section. In summer, it is open weekdays from 10 am to 7 pm, on Saturday from 9 am to 2 pm and on Sunday from 11 am to 3 pm. In winter, opening hours are slightly longer. Carelia House, at the university, also has an excellent library, which is open Monday to Friday.

Books & Maps Akateeminen Kirjakauppa, Suomalainen Kirjakauppa, and Sokos are all near the market. They all sell imported magazines. Sokos currently has the best choice, although Akateeminen is the best when it comes to books in English.

Travel Agencies Joensuun Kongressi ja Matkailupalvelu Oy (☎ 129 141) has a weekly program of tours in summer, including tours to Russia, which require a visa and should be booked well in advance. Local tours can be booked the previous day. Contact the office at the town hall at Rantakatu 4, 80100 Joensuu.

Left Luggage There are cheap lockers at the railway station, and the luggage room charges 10 mk per piece.

Emergency Services In a general emergency call ☎ 112; for a doctor ☎ 10023. Pharmacies are at Siltakatu 14, Koskikatu 7 and Kirkkokatu 18.

North Karelian Museum

This small museum, on the island of Ilosaari in the Pielisjoki River, features old furniture and artefacts from Russian and Finnish Karelia, although it is inferior to Pielisen Museo in Lieksa. It's open noon to 4 pm on Tuesday, Thursday and Friday, noon to 8 pm on Wednesday and 11 am to 5 pm on Sunday. Admission is 5 mk (more during special exhibitions) but it's free on Sunday.

Joensuun Taidemuseo

The Joensuu Art Museum has art from Finland, Greece and Egypt, including a few old icons. Opening hours are from 11 am to

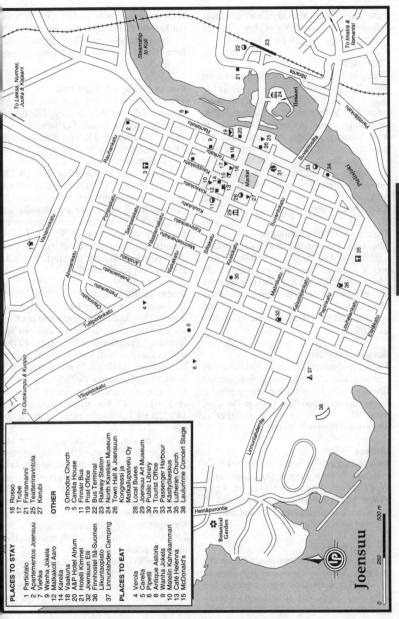

NORTH KARELIA

PLACES TO STAY
1 Partiotalo
2 Apartementos Joensuu
7 Viehka
9 Wanha Jokela
12 Matkakoti Aaro
14 Karelia
18 Vaakuna
20 A&P Hotel Atrium
21 Hotelli Kimmel
32 Joensuun Elli
36 Finnhostel Itä-Suomen Liikuntaopisto
37 Linnunlahden Camping

PLACES TO EAT
4 Verola
6 Carelia
8 Pipetti
9 Antique Astoria
9 Wanha Jokela
10 Matelin Kahvikammari
13 Café Helenna
15 McDonald's
16 Rosso
17 Trube
21 Fransmanni
25 Teatteriravintola
27 Kerubi

OTHER
3 Orthodox Church
5 Carelia House
11 Finnair Bus
19 Post Office
22 Bus Terminal
23 Railway Station
24 North Karelian Museum
26 Town Hall & Joensuun Kongressi ja Matkailupalvelu Oy
28 Local Buses
29 Joensuu Art Museum
30 Public Library
31 Tourist Office
33 Passenger Harbour
34 Käsityökeskus
35 Lutheran Church
38 Laulurinne Concert Stage

To Lieksa, Nurmes, Juuka & Kajaani

To Outokumpu & Kuopio

Steamship to Koli

To Imatra & Ilomantsi

Iltarinta

Ilosaari

Botanical Garden

Heinäpurontie

Joensuu

0   250   500 m

4 pm daily except Monday. Entry is 15 mk. Admission is free on Wednesday when the museum is open until 8 pm.

Churches

The most interesting church in Joensuu is the wooden Orthodox Church of Sankt Nikolaos, built in 1887. The icons were painted in St Petersburg in the late 1880s. Open to the public in summer from 10 am to 8 pm Monday to Friday, the church is at the northern end of Kirkkokatu (Church Street).

Symbolically, at the other end of Kirkkokatu is the Lutheran Church. The interior and stained-glass windows are worth a look. It's open early June to mid-August, daily from 10 am to 6 pm.

Trooppinen Perhospuutarha

The world's northernmost tropical butterfly garden is at Avainkuja 2, in industrial quarters a little to the north of Joensuu. In addition to butterflies and other insects, there are exotic plants and stones. It's open Monday to Friday from 10 am to 6 pm, and on weekends from 10 am to 4 pm. Admission is 30 mk.

Botanical Garden

The greenhouses of Joensuu University contain almost 1000 plant species. At Heinäpurontie 70, near the camping ground, the gardens are open daily (except Tuesday) from 10 am to 6 pm (closing earlier in winter). Admission is 20 mk.

Cruises

Saimaa Ferries Oy runs three cruises from mid-June to early August from Monday to Wednesday. These cruises, on Lake Pyhäselkä, take about two hours and cost 60 mk. Check current timetables and rates at regional tourist offices.

Joensuu Festival

This week-long event transforms the streets, and is by far the best reason to visit Joensuu in June. There are always free concerts and something happening at the market. High-class concerts are held in the modern Carelia

Hall, at the university. Tickets are sold at the market and at Pilettipuoti in the town hall, which is normally open Monday to Friday from 10 am to 5 pm (but a little longer during the festival).

Places to Stay – bottom end

There are two youth hostels in Joensuu, open in June, July and August only. The dilapidated boy scouts' house, *Partiotalo* (☎ 123 381) at Vanamokatu 25, open from 1 June to 31 August, certainly has character. Dormitory beds start at 35 mk.

Another option, *Joensuun Elli* (☎ 225 927) at Länsikatu 18, is a student apartment building, open to travellers from 1 June to 31 August. It has clean four bed dormitories, with a bathroom and a kitchen in each room. Beds are good value, at 45 mk for HI members. Summer hostel rooms cost 200/260 mk, including breakfast, with a 15 mk discount for HI members.

Places to Stay – middle

Linnunlahden Camping (☎ 126 272) has a superb lakeside location near a vast open-air stage, so expect occasional free concerts and lost sleep! There are huts for 160 to 240 mk, with at least four beds in each. Pitching a tent is expensive, starting at 55 mk. A sauna bath costs 50 mk but is free for lodgers from 7 to 10 am. *Apartementos Joensuu* (☎ 224 886) at Torikatu 47 has singles/doubles for 140/220 mk but discounts are available for consecutive nights.

Very central is *Matkakoti Aaro* (☎ 148 1051) at Kirkkokatu 20, with singles/doubles for 140/220 mk. *Wanha Jokela* (☎ 122 891) at Torikatu 26 is a small private hotel with a few singles/doubles for 150/250 mk, though it's known more as a popular evening pub. *Viehka* (☎ 221 450) at Kauppakatu 32 has singles/doubles for 210/300 mk in summer; a little more at other times. Breakfast is included.

Finnhostel Itä-Suomen Liikuntaopisto (☎ 167 5076) at Kalevankatu 8 is a school building that serves as a youth hostel. Rooms cost 260 mk; HI members get a 15 mk discount.

The tourist office also arranges accommodation in private homes, at 120 mk per night.

Places to Stay – top end

There are several good hotels in Joensuu:

Hotelli Kimmel (☎ 1771). Opposite the railway and bus stations, this is the largest hotel in Joensuu, with 500 beds. In summer and on weekends, all rooms are 465 mk. At other times, singles/doubles cost 520/655 mk.

A&P Hotel Atrium (☎ 126 911) at Siltakatu 4 has 53 rooms, a restaurant and a sauna. Singles/doubles cost 350/460 mk.

Karelia (☎ 224 391), at Kauppakatu 25 right in the town centre, has rooms for 335 mk.

Vaakuna (☎ 227 311) at Torikatu 20 has recently renovated rooms for 370 mk in summer; 425/510 mk at other times.

Places to Eat

For snacks and local specialities, *lörtsy* and *karjalanpiirakka* pies at the market are something of a must. Pastries cost 3 to 7 mk but you can bargain a bit. *Marttakahvio* is one of the more popular cafés.

The University of Joensuu has several student cafés. *Carelia* in the main building is open for lunch Monday to Friday until 2 pm. A decent meal costs less than 20 mk, milk, bread and salad included, but no discount is available for ISIC holders. Also, *Kurniekka*, *Verola*, and *Pipetti* remain open in summer, from morning until early afternoon.

Lunch is served in restaurants from 11 am to 2 pm. *Wanha Jokela* at Torikatu 26 is an attractive budget restaurant and, in the evening, the only really popular place among locals. The best place to wine and dine is reputedly *Fransmanni* in the Hotel Kimmel, opposite the railway station. The menu is in English but there are no discount lunch specials. *Rosso* near the market is popular, and has a menu in English.

Teatteriravintola at Rantakatu 4 is one of the fine restaurants situated in the imposing town hall. It is snobbish and a bit overpriced yet popular. Ask for Karelian specialities, or check out the beer terrace in summer.

Antique Astoria, in the small riverside building at Rantakatu 32, is an intimate Hungarian restaurant with a terrace and live music.

Café Helenna at Siltakatu 16 and *Trube* at Torikatu 23 have tempting cakes and sweets. A good alternative is *Matelin Kahvikammari* at Niskakatu 9. It has heaps of tradition plus handicrafts for sale.

Things to Buy

An interesting collection of the work of local artists can be seen at the sales exhibition of Käsityökeskus at Rantakatu 2. There's also a summer sales point at Siltakatu 20. Handicrafts are sold at the market too – bargaining may help get the price down a bit. For bicycle repairs or spare parts, try the sports shops at Torikatu 37B, or Merimiehenkatu 27. Joensuun Retki ja Pyörä at Koskikatu 9 sells bicycles and trekking gear.

Getting There & Away

Air Finnair, Karair and Finnaviation operate several flights a day between Helsinki and Joensuu.

Bus Regular buses to all destinations in North Karelia and Savo depart from the modern bus terminal, where there is a 24 hour restaurant. Tickets are sold from 8 am to 4 pm Monday to Friday, but you can pay the fare on the bus.

Train There are five trains a day to Joensuu from Helsinki, and four trains from Turku. There are also two trains a day to/from Nurmes, with bus connections between Nurmes and Oulu. You'll find a VR Matkapalvelu 'travel service' booth at the ticket office.

Boat The MS *Vinkeri II*, run by Saimaa Ferries Oy, sails twice a week (Thursday and Saturday), departing at 9.30 am from Joensuu to Koli and Nurmes. The interesting trip takes all day and costs 120 mk to Koli and 150 mk to Nurmes. The ship returns on Friday and Sunday.

Getting Around

The Joensuu town centre is small enough to

NORTH KARELIA

walk around. Local buses run infrequently from a station near the market. Taxis are expensive. The Matkatavara left-luggage office at the railway station, open all day, rents bicycles and mountain bikes. There is a Finnair bus to the airport 35 minutes prior to each departure. It departs Joensuu at Kirkkokatu 25.

Around Joensuu

SAILING THE PIELISJOKI RIVER
Every Thursday and Saturday in summer, the MS *Vinkeri II* sails north from Joensuu to Koli on the Pielisjoki River. It's a scenic route that stops at canals and other attractions.

After surviving the canal, and passing under the bridges of Joensuu, the ship sails along the river, which flows rapidly from Lake Pielinen. **Kuurna**, the first canal lock, has an elevation of seven metres. It's a power station too. **Jakokoski** is a *museokanava*, or museum canal, with several old river boats and other paraphernalia of river navigation. The museum is officially open from 11 am to 8 pm, but you can see the boats at all times. There's also a camping ground. **Kaltimo** is also a power station, with an elevation of 10 metres; here the lock is more dramatic.

Other sights include the massive pulp factory in **Uimaharju**, and the scenic islands and headlands of **Ahveninen**, which mark the beginning of Lake Pielinen.

Places to Stay
Jokipirtin Majatalo (☎ 774 607) is a youth hostel in Paukkaja, approximately eight km north of Eno. It is visible from the river and accessible via road.

OUTOKUMPU
Outokumpu (population 9000), about 50 km west of Joensuu, was a wealthy mining town until the 1980s, when all three mining operations were permanently closed. Outokumpu was on the verge of becoming a ghost town. Its property prices plunged to the lowest level in Finland and its unemployment rate exceeded the national average. However, a new industrial area attracted several companies to the town, and employment figures are now close to the national average. The excellent mining museum is worth a visit.

Information
Outokummun Matkailu (☎ 554 793) at Kiisukatu 6 is the tourist information office of Outokumpu. The library is open Monday to Friday from 1 to 7 pm.

Vanha Kaivos
On a hill overlooking the town centre lies an abandoned mine, which was reopened to the public in 1985. There is an extensive mining museum and an adjacent tunnel with mining equipment. You can climb the tower for a superb view, or watch the hourly slide show. For children, there is a fun park at the bottom of the valley. An underground restaurant and a café with a good view offer refreshment. The entire area takes several hours to explore. It's open daily from 10 am to 6 pm. Admission to the museum is 5 mk, or 35 mk for all attractions. Discounts are available for children and students.

Lake Sysmäjärvi
One of the best bird-nesting lakes in Finland lies south of Outokumpu. Sysmäjärvi was declared dead in the 1950s, due to polluted mining deposits that flowed freely into the lake. Since recovered, the lake is now surrounded by lush vegetation, and birds have returned here in large numbers: a recent study found 72 species and unusual density figures. There are birdwatching towers. May and June are the best months to visit.

Places to Stay & Eat
Särkiselän leirintäalue (☎ 553 037), a camping ground some five km north-west of town, has cottages from 110 mk. It is open from 1 June to 31 August only.

The only hotel in Outokumpu, *Malmikumpu* (☎ 550 333) at Asemakatu 1 in the town centre, is easy to find. A double room starts at 340 mk. The hotel also serves

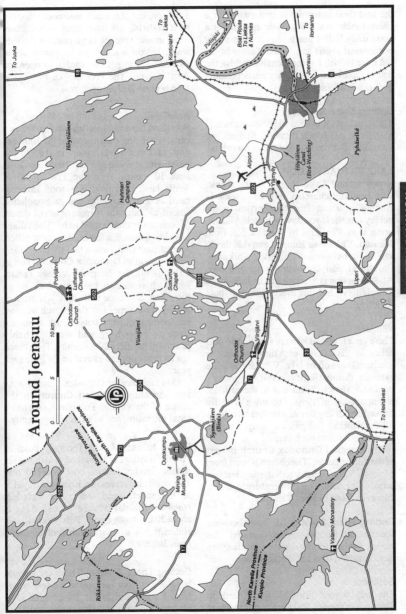

the best food in town. Go downstairs for a cheap lunch on weekdays, or upstairs for a good daily buffet lunch. Apart from a few economical *grillis* and *Vanha Kaivos* in the old mine (which has inexpensive meals), the rest of Outokumpu's eateries are depressing beer-drinking joints.

Getting There & Away
The train station nearest to Outokumpu is at Viinijärvi. All buses between Kuopio and Joensuu call at the Outokumpu bus terminal.

LAKE VIINIJÄRVI LOOP
Roads around Lake Viinijärvi are scenic, with beautiful churches and old houses. In August, you can find blueberries in the nearby forests. If you have a bicycle, you can bring it to Viinijärvi by train or bus from Joensuu, Varkaus or Kuopio, and ride the 60 km loop between Viinijärvi, Sotkuma, Polvijärvi and Outokumpu in one day. Another option is to take a bus from Joensuu to Polvijärvi, but this means you'll bypass Sotkuma.

Viinijärvi
There are a few banks, many shops and a post office in the village of Viinijärvi, on the southern shore of the lake. Viinijärvi is quite famous domestically, as its women's *pesäpallo* (baseball) team won the national championship in 1990. The town is really packed on Sunday during matches. A colourful Praasniekka (religious holiday) Festival is held on 26 June each year.

The beautiful **Orthodox Church** is west of the village centre. The church is open from 11 am to 3 pm Tuesday to Saturday, but few services are held. The 19th century icons are copies of those in Kiev Cathedral.

Getting There & Away All buses between Joensuu and Kuopio stop in Viinijärvi. The café at the bus terminal serves meals every day. Viinijärvi also has a train station.

Sotkuma
The narrow road from Viinijärvi north to Sotkuma is scenic. Sotkuma is not much of a village, but the small *tsasouna* (chapel), built in 1914, has interesting 19th century icons inside; note the large ones on the side walls. If you want to go in, phone ahead (☎ 638 522) to get the warden to open the door for you. The Praasniekka Festival is held here on 20 July each year.

Polvijärvi
Polvijärvi has an interesting history. When a canal was being constructed at the southern end of Lake Höytiäinen in 1859, the embankment collapsed and the water level sank 10 metres, revealing 170 sq km of fertile land. Polvijärvi was soon incorporated as a municipality and its population soared, although the current figure of almost 5800 is lower than it used to be. The village has a bus terminal, a few banks, a post office, several food stores and a taxi (☎ 631 066).

The beautiful **Orthodox Church**, built in 1914, is not far from the village centre. Mutakatti restaurant keeps the key, so go there first. Someone will show you around, if they have time, but the church is most interesting from the outside. Its icons are from St Petersburg and were probably painted in the early 20th century. The church has its Praasniekka Festival on 24 June each year.

Don't mistake the Orthodox church for the less appealing **Lutheran Church** in the centre of the village. Polvijärvi also has a **local museum**, north of the village centre.

Places to Stay & Eat The only hotel in Polvijärvi village is *Mutakatti*, which has six rooms. Singles/doubles cost 160/230 mk. This place also serves lunch on weekdays for 35 mk, salad, bread and coffee included. *Huhmari Holiday Village* (☎ 635 571) is about 20 km south-east of Polvijärvi village. Huhmari has a great number of cottages, from 360 mk.

Getting There & Away There are several buses a day from Joensuu and a few others from Kuopio and Juuka. Buses from Outokumpu run on school days only.

South of Joensuu

The area south of Joensuu, usually referred to as Central Karelia, includes the municipalities of Rääkkylä, Kitee, Kesälahti, Tuupovaara and Värtsilä.

RÄÄKKYLÄ

This small isolated place (population 3400) boasts beautiful scenery on the shores of Lake Orivesi. The large church from 1851 seats 1200 people and is open daily in summer from 10 am to 6 pm. Kihaus, a four day folk music festival in July is by far the best time to visit Rääkkylä. The festival features the band Värttinä, Rääkkylä's own contribution to the world music scene. There's music well beyond midnight during the white nights.

If you have an interest in birds, there are several observation towers at good locations in Rääkkylä, including Ruokosalmi (five km from the main centre), and at Lake Kiesjärvi, where a two km trail has been set up.

Places to Stay & Eat

Koivuniemen Lomakylä (☎ 661 182) near the main village, is an attractive place with a fine mansion which also serves meals. Cottages are available for 130 to 220 mk; beds in rooms for 100 mk per person, including breakfast.

Bonne Femme is the best restaurant in the village.

Getting There & Away

Rääkkylä is a 31 km side trip from the busy Imatra to Joensuu road No 6. There are four buses a day, Monday to Friday, from Joensuu 66 km north. You can also catch a post bus from Kitee, 40 km away, from Monday to Friday and usually at 1 pm or so.

VÄRTSILÄ

This tiny area right on the Russian border shares the fate of Uukuniemi (having lost most of its territory to the Soviet Union in WWII), but the population of 769 has grown recently. The territorial loss was enormous and included the famous factory area.

There's a bird observation tower on the shores of Lake Sääperi. Although it's close to the border, access is allowed without a special permit. The best time to visit is the migratory time, usually late May for Arctic birds.

Places to Stay & Eat

Hotelli Sinilintu (☎ 629 481), also a restaurant, is mostly a local haunt. There are four doubles at 170 mk.

North on road No 500, past the crossing towards Tuupovaara, *Rajahotelli Korpiselkä* (☎ 866 171) is one of the fine Karelian wooden houses that have sprung up during the last decade along the eastern border road. It's a roadhouse, a hotel, a restaurant serving traditional Karelian specialities and a nice place to unwind.

Getting There & Away

There's no reason to go to Värtsilä as such, but the busy border post of Niirala just to the south is open to both Finnish and Russian citizens. The situation for all other nationals has been volatile, but could become more flexible in the near future. Always check the current situation in advance.

There are regular buses from Joensuu to Sortavala and Petrozavodsk (Finnish: Petroskoi) in Russia via Vyartsilya (the old centre of Finnish Värtsilä). At the time of writing, tickets had to be paid for in advance at post offices in North Karelia.

Finnish buses run from Joensuu to Värtsilä on Saturday only.

KITEE

Kitee, a small town south-west of Värtsilä (population: 11,000) was awarded the flattering title of *kaupunki* (city) on 1 January 1992 although the place is not very urban.

The huge **church**, among the 10 largest in Finland, seats 2200. Made of grey stone, it was built in 1886 and is open June to August, daily from 9 am to 5 pm. The **local museum** on the main road in the centre is open mid-June to mid-August, daily (except Monday and Saturday) from noon to 4 pm. Just next door, downstairs at the town hall, **Pienoisrautatie** is a 250 metre long model railway that you can see daily in July and from 10 am to 4 pm weekdays between 12 June and 11 August. Entry is 10 mk.

About four km from the centre is **Savikon maakauppa**, the oldest general store in Finland. It is open for tourists mid-June to early August, Monday to Friday from 10 am to 4 pm.

Well signposted from road No 6 but located between the two access roads to the town centre, **Vanhahovi**, in the village of Suorlahti, is an old house that once belonged to a tax collector. It's a relatively interesting place to visit, open 1 July to mid-August daily from noon to 7 pm. Admission is 10 mk. An old smoke sauna is yours for 300 mk per session.

Places to Stay & Eat

If you get off at the railway station, *Neste* petrol station along road No 6, just 200 metres away, has meals and snacks until quite late.

Nearby, *Likolampi* (☎ 422 222) is a fine camping ground approximately 1.5 km from the train station along road No 482 towards Rääkkylä. The cottages for two/three/four people cost 100/130/160 mk, and you can camp for 60 mk. There's a small lake and you can rent a boat or bathe in one of the two lakeside saunas for 50 mk. The reception doubles as a restaurant.

In the town centre at Rinnepolku 2, *Matkakoti M Ilvonen* (☎ 411 137) is the cheapest place to stay. *Arctia Hotel Kitee* (☎ 412 221), at Hovintie 2 in the town centre, is the top-end establishment, with 34 rooms, two saunas and food and dance almost daily.

There are several restaurants in the town centre, including *Karhu* and *Rebekka*.

Getting There & Away

All trains stop at Kitee railway station (the place is also known as Tolosenmäki), but it is far from the town centre. The station is open daily and sells tickets. You need a Tele phone card for the public phone at the station.

There are direct buses to Kitee from Savonlinna (88 km west) and Joensuu (67 km north). Most of them go via Tolosenmäki.

HEINONIEMI

This small village, officially part of Kitee municipality, has its own church and a variety of attractions in summer. The highlight is **Kalevala Forum** (☎ 423 211), which was established in 1980 in Uukuniemi and transferred to several places until it found a suitable location in an old school building here. Mr Samppa Uimonen sings and recites old Karelian poems and songs from the Kalevala. There's also an exhibition. The place is open from 20 June to mid-August, daily from noon to 8 pm. Entry costs 30 mk and includes a welcome drink, a concert, and apparently much individual attention from the eccentric host. Nearby, **Leo Karppasen Ateljee** is the studio of a sculptor who works with wood. The studio is open daily except Monday and Thursday from noon to 8 pm (Saturday to 3 pm). **Viitakoru** is a sales exhibition on Majakummuntie, with products made of wood and gnarl. Even here you have to pay to get in, but just 5 mk.

Getting There & Away

You will need your own wheels. The Savonlinna to Puhos road (No 71) is the access road; you need to turn off and a further 10 km to reach Heinoniemi.

KESÄLAHTI

Kesälahti, in the southern corner of the province, is a quiet place between two lakes. The village centre has various services, including a library. *Myllytupa*, the local museum not far from the church, is open in summer daily and worth a visit. There's also a café.

Places to Stay & Eat

Karjalan Kievari (☎ 371 421) at Lappeenrannantie 18 (on road No 6), not far from the railway station, is a busy roadhouse. The restaurant serves a daily special costing around 35 mk. In summer, there's a tourist information hut open Monday to Friday from 10 am to 6 pm, on Saturday until 2 pm and on Sunday until 4 pm. The Shell petrol station sells many items. A motel has rooms for 220/290 mk and *Camping Puruvesi* has red cottages from 140 mk. You can take a smoke sauna or rent a bicycle or boat. A separate Kalastuspuisto (Fishing Park) lets you catch a fish (and prepare it) but you have to pay for it. There's also the Kotieläinpuisto (zoo).

Pivanka, at the northern crossing on the main road, is a restaurant at Esso petrol station. Opposite the petrol station, there's a crossing to road No 480, and a few places are signposted on road No 6. *Mäntyranta* (☎ 374 153), four km from the crossing, has cottages from 250 mk plus tax, as well as camp sites. *Karjalan Lomakeskus* (☎ 378 121) further north (access also from road No 71), has cottages for 120 to 400 mk and a great variety of activities.

Getting There & Away

Almost all trains stop at Kesälahti railway station but the actual station building is closed, so you will have to buy your ticket on the train. You need a Tele phone card for the public phone at the station.

Lieksa

If you're looking for wilderness, Lieksa has more to offer than any other place in North Karelia. This vast area (administratively, a city) boasts such natural attractions as Ruunaa, Jongunjoki, the Koli and Patvinsuo National Park. Lieksa is probably the only 'city' in the world with a 100 km border with Russia, and with a city ferry service across a 30 km wide lake (Lake Pielinen). Over the last 30 years, the population has dwindled by 10,000 to 17,000, half of whom are engaged in service industries.

Sami people inhabited Lieksa over 500 years ago, but immigrant Karelians pushed them further north.

LIEKSA TOWN

Count Per Brahe founded the town of Brahea in 1653 but it didn't survive long. The present Lieksa township was founded in 1936 and incorporated as a town in 1972.

Information

Tourist Office Tourist information services are provided by Lieksan Matkailu (☎ 520 2400) at Pielisentie 7. In summer, the office is open on weekdays from 8 am to 6 pm, on Saturday from 9 am to 2 pm and on Sunday from 11 am to 3 pm.

Post & Telephone The post office is at the northern end of Pielisentie, the main street. It's open 9 am to 4.30 pm, Monday to Friday.

Library A good public library at the market square, near the post office, is open Monday to Friday from 10 am to 7 pm. An upstairs section contains travel books, and there are imported magazines and 1:20,000 regional maps. If you would like to listen to music, there is a large compact disc collection to choose from.

Travel Agencies Lieksan Matkailu (see above) is also an agent for almost anything in Lieksa, including the Koli area. Services include phone calls, bookings for accommodation and assistance with transport. Mari Palosaari, the wilderness guide, has developed ecotourism in Lieksa like no-one else, and her Metsäväki group of wilderness guides is becoming an environmentally conscious movement. (Rejection of plastic cups is one thing that has proven surprisingly hard to achieve among local entrepreneurs.) Practically all tours are tailor-made. Nurmes and Ilomantsi may be included in the itinerary.

Matka-Harila is a general travel agent. Tours to Russia require a visa.

Pielisen Museo

This is without doubt the best open-air museum in Finland. More than 70 traditional houses contain tools and artefacts. The area has been divided into several sections, according to the century or trade featured.

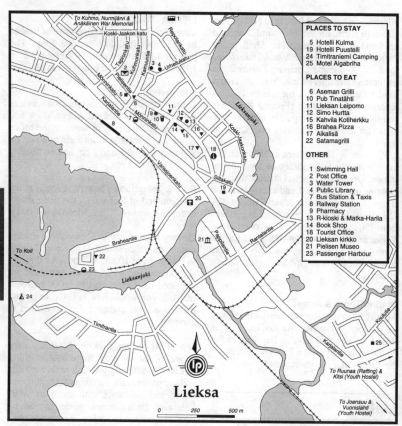

To Kuhmo, Nurmijärvi & Anäkäinen War Memorial

PLACES TO STAY

5 Hotelli Kulma
19 Hotelli Puustelli
24 Timitraniemi Camping
25 Motel Aigabriha

PLACES TO EAT

6 Aseman Grilli
10 Pub Tinatähti
11 Lieksan Leipomo
12 Simo Hurtta
15 Kahvila Kotiherkku
16 Brahea Pizza
17 Aikalisä
22 Satamagrilli

OTHER

1 Swimming Hall
2 Post Office
3 Water Tower
4 Public Library
7 Bus Station & Taxis
8 Railway Station
9 Pharmacy
13 R-kioski & Matka-Harila
14 Book Shop
18 Tourist Office
20 Lieksan kirkko
21 Pielisen Museo
23 Passenger Harbour

Lieksa

0   250   500 m

The new building has a large indoor museum, with artefacts organised along similar divisions. Get yourself an English-language guide map, as there are almost 100 distinct attractions in the area. The museum is open mid-May to mid-September from 9 am to 6 pm daily.

In winter, only the exhibition hall stays open, from 10 am to 3 pm Tuesday to Sunday. Entry is 15 mk and includes the map.

Lieksan Kirkko

The modern Lutheran Church of Lieksa (also known as the Church of Lake Pielinen) was built in 1982 to replace the old wooden church that burnt down on a freezing New Year's night in 1979. It was designed by Reima and Raili Pietilä, who are among the most famous contemporary Finnish architects. The huge cross-shaped ceiling dominates the hall, and large windows at the altar enable you to view the surviving bell tower.

The wood sculptures are by local talent Eva Ryynänen. The church is open from June to mid-August, daily from 11 am to 7 pm.

Festivals

The Lieksa Brass Festival, held in late July, attracts quite a number of international players. There are several concerts each day, with prices ranging from 30 to 60 mk. For further details, contact Lieksan Vaskiviikko, Koski-Jaakonkatu 4, 81700 Lieksa.

Places to Stay

Lieksa does not have a large variety of budget accommodation. For camping and bungalows, go to *Timitraniemi Camping* (☎ 521 780), three km from the town centre. It is off the main road, south of Lieksajoki bridge. Open from 1 June to 31 August it has two bed huts for 170 mk and four bed cottages for 240 to 370 mk. Prices are lower before mid-June and after mid-August. Camping costs from 25 mk per person.

Hotelli Puustelli (☎ 525 544) is the best hotel in Lieksa. Modern and convenient, it generally has lower prices in summer than in winter. In summer, accommodation costs 300/380 mk per night, including sauna and breakfast. *Hotelli Kulma* (☎ 522 112), on the main street, is a sleazy pub that will probably put you off, but there are eight rooms, at 180/300 mk, and it's nearest to the railway station. *Motel Aigabriha* (☎ 522 922), three km south-east of the centre, has 20 singles/doubles for 240/320 mk, including breakfast and sauna.

Places to Eat

Most restaurants are on Pielisentie, including *Aseman Grilli*, opposite the railway station. *Brahea Pizza* serves until 10 pm or later and pizzas start at 30 mk. At the harbour, *Satamagrilli* is open until late at night, serving your typical choice of junk food. Locals gather here, especially for the drive-in service.

Among the pubs, *Simo Hurtta* also serves proper meals, even if it's a bit too dark inside. *Pub Tinatähti* has cute decor inspired by American westerns.

Lieksan Leipomo is the most popular of Lieksa's bakeries but *Kahvila Kotiherkku* serves lunch too, although it may be too smoky to be attractive. *Aikalisä*, in the Oltermanni supermarket, is another lunch restaurant. Speaking of supermarkets, they are enormous in Lieksa.

Getting There & Away

Bus There are two buses a day from Joensuu airport and up to 10 buses from Joensuu. Regional bus services are better during the school season; in summer, there are fewer services. Southern Lieksa is well served by buses to/from Joensuu. Ruunaa should still have a subsidised mini-bus service twice a day. The daily bus to Kuhmo via Nurmijärvi and Teljo departs Lieksa at 1.55 pm Monday to Friday, and Kuhmo at 6 am. Towards Ilomantsi along Runon ja rajan tie on weekdays, you can get only as far as Lehmivaara, which is 10 km short of the Loma-Kitsi youth hostel.

Train There are two trains a day to Lieksa from Helsinki (via Joensuu) and Nurmes. The night train from Helsinki has a bus connection at Joensuu.

Boat In summer, the MF *Pielinen* (run by Saimaa Ferries Oy) sails twice a day from Koli to Lieksa, leaving Koli at 11.30 am and 5 pm, and Lieksa at 9.30 am and 3 pm. Check current timetables in advance to avoid disappointment. At the harbour, Satamagrilli has a telephone, and will book you a taxi for 2 mk.

TIENSUU

Not very far south of Lieksa, Tiensuu is becoming an area that offers a great variety of attractions to visitors. Even if you have to make some arrangements at the tourist office, you can experience quite a lot in this area.

Loma-Ravila

This farmhouse specialises in wilderness pony trekking. On an Iceland pony and with a guide you get to see the superb scenery and forests around Lake Pielinen and go to places you could never find alone. Loma-Ravila

NORTH KARELIA

(☎ 535 123) is 11 km from Lieksa. Assistance and bookings are provided by Lieksan Matkailu, the tourist office.

Sarkkilan Hovi

The privately owned Sarkkila Manor has been carefully renovated. Dating back to 1840, it was purchased in a dilapidated condition by the Kilpeläinen family, the present owners, in 1978. All houses on the estate have been meticulously cleaned, rebuilt and decorated. In summer, when the estate is open to visitors, there's also an exhibition. The entry fee is 30 mk.

Places to Stay

Lieksan kotitalousoppilaitos (☎ 680 3700) at Märäjälahdentie 19, seven km south of Lieksa, is a household management school, open to guests from June to mid-August. Doubles are 180 mk.

Nuutila (☎ 535 189), a nice farm estate by Lake Pielinen on the way to Sarkkilan hovi, offers accommodation in three buildings, including the charming old Riihi-Iglu, at 250 mk per night. Weekly rental is the rule here.

Getting There & Away

Driving south from Lieksa, you can turn

right at the first sign that says 'Tiensuu'. However, it's easier to find the attractions if you continue along the main road, and turn right onto Tiensuuntie in the direction of Märäjälahti.

PATVINSUO NATIONAL PARK

Patvinsuo is a large marshland area just where the municipalities of Lieksa and Ilomantsi meet (see the Around Lieksa map). Swans, cranes and other birds nest here, and bears and other mammals can be seen if you're lucky. With the excellent *pitkospuu* (boardwalk) network, you can easily hike around, observing the life of a Finnish marshland.

If you have little time, go to the southern shore of Lake Suomu. It is 3½ km from the main road to Teretin lintutorni, a birdwatching tower. This is a good walk through forests and wetlands, and you will see some birds. Get a free map at the park headquarters and use it for planning. There are lakes and pine forests between the wetlands. Come in May or June to hear birds sing, or from June to September for the best trekking conditions.

There are three nature trails and several good hiking routes along the boardwalk path. You can walk around Lake Suomujärvi or follow pitkospuu trails through the wetlands.

Places to Stay

Suomu Park Centre has a warden in attendance from May to mid-September, for advice, fishing permits and free maps. There is a dormitory with nine beds available for a mere 25 mk per person, including the use of a small kitchen. You can use the telephone and the sauna for a fee. There are seven camp sites and one *laavu* (an open shelter with sloping roof) within the park boundaries, all have toilets and firewood and are free of charge.

Loma-Kitsi (☎ 539 114) is a youth hostel with a beautiful view from a hill 20 km north of the park centre. It is 10 km east of Lehmivaara village and not the friendliest place. Dormitory beds start at 50 mk. The place is open from 15 May to 15 October but is often booked up by groups, so call ahead.

Getting There & Away

There is no public transport. From Lieksa, drive 18 km east towards Hatunkylä, then turn right to Kontiovaara. It is a dangerously narrow but very scenic road, which runs along small ridges. Midway, there is a small nature reserve with a 5.2-km-long marked path. When you reach a sealed road (Uimahar-juntie), turn left, drive a few hundred metres and turn right. If you drive along the eastern Runon ja rajantie route, turn west as you see the small 'Uimaharju' sign, just south of the Lieksa-Ilomantsi border. If you are trekking, Bear's Path and Suden taival (Wolf Trail) both lead here, as the park is where these trails meet.

RUUNAA

Ruunaa, north-east of Lieksa, is currently the most popular destination east of Lake Pielinen. A great variety of outdoor activities make Ruunaa a rewarding place to visit. It boasts 38 km of waterways, five relatively difficult rapids, reputedly the least polluted wilderness in Europe, excellent trekking paths and good fishing. The area is run by the Forest and Park Service, which puts over 6000 kg of fish into the waters every year. Campfire sites are also provided and maintained.

Huge ant hills are a feature, and there's an observation tower at Huuhkajavaara.

Information

Ruunaan opastuskeskus (☎ 533 165) near Naarajoki is the main information centre. It's open in summer, daily from 9 am to 7 pm (until 9 pm in July). It's an excellent place to visit: there are exhibitions, maps, a library and a slide show in English. Entry is free.

In Neitikoski there's a coin-operated phone and a mail box too.

Activities

Ruunaa is busy all year round, as it hosts skiing and other snow sports in winter.

Boating & Canoeing In summer, people shoot the rapids in wooden motorboats. Canoeing is also possible. The rapids aren't really that big, but beware: in 1990, four people died in two separate canoeing accidents. None of them wore a life jacket. Get one, and a helmet too, if you plan to try your canoeing skills in Ruunaa.

Fishing Ruunaa is one of the most popular fishing spots in North Karelia. Those using a wheelchair can reach the water along a long wooden road. One-day fishing permits cost 40 mk and are available in Lieksa town from R-kiosks and Kesport, as well as many Ruunaa area locations. There is also a fishing permit machine near the Neitijoki rapids. Fishing is allowed from 1 June to 10 September and from 16 November to 31 December.

Trekking There are basically two trekking routes in the Ruunaa area. *Bear's Path*, a longer trekking route, runs across Ruunaa. You will find it just 50 metres north of the Naarajoki bridge. The path is marked with round orange symbols on trees.

Around the river system, and over two beautiful suspension bridges, runs *Ruunaan koskikierros*, a 29 km loop along good *pitkospuu* paths, with good signs along the way and beige paint on trees. If you have more time, there are another 20 km of side trips you can take.

If you start at the Naarajoki bridge, you will have to walk five km along the Bear's Path to reach the Ruunaan koskikierros trail. Another 3.3 km brings you to the Neitikoski rapids, where you'll find commercial services. Neitikoski has road access.

Organised Tours
At least six operators run long wooden motorboats along the Ruunaa waterways. The boats are safe, unlike small canoes. Operators provide participants with life jackets and waterproof jackets and pants. During the tour, you go ashore to enjoy a feast of local food. There are daily departures at 10.30 am in summer, but times vary; enquire at Lieksan Matkailu in Lieksa or go

to the Naarajoki bridge, where all tours start. Prices range from 150 to 160 mk, depending on the quality and quantity of the food. The easiest way to organise a tour is to go to Lieksan Matkailu, as they can bargain a bit for you. Transport is available from Lieksa to Naarajoki bridge, and on to the boat launch. If you would like to return to Lieksa, that can be arranged too.

Highly recommended is Ismo Räsänen (☎ 533 111), who is something of a Crocodile Dundee of the Karelian wilderness. He is flexible, according to your needs, and has a picturesque island for the meal stop. His family prepares *lanttukukko* and karjalanpiirakka pies and other food, and he catches his own salmon. He also manufactures boats. Other operators are the Ruunaan Matkailu (☎ 533 130), which has a kiosk near the bridge, and Kari Sainio (☎ 531 547), with two daily departures. Karjalan Kuohu (☎ 535 201) arranges white-water rafting for 150 mk per person.

Places to Stay
There are at least 10 laavu shelters and another 10 camp sites in the area. Camping and sleeping in laavu is free of charge. Get the free *Ruunaa Government Hiking Area* map and guide for accommodation information. You will need a lightweight mattress, a sleeping bag and some mosquito repellent. Lighting a fire is allowed, except during fire alerts.

Sillankorva (☎ 533 121) offers superb accommodation right at the Naarajoki bridge. The large house is yours for 640 mk, or either floor for 320 or 430 mk. Everything is extremely clean and nice with wood panelling on the walls. The cheapest option is a room for 160 mk. The smoke sauna can be heated for 370 mk.

Ruunaan Matkailu (☎ 533 130) has several huts five km east of Naarajoki bridge.

Near the Neitikoski rapids, *Ruunaan retkeilykeskus* (☎ 533 171) has several deluxe bungalows, each with six beds, air-conditioning, designer crockery and a sauna. They can be rented for 400 mk in the low season, 550 mk in summer. You can pitch your tent there for 35 mk. This is a modern place, with public telephones and a TV, and you can use the kitchen, washing machines and showers at no extra cost. Use of the sauna costs 35 mk per person. There are mountain bikes and rowing boats for hire (95 mk per day). Canoes and kayaks cost a hefty 125 mk per day, but free transportation is provided within 10 km. You can eat in the reception building or buy sausages and other items at the shop.

Getting There & Away

In 1995, public mini-buses served the area twice a day from various places in Lieksa, including the railway station. Enquire at the tourist office. If you drive, follow the 'Ruunaa 27' sign east of the Union petrol station, two km south of the town centre. This is also the place to start hitchhiking, with a likely change of vehicle right after Pankakoski, six km away.

NURMIJÄRVI AREA

Known for its canoeing routes and generally called northern Lieksa, the Nurmijärvi area is wild and remote, with quite a few interesting places to visit. Nurmijärvi village has enough services to get you to the Jongunjoki River or Lieksa River canoeing routes, or to the Änäkäinen area for fishing, trekking and exploring WWII ruins.

Places to Stay & Eat

Erästely Ky (☎ 546 550), the main canoe rental company, has 20 beds in the village, between Aunen kahvila and the shop. Beds cost just 50 mk, including a sauna bath, but bring your own sheets.

If you come by bus, you can walk to *Jongunjoen Lomapirtti* (☎ 545 531), two km from the main road towards Änäkäinen and the Russian border. There is also a connecting five km path from the Bear's Path to the Lomapirtti. The overnight charge is 100 mk per person in spotless four-bed rooms, even if you have the room alone. You can camp for 20 mk, with use of showers and toilets. There are two smoke saunas available, as well as bicycles, canoes and boats for rent.

The nearby *Eräkeskus* (☎ 546 541) is a good base for activities. The cheapest beds are 100 mk, singles/doubles 300/370 mk, including sauna and breakfast.

Aunen kahvila is a popular roadside café in Nurmijärvi, 15 km from the Russian border. It is visited by local authorities as well as by tourists. Aune offers home-made meals (30 mk), sells fishing permits and has keys for the Änäkäinen rented fishing boats (see below). Aunen kahvila is open every day till 7 pm.

Änäkäinen

Änäkäinen saw fierce fighting during the early weeks of the Winter War in December 1939. Finnish soldiers held their positions here, leaving a large number of Russian soldiers dead. In order to stop enemy tanks, the Finns built large rock barriers; when the war erupted again in 1940, even larger rocks were added. The area is now a government fishing area, with the Bear's Path running through it. To get there, turn right as you drive north from Nurmijärvi, and proceed six km. To your left is the fishing area, with a *korsu* (a rebuilt underground bunker used by Finnish soldiers during WWII), and the Korsukierros area, with *juoksuhauta* (circular) trenches opposite the korsu.

Probably the best thing to see in Änäkäinen is a cave that has been dug on the other side of the main road. Rocks from the cave were brought to the front in 1940 to block the tanks. Follow the 'korsukierros' sign to the entrance, up on a hill. Bring your torch, as it is totally dark and you will have to climb two ladders inside. The exit is narrow, so your clothes are likely to get a bit dirty.

Fishing The Forest and Park Service controls fish quantities in three lakes in the area. Fishing is allowed all year round, except in May. The Aunen kahvila, the Karjalan Eräkeskus and the Jongunjoen Lomapirtti have boats and fishing permits for 40 mk per day. Permits are also available in Lieksa.

Places to Stay The Änäkäinen area has free

accommodation for trekkers. It is possible to stay overnight in one of the three laavu shelters, or inside a *luppokota* cabin, which can take up to five people for one night. Camping is also possible. You can even stay overnight inside the korsu, but clean it first, as it is usually filthy.

Canoeing the Pankasaari Route

While in Nurmijärvi, you can rent a canoe from the Erästely Company (☎ 546 550) at Nurmijärventie 158A. The route starts across the road. Get yourself a free route guide, which is widely available at brochure outlets (tourist offices or roadside shopping areas), or at Lieksan Matkailu. The route follows the Lieksajoki River downstream to Lake Pankajärvi. From there, you paddle southeast under a road bridge to Lake Pudasjärvi. Avoid the dangerous Pankakoski power station in the south and paddle upstream to the upper part of the Lieksajoki River. Heading north-west from this point, you first reach Naarajoki at Ruunaa and then pass a few tricky rapids, especially Käpykoski (pull the canoe with a rope here, unless you are experienced), before returning to Nurmijärvi.

Canoeing the Jongunjoki River

This beautiful wilderness river has over 40 small rapids, but none of them are very tricky. Lieksan Matkailu has a good English-language guide to the route. You can start at Jonkeri up north (in the municipality of Kuhmo), or further south at Teljo bridge, or at Aittokoski, or even at Lake Kaksinkantaja. Allow four days if you start at Jonkeri and one day from the last point. The Räsänen shop in Nurmijärvi will take two people and a canoe to Jonkeri for 230 mk, to Teljo for 175 mk and to Kaksinkantaja for 90 mk. Canoe rental charges are 240 mk per day.

Getting There & Away

The Nurmijärvi area can be reached by catching the bus from Lieksa to Kuhmo which departs at 1.55 pm each weekday. It passes Nurmijärvi village and the Änäkäinen turnoff, and past Teljo and Jonkeri villages. From Kuhmo, the bus departs at 6 am. To hitchhike to Nurmijärvi from Lieksa, walk two km towards Nurmes to the road crossing. In Nurmijärvi, you can hire a taxi from Räsänen shop (50 mk to Änäkäinen, 70 mk to Kaksinkantaja).

VUONISLAHTI

Often referred to as southern Lieksa, Vuonislahti, a completely rural village, has a railway station, a youth hostel (one of only two in the Lieksa area) and a host of interesting attractions.

There is a **war memorial** on a small hill

The Bear Hunter

Now for something completely different: you may not like it, but Väinö Heikkinen has killed almost 40 bears since July 1948. His collection of bear skulls at Kaksinkantaja is the result of a lifetime of traditional hunting, not sport. Situated just 10 km from the Russian border, his old house typifies Karelian isolation – the nearest house is one km away and abandoned.

If this appeals, pay Väinö five mk when you visit, but don't expect any stories, except in Finnish. His farm is quite an authentic piece of traditional Finnish life. To get there, follow the signs along gravel roads before the Änäkäinen area. If you are travelling by canoe, you can reach the house easily by stopping when you see the 'Kaksinkantaja, Karhunkaatajan koti' signs halfway along the Jongunjoki route.

Väinö can even put you up for the night. Ask if the double room in the *aitta* is available – the charge is a mere 20 mk per person. The bear hunter will heat his sauna (for 10 mk) or prepare game food, if you let him know you're coming. Lieksan Matkailu (see Travel Agencies in Lieksa Town) can make the phone call for you. ■

across the road, as you come from the railway station. This is where Russians were stopped by Finnish soldiers in 1808. On Saturday in July, a village market is held near the war memorial, and the nearby *tanssilava* house has dancing in summer on Saturday evenings.

Paateri

Paateri is best known for the gallery of Eva Ryynänen, a respected woodcarver. Born in 1915, she has been a sculptor since her teens and is still active. This isolated property, surrounded by pine trees, is the childhood home of her husband, Paavo. Together, they have embellished their residence with woodcarvings. The latest work is an impressive wilderness church, opened in 1991, with walls and floor made of Russian pine, and huge doors carved from Canadian cedar. The altar was created using a stump that once belonged to the largest fir tree in Finland. The place also has a café. The gallery is open June to August, daily from 11 am to 6 pm. Entry is a hefty 20 mk, 5 mk for children.

Getting There & Away The most exciting way to get to Paateri is to row a boat from the Herranniemi youth hostel nearby. Ask for a map to avoid getting lost. If you are driving or cycling, follow the road signs from the main road or from the secondary road north of Vuonislahti. You can also rent a bicycle at the Herranniemi youth hostel.

Pikku-Kili

If you're looking for something extremely weird and absurd, get to this place. A long, narrow, twisting gravel road leads to this isolated hill-top farm estate, run by the Leinonen family. The views are excellent and there is no trace of humans in the surrounding wilderness. There are peacocks, ostriches and a great number of unexpected animals caged in this large area. An artificial lake has fish, and there are horses that will take you around the wilderness. The address is Salokyläntie 90, east of Vuonislahti, and the place is well signposted from road No 73.

Pikku-Kili is open from 15 May to 30 August, daily from 10 am to 9 pm (6 pm on Saturday). Entry is 30 mk and worth it. Children get a discount (and young children won't want to leave). You can get coffee and snacks, and staying overnight is possible in some of the old buildings. This should not cost more than 100 mk.

Places to Stay & Eat

Herranniemi (☎ 542 110), south of Vuonislahti, is a very quaint youth hostel, open from mid-May to mid-October, and a good choice for those wanting to stay in an old farmhouse. The main building is over 200 years old. There are cheap dormitories in an old *aitta* (storage) building; beds cost 45 mk with an HI card. There are also hotel rooms (more expensive and less attractive) and a few huts. The place sells coffee and snacks, exhibits local handicrafts and rents bicycles (35 mk per day) and boats. You can also bathe in a sauna. To get to Herranniemi, walk straight from the Vuonislahti train station to the main road, turn left and proceed 500 metres to the sign.

Another option is *Isäntärenki* (☎ 543 114) on main road No 73, a bit far away from the train station but convenient if you drive. The accommodation is basic but most people stop here for the buffet lunch (50 mk) that features mutton and Karelian specialities. There are also handicrafts for sale and some local paintings displayed.

Getting There & Away

There are two trains a day to Vuonislahti from Joensuu, and three from Lieksa. The small Vuonislahti train station doubles as a post office. Even though the station is closed on Sunday and on Saturday afternoons, you can buy tickets on the train.

Lake Pielinen

Some of the most interesting attractions in North Karelia are around this lake, one of the largest in Finland.

KOLI

Koli Hill, south of Lieksa across Lake Pielinen, has been dubbed the first-ever tourist attraction of Finland. Several Finnish artists of the National Romantic era drew their inspiration from this place. Jean Sibelius, the composer, is said to have brought a grand piano to the top of the hill to celebrate his honeymoon. In 1991, the Koli hill was declared a national park, after hot debate between environmentalists and land-owners. The owners agreed to sell their land and environmentalists dropped their demand that the Koli Hotel, up on the hill, be closed down and demolished. Most of the area is still untouched and there are many walking tracks on the hill.

Things to See & Do

Near the hotel on the hill is **uhrihalkeama**, a large crack in the rock that has served as a sacrificial site since time immemorial.

Ukko-Koli is the highest point and 200 metres further is **Akka-Koli**, another peak. **Mammutti** is a huge stone with a 'Temple of Silence', which is used for religious events. The solid rock peak nearby is called **Pahakoli**, or 'Evil Koli'. Further south, the path runs via pleasant meadows and climbs up to **Mäkrävaara**, a hill which has the best views.

For caves, continue to **Pirunkirkko** ('Devil's Church'), an area of rocks, cliffs and small caves. The site, south of the Koli area on the lakeside road, is signposted.

Places to Stay – bottom end

You can stay one night free in the cosy *Ikolanaho* hut with a pleasant meadow setting in the national park. The door is locked, but you should have no problem signing for the key at Hotelli Koli. There are four bunks with mattresses, a fireplace and wood.

The youth hostel, *Kolin retkeilymaja* (☎ 673 131), is in an old school building. This is one hostel that stays open all year round but it is five km from the main road and the bus, so you have to hitchhike or walk; however, the road is scenic. This magnifi-cent, quiet youth hostel must be one of the most relaxing places to stay in Finland. A bed costs 40 mk for HI card holders; sheets are extra. Bring food to prepare in the kitchen.

For near rock-bottom prices, *Lohikeidas*, three km out of Koli village towards Ahmovaara, is a tasteless salmon-fishing business. It has four huts, at 50 to 80 mk each. You can try to catch salmon for 35 mk per kg. Another bargain place is *Loma-Aitat* (☎ 672 257), in the backyard of a farmhouse a few km further from the harbour crossing. The elderly couple doesn't speak much English. You can get a two bed aitta room for 100 mk, or less if you are alone and bargain a little. You have to clean the room before you go.

Places to Stay – top end

Hotelli Koli (☎ 672 221), at the top of Koli hill, is a typical 1970s concrete box with singles/doubles for 310/400 mk. Services are good and abundant and views from the café and restaurant are great.

Loma-Koli (☎ 673 211), at Merilän-rannantie 68, was previously known as Kolin Hiisi until it was renamed after bankruptcy. It is near the Hiisi Hill slopes, and there is downhill skiing nearby. Singles/doubles are 250/350 mk; four bed apartments are 600 mk.

Loma-Koli Camping (☎ 673 212) nearby has excellent camping facilities, including four bed cottages from 160 mk.

Getting There & Away

Bus The Koli area is served by regular buses from Joensuu, Juuka and Nurmes. If you drive, the village of Koli is some 10 km east of Ahmovaara village, near the main Joensuu to Nurmes road.

Boat In summer, the MF *Pielinen* of Saimaa Ferries Oy sails twice a day across Lake Pielinen, leaving Koli at 11.30 am and 5 pm, and Lieksa at 9.30 am and 3 pm. Check current timetables in advance to avoid disap-pointment. The journey takes 100 minutes and costs 55 mk, plus 10 mk for a bicycle or 30 mk for a car. The return trip is cheaper.

Food and snacks are available. There are also boats from Joensuu and Nurmes twice a week in summer.

Getting Around

Bus If you arrive at the Koli pier by ferry, a bus will be waiting to take you to the Koli hilltop, via Koli village, for 7 mk.

Bicycle The Loma-Koli camping ground rents mountain bikes on an hourly or daily basis (50 mk per day).

KELVÄNSAARI

There are tours to this beautiful island in Lake Pielinen, nine km from the Koli pier, for 300 mk per person. The price includes transport, dinner, smoke sauna, accommodation, and breakfast. There are also cottages on the island. Enquire at the Lieksa tourist office (☎ 520 2400).

JUUKA

Juuka is a vital link on the route around Lake Pielinen. There are excellent places to stay, a great variety of attractions and probably the most beautiful natural scenery in the region, but you have to look around for it.

The municipality of Juuka (population 7100) covers an area of 1503 sq km on the western side of Lake Pielinen. Famous for its soapstone mining and handicrafts, Juuka is a little way off the tourist routes but that may be the main reason it's worth a visit. It has two excellent museums and a small, wooden old town. Juuan kirkonkylä, the village itself, is off main road No 18, equidistant from Nurmes and Koli. The best views can be enjoyed from a narrow parallel road that runs from Juuka south to Nunnanlahti village, and also along the Vuokko road north of Juuka.

Information

Go to Kolinportti at Ahmovaara for tourist information, or call ☎ 470 650 for the municipal office at Poikolantie 1. The public library at Poikolantie 6, one of the highlights of the modern architecture in the village of Juuka, has a great variety of books and mag-

azines. It's open in the afternoons, Monday to Friday only.

Puu-Juuka

Puu-Juuka (Wooden Juuka) in the village has at least 60 wooden houses, some over 100 years old. They were preserved from demolition largely through the efforts of individuals. Many have been beautifully renovated. Juukeli, one such house, has an art exhibition, Piennaali, every odd year.

Also part of Puu-Juuka is **Myllymuseo**, the mill museum, located in a beautiful natural riverside setting. The museum includes an old grain mill, which has served the villagers since 1870. There are four buildings, with old tools and machines, including a genuine smoke sauna. In the old days, logs were floated downriver past the rapids, through the *uittoränni* (a specially constructed chute for floating logs past rapids). The museum is open 1 June to 31 August daily from 10 am to 6 pm. Entry is 10 mk, and the ticket is also valid in Pitäjänmuseo.

Pitäjänmuseo

Visible from the main road, this big red wooden house with 'Museo' written on it houses the Juuka village museum. An interesting construction, built in 1825 with double walls to prevent thieves from stealing the grain that was stored inside, the museum has an impressive collection of local and regional artefacts, some up to 200 years old. Opening hours are similar to the mill museum.

Architecture

In addition to many fine old buildings in Puu-Juuka, there are several interesting public edifices that Juuka has recently invested in. The **civic centre** has many fine examples of modern architecture. Local soapstone from Nunnanlahti has been used in most public buildings, combined with wood and white walls. **Kunnantalo**, the municipal centre designed by Erkki Helasvuo, was built in 1984. The library, designed by Kaj Michael, was finished in

1993. Other recent additions are the Kotikallio building (home for old people) and the health care centre nearby.

Other notable buildings in the Juuka area include **Kivikylä** in Nunnanlahti, and **Kolinportti** in Ahmovaara.

Places to Stay

For pleasant accommodation on the shore of Lake Pielinen, go to *Piitteri* (☎ 472 000), which has simple but clean two bed huts at 180 mk, four bed cottages at 220 mk and camping at typical prices. Piitteri also owns a laavu on an island that you can reach by rowing boat. There is also a typical Finnish *huvilava* (dancing stage), where minor Finnish celebrities sometimes sing on Saturday nights. Tickets cost about 50 mk. For further information on Piitteri tours, write to Piitteri Oy, FIN-83900 Juuka.

In the village of Juuka, *Rikas Rouwa* (☎ 472 010) has three excellent rooms for rent, but they are a bit overpriced at 250/350 mk, including breakfast. Meals and snacks are also available. The place is the most homely in Juuka. Also in the village, *Hotel Petra* (☎ 472 700) has five rooms, with singles/doubles for 240/290 mk. *Juuan Elli* (☎ 470 360), along road No 18, has just three rooms, with singles/doubles for 220/280 mk.

Many private cottages around Juuka are available for weekly or even daily rental; enquire at the Juuka tourist office.

Places to Eat

The best value is *Katrilli* at Väyryläntie 9, in the Kotikallio building near the fire brigade. Inexpensive meals are available Monday to Friday until 6 pm only. *Hotel Petra* offers fine dining, and across the street, *Murkina* serves lunch, although it is more of a beer joint.

You can also find something decent at Shell and Esso petrol stations, or at *Juuan Elli* which is associated with the SEO petrol station along road No 18.

Getting There & Away

Regular buses between Joensuu and Nurmes will drop you off in Juuka. Hitchhiking along the main road is relatively easy, as there is a lot of traffic.

PAALASMAA

The largest island in Lake Pielinen is connected to the mainland by a free *lossi* ferry and a causeway through small islands. Noted for its scenery and peaceful atmosphere, the island was isolated until a few decades ago, when the road was constructed. This happened after a disastrous boat accident on 4 October 1959, in which 15 people perished. Locals haven't forgotten this – a memorial stone was recently erected near the camping ground – but boats are still used by everyone. One particular member of the community refuses to use the new bridge between Toinensaari and Paalasmaa. To go shopping, he rows his boat across the strait to the camping ground, and walks from there to the shop.

Paalasmaa is the highest island in Finland; its tallest point is 132 metres above the lake's water level. A wooden observation tower was recently constructed. If you follow the signs that say 'tornille', you will see old houses that tell of the long history of Paalasmaa. **Ritoranta** is a *savipaja* (a small pottery studio) before the ferry terminal on the mainland, 2 km from road No 18. Soapstone is mixed with local clay here. You can purchase handicrafts made by local artists.

Places to Stay & Eat

Ritoranta on the mainland (☎ 470 824) has two rooms at 150/200 mk and a nice lakeside sauna. Although the place is archaic, you'll probably sleep well. You can also have coffee and simple meals. On the island itself is a shop (with food), which is open every day in summer.

At the east end of the island there's *Paalasmaan Lomamajat Camping* (☎ 479 516). It's located at a nice lakeside spot. There are eight two/four bed cottages that cost 150/220 mk and two saunas that can be rented for 40 mk per hour. The three km trek to the lookout starts from here and is one of the things to do in addition to boat tours and fishing.

Getting There & Away

To get to Paalasmaa, drive two km north of Juuka village and turn right. It is 15 km to the island and there is a free ferry to take you. The road continues to Toinensaari ('Second Island'), which has a few farmhouses.

VUOKKO

The northern bicycle route from Juuka follows the parallel road through Keski-Vuokko. It's a scenic route; you should stay in one of the cottages at the camping ground. Keski-Vuokko was used as the beautiful setting in the 'blockbuster' Finnish movie *Kivenpyörittäjän Kylä*, and this fact may still be heard once you get to know locals.

The old Orthodox monastery at Pyötikkö, south of Vuokko, has long gone but the old cemetery now boasts a fine tsasouna, which is open in summer daily.

Places to Stay & Eat

Vuokonjärven Loma (☎ 477 096) has probably the best location in the Juuka area. There are just 10 cottages hidden among trees and the shallow lake is pleasant to swim in if the weather is warm. Rent a rowing boat and visit the cave in the steep cliff on an island across the strait. Two bed cottages are 150 mk, camping costs 55 mk. There are several saunas. A smoke sauna will be heated for 200 mk but make sure to book the day before. There are showers, a very nice kitchen in the service building and a laundry that is a bit overpriced at 30 mk per load.

Kosken kioski sells food in the village of Keski-Vuokko; the camping ground can provide you with more. Bring enough food with you.

Getting There & Away

Fortunately, one of the afternoon buses travelling north from Juuka to Nurmes passes Vuokko. But a bicycle or car is more recommendable.

NUNNANLAHTI

Nunnanlahti, south of the village of Juuka, is known for its soapstone (Finnish: vuolukivi). If you ignore the mountains of

rock residue, the village is one of the highlights of the Lake Pielinen region. Don't miss the huge quarry pit, it's an awesome sight.

The soft material was discovered at the end of the 19th century and the first company was founded in 1893 to exploit the deposits. Art Nouveau architecture found soapstone a useful material. In the 1980s soapstone became fashionable again.

The small village along the narrow parallel road has a few attractive wooden buildings. There's currently no place to stay in Nunnanlahti.

Kivikylä

Tulikivi Oy is probably the more successful of the two local quarries that compete here. Avoid buying souvenirs here unless you have a car (or a truck!). Soapstone is extremely heavy.

Modern architecture in Kivikylä includes the restaurant-cum-exhibition building where you can learn about soapstone products. The red wooden building at the back is **Vuolukivimuseo**, the Soapstone Museum, displaying products and old tools. The museum is open mid-June to mid-August from 9 am to 10 pm. Entry is free.

Places to Eat *Sinikko*, in the restaurant building at Kivikylä, serves snacks and meals; you should try meat or fish served on a soapstone hotplate. Try also the whitefish dish, Tillinen muikkupata.

From 9 am, Karelian pies are prepared in the restaurant. You can watch, or prepare and cook your own pie in the large soapstone oven – a practice locally referred to as the Karelian Pie University.

AHMOVAARA

The main information office for both Juuka and Koli is at Kolinportti (☎ 671 333) in the village of Ahmovaara along road No 18. The place is known (and hated) for its modern architecture (which has been called 'modern Karelianism') but it remains very popular with locals and visitors alike. You can eat, stock up on provisions, or buy souvenirs.

NORTH KARELIA

There's also an exhibition on natural attractions in the Lake Pielinen region.

Tuomelan Tupa is a small museum devoted to a local poet, Mr Viljo Tuomela, who lived here from 1895 to 1977. The house, some two km from the main road, is open June to August from 10 am to 4 pm, Tuesday to Sunday. Entry is free.

South of Ahmovaara, *Future Freetime* (☎ 674 201) has large rooms for 125 mk per person, including breakfast.

VAIKKOJOKI RIVER

The 50 km Vaikkojoki route has been restored to its original state and is no longer used for floating logs. It is now promoted as a canoeing route from Juuka to the municipality of Kaavi. There are 40 rapids of varying difficulty and a few accommodation options along the route. Get a free copy of the *Vaikkojoki* brochure (English and German text) or buy a waterproof route map (25 mk) at the Juuka tourist office. The route starts 25 km west of Juuka village, at the Ahmonkoski rapids, and ends near the village of Kaavi. You can rent canoes at holiday villages in Kaavi or Juuka.

NURMES

Nurmes (population 10,700), at the northwest tip of Lake Pielinen, is probably the most pleasant of the eastern towns that claim to embody the Karelian heritage. The terraced old town is attractive, with its beautiful wooden houses and views of two surrounding lakes. Nurmes was founded in 1876 by Tsar Alexander II of Russia and the old town still has the character approved of by the 19th century Russian ruler. The town of Nurmes is overshadowed by a sawmill, but the municipality area features genuine wilderness and good fishing waters.

Orientation

Train and bus stations are in the town centre, opposite the Kauppatori market square. The main street is Kirkkokatu, with its beautiful birches. Old Nurmes is north-west of Kauppatori. The Bomba (a Karelian theme village) and most places to stay are a few km

to the east. Porokylä in the north is becoming the de facto commercial centre of Nurmes, although it is not enormously interesting.

Information

Tourist Office The excellent tourist information services and most of the commercial tourist services for that matter are run by the semiprivate company Loma Nurmes (☎ 481 770) at Hyvärilä. The railway station has an information booth, open 1 June to 10 August, daily from 9 am to 9 pm. You can also get tourist information from Saimaa Ferries Oy (☎ 481 244), the local shipping company. Their office, at Kirkkokatu 16, is open Monday to Friday from 9 am to 4 pm.

Post & Telephone The main post office is at Torikatu 14 and is open Monday to Friday from 9 am to 4.30 pm.

Library Officially called the Nurmes-talo, the public library at Kötsintie 2 has a good range of travel books and maps, including regional 1:20,000 maps in the käsikirjasto section, as well as a local museum. There is a collection of the *Kalevala* in various languages and an Internet terminal.

Churches

The vast Lutheran Church from 1896 is the largest in North Karelia, with 2300 seats. There are miniature models of earlier Lutheran churches. The church is open in summer from 10 am to 6 pm. The small Orthodox church, east of the town centre, is open only during services. It offers little of interest.

Puu-Nurmes

In Puu-Nurmes (the old wooden town northwest of the train station), there are idyllic wooden houses which are protected by law and surrounded by birch trees. Harjukatu, Työväenkatu and Rajakatu are three streets that constitute the most interesting area.

Nurmes-Talo

This fine building houses a library, a theatre, a gallery section with excellent views from

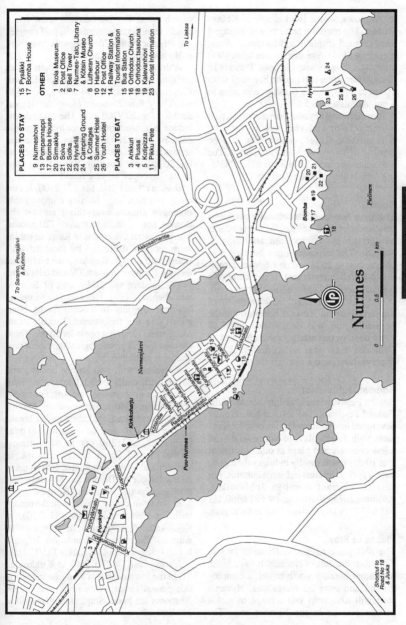

PLACES TO STAY

9 Nurmeshovi
13 Pompannappi
17 Bomba House
20 Sirmakka
21 Solka
23 Hyvärilä
24 Camping Ground & Cottages
25 Summer Hotel
26 Youth Hostel

PLACES TO EAT

3 Ankkuri
4 Plussa
5 Kotipizza
11 Pikku Pete

15 Pysäkki
17 Bomba House

OTHER

1 Ikola Museum
2 Post Office
6 Bell Tower
7 Nurmes-Talo, Library & Kötsin Museo
8 Lutheran Church
10 Harbour
12 Post Office
14 Railway Station & Tourist Information
15 Bus Station
16 Orthodox Church
18 Orthodox Isasouna
19 Kalevanhovi
23 Tourist Information

NORTH KARELIA

its windows, and a local museum, **Kötsin Museo**. The museum features well arranged local cultural displays and historical items, including Stone Age discoveries from 4000 years ago. The museum is open Tuesday to Friday from noon to 6 pm, on Saturday from 10 am to 3 pm, and on Sunday from noon to 4 pm. Admission is 5 mk.

Proceed north beyond the main street, past Nurmes-Talo, and continue to the low Kirkkoharju Ridge, which has a large number of tombstones and sculptures. The red bell tower from 1773 is the oldest building on this side of Lake Pielinen.

Bomba

This large house and its culturally conscious surroundings, two km east of the centre, is by far the most important attraction in Nurmes. The imposing main building was constructed in 1978 and now houses a traditional Karelian restaurant. It is a copy of a typical Karelian family house that was built in 1855 by Jegor Bombin, a farmer from Suojärvi (now in Russian Karelia), but the original house was demolished some 80 years later. In this area you will also find an Orthodox tsasouna, an exhibition house (Kalevanhovi) and a summer theatre.

Bomban Juhlaviikot

Bomba Festival Week, in July, is one of the Finland Festivals. The festival has recently developed into a Finno-Ugrian cultural spectacle, with theatre plays in Nurmes-Talo and a few concerts and plays at other locations. The 10 day event mostly indulges those who have a special interest in Finnic cultures. For details, contact Bomban Juhlaviikot, Kötsintie 2, 75530 Nurmes (☎ 681 6460, fax 681 6494), or any tourist office in the region.

Places to Stay

The best place to stay is *Hyvärilä* (☎ 481 770), four km east of Nurmes. It has a hotel, a summer hotel, a youth hostel, a camping ground and over 30 bungalows. Hyvärilä staff will also help you arrange to rent a private cottage in the Nurmes area. The superb, quiet Finnish lakeside scene has a beach, tennis courts, mini-golf, golf courses and other activities. You can walk from here to Bomba along jogging routes.

A dormitory bed in the old youth hostel building starts at 55 mk with an HI card. *Kartanohotelli* has just 14 rooms, from 380 mk. The yellow *Pehtoori Hotel* has singles/ doubles for 200/300 mk. The bungalows, hidden in a forest, house three to four people and cost 180 to 280 mk per day. You can rent saunas and hire bicycles, canoes and boats for 20 mk per hour or 100 mk per day. Hyvärilä is open all year round.

Bomba (☎ 687 200, fax 687 2100) is currently run by a large holding company that manages almost everything around the Bomba house, including over 120 rooms. The very attractive rooms in Karelian cabins were recently decorated by local artisans. Being built of logs, they keep the traditional feeling. Each room has a TV and telephone.

The modern spa *Sotka*, east of Bomba, was opened in 1991. It has its own reception but there are only 16 modern rooms. Non-guests can use the saunas, Turkish steam rooms and swimming pools for 50 mk. There are also special physiological treatment programmes available.

Sirmakka, with two storey houses, and *Soiva*, with earth-roofed houses, are both near Sotka in the woods and offer comfortable cottage-style accommodation. Rooms in the Bomba area, including buffet breakfast, cost 470 mk in summer and at Christmas, and 390 mk at other times. Sirmakka and Soiva charge 590 mk in summer and 510 mk in winter. Spa usage is 20 mk for guests. Bomba has a weekly programme of activities around Nurmes.

In the town centre, the student dormitory building *Pompannappi* (☎ 481 770), at Koulukatu 16, is open from 1 June to 10 August. There are discounts for HI card holders. Singles/doubles start at 135/170 mk.

Nurmeshovi (☎ 480 750) at Kirkkokatu 21, in the town centre, is a bit of a travelling salesperson's joint, with a smoky bar, but the 30 rooms are good. Singles/doubles start at 310/360 mk.

Places to Eat

In the town centre, you can rely on the nearest grilli, or do your grocery shopping at reasonably priced supermarkets. You will find *Pysäkki* at the bus station; *Pikku Pete*, the local pub, is on Kirkkokatu.

For a splurge, *Bomba* (in Bomba House) has a Karelian smorgasbord abounding in Karelian pies, fried muikku (whitefish) and varieties of karjalanpaisti (stew). The buffet (80 mk) is served all day, and is good value. Bomba is generally open daily from 7 am to late at night. The *Hyvärilä* centre has a restaurant in the hotel building with a buffet for 35 mk. There's also a summer café.

In the commercial centre of Porokylä, you will find the most choice. On Porokylänkatu there is *Kotipizza* and *Plussa*. *Bella* near the post office is the best for lunch, but it doubles as a pub. *Ankkuri* is another local pub, as is the *Hip Hop Pub* nearby.

Getting There & Away

Bus Buses run regularly to Nurmes from Joensuu, Juuka, Kuhmo, Kuopio and Lieksa. There are fewer buses on weekends.

Train Nurmes is currently the terminus for the eastern railways, although light rail services to Kajaani are scheduled to resume by 1997. There is a scenic train journey from Joensuu to Nurmes twice a day. Connections from Kajaani are currently run by buses but train passes are valid. There are no lockers at the station but many people keep their luggage in one of the rooms there. It is free, if you ask politely.

Boat Saimaa Ferries Oy runs passenger ships from Joensuu via Koli twice a week from mid-June to early August. The MS *Vinkeri II* leaves Joensuu at 9.30 am on Thursday and Saturday, and arrives in Nurmes at 8 pm. A one-way ticket is 150 mk from Joensuu and 100 mk from Koli. Current timetables are available from most local tourist offices in Finland.

Getting Around

Local buses run from the market to the Hyvärilä crossing a few times each morning on weekdays. Timetables are available. The taxi stand is opposite the train station.

AROUND NURMES
Saramo

This small, remote village, 24 km north of Nurmes, is where the Korpikylien tie ''Road of Wilderness Villages'') begins. At the far end of the village, the Kalastajatalo, or 'Fisher's House' (☎ 434 066), serves as an information centre and restaurant. Kalastajatalo is open 1 June to 20 August, daily from 10 am to 9 pm. It is open on weekends from 10 am to 6 pm during the rest of the year. There is a shop and a post office in Saramo.

Saramo Jotos Trek Saramo could be used as a base for this 75 km trekking route, which covers all the interesting places around Saramo. Between Saramo and Peurajärvi, there are two campfire sites in addition to Kourukoski, a spot named after rapids there. Between Peurajärvi and road No 75, at Jalasjärvi, there's a laavu. Between road No 75 and Lake Mujejärvi, there are three laavu sites. South of Lake Mujejärvi, there's a laavu at Markuskoski and cottages for rent at Paalikkavaara. The marked trail was established in early 1996. Ask for details in Nurmes or Saramo.

Canoeing the Saramojoki River There are two possible routes. Peurajärvi is not a bad lake to start paddling from (there are few difficult rapids), although July might not be the best month because of low water levels. If you start from Lake Mujejärvi, beware of Pitkäkoski rapids. The river drops 19 metres over 900 metres, so carry your canoe. Just half a kilometre later at Louhikoski, there's another drop of five metres. Other than these two rapids, this route is fine. Contact Kalastajatalo in Saramo for canoe rentals – expect to pay 120 mk per day and 60 mk for transport.

Getting There & Away Some 17 km north of Nurmes, turn left and hitchhike or walk the seven km to Saramo village. Buses run infrequently and charge 37 mk from Nurmes. A shared taxi may be cheaper if there are four of you. A taxi ride 14 km further to Peurajärvi should cost no more than 80 mk.

Kourukoski
Some six km further north, in a totally isolated spot, is the small business of Mr Kauko Timonen (☎ 434 050). He has a salmon-fishing pond, smoke sauna and free accommodation. To fully enjoy the place, fish for salmon (40 mk per kg), get Kauko to prepare it on the campfire, then rent the smoke sauna (about 200 mk for the entire evening) and sleep for free under an open-air laavu at the riverside. This is a very informal place, so you can negotiate all prices.

Peurajärvi Fishing Area
Carefully planned and well kept, this area has good, economical services to keep you busy for days and enough peace and quiet to keep you relaxed for weeks. Go first to the service cabin (☎ 453 011), which has a café and an information booth. It's open from 1 June to 18 August, noon to 9 pm every day. Fishing is not allowed in May. Three hour fishing permits (20 mk) allow you to catch one salmon and unlimited numbers of other species, or you can get a one day permit for 40 mk. You will need to rent a rowing boat in order to catch anything. The service-cabin rents rowing boats (30 mk per day) and there's a lakeside sauna (35 mk per hour). The fishing area is managed by the Forest and Park Service, which releases 6000 kg of salmon into the local waters every spring, for the benefit of licensed amateur fishers.

Apart from the fishing, there's a network of trekking routes (marked by orange paint on trees) running west to Hiidenportti National Park, east to the main road and further to Lake Mujejärvi.

Places to Stay Camping is allowed in many places – get a free map that shows the locations. Peurajärvi centre (☎ 453 011) has a large room in the main building for 230 mk and several six bed cottages for 380 mk. You

must reserve in advance. There are *luppokota* huts, small Lappish-style houses with room for three trekkers, at the southern and northern end of Lake Peurajärvi and at the shores of Lake Iso-Valkeinen. They can be used for free all year round and are always open.

Getting There & Away Peurajärvi is west of the Nurmes to Kuhmo highway. From Peurajärvi, a marked trail due east crosses the highway; from there, you can hitchhike or catch a bus to Nurmes or Kuhmo. The only sealed road is road No 75.

Lake Mujejärvi
This area, north-east of Nurmes, is being developed for wilderness trekking. *Tammikämppä*, a hut which sleeps eight, is always open. The area is east of road No 75 and can be reached by following the Saramo Jotos track.

Ilomantsi

Ilomantsi, Finland's most Karelian, Orthodox and eastern municipality, is one of the three regions in Finland with a non-mainstream indigenous culture (the two others being Åland and the Sami culture of north Lapland). Its inhabitants are probably the friendliest people in Finland, and its forests contain bears and other big animals. The large land area (2770 sq km) is home to some 7900 people. Be forewarned, however, that the main commercial centre of Ilomantsi happens to be one of the ugliest such centres in Finland, and has nothing to do with the Karelian heritage. Go to the tourist office and find out how to explore the interesting wilderness in the frontier area.

Information
The tourist information office (☎ 881 833 or 881 707), right in the village centre at Mantsintie 8, 82900 Ilomantsi, is managed by Ilomantsin Matkailu Oy. The office is very helpful and will provide quite a lot of

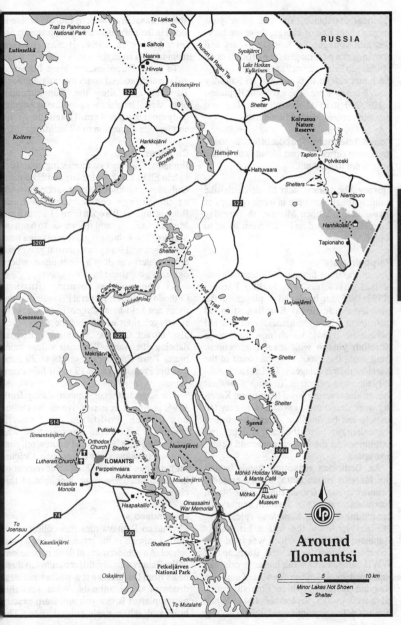

Around Ilomantsi

0   5   10 km

Minor Lakes Not Shown

➤ Shelter

practical assistance. You can leave your luggage here free of charge, there are bicycles and cottages for rent, and tours and bookings can be arranged. The office is open Monday to Friday from 9 am to 4 pm. In July, the hours extend to 6 pm, and on Saturday from 9 am to 2 pm. The excellent Ilomantsi 1:100,000 map shows all trekking and canoeing routes around Ilomantsi.

Post & Telephone The post office, opposite the tourist office, is open Monday to Friday from 9 am to 4.30 pm.

Library The library, next to the castle-like municipal hall, has little in terms of maps or magazines. It's open Monday to Thursday from 1 to 7 pm, and on Friday from 10 am to 3 pm.

Parppeinvaara

One of the most famous of Ilomantsi's historical characters was Jaakko Parppei (1792-1885), a bard and a player of the *kantele*, a traditional Karelian stringed instrument. He is the namesake of this hill (where he lived), which now features a **Karelian village** with several attractions. Built since the 1960s, it is the oldest of the Karelian theme villages in Finland and probably the most attractive. To qualify for their job, guides wearing *feresi* (traditional Karelian work dress) must know how to play the kantele and be fluent in several languages. Runonlaulajan pirtti, the main building, has exhibitions on the *Kalevala* epic and Orthodox arts.

An **Orthodox tsasouna** stands behind the **Matelin museoaitta**, a tiny museum commemorating female rune singer Mateli Kuivalatar, famous in the 19th century for her renditions of the *Kanteletar* epic.

Finally, down the hill a bit stands **Rajakenraalin maja**, which was used as a command centre by General Raappana of WWII fame. Part of the house is original, first built in Rukajärvi (east of Kuhmo in Russian Karelia), where Finnish troops advanced on 15 September 1941. When Finnish defeat was imminent, the house was quietly transferred back to Finland where it stood in the Patvinsuo area until it was transferred here in 1984. It now houses memorabilia from the war.

To get to Parppeinvaara, leave Ilomantsi village and proceed south towards Joensuu. Turn left and follow the 'Runonlaulajan pirtti' sign. The place is open June to August, daily from 9 am to 8 pm. Tickets are 15 mk and include admission to all buildings.

Churches

Ilomantsi features two interesting churches. Pyhän Elian Kirkko is the large and beautiful Orthodox church of Ilomantsi, one km west of the village centre, towards Lake Ilomantsinjärvi. It's open from 11 am to 6 pm Monday to Friday and from noon to 6 pm on Sunday. The *kalmisto* (graveyard) sign near the church will lead you to the old graveyard at the waterfront. It is a silent place, where old trees give shade to a few graves.

As Ilomantsi has so many (Russian) Orthodox believers, several Praasniekka festivals are held here. Originally, these were strictly religious events, but these days they also attract tourists. Sometimes there is dancing afterwards. Ilomantsi village celebrates Petru Praasniekka on 28 to 29 June and Ilja Praasniekka on 19 to 20 July every year.

The large Lutheran Church, dating from 1796, is almost as impressive as the Orthodox Church. Following the Swedish conquest, a Lutheran congregation was established here in 1653 and the new religion soon overshadowed the eastern one. Colourful paintings from 1832, an achievement of Samuel Elmgren, are the highlight of this church.

Eläinmuseo

Mr Jaakko Rautava runs this collection of stuffed animals in the ground floor of a local school. An achievement of three generations of the Rautava family, this museum has three bears from Ilomantsi, a few wolves and hundreds of other animals. What sets this museum apart is that you will learn exactly how and when each animal died. The museum is open daily in summer from 10 am to 5 pm. Admission is 10 mk.

Viinitorni

The local water tower was reborn as Viinitorni (Wine Tower) when Peltohermanni, a local agricultural company, started its café at the top in 1994. Typically of Finland, production, marketing and retail selling of domestic wine was strictly forbidden. Three energetic young men were determined to overcome bureaucratic obstacles and produce and sell something that people like to consume. Strawberry and blackcurrant are used as raw materials to produce a wine that has an alcohol content of 12%. Viinitorni is open from 10 am to 6 pm daily and the entry fee of 10 mk includes coffee. Climb the 188 steps to the top, or use the elevator. If you don't care for wine, come for the fantastic view.

Places to Stay

All bottom-end places are outside the centre. *Ruhkaranta* (☎ 843 161) is a camping ground nine km east of Ilomantsi. Located in a salubrious pine forest, it has spectacular views of several lakes and clean cottages. Cottages for two/three/four people are 100/190/330 mk, with discounts outside the high season. The place is open from May to September. Its traditional smoke sauna is certainly worth the experience but expensive at 900 mk for four hours. A large restaurant is open daily and serves as the reception outside the high season.

Haapakallio (☎ 843 107) is a youth hostel with over 40 beds available all year round. Prices for HI members range from 50 to 125 mk and bicycle rental costs 40 mk per day. The house is seven km south-east of the village of Ilomantsi, or two km from the Möhkö road. Views from the hill are superb; you can see some Russian territory too. To get there, turn onto Kuuksenvaarantie from the Ilomantsi to Möhkö road.

On a hill three km south of the village centre towards Joensuu, 500 metres off the main road, is *Anssilan Monola* (☎ 881 181), where a very friendly family rents rooms in their farmhouse. Singles/doubles are 80/160 mk (bring your own sheets). There are cows, so fresh milk is served at breakfast (25 mk per person). Bicycles can be rented for 30 mk per day.

There are two expensive places to stay in the village itself. *Hotelli Ilomantsi* (☎ 882 533), in the main street, is a pleasant and clean hotel with three separate buildings. Singles/doubles cost 345/425 mk.

Pääskynpesä (☎ 682 7405 or 682 711), at Henrikintie 4, is an enormous establishment behind the Lutheran Church on the lakeside. The price, 310/420 mk, includes breakfast and use of the sauna and pools. Ask for summer discounts. The 25 metre pool is a public swimming pool, with inexpensive admission. There are bicycles and many kinds of boats for rent.

Places to Eat

The best value is *Kelopirtti* on the main road, just outside the village. A substantial buffet is served for 35 mk but later in the afternoon and evening à la carte prices apply. For a real Karelian buffet, called *pitopöytä*, go to *Parppeinpirtti* in Parppeinvaara. The Karelian buffet is a bit expensive, at 70 mk, but for 40 mk you can eat the ordinary buffet. Taste the excellent mushroom salad and vatruska pies, and the slightly sweet vuašša malt drink.

In the centre, most eating places are along the main street. *Sirmakka* is a dark pub frequented by locals but simple meals are also available. Places at the bus terminal include *10 Burger* and *Baari*, both nothing special. *Kahvila Leipomo* is a local bakery that serves coffee. For junk food, *Kassakka* at the market serves hamburgers and other snacks until 10 pm. For self-catering, there are several budget food stores along the main street in the village.

Things to Buy

Kelopirtti has a large variety of local handicrafts and is certainly worth a visit. Piirolan piha at Kauppatie 26 is a pleasant handicrafts centre with local flavour. There are several exhibitions and a café. Piirolan piha is open daily mid-June to mid-August but the sales exhibition is open Monday to Thursday all year round.

Getting There & Away

Buses run throughout the day, Monday to Friday, from Joensuu to Ilomantsi village. There are fewer buses on weekends, so plan ahead. The bus terminal in Ilomantsi is right in the village centre. From here, there are several connections to Möhkö, Hattuvaara and Naarva villages but most buses run only on school days; during the summer holidays, there is usually just one daily departure, Monday to Friday. Taxis depart from near the bus terminal.

Transport services from Ilomantsi to other villages have deteriorated since the first edition of this book. A tip: contact the tourist office. There might be a guesthouse owner going your way, or if you promise to wait at a particular place, the owner might come and pick you up. Ilomantsi certainly has more to offer than the central village.

HATTUVAARA

Hattuvaara, north-east of Ilomantsi, is a convenient base for tours to the easternmost region in Finland. The village is the main landmark along the little-travelled Runon ja rajan tie route. Experiencing a summer night in this quaint little village is a highlight: birds sing, cow bells sound and wild flowers bloom. Winter is quieter, with a great deal of snow falling.

Gold was recently discovered on both sides of Hattuvaara village, so mining activity may grow during the next couple of decades.

Mr Jouni Puruskainen runs much of the village and almost any tour around the region. His wife speaks English and they can be contacted at Taistelijan Talo (see below).

Orthodox Tsasouna

Hattuvaara has the oldest Orthodox tsasouna in Finland. Built in the 1720s, it has several old Russian icons inside. Its small tower was used as a watchtower during WWII. In summer, the small chapel is open from noon to 6 pm Tuesday to Sunday. On 29 June, a colourful Praasniekka festival takes place here, with a *ristinsaatto* (Orthodox procession commemorating a saint) beginning at the tsasouna.

Behind the chapel, many of the old graves at the **kalmisto** (graveyard) have a wooden *grobu* (marker) above them, shadowed by surprisingly thick trees. A path leads from here to **Hoskosen pihapiiri**, a number of old houses visible from the main road. Renovation work is under way.

Taistelijan Talo

The modern 'Fighter's House' is down the road from the tsasouna. Designed by Joensuu architect Erkki Helasvuo, this house symbolises the meeting of East and West. There is a WWII museum downstairs, with interesting photos, guns and handicrafts *(puhde-esineitä)* made by Finnish soldiers in moments of wartime stalemate. There is more to see in the backyard. The house serves food and is open Monday to Friday from 10 am to 6 pm, and on weekends until 5 pm. Entry to the museum costs 18 mk.

Places to Stay & Eat

Arhipanpirtti (☎ 830 138) is the only place to stay in Hattuvaara, but go to Taistelijan Talo (☎ 830 111) for reception. There are 10 rooms in several buildings. The superb cottage accommodates at least six people and costs 400 mk per night and 2000 mk per week. A bed in an aitta building starts at 60 mk per night. Better rooms in *Sergein tupa* are 90/180 mk, including a kitchen and a sauna. Bicycles are a bargain at 20 mk per day; boats and canoes are also available.

For a good buffet, go to *Taistelijan Talo*; for 50 to 65 mk you can eat as much as you like. In summer, the place serves food all day until 10 pm. You can get food supplies at the only shop in the village, Hatun Puoti, near the tsasouna.

Getting There & Away

Hattuvaara is by far the largest village between Ilomantsi and Lieksa along the Runon ja rajan tie route. There is a bus from

Ilomantsi village at 1.20 pm, Monday to Friday, and a few more buses on school days.

AROUND HATTUVAARA
Far East

Lake Virmajärvi, the easternmost point of Finland (and the European Union) is now open to visitors. You must go there with Jouni Puruskainen, who will arrange a special permit at the Border Guards' Station next to Taistelijan Talo. You must provide the authorities with passport details. The permit is free and usually provided in less than 24 hours.

Jouni has a 4WD minibus that takes seven people. The minimum charge is approximately 200 mk; to reduce costs, try to join a group or wait until enough people show up. It seems Jouni is willing to include a meal in the wilderness with the tour so negotiate first. It's an interesting journey, passing a few WWII *sotapaikka* (battle locations) at Sikrenvaara, and the *hauta* (grave) of a Russian female soldier. Ask for these, as Jouni speaks little English.

Tapion Taival

The easternmost trekking route in Finland gives you the choice of a 13 km wilderness track along the Koitajoki River, or an eight km northern extension across the Koivusuo Nature Reserve, or yet another extension north of Koivusuo to Kivivaara. The Koitajoki section is certainly the highlight. The path is marked by orange paint on tree trunks.

The Koivusuo track starts at the northern end of Koivusuo Reserve, on an old gravel road that takes you via Pirhu Research Station (everything's locked), and through an open bog that is the only thing really worth seeing along the Koivusuo leg.

South of Koivusuo, you join the original Tapion taival path near the Polvikoski rapids. After the first campfire place (20 minutes or so), you reach the river and follow its twists and turns thereon. There are unusually large trees, mostly pine and fir, varied vegetation and abundant birdlife. There are rumours of bears and other big mammals. After Hanhikoski, the track leaves the river (which flows to the border area and further into Russia) and crosses a few bogs until it parallels the yellow-marked border. Do not cross it. A parking area marks the end of the trek at Tapionaho.

Places to Stay Technically, there are four places where you can find shelter but only one is suitable for staying overnight in. Heading down from the Polvikoski bridge in the north, walk 30 minutes or more to *Karanteenipudas*, which is a very basic laavu offering temporary shelter. Another half an hour will take you to *Sammalpuro*, a low-built hut where you can sleep, but do not light a campfire inside even if there is a place to do so. Just 15 minutes away is *Niemipuro*, an excellent hut with several mattresses and space for five people. An oven heats the hut but doesn't boil the water.

Hanhikoski, one of the easternmost buildings in Finland, is the one where you can legally stay overnight, and it's absolutely free. This hut is a sauna, so sleeping is not comfortable. There often seem to be more mozzies inside the hut than out. You can swim in the river. Hanhikoski is an hour's trek from Niemipuro.

Getting There & Away You may have to negotiate with Jouni Puruskainen in Hattuvaara about transport and its price, especially if you want to do the Koivusuo leg first. You can trek the 10 km from Hattuvaara to the northern end of the original Tapion taival; there are some WWII memorial stones along the way. Starting from Möhkö further south, you can combine Susitaival with Tapion taival and turn right from Kivilampi to Koivuvaara (seven km) and further to Tapionaho (20 km). You will need a map for these roads.

Coming from the Ilomantsi to Hattuvaara road, the southern end of the route (Tapionaho) is reached by following the sign that reads 'Niemijärvi 15'.

Hoikan Kylkeinen

For fishing, try Lake Hoikan Kylkeinen, a bit

further north of the Koivusuo Nature
Reserve. Salmon are released into this lake.
The Hatun Puoti and the Taistelijan Talo,
both in Hattuvaara, sell fishing permits. You
can also rent a boat from Taistelijan Talo.

En route from Hattuvaara, **Pirun kallio** is
a large rock. Follow the sign from the
parking area in the nature reserve.

MÖHKÖ

In the last century, Möhkö was a busy village
with an ironworks. Ludvig von Arppe, a
clever industrialist, employed 2000 people
in his plants, and even printed his own
money to pay his employees. Local shops,
also owned by Mr Arppe, only accepted his
money. Russian soldiers destroyed most of
the town during WWII but an interesting
museum and a few other sights remain.
Möhkö, just two km from the Russian
border, has only 200 inhabitants today.

Möhkö is a Sami word for a river curve –
the Koitajoki River, flowing from Russian
territory, curves here. There's a shop and a
post office in the village. The longest trekking route in Ilomantsi, Suden taival, starts
from Möhkö.

Ruukki

Ruukkimuseo, the museum of Möhkö, is in
an old Pytinki house, built in 1849. It has old
furniture and exhibitions illustrating old
techniques used in the iron and paper industries. There are sections on WWII and
logging culture, a renovated canal and other
old constructions, as well as a two km
lemmenpolku ('romantic trail') around the
area. The museum, which is well worth a
visit, is open from mid-June to mid-August,
Sunday to Friday from 10 am to 6 pm and on
Saturday from 10 am to 4 pm. Entry is 10
mk.

Places to Stay & Eat

Möhkön Karhumajat (☎ 844 180), the
easternmost holiday village in Finland, is
open March to October. It has good huts for
rent and camping is possible. Although the
service is not especially good, the location is
definitely something special. The cheapest

doubles start at 150 mk. There are boats for
rent and you can buy fishing permits.

Manta, near the bridge, is an old barge that
once accommodated factory workers. It is
now a café serving coffee and real Karelian
vatruska and *kukkonen* pies.

Getting There & Away

Möhkö is well connected by sealed road to
Ilomantsi. In summer, there are taxi buses
twice daily on Monday, Wednesday and
Friday. Contact the tourist office in Ilomantsi
for bookings. During the school season,
buses run four times a day, Monday to
Friday. If you have a car, an interesting loop
is Ilomantsi to Möhkö to Hattuvaara.

PETKELJÄRVI NATIONAL PARK

Petkeljärvi, south-east of Ilomantsi, is one of
the smallest national parks in Finland.
Founded in 1956 to protect an attractive
piece of ridge and lake scenery, the emphasis
is more on recreation than nature preservation. There is a sealed road through the park
and many clearly marked trails. To appreciate Petkeljärvi, take mosquito repellent,
walk to an isolated spot, sit down and listen
to what nature has to say. There are wilderness bird species such as the black-throated
diver and some owls. The best time to see
birds is April to June, but all summer is fine.

This is also a good place to get some
serious *löyly* in the lakeside sauna.

Things to See

There are reconstructed WWII sites at the
southern tip of Petraniemi, near the park
headquarters. The *korsu* bunker was where
soldiers slept while their comrades guarded
the other side of the lake. No fighting took
place here. There is a large war monument
on the main road at Oinassalmi.

Places to Stay & Eat

Petkeljärven leirintäalue (☎ 844 199) is a
camping ground at the National Park Centre,
six km from the main road. The modern
building offers accommodation in superb
rooms. Prices range from 55 to 80 mk per
person, according to the size of the room, and

one single is available for 150 mk. Camping costs 35 mk for one person, 60 mk for two or more. You can hire boats and canoes, buy fishing permits or rent the sauna (55 mk per hour). A buffet breakfast is available, by order, but it may be cheaper to bring your own food and prepare it in the kitchen.

Getting There & Away

Möhkö buses run along the good road from Ilomantsi. A sealed road (no bus) takes you the six km from the main road to the park headquarters. If you want to trek, follow the 26 km Taitajan taival ('Expert trail') from Putkela village, five km north of Ilomantsi village. You can also join the path from the Möhkö road (the turn-off is signposted), a 13 km hike.

TAITAJAN TAIVAL

This 26 km trekking route from Petkeljärvi National Park to Petkula (north of Ilomantsi) is very different from the Tapion taival wilderness track. Crossing paved roads and passing inhabited areas and unpleasant logging sites, Taitajan taival (also known as 'Putkela-Petkeljärvi retkeilypolku') also takes you to spectacular ridges and to small idyllic lakes. The track can be done as a light-gear trip in one or two days.

Ruhkaranta camping ground (see Ilomantsi) serves as a midway pit-stop with food, drinks and inexpensive accommodation in comfortable cottages. There are also laavu shelters every five km or so, where you can make a campfire and rest.

Probably the best starting point is the village of Putkela north of Ilomantsi (catch the afternoon bus to Hattuvaara), because you can stay overnight at Petkeljärvi after completion of the trek. The track is marked by yellow paint on trees.

MUTALAHTI

This tiny place to the south of Ilomantsi can be reached by an eastern canoe route that will take you through some attractive scenery. **Juustola** (☎ 841 110) is a private dairy that produces cheese. It is run by Jussi Aellig from Switzerland and his wife. The place

should be open on Sunday. Check at the Ilomantsi tourist office for details.

NAARVA

Mostly appreciated for fine Karelian scenery and peace and quiet, Naarva, north-west of Hattuvaara, is a tiny village that can be visited as a side trip from the quiet Runon ja rajan tie route. Naarva has a bank and a shop where you can buy petrol.

From Naarva village, there are good views of the surrounding wilderness. As you drive along the road through the village, a sign reading 'asepajamuseo' indicates a **gunsmith's museum**. The grey building was built in 1790 and looks as if it's about to collapse. It is normally closed but you can see through the windows or ring the bell in the hope that someone might come from the house nearby to open the door. Admission is 5 mk.

Places to Stay & Eat

One reason to visit Naarva is to stay in an old farmhouse and relax for a few days. The owners speak good Finnish but with an eastern accent, so bring your phrasebook. *Hirvola* (☎ 831 131), classified as *maatila-majoitus* (farm accommodation), a short distance past the village shop, has four rooms. It is run by an elderly Karelian couple who prepare traditional food. Prices are negotiable, but expect to pay 60 mk per person, sauna and sheets included, or 300 mk for a house with eight beds. Another place, two km off the main road, is *Salhola* (☎ 831 106). There are two four bed houses, at 60 mk per person. Try to get the red *mummon-mökki* (grandmother's house) behind the spruce trees – it is very quiet. Views from both places are splendid.

Getting There & Away

Naarva is seven km west of the Runon ja rajan tie route, and 50 km north of Ilomantsi. There is a bus from Ilomantsi village from Monday to Friday at 2 pm but only on school days. In summer, enquire at the tourist office in Ilomantsi. If you walk the Susitaival trail, you'll get to Naarva.

LAKE KOITERE

This scenic lake in the north-west corner of Ilomantsi municipality can be visited by staying at *Koitereen Helmi* (☎ 832 440) on Kivisalmentie, on the western shore of Lake Koitere. There are 23 cottages of various size, ranging from 170 mk for doubles to 300 mk for a six bed cottage. Camping costs from 40 mk person. There are bicycles, canoes and boats for rent. Canoes can be transported; look for interesting canoeing routes from here. The place is located midway between Uimaharju and Patvinsuo National Park.

Pohjanmaa

Pohjanmaa, known as Österbotten in Swedish and sometimes as Ostrobothnia (from the Latin), is the great secret of Finland.

For many travellers this flat region may be one of the ugliest parts of the planet they have ever seen. This first impression is a pity because the West Coast has some of the most interesting historical sights in Finland, from colourful old Catholic churches to more recent wooden towns that have been surprisingly well preserved.

The West Coast also has a unique Swedish-speaking population whose customs are quite different from those of other Finns. You can forget about the flat plains, but missing the coastal towns, from Kristinestad in the south to Raahe in the north, would be a serious mistake for anyone wanting to get a full picture of Finland.

HISTORY
Some 7000 years ago, most of today's Pohjanmaa was covered by the waters of Lake Litorina. The heavy ice layer that had covered all of Scandinavia, including Finland, compressed the landmass. As the ice melted, the land slowly expanded.

Even today, it is estimated that the land continues to rise almost one cm each year, revealing more sea bed as time goes by. Prehistoric remains and records of early settlement are abundant.

Swedish fishers established settlements along the coast. They were soon followed by Häme people who settled in the interior of Pohjanmaa, and the language boundary that emerged is still strongly evident.

Throughout history, Pojanmaa's busy harbours have attracted a great number of visitors, many of whom enriched the social fabric.

Närpes, Vaasa, Isokyrö, Pedersöre (near Pietarsaari) and Karleby (Kokkola) once flourished as Catholic centres and plenty of

Highlights
- The pleasant seaside town of Vaasa, with its fine museums.
- The old wooden towns and distinctive culture along the Swedish Coast.
- Stundars, a living museum of Swedish culture, near Vaasa.
- Narrow riverside roads in central Pohjanmaa, ideal for cycling.
- Isokyrö Church, the oldest in Pohjanmaa.
- Alvar Aalto architecture in Seinäjoki.
- The trip to Maakalla Island, off Kalajoki.

medieval churches have survived. Over the centuries, a proud farming culture grew in the flat but fertile Pohjanmaa, and Swedes developed trading towns on the coast in the 17th century to exploit the rich forests – sources of tar for Sweden's war fleet.

Some of Finland's bloodiest wars, both civil and international, have been fought in Pohjanmaa. In the early decades of Finnish independence, the extreme right had its base here; today the right is focused on the upholding of traditional and cultural values.

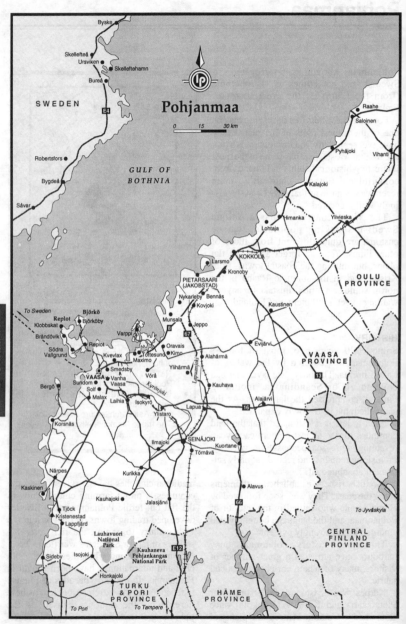

POHJANMAA

Vaasa

Vaasa (Swedish: Vasa), the largest town in Pohjanmaa, has a culture all of its own. Some 27% of the population of 55,000 speak Swedish and the surrounding countryside is largely inhabited by Swedish speakers, making Vaasa the largest distinctively bilingual town in Finland. This is one of its attractions. Vaasa can be reached from Sweden by regular passenger ferry.

During the Vaasa Carnival in early August, there is dancing, music and beer drinking. Many of the Korsholm Music Festival concerts are held in Vaasa.

History

Vaasa began in the 14th century as a village called Korsholm. It had an important harbour, now in ruins, near today's Old Vaasa. It gained town rights in 1606 and became the capital of Pohjanmaa. It was renamed after the royal Swedish Wasa family. The town was to become important for administrative and military reasons. During the Civil War that followed Finnish independence, Vaasa was the capital of the 'Whites'.

Orientation

Nearly half of the central grid is occupied by commercial companies, a great number of which are in Hovioikeudenpuistikko, the main street. The market square is the centre point of Vaasa. Vaskiluoto to the west and Pikisaari to the north are two islands connected to central Vaasa by bridges.

Information

Tourist Office The tourist office (☎ 325 1145) at Hovioikeudenpuistikko 11 is open from June to August on weekdays from 8 am to 7 pm and on weekends from 10 am to 7 pm. At other times, it's open Monday to Friday from 8 am to 4 pm.

Post & Telephone The main post office is opposite the train station at Hovioikeuden-

puistikko 23A. Tele is at Pitkäkatu 44. Vaasa's postcode is 65100.

Library The public library is at Kirjastonkatu 13 near the railroad tracks. The library is open Monday to Friday from 11 am to 8 pm and on Saturday from 10 am to 3 pm.

Books & Maps Suomalainen Kirjakauppa in the Rewell Shopping Centre is the largest bookshop in town.

Left Luggage Lockers at the railway station cost 10 mk.

Emergency Services In a general emergency call ☎ 112; for a doctor, ☎ 10023. There are pharmacies at Hovioikeudenpuistikko 9 and 20.

Churches

Vaasa Church is an impressive red brick building with an interior of beautifully carved wood. Three 19th century painters created the works at the altar. The church is open June to August, Tuesday to Friday from 10 am to 3 pm and on Saturday from 6 to 8 pm. During the rest of the year, it's open Tuesday to Friday from 1 to 3 pm.

At the other end of Kirkkopuistikko (Church Street), the **Orthodox Church**, also made of red brick, has old icons, some of them brought from St Petersburg. It's open from late June to early August, daily from 10 am to 2 pm.

Pohjanmaan Museo

This regional museum on Museokatu is one of the best museums in Finland. The Hedman collection upstairs is one of the best collections of art from Finland's Golden Era. The general collection displays some of the cultural wealth for which Pohjanmaa is famous: decorations, traditional wedding items and colourful artefacts. The museum is open on Monday from noon to 4 pm, Tuesday to Friday from noon to 8 pm and on weekends from 1 to 6 pm. Admission is 10 mk for adults and 5 mk for students and children.

POHJANMAA

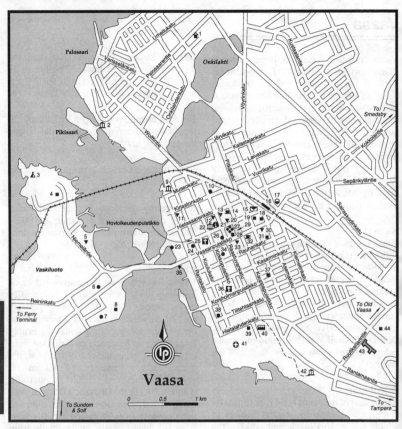

Vaasa

0   0.5   1 km

To Sundom
& Solf

Brage

This open-air museum has a dozen buildings and features an original farmyard from the Närpes municipality. You may have to ask the warden to show you some of the other exhibits, such as the Seal-Hunting Museum and the old saunas. The museum is one km south of the town centre. It is open Tuesday to Friday from 1 to 6 pm and on weekends from noon to 4 pm. Entry is 10 mk for adults and 5 mk for students.

Other Museums

Nautical Museum This museum in the Pal-

osaari area exhibits old vessels and artefacts recovered from sunken boats. It's open from late May to mid-August, weekdays from 11.30 am to 6.30 pm. Admission is 5 mk.

Ostrobothnia Australis This very centrally located collection of stuffed animals at Hovioikeudenpuistikko 9 is open Wednesday to Sunday from noon to 5 pm. Admission is 10 mk.

Taidehalli The art gallery in the town hall has temporary exhibitions. It's open

PLACES TO STAY	11	Bacchus	15	Post Office
	12	Gustav Wasa	16	Railway Station
1 Tekla	13	Koti	17	Bus Station
3 Wasa Camping	14	Maipin Café	21	Tourist Office
4 Hotel Fenno	20	McDonald's &	22	Ostrobothnia Australis
8 Sokos Hotel		Konditoria	23	Flea Market
Tropiclandia		Kotileipomo	24	Tikanoja Art Gallery
18 Hotelli Vallonia City	30	Chilli Pepper &	25	Vaasa Church
19 Sokos Hotel Royal		Vaasan Panimo	26	Town Hall & Taidehalli
Waasa	32	Tom Café &	27	Rewell Shopping
28 Sokos Hotel Vaakuna		Kauppahalli		Centre
31 Olo	33	Bertels Panorama	29	Market Square
37 Motel Teboil	35	Faros	32	Kauppahalli Indoor
38 Evankelinen				market
Kansanopisto	**OTHER**		34	Water Tower
39 Kesähotelli			36	Orthodox Church
44 Hotel Silveria	2	Nautical Museum	40	Swimming Hall
	6	Wasalandia	41	Hospital
PLACES TO EAT	7	Spa	42	Brage Museum
	9	Pohjanmaan Museo	43	Kuntsi Collections of
5 Segeli	10	Public Library		Modern Art

Wednesday to Sunday from noon to 5 pm. Admission is 5 mk.

Tikanoja Art Gallery The Tikanojan taidekoti on Horioikeudenpuistikko has a good collection of Finnish and foreign paintings. It's open Tuesday to Saturday from 11 am to 4 pm and on Sunday from noon to 5 pm. Entry is 10 mk; free for students.

Kuntsi Collection of Modern Art This museum, at Ruutikellarintie 9, is on the premises of a business school. You will have to talk to the people at the Tikanoja Art Gallery re admission. Entry is free.

Wasalandia

This typical amusement park, on the island of Vaskiluoto, is open from 16 May to 12 August daily, and from 30 April till early September on weekends. In addition to the 70 mk pass, valid for all park facilities, there is a small entry fee in the high season.

Places to Stay – bottom end

Wasa Camping (☎ 317 3852) on the island of Vaskiluoto, some two km from the town centre, is open from late May to late August. The four-bed bungalows cost 170 mk (220 mk in July). The camping ground is well kept

and has good kitchens, showers and toilets. It also rents bicycles and boats. *Tekla* (☎ 327 6411), at Palosaarentie 58 on Palosaari Island in northern Vaasa, is the only youth hostel in Vaasa. From 1 June to 15 August beds start at 85 mk. During the rest of the year singles/doubles cost 195/250 mk.

Places to Stay – middle

Olo (☎ 317 4558) at Asemakatu 12, not far south of the railway station, has singles/doubles for 100/150 mk. *Evankelinen Kansanopisto* (☎ 317 4903) is an evangelical folk school at Rantakatu 21-22, with singles/doubles for 210/260 mk. Rooms have to be reserved in advance.

Motel Teboil (☎ 317 6422) at Pitkäkatu 62 is a petrol station motel with singles/doubles for 210/280 mk. The price includes sauna and breakfast. *Kesähotelli* (☎ 9400-668 521) is a summer hotel at Hietalahdenkatu 6, with singles/doubles for 100/170 mk. It's open for a few weeks in June and July only.

Places to Stay – top end

Many of the more expensive hotels in Vaasa offer special discount rates in summer. Hotels in the top price bracket include:

Sokos Hotel Vaakuna (☎ 327 4111) in the Rewell

POHJANMAA

Centre charges 375 mk for all rooms but in winter prices are higher.

Sokos Hotel Royal Waasa (☎ 327 8111) is on Hovioikeudenpuistikko 18. This fine hotel near the railway station accommodates people in two buildings. All rooms are 425 mk in summer; more at other times.

Hotelli Vallonia City (☎ 317 6200) at Asemakatu 4 has only 32 rooms, but there's a restaurant and a sauna. The lobby restaurant is pleasantly decorated. Singles/doubles cost 460/540 mk, 360/430 mk in summer. Rooms with their own sauna cost approximately 100 mk more.

Hotel Fenno (☎ 312 1055) is in Vaskiluoto. Singles/doubles cost 280/370 mk in summer.

Sokos Hotel Tropiclandia (☎ 325 7111) is at Lemmenpolku 3 in Vaskiluoto. A large spa hotel, it has singles/doubles from 490/530 mk.

Hotel Silveria (☎ 326 7511) at Ruutikellarintie 4 is a fine hotel school. Singles/doubles are 320/380 mk, and this includes breakfast, morning sauna and a swim.

Places to Eat

There are several *grillis*, pizzerias and hamburger restaurants near the market square and in the Rewell Centre. The market area is especially good on sunny days.

There are two nice lunch restaurants on Vaasanpuistikko with a panoramic view over the market square. On the third floor at Vaasanpuistikko 16, *Bertels Panorama* is older and more popular but it is open only on weekdays till 5 pm. *Tom Café* is newer and offers a similar lunch package. Also on Vaasanpuistikko, *Chili Pepper* at No 20 serves hamburgers, while *Vaasan Panimo* at No 22 serves Tumma and Vaalea beer made in their own brewery. The indoor *Kauppahalli market* has a few cafés selling fresh bakery products.

There are several popular places near the market, including *McDonald's* and *Konditoria Kotileipomo*, which has a terrace in summer, and the pleasant *Maipin Café* on Kauppapuistikko.

Around the corner from the tourist office, *Gustav Wasa* at Raastuvankatu 24 is a cellar restaurant with brick walls and steep prices for fine evening dining. Across the street, but certainly not as chic, is *Koti* which translates as 'home'; a brief look in will probably explain why this very old pub feels like home to its clientele. *Bacchus*, in the basement of a fine wooden house at Rantakatu 4 near the waterfront, also serves good cuisine. Well seasoned meat is the speciality.

Faros, a boat restaurant near the bridge that leads to Vaskiluoto, is quite special, and always packed when the sun is shining.

Vaskiluoto has a few summer restaurants, such as *Segeli* at Niemeläntie 14, south-east of the camping ground. It offers a buffet lunch from 11 am to 2 pm for 34 mk.

Things to Buy

The market square is bustling on weekdays till 5 pm and on Saturday till 2 pm. The old Kauppahalli market, near the market square, sells foodstuffs, glassware and handicrafts. The Rewell Centre is a modern shopping centre also near the market square. There are some bargains here, if you look. A delightful flea market can be found on the waterfront at the end of Hovioikeudenpuistikko. People come to sell bric-a-brac and you have to bargain. The market is in operation daily till September.

Getting There & Away

Air There are several flights a day from Helsinki to Vaasa. There are also flights to/from Kokkola.

Bus There are daily bus services from all major western and central towns, and several express buses a day from Helsinki and Turku via Pori. Buses run along the west coast on weekdays almost hourly.

Train Vaasa is off the main railway lines, but there is a connecting line from Seinäjoki to Vaasa and there are half a dozen trains per day. The fastest IC train from Helsinki covers the 420 km in four hours.

Getting Around

Bus Although the town centre is small enough for you to walk around, local buses come in handy if you want to reach more distant places. Take bus No 10A/B to the harbour or to Old Vaasa, and bus No 2 to the youth hostel. Buses accept the 10 km Coach Holiday Ticket coupon.

Bicycle Bicycles can be rented at the tourist office for 10 mk per day. Tekla and Vaasa Camping rent bikes too.

AROUND VAASA
Vanha Vaasa

The old town of Vaasa developed around a harbour that became unfit for vessels as the Bothnian landmass rose. The medieval church is now in ruins, and although the old fortress area has been protected not much remains. **Köpmanshuset Wasastjerne**, a museum at Kauppiaankatu 32, has been renovated for educational exhibitions. It's open from mid-June to mid-August, daily from noon to 6 pm (and on Sunday only until early September). Admission is 10 mk. Probably the most interesting sight is the **Church of Korsholm**, built in 1786. It looks very pompous; it was originally a judges' palace.

Korsholm

This unusually shaped municipality (Finnish: Mustasaari) surrounds Vaasa on almost all sides. Consequently, much of it can be seen on day trips from Vaasa by bus. Almost 75% of the population of 16,200 speak Swedish.

One of the centres, Smedsby, is a modern administrative and business centre just outside Vaasa. *Hotel Vallonia Garden* (☎ 322 2200) at Keskustie 3 has rooms for 400/500 mk, which includes breakfast.

Sundom

A quaint little village to the south of Vaasa, Sundom has red houses and a little yellow church on a hill. The local **museum** (☎ 357 1042) is open by appointment in summer. *Sundom Hallen* serves coffee and sells handicrafts, and is open Monday to Saturday.

Solf

One of the most attractive villages in Finland, Solf (Finnish: Sulva) is best known for its museum, Stundars.

Stundars This fantastic open-air museum, with around 50 buildings, comes alive in summer. There are several days when people dress up in national costume, most notably on Kalas Day (check dates at tourist offices). Lots of handicrafts are available, and you can see how wool is dyed or wood is carved. The museum precinct is open from 15 May to 15 August, daily from noon to 6 pm; 15 mk will admit you to everything and includes a guided tour. Nearby, **Tryckerimuseum** includes old printing machines from a local newspaper, and with luck you'll see how it used to be printed. There are exhibits and a café in the houses nearby.

Solf Church This wooden church was constructed in 1786. The fantastic 17th century altar decoration was purchased from the town of Hudiksvall in Sweden. The church is open in summer from 9 am to 4 pm.

Places to Stay & Eat *Solf Gästgiveri* (☎ 344 0999) is a meticulously renovated old house. Pleasant rooms cost 250/300 mk and include breakfast and sauna.

Fredrikas, the local restaurant not far from the church, is not easy to spot. *Söderfjärden* is a restaurant a few km from Solf towards Sundom, near the main road.

Getting There & Away Make sure you travel the scenic route to Solf from Vaasa, via Vaskiluoto and Sundom. Buses from Vaasa make the 16 km trip to Stundars.

Replot

Replot (Finnish: Raippaluoto) is a large island off Vaasa and one of the day tours you can take from Vaasa. It is also a worthwhile destination if you have a bicycle.

There are several small fishing communities in addition to the main village, which is also called Replot. A ferry connects Replot with mainland Finland. However, in 1997 a bridge 1040 metres long (the longest bridge in Finland) will connect Replot with the mainland.

Bullerås The small village of Bullerås is at

The whimbrel, a common bird in Pohjanmaa

the south-west corner of the island, some 10 km from the village of Replot. It has a museum. The holiday village (☎ 352 7613) has cottages from 150 mk and a restaurant in a 1920s villa.

Klobbskat A village at the western end of the island of Replot, Klobbskat is in a Lappish-like setting. At *Kalle's Inn* (☎ 312 3863) you'll pay about 390/700 mk for singles/doubles. Bookings are essential.

Bjököby
This little village on Björkö, an island northwest of Replot, was previously part of an independent municipality. The museum area has a few old houses scattered around, including an old house at the fishing harbour of Bodback, three km from the actual museum. In 1617, locals were given the responsibility for mail transport in exchange for tax deductions and an exemption from military service.

Kvevlax
This little village north of Vaasa has a nice yellow church with a separate bell tower. The church, originally built in 1693, was rebuilt during the 18th century. There is a small museum across the road. You can eat at *Café Anneli* or at *Sofia Grillkiosk* up the road.

Central Pohjanmaa

Probably the most interesting part of Pohjanmaa lies between the busy towns of Vaasa and Seinäjoki. It is here that prehistoric discoveries and a few medieval churches are to be found. Several significant rivers that cross the landscape and spending some time cycling or paddling along them is an interesting option.

SEINÄJOKI
Seinäjoki (population 29,000), the most important town in this part of Pohjanmaa, is known for the architecture of Alvar Aalto. There is also an unusually interesting museum area at the southern edge of town.

The best time to visit is during festivals, such as Tango markkinat or Provinssi rock. Both these events attract some of the largest crowds at Finnish summer festivals.

History
Human settlement in the Seinäjoki region extends back some 4000 years. Seinäjoki started its slow growth with the founding of ironworks in 1798 at Törnävä near the Östermyra estate. Törnävä, also the name of the mansion on the estate, was built in 1806 by the Wasastjerna family. Other buildings in the village of Törnävä constitute one of the largest museum complexes in Finland.

Alvar Aalto designed the famous civic centre and in 1960 Seinäjoki was incorporated as a town. It is now the commercial centre of the region and rivals Vaasa as the busiest town in Pohjanmaa. In contrast to Vaasa and the Swedish coast, only 0.2% of locals speak Swedish.

Although Seinäjoki is a modern town, it is emerging as a rival to the more historic Vaasa. In addition to linguistic quarrels, there is economic jealousy. For people from Seinäjoki, Vaasa is merely their maritime harbour, while those from Vaasa regard Seinäjoki as nothing more than a railway junction.

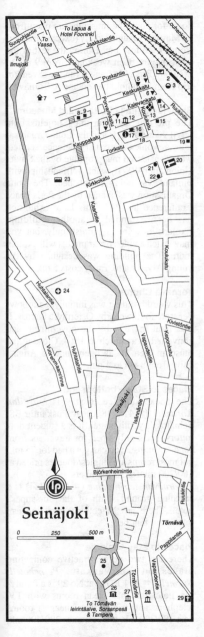

Seinäjoki

0 250 500 m

PLACES TO STAY

7 Marttilan Kortteeri
8 Matkustajakoti Vuorela
9 Perhehotelli Nurmela
14 A&P City Hotel
15 Cumulus
18 Hotel Sokos Vaakuna
19 Sokos Hotel Lakeus

PLACES TO EAT

4 Sokos Kahvio
5 Rosso
6 Kebab Center
10 Kotipizza
11 Kotipulla
16 Hesburger & Creps Café

OTHER

1 Post Office
2 Railway Station
3 Bus Station
12 Suojeluskunta ja Lotta Svärd Museum
13 Epstori Shopping Centre & Hanna ja Kerttu
17 Tourist Office & Torikeskus
20 Lakeuden Risti Church
21 Town Hall
22 Public Library
23 Swimming Hall
24 Health Care Centre
25 Törnävä Island & Park
26 Östermyra mansion
27 Agriculture Museum
28 Törnävä Museum Area
29 Törnävä Church

POHJANMAA

Orientation

Seinäjoki has three centres. The newest one, where all shops and services can be found, is near the railway and bus stations. The monumental Aalto Centre, one of the main works of the architect from whom it takes its name, is to the south. Further south is the suburb of Törnävä, the original township, which has several museums.

Information

Tourist Office The tourist office (☎ 416 2184) is on the second floor of the Torikeskus Shopping Centre in the market square. It's open Monday to Friday from 9 am to 5 pm.

Post & Telephone The main post office is

near the railway station, at Valtionkatu 1. Seinäjoki's post code is 60100.

Library The public library is opposite the church at Koulukatu 21. It has loads of travel literature and is also worth a visit for its gorgeous architecture. It is open Monday to Friday from 10 am to 7 pm, and on Saturday from 11 am to 3 pm.

Books & Maps Suomalainen Kirjakauppa is in the Epstori Shopping Centre. Info is the other option at Koulukatu 20.

Emergency Services In a general emergency call ☎ 112; for a doctor ☎ 10023. There are pharmacies at Keskuskatu 3 and Koulukatu 11.

Aalto Centre

The Aalto Centre's monumental buildings include the Lakeuden Risti Church, the town hall and the library. The massive church is the most famous building of them all, though its decorations are minimal. The church, dating from 1960, is open daily from noon to 6 pm. Most of the other buildings can be seen weekdays until 3 pm.

Törnävä Estate

Törnävä is a very different area and looks almost idyllic when the weather is fine. The Östermyra mansion is the main feature of this riverside estate. The small island in Törnävä is perfect for a picnic. A large number of buildings, including some that have been transferred from elsewhere, constitute a large museum area. There are buildings on both sides of busy road No 64 so be careful if you have children! On your right, when coming from the town centre, is the large **Agriculture Museum** and a mill museum. On your left in the old yellow building is the **Gunpowder Museum**. Behind it is a large open-air museum with a smoke house and a smith's house from the 17th century. The main building, **Liinamaan tuparatu**, dates from 1837. The old Kauppapuori (local dialect for shop) exhibits old merchandise. Ask someone to open the

doors for you. The museums are open from 15 May to 31 August, daily (except Monday) from 11 am to 7 pm. During the rest of the year, they're open weekdays from 9 am to 2.30 pm. Bus Nos 1 and 5 run the seven km trip from Seinäjoki bus station to Törnävä.

Suojeluskunta ja Lotta Svärd Museum

The pre-war and wartime Suojeluskunta (civil guard) troops and the Lotta Organisation, a women's auxiliary defence service, were considered inappropriate by the Soviet Union after WWII, when a 'friendship' with Finland was being established. The Lotta Organisation was banned by the Paris Peace Conference in 1947. This large exhibition has been extended to another building. Explanations are in Finnish only, but you may watch a video program that will explain more. The building was designed by the young Alvar Aalto. Entry costs 5 mk.

Törnävä Church

This weird building was initially a gunpowder store for the nearby Östermyra factory. It was built in 1827 by the government and converted to a church in 1864. Close to the museum area, it is open June to August daily from 8 am to 4 pm.

Places to Stay – bottom end

The cheapest place to stay is *Marttilan Kortteeri* (☎ 414 4800) at Puskantie 38, Seinäjoki's youth hostel. It is a student dormitory, so is only open for travellers from June to August. You can get a bed for 75 mk, but most rooms are singles/doubles priced at 160/200 mk for HI members.

Törnävän leirintäalue (☎ 412 0784) is a camping ground south of the Sorsanpesä hotel. There are 18 cottages and you can pitch your tent here.

Places to Stay – middle

There are two very attractive competing places on Kalevankatu. *Perhehotelli Nurmela* (☎ 414 1771) at No 29 is a family-run hotel that has clean rooms with TV, telephone and fridge. The cheapest rooms cost 180/300 mk, the best ones 280/400 mk, and both rates include breakfast. Cheaper and more basic is *Matkustajakoti Vuorela* (☎ 423 2195) at No 31, run by an elderly lady. There are just 15 rooms (each with a TV) priced at 150/240 mk, which includes a sauna and a very good breakfast.

Places to Stay – top end

The high rates in the best hotels reflect the significance of Seinäjoki as a regional business centre, but you can save some money on weekends or in summer. Choices in this price bracket include:

A&P City Hotel (☎ 414 2111) at Kalevankatu 2 has 49 rooms, six restaurants/bars and two saunas. Singles/doubles cost 360/450 mk.
Cumulus (☎ 418 6111) is at Kauppakatu 10. There are 71 rooms, three restaurants and two saunas. Singles/doubles start at 395/450 mk.
Sokos Hotel Lakeus (☎ 419 0111) is at Torikatu 2. There are 111 rooms, five restaurants and two saunas. Singles/doubles start at 350/450 mk.
Hotel Sokos Vaakuna (☎ 419 3111) is at Kauppakatu 3. This is the largest hotel in central Seinäjoki, with 143 rooms, four saunas and a number of restaurants, some of which are popular evening places. Singles/doubles start at 350/350 mk, but there are more expensive rooms.
Sorsanpesä (☎ 419 9111) at Törnäväntie 27, south of Törnävä and inconveniently far from the town centre, is a round building with 158 rooms. It costs 280/380 mk in summer; 370/470 mk at other times.
Hotelli Fooninki (☎ 414 6900) at Kaarretie 4, three km north-east of town on the Seinäjoki to Lapua road (No 67), has 30 rooms beginning at 220/280 mk in summer.

Places to Eat

Just opposite the railway station, *Kebab Center* serves Turkish delights. *Sokos Kahvio*, upstairs in the Sokos Department Store, has inexpensive food until 6 pm; expect to pay 30 mk for a meal that includes coffee and salad. *Rosso* at Keskuskatu 7 has a standard menu, available in English. Other national restaurant outlets include *Hesburger* at the Torikeskus Shopping Centre, and *Kotipizza* at Kauppakatu 19.

Seinäjoki has surprisingly good cafés. Near Torikeskus, *Creps Café* serves crêpes with coffee. *Kotipulla* at Kalevankatu 14 is a bakery which also serves hot coffee. Ask about the offer of a bowl of soup for a mere 10 mk. *Hanna ja Kerttu* inside the Epstori shopping arcade is another good café.

Getting There & Away

Bus There are excellent connections to towns and villages both near and distant.

Train Seinäjoki is the train hub of Pohjanmaa. The fastest trains from Helsinki cover the 346 km in three hours.

Getting Around

The Seinäjoki town centre is small enough for you to get around by foot. Local bus Nos 1 and 5 will take you to Törnävä, south of the centre.

LAIHIA

Laihia, south-east of Vaasa, is an interesting place to visit, although its magnificent Nuorisoseuran talo building was destroyed in a disastrous fire in 1994. The building, erected in 1914, is being renovated to house a youth movement museum.

The people of Laihia have a reputation for thrift. A celebration of the local trait is the tiny **Nuukuuren museo**, or Museum of Stinginess. It offers good hints for budget travellers. The museum is three km from the centre on road No 6871, near **Laihian museo**, the local museum. The main building of the local museum, Rapilan talo, dates from 1827 and has plenty of interesting items, including a small collection of local prehistoric discoveries. There are presently over 3000 prehistoric sites in the Laihia area. Both museums are open on Sunday only, from noon to 3 pm.

Places to Stay & Eat

Gasthaus Laihia (☎ 477 1188) at Kauppatie 5 is the only place to stay in Laihia. *Penninvenyttäjä Pub* serves beer, while *Katukeittiö* has hamburgers.

Getting There & Away

Laihia is located at the intersection of road Nos 3 and 16, and many regional buses will take you there. The railway station is four km north-east of the village.

ILMAJOKI

The small village of Ilmajoki is recommended as a side trip from Seinäjoki. It offers fine museums and a few interesting events on the banks of the Kyrönjoki River. The Ilmajoki Music Festival in June features song and opera. Further information is available from Ilmajoen Musiikkijuhlat (☎ 424 7049, fax 424 7171) at Kauppatie 26, 60800 Ilmajoki.

A total of 12,000 people live in the municipality.

Yli-Laurosela Museum

This large house, built in 1849, has been carefully renovated by the National Board of Antiquities. It now houses exhibitions, including old furniture. An exhibition in an old cow shed explains house renovation. It is open from 2 May to 30 September, daily from 11 am to 5 pm. For the rest of the year, it's open on weekends from 10 am to 4 pm. Entry is 10 mk.

Ilmajoki Museum

Across the 'Ilkka Field' (named after a local hero), this church-shaped museum has 15,000 items on display. The museum is open June to August daily from 9 am to 5 pm. Admission is 10 mk, which includes the Merita Bank money collection (see below).

Money Collection

Visit Merita Bank in the centre of town during opening hours and contact Mr Koskenkorva (or whoever is in charge). He will show you a unique collection of old Roman coins (at least one for each emperor) and a large number of German, Russian, Finnish and other European banknotes from between WWI and WWII. Admission is 10 mk and includes entry to the Ilmajoki Museum.

Ilmajoki Church

This beautiful church dating from 1766 is worth a visit for its statues, paintings and the old clock that was manufactured by the famous Könni people (from the nearby village of the same name). The church is open in summer, daily from 9 am to 3.30 pm (on Friday to 2.30 pm).

Places to Stay & Eat

Ilmajoki has an excellent youth hostel, *Palonkortteeri* (☎ 424 6490), open all year round. There are rooms in new student apartments, and the modern *Art Rock Café* is complemented by an old dining hall that occasionally features live music.

You can also stay at the *Viitala* (☎ 422 7657) a youth hostel in the village of Huissi, 10 km north-west of the main centre. Beds cost 35 mk for HI members, 60 mk for non-members.

Shell and Esso both have some food available, but *Kantri* in the town centre serves a decent lunch from 35 mk, and there's a *Kotipizza* across the street.

Getting There & Away

The village is a few km off the main Seinäjoki to Kurikka road. There are regular buses from Seinäjoki, 15 km away.

ISOKYRÖ

Stop at this historical village if you want to look at the old church and the local museum. The population is 5350.

Information

Tourist information (☎ 470 1111) is available at Pohjakyröntie 136 Monday to Friday from 8 am to 3 pm.

Isokyrö Church

This venerated **medieval church** is impressive from a distance (the best view is from across the river) as well as from inside. It was probably built in the late 14th century but locals maintain that the year of construction was 1304. During the Catholic era, this was the 'mother church' of Pohjanmaa, where people gathered from far away. Its unique paintings, 114 in all, date from the 16th century and are the main reason for a visit.

The church is open daily from 15 May to 31 August.

A newer church (built in 1877) holds 1300 people.

Local Museum

Close to the church, this museum has over 10 buildings and some 4000 artefacts. It's open May to October, Tuesday to Friday from noon to 6 pm, till 4 pm on weekends.

Napue

At Napue, three km east from the main village, there's a statue commemorating battles in 1714 when Russians attacked Finland. The nearby bridge over the Kyrönjoki River takes cars. Built in 1909, it is the oldest suspension bridge in Finland.

Places to Stay

Sarin Trafteerikortteeli (☎ 472 4808), near the Isokyrö train station, offers accommodation for 130 mk per person, breakfast included.

Getting There & Away

Isokyrö is on the main Seinäjoki to Vaasa road; a bus from either end costs 22 to 25 mk. Isokyrö's railway station is several km from the village (and the church). Most trains stop at Isokyrö station and all trains stop at Tervajoki station.

TERVAJOKI

This village on the border between the municipalities of Isokyrö and Vähäkyrö is the most American looking village in Finland. It has huge car sales halls (most of them empty at last visit) and other box-shaped buildings. The village has a factory sales outlet for sheet-metal household items, which are exhibited in the **Pläkkyrimuseo**. The museum is open from June to mid-August, weekdays from 9 am to 8 pm; on Saturday from 9 am to 4 pm; and on Sunday from 11 am to 8 pm.

YLISTARO

This small place with almost 6000 people is another landmark along the Kyrönjoki River.

The local church is one of the largest in Finland. It was built in 1851.

LAPUA

With 14,500 inhabitants, Lapua is one of the larger centres in this part of Pohjanmaa. Lapua is best known for its religious movement, the Lutheran Herättäjäyhdistys.

Lakeus

This name means wide flat landscape, of which there is plenty around Lapua one of the highlights of Pohjanmaa. The place to observe the flat countryside with its old hay barns is along the dirt road north of Lapua along the Lapuanjoki River. Drive a few km north from Lapua centre until you reach main road No 16. If you followed the western bank of the river, continue over road No 16 to the gravel road. If you followed the eastern bank, turn left, cross the bridge and turn right at a sign saying 'Kaunissaari'. Drive more than five km and you will reach typically flat scenery. Locals love it here.

Places to Stay & Eat

The cheapest place is *Gasthaus Tiitu* (☎ 438 7690) at Liiverintie 2, one km east of the town centre. Singles/doubles cost 150/250 mk. *Tervaranta*, on Myllytie not far from Gasthaus, (☎ 438 4057) is a small camping ground, which also has some inexpensive cottages. *Kantarellis* (☎ 433 1122) is a top-end hotel right in the village centre, but it collects much of its income from locals who converge here to dance to live music. Rooms cost from 200 to 440 mk. Kantarellis has a reputable restaurant and there are also *grillis* in Lapua.

Getting There & Away

Lapua is on the Helsinki to Oulu railway line.

HÄRMÄ

This region north of Lapua has one of Pohjanmaa's richest folk traditions. These days the flat landscape is administered by two municipalities: Alahärmä, or lower Härmä, and Ylihärmä, or upper Härmä. The

POHJANMAA

Härmä area has been one of the main sources of Finnish emigration to America and the people of Härmä have always maintained a tradition of travel. Surprisingly, Härmä has become synonymous with Finland (the down-to-earth type of Finnish culture that is, rather than that of posh Sibelius or the Kalevala).

There's a local museum in both Alahärmä and Ylihärmä, open Wednesday to Sunday in the afternoon.

Places to Stay
Härmän Kuntokeskus (☎ 483 1111) is a huge spa on the main road in Ylihärmä. There are 125 rooms beginning at 310/360 mk.

KAUHAVA
In the small centre of Kauhava (population 8500), knife industries are the main attraction. You can purchase a knife that may be useful during treks in the wilderness. There's also a museum devoted to local knives in the library building on Kauppatie. Another feature is the flat landscape with hay barns scattered around fields. The large church dates from 1925.

Places to Stay & Eat
Tuppiroska (☎ 431 5350) at Kauppatie 109 is a youth hostel in a school apartment building, open from 1 June to mid-August. There are rooms for 175/230 mk; 15 mk off for HI members.

Getting There & Away
Most trains on the Helsinki to Oulu line stop at Kauhava railway station, which is one km west of the centre.

South Pohjanmaa

The south is not quite typical of Pohjanmaa scenery and can be considered a drive-through region with two possible routes. The eastern route follows road No 66, a continuation of the famous North Häme route, and includes an architectural detour to Alajärvi,

where Alvar Aalto once lived and worked. The western route largely follows the Kauhajoki River, until it reaches the Kyrönjoki River south of Kurikka.

ALAVUS
The people of Alavus were recently flattered by their town's ascension to the status of a city. Over 10,000 people live in Alavus, the gateway to the flat Pohjanmaa region. There are several shops but hardly anything of interest, except the local museum near the church. If you are approaching Alavus from the south, a drive around Lake Alavudenjärvi could be interesting.

Places to Stay & Eat
The cheapest place in Alavus is *Matkustajakoti Kirmanen* (☎ 511 1866), north of the cemetery at Lähteentie 14. Singles/doubles cost 140/220 mk. *Puustelli* (☎ 511 2881) is the local hotel right in the town centre at Järviluomantie 4. Rooms cost 300/400 mk. South of Alavus near road No 66, *Sapsalampi Camping* (☎ 514 5352) has cottages and inexpensive camping facilities.

Isokangas is a very nice café on the main road, but if you want to dine, go to the hotel and try the lunch for 45 mk. *Ittellismies*, the local pub, is not really that bad. South of Alavus at a crossroads, *Harrin pikapala* sells hamburgers and provides tourist pamphlets on Alavus.

Getting There & Away
Alavus is on historic Route 66, a popular route with plenty to see. Trains stop at the station several km north of the main village.

KUORTANE
Kuortane, north of Alavus, is one of the more interesting centres in this part of Pohjanmaa and certainly worth a visit. Kuortane was Alvar Aalto's birthplace. However, his childhood house, at Mäenpääntie 23 south of Kuortane village, is privately owned and off-limits to visitors.

Kuortane is surrounded by a wealthy region with several examples of the typical *kaksifooninkinen* farmhouse ('one with two floors'). For those with time, a trip around Lake Kuortaneenjärvi is highly recommended, and might also include **Ruukin Runni**, an old copper mine 1.2 km from road No 6991. Further south, the village of Mäyry has a summer exhibition featuring the paintings of Ms Soile Yli-Mäyry, who has exhibited her work around the world.

Kuortane Church

This old wooden church is exceptionally beautiful and dates back to 1777. The yellow bell tower is equally attractive, and there's an old longboat in the church precinct. The church is open in summer, daily from 9 am to 3.30 pm. Find your way to the beach nearby.

Museums

Kuortane has two museums not far from the church. **Talomuseo** is a collection of a dozen old houses, including one from the 16th century. Across the road, **Klemettimuseo** displays the personal memorabilia of Mr Heikki Klemetti, who was a nationally known local composer in the first half of the 1990s. Both museums are open Tuesday to Friday from 10 am to 6 pm and on weekends until 5 pm. The 10 mk ticket includes both museums.

Places to Stay & Eat

The cheapest place is the local camping ground *Aholankankaan leirintäalue* (☎ 525 4104) north of the church. There are youth hostel beds for 36 mk in an attractive old house, as well as 10 cottages and a sauna.

Nokiotta (☎ 525 4177) is close to local nightlife. Singles/doubles cost 150/200 mk including breakfast.

About two km north of Kuortane centre, *Kuortaneen Urheiluopisto* (☎ 516 6111) is an enormous edifice that serves as a national sports institute. There are hundreds of beds and visitors are welcome to stay, though prices are of the top end variety.

Matkabaari, a café and bar, also serves as the local bus terminal and has snacks. A short distance south of the commercial centre,

Masan Grilli, *Honkatupa* and *Nokiotta* do their best to attract thirsty and hungry locals.

Getting There & Away

Kuortane is on Route 66, and there are buses from more central towns in Pohjanmaa.

ALAJÄRVI

Alajärvi is best known as the small town (population 10,000) where Alvar Aalto worked as a young architect. Most of the houses and the war cemetery that he designed here are of limited interest, especially if you're expecting fine examples of functionalism.

The church dates from 1836. Nelimarkka Museum, at Pekkola across Lake Alajärvi, is an art museum displaying the works of Eero Nelimarkka, a local whose paintings depict the flat Pohjanmaa countryside.

Places to Stay

Matkustajakoti Pöntinen (☎ 557 2274) at Hirsikankaantie 5 is cheaper than the more centrally located *Hotelli Kitronhovi* (☎ 557 2455) at Paavolantie 1.

Getting There & Away

Buses running between Jyväskylä and Vaasa stop at Alajärvi a few times daily. There are also connections from Seinäjoki, 70 km west.

LAUHAVUORI NATIONAL PARK

This national park (36 sq km) was founded in 1982 around Lauhavuori Hill, which rises 231 metres above sea level and over 100 metres above the surrounding landscape. The observation tower at the top, open daily from 5 am to 10 pm, is well worth climbing. In summer, you may find someone selling snacks here.

Two walking tracks have been established: one to Lake Kaivoslampi in the north and one to Lake Spitaalijärvi in the south (camping is permitted at both lakes). From Lake Spitaalijärvi, an extension to the west takes you via wet marshland to **Kivijata**, a prehistoric seashore. You can stay at *Lauhan kämppä* (☎ 448 1821), one km north of the tower, if you reserve the whole hut in advance.

East of Lauhavuori, Kauhaneva-Pohjankangas National Park consists largely of open bog and is of less interest.

Getting There & Away

If you want to get to the national park by public transport you'll have to walk five km from the Honkajoki to Kauhajoki road (No 669) or 12 km from Isojoki, via Sarviluoma. There are buses to both crossings.

KAUHAJOKI

Kauhajoki, south-east of Seinäjoki, is the largest municipality in this part of Pohjanmaa, both by area and population, but does not enjoy town status. Of the 15,000 people who live here, only 0.2% speak Swedish.

The Kunnantalo on Puistotie is the local administrative building. It houses the tourist office (☎ 231 8203), where local and regional advice is given weekdays from 8 am to 4 pm. Topeeka is the unusual name of the main street.

Things to See & Do

Kauhajoki is best seen on Sunday in July when all its museums are open. **Eduskuntasalimuseo**, a small museum in a school in the centre, is devoted to the fact that the Finnish Parliament functioned in Kauhajoki during WWII. The museum is open daily except Saturday from 3 to 6 pm. **Veteraanimuseo** nearby is a war museum, open on weekends from noon to 3 pm. Behind these museums, the **local museum** is open on Sunday only until 3 pm.

Several km south of Kauhajoki, **Hämes-Havunen** is a traditional Pohjanmaa house, open to the public in summer on Sunday from noon to 6 pm. A traditional buffet is available until 3 pm, though it's not cheap.

Places to Stay & Eat

In the centre of Kauhajoki, *Hotelli Krouvi* (☎ 231 1644) at Topeeka 30 has 17 rooms for 320/390 mk, which includes a sauna and breakfast. Prices are lower on weekends.

Susannan Grilli serves hamburgers. *La Linda* is a pizza restaurant across the street. Most locals love to drink their coffee with something from *Ojalan Pakari*, the local bakery. It's an old, yellow building on Topeeka, the main street. There's also a café at the bus station

Getting There & Away

There are direct buses from Tampere, 190 km away, every two hours or so during the week, but less frequentlyon weekends. The closest railway station is at Seinäjoki, 60 km away. If you drive, choose either of the scenic roads along the Kauhajoki River.

KURIKKA

Kurikka, 34 km south-west of Seinäjoki, is an excellent place to learn something about Pohjanmaa's traditions. The local museum has an extensive coverage of local traditions, including a collection of *kurikka* tools, items used to dry clothes. Mr Samuli Paulaharju, an important 'cultural explorer', was born in Kurikka in 1875 and there's a special room devoted to his travels. The museum is behind the village on Museotie, and is open June to August, Monday to Friday from 11 am to 4 pm, and on Sunday to 3 pm. Entry is 5 mk.

The church, designed by CL Engel, dates from 1847, but the bell tower (and one of the paintings in the church) date back to 1794. The church is open weekdays from 9 am to 3 pm (from noon to 6 pm on weekends).

Places to Stay & Eat

Cactus (☎ 450 2655) near the church is actually a cellar restaurant, but there are also four rooms available at 180/280 mk.

Across the river, *Pitkä-Jussi* (☎ 450 3500), Kurikka's top-end hotel, is named after Mr Juha Mieto, a local skiing champion whose medals and other memorabilia are exhibited. This hotel has a lively nightlife, at least by local standards. Rooms start from 375/495 mk.

There are several restaurants. *Eveliina* is a decent lunch restaurant in the post office building. The two nearby cafés, *Suklaasydän* and *Mocca*, create tempting bakery products.

Behind the church and across the river, *Jokikettu* is also nice.

Getting There & Away

There are plenty of buses from Seinäjoki.

JALASJÄRVI

Although Jalasjärvi, south of Seinäjoki on road No 3, is not a very interesting town, **Jalasjärven museo** is one of the largest local museums in Finland. There are almost 20 buildings, many housing special exhibitions. The museum is open June to August daily from 11 am to 4 pm (to 5 pm on weekends).

Swedish Coast

The term Swedish Coast here refers to the predominantly Swedish-speaking communities south and north of Vaasa. Here Swedishness is something like a regional identity and is officially recognised by the new administrative framework.

The landscape is typically flat but there are dense forests and hundreds of islands off the coast. Very neat old houses typify the coastal region, as do numerous long houses where animals that will eventually be slaughtered for the annual fur auctions near Helsinki are reared. Language is the distinctive feature here; a magazine booth in a local supermarket will have a collection of imported Swedish papers that keep locals gossiping about Sweden's TV stars, and the grooving radio station is more likely to be Stockholm's 'P3' than the Finnish Rundradion.

The area of Swedish-speaking Finns spans from Sideby in the south to Kokkola (Swedish: Karleby) in the north. People from Sweden treat this region of lost brethren with curiosity and call it *Parallelsverige*, or 'Parallel Sweden'. Swedes can understand the local dialects.

SIDEBY

The small village of Sideby (Finnish: Siipyy), once an independent municipality, is now part of the very large municpal area of Kristinestad. Sideby has for centuries been the most southerly village in the Swedish-speaking region. It was here that the ancient Häme (interior in Finnish) people lived side by side with Swedish fishers. Later the area south of Sideby became known as Satakunta, and these days there is a provincial border separating the two. Pronounce Sideby as SEE-deh-BEW.

Kilens Museum

With its old buildings and historical items, this seaside open-air museum at Kilstrand (Finnish: Kiili) is the main attraction in Sideby. The most interesting building is a wooden chapel. The museum is open in June and the first half of August from 10 am to 6 pm; in July from 10 am to 8 pm. It's closed on Monday in August. Admission is 5 mk.

Places to Stay

Kilstrand (☎ 222 5611) is a youth hostel just east of the museum and the sea. There are just nine rooms, and HI members pay 70 mk. The hostel is open from 1 June to 15 August, and there are canoes for hire.

KRISTINESTAD

Kristinestad (Finnish: Kristiinankaupunki) is a small, idyllic town. Like other towns in the area, it is bilingual. Some 57% of the 8600 inhabitants speak Swedish.

History

Kristinestad, named after Queen Kristina of Sweden, was founded in 1649 by Count Per Brahe. By the 1850s, the town had become one of the main ports in Finland and an important centre for shipbuilding. With the arrival of steamships, Kristinestad's importance declined and many of its inhabitants moved to Sweden. The immigration came to an end only in the 1970s when the opening of several industrial plants provided a long-needed stimulus for the town. Recently, however, the population has again dwindled.

Information

Tourist Office The tourist office (☎ 221

POHJANMAA

POHJANMAA

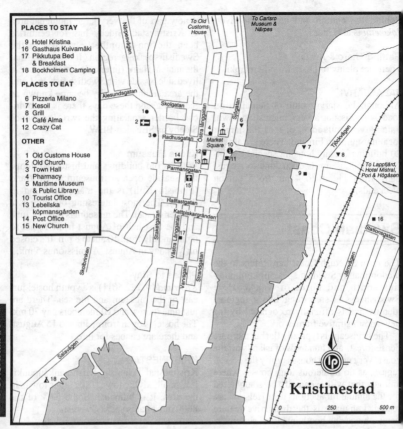

PLACES TO STAY
9 Hotel Kristina
16 Gasthaus Kuivamäki
17 Pikkutupa Bed
   & Breakfast
18 Bockholmen Camping

PLACES TO EAT
6 Pizzeria Milano
7 Kesoil
8 Grill
11 Café Alma
12 Crazy Cat

OTHER
1 Old Customs House
2 Old Church
3 Town Hall
4 Pharmacy
5 Maritime Museum
   & Public Library
10 Tourist Office
13 Lebellska
   köpmansgården
14 Post Office
15 New Church

Kristinestad

6278), at Sjögatan 8 near the bridge next door to Café Alma, is open in summer on weekdays from 10 am to 5 pm, and to 3 pm on Saturday.

Post & Telephone The post office is at Parmansgatan 11. Kristinestad's postcode is 64100.

Library The public library is in the market square at Salutorget 1.

Emergency Services In a general emer-

gency call ☎ 112; for a doctor ☎ 10023. There's a pharmacy at Salutorget 3.

Old Town

The most interesting thing in Kristinestad is the town itself. In olden times, every traveller entering the town had to pay customs duty, which was collected at one of two houses: the one near the old church dates from 1720, and the other one, at the northern end of the town, from 1680.

The narrowest street in town, Kattpiskargränden (Cat Whipper's Alley) is only 299 cm wide. In the 1880s the town employed a cat catcher, whose job was to kill sick cats in order to prevent the spreading of plague, hence the name of the street.

Lebellska Köpmansgården This house museum at Strandgatan 51 was once home to a wealthy merchant. Dating from the early 19th century, it's an excellent representation of upper-class life in old Kristinestad. Ask for the English-language brochure. The museum is open daily (except Monday) from noon to 4 pm. Admission is 10 mk.

Churches
The fantastic **old church** on Staketgatan dates back to 1700 and is among the oldest wooden churches in Finland preserved in its original form. The church is named after the 17th century Swedish Queen Ulrika Elenora, wife of Karl XI. The church is open from mid-May to 31 August, Tuesday to Friday from 10 am to 5 pm, and to 2 pm on Saturday. The **new church** on Parmansgatan was built in 1897 and has similar opening hours.

Sjöfartsmuseet
The Maritime Museum at Salutorget 1 displays a private collection of sea-related items collected by an old sea captain. The sailboat *Fides* from Kristinestad was caught in a storm near South Australia in 1860. The boat sank and 10 of the sailors drowned. In the 1980s, a man from Kristinestad visiting relatives on Kangaroo Island, off the South Australian coast, told the story of the *Fides* to locals. The site was found, over 100 years after the accident, and a memorial stone was sunk there. The museum has a copy of the memorial and pictures from Kangaroo Island. It's open from 1 May to 31 August, daily (except Monday) from 11 am to 3 pm. Admission is 5 mk.

Places to Stay
The cheapest place to stay in Kristinestad is *Rockholmen Camping* (☎ 221 1484) on Kalavägen, 1.3 km from the town centre. This pleasant place at a small beach is open from 1 June to 15 August. Cottages for two

cost 110 mk, cottages for four are 150 to 200 mk. Camping is typically priced. There are bicycles for rent.

Similarly inexpensive is *Pikkutupa Bed & Breakfast* (☎ 221 2632) in the old town at Västra Långgatan 32. It has accommodation at 125 mk per person in an old house in the back garden.

Gasthaus Kuivamäki (☎ 221 2878) outside town at Järnvägen 4, on the western side of the bay, has singles from 145/230 mk. Breakfast costs an extra 15 mk. One km away and run by the same family, *Högåsen* is open in June and July. Reception is at Gasthaus. Singles/doubles are 135/220 mk, including breakfast, but a kitchen is also available for guests.

Hotel Kristina (☎ 221 2555), across the bridge from the town centre, offers comfortable accommodation with a great view over the bay. Singles start from 270/360 mk in summer, slightly more in winter. There is dancing and live music in the evenings.

Hotel Mistral (☎ 222 1421) is near the main road (No 8) at Lålby, halfway between Kristinestad and Lappfjärd.

Places to Eat
Café Alma is a pleasant café at the tourist office building near the bridge. The main attraction here is a 1:8 scale model of the ship *Alma*. A few hundred metres north at the waterfront, *Pizzeria Milano* serves good pizzas and other meals. *Crazy Cat* near the market square serves alcohol and passes for a nightspot. On the other side of the bridge, you'll find a *grill* where hamburgers are served and, at the Kesoil petrol station, a restaurant.

Getting There & Away
Five buses a day running between Pori and Vaasa stop at Kristinestad. The trip from either Vaasa or Pori takes approximately 1½ hours. There are two buses a day from Tampere, a trip of over five hours.

AROUND KRISTINESTAD
The area of Kristinestad was originally just 34 sq km but grew 20-fold in 1973 when the

municipalities of Tjöck, Lappfjärd and Sideby (Finnish: Tiukka, Lapväärtti and Siipyy) were incorporated. There are a few attractions near Kristinestad.

Carlsro Museum
Easily the most delightful museum in Finland, this old villa displays a collection of bric-a-brac from the tsarist era. The museum is five km north of town (two km from road No 662), and is open Tuesday to Sunday from noon to 6 pm.

Lappfjärd
Lappfjärd, east of Kristinestad, was previously the centre of a large municipality. A number of old houses bespeak of a proud past. The church, built in 1851 and originally designed to seat 3000 people, is huge in relation to the present-day size of this little village. It's open May to August, daily from 10 am to 5 pm. Some eight km north-east of Lappfjärd, Pyhävuori Hill is the highest in the region, measuring a whopping 130 metres above sea level. The view is good from here and you can take shelter in a hut at the top. The field of rocks here is a remainder of the prehistoric water level. A cave at the Susivuori Hill is 30 metres deep, but may be difficult to find.

Tjöck
A drive along the Tjöckå River on the gravel road offers rural scenery. You can rent a canoe for 80 mk in Tjöck Bilservice (☎ 222 3771) on road No 8 at Tjöck and paddle the seven km along the river to Kristinestad. There are a few rapids along the route and lots of fish in the river. Ask for further details and fishing permits at the tourist office in Kristinestad or the petrol station in Tjöck.

KASKINEN
If you want to visit a really small and quiet town, Kaskinen (Swedish: Kaskö) is the place to go – it is Finland's smallest town, with a population of 1650. Look for especially beautiful houses; the police station tops the list. Finnish is spoken by the majority of people, many of whom work in the

enormous pulp factory at the south end of Kaskinen. This may be the only factory area in Finland which is actually larger than the town itself.

Information
Kaskinen is on an island of 10 sq km, and two bridges connect the town to the main land. There is no tourist office, but you can get advice and brochures from the town hall at Raatihuoneenkatu 34 Monday to Friday from 8 am to 3 pm. You can also get information at the youth hostel. There's a public library, a bookshop and pharmacy in town.

Things to See
A **museum** exhibiting old buildings and other items is at Raatihuoneenkatu 48. It's open in summer on Sunday and Wednesday from 2 to 5 pm. The small **Fishing Museum** at Kalaranta is open in summer on Sunday only from 2 to 4 pm. The old boat sheds at Kalaranta are also worth a look.

Places to Stay & Eat
The *camping ground* (☎ 222 7589) is small but pleasantly located by the seaside at the north-eastern corner of Kaskinen. Camping costs 50 mk per family and 25 mk for single travellers. Four bed cottages cost 120 to 150 mk. *Björnträ* (☎ 222 7007) at Raatihuoneenkatu 22 is a very nice youth hostel, with rooms almost of hotel standard costing only 40 to 60 mk for members. There is also a kitchen for guests. The best of the bunch is the top-end *Hotel Kaske* (☎ 222 7771) at Raatihuoneenkatu 41-43.

Pizzeria Kaskemari is associated with Hotel Kaske and serves meals as well as pizza. *Pub New York*, opposite the Shell petrol station on Bladintie, is a beer joint with a grossly inappropriate name. Shell has a café.

Getting There & Away
Kaskinen is 12 km south of Närpes. There are a few buses daily, mostly on weekdays.

NÄRPES
Närpes (Finnish: Närpiö), south-west of

PLACES TO STAY

1 Camping ground
7 Hotel Kaske
14 Björnträ

PLACES TO EAT

6 Pizzeria Kaskemari
12 Pub New York

OTHER

2 Fishing Museum
3 Museum
4 Public Library
  & Pharmacy
5 Post Office
8 Police
9 Church
10 Town Hall &
   Tourist Information
11 Book Shop
13 Bus Station &
   Shell Petrol Station
15 Pottery Maker

To Närpes & Vaasa

Kalaranta

Kaskinen

0   125   250 m

Sulkukatu

Luotsinkatu

Prinssi Erikinkatu

Kalastajankatu

Pyhäneskilinkatu

Puistokatu

Kuningas Kustaan Aukio

Koulukatu

neenkatu

Aleksanterinkatu

Blädniie

Ruotsinkatu

Raatihuo

Suutarinkatu

Salamakatu

Tervahovinkatu

Kneiffinpolku

Kirkkokatu

Vuorikatu

Närpiönkatu

Hudikinkatu

Roopertinkatu

Marian-rannankatu

Lampurinkatu

To Seinäjoki, Vaasa & Pori

Hermansintie

POHJANMAA

Vaasa and the tomato basket of Finland, has one of the highest rates of Swedish speakers in the country – 93% of the 10,000 inhabitants speak Swedish as their native language, with a local accent that is hard to understand. There are a few nice places to visit.

Närpes Church

Some 150 unique *kyrkstallar*, or 'church stables' (though they are in fact for the use of people not horses), surround the medieval church of Närpes. This is the only place in Finland where these temporary shelters have been preserved. In the past, people from outlying districts used to stay overnight when visiting the church. The interior of the church is beautifully decorated, although the small red houses are clearly the highlight.

Öjskogsparken

Just down the road from the church, this attraction includes a dozen old houses (which constitute a local museum of traditional living), two other museums in a modern house, a pharmacy museum and a 'country store' with goods that are 100 years old. Admission is 10 mk.

Places to Stay & Eat

Gästgivars (☎ 41421) is the local hotel on Närpesvägen in the middle of Närpes. It has singles for 200 to 320 mk, and doubles from 280 to 440 mk depending on the season and the age of the room. A lunch buffet is served on weekdays until 5 pm.

Across the river to the east, *SÖY* (☎ 224 3151) is a summer hotel (June and July) in the premises of a school. There are singles/doubles for 150/200 mk. Make your reservation before 3 pm. *Söff* (☎ 225 6441), another summer hotel eight km north of Närpes in Yttermark, has B&B for 130 mk per person.

Tjärlax Camping, several km south-west of town, has four-bed cottages for 150 mk and larger ones for 250 mk. The camping ground is open from 1 June to 31 August.

All eateries in Närpes are along Närpesvägen, the main road. *Pizzeria Casa* and *Kotipizza* are at the northern end. *Wilson* is a

café. *Grillbaren* is at the police station and *Hockey Grillen* at the bus station. Down at Öjskogsparken, *Vrid-In* serves a daily buffet lunch until 4 pm.

Getting There & Away

You can get to Närpes by taking a bus from Turku to Vaasa. There are four buses a day, and the same buses also go via Kristinestad and Pori.

KORSNÄS

Korsnäs, south-west of Vaasa, is one of the most Swedish communities anywhere in the world, as 98% of the local population of 2300 speaks Swedish as their first language. This anomaly can be experienced along the coastal road No 673. Korsnäs has no Finnish name at all. It is also the westernmost place in continental Finland.

Hembygdsmuseum is open between mid-May and 31 July, daily except Saturday from 1 to 5 pm. **Prästgårdsmuséet**, a large house that shows how Lutheran clergy lived, provides a good introduction for those who want to learn about the traditions of Korsnäs. It is open from late May to late August, and admission is 5 mk. The **church**, built in 1831, is also worth a look. It has 17th century paintings from the church it replaced.

Places to Eat

S-Market near the church and *K-Ankare* further south sell foodstuffs. *BG Grillen*, a grill, usually opens at 5 pm. There's a restaurant at the petrol station on the main road.

Getting There & Away

Road No 673 is interesting and takes you to this beautiful area from Malax. There are buses from Vaasa.

MALAX

This small municipality (Finnish: Maalahti) just south of Vaasa is home to 5800 people of whom almost 90% speak Swedish. The centre, also known as Köpings, has old houses scattered around a flat landscape. The church, almost two km from the main road on Kyrkbacken, is beautiful and impressive although there are no treasures. It's open June to August from 8 am to 6 pm.

Places to Stay & Eat
Charley's (☎ 365 1104) serves lunch at noon and pizza and beer at other times. There are also four rooms costing 120/200 mk. *Neste* petrol station has a café.

Getting There & Away
There are a few daily buses that run between Vaasa and Korsnäs, via Malax, or between Vaasa and Seinäjoki, but neither service operates on the weekend.

BERGÖ
This little island off Malax was previously a small fishing community where over 99% of the population spoke Swedish and just one family spoke Finnish. Now incorporated into Malax, Bergö is no longer an extremely busy place but offers quaint archipelago vistas. The church, dating from 1802, was rebuilt in 1853. The local museum in Bergö is open on Wednesday from 6 to 8 pm. Hand-arbetsstugan sells handicrafts and is open Monday to Saturday during normal office hours.

At a scenic seaside location a few km west of Molpe, *Strand-Mölle* serves meals until quite late. It's the last place to stuff yourself before the Bergö ferry.

Getting There & Away
A bus departs Vaasa Monday to Friday at 2.10 pm. It arrives at Bergö, 53 km away, two hours later, having stopped at Solf and Malax. If you are driving, go via Molpe. There's a ferry across the strait to the island. It runs continuously, but you should still push the button to call the ferry.

Central Swedish Belt

The rural area between Vaasa and Nykarleby contains several small communities where Swedish is spoken and Finnish is hardly

understood. The area is scenic, and includes a large archipelago north of Maxmo.

MAXMO
Maxmo (Finnish: Maksamaa) is the most Swedish municipality north of Vaasa with over 94% of people speaking Swedish as their first language. There are only 1100 inhabitants. The church, dating from 1824, has a large altar piece and opens from 10 am to 8 pm.

Three km from the village, **Tottesunds herrgård** is an old 17th century manor that is home to a ghost called the White Lady. The manor is open during office hours, but the ghost can be met later, especially around midnight. The composer Jean Sibelius and Aino Järnefelt were wed here in 1892. The road continues north to the islands and all the way to Österö, 24 km from Maxmo.

Places to Stay & Eat
Klemetsgårdarna (☎ 345 0122) right on the main road (northern crossing) is worth a visit, at least for the exhibitions. The café serves as an excellent information and reception point for cottages that are scattered around Maxmo's archipelago. There are a few of them within 500 metres from the place, but some are 30 km away, with prices from 230 mk per night. *Varppi* (☎ 345 5065) is one particularly attractive place, 22 km north from here.

Café Grillhörnan in Maxmo village has coffee, beer and food.

Getting There & Away
A few buses run from Vaasa to Maxmo and further north from Monday to Friday. There's a bus connection to Österö, 24 km north of Maxmo in the archipelago, departing Vaasa from Monday to Friday at 2.05 pm.

VÖRÅ
This small, wealthy town (Finnish: Vöyri) features large wooden houses, and a private garden with home-made, life-sized sculptures of animals and people. The main sight here is the wooden church, built in 1627, the oldest surviving wooden church in Finland.

POHJANMAA

It is well preserved, with its old pulpit and wall paintings, and can seat 1000 people. The church is almost three km north of the commercial centre. In all, Vörå has 3750 inhabitants, 85% of whom speak Swedish.

Places to Stay & Eat
Norrvalla Rehab Center (☎ 383 1511) is a war veterans' rehabilitation centre and, if you need a place to stay, excellent doubles start from 340 mk per person. The institution is north of the town centre towards Oravais.

In the centre of Vörå, *Anitas Grill-Bar* is where local youngsters plan their future, and *Torggrill* is where they waste it.

Getting There & Away
Vörå is 36 km from Vaasa, and there are several buses a day from Monday to Saturday.

ORAVAIS
This municipality (Finnish: Oravainen) is known for its Vallonic (Belgian-French) minority, now assimilated, who arrived during the 17th century to develop ironworks in the village of Kimo. As many as 85% of the local population of 2450 speak Swedish. The village has an impressive church (built in 1797) on a hill, which is open from 9 am to 6 pm.

The **Oravais Slagfält** site two km from the village commemorates the battle of 14 September 1808 in which Finnish and Swedish soldiers fought Russians. At least 12,000 soldiers fought here and hundreds lost their lives. **Furirbostället** is a historic house that has a café and shows a film for a fee. The house and a few memorial stones are on the **Minnestods Road**, which is a protected museum road.

Places to Eat
The SEO petrol station along the main road serves pizza and snacks.

Getting There & Away
There are several buses daily between Vaasa and Pietarsaari that stop at Oravais, 48 km from both.

KIMO
Several km south of Oravais, Kimo has a well-preserved, quaint riverside *bruk* with red wooden houses, a power station and the ruins of the original ironworks. **Kimo Bruks Museum** includes a gallery and is open daily, except Monday, from noon to 6 pm. Admission is 10 mk.

Kimo is seven km from Oravais. The direct gravel road from Vörå is a slow short cut.

NYKARLEBY
Nykarleby (Finnish: Uusikaarlepyy) is a small, old town south of Pietarsaari. It is a pleasant place to spend a day exploring the streets and museums. Some 7600 people live here and almost 91% of them speak Swedish, making it the most Swedish of all Finnish towns. In 1995 a Finnish newspaper estimated that the happiest people in Finland live in Nykarleby. The town was founded in 1620, the same year as its namesake Karleby (Kokkola), but what makes this town 'newer' than Kokkola is not quite clear. These days Nykarleby certainly retains more of the old atmosphere than the bustling Kokkola, even though most of the old town burned down in 1858.

Orientation
The town centre is on the left bank of the Nykarleby River, which divides the town into two parts. The bus terminal, post office, banks, pharmacies, shops and library are all on the small central square, which is bisected by the main street, Topeliusesplanaden. There are good views from the café on top of the water tower. It's open till 6 pm.

Information
In summer, you can get tourist information and excellent maps from the Kyrktuppen café. Gold Coast Travels (☎ 764 550) at Bankgatan 6, 66900 Nykarleby, arranges trips in the region.

Nykarleby Church
The beautiful yellow church on the riverside was built in 1708. Its walls, pulpit and ceiling

are covered by 18th century paintings and it has many chandeliers. It's open daily in summer from 9 am to 6 pm.

Nykarleby Museum
Also known as Herlers Museum, this old red house, to the north along the main street, has plenty of local flavour. It features bric-a-brac, old costumes and furniture, and is open Sunday to Friday from noon to 5 pm.

Kuddnäs Museum
This museum is located at the birthplace of Zacharias Topelius. Born in 1818, his fairy tales are much loved. The exhibits are interesting and there are several buildings and a nice garden. The large house is especially attractive and has fantastic furniture. Note the WC that is actually a misnomer as it contains no water. See the two seater toilet and figure out how it's used! The place is open May to August, daily (except Monday) from 10 am to 5 pm. Admission is 10 mk.

Places to Stay & Eat
The only place to stay in Nykarleby is *Juthbacka* (☎ 220 677), one km south of the town centre along the main street; it has a hotel, huts and camping. Camping costs 40 mk for one person, or ask for cottages from 110 to 310 mk. For greater comfort, there are singles/doubles for 280/370 mk and there's also a separate summer hotel. The place also rents bicycles (50 mk per day). The daily lunch includes drink, bread and coffee and costs 38 mk.

The town centre has a few *grillis*, and the very nice *Restaurant von Döbeln* at Bankgatan 7 has lunch for 40 mk. *Café Kyrktuppen* is a pleasant little café nearby, and equally worth a visit is *Brostugan*, across the river opposite the church. Good våfflor, with cream and strawberry jam, is the speciality, and there are paintings from 1941 that depict local history. *Vegana* is a new vegetarian restaurant at Jakobstadsvägen 1, north of the centre.

Getting There & Away
Kokkola, Pietarsaari and Vaasa are the main gateways to Nykarleby; there is a regular bus service from all these towns. Nykarleby is seven km off the main road, which makes hitchhiking slightly difficult.

AROUND NYKARLEBY
The Nykarleby municipality includes the villages of Jeppo, Munsala and Kovjoki, which have their own churches and local museums.

Munsala
Finland's Svenska Skolmuseum is a museum devoted to Swedish schools in Finland. The museum is open in July, only on weekends from noon to 4 pm. The local museum is open on Sunday in summer from 11 am to 3 pm. Munsala has a church that is open daily in summer.

Jeppo
The local museum in Jeppo (Finnish: Jepua) is open from mid-June to late August on Wednesday from 5 to 8 pm, on Saturday from 2 to 6 pm and on Sunday from noon to 4 pm. The church is open daily.

Kovjoki
A museum railway was constructed during the 1980s in the spirit of the original narrow-gauge railway between Kovjoki and Nykarleby that was inaugurated in 1899. The station is home to *Pufetti café* and several old locomotives. You can ride a steam train in July on Sunday, but the place is also open for viewing only from noon to 4 pm on weekdays. Kovjoki also has a museum that is open only in July on Sunday from 1 to 3 pm.

Stubben
This lighthouse here, built in 1954, is probably the only lighthouse in a Scandinavian country to offer accommodation. There are five floors, five rooms, a kitchen and a sauna. Enquire at Gold Coast Travels in Nykarleby.

LARSMO
This Swedish-speaking community (93% of almost 4000 people) live in a rural area along the Pietarsaari to Kokkola road (No 749), a

POHJANMAA

good alternative to the boring road No 8. Finns call this place Luoto.

There's a large church 2.6 km from main road No 749, and a small museum half-way between the two. There's a camping ground (☎ 728 5151) south of Larsmo, with cottages from 130 mk, and plenty of space for tents and caravans.

KRONOBY

Unless you read about Larsmo and the alternative road, you are likely to be travelling along road No 8 through this Swedish-dominated place, where 87% of locals speak Swedish. The airport here serves both Kokkola and Pietarsaari.

Kronoby (Finnish: Kruunupyy) is a nice little village with a yellow wooden church from 1822. The paintings from the 1750s, and the pulpit, are from the previous church. Kronoby also has a museum, but it's not always open when it should be. There are a few shops here, and *Snåres bageri* has fresh bread and coffee.

BENNÄS

There is a bus service to Pietarsaari, 11 km away, from the old train station of Bennäs (Finnish: Pännäinen). Most trains stop at this tiny village, which has several beautiful wooden houses, a bank and a post office. Bennäs, one of the townships of Pedersöre, boasts over 10,000 inhabitants, over 90% of which speak Swedish.

At Kollby, 10 km from Pietarsaari, *Hotel Polaris* (☎ 766 7671) at the crossing on road No 8, has singles/doubles for 380/460 mk.

PIETARSAARI

Pietarsaari (Swedish: Jakobstad) would be one of the most pleasant coastal towns in Finland, if it were not for the huge pulp factory that gives the town its distinctive bad smell. This shouldn't put you off visiting Pietarsaari, which has great museums and some idyllic small towns. Over 55% of the 20,000 inhabitants speak Swedish. Pietarsaari can be reached from Sweden by regular passenger ferry.

History

Jakobstad was a Swedish town, founded in 1652 by Ebba Brahe, wife of war hero Jacob de la Gardie, who is the namesake for this town. He had been involved in Swedish administration while the Swedish Queen Kristina was too young to assume absolute power. The surrounding region, Pedersöre, gave the town its Finnish name, which translates as Peter's Island.

Once Jakobstad was founded, unfavourable trading rights hampered growth, and Russians destroyed Jakobstad twice in 1714. The national poet of Finland, JL Runeberg,

was born here in 1804. The harbour has always been important: Finland's first round-the-world sailing expedition started here in 1844. Later, industries were founded in and around Pietarsaari, although today Pietarsaari is known more for its museums.

Orientation

Pietarsaari is a large town. The main street, Storagatan, takes you from the market square to the grid of Skata, the old town. Intersecting Kanalesplanaden is a popular pedestrian street.

Information

Tourist Office The tourist information office (☎ 723 1796) is near the market square. It is open Monday to Friday from 8 am to 6 pm and on Saturday from 9 am to 3 pm. In winter it is open weekdays from 8 am to 4 pm.

PLACES TO STAY

1	Hotel Pool
6	Westerlund Resandehem
8	Park Hotel Vanadis
12	Hotel Fontell
24	Bodgärdet

PLACES TO EAT

11	Calles Konditori
15	Pizzeria Hambis
16	Sesam
18	Café Johan Ludvig
19	Konditori Fredrika
21	Musikcafé After Eight

OTHER

2	Guest Harbour
3	Orthodox Chapel
4	Jacobstads Wapen
5	Passenger Pier
7	MC Museum & Vapen Museum
9	Pietarsaari Church
10	Westmansmors stuga
13	Tobaksmagasinet
14	Jakob Lines & Tourist Information
16	Public Library
17	Town Hall
20	Bus Station
22	Jakobstads Museum
23	Pedersöre Museum
25	Pedersöre Church

Post & Telephone The main post office is at Stationsvägen 4.

Pietarsaari's post code is 68600.

Library The central public library at Rådhusgatan 3 is open in summer Monday to Friday from 11 am to 7 pm.

Books & Maps There's a bookshop at Storagatan 11. Holländer at Storagatan 13 sells imported magazines.

Left Luggage Ask at the tourist office.

Emergency Services In a general emergency call ☎ 112; for a doctor ☎ 10023. There are pharmacies at Köpmansgatan 16, Storagatan 16 and Skolgatan 21.

Skata

The old town is the premier sight in Pietarsaari and should not be missed. This large section of town has been beautifully preserved. Most of the 300 houses were built in the 19th century; the 18th century houses along Hamngatan are the oldest in town.

Museums

There are several museums in Pietarsaari. They generally open at noon and close four or five hours later, so you have to plan ahead if you only come for a day.

Jakobstads Museum This excellent museum at Storagatan 2 includes the old main building, Malmin talo, and several separate private collections in other houses. The main exhibition has furniture, old paintings and objects relating to local maritime culture. It is open daily from noon to 4 pm, and also on Tuesday and Thursday evenings from 6 to 8 pm.

MC Museum This museum at Alholmsgatan 8 is a private collection of over 120 motor cycles and hundreds of motors.

In addition to a few old Harley Davidsons, there are also funny little motor-powered bicycles. The museum is open daily except

POHJANMAA

Monday from noon to 5 pm (to 4 pm on weekends). Admission is 20 mk.

Vapen Museum This small private collection of over 200 old guns can be viewed with the help of a guidebook in English, available at the museum. The oldest gun dates back to the 1740s.

This exhibition near MC Museum is open in June and July, Tuesday to Sunday from noon to 6 pm. At other times, call ☎ 723 2974. Admission is 20 mk.

Westmansmors Stuga This small museum was once a private school dating from 1794. The *vindskammare* (upstairs room) was where JL Runeberg, Finland's national poet, was taught.

The small museum is at Visasbacken 4, and is open Tuesday to Sunday from noon to 4 pm. Admission is 5 mk. The house next door has handicrafts by Hemslöjdens vänner for sale, and is open during normal shop hours.

Pedersörenejdens Bygdemuseum This monster name denotes a regional museum. The museum is in a few houses, including a former cow shed at an old mansion on Masaholmsvägen. In contrast to Jakobstad Museum nearby, here fine, grey dust covers old tools and other items that are exhibited. Admission is free, and the museum is open in summer from noon to 4 pm (on Sunday to 3 pm).

Cikoriamuséet This unusual museum explains how the roots of the blue-flowered chicory were used in wartime Finland to improve the taste of coffee. The factory near the harbour at Alholmen was founded in 1892. By 1960 coffee supply was back to normal and an additive was no longer needed. The renovated factory is now open in summer, Tuesday to Friday from noon to 4 pm. Admission is free.

Tobacco Museum Associated with the local industry, this museum (☎ 723 0333) displays old products and techniques. Call ahead for admission.

Jacobstad Wapen This new vessel was constructed according to a 17th century design. It is open to visitors when in dock. Admission is 10 mk. Eventually, there will be a maritime museum here. Cruises depart from the harbour, Gamla Hamn, in summer. Enquire at the tourist office.

Nanoq This fine Arctic museum is located seven km west of Pietarsaari in the village of Fäboda. The turf-roofed construction and the collection are the private achievement of Mr Pentti Kronqvist who has made several expeditions to the Arctic. *Nanoq* is Greenlandic for polar bear. The museum is open in summer, daily from noon to 7 pm, and at other times Monday to Friday to 5 pm. Admission is 20 mk.

If you get this far, it's certainly worth the effort to continue to the seaside to look at the fine beaches of Fäboda.

Skolparken
The Skolparken (School Park), a botanical garden, is one of the most delightful attractions in central Pietarsaari, and it's free. One of the finest sections is named after Versailles. There's much to explore.

Fanta Sea Park
This amusement park has water slides, and other attractions that won't get you wet. The park is open in summer, daily from 11 am to 7 pm. Admission is 15 mk, 10 mk for children.

Churches
The highlight is **Pedersöre Church** next to the Bodgärdet summer hotel. It was originally built in the 1400s, but during the reign of King Gustav III it was extended to become a cross-shaped church. The architect partly deviated from the king's plan and saved the 85 metre spire. A separate bell tower from the 1760s also remains. The church is open in summer from 9.30 am to 7 pm.

In the town centre, **Pietarsaari Church,**

dating from 1731, has many old chandeliers, and is open in summer, daily from 9.30 am to 4 pm. The Orthodox chapel on Alholmsvägen is open by appointment.

Places to Stay

A good place to stay is *Svanen* (☎ 723 0660). Known as 'Joutsen' in Finnish, this youth hostel is six km north of town, in Nissasörn. There are two old houses with dormitory beds for 30 mk. You may have to negotiate to be accepted if it is already 'full'. Two bed huts start from 90 mk. You can hire bicycles (25 mk per day), boats and canoes, or wash your laundry here. Camping costs 30 mk. To get to Svanen, take a local bus from the station.

One km south of the town centre is *Bodgärdet*, a hostel on Sockenvägen near Pedersöre Church. Beds in double rooms cost just 65 mk, if you have your own sheets. There are also more expensive hotel rooms. It is only open from 1 June to 31 July.

For accommodation in old Pietarsaari, try *Westerlund resandehem* (☎ 723 0440) at Norrmalmsgatan 8. This homely, spotless place is run by a friendly Swedish-speaking lady. Singles/doubles are 130/210 mk, including breakfast.

Top-end possibilities include the small *Park Hotel Vanadis* (☎ 723 4700), at Skolgatan 23 just on the edge of the old town, which has singles/doubles for 430/530 mk. There is also *Hotel Fontell* (☎ 786 4111), at Kanalesplanaden 13 one block from the central square, where singles/doubles cost 470/590 mk. *Hotel Pool* (☎ 723 5235), at Alholmsvägen north from Gamla Hamn, is not a very attractive place to stay, but it has a quiet location and singles/doubles from 370/470 mk.

Places to Eat

There are quite a few grillis and restaurants to choose from. *Pizzeria Hambis* at the market square has a large pizza special (35 mk) from 11 am to 2 pm. The price includes a drink, salad and coffee. *Saigon City* at Alholmsvägen 6 is an Asian restaurant, and has similar prices. *Sesam* is an Indian restaurant right at the market square on Rådhusgatan. *Visa Grande* at Storagatan 20, near the church, serves pizza at reasonable rates.

Calles Konditori at Storagatan 14 serves excellent strawberry tarts and coffee. There are also a few cafés near the bus station, including *Café Johan Ludvig* at Köpmansgatan 8, and *Konditori Fredrika* at Köpmansgatan 6. *Musikcafé After Eight* at Storagatan 6 is open in July from Wednesday to Saturday and from August to June on Saturday only. It is an unusual place as no chair is similar.

Getting There & Away

Bus There are regular express and ordinary buses to Pietarsaari from Kokkola, Vaasa and other coastal towns.

Train Bennäs (Finnish: Pännäinen), 11 km away, is the closest railway station to Pietarsaari. A shuttle bus meets arriving trains.

Ferry Jakob Lines (☎ 723 5011) shares an office with the tourist office. There are a few regular ferry connections from Skellefteå and Umeå (in Sweden) to Pietarsaari. In both Swedish towns, bus transport to the harbour is available. The Pietarsaari harbour is six km north of the town centre, and buses to each departing ferry leave the market square 30 minutes prior to the ferry's departure.

Getting Around

The tourist office rents bicycles for a bargain 20 mk per day. There are also local buses.

North Pohjanmaa

The northern flat plains contain plenty of undiscovered territory; few travellers ever visit these areas. The coastal road (No 8) is the recommended route: it takes you past several villages at the mouths of Pohjanmaa's rivers.

EVIJÄRVI

The **Järviseudun museo**, or Lake District Museum, some 10 km west of Evijärvi village, is one of the largest open-air museums in Finland. On display are several houses, dating from the 1600s to the mid-1800s, and thousands of artefacts. The museum is open in summer, or by appointment in winter. There are some small hotels in Evijärvi.

Getting There & Away

Unless you have a vehicle, you will have to hitchhike. Buses from Pietarsaari depart at 4.10 pm on weekdays. If this is too late, you can catch early morning buses from Kokkola or Seinäjoki to the village of Evijärvi and hitchhike from there.

KAUSTINEN

Kaustinen (population 4500) is a small village south-east of Kokkola. There isn't much to see in the village itself, but the Kaustinen Folk Music Festival livens things up, so it is recommended that you visit then. Incidentally, the Peanuts cartoon character 'Woodstock' is called 'Kaustinen' in the Finnish version.

Orientation

The bus terminal and most shops and banks are along Kaustintie in the village centre and can be reached on foot.

Information

The tourist information office (☎ 612 201) is close to the main road, at Kaustintie 1. During festivals, go straight to the festival office for free maps and accommodation reservations.

Folk Music Instrument Museum

This small but interesting museum in the festival square, off the main street, is open in summer from 10 am to 7 pm. Admission is 5 mk. In winter, you can see the museum during office hours, if the warden is in his office. There is also a small local museum at Siltatie 7, near the church.

Pauanne

Don't miss this strange place on a small hill above Kaustinen. It is a weird, off-beat centre that combines shamanism, handicrafts and much more. The architecture is also unique. Rock-bottom accommodation is available, and baths in the popular smoke sauna can sometimes be had for a mere 10 mk per person. Visit Pauanne and see what is currently going on. It's about three km from the centre of Kaustinen.

Festivals

The Kaustinen Folk Music Festival is one of the most loved summer festivals in Finland. It attracts huge crowds and many musicians from both Finland and abroad. At any time from 10 am to midnight and beyond, there are several official venues and half a dozen impromptu jam sessions going on. Bring your own instrument if you would like to join in.

To enter the area, you have to purchase a festival pass which gives unlimited admission for one day. Prices range through the week from 50 to 90 mk. Several concerts require additional admission tickets, but attending these is not essential to get into the mood. The festival lasts a full week (or more) in July. For details, contact Kaustinen Folk Music Festival (☎ 861 1252, fax 861 1977) PL 24, 69601 Kaustinen.

Places to Stay & Eat

The festival office organises all accommodation during the busy periods. There are two hostel accommodation locations, offering beds for 60 mk per person, home accommodation at 175/240 mk for singles/doubles, and hotel-style doubles for 320 mk. Camping is expensive, at 60 mk.

At other times, the best value is *Pauanteen Majatalo* (☎ 861 1881) up at Pauanne. There are 13 doubles, and each bed costs approximately 50 mk. *Koskelan Lomatalo* (☎ 611 338) at Känsäläntie 123 is another youth hostel five km north of Kaustinen, open all year round. Beds cost from 45 mk for HI members. A small motel, *Motelli Marjaana* (☎ 611 211), across the main road, is also open all year round. Rooms are 180/250 mk. The best hotel is *Kaustisten Terveyshotelli* (☎ 861 2131) at Pajalantie 24. Singles/doubles cost 280/360 mk, which includes breakfast.

The festival area has a busy restaurant, which serves down-to-earth meals for around 40 mk. Kaustinen also has a grilli, a bar and a few restaurants.

Getting There & Away

Catch a bus from Kokkola, which has a railway station and is just 47 km away. There are several buses every day. There are also daily express buses from Jyväskylä to Kokkola via Kaustinen.

KOKKOLA

Seen from the train station, Kokkola (Swedish: Karleby) looks very boring, but an interesting old town is hidden behind the box-like supermarkets, and the seaside is quite scenic. Kokkola serves as a jumping-off point for train travellers who want to explore Pohjanmaa by bus. Of the town's 35,500 inhabitants, 20% speak Swedish.

History

In 1620, Kokkola was founded as Karleby on the west coast of Finland. The importance of this village increased with the tar trade, which flourished in the 17th century. The rising land threatened Kokkola's excellent harbour, but dredging made seafaring possible. In the 1850s, during the Crimean War, the British attacked the harbour of Kokkola; they lost, and one barge was confiscated. This boat is still on display near the river, despite efforts by the British to buy it back.

Orientation

It's a short walk from the train station to the centre of Kokkola. Although the market square is the heart of Kokkola, Rantakatu is the main street. The river continues all the way to the seaside area of Suntinsuu.

Information

Tourist Office The tourist office (☎ 311

902) is in the heart of Kokkola, on Mannerheiminaukio.

Post & Telephone The main post office, at Rantakatu 4, is open weekdays from 8 am to 5 pm. The Tele office is at Sairaalankatu 9. Kokkola's postcode is 67100.

Library The busy library is one block north of the railway station at Isokatu 2. It's open in summer from 11 am to 7 pm.

Books & Maps The two book shops compete on Rantakatu near the market. Torikioski at Torikatu 27 has a wide variety of imported magazines and newspapers.

Left Luggage The lockers at the railway station cost 15 mk. The bus station has 10 mk lockers and closes at 7 pm.

Emergency Services In a general emergency call ☎ 112; for a doctor ☎ 10023. There are pharmacies at Rantakatu 10, Mannerheiminaukio 1 and Mariankatu 19.

Neristan

The entire old town is worth a close look. It is a quiet, solitary place. The most interesting streets are Itäinen Kirkkokatu, Läntinen Kirkkokatu and Isokatu.

Museums

All museums in Kokkola centre are on Pitkänsillankatu and have free admission. They are open Tuesday to Friday from noon to 3 pm and weekends from noon to 5 pm. On Thursday, museums also open from 6 to 8 pm.

The **Historical Museum**, in an old house at Pitkänsillankatu 28, has several exhibitions. The **Renlund Art Gallery** at Pitkänsillankatu 39 displays Finnish art, and adjacent to the gallery, the **Camera Museum** has an impressive collection of old cameras. There is also the **Museum of Natural History** at No 1.

Other Attractions

An old British **barge** captured in the

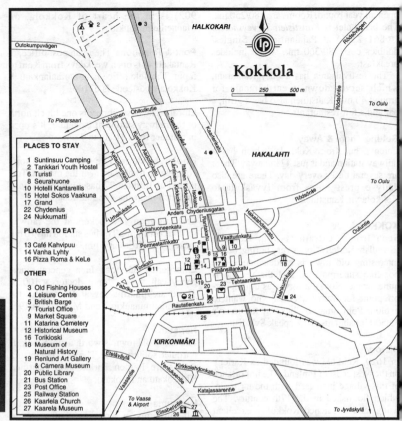

Kokkola

PLACES TO STAY
1 Suntinsuu Camping
2 Tankkari Youth Hostel
6 Turisti
8 Seurahuone
10 Hotelli Kantarellis
15 Hotel Sokos Vaakuna
17 Grand
22 Chydenius
24 Nukkumatti

PLACES TO EAT
13 Café Kahvipuu
14 Vanha Lyhty
16 Pizza Roma & KeLe

OTHER
3 Old Fishing Houses
4 Leisure Centre
5 British Barge
7 Tourist Office
9 Market Square
11 Katarina Cemetery
12 Historical Museum
16 Torikioski
18 Museum of Natural History
19 Renlund Art Gallery & Camera Museum
20 Public Library
21 Bus Station
22 Post Office
25 Railway Station
26 Kaarlela Church
27 Kaarela Museum

Crimean War is at the riverside. For a nice walk, visit the row of old boathouses north of the town centre. The historic **Katarina Cemetery**, to the west of the old town, is an old park.

Kaarlela Church, the oldest in Kokkola, is a long walk south of the railway station. The altar is especially fine. Hours are 10 am to 6 pm daily, and a guide is available in summer. The **local museum**, near Kaarlela Church, exhibits local tools and artefacts. It is open from 15 May to 31 August, Tuesday to Sunday from noon to 6 pm. Admission is 2 mk. There is also a small Tannery Museum

in the area. The Chydenius Memorial Room can be seen only on request.

Tankari

The island of Tankari is a pleasant place to visit from Kokkola harbour. It has a seal-hunting museum and an old chapel dating from 1754. Regular cruises will take you there in summer on Monday and Saturday. A return ticket is 65 mk.

Places to Stay – bottom end & middle

The cheapest place in Kokkola, *Tankkari youth hostel* (☎ 831 4006) at the camping ground, is open from 1 June to 20 August. Dormitory beds cost 65 mk, sheets included. *Suntinsuu Camping* (☎ 314 006) itself has cottages from 140 mk. The best cottages take four people and cost 280 mk.

Turisti (☎ 831 8968) at Isokatu 22 is a guesthouse with rooms for 85/170 mk but it is closed during summer. It is open during the rest of the year. *Grand* (☎ 831 3411) at Pitkänsillankatu 20B is the cheapest hotel in Kokkola with rooms for 180 mk.

North of Kokkola on a promontory at Trullevi, *Lomakylä Trullevi* (☎ 822 4637) has six bed cottages for 30 mk per person in addition to the 200 mk price tag (lower in winter, spring and autumn).

Places to Stay – top end

Kokkola has several top-end hotels. Most are expensive, but there are often special prices on weekends:

Nukkumatti (☎ 831 0890) has singles/doubles from 220/300 mk. It's on Rautatienkatu adjacent to the Kesoil petrol station to your right from the railway station.

Chydenius (☎ 831 4044) is at Rautatienkatu 6. Just opposite the railway station, this place is currently operated by Sokos Hotel Vaakuna (see below).

Hotelli Kantarellis (☎ 822 5000) has a very central location at Kauppatori 4. There are 122 rooms, four restaurants and three saunas. Singles/doubles are 420/520 mk.

Seurahuone (☎ 831 2811) at Torikatu 24 opened in 1943 and is the oldest hotel in town. Singles/doubles cost 200/250 mk.

Hotel Sokos Vaakuna (☎ 827 7000) is at Rantakatu 16. Singles/doubles are 420/520 mk.

Places to Eat

There are quite a few restaurants in town, most of which offer a discount lunch at noon. *Vanha Lyhty* at Pitkänsillankatu 24 is decorated in the spirit of the old town, and offers meals and beer. *Kellariravintola Lyhty* is an annex in the basement next door. It's equally interesting and recommendable. Around the corner on the pedestrian street, *Café Kahvipuu* at Isokatu 11 is a tasteful little café with home-made pastries and a summer terrace which serves beer.

In addition to restaurants in the three hotels around the market, there are a few other places in the area, including *Pizza Roma* and *KeLe* , which is a bakery and a café. Both these places are on Torikatu.

Getting There & Away

Air The nearest airport serves both Kokkola and Pietarsaari. There are several flights a day from Helsinki.

Bus Regular buses run to/from all coastal towns, especially Vaasa and Pietarsaari. The bus station is close to the railway station.

Train There is a major railway station in Kokkola and all trains using the main western railway line stop here. The journey from Helsinki takes less than five hours in daytime.

Boat Silja Line suspended ferry connections between Kokkola and Sweden in 1995 but the situation may change. The tourist office on Mannerheiminaukio may also offer a check-in facility and shuttle service to Pietarsaari one day.

Getting Around

The youth hostel rents bicycles for 50 mk per day or 180 mk per week.

LOHTAJA

Most visitors to this quiet village (population 3100) 33 km north of Kokkola come to see the old wooden **church**, built in 1768. There are several paintings by Mikael Toppelius inside the yellow church. The separate bell tower dates from 1732. The nearby museum is also worth a look, if it is open. The Vexila Regis Church Music Festival takes place during the second week of July.

There's a post office and a library opposite the Neste petrol station, which also serves as a local bus terminal and café. *Ravintola Ohtakari* is the local restaurant nearby.

Getting There & Away

The Oulu to Kokkola bus will take you to

POHJANMAA

Lohtaja, or catch a direct Kokkola to Lohtaja bus.

HIMANKA

Himanka is a small village north-east of Lohtaja along the Lestijoki River rapids. The typical riverside scenery can be explored along the two parallel roads that run south-east from Himanka towards Kannus and Toholampi. The small wooden church, dating from 1794, is worth a photo, but the tiny museum south of the village is generally closed.

Roiman maja has a few cottages from 160 mk, but *Sautinkari* (☎ 875 099) is larger and is open all year round. Four bed cottages start from 200 mk. You can stop for lunch or a drink at *Koski-Hovi* right above the rapids.

The bus terminal is located near road No 8 next to *Matka-kahvio*, which serves snacks and coffee.

KALAJOKI

Most Finns know Kalajoki for its sandy beaches. Over the years, as package charter flights to Spain have become cheaper than a holiday in Kalajoki, the region has sought new ways to attract Finnish tourists. Consequently, Kalajoki provides many services for tourists, including an amusement park and expensive hotels. Skip all this, if you like, but don't miss the side trip to the autonomous Maakalla Islet. Almost 10,000 people live in the municipality.

Orientation

You'll find the bus terminal, supermarkets, banks, a post office and a pharmacy in Kalajoki village, on the banks of the Kalajoki River. The large Kalajoki Beach area is six km south of the village.

Information

The tourist office is off the main road, at the southern end of the beach area. It's open in summer on weekdays from 10 am to 6 pm and on weekends from 11 am to 6 pm.

Museum

The local museum, one km south of the bus terminal, is open from 21 June to 9 August and from noon to 4 pm Tuesday to Sunday.

Plassi

One km north of Kalajoki village, the Plassi area has old wooden houses and a small fishing museum (Kalastusmuseo), which displays fishing and seal-hunting equipment. It is open daily (except Monday) from 10 am to 4 pm, with a lunch break at noon. Entry costs 2 mk. In the red house opposite the museum you can find a guide who will show you around the area.

Kalajoki Särkät

One of the most popular holiday spots for Finns is Kalajoki Beach, some six km south of Kalajoki village. It has a lot to offer: the JukuJuku Fun Park, a spa, a golf course, holiday villas, sandy beaches, restaurants and cafés, good hotels and discos. If you want to have a Mediterranean-style holiday experience at a latitude of 64°, this is the ticket.

Places to Stay – Kalajoki

There are two places to look for accommodation: the village itself and the beach area six km south. In the village of Kalajoki, try *KaJu* (☎ 462 933), the youth hostel at Opintie 1. It is a student apartment building. Because the staff don't like to mix people, you get a whole room for 55 mk (70 mk for nonmembers). The place usually fills up, partly because of this strange policy. It is not the cleanest place in Finland, but it's quite OK, with a common kitchen available free of charge.

Places to Stay – beach

The Särkät area has great variety. For individual cottages, contact Hiekkasärkkien Majoituspalvelut (☎ 466 682), which rents out 40 cottages in various locations. Hotels and holiday villages include:

Tapion tupa (☎ 466 622), near the main road, is a HI associated hostel with beds from 100 mk per person, and good rooms from 400 mk (100 mk less during off-season weeks).

Camping Hiekkasärkät (☎ 469 2380) has almost 80 cottages. Prices range from 195 to 565 mk, depending on the quality and the number of inhabitants.

Aurinkohiekkojen lomakeskus (☎ 466 642) runs almost 50 cottages, with prices from 270 to 420 mk.

Hotelli Rantakalla (☎ 466 642) has over 30 rooms, with singles/doubles from 350/460 mk in summer, or 300/320 mk at other times.

Sanifani (☎ 469 2400) has 35 rooms starting at 340 mk in summer, or less at other times.

Getting There & Away

There are several buses a day from Oulu, Raahe, Kokkola and other coastal places to Kalajoki and the beach. There are weekday bus connections from both Oulainen and Ylivieska railway stations.

MAAKALLA

This is recommended as a side trip from Kalajoki Beach. An isolated islet that has only existed since the 15th century, Maakalla has retained a genuine fishing-village image. There are no roads, shops or electricity, but you will find an interesting wooden **church**, abundant plant and bird life and some red fishing huts. Maakalla is protected and has an autonomy of sorts, even though there aren't any permanent inhabitants. The owners of the tiny fishing huts gather regularly and vote to keep the islet as it is.

For the most isolated accommodation in Finland, ask the boat operator for rooms on the island of Ulkokalla, a rocky islet five km west of Maakalla. Rooms cost 250/350 mk and sleep two/four people. There is no electricity, and fresh water for the sauna stove is brought from the mainland! To get to Maakalla and Ulkokalla, book a return boat ride (60 mk) at Kallan Matkailu (☎ 465 223) or at the pier. From 5 June to 9 August, boats depart daily at 2 and 6 pm. In July there is an extra departure at 10 am.

PYHÄJOKI

The river-mouth village of Pyhäjoki, northeast of Kalajoki along the coast road (No 8), once had more significance than it does today. There is a new town centre where

essential services are available. South of the centre, the Pyhäjoki River has two rapids and the island between the rapids contains a camping ground. An old bridge has been preserved as a museum bridge.

Annala is the local museum a little way off the main road opposite the commercial centre. It has been an important estate since the 17th century; it now has 17 houses, with over 7000 items on display. In summer, the museum is open daily from noon to 6 pm. In winter, call ☎ 439 0246 to get someone to show you the place. Entry costs 5 mk.

Places to Stay & Eat

Apart from the camping ground on the island, *Kielosaaren Lomat* (☎ 433 212) south of the village is open all year round and has several cottages. Two bed cottages start from 140 mk, and there are four-bed cottages from 200 to 350 mk.

Nuotta is a local restaurant next to the bookshop that also serves as the bus terminal. Daily lunch is available. The Shell petrol station, situated between the two rapids, also serves meals.

Getting There & Away

Buses between Oulu and Kokkola stop at Pyhäjoki. You can also try your luck and hitchhike here as the village is right on road No 8.

RAAHE

Raahe used to be an important port, and you will still see evidence of its glorious past. Founded in 1649 by Count Per Brahe (hence the name), Raahe is now a sleepy little town with 17,800 inhabitants. A huge steel plant south of the town dominates the local economy and it shows; the ice hockey stadium and the three water towers are made of local steel. Not many travellers come here, but it is actually the most interesting place along the coast between Kokkola and Oulu.

Orientation

Raahe is divided into an old and a new town. The bus terminal and most of the shops are in the new town. Laivurinkatu is the main commercial street in the new town and has become a pleasant pedestrian street. Kirkkokatu connects the new and old towns, and Rantakatu runs along the waterfront.

Information

Tourist Office The tourist information office (☎ 299 2268) is near the church at Brahenkatu 10. The office is open in summer, on weekdays from 9 am to 5 pm and on Saturday until 1 pm. In winter the hours are 8 am to 3.30 pm.

Post & Telephone The main post office is at Fellmaninpuistokatu 2. Raahe's postcode is 92100.

Library The public library at Rantakatu 49 also has a café.

Emergency Services In a general emergency call ☎ 112; for a doctor ☎ 10023. There are pharmacies at Laivurinkatu 24 and Kauppakatu 31.

Things to See & Do

Old Town Many wooden houses have been restored in the old town, which remains quiet and attractive. The church, dating from 1914, was designed by Josef Stenbäck, the famous Art-Nouveau architect.

Museum The local museum, on the waterfront, is mostly devoted to maritime and religious paraphernalia. Highlights include the world's oldest diving suit (the British Museum has attempted to purchase it, in vain) and some old wooden religious sculptures. It is open from noon to 6 pm daily. Entry is 10 mk, 5 mk for students.

Island Cruises Boats to islands outside Raahe depart from behind the museum. In summer cruises are available daily (except on Monday) at 1 and 5 pm.

Places to Stay

The *camping ground* (☎ 299 270) in the northern part of Raahe is the cheapest place in town unless the youth hostel reopens.

Hotelli Tiiranlinna (☎ 223 8701) remains the only hotel in Raahe. Located one km south of the centre towards Kokkola, it has two restaurants and two saunas.

Places to Eat

Kahvila Sapuska at the bus station is currently the cheapest place for a very simple lunch; there are sandwiches and coffee for sale. Also near the bus station, *Leipä ja pullapuoti* at Kumpeleenkuja 20 is a café and a bakery. More choices await on Laivurinkatu, the pedestrian mall, including *Blues Moon* and *Kotipizza* at the small shopping centre, and *Ramos* on the other side of the street.

In the old quarters, *Alto Mare* at Kirkkokatu 27 has set weekly pizzas at a discount. The popular *Klubiravintola*, near the museum at Rantakatu 24, has good live music on weekends.

Getting There & Away

Bus There are several daily buses from Oulu to the north-east, and a few connections from Kokkola to the south-west.

Train Vihanti, 36 km away, is the closest train station to Raahe. A shuttle bus meets most arriving trains. Railway tickets, including train passes, are valid on the bus.

AROUND RAAHE
Saloinen

This previously independent municipality has a church from 1932. The large **Saloisten kotiseutumuseo**, a nice open-air museum open in summer, has several old houses. It's right on road No 8.

Pattijoki

This independent municipality has its centre very near Raahe. The **church** was constructed in 1912 and was designed by Josef Stenbäck, and the **Pattijoen silta** bridge is protected. There are several restaurants here.

Kastelli

This mysterious stone structure measures 58 by 36 metres, and is located 53 metres above sea level. That's where the sea shore was located approximately 4100 years ago. The width of the walls is almost ten metres, and the height almost two metres, and there's a lower area in the middle of the construction. Nobody knows for certain whether Kastelli is a natural phenomenon or made by prehistoric seal hunters. You can come to your own conclusion by driving south-east from Saloinen along road No 88 (and turning left), or from Pattijoki along road No 8121 (and turning right). Kastelli is the best-known of at least ten such stone-fortress structures in the Raahe area.

VIHANTI
If you have time to spend, see the old red **church** dating from 1748, which is a good example of the region's architecture. Buses to Raahe depart from outside the Vihanti railway station. Vihanti, south-east of Saloinen, has 3800 inhabitants.

YLIVIESKA
This railway junction, south-east of Kalajoki on the banks of the Kalajoki River, could come in handy for those who wish to visit the Kalajoki area. The bus and taxi stations are near the train station and a few buses are always waiting when the train arrives. There is a restaurant at the bus terminal and a left-luggage office at the railway station. Supermarkets are to be found close to the river. Ylivieska is one of the region's commercial centres. It has 13,500 inhabitants, and it services a wider population of 40,000.

POHJANMAA

Oulu Province

The large Province of Oulu can easily be divided into three regions. The town of Oulu, the provincial capital, is surrounded by a flat region with many historical attractions. Kainuu, to the east, is a wilderness area with a recorded history going back to the 16th century. Koillismaa, literally 'north-eastern land', is the transitional region between the south and Lapland and includes the rugged Kuusamo area, one of the natural highlights of Finland.

The south-west of Oulu Province is covered in the Pohjanmaa chapter of this book.

Oulu

Oulu (Swedish: Uleåborg) is the largest town in north Finland and the regional centre. It is a busy place with a large university campus and a host of high-technology industries. Unfortunately, the stinking pulp factory nearby is too visible to be ignored. Despite this, Oulu is a pleasant town to visit in summer, with good parks, lively markets and a host of attractions. In June and July, it never gets dark in Oulu, even at night.

Locals often say that Oulu is the only town with 'a university built on a swamp, a theatre on the sea, a ship in the marketplace and a science centre in a factory'. Sadly, many of Oulu's fine old wooden buildings have been demolished in recent years to make way for modern constructions.

The Oulu School of Architecture is an example of regional postmodern architecture (featuring small towers, porticoes and other decorative elements). Another of the many examples in the area is the town hall of Oulunsalo, south of Oulu.

History
Oulu has a long history of tar production. The town was founded in 1605 soon after

Highlights
- The market and museums of Oulu.
- The chamber music festival in Kuhmo.
- Wilderness trekking and camping on the Karhunkierros route.
- Birdwatching at Liminka Bay, near Oulu.
- Canoeing down the Kitkajoki and Oulankajoki Rivers in Kuusamo.
- Murals and ceiling paintings in the 'picture churches' at Haukipudas, Kempele and Paltaniemi.
- Fishing and trekking at Hossa, Finland's fishers' paradise.

Sweden expanded its territory to the wilderness of Kainuu. Hard-working pioneers of the Kainuu forests floated barrels of tar to Oulu, where this essential raw material (used in the building of wooden ships) was traded. In 1869 Oulu had the largest fleet in Finland. Tar eventually lost its significance in shipbuilding but paper and pulp still contribute to the local economy.

Oulu is also banking on a host of new technologies. The Oulu school of technologies is one of the most advanced research and

Oulu Province

development institutions in Finland. Today Oulu is the fastest growing urban area in Finland, with 107,000 inhabitants.

Orientation

Oulu is situated at the mouth of the Oulujoki River, with bridges connecting the riverbanks and several islands. You can easily walk from the railway and bus stations to most places in the town centre. Kirkkokatu is the main street and it has a pedestrian section called Rotuaari. The market square is another centre of activity.

The islands on the Oulujoki River are connected by bicycle bridges, and there is a lot to explore. Linnansaari (Fortress Island) has a historical exhibition in the basement of Tähtitorni, the wooden tower. Nearby is the pleasant relaxation spot Hupisaaret (Fun Islands).

Information

Tourist Office The tourist information office (☎ 314 1295) at Torikatu 10 is open Monday to Friday from 9 am to 4 pm. From July to mid-August, it's open daily till 6 pm, except on Sunday, when it closes at 4 pm.

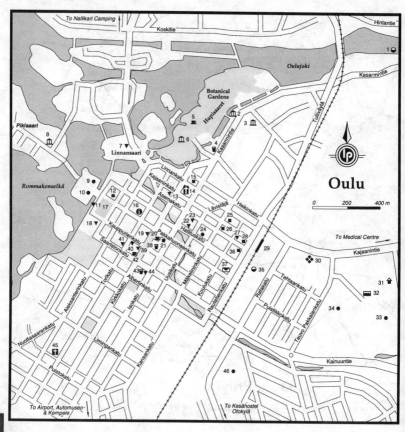

Post & Telephone The main post office, near the train station at Hallituskatu 36, is open from 9 am to 5 pm Monday to Friday. The telephone office is next door. The poste restante address is 90101 Oulu.

Library The new public library building was erected on reclaimed land at the market. There is an excellent choice of magazines on the 1st floor, travel books on the 2nd floor and the *käsikirjasto* (reference) section on the 3rd floor has 1:20,000 maps of the entire Province of Oulu. The library is open from

10 am to 8 pm Monday to Friday, with shorter hours on Saturday and Sunday.

Books & Maps Akateeminen Kirjakauppa at Kirkkokatu 29 also sells imported magazines.

Travel Agencies The student travel bureau Kilroy travels (☎ 372 720) is at Pakkahuoneenkatu 8. VR has a travel bureau at the railway station.

Left Luggage The railway station will be

PLACES TO STAY		19	Botnia Emigrants &	2	Art Museum
			Bisketti	3	Tietomaa
12	Vaakuna	20	Café Antell	6	Ainola
15	Rantasipi	21	Hesburger	7	Oulu Castle Exhibition
21	Arina	22	Zakuska & Never Grow	8	Merimiehen Kotimuseo
25	Cumulus		Old	9	Library
26	Apollo	23	Da Mario	10	Theatre
28	Lanamäki	27	Coq	14	Cathedral
31	Välkkylä	30	Pikantti	16	Tourist Information
36	Turisti	38	Oulun Panimo	17	Market Square
		39	Villa Pekuri	24	Finnair
PLACES TO EAT		40	Jumpru	29	Railway Station
		41	Da Mario	30	Raksila Supermarkets
4	Rauhala	42	Café Antell	32	Swimming Centre
5	Tuomenkukka	43	45 Special	33	Sports Centre
7	Tähtitorni	44	Carrols	34	Indoor Skating Rink
11	Neptunus			35	Bus Station
13	Franzén	OTHER		37	Post Office
18	Kauppahalli			45	Orthodox Church
		1	Waterbus	46	Concert Hall

your best bet. Lockers and the storage room cost 10 mk per day.

Emergency Services For general emergencies, phone ☎ 112; for a doctor, phone ☎ 10023. There are pharmacies at Kirkkokatu 11, Hallituskatu 11, Isokatu 27 and Ratakatu 8.

Market

At the market square (*tori*) you'll notice the *Toripolliisi* statue, a humorous representation of the local police. The old red storehouses at one end, and the slightly newer houses at the other (notably the Hirvosen Vanha Makasiini), are fascinating to see, even if you don't want to buy anything. Nearby are two of the above mentioned Oulu oddities: the ship and the theatre.

Oulu Cathedral

The landmark cathedral from 1777 was rebuilt in 1832 after the great fire. The hall is dark inside but the oldest portrait in Finland (from 1611) can be seen in the vestry. The church is open in summer from 10 am to 7 pm, at other times from noon to 1 pm.

Tietomaa Science Centre

This is the oldest science centre in Finland. It's not particularly special in terms of scientific discoveries, but its location, in an old factory building, makes Tietomaa special. There is a corny UFO exhibition and a valuable collection of uniforms and medals, many dating from WWII. An Omnimax film is shown at noon, 2 and 4 pm daily, but the main film and many of the exhibits are in Finnish only. Tietomaa is open from 1 April to 31 August from 10 am to 6 pm, closing at 4 pm on weekdays. Entry is 75 mk for all attractions, less for students, children or for limited admission.

Ainola Provincial Museum

This is the best museum in Oulu and can be found on Hupisaaret Island. The four floors house well-displayed collections dealing with everything from seal hunting and old coins to home interiors and Sami culture, and there's also a temporary exhibition. Don't miss this place, and set aside several hours to see everything. No English-language presentation is provided. The museum is open Monday to Thursday from 10 am to 6 pm, on Saturday to 4 pm and on Sunday to 5 pm. Entry is 10 mk, but the ticket is also valid at the Merimiehen kotimuseo in Pikisaari.

OULU PROVINCE

Other Museums

The **Oulu Art Museum** is a modern building at Kasarmintie 7, near Tietomaa. It has a permanent collection of modern art plus temporary exhibitions. It's open daily (except Monday) from 11 am to 6 pm. Admission is 10 mk, but there's free entry on Wednesday from 6 to 8 pm.

The small exhibition on the old Oulu castle is in the basement of **Tähtitorni** on Linnansaari Island. The tower is a good place to try some local food although it ain't cheap here. You can walk here from the market, as well as from Hupisaaret.

Across the bridge on Pikisaari Island, the small **Merimiehen kotimuseo** at Pikisaarentie 6 is a museum, formerly the home of a local sailor. The house, known as Matilan talo, is the oldest house in Oulu, built in 1737 and transferred here from the centre in 1983. It is open in summer daily except Friday from 10 am to 6 pm (until 4 pm on Saturday and 5 pm on Sunday). Admission is 5 mk.

Turkansaari Island

This island in the Oulujoki River, 10 km from the centre of Oulu, has an open-air museum that should not be missed. If the weather is fine, and you have the time to get there, Turkansaari Island makes an excellent day trip from Oulu. Originally a trading post for Russians and Swedes, it has a 17th century church and quite a number of old houses, with various items on display. Bring some mosquito repellent on hot summer days. On Sunday there is a Lutheran service on the island at noon and cultural shows at 3 pm. On Saturday, you may see a wedding in the little church.

To get there, drive about 10 km towards Muhos and follow the 'Turkansaari' signs. Hourly buses from Oulu will drop you off at the crossing 1.7 km from the museum, and three buses a day pass close by. You can make the trip by boat, along the Oulujoki River. This costs 60 mk return, museum admission included. Otherwise, entry to the museum costs 10 mk, or 3 mk for students.

The museum is open in summer daily from 11 am to 8 pm.

Automuseo

This weird building features over 30 old vehicles, ranging from the German Vomag (from around 1910) to nostalgic Chevys and East German cars. The museum is run by a local motoring organisation, and was opened in 1986. There are over 100 members, and practically all cars are privately owned. It's open in summer, daily from 9 am to 7 pm and admission is 25 mk. The place also serves an excellent all-you-can-eat lunch for 30 mk. The museum is along the Oulu to Kempele road, about five km south of Oulu.

Places to Stay – bottom end

Välkkylä (☎ 377 707) at Kajaanintie 36, the only official youth hostel in Oulu, is only open from 2 June to 30 August. Dormitory beds start from 50 mk. Välkkylä is also a summer hotel, with student apartment rooms from 160 mk a double. Each room has a kitchen but you can get a buffet breakfast for 25 mk.

Kesähostel Otokylä (☎ 530 8413) at Haapanatie 2, three km south-east from the railway station, is a student apartment building, open to travellers from mid-May to mid-August. There are beds from 50 mk and more expensive single rooms.

You can camp or rent a hut at *Nallikari Camping* (☎ 554 1541), open May to October. It is a busy, well-established camping ground five km north from the town centre. To get there, take bus No 5 ('Eden' bus) or the more expensive Potnapekka bus. There are 50 huts for one/two people, costing 150/220. In May, September and October, huts cost 130/180 mk. Camping charges are 30 mk per person.

Places to Stay – middle

Turisti (☎ 375 233) is easy to find opposite the railway station. It has singles/doubles at 185/260 mk and sometimes offers special prices.

Next door is *Lanamäki* (☎ 379 555), named after its owner, a colourful local figure who owns a number of waterholes but is shunned by some locals, who consider him racist. This establishment is currently over-priced at 460/520 mk but check discounted summer prices.

Associated with Lanamäki and also close to the station, *Apollo* (☎ 374 344), at Asema-katu 31-33, has singles/doubles from 275/330 mk in summer, but the best rooms are considerably dearer at other times.

Places to Stay – top end

Oulu has an excellent choice of expensive accommodation, and some of these places attract large crowds of locals for their lively nightlife.

Vaakuna (☎ 372 666), Hallituskatu 1. The Vaakuna is ugly but is located right at the waterfront, with good views from rooms. Prices start at 510 mk

Sokos Hotel Arina (☎ 311 4221), Pakkahuoneenkatu 16. This is the most central hotel in Oulu. Room prices start from 400 mk.

Cumulus (☎ 316 7111) at Kajaaninkatu 17 is a large hotel with 202 rooms for 450/520 mk, or 355 mk in summer for any room.

Rantasipi (☎ 313 9111), Kirkkokatu 3. The most modern hotel in Oulu, Rantasipi has singles/doubles from 450/520 mk (all rooms are 355 mk in summer). There are 154 rooms, 12 of which have their own sauna.

Kylpylähotelli Eden (☎ 550 4100). This modern spa, several km away in Nallikari, has 101 rooms, six restaurants, seven saunas, pools, water slides and physical treatment programmes. Singles/doubles are 420/610 mk, but there are special two day offers, especially from Sunday to Tuesday. All prices include unlimited use of pools and saunas.

Places to Eat

Cafés *Café Antell* is an Oulu institution which prepares tempting cakes and serves hot coffee. There are two outlets on Rotuaari and a few more in the suburbs. There's also *Bisketti* on Rotuaari. *Tuomenkukka* is a nice café in the botanical gardens on Hupisaaret Island. Another place to have a cup of coffee is the nearby *Tähtitorni*, the wooden tower on Linnansaari Island. It is hard to miss and is recommended more for the atmosphere and the view than for quality or prices. *Villa Pekuri* on Rotuaari (Kirkkokatu 12) is a fine

café, although a bit dear. The Steakhouse upstairs serves good meals.

Restaurants You'll find good, cheap pizza at *Kotipizza* at Torikatu 9, or at *Da Mario* at Torikatu 24 or Asemakatu 10. *Jumpru* bar at Kauppurienkatu 6 serves lunch for 36 mk, including salad, a drink, bread and coffee. *Döner Kebab*, opposite, offers a substantial 28 mk plate. The daily lunch at *Botnia Emigrants*, along Rotuaari, is more expensive. *Neptunus*, the ship at the market, is recommended for its food and service, but be warned: a proper meal may be costly.

Franzén at Kirkkokatu 2 is probably the finest place to dine in Oulu, and includes a German-style beer cellar. The house dates back to 1829. *Zakuska* is a Russian restaurant at Hallituskatu 13 with fine cuisine at higher prices. *Coq*, at Asemakatu 39 near the railway station, offers cheap lunch packages.

Pikantti in Citymarket Superstore at Raksila, not far from the bus station, has ready meals at reasonably prices. Even cheaper may be *Carrols* and *Hesburger* in the town centre.

Bars The people of Oulu enjoy their cold beer sitting out on the patios in good weather. The patio at *Jumpru* is the most popular of them all, though the beer is a bit dearer here than elsewhere. *Oulun Panimo* brews its own beer and is located near Rotuaari. *Rauhala*, in an attractive wooden building at Mannenkatu 1, is occupied by local students from 2 pm. The occasional live program makes up for the lack of food. There's a summer patio whenever weather permits.

Near Akateeminen Kirjakauppa, *45 Special* has live music, and there are several other places nearby for late night entertainment. *Never Grow Old* is a reggae pub at Hallituskatu 13 with occasional live music. Also worth trying is *Red Neck*, at Hallituskatu 13.

Self-Catering Oulu specialities include rieska (thin chapati-like bread), leipäjuusto (large baked cheese loaf), and lohikeitto (salmon soup). These food items can be found at the marketplace or the Kauppahalli (indoor market). The cheapest food can be found in three competing supermarkets at Raksila, near the stations.

Things to Buy
On Rotuaari, the pedestrian section of Kirkkokatu, there is a good range of shops, plus street musicians and other events in summer. Look for handicrafts and souvenirs with hints of Lapland exoticism at the market. For cheap food and bargains, try the three large, competitive supermarkets in Raksila, just next to the bus terminal.

Getting There & Away
Air Oulu airport is the second busiest in Finland. There are flights from Helsinki every two to three hours or so.

Bus Buses depart from near the railway station, and each destination has its own platform. There are seven buses to Kuusamo each day. To reach nearby villages, catch a local Koskilinjat bus from the town centre.

Train The train station is close to the town centre. Six to 10 trains a day run from Helsinki to Oulu, the fastest trains covering the 680 km in a little over six hours. There are also trains via Kajaani.

Getting Around
To/From the Airport The airport is a few km south of the centre. Arriving flights are met by a Finnair bus to Oulu.

Bus There is a large network of local buses. Each ride costs about 9 mk, and route maps are displayed at bus stops.

Bicycle There are bicycles for rent at the railway station, or check Laatupyörä at Saaristonkatu 27, where bicycles cost 45 mk per day. The cheapest rental bicycles can be found at Nallikari Camping. Oulu is said to have the best local bicycle routes in Finland.

Around Oulu

The area around Oulu was a sea bed after the Ice Age, until a few thousand years ago. These days, it is relatively fertile farmland, which is still rising one cm every year.

The main arteries from Oulu are oversized motorways (freeways) which are off-limits to cyclists and offer little interest to motorists. Beyond the asphalt, concrete and pulp factories is a fragile natural environment, fine museums and old churches.

HAILUOTO ISLAND
Hailuoto (population 970) didn't even exist 2000 years ago – it is a product of the rising up of the land in western Finland. This flat island has a fragile yet well-preserved natural environment on an area of 200 sq km (and growing). Its population, mainly fishers, has been isolated for centuries, and these days, Hailuoto's main appeal is quaint villages and peace and quiet, as its traffic is effectively regulated by ferries. Many artists come here to seek inspiration – the island's old rural scenes have escaped the bulldozers that have changed most of Finland over the last couple of decades. Most of Hailuoto can be explored only on foot. April, May and September are the best months to see the 'great bird migration'.

Grey lichen, used for reindeer food on the mainland, is the main produce of Hailuoto.

Orientation & Information
The island is 30 km long and has just one main road. Hailuoto village has shops, a bank and a library. The tourist information office (☎ 810 1133) at the ferry harbour has maps.

Hailuoto Church
The modern church near Hailuoto village was built in 1972 after a fire, probably deliberately lit, destroyed the 300-year-old wooden church. It is a bit of a disappointment, with its concrete walls, but there is an exhibition of old religious artefacts inside.

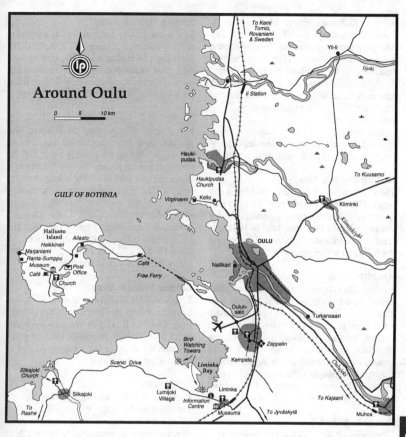

Around Oulu

0   5   10 km

The church is open on Monday, Wednesday and Friday from 11 am to 3 pm.

Kniivilä Museum

This open-air museum, a little to the west of the church, is an interesting collection of old houses, complete with furniture, lots of rusty tools and the like. It's open in June and July only, daily from 10 am to 3 pm (on Sunday to 4 pm). Admission is 5 mk.

Marjaniemi

The westernmost point of Hailuoto has a lighthouse and a cluster of old fisherfolk's houses. There is also a *luontopolku* trail, if you want to see more of the countryside.

Places to Stay & Eat

Ranta-Sumppu Camping (☎ 810 0690) has the largest capacity on Hailuoto. It is at the far end of the island, 30 km from the ferry. There are 17 cottages for rent, and camping is possible too. A buffet lunch is available for 50 mk.

Ailasto (☎ 810 0384) is the first place along the road from the ferry. Run by a Polish man who plays his keyboards on weekends, it has five modern, four bed cabins at 300 mk per day. Rather expensive meals are available. *Maatilamajoitus Heikkinen* (☎ 810 0349) is a few km further on. This farmhouse has been an inn since 1766, and the half dozen rooms for rent have plenty of character. Accommodation costs a mere 60 mk per person in three-bed rooms. The kitchen and other facilities are in an old cowshed. Bring your own food.

You may save a bit by buying food at stores in the main village. *Saaren leipä*, a few km west of the church, sells fresh bread.

Getting There & Away

There are two or three buses (No 18) a day from Oulu to Marjaniemi and Ranta-Sumppu. A free *lossi* (ferry) makes the 6.8 km journey from the mainland to Hailuoto. It takes 60 cars and is seldom full, but expect delays when returning on weekends.

HAUKIPUDAS

Haukipudas (population 14,600) is an Oulu suburb to the north, located at a scenic spot along the Kiiminkijoki River. The main attraction is the particularly interesting church, one of the most notable 'picture churches' in Finland. It has superb naive frescoes on the walls and a small wooden *vaivaisukko* (pauper statue) outside, begging for alms. It's open Monday to Friday from 10 am to 6 pm.

Places to Stay & Eat

Virpiniemi (☎ 401 222), at the seashore near Kello village, is six km from the main road and 23 km from Oulu. It is classified as a Finnhostel and is open all year round. There are large dormitories, with beds available from 45 mk for HI members. *Kello*, a grilli, and the Shell petrol station have food.

Särkyneen pyörän karjatila is just near the main road in Haukipudas village. It is a 150-year-old cowshed, now wonderfully transformed into a cosy restaurant. There is a special lunch menu and meals until late. You can also find something inexpensive at the two grillis in the modern Haukipudas centre, or in the café at the nearby Esso petrol station.

Getting There & Away

Trains no longer stop at the Haukipudas railway station, but buses run almost hourly from Oulu to Haukipudas. The new motorway past Haukipudas makes hitchhiking more difficult. A local bus from Oulu will be your best bet.

II

Ii is a small village along the Ii River. The unusual name may come from a Saame word for 'night'. If you are passing by, it may be worth stopping to see the **Iin Hamina**, a historical area with a handful of attractive old houses. The riverside has an old cemetery and quaint old wooden buildings, one of which houses the Musta Lintu clay pot studio, on the northern shore of the river. The village of Ii offers all kinds of services. *Iin Sillat* (☎ 817 3300) is a local hotel that has rooms from 220 mk in summer.

Getting There & Away

Trains stop at Ii railway station (four km from the centre), and buses run almost hourly from Oulu to Ii. If you want to hitchhike north from Oulu, Ii would be the best place to catch a bus to (to see local sights and to get past the motorways).

KEMPELE

Kempele is today known for Zeppelin, its oversized roadside shopping complex; it's a bit of a white elephant. There's also a commercial centre in Kempele, to the south of Oulu, but the two churches are the main attraction. Kempele has a population of just over 10,000.

Churches

There are two churches one km west from the commercial centre (or three km from Zeppelin). The new church was finished in 1993, and was designed by Jorma Teppo from Oulu. The outside is probably more interesting than the inside. The old church, built in 1688, has 10 colourful paintings by Mikael Toppelius, dating from 1785-95. What is unusual is that many of the paintings include the sponsor's name. The bell tower was built in 1733. A guide is in attendance in the new church daily from noon to 6 pm (on Saturday from 3 pm), and will open the doors for you.

Places to Stay

Pohjan Kievari is a motel-style establishment. The doors open at 4 pm, and accommodation costs 110 mk, including breakfast. *Kempele Camping* (☎ 515 455) has cottages for 80/120 mk.

Getting There & Away

The hourly bus No 9 will take you to Kempele from Oulu.

KIIMINKI

This modern village north-west of Oulu has a pleasant modern library and shops. One of the Finnish 'picture churches', located approximately one km past the library and shops, is open in July, Monday to Friday from 11 am to 1 pm. At other times, call ☎ 816 1003. The altar has naive frescoes by Mikael Toppelius, painted directly onto the logs. The church was built in 1760 and renovated in 1954.

Kiiminki has 9200 inhabitants.

You can eat at *Tikankontti*, or check *Grilli-Kioski* or the Teboil petrol station, both on the main road at Kiiminki.

Getting There & Away

Kiiminki is on the main Oulu to Kuusamo road. Bus No 8 makes the trip from Oulu every hour in summer, every 30 minutes in winter.

LIMINKA

Liminka is famous for its many hay barns. The town used to be on the sea bed, but the area is now the largest individual plateau in the Oulu region. Liminka has always been a wealthy municipality, so it has many attractive old buildings, especially at the well preserved Limingan Ranta, the old centre that now features a museum area. In the 17th century, Liminka was the centre of an area covering half of the present Province of Oulu. Now it has only 5400 inhabitants. The

bird sanctuary has more species than any other similar place in Finland.

There are few places to stay or eat in Liminka, although you can pitch your tent at the Liminganlahti information centre. The town centre has a wide range of services, including supermarkets.

Liminka Church

This large but rather lonely church is at the back of the modern centre. It was completed in 1826, but contains items from an earlier church, built in 1727, including a colourful pulpit.

Museums

You'll find three museums in the Museoalue, or 'Museum Area', 500 metres off the main road. Getting there along the river, past bridges and beautiful manors, is half the fun. Tickets cost 10 mk and are valid for the two museums that charge a fee. In **Lampi Museo** there are paintings by Vilho Lampi a local artist. **Muistokoti Aappola** features furniture and other items once owned by an opera singer, Abraham Ojanperä. The third museum houses a local collection. The museums are open June to August, daily from noon to 6 pm.

Liminganlahti (Liminka Bay)

The large sea bay is protected and funded by the World Wide Fund for Nature (WWF). There are four birdwatching towers, and several rare species of birds nest here. The 'great bird migration' is best seen in May, August and September. Several km west from Liminka towards Lumijoki, the *opastuskeskus* (information centre) is 600 metres off the road, with a guide (☎ 382 842) in attendance May to August, daily from 9 am to 5 pm. You may borrow the telescope and walk just 400 metres to the nearest tower. Up to 70 species of birds can be seen in a single summer day.

Getting There & Away

Several Raahe-bound buses make the 30 km trip from Oulu to Liminka each day, and pass the Liminganlahti turn-off.

OULU PROVINCE

LUMIJOKI

This small place (literally Snow River) has a church dating from 1890 and a small museum, but they are usually closed. One of the Liminganlahti bird towers is west of here. *Lumibaari* is a local place for beer, and *Grilli Snö* serves hamburgers. There are three supermarkets.

SIIKAJOKI

This very small place on the shores of the Siikajoki River has very little to offer. The beautifully decorated church dating from 1701 is three km north of the village centre. There's also a large monument that commemorates the war with Russia in 1808. It would be possible to explore the riverside along the two parallel roads that run south-east from here towards the small villages of the Ruukki municipality.

TYRNÄVÄ

If you want to see a really flat landscape, drive to this very small place south-east of Oulu, which also boasts a museum and a church dating from 1873 (both are usually kept locked). A very fine dairy building from 1919 is really the only thing to see.

OULU TO KAJAANI

The Oulujoki River has been important since pioneers entered Kainuu to exploit its forests. For centuries it was the only transport route for tar barrels. While the river is no longer navigable due to hydroelectric power plants, you can still enjoy the scenery from the main road (No 22) and the parallel railway line.

There are large farm estates and a surprisingly large number of horses in this region. After completing this route, you can visit Kajaani Museum to learn more about the tar trade.

Muhos

Muhos is a modern little village but it has an interesting wooden church, built in 1634 (and thus the third oldest in Finland, after those in Jokioinen and Vörå). It is open June to August, daily except Friday and Sunday from 10 am to 3 pm.

Emma (☎ 533 1445) is the local hotel with rooms for 290/380 mk.

Muhos is 37 km south-east of Oulu. All buses and trains from Oulu to Kajaani will take you to Muhos.

Utajärvi

This village 60 km from Oulu has a wooden church from 1762 and a fine modern library.

Rokua

Rokua is a small national park covering a mere four sq km. It was established in 1956 to protect its grey lichen vegetation which covers the ground everywhere. There are rolling hills and salubrious pine forests. If you like walking in the forest and relaxing, you will enjoy Rokua. However, unless you want to discuss WWII or other people's problems in Finnish, don't stay for weeks.

Private land here is devoted to sports, commercial tourism and spa activity. There is even a miniature railway. The park is 2.5 km from the main hotel.

Places to Stay There are several places here. The main institution is *Rokuan kuntokeskus Spa* (☎ 542 3100), a white elephant (financed by compulsory retirement payments and taxes) frequented by war veterans. For cheaper prices, try *Rokuan lomamökit* and its cottages, or *Hotelli Rokuanhovi* (☎ 542 4600).

Getting There & Away Make sure that the bus from Oulu actually makes the detour to Rokua from the main road.

Vaala

This small and somewhat isolated village on the shore of Lake Oulujärvi has a certain quiet appeal. The population is 4400.

Places to Stay The cheapest place is *Gasthaus Seppänen* (☎ 536 1183) with doubles for approximately 200 mk. Better is *Hotelli Siitari* (☎ 536 1170) with singles/doubles for 200/320 mk.

Murkina Baari, near where the bus stops, serves meals. You can also eat at the hotel, or at *Zapuki* on Järvikyläntie.

PIIPPOLA
There is absolutely nothing interesting about Piippola, except that it happens to be in the centre of Finland. Also, it was 'the grandpa of Piippola' (not Old MacDonald) who had a farm in the Finnish version of the famous children's song. Some 1500 people live in Piippola.

RUUKKI
This small community is not often visited by travellers but there are two mysterious stone 'fortresses' nearby, Linnakangas and Pesuankangas.

These *jätinkirkko* (Giant's Church) formations have baffled archaeologists for a long time. It is thought that they may have been formed by waves and ice movements. They are situated over 50 metres above sea level (where the sea shore was over 4000 years ago). They have thick walls that look as though they were constructed by humans. The Linnakangas formation, near Paavola, measures 58 x 36 metres, while the Pesuankangas formation is smaller. There are a number of these formations in this part of Finland; the ones near Raahe are more accessible.

The oldest church in Ruukki is from 1756 and is located in the village of Paavola. The church in Revonlahti village is from 1775.

Kainuu

The large wilderness area to the east of the flat Oulu region has been exploited over the centuries as a source of timber and tar. It boasts extensive forests and several stories of heroic survival. Kainuu is in the process of changing from a poor backwater to a more developed region. One of the least known areas among travellers, Kainuu offers much to explore, both in its villages and desolate wilderness.

HISTORY
There is evidence of settlements in Kainuu dating back some 6000 years, and there are traces of Sami people and probably Karelian hunters.

Following Swedish expansionist policies, Finns entered this region in the 16th century, violating the earlier border treaty between Sweden and Russia. After bloody wars, Swedish territory was pushed further east, to where the border stands today. After occasional Russian attacks, all Finland was ceded to Russia in 1809, and things calmed down enough for Elias Lönnrot to research part of the *Kalevala* epic, which includes much oral poetry from the region.

Famine and disease plagued the pioneers, and there are records of ice-cover on lakes as late as midsummer during the most desperate years. Tar became the salvation of this poverty-stricken region, but the hard-working Kainuuites were grossly exploited by the business people of Oulu.

During WWII, bloody battles were fought against the Red Army in Kuhmo and Suomussalmi, and soon after the war an enormous flood of emigrants escaped to Sweden and elsewhere from the poverty of the wilderness villages around Kainuu. Kainuu has only recently recovered economically and now offers plenty of modern delights amidst real wilderness.

KAJAANI
Kajaani (population 37,000), the undisputed centre of the Kainuu region, is a good starting point for visits to other places in the area. The locals are proud of their town, which boasts good fishing in the town centre as well as the only tar-boat canal in the world. The town has long been an important link in the Oulu-based tar-transporting business.

History
In the late 16th century, Kainuu witnessed fierce frontier wars between Russians and the coastal people, then citizens of the Swedish Empire.

King Karl IX had a castle built on an island in the Kajaaninjoki River. In 1651, when the

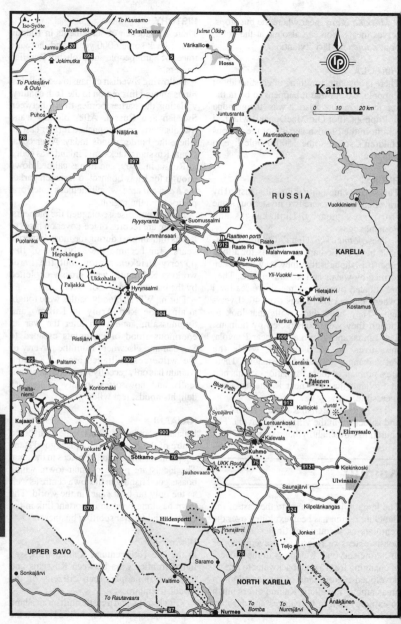

castle was still being constructed, Count Per Brahe founded the town of Kajaani. Russians attacked in 1716, and destroyed the castle after five weeks of fighting.

Kajaani has been home to some colourful personalities. Elias Lönnrot, creator of Finland's national epic, the *Kalevala*, stayed here. The long-reigning president Urho Kekkonen lived here as a student. More recently, newspaper editor and presidential candidate Keijo Korhonen, who has lived for years in the US, ran his anti-EU campaign from here and gained substantial local support.

Orientation

Kauppakatu is the main street. The railway station is at the southern edge of the town centre. The bus terminal is close to the centre of town.

Pulp Fiction & Fact

On the surface, Finland appears to be an ecologically conscious country. According to the Finnish Forest Industries Federation (FFIF), Finland's forests are in a healthy, natural state, and their many species of flora and fauna are thriving. Any logging which goes on, FFIF argues, merely imitates the effects of natural forest fires.

But according to environmentalist groups, the reality is rather different. Over the past 30 years or so, the ancient woodlands have been logged heavily – all that's left of Finland's original old-growth forests is mainly in the sparsely populated areas of Kainuu, North Karelia and Lapland. According to the World Wide Fund for Nature (WWF) and Finland's environment ministry, only about 3% of Finland's native woodlands maintain the biodiversity of the ancient forests. Most of the ancient forest has been replaced by trees of commercial value, such as pine and birch.

The WWF and Greenpeace argue that this practice has placed some 692 species at risk of extinction. These include the flying squirrel, osprey and white-backed woodpecker, as well as the fungi, mosses, lichens and invertebrates which need a variety of tree species of all ages, plus large quantities of dead or decaying wood, in order to survive.

Much of the paper produced from Finnish timber bears the eco-friendly label: 'This comes from sustainably managed Finnish forests'. The WWF argues the word 'sustainable' is used in the narrowest of senses – by concentrating on a couple of commercial species, the Finns have been able to maintain their timber yield but they certainly aren't sustaining the forest as a whole.

The mid-1990s witnessed some signs of change. Demonstrations against environmentally damaging forestry practices in Scandinavia took place throughout Europe in February 1995. Finland's Forest and Parks Service worked on a forest inventory to find out which areas needed to be protected on conservation grounds. The environment ministry also pushed for protection of old-growth forests and for tighter controls on logging practices elsewhere.

Environmentalists have remained cautious, pointing out that similar guidelines, issued in 1985, were largely ignored. They also argue that the restrictions don't apply to private forest land (which makes up some 72% of total forest in the south) or to timber imported from Russia. And as the timber export trade brings in billions of dollars each year, conservation measures are always likely to be unpopular in many quarters.

The WWF believes that if Finland is serious about conservation, then it has one major advantage over many other countries. 'Finland is in the unique position of growing only native species,' WWF forestry specialist Jean-Paul Jeanrenaud told *New Scientist* in 1995. 'This means there's a real opportunity to start rebuilding natural forest, using management systems which mimic the natural processes.'

As the *New Scientist* concluded, if Finland's forestry can make the changes needed to preserve the ancient forests, that label on Finnish paper will have real meaning after all.

Finnish environmental groups include:

Greenpeace, Kirkkokatu 2B, 00170 Helsinki (☎ 661 992, fax 661 899)
Luonto-Liitto, Perämiehenkatu 11A, 00150 Helsinki (☎ 630 300, fax 630 414)
Suomen Luonnonsuojeluliitto, Kotkankatu 9, 00510 Helsinki (☎ 228 081, fax 2280 8200) ∎

Information
Tourist Office The tourist office Kajaani Info at Pohjolankatu 16 (☎ 615 5555) gives information, arranges hotel reservations and sells fishing permits. The office is open Monday to Friday from 9 am to 5 pm. In summer it stays open weekdays until 6 pm, and on Saturday until 1 pm.

Post & Telephone The post office is at Sammonkatu 13.

Library The library is at Kauppakatu 35, and opens Monday to Friday from noon to 7 pm.

Books & Maps Suomalainen Kirjakauppa on Kauppakatu has the widest choice of imported magazines and newspapers and a good selection of maps.

Churches
The wooden **cathedral** from 1896 is worth a look, both from outside and inside. It's open in summer, daily from 10 am to 8 pm, and there is a guide inside. The **Orthodox church** nearby is open in summer daily from 1 to 7 pm.

Kajaaninjoki River
The river drops 15 metres in Kajaani. The lower Ämmäkoski waterfall has a unique **tar-boat canal**, a type of lock built in 1846 to enable the boats laden with tar-barrels to pass. Demonstrations are held on Tuesday and Sunday in summer, usually at 5 pm. The old wooden **Lussitupa house** has related exhibitions and is open in summer from noon to 6 pm daily except Monday. Under the river bridge stands **Kajaani Castle**, built in the 17th century and damaged by war, time and some more recent mischief. It can be explored at all times. Admission is free.

Kainuun Museo (Kainuu Museum)
The museum at Asemakatu 4, near the railway station, is worth visiting. There is an extensive exhibition about the old tar trade, plus displays about WWII and traditional lifestyles. The museum is open daily (except Saturday) from noon to 3 pm, but closes at 8 pm on Wednesday and 5 pm on Sunday. Admission is 5 mk, or 2 mk for students (free on Wednesday evenings). There is no information available in English.

Other Attractions
There's an **art museum** at Linnankatu 14, closed on Saturday. The old **town hall** nearby is not open to the public, but deserves a look. It was built in 1831. The **railway station** is probably the finest in Finland. It was built in 1904 in Art-Nouveau style and has been meticulously renovated. Walking tracks can be found around Pöllyvaara Hill just above Kartanohotelli Karolineburg. In summer, enquire about boat launches that depart from the market and cost approximately 30 mk per person. They used to do trips to Sotkamo.

You can swim and bathe for 12 mk at the **swimming hall** (Uimahalli) at Urheilukatu 7. It's open daily until 9 pm.

Places to Stay – bottom end & middle
There are no rock-bottom accommodation options in Kajaani, unless you take advantage of the right of public access and pitch your tent in any forest *outside* the inhabited town area. For groups, *Onnela Camping* (☎ 622 703) is the best value in Kajaani. Not far from the train station, it has huts for two/six people (140/270 mk). There are also four-bed rooms for 170 to 220 mk. Camping is 65 mk. The place rents boats, canoes and bikes.

Matkustajakoti Nevalainen (☎ 622 254) at Pohjolankatu 4, near the railway station is now associated with the Finnish hostels association (SRM), and has singles/doubles for 145/200 mk, including breakfast. Lower prices are available on weekends and for HI members.

Places to Stay – top end
There are several top-end hotels in Kajaani.

Hotelli Kajaani (☎ 61531) is near Onnela Camping. There are singles/doubles for 320/400 mk.
Arctia Hotel Kajanus (☎ 61641), Koskikatu 3. Across the river, this is the largest and one of the best

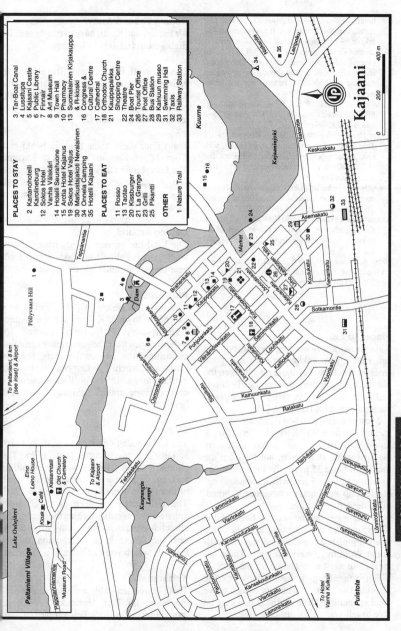

Kajaani

0   200   400 m

Kajaaninjoki

Kuurma

Pöllyvaara Hill

To Paltaniemi; 8 km
(see inset) & Airport

Paltaniemi Village

Lake Oulujärvi

Eino Leino House
Old Church & Cemetery
Keisarintalli
Kiosk • Café

Pappilanniementie
"Museum Road"

To Kajaani & Airport

Kaupungin Lampi

Puistola

To Hotel Vanha Kulkuri

PLACES TO STAY

2   Kartanohotelli Karolineburg
12 Sokos Hotel Vanha Valskäri
14 Hotelli Seurahuone
15 Arctia Hotel Kajanus
19 Sokos Hotel Valjus
30 Matkustajakoti Nevalainen
34 Onnela Camping
35 Hotelli Kajaani

PLACES TO EAT

11 Rosso
13 Taotao
20 Kissburger
21 La Grange
23 Grilli
25 Pikantti

OTHER

1   Nature Trail
3   Tar-Boat Canal
4   Lussitupa
5   Kajaani Castle
6   Public Library
7   Finnair
8   Art Museum
9   Town Hall
10 Pharmacy
13 Suomalainen Kirjakauppa & R-kioski
16 Congress & Cultural Centre
17 Cathedral
18 Orthodox Church
21 Kauppapäikka Shopping Centre
22 Theatre
24 Boat Pier
26 Tourist Office
27 Post Office
28 Bus Station
29 Kainuun museo
31 Swimming Hall
32 Taxis
33 Railway Station

OULU PROVINCE

hotels in North Finland, with 237 rooms, five restaurants and five saunas. It has rooms for 450 mk, or 390 mk on weekends and in summer.

Kartanohotelli Karolineburg (☎ 613 1291) is an elegant old manor across the river. This expensive hotel provides accommodation in singles/doubles for 330/450 mk, but there are better rooms and suites.

Hotelli Seurahuone (☎ 623 076), Kauppakatu 11. Singles/doubles start at 275/375 mk, or new rooms at 390/450 mk.

Sokos Hotel Valjus (☎ 615 0200), Kauppakatu 20. This is the finest hotel in the town centre, with refurbished rooms and a noisy disco. Rooms start at 370/490 mk, but there are discounts in summer and on weekends.

Sokos Hotel Vanha Välskäri, Kauppakatu 21. Rooms cost 250 mk, which includes breakfast and sauna. The reception is at Sokos Hotel Valjus.

Asuntohotelli Vanha Kulkuri (☎ 629 151), on Reissumiehentie. This hotel, two km west of the railway station, has singles/doubles for 230/290 mk.

Hotel Kainuun Portti (☎ 613 3000) is several km south of Kajaani on road No 5. The price, 275/290 mk, includes breakfast and sauna.

Places to Eat

Kajaani market is nothing special, but you can find a few kukko varieties and good smoked fish here. For those on a budget, the cheapest options are the several *grilli kiosks* and fuel station *cafés*, or try *Kissburger* at Kauppakatu 9 for fast food.

Most restaurants are on Kauppakatu. They include *Rosso* at No 21, which offers a 50 mk lunch, and the Chinese *Taotao*. Definitely the best value is *Pikantti*, not far from the market. It has a 35 mk buffet lunch Monday to Saturday until 5 pm, which includes vegetable soup and a main course, salads, bread, milk, dessert and coffee.

La Grange, on the second floor of the Kauppapaikka shopping centre, is one of the many Finnish places decked out in traditional Western (American) style. There are meals, but most locals come for the beer.

For something different, look for the *Kainuu à la carte* restaurants, which serve local specialities. The tourist office may be able to tell you which ones they are.

Getting There & Away

Air Finnair and Karair have two to three daily flights from Helsinki to Kajaani.

Bus Kajaani is the major travel hub in Kainuu. There are frequent departures for Kuhmo and Suomussalmi during the week, but few departures on weekends. The bus terminal has timetables.

Train Four daily trains from Helsinki (via Kouvola and Kuopio) take you to Kajaani. The fastest train takes less than seven hours. A night train takes over nine hours, enough time for a good rest. The same trains return from Oulu.

Getting Around

The local bus service is only useful if you want to visit Paltaniemi. Taxis depart from near the bus terminal but are expensive.

PALTANIEMI

Although the village of Paltaniemi is now part of the town of Kajaani, it has a distinctive history. Paltaniemi carved its independence from the once strong Liminka, becoming the regional centre for the Lutheran Church. The first church here was built as early as 1599. You'll see some of the most exciting church paintings in Finland here.

Church

The old wooden church was built in 1726, and its bell tower dates from 1776. The church is known for its wonderful murals and ceiling paintings. Unfortunately, some of them were altered and repainted in 1940. The Hell scene has been partly covered, apparently to avoid disturbing the locals. The church is open in summer, daily from 10 am to 6 pm. There is an information tape in English, which you can listen to on request.

Keisarintalli

This old wooden stable was used as a boarding house for Tsar Alexander I when he toured Finland in 1819. This simple building was actually the best available for the visitor. The keys to the stable are kept at the church.

Eino Leino Talo

This house was built in 1978 to commemorate the centenary of the birth of Finland's famous poet Eino Leino, who was born in Paltaniemi. There is little to see, but the house has a café. It's open from mid-June to the end of July, daily from 11 am to 6 pm. Admission is free.

Museotie

This old three km road has been declared a 'museum road'; it runs west from Paltaniemi. There are old trees, some of them over 500 years old and good views at the end of the road.

Getting There & Away

There is a regular town bus service from Kajaani to Paltaniemi (bus No 4), leaving hourly on weekdays. There are half a dozen buses on Saturday and four on Sunday.

SOTKAMO

Sotkamo is famous for its Vuokatti sports and tourist centre, and also for its *pesäpallo* (baseball) team, Sotkamon Jymy. The village centre is modern but offers little of interest: what makes Sotkamo special is its setting. Surrounded by lakes on all sides, the area between Kajaani and Kuhmo is a beautiful region to travel through. There are good beaches around the village, which are quite popular when the weather is fine. All shops, banks, the post office and the bus terminal are in the village centre. Over 11,500 people live in the municipality.

Information

There is a tourist information office (☎ 666 0055) on your right as you arrive in the village from Kajaani. The place stocks quite a number of brochures detailing Sotkamo's services.

Things to See

The tiny local **museum**, just off the main Kuhmo road, has few interesting exhibits;

entry costs 5 mk. The wooden **church** east of the village centre can seat 1500 people, and has large paintings. It is open in June, July and August, daily.

There is an **elk sculpture** on an island along the Kajaani road, recently erected in honour of Veikko Huovinen, the famous Sotkamo author. A quote from his best-known book is carved into the rock: 'Man has the authority of an ant in this universe'.

Places to Stay & Eat

The youth hostel, *Matkakoti Tikkanen* (☎ 666 0541), is at Kainuuntie 31. It has dormitory beds for 45 mk in triples, but there are also singles/doubles at 100/110 mk for HI members (15 mk extra for nonmembers). Bring your own sheets, or pay 25 mk more. *Hotelli Tulikettu* (☎ 666 1111) above the village is a spa centre and the best place to stay. Singles/doubles cost 450/550 mk, or ask for special two day packages, including many extra services.

There are a few restaurants in Sotkamo offering inexpensive meals at lunchtime. *Caramia* at Kainuuntie 14 is popular for lunch. *Cairo* at Akkoniementie 3 is a local pub.

Getting There & Away

Buses between Kajaani and Kuhmo pass through the village of Sotkamo. It's also easy to hitchhike along this road.

VUOKATTI

Vuokatti is home to some excellent sports facilities. Vuokatti Hill has several downhill skiing slopes, and the whole area is criss-crossed by jogging and skiing trails. Recent developments include a spa and an international time-sharing village, the Katinkulta. The area caters mostly to professional and amateur Finnish athletes, but you can rent a room or a cottage anywhere. The unpolluted environment and good facilities make this a pleasant place to stay and to engage in sports. Vuokatti village is small, with a post office, banks and shops.

Places to Stay

Vuokatinranta (☎ 640 261) is a Lutheran holiday centre, and religious events are held here. The simplest cottages are available from 180 mk per night and sleep three people, but they are often full, so ask early. *Vuokatinhovi* (☎ 669 8111), surrounded by pine forests, is in a quiet lakeside location. The cheapest rates start from 160 mk, but there are also more expensive hotel rooms and cottages. You can rent practically any sports or fishing equipment here, including bicycles. *Vuokatin urheiluopisto* (☎ 669 1111), the sports institute of Vuokatti, has singles/doubles from 390/470 mk, including breakfast and use of facilities. The place rents canoes, boats and any other equipment you might need.

Off the road to Vuokatinranta is *Suvikas* (☎ 664 0401). This place is recommended if you are looking for high-quality Swiss-style family accommodation. Singles/doubles cost 380/500 mk, but there are always lower summer rates. There is a good restaurant here. *Katinkulta* (☎ 647 711) includes a holiday village, sports facilities and a spa. Opened in late 1991 in the midst of the recession, the resort has a rather yuppie flavour, with superb facilities. Doubles cost 550 mk, or special packages are available through Finnair.

Getting There & Away

Buses run frequently from Kajaani, but you have to get off along the main road and walk to the place of your choice. If you plan to hitchhike, be warned: cars drive fast here.

KUHMO

Kuhmo, with an area of 5458 sq km, is the largest city in Finland. Of course, this is just a technical definition, as there could hardly be an area more remote than the 'suburbs' of Kuhmo, along the Russian border. Kuhmo is famous for its annual chamber music festival and for several WWII battlefields, as well as for its indigenous forest reindeer population, which reaches 600 head in winter and 400 in summer. The population of Kuhmo is 12,500, of which 7500 live in the town of Kuhmo.

Information

Tourist Office The helpful tourist information office (☎ 655 6382) is right in the town centre, on the main street. It's open in summer, Monday to Friday from 8 am to 6 pm, on Saturday from 8 am to 4 pm, and in winter, Monday to Friday from 8 am to 5 pm. The office stocks good maps and walking guides to the region.

There is also a national park information centre near the Kalevala theme park.

Post & Telephone The post office is near the market.

Public Library Don't miss the beautiful library at Pajakkakatu 2. Opened in 1988, it is typical of the most inspirational modern Finnish architecture. There are magazines and travel books, and you can listen to compact discs. It's open Monday to Friday from 10 am to 7 pm and on Saturday from 9 am to 3 pm.

Travel Agencies Kainuun Matkatoimisto (☎ 652 0421) at Koulukatu 12 and Matka-Kyllönen (☎ 652 0771) at Kainuuntie 84 arrange tours to Russia, but you must get your visa in advance.

Lutheran Church

The large wooden Lutheran Church in the town centre has been beautifully repainted. Concerts are held there during the chamber music festival, but at other times admission is free. It is open from early June to mid-August, daily from 10 am to 6 pm.

Orthodox Church

More interesting is the Orthodox Church, one km outside the centre towards the suburb of Kalevala. There are several 18th century icons, which were painted in the Valamo Monastery, annexed by the former Soviet Union, and a 300-year-old Madonna icon in the inner sanctuary. The church is open on request only; enquire at the tourist office.

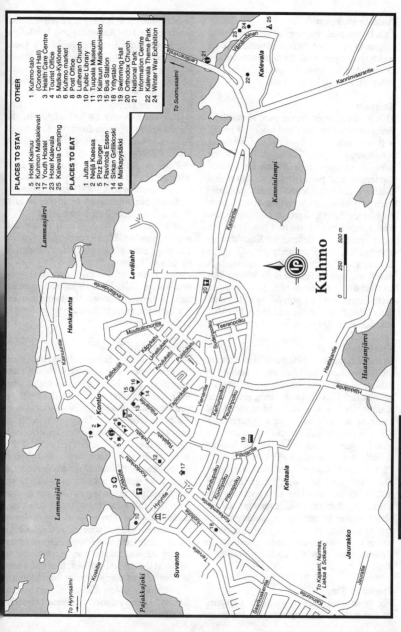

PLACES TO STAY

5 Hotel Kainuu
12 Kuhmon Matkakievari
17 Youth Hostel
23 Hotel Kalevala
25 Kalevala Camping

PLACES TO EAT

1 Juttua
2 Neljä Kaesaa
7 Pizz Burger
14 Ravintola Essen
15 Sirkan Grillikioski
16 Matkapysäkki

OTHER

1 Kuhmo-talo
   (Concert Hall)
3 Health Care Centre
4 Tourist Office
6 Matka-Kylönen
8 Kuhmo market
9 Post Office
10 Lutheran Church
11 Public Library
12 Tuupala Museum
13 Kainuun Matkatoimisto
15 Bus Station
18 Yritystalo
19 Swimming Hall
20 Orthodox Church
21 National Park
    Information Centre
22 Kalevala Theme Park
24 Winter War Exhibition

Kuhmo

0   250   500 m

OULU PROVINCE

Tuupala Museum

This homestead museum at Tervatie 1 was originally a prosperous farmhouse. The main building is open June to September, daily except Monday, from 10 am to 4 pm (in July to 6 pm). Admission is 10 mk.

Kalevala

This *Kalevala*-epic theme park shows how Finns used to live, hunt and work in Karelia. It is not only a museum – there is always something going on. Tickets are 40 mk to the museum precinct, plus 20 mk for a guide (optional). The park is marked with a sign that says 'Kalevalakierros', and is open daily from May to September. Hours from June to August are 9 am to 6 pm; at other times, the park is open from 8 am to 4 pm. Three km from the centre of Kuhmo, the Kalevala area also has a hotel, a camping ground, sports facilities and a children's playground. A recent addition to the area is the **Winter War Exhibition**, open from May to September, daily from 9 am to 7 pm. Many of the artefacts were found in the Kuhmo wilderness. Admission is 20 mk.

Festivals

Of the several annual events held in Kuhmo, the international chamber music festival in July stands out. Over 100 acclaimed international musicians make the long journey to Kuhmo for the two weeks of music. Most concerts are held in the new concert hall. There is usually just one concert at any one time between 11 am and 11 pm, so you can actually hear everything. Tickets cost 20 to 75 mk, with student discounts available. There are also free concerts every day. The festival gives musicians an opportunity to meet and collaborate, and several groups can play together in one venue. Weekly passes are available. For further information, contact the Kuhmon Kamarimusiikki in Kuhmo (☎ 652 0936), Torikatu 39, 88900 Kuhmo.

Places to Stay

For those on a budget, *Kalevala Camping* (☎ 655 6388) offers the cheapest dormitory beds in Finland. It is three km from the town centre, behind the Kalevala park. Ask for the 'Tervapirtti' (the dormitory building). There are 24 beds available, at 16 mk, and cottages for 150 mk. Camping costs 25 mk for one person. You can rent a rowing boat or a canoe for 20 mk per hour (you may be able to negotiate the price).

The *youth hostel* (☎ 655 6245) in the Piilola school is open from 10 June to 10 August. Dormitory beds start from 35 mk. A sauna will cost you a mere 10 mk.

Kuhmon Matkakievari (☎ 655 0271) at Vienantie 3 is clean but a bit tacky. Singles/doubles cost 140/190 mk, breakfast included, but prices are a bit higher in July. Rooms don't have their own toilets.

Hotel Kainuu (☎ 655 1715) is the best place to stay in the town centre, with singles/doubles from 280/360 mk. *Hotel Kalevala* (☎ 655 4100) looks better in reality than in photographs. Comfortable, modern singles/doubles are 425/570 mk. This place handles most of the rental services, including canoes. For bicycles, though, there are better options in the town centre.

Places to Eat

The small market is busy all summer, until the first snow comes; there are stalls till late afternoon. This is the place to bargain for fresh karjalanpiirakka pies or rönttönen, if you happen to like them.

Cheap food is available from cafés or petrol stations, or from *Sirkan Grillikioski* or *Matkapysäkki*, near the bus terminal. If this is not your style, there are a few typical restaurants in Kuhmo. *Pizz Burger* on the main road serves a good buffet-style set lunch from 11 am to 4 pm. You can choose soup or a full meal, salad, bread, drink and coffee included. *Ravintola Essen* is almost opposite on the main street. If you're looking for nice cafés, compare *Neljä Kaesaa* on the corner of Koulukatu and Kainuuntie to *Juttua* at the concert hall near the lake. There is also a traditional buffet lunch/dinner (70/90 mk) at *Hotel Kalevala*, with several fish and kukko (stuffed rye bread) varieties on offer.

Top: Petkeljärvi National Park, Ilomantsi
Left: Small sauna on a lakeshore, North Karelia
Right: Orthodox Church, Ilomantsi

Top: The Skata (Old Town), Pietarsaari
Bottom: Lone painter in the open-air Kilens Museum, near Sideby

Things to Buy

For handicrafts, see what is currently on sale in the Kalevala area. In the theme park, you can talk to artists in the Pohjolan talo or at Taidepaja, and the smith in the Ilmarisen paja (workshop) sells what he makes.

The Yritystalo building has an exhibition and sales, and the Kuhmo market has some handicrafts, including items made of birch bark.

Getting There & Away

Kajaani is the main gateway to Kuhmo. A minibus runs from Kajaani airport to Kuhmo village after the arrival of each flight. The fare is 100 mk per person. Many trains are met by a bus from Kajaani station to Kuhmo. There are 12 buses a day from Kajaani to Kuhmo, and a few buses from Nurmes and Oulu. Hitchhiking is easier if you walk out of town first, whichever direction you're heading in.

AROUND KUHMO
Lentuankoski

White-water rafting is arranged daily from 1 June to mid-August at the Lentuankoski rapids, some 15 km north of Kuhmo. Prices range from 25 to 40 mk per person, depending on the size of the group.

Lentiira

Lentiira is the biggest 'suburb' of Kuhmo, and is known for the 'axe people', skilful builders who finished the fourth consecutive wooden church here in 1992. Although the first three churches all burned down, the new one is made of local wood.

Lentiira is a good location from which to start paddling towards Kuhmo. You could also consider a mountain-bike tour along the Urho K Kekkonen (UKK) route, as it may be suitable for that purpose by now.

Places to Stay Lentiiran Lomakylä (☎ 650 141), three km from the village crossing, has good cottages (from 270 mk for two, plus 50 mk for each additional person). There is also a seasonal supplement from mid-June to

July. Boats, canoes and mountain bikes can be hired here.

Syväjärvi

This fishing area, some 17 km north-west of Kuhmo, is controlled by the Forest & Park Service. Trout and salmon are released into the waters here every year. There are walking tracks around Lake Syväjärvi; camp sites and a *laavu* (open shelter with sloping roof) provides basic (and free) accommodation. Fishing is allowed all year round, except in May. The reception building (open from late May to 31 August) has a café, sells fishing permits and hires rowing boats (35 mk for 12 hours). Fishing permits are also available in Kuhmo and Sotkamo.

UKK Trekking Route

Kuhmo has pockets of the now-rare Finnish wilderness, best preserved along the eastern border of Finland. There are over 230 km of trekking trails around Kuhmo. The recommended options, starting from the town of Kuhmo, are the two legs of the enormously long UKK route, east and north to Lentiira, or west and south to Hiidenportti. In the Kuhmo area, the trail is well maintained. Every 10 to 20 km, you will find a waterfront laavu shelter area. Carry a sleeping bag and mosquito repellent to take advantage of this free open-air accommodation. Each laavu has an established campfire place, firewood and a simple toilet. The trail is marked with occasional blue plastic ribbons on trees, and there are clear signs when the path forks. Get a free copy of the route map at the tourist office in Kuhmo, or other brochure outlets in the region.

Kuhmo to Lentiira This long section of the UKK route first heads east, almost to the frontier, then continues north-west to Lentiira village. The trek takes at least four days, but you can spend eight days on this route if you stay at each shelter along the way. The scenery is better here than along the south-western leg of the UKK route. Highlights include the two pockets of the Finno-Russian Friendship Park, Elimyssalo

OULU PROVINCE

and Iso-Palonen. To shorten the route (and to avoid walking along the main road), hitch-hike or catch a bus to the northern entry point on highway No 912.

Kuhmo to Hiidenportti This interesting section of the UKK route follows the small park trails in the nature reserves through which it passes. It is recommended that you add the Hiidenportti National Park, the Peurajärvi fishing area and even the Mujejärvi area to this route (see the Nurmes section for details of these areas).

Other Trekking Areas
Elimyssalo This park has an indigenous deer population. There is a parking place off the unsealed Juntti road, and a laavu shelter and a few camp sites inside the park.

Iso-Palonen North of Elimyssalo, this government trekking area has several walking tracks, shelters and campfire places. You can rent cabins here; enquire at the tourist office.

Jauhovaara The area around this hill (253 metres) is a nature reserve. It has a three km trail with a camp site and shelter. Many of the trees were brought from abroad and planted in the 1930s.

Road of Wilderness Villages
Recommended for vehicles and cyclists alike, this circular route east of Kuhmo (known as 'Korpikylien tie' among locals) features some interesting WWII battlefields, desolate farmhouses and real wilderness. It is also possible to combine hitchhiking or trekking with travel on the twice weekly bus that runs through Saunajärvi and Korkea.

Sivakka The old school building near the road crossing is run by *Erämatkailu Piirainen* (☎ 535 107) with beds from 50 mk per person. The place organises all kinds of activities.

Saunajärvi This place has several WWII sites. The old *korsu* (bunker) has been refurbished; take matches from the letter box and light a candle downstairs. You can sleep inside the korsu, as Finnish soldiers did during the war, but it's cold and unpleasant. See also the watermill, marked by a 'Vesimylly' sign, at the river. It is still used sometimes for making flour. The small kiosk at the bridge rents boats for use on the lake, where you can fish if you have a permit (which costs 5 mk per week).

Kilpelänkangas Some 10 km off the Korpikylien tie, towards the border, is the largest WWII memorial on this route. There is also a three km trail (Retkeilypolku) along the river where you can see the old floating wooden chutes used for transporting logs past the rapids.

Kiekinkoski The large house (☎ 658 019) rents cabins on a weekly basis, but you have to call ahead. Rates for four bed cottages start at 1200 mk per week. The place also rents boats and sells fishing permits.

Elimyssalo Follow the 'Juntti' sign north along a gravel road. See the UKK Trekking Route section above for park information. It is one km from the road to the parking area and a further 600 metres to the nearest lakeside campfire place, or five km to the nearest laavu.

Juntti Climb the fire observation tower for an unforgettable view over the Kainuu wilderness. Bring binoculars to scan the marshland for deer. The road here is very bad, so if you have a camper, skip this one and take the alternative western route.

Kalliojoki There are several farmhouses here, which rent boats and sell fishing permits, but there are no signs. The fuel tanks a bit further on belong to a shop which is hidden in the house behind.

HYRYNSALMI
The small village of Hyrynsalmi is some 500 metres off the Kajaani to Ämmänsaari road (No 5). The old church near the main road is one of the few buildings that escaped

German destruction during WWII. The population of the municipality is just 3900.

There are two ski centres west of Hyrynsalmi. Ukkohalla has the longest slopes in Kainuu. Another option in the region is Paljakka. There are hotels in both places.

Places to Stay

Hyrynsalmi Youth Hostel (☎ 741 811) is just at the crossroads in a school building. It's open from late June to 31 July, but come before 10 pm to get in. Beds cost 45 mk for HI members.

PUOLANKA

This large municipality is the most sparsely populated area outside Lapland, with just 4350 people, or 1.7 people per sq km. The highest waterfall in Finland is **Hepoköngäs** (24 metres), off the Puolanka to Hyrynsalmi road.

KUIVAJÄRVI

This small village on the border with Russia is in a beautiful setting, surrounded by lonely lakes. Once an important settlement of Russian Karelians, linked culturally to more eastern villages, it is now a decaying place linked by a gravel road to the Suomussalmi municipality.

There is little left of the archaic Karelian culture here, although the fine wooden Orthodox *tsasouna* (chapel) has an 18th century icon from Novgorod.

Treks

You can do plenty of walking in the forests near Kuivajärvi. A few km east of the Domnan pirtti youth hostel, there's a small parking area. The track leads to the Saarisuo area where there's a shelter on the shore of small Lake Kirnulampi. You can also walk further north towards Malahvianvaara, to reach the fishing area of **Yli-Vuokki**, where you need all the appropriate licences before you can catch your lunch.

Places to Stay

There are currently two attractive and clean places to stay. They both give excellent value

for money. *Domnan pirtti* (☎ 723 179) is one of the most attractive youth hostels in Finland, with good beds in partitioned dorms. It is named after Ms Domna Huovinen (1878-1963), a native Russian Karelian and mother of 11 children, who was one of the most notable singers of traditional *Kalevala*-inspired poems and of itkuvirsi ('cry psalm') songs. Dormitory beds cost 55 mk, and singles/doubles are 125/200 mk. Further east, *Kuivajärven leirikeskus* (☎ 723 167 or 723 171) has superb dorms for a mere 30 mk per person, or 200 mk per week. You should bring your own sheets. Meals are available if you give notice, and there is a sauna, which will cost extra.

Getting There & Away

Kuivajärvi is 75 km from Ämmänsaari. There are no buses, but those with private vehicles will have no trouble getting there.

The main road (No 912) runs between Kuhmo and Ämmänsaari. You can hitchhike from both places. Kuivajärvi is 20 km from road No 912. There is little traffic so start walking while waiting for friendly BMWs to come along.

Another option is to hitch to Vartius (or take the bus), which should be no problem if you start from Kuhmo. This is a relatively busy border crossing to the Russian town of Kostomuksha (Kostamus in Finnish). There is a railway station in Vartius but no passenger trains. There is a pub near the station. From Vartius, walk under the bridge, turn right, follow the tracks for some time and then follow the gravel road which runs parallel to the border. Halfway there is a fence, which separates the southern deer population from the northern reindeer stock. Border patrols drive along this road. It is approximately 20 km from Vartius to Kuivajärvi, so you should allow at least five hours. Carry some food and drink from the lakes. When you finally hit the 'main road' turn right to reach Kuivajärvi.

ÄMMÄNSAARI

Ämmänsaari is the 'capital' of Suomussalmi, one of the largest municipalities in Finland, which has always been a bit of a backwater. Many people have left their homes here and emigrated to the south, or to Sweden, to escape poverty. Some 12,200 people live in Suomussalmi these days, half of them in Ämmänsaari, the commercial centre. Suomussalmi has declared itself an *eko*-municipality, signifying its concern with all things 'green'.

Information

The tourist office (☎ 719 1243) is in the Kiannon Kuohut spa, at Jalonkatu 1. It's open in summer from 8 am to 6 pm Monday to Friday, from noon to 6 pm on Saturday and till 4 pm on Sunday. All other services are near the bus terminal, as is the tourist office.

Cruises

From late June to mid-August, there are daily cruises to Turjanlinna House, departing at 11 am and 3 pm. The two hour cruise costs 40 mk.

Places to Stay

The cheapest place to stay in Ämmänsaari is *Matkakoti-Kianta-Baari* (☎ 711 173) at Ämmänkatu 4, with singles/doubles for 130/210 mk. *Kiannon Kuohut* (☎ 710 770) has singles/doubles at 450/550 mk, including breakfast and swimming. Several bungalow villages around Ämmänsaari offer accommodation from 100 mk per night, such as *Ämmänsaaren lomakylä* (☎ 712 525) some six km towards Kajaani.

Places to Eat

Kultainen kukko at the K supermarket has lunch from 30 mk. *Tervareitti* at Keskuskatu 24 has meals but is less attractive. *Hotel Kiannon Kuohut* at Jalonkatu 1 has higher prices and better service. *Pizza Mafia* serves decent pizzas, and *Auto-Grilli Rasti* is a typical junk-food joint.

Esso, Shell and Teboil all have cafeterias, but they are outside the town centre. Eight km north of Ämmänsaari on road No 5, *Ryysyranta* has a fish pond (you can catch and prepare the fish), a licensed restaurant and a dance floor.

Ämmänsaari has four enormous supermarkets within 100 metres or so of each other, each staying open until 8 pm on weekdays. Now that's impressive.

Getting There & Away

Up to 10 buses from Kajaani, four from Kuusamo and one from Oulu travel to Ämmänsaari each weekday, and there are several buses on weekends.

AROUND ÄMMÄNSAARI
Suomussalmi

The old centre of Suomussalmi is sadly decaying while Ämmänsaari booms. The modern church from 1950 marks the turn-off for the 2.3 km road to the local museum, which is on an island connected by a causeway. This scenic spot was the site of the 18th century church that was destroyed during WWII. The museum itself consists of several buildings, with exhibitions varying from prehistory to local tools. The museum is open daily in summer from 9 am to 7 pm; admission is free.

Places to Stay *Wanhan Kalevan Majatalo* (☎ 715 018) at the Matkahuolto (bus stop) has five rooms priced at 150/230 mk. There are also snacks and coffee available.

Raate Road

Almost 40,000 Russian soldiers attacked the Suomussalmi area in early December 1939, approaching along the Raate road. In a week, they advanced to the village of Suomussalmi. The Russians apparently aimed to cut Finland in two and started here. Finns used the tactic of encirclement, or *motti*, to trap entire divisions and by the end of January, the Russians were defeated. Some 22,500 Russians were buried along the road by the summer of 1940, and 6500 Finns were left dead or wounded. Don't miss the **Raatteen Portti**, 24 km east of Ämmänsaari. There is a war exhibition and a restaurant here. It's open from 1 May to 27 September from 9 am to 4 pm daily, and in summer from 10 am to 8 pm. Admission is 15 mk.

Ala-Vuokki

Some 60 km from Kuivajärvi, this village has grown up on both sides of Lake Vuokkijärvi. Several farms rent rooms and serve home-made food.

Juntusranta

Located at a scenic lakeside setting north-east of Ämmänsaari, Juntusranta has a modern church and many WWII sites to visit. There are some shops that sell food.

Martinselkonen

This isolated area approximately 30 km south-east of Juntusranta (60 km from Ämmänsaari) offers walking tracks, with two wilderness huts providing free accommodation. The area may become a national park in the future.

Martinselkosen eräkeskus (☎ 736 160) is the only service business in the area, located at the old border guards' station 14 km from road No 913 on Pirttivaarantie, not far from the Russian border zone. There are activities, rooms and meals available. Rooms start from 100/125 mk, and there are also wilderness cottages for rent by the day or week. Use of the smoke sauna is relatively inexpensive here.

HOSSA

Hossa, dubbed the 'fisher's paradise', is one of the most carefully maintained fishing areas in Finland. Trekking is also excellent, and some of the paths take you to beautiful ridges between lakes.

You will need to do some planning, to decide where to purchase fishing permits and where to stay, but once you get started, you can enjoy some excellent scenery in and around Hossa.

Information

The excellent information centre (☎ 732 361) will explain everything, rent anything and help make your stay successful. Free *Hossa* maps are also available from regional tourist offices. You are allowed to drive a motor vehicle in the Hossa area.

Värikallio

Colour Rock, in the north-west corner of the Hossa area, features one of the most appreciated rock paintings in Finland. It is estimated to be 4000 years old. You can only reach the site via the marked trail.

Places to Stay

In the south, *Lomamökit Paasovaara* (☎ 732 319) has a number of cottages from 200 mk. There are meals for 45 mk, breakfast for 25 mk and a sauna. You can rent a bicycle here.

Further north, two companies compete side by side. *Erä-Hossa* (☎ 732 310) has a number of cottages from 160 to 380 mk (the best cottages have a TV, a sauna and a microwave oven). Canoes are available for 90 mk per day. *Hossan Lomakeskus* (☎ 732 322) is a large establishment near the road, with hotel doubles in summer for 320 mk, and many kinds of cottages at the waterfront. Buffet lunch is available for 60 mk.

Hossan Retkeilyalue (☎ 732 361) is an information centre run by the Forest & Park Service. Its services include *Karhunkainalon Leirintäalue*, a camping ground with rates from 35 mk for a single traveller, or 70 mk for a tent. You can also rent one of the several rustic cottages in Hossa. The information centre takes care of daily or weekly rental and rates start from 280 mk per day from 20 February to 30 September, and from 230 mk at other times. Closest to the information centre, *Iikoski* is located at rapids of the same name. *Jatkonsalmi* is the largest house, with 46 beds in two rooms. It costs 490 mk per day for the smaller room. *Lounatkoski* is at the rapids of the same name. *Tolosenvirta* further west is a fine house with five small rooms for 490 mk per day. *Peurapirtti* and *Hirvastupa* are at Lake Iso-Valkeinen.

Wilderness Huts There are five huts in Hossa that can be used free of charge. Remember that the first person to arrive should be the first one to leave. All huts are suitable for staying in overnight in winter. In addition to huts, there are several laavu shelters in Hossa. You can visit them and light a

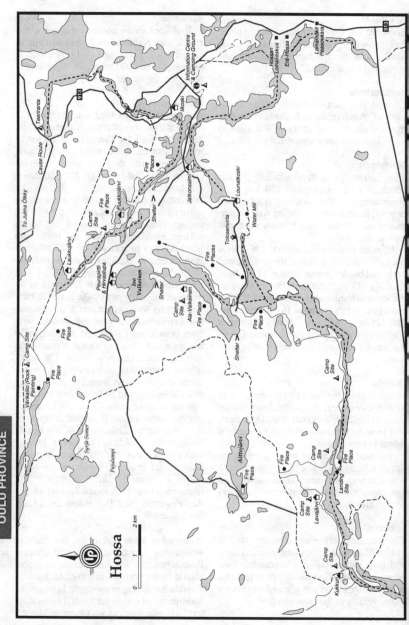

camp fire and you can stay overnight, although it's not very luxurious.

Kukkuri – This hut in the far west of the area has room for seven people.

Lavajärvi – This ex-sauna now houses five people on the shore of Lake Lavajärvi, in the western part of Hossa.

Ala-Valkeinen – By Lake Ala-Valkeinen, this hut has room for six people.

Laukkujärvi – Close to the prehistoric paintings, this small hut can sleep four people.

Puukkojärvi – This small hut for three people, north-west from the information centre, is well located between Lake Puukkojärvi and Lake Suottajärvi.

Getting There & Away

There are daily post buses between Ämmänsaari and Kuusamo, via Hossa. Another bus runs from Ämmänsaari to Hossa on weekdays, departing from Ämmänsaari at 2.45 pm.

KYLMÄLUOMA

This is another fishing and trekking area, some 30 km from Hossa, which can be reached from Hossa by following the marked trail that starts from near the Värikallio. *Kylmäluoma* sketch maps are available in several regional tourist offices, free of charge.

Koillismaa

The distinctive Koillismaa region, literally 'north-eastern land', is a transitional region between Oulu and the Russian border, and buses run through it. Koillismaa is one of the poorest areas in Finland. Without the winter sports activity and related services, there would be little reason to visit.

The Kuusamo area in eastern Koillismaa, however, is unique. A variety of regional characteristics meet here: the fells and reindeer of Lapland, the lakeland of Savo, the Kainuu-type wilderness and the Karelian scenery. This region is blessed with an abundance of water, has a rugged landscape and records the 'worst' earthquakes in (geologi-cally stable) Finland. Rivers from the many lakes run in all directions: Kuusamo is a watershed area. This is also where northern and southern fauna meet, and there are more species to be found in Kuusamo than almost anywhere else. Add to this the fierce local pride and excellent services and you have a most interesting region to explore. Consequently, Kuusamo ranks high on the list of popular holiday destinations among Finns.

KUUSAMO TOWN

There is little to see in the town of Kuusamo, but the place serves as an excellent base for obtaining information and planning treks in the large municipality of Kuusamo. Locals consider Kuusamo a town rather than a village, and indeed, it has grown considerably over the last decade. There are good services, including a well-stocked library with books on the area.

There are 18,700 inhabitants in the 5,805 sq km area of Kuusamo, with 11,000 of them scattered around the main town.

History

A Lutheran parish for over 300 years, Kuusamo was incorporated as a municipality in 1868. By 1900, its population had grown to 10,000, and relations with nearby Russia were close. During WWII, the village was a command centre for German troops, who also supervised the construction of the 'Death Railway' that operated for just 242 days. When the Soviet army marched into Kuusamo on 15 September 1944, the Germans burned down the entire town and blew up the railway. The Soviets retreated, after occupying Kuusamo for about two months, and the inhabitants of Kuusamo returned to their destroyed town. A large number of refugees from the annexed Salla region were settled around Kuusamo after WWII, and the last phase of the Finnish land reform was carried out in Kuusamo.

Information

Tourist Office Excellent tourist services are available at the Karhuntassu Tourist Centre (☎ 850 2910 or 850 6777; fax 850 2901) at

OULU PROVINCE

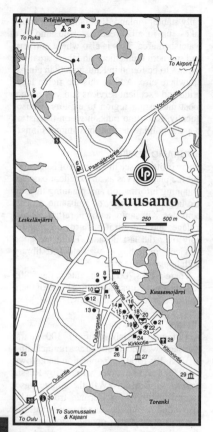

Kuusamo

PLACES TO STAY

1   Matkajoen leirintä
2   Rantatropiikki Camping
3   Kuusamon Tropiikki
11 Kuusamon Kansanopisto
14 Hotel Viikinki
24 Hotel Martina
26 Sokos Hotelli Kuusamo

PLACES TO EAT

8   Lunch Bar Ali-Baba
16 Ampan Pizza Bar
18 Rolls & Café Green
19 Pub Jalopeura & Shaman
22 Karhunkierros

OTHER

2   Kuusamon Erä-Safari
4   Dairy Shop
5   Kuusamon Uistin
6   Neste Petrol Station
7   Swimming Hall
9   Kuusamotalo House
10 Bus Station
12 Public Library
13 Water Tower & Café
15 Matka-Ruka Travel Agency
17 Bjarmia Ceramics Factory
18 Kauppakulma Shopping Centre
20 Post Office
21 Health Care Centre
23 Market Square
25 The White Studio (ceramics)
27 Porkkatörmä Gallery
28 Church
29 Museum
30 Tourist Office

Torangintaival 2, two km from the centre on the main highway (No 5). It's open in summer from 9 am to 7 pm, and in winter from 9 am to 5 pm Monday to Friday. Get a copy of *Kuusamo the Green Adventure*, which has an extensive range of useful information and glossy photos. The services here include the café *Kuukkeli*, which has souvenirs for sale, and the office of the Finnish Forest & Park Service, with information available on national parks.

Post & Telephone The post office is right in the centre. The telephone office, near the

Sokos Hotelli Kuusamo, is open from 8 am to 5 pm Monday to Friday.

Travel Agencies Matka-Ruka (☎ 850 6777, fax 852 2015) at Kitkantie 15 is a regular travel agency, but they also arrange reservations at any of over 600 accommodation units scattered around Kuusamo. For whitewater rafting and safaris, there are several operators such as Kuusamon Erä-Safari (☎ 853 196) at Rantatropiikki Camping at Kitkantie 71, or Lapin Luonto-ja erämatkat (☎ 852 2818) at Torankijärventie 2A.

Library The public library is opposite the bus terminal, at Kaiterantie 22. It has 1:20,000

maps of the Kuusamo area, available in self-service drawers in the käsikirjasto section. It's open from noon to 7 pm, Monday to Friday.

Museum

Some 500 metres beyond the church is the museum, featuring several old grey buildings and some artefacts. It's open from mid-June to mid-August from noon to 6 pm daily, and from mid to late August from 9 am to 3 pm Monday to Friday. Admission is free.

Other Attractions

The **water tower** on Joukamontie has an observation platform with a good view over Kuusamo. There's a café there with snacks available. The tower is usually open from noon to 8 pm.

The large white **Kuusamotalo House** (☎ 850 6028) at Kaarlo Hännisentie 2 was finished in 1996. It has exhibitions, concerts and a café.

Places to Stay – bottom end

Kuusamon Kansanopisto (☎ 852 2132) at Kitkantie 35 is a youth hostel, open from 1 June to 31 August. Conveniently located across the street from the bus terminal, it has dormitory beds from 40 mk. There is a kitchen and a satellite TV in the common room.

Places to Stay – middle

Hotel Martina (☎ 852 2051) at Ouluntie 3 has 32 rooms at 290 mk for one to four people. *Hotel Kultainen Joutsen* (☎ 851 2701) at Haapanantie 1 is a bit out of the centre, but offers a quiet location and singles/doubles at 200/300 mk.

There is a cluster of three camping areas five km north of Kuusamo. *Rantatropiikki* is by far the most comfortable of these. It is associated with the neighbouring spa, and its cottage rates include use of the spa facilities. Rates for bungalows are lower at *Matkajoen leirintä* and at *Petäjälammen leirintäalue*. The latter also has cottages available close to the main road and a camping area 500 metres from the road.

Places to Stay – top end

Hotel Viikinki (☎ 852 3619) at Juhantie 10, not far from the bus station, has 16 apartments, most of which include a sauna. Rates are 250/300 mk.

Sokos Hotelli Kuusamo (☎ 85920) at Kirkkotie 23 is a concrete box-like structure and has 182 rooms; the *kota* (traditional Lappish hut) structure is quite impressive. This is also where you'll find the most interesting nightlife in Kuusamo. Doubles start at 440 mk.

Some five km north of Kuusamo, near the camping grounds, *Kuusamon Tropiikki* (☎ 85960), is a superb modern spa and hotel with 81 rooms and a plastic tropical wonderland with a 45 metre water slide. There are singles/doubles from 325/430 mk, including breakfast and use of the pool and saunas. For nonguests, a two hour visit to the spa costs 60 mk.

Places to Eat

Kitkantie, the main road, has a few options. *Ampan Pizza Bar* at No 18 supplies just about what you'd expect from a place with such a name. At No 1, there are two evening pubs; *Pub Jalopeura* opens at 5 pm, and *Shaman* as late as 9 pm (closed on Monday). Opposite Shaman in the Kauppakulma shopping centre, you can check out *Café Green*, and *Rolls*, which serves sandwiches.

Lunch Bar Ali-Baba, also known as *Lopotti*, is near the bus station at Kaarlo Hännisentie 2, with inexpensive lunches available until 5 pm. Something cheaper but not that chic is the petrol station *Cafe-Kesoil Kuusamo* with home-made meals and an English menu.

The two hotels, Martina and Sokos Hotelli Kuusamo, have large restaurants with busy terraces in summer. There are also a few *grilli kiosks* at the market, which are open well past midnight. The market itself is busy till 3 pm.

Things to Buy

There are some good buys in Kuusamo. Bjarmia is a ceramics factory with a café and a discount section at Vienantie 1, right in the centre. You can watch the manufacturing while tasting the pies. Another studio that makes ceramics is the White Studio on Pajatie, to the west from the main road. The artist is from Britain.

Sokos Kuusamo and Kesport Intersport sell trekking gear and other sports equipment. Outside the centre, to the north on the main road (No 5), Kuusamon Uistin sells lures and sheath knives from its factory. Some of these products are exported throughout the world under the brand name Kuusamo.

Getting There & Away

Air Finnair has daily morning and evening flights from Helsinki to Kuusamo.

Bus Several bus companies run daily express buses from Oulu to Kuusamo. There are also regular connections from Rovaniemi. Buses from Kemijärvi run regularly only during the school year.

Car Rental Hertz (☎ 851 4683) is at the airport and open 24 hours.

KARHUNKIERROS TREKKING ROUTE

Karhunkierros, one of the oldest and most established trekking routes in Finland (often translated as Bear's Ring), offers the most varied and breathtaking scenery in Finland. It's very popular during the *ruska* (autumn) period.

Because the loop runs through some isolated areas within Oulanka National Park, getting there will require some strategic planning. There are four possible starting points and a short, marked loop trail from Juuma. The best section of the trail runs between the northern starting-point and Juuma.

Information

There is a useful visitor's centre in the middle of Oulanka National Park, accessible by car or by bus. There are exhibits, a library, video programs and a slide show that can be seen daily in summer from 10 am to 8 pm. Snacks and drinks are available at the centre

in summer till 31 October. Get a copy of the 1:40,000 *Rukatunturi-Oulanka* map (50 mk), which is useful for a trek of any length.

Trekking

The track is in excellent condition and can be walked in light shoes on dry summer days.

Day 1 – Start your trek at the northern parking area near Ristikallio. After 15 minutes you will reach the national-park border. You can stop at a campsite at Aventojoki or proceed further to Ristikallio, which offers some breathtaking scenery. You can either stay here or proceed less than one hour further to Puikkokämppä at a small lake, or one km to Taivalköngäs. Taivalköngäs waterfall (near the wilderness hut of the same name) actually has two rapids, and three suspension bridges for a better view.

Northern extension – If you start trekking from Hautajärvi, you'll have to walk a further 20 km through an unimpressive landscape until the path reaches the Savinajoki River. The highlight here is the deep Oulanka Canyon. There's a wilderness hut at the Oulanka riverfront near Lake Savilampi. The distance between the *Savilammin kämppä* hut and Taivalköngäs is four km.

Day 2 – The first leg is an eight km trek from Taivalköngäs through some ordinary scenery although there are a few beautiful lakes. At 4.2 km, you can camp at Lake Runsulampi; there's dry wood available. Four km further east, you can stay overnight at a camping ground, or just continue to the information centre and stock up on provisions. The Kiutaköngäs rapids, just 800 metres from the visitor centre are noted for their rugged cliffs nearby. It's possible to reach Ansakämppä by early evening from here, or even Jussinkämppä on Lake Kulmakkajärvi.

Day 3 – A relatively easy hike through ridges and forests (and boardwalk across wetlands), takes you to the Kitkanjoki River, in another deep gorge. After following the river, you can choose between several routes, either walking directly to Juuma or crossing the river at Myllykoski to see the mighty Jyrävä waterfall (three km from Juuma) that has an elevation of 12 metres. There's a hut at Jyrävä.

Ruka extension – Juuma is a convenient end point to the trek. It is also possible to walk 23 km further to Ruka, which has an excellent choice of accommodation and better road connections to Kuusamo. There are free huts en route (see below).

Places to Stay

There is a good network of wilderness huts

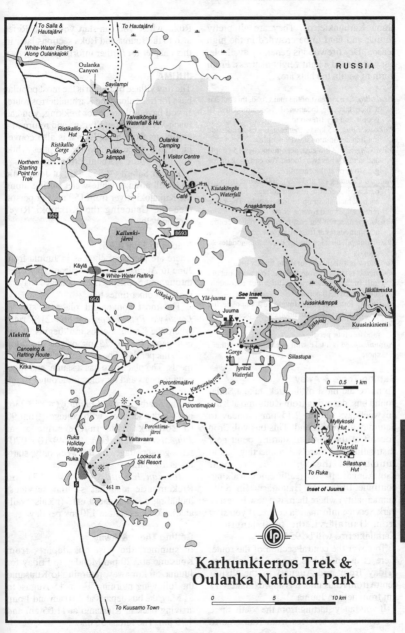

RUSSIA

To Salla & Hautajärvi
To Hautajärvi
White-Water Rafting Along Oulankajoki
Oulanka Canyon
Savilampi
Taivalköngäs Waterfall & Hut
Ristikallio Hut
Oulanka Camping
Ristikallio Gorge
Puikko-kämppä
Visitor Centre
Northern Starting Point for Trek
950
Café
Kiutaköngäs Waterfall
Ansakämppä
8693
Kallunki-järvi
Oulankajoki
Käylä
White-Water Rafting
Jäkälämutka
Kitkajoki
Ylä-juuma
Jussinkämppä
Juuma
Kuusinkiniemi
Alakitta
Kitkajoki
See Inset
Canoeing & Rafting Route
Gorge
Siilastupa
Kitka
Jyrävä Waterfall
Porontimajärvi
Karhunkierros
Porontimajoki
0   0.5   1 km
Porontima-järvi
Myllykoski Hut
Ruka Holiday Village
Valtavaara
Waterfall
Ruka
Lookout & Ski Resort
Siilastupa Hut
5
To Ruka
461 m
Inset of Juuma

OULU PROVINCE

Karhunkierros Trek & Oulanka National Park

0   5   10 km

To Kuusamo Town

along Karhunkierros. They are all pretty similar and tend to be crowded in the high season. Dry firewood is generally available, but you'll need a lightweight mattress. From north to south, the huts are:

Ristikallio, five km east of the main road, this hut has a nice lakeside location. It accommodates 10 people and dry firewood.

Puikkokämppä, 2.5 km further east, is a basic lakeside hut that accommodates 10 people.

Taivalköngäs, 1.3 km east, accommodates 15 people and actually has two floors. You can cook on the gas stove or at the campfire.

Oulanka Camping (☎ 863 429), 500 metres from the park visitor centre, has ten cottages for 200 mk each, which sleep up to four people. The place rents canoes and rowing boats.

Ansakämppä, seven km east from the visitor centre, accommodates at least 10 people.

Jussinkämppä, nine km further on, accommodates 20 people.

Kotalaavu is a shelter several km further on.

Myllykoski is two km from Juuma. This worn-out old mill building has few facilities but accommodates at least 10 people.

Siilastupa, four km from Juuma just opposite the Jyrävä waterfall, accommodates 12 people.

Porontimajoki, eight km south from Juuma, accommodates four people.

Porontimajärvi is a lake with a laavu on its northern shore.

Getting There & Away
To make the most of the trek, take a Salla-bound bus, departing from Kuusamo at 8 am on weekdays and at 2.15 pm Monday to Saturday all year round. This bus will drop you off at the northern starting point near Ristikallio, and there's a connecting bus to Juuma and the visitor centre near Kiutaköngäs. If you really enjoy walking, continue further to Hautajärvi (in Salla municipality) where there is a new Forest & Park Service information centre. If you start from Hautajärvi, the total length of Karhunkierros will be 95 km.

To cover the central section of the route, there is a school bus service (Monday to Friday from mid-August) to the visitor centre from Kuusamo. It is approximately 17 km from here to Juuma.

If you fancy starting from the south, there are regular bus services from Kuusamo to

Ruka, where you can start your trek. Refer also to the Juuma and Ruka sections later in this chapter for further information.

JUUMA
The tiny village of Juuma is the most popular base for treks along the Karhunkierros route. If you have little time for trekking, you can reach Myllykoski and Jyrävä and return in a few hours from here. Juuma is also convenient as a place to shop for supplies while doing the entire Karhunkierros route.

Kitkan Safarit (☎ 853 458) at Juumantie 134, will arrange white-water rafting along the Kitkajoki River from 150 mk per person (see the Canoeing the Kitkajoki River section below).

Places to Stay & Eat
There are plenty of choices in Juuma from June to August, and some places stay open throughout September, but cottages may be rented at other times too.

The most convenient place to stay is *Lomakylä Retki-Etappi* (☎ 863 218) right where the Karhunkierros trail begins. It has cottages at 130 to 275 mk, or you can camp at 50 mk per day. The café serves snacks and meals. The place also has a sauna, and rents rowing boats and bicycles for around 50 mk per day.

The nearby *Jyrävä Camping* (☎ 863 236) has similar services, with cottages from 90 to 200 mk. Also in the same area, *Juumajärven lomakylä* (☎ 949-106 070) rents good cottages by the week only, starting at 1000 mk per week.

Juuman leirintä (☎ 863 212) on Riekamontie also has similar services, including a sauna and a café (meals available). Cottages start at 130 mk per day.

Getting There & Away
In summer, the post bus departs from Kuusamo at 2.20 pm Monday to Friday for Juuma, 50 km away, returning to Kuusamo the following morning. From 15 August to 31 May, the bus departs at 7.10 am and 1 pm, arriving back in Kuusamo at 11.05 am and 4.35 pm. The fare is 56 mk.

KÄYLÄ

The village of Käylä is the starting point for white-water rafting along the Kitkajoki River. There is a shop, a fuel station and a post office. Accommodation is available at *Kitkajoen lomatuvat* (☎ 864 149) and in a handful of other places. Further information is available at the Kuusamo tourist office.

CANOEING THE KITKAJOKI RIVER

The rugged Kitkajoki River offers some of the most challenging canoeing (or kayaking) in Finland. Although the VI-classified Jyrävä is definitely a no-no waterfall, there are plenty of tricky rapids, including the 900 metre Aallokkokoski, with a IV classification to scare you shitless.

You can start the trip from either Käylä or Juuma. From Juuma it's about a 20 km trip to Jäkälämutka near the Russian border.

Käylä to Juuma

The first 14 km leg of the journey is definitely the easier of the two and does not involve any carrying at all. You start at the Käylänkoski rapids, and continue some three km to the easy Kiehtäjänniva, and a further one km to Vähä-Käylänkoski rapids. These are both in the easy category I. After a bit more than a km, there are three category II rapids every 400 metres or so. After a further one km, there's the trickiest one, the category III Harjakoski, which is 300 metres long. The rest of the journey, almost seven km, is mostly lakes. The road bridge between lakes Ylä and Ala-Juumajärvi marks the end of the trip. It is one km to Juuma from the bridge.

Juuma to the Russian Border

This 20 km journey is the most dangerous river route in Finland, which means you *must* carry your canoe at least once. I have met one person who has come down the 12 metre Jyrävä waterfall (alive), but it was done in a rubber raft and under supervision. Do inspect the tricky ones before you let go and ask for local advice in case the water level is unfavourable.

The thrill starts just 300 metres after Juuma, with the category II Niskakoski.

From here on, there is one km of quiet water. Myllykoski, known for its water-mill, is a tricky category IV waterfall. If you are not experienced (and don't want to get all your experience right here and now), you may have to carry your canoe over one km, well beyond the Jyrävä waterfall. Right after Myllykoski, the 900 metre Aallokkokoski means quick paddling for quite some time. What is risky, though, is the fact that Jyrävä comes right after this long section. Do not keep paddling like a maniac after the rapids slow – pull aside 80 metres before Jyrävä, and carry your canoe. Do *not* even think of paddling down Jyrävä. After Jyrävä things cool down considerably, although there are some category III rapids. After some six kms or so, there is the Päähkänäkallio hut, where you can have a break. When you meet Oulankajoki River, seven km from the hut, you can either paddle upriver to Jäkälämutka, or continue right to the border zone and look for the Kuusinkiniemi forest road some hundred metres upstream. You should arrange return transport beforehand for this stage.

CANOEING THE OULANKAJOKI RIVER

Equally impressive, and demanding, among the great Kuusamo River routes, the Oulankajoki River gives you a chance to see the mighty canyons from a canoe. You *must* still carry your canoe at least four times, past parts of the Oulanka Canyon, Taivalköngäs, Kiutaköngäs and another waterfall.

The first leg, an 18 km trip, starts from road No 5, north of the ordinary Karhunkierros starting point. The first seven km or so is relatively calm paddling, until you reach the Oulanka Canyon. The safe section is about one km, after which you should pull aside and carry past the dangerous rapids. Fortunately, there's the Savilampi hut for staying overnight. You will have enough time to check the rapids beforehand (and appreciate the scenery), so take it easy. Many people consider the canyon the most impressive part of the journey. Some three km after Savilampi are the Taivalköngäs rapids. You'll need to carry your canoe, and there's a hut here, too. The next six kms are quiet, until you reach the Kiutaköngäs area (with its camping area and visitors' centre).

The second leg of the journey, a full 20 km long, starts *past* the Kiutaköngäs waterfall. Don't bother risking your life. When you finally reach some quiet waters, there's another waterfall after 500 metres or so, and it's carrying-time again! But after this, the river becomes smooth and there is little to worry about as far as rapids go. This leg is suitable for families with children.

RUKA

Ruka is a protected nature area, and one of the most popular winter-sports centres in Finland (it has won several awards). Prices and demand for accommodation keep it off-limits for budget travellers in winter, but in summer, it is a good place to start the s trek because there are good bus connections from Kuusamo. There is also the monster toboggan slope in summer for speed lovers – each ride is approximately 20 mk.

Information

The annual Ruka booklet is a good source of information (in Finnish).

Post Office The post office is near the main road, three km from the Ruka centre.

Travel Agencies There are several tour operators in Ruka, such as Ruka Safaris (☎ 868 1494) at Rukarinteentie 7. Rukapalvelu Oy (☎ 868 1526) operates from the new Safaritalo building, and arranges fishing tours, canoe safaris, white-water rafting and guided treks. Tours to Lake Paanajärvi (across the border in Russia) can be arranged but require a Russian visa.

Valtavaara

This hill is a continuation of Ruka hill. Several unusual birds nest around the hill, and an annual birdwatching competition is held in the area. In this competition (called 'Pongauskilpailu', from the Swedish *poeng*, meaning 'point'), you score a point for every

bird species you spot. There are over 100 species in this area, so in theory, you could score over 100 points.

The 1995 competition was held in June. If you have any interest in birds, this is the best place in the region.

Skiing

There are 25 downhill ski slopes around the Ruka hill. The ski season is approximately between 1 November and 2 May, depending on snowfalls. A ride up on the ski lift costs 10 mk, or buy a day pass for about 100 mk. You can rent slalom equipment (about 100 mk per day) and cross-country skiing equipment (50 mk per day).

Places to Stay

Ruka is a very busy winter sports centre, and that is the time when it may be hard to find a bed, especially at reasonable prices. Summer is also busy but not impossible.

Rantasipi Ruka (☎ 85910) is the largest hotel in Ruka with 75 rooms and three saunas. Doubles start at 380 mk. Nearby, *RukaKlubi* (☎ 868 1231) has apartments, a sauna and a café (closed in summer). There are also any number of luxurious cottages available, but in summer prices are somewhat lower and within reach of budget travellers, especially for those in a small group.

Just north of Ruka, *Motelli Ukkoherra* (☎ 868 1121) has doubles from 200 mk. *Rukatupa* (☎ 949-431 856) at Ukkoherrantie 18 has small two or three bed cottages at 150 mk. *Rukan Lomapalvelu* (☎ 852 2082 or 9400-386 414) at Lake Salmilampi has just eight cottages, from 280 mk. Some two km from Ruka, *Rukan Kuukkeli* has some fine apartments from 230 mk (enquire at Kuusamo agencies).

Also, there is *Viipus Camping* (☎ 868 1213) at Lake Viipusjärvi, several km north of Ruka, with small cabins from 140 mk, and better six bed cottages at 300 mk. You can camp there for a fee, and there's a shop, a sauna and boats for hire.

Places to Eat

Pizzeria Ruka serves pizza, and *Riipisen Riistakahvila* nearby specialises in wild boar and bear, but these are expensive (cheaper meals are available). This log house is nationally known and celebrities are often seen here in winter. In the main square in Ruka, *Pitäjän-Pirtti* serves coffee and sells souvenirs, and *Rantasipi Ruka* has a large restaurant with 500 seats. *Rukakeskus Hillside* is a hamburger restaurant.

Getting There & Away

Most regular bus services to Kuusamo continue further north to Ruka. Ruka is on main road No 5, and there is enough traffic to hitchhike.

JULMA ÖLKKY

This narrow gorge lake in southern Kuusamo is a good reason to make the 8.5 km detour from road No 913 when travelling north from Hossa. The turn-off is south of Teeriranta but the access road is gravel.

The lake can be seen on daily boat tours. From 15 June to 15 August, there are boat operators near the lakeside road from 9.30 am to 8 pm. The 30 minute boat tour costs 30 mk for adults and 15 mk for children under 12 (free for children under five). At other times of the year, call ☎ 949-389 345 for boat tours. It is also possible to walk.

Places to Stay

Teeriranta Camping (☎ 861 341) is on road No 913 in the village of Teeriranta, and they will help you to get to Julma Ölkky – or at least help you to pronounce the name. There are cottages for two to eight people, a camping ground, a small shop and saunas. It is open all year round.

TAIVALKOSKI

A large municipality between Kuusamo and Pudasjärvi, Taivalkoski does not have a major tourist attraction. There are rapids and a local museum in the main village, and Taivalvaara is a local skiing centre, dwarfed by higher hills further north. Most Finns go to Taivalkoski to see Kallioniemi, the home of Kalle Päätalo, one of the most productive authors in contemporary Finnish literature.

Taivalkoski has 5600 inhabitants. It recently suffered a record unemployment level of 35%.

Places to Stay

Although Taivalkoski is not really an interesting place to visit, you may need a place to stay overnight. There are a few places in the main village. *Asuntohotelli Ruska* (☎ 842 561) at Kauppatie 37 is central, and the cheapest with singles/doubles for 165/260 mk. *Hotelli Joki-Jussi* (☎ 841 021) has 13 rooms with similar prices and a restaurant. At the ski centre, *Hotelli Taivalvaara* (☎ 841 661) is a grandiose building that doubles as a cultural centre. There are 15 rooms (doubles 350 mk) and ten cottages (400 mk each).

There are several other possibilities around the large municipal area. *Kolmiloukon leirintäalue* (☎ 841 471) just four km west from Taivalkoski has five cottages at 140 to 270 mk. *Jokimutka* (☎ 845 762) is a youth hostel to the west of Jurmu, six km from the main Oulu to Kuusamo road (No 20). There are beds at 50 to 85 mk, or 15 mk more for nonmembers. *Ooka-Stoppi* (☎ 845 777) is a restaurant and a petrol station further west with three cottages for 320 mk each.

PUDASJÄRVI

The centre of the large municipality of Pudasjärvi is not the most interesting village in Finland, but it is the biggest place along the main Oulu to Kuusamo road. Visit the local tourist office, Pudasjärven Matkailu Oy (☎ 23400) at Varsitie 7, for more information. The population of Pudasjärvi is 11,000, or two people per sq km.

Things to See

The six km side trip from the main Oulu to Kuusamo road is worth the effort. The **museum** here, one of the largest open-air museums in North Finland, can be found off the Pudasjärvi to Ranua road, some seven km from the village of Pudasjärvi. The museum guidebook is in English. The museum is open late June to mid-August from 10 am to 6 pm Tuesday to Friday and 11 am to 6 pm on Sunday. Admission is 5 mk.

The Pudasjärvi **church** is close to the museum. Built in 1781, it is not very different from many churches in the Oulu area, except for the bell-tower wall paintings by the famous Mikael Toppelius. The unusually long fence around the cemetery was built of horizontally laid logs and covered by a roof, and the only explanation for this lavish spending is that the fence kept wolves from digging up the dead bodies. The church is generally open from noon until late afternoon. Enquire at the museum.

Places to Stay & Eat

The cheapest place to stay is *Pudasmaja* (☎ 823 220), the youth hostel close to the main Oulu to Kuusamo road, with beds from 85 mk. It's clean, and many rooms have their own shower. Breakfast can be had for 25 mk. The best place in the village is *Hotel Kurenkoski* (☎ 821 400) at Kauppatie 7, just behind the bus terminal. Singles/doubles start at 190/250 mk. You can eat here too. For small groups, there are attractive cottages at *Jyrkkäkoski Camping* (☎ 822 550), some five km north of Pudasjärvi.

Along the main road, you can eat at the Teboil and Shell petrol station cafés, or the tacky *Café Burger* at Neste petrol station north of the village. In the village itself, *Texas* serves an economical weekday lunch in a semi-American setting. *Sivakka* at the bus station is another possibility.

Getting There & Away

Pudasjärvi is on the main Oulu to Kuusamo road, and several buses a day make the 1½ hour trip from Oulu.

SYÖTE

Just a decade ago, the Syöte, the most southerly fell in Finland, was covered by virgin forest. Not any more. Syöte's twin peaks, the Iso-Syöte and the Pikku-Syöte ('Big Syöte' and 'Small Syöte', respectively) now have several downhill slopes, ski lifts, hotels and restaurants.

In addition to its winter-sports facilities, the Syöte area offers the visitor access to the protected government recreational area to the north and south-west of the Iso-Syöte. This area has walking tracks and a few comfortable wilderness huts.

Information

Practically all accommodation in the Syöte region can and should be arranged by Pudasjärven Matkailu Oy (☎ 823 400, fax 823 421) at Varsitie 7 in Pudasjärvi. If you plan to stay, you can choose either a daily or a weekly rate. The *Syöte* brochure features about 50 individual lodging options.

Activities

Trekking Only a few trekkers a week seem to take advantage of the excellent facilities along the walking tracks around Syöte, provided free of charge by the Forest & Park Service. There are a number of walking routes in the area. Most trekkers use the Ahmatupa hut as a base, and do a loop around the northern part of the trekking area.

Another route, indicated by yellow markings on trees, makes a loop around Iso-Syöte Hill. Also, the long UKK Route, marked with blue paint on trees, runs from Puolanka to Posio, via Syöte. New shelters and boardwalks are being constructed along this route.

Fishing There are three fishing areas around Syöte, and the Forest & Park Service adds fish to all of them. Along the Pärjänjoki and Livojoki rivers, fishing is allowed from 1 June to 10 September. In lakes Hanhilampi, Kellarilampi and Lauttalampi, near the Iso-Syöte, you can fish at any time except May.

Skiing Some 90 km of skiing tracks are regularly groomed with a snowmobile. Getting lost is practically impossible, and there are good signs when tracks fork.

The best place to start is the ski stadium, at the foot of Iso-Syöte. For downhill skiing, the more popular Iso-Syöte has an elevation of 195 metres. You can rent skiing equipment and purchase a three hour lift pass at the Romekievari station.

Places to Stay

The cheapest place to stay is *Kuntosyöte*, in the village of Syötekylä. In summer, rooms and cabins cost 120 to 130 mk per night for one or two people, plus 30 mk for each additional person.

Some of the most luxurious *kelo* (pine) log cabins on top of Syöte Hill have microwave ovens and TVs. In the spring high season, these cabins cost 500 to 640 mk per night, or 2900 to 3700 mk per week (900 to 1350 mk per week in summer). They accommodate six people.

Wilderness Huts There are three huts and several kota or laavu shelters around the Syöte area. One of the best wilderness huts in Finland, *Ahmatupa* hut takes at least six people. It has gas, comfortable mattresses and a stove. During the winter high season, there is a café, open till 4 pm. Just 50 metres away is *Ahmakota*, which gives shelter when the hut is fully occupied. Outside the 'official' trekking area, there is the *Toraslampi* hut, at the lakeside, and the *Romesuvanto* hut, near the Pärjänjoki River, which is popular with fishers. All these facilities can be used free of charge.

Places to Eat

You should bring food with you in summer. Restaurants around the downhill slopes are busy in winter, and there are grillis and a few grocery stores in the village of Syötekylä.

Getting There & Away

Buses for Syöte depart from Oulu, 140 km away, at 2.40 pm on weekdays. The trip takes about 2½ hours and costs 63 mk.

Getting Around

In winter, snowmobiles can be rented near the Iso-Syöte slopes. You must use established routes. A taxi is available (☎ 949-287 080).

Lapland

Covering almost half of the entire country, sparsely populated Lapland is *the* great adventure in Finland. It is a highlight of any journey, whether you just drive through it or do extensive trekking around the region. Both options are rewarding, but if you set aside enough time to get off the main roads and into the wilderness, Lapland will provide unforgettable experiences, and some of the best free accommodation available anywhere in the world.

The Province of Lapland has a population of 200,000, or 2.1 people per sq km. Much of the population lives in towns in south Lapland.

HISTORY

Finnish Lapland has not been quite as busy as the Finnmark region in northern Norway was over 5000 years ago. Discoveries have been made dating back to the Stone Age. When Sami peoples were pushed north by migrating Finns, traditions evolved and developed. Many legends remain, including those of miracle-working witches who could fly and transform themselves into strange creatures. Conspicuous lakes or rocks became *seita* (holy sites), the island of Ukko on Lake Inarinjärvi being the best known of these.

The banks of Tornionjoki River, as well as the mouth of the Kemijoki River nearby, developed into busy trade centres during medieval times. Some traces of Viking contacts have been found. The king of Sweden granted the Pirkka people (of Häme) exclusive rights to collect taxes among Lapps in the 13th century, and their centre grew at Tornio. Catholic churches remain in Keminmaa and Alatornio. Finns moved farther north along the rivers.

Inari was an important Sami trade centre from the early 1500s, and there were Sami settlements around the vast territory. During the 1600s, Swedes increased their presence throughout northern Finland (the Tor-

Highlights

- Excellent fell-walking, especially in the north of Lapland.
- Well-maintained wilderness huts, absolutely free.
- Inari, the centre of Sami culture.
- Reindeer-spotting.
- Husky and reindeer tours, especially during winter twilight.
- Snowmobile safaris.
- The Tornionjoki River – rafting or watching fishers at the Kukkolankoski rapids.
- Tornio and its attractions, including midnight golf.
- The Arktikum Museum in Rovaniemi, specialising in Arctic life and Lapland.
- The church in Keminmaa, the only preserved medieval church in Lapland.

nionjoki River Valley remained Swedish until 1809). In 1670, cult sites and religious objects of the Sami were destroyed by one Gabriel Tuderus, who represented the Lutheran Church. Wooden churches were built throughout Lapland, the oldest remaining in Tornio, Sodankylä and Tervola.

During the next centuries, more Finns

Pirkka tribe in Lapland, 13th century. The king of Sweden granted the Pirkka people (from Häme) the right to collect taxes from the Lapps.

were attracted to the vast province, adopted reindeer herding and were assimilated into the Sami communities (or vice versa), especially in southern Lapland. In 1800, there were 463 Samis in Inari and only 18 Finns. One hundred years later, there were 800 Samis and 585 Finns. At that time, there were only paths to the northernmost parts of Lapland. The first gravel road to Ivalo was built in 1913, to Inari in 1924 and to Karigasniemi during WWII.

The area of Petsamo, north-east of Inari, was annexed to Finland in 1920 as a result of the Treaty of Tartu and a nickel mine was opened in 1937. Russians attacked the area in the Winter War and the whole area was evacuated on 4 September 1944. The Soviet Union annexed the mineral-rich area and has kept it ever since. The Scolt Samis from Petsamo were settled in Sevettijärvi, Nellim and Virtaniemi in north-eastern Lapland.

When the peace agreement between Finland and the Soviet Union stated that Germans had to leave Finnish territory immediately, the troops of Nazi Germany burned and destroyed all buildings they had access to while retreating to northern Norway. In addition to a few churches and a few villages (such as Suvanto near Pelkosenniemi), only a few isolated houses in Lapland date back to the period before WWII.

The province has had trouble recovering from the destruction caused by the devastating Lapland War. Now, however, with facilities ranging from tacky box-like structures in overnight villages to oversized luxurious skiing resorts on every hill with road access, Lapland is emerging as one of the most affluent regions in Finland, benefiting from booming tourism and generous subsidies from the south.

Although new areas are being threatened with flooding to create dam reservoirs, mining rights are being granted to multinational mining companies (even for land in protected areas), and clear felling of fragile northern forests continues, Lapland still has some of the best preserved wilderness in Europe.

SAMIS

Samis (Lapps) have traditionally been nomads, herding their reindeer in the large area of Lapland spanning from the Kola peninsula in Russia to quite southern ranges of Norwegian mountains. National borders have played no part in defining the areas they inhabit. Their traditional dwelling, the *kota*, resembles the tepee or wigwam of native North Americans, and is easily set up as a temporary shelter. Now that old traditions are vanishing, most Samis live in houses and use motor vehicles while still herding their reindeer.

Reindeer wander free around the large natural areas within each *paliskunta* (reindeer cooperative), which is bordered by enormous fences that cross the wilderness. Reindeer are slaughtered after the annual reindeer roundup, during which each family recognises its own stock by ear marks. Reindeer escape insects in July by moving to the

windy hills (or sometimes to roads), but spring and autumn are the best months to see reindeer near roads. That's also the dangerous time for drivers (see the Getting Around chapter). Some Finns also herd reindeer in Lapland, but it is especially to the Samis that a large reindeer stock brings prestige.

The loud *yoik* singing is the traditional music style that has been recently made famous by Angelin tytöt, a small group that has performed with a Finnish hard rock group. This crossover music has been seen on international charts.

Samis have been subjected to humiliation in the past, just like any minority that can be defined as belonging to the 'Fourth World' (such as Hill Tribes in Thailand). Samis inhabited all of Finland 6000 years ago but have been pushed farther north ever since. They were forcibly converted to (Protestant) Christianity in the 1600s, and their religious traditions were made illegal. This has led to an awkward situation whereby many Samis define themselves not as Samis but as ordinary Finns.

Officially, Samis in Finland number about 4000, and speakers of Sami languages about

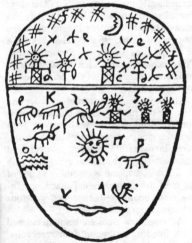 

Sami witch drums, 16th century. When the Samis were forcibly converted to Christianity in the 17th century, their religious traditions were outlawed.

1730, but the actual number may be larger. These days, Sami rights are defended, and their language is prominently displayed officially in Sami regions in Finnish Lapland.

The universal right to 'Sami territory' (a somewhat blurry definition) is continuously disputed. No 'homeland' or 'reservation' has been created so far. The Sami area of Finland is larger than, say, Belgium.

Norway is the strongest preserver of Sami culture today, and Finnish Samis keep close contacts with their Norwegian counterparts across the border. The National Museum in Helsinki, Arktikum in Rovaniemi, Ainola in Oulu, Maakuntamuseo in Tornio and Saamelaismuseo in Inari are some of the museums that cover Sami culture extensively.

SAMI LANGUAGES

Sami languages are related to Finnish and other Finno-Ugric languages. There are three Sami (Lapp) languages used in Finland today, although there are just 1730 regular users. Sami is taught in local schools, and legislation grants Samis the right of Sami usage in offices in North Lapland. In Utsjoki Sami speakers constitute almost the majority of the population, and there are several users in Inari and Enontekiö municipalities, as well as in Vuotso north of Sodankylä. You will find another seven Sami languages in Norway, Sweden and Russia.

Fell Sami

The most common of Sami languages, also known as Northern Sami or Mountain Sami, Fell Sami is spoken by Utsjoki and Enontekiö Samis, and tens of thousands of Samis in Norway. Fell Sami is considered the standard Sami. There is plenty of literature, printed in Utsjoki or Karasjok (Norway).

Written Fell Sami includes several accented letters but does not directly correspond to spoken Sami. In fact, many Samis find written Sami difficult to learn. For example, *giitu* (for 'thanks') is pronounced 'GHEECH-too', but the strongly aspirated 'h' is not written. Likewise, *dat* is pronounced as 'tah-ch'. You should ask Samis

to read out loud these words to learn the exact pronunciation; this flatters many Samis.

Hello	*Buorre beaivi*
Hello (reply)	*Ipmel atti*
Goodbye (to the one who leaves)	*Mana dearvan*
Goodbye (to the one who stays)	*Báze dearvan*
Thank you	*Giitu*
You're welcome	*Leage buorre*
Yes	*De lea*
No	*Ii*
How are you?	*Mot manna?*
I'm fine	*Buorre dat manna*
library	*girjerádju*
airport	*girdingieddi*

1	*okta*
2	*guokte*
3	*golbma*
4	*njeallje*
5	*vihta*
6	*guhta*
7	*čieza*
8	*gávcci*
9	*ovcci*
10	*logi*

Inari Sami

Although spoken by several people in the region around Lake Inarinjärvi, Inari Sami is rarely written and the whole language may become extinct in the future. There are many loan words.

Hello	*Tierva*
Goodbye	*Mana dearvan*
Thank you	*Takkâ*
Yes	*kal*
No	*Ij*
How are you?	*Maht mana?*
I'm fine	*Pyereest mana*

1	*ohta*
2	*kyeh'ti*
3	*kulma*
4	*nelji*
5	*vitta*
10	*love*

Scolt Sami

This rare language (Finnish: *kolttasaame*) is spoken by approximately 600 Sami people who live in Sevettijärvi and Nellim villages. Being refugees from the Petsamo region (which was annexed by the Soviet Union), they maintain Russian Orthodox traditions. Scolt Sami contains some Russian loan words.

Hello	*Tiõrv*
Goodbye	*Kuáddu teárvan*
Thank you	*Spässep*
Yes	*Kaéll*
No	*Ij*
How are you?	*Mä'htt maan?*
I'm fine	*Puârast maan*

1	*õhtt*
2	*kue'htt*
3	*koumm*
4	*nellj*
5	*vitt*
6	*kutt*
7	*čiččâm*
8	*kääu'c*
9	*ååuc*
10	*loé*

WARNING

Since German troops practically destroyed Lapland during WWII, Lapps have had reason to treat foreigners with suspicion. Even though Finnish trekkers may cause more harm, it is always foreigners who are accused.

With this in mind, visitors to Lapland should be on guard – both the people and the environment are sensitive to the influx of the masses.

Don't exploit the availability of free accommodation, be careful with fire, and replace all wood and food you take from open huts. Remember that all rubbish must be carried out from the wilderness. And don't tease the reindeer.

Rovaniemi

Rovaniemi has enjoyed a stream of wealthy visitors recently, making it something of a boom town for tourism. It's also a friendly place for a budget traveller. Rovaniemi has many good sources of information and is the best stepping stone for practically all trips to Lapland.

Rovaniemi today has 35,000 inhabitants but its businesses cater to almost 60,000 regional customers. There are 10 major hotels with almost 1000 rooms, enjoying healthy occupancy rates yet charging reasonable prices (recently 290 mk per room). There are also plenty of inexpensive options for budget travellers.

A staggering 80% of the population is engaged in service industries.

History

Rovaniemi was classified as a *kauppala*, or a trade centre, until it was completely destroyed by Germans in autumn 1944. A five-storey administrative edifice disappeared completely, as did 1000 or so of Rovaniemi's 1200 prewar houses. Every single axle in all railway carriages had an individual explosive planted by the meticulous Germans.

Hidden landmines remained for years after, injuring and killing civilians. Amidst the total devastation, locals started rebuilding a town in which only skeleton chimneys remained standing.

The new Rovaniemi was envisaged as the centre of all Lapland. Over the decades, Rovaniemi gained admiration for its modern architecture. Indeed, some of the works of Alvar Aalto are still appreciated, but much of the earlier excitement has already faded. Arktikum, however, is a recent addition to the city's collection of architectural wonders.

Orientation

Rovaniemi is built along the Ounasjoki River, near where it joins the Kemijoki River. The town centre is on the western

Rovaniemi

OTHER

1 Arktikum
3 Lauri-tuotteet
6 Rovaniemi Art Museum
9 Pharmacy
9 Post Office
10 R-kioski
14 Arctic Safaris & Europcar
15 Lapin Safarit
18 Hertz
19 Tourist Office & Lapin Matkailu Oy
21 Avis
28 Bookshop
33 Bus Station
35 Pharmacy
38 Main Post Office
39 Railway Station
40 Lappia-talo
41 Public Library
42 Karttakeskus Map Shop
44 Rovaniemi Church

PLACES TO STAY

2 Hotel Rudolf
4 Hotel Lapinportti
7 Hotelli Lapponia
11 Hotelli Oppipoika
16 Sokos Hotel Vaakuna
17 Pohjanhovi
20 Pohjanhovi Annex
23 Hotel Polar
27 City Hotelli
30 Matka Borealis
31 Domus Arctica
33 Summer Hotel
34 Outa
37 Youth Hostel

43 Ounaskosken leirintäalue

PLACES TO EAT

5 Kotipizza
12 Kisälli & Oppipoika
13 Sampo
22 Kotipizza
24 Sandwitz & Rovaniemen Panimo
25 Pub Roy
26 Hesburger
29 Walentina
32 Torikeidas
36 Boswell

bank of the Ounasjoki, and Rovakatu is the main street. Administratively, Rovaniemi is divided into two municipalities: the town of Rovaniemi (Rovaniemen kaupunki) and rural Rovaniemi (Rovaniemen maalaiskunta).

Information

Tourist Office The tourist office, in an annex of the hotel Pohjanhovi at Koskikatu 1 (☎ 322 2279), is open from June to August Monday to Friday from 8 am to 6 pm and Saturday from 11.30 am to 4 pm. At other times it's open weekdays only from 8 am to 4 pm.

Post & Telephone There are two handy post offices in Rovaniemi. The one at Postikatu 1 (96100), near the railway and bus stations, is the main one. The 96200 post office, which is conveniently central at Rovakatu 36, is open Monday to Friday from 9 am to 5 pm. The Tele office is at the main post office.

Travel Agencies There are many small tour operators near the main hotels for river cruises, white-water rafting, fishing or visits to reindeer farms, ranging from 100 to 600 mk per person. Mr Matti Laurila (☎ 399 244) has been recommended for small groups, but there are currently almost 10 options to choose from. Lapin Safarit (☎ 312 304) is at Harrikatu 4. Lapin Matkailu Oy (☎ 346 052; fax 312 743), next to the tourist office in the hotel Pohjanhovi annex at Koskikatu 1, is a marketing organisation for tourist services in Lapland. You can book hotel rooms and arrange tours there. This office is open Monday to Friday until 5 pm.

Library At the public library at Hallituskatu 9, you can find books about Lapland and the Sami people. The library is open Monday to Friday from 11 am to 7 pm, and Saturday from 10 am to 3 pm.

Books & Maps Suomalainen Kirjakauppa monopolises the local book scene at Rovakatu 24. Karttakeskus has a map shop at Hallituskatu 1-3 C near the library. R-

kioski sells imported magazines at the railway station, and on Koskikatu.

Left Luggage There are large 10 mk lockers at the railway station. The bus station has smaller lockers and a more expensive luggage room.

Camping Equipment See Kesport at Koskikatu 25.

Emergency Services In a general emergency, ring ☎ 112. For a doctor, call ☎ 10023. There are pharmacies at Rovakatu 11 and 27.

Arktikum

Arktikum is the prized building that is as much an architectural wonder as the home of two excellent museums. The Arctic Centre covers all Arctic peoples and their cultures in its interesting displays. The Provincial Museum of Lapland includes traditional items and covers more recent culture. Arktikum is open in summer daily from 10 am to 6 pm (in other seasons it is closed on Monday). Admission is a hefty 45 mk, but there are discounts.

Rovaniemi Church

The fresco above the altar depicts a Christ figure emerging from Lappish scenery. The church was completed in 1950, replacing the one destroyed during WWII. Donations from abroad helped in financing the new building. It's open from 15 May to 30 September daily from 9 am to 9 pm.

Rovaniemi Art Museum

This museum, at Lapinkävijäntie 4, has temporary art exhibitions. It is open Tuesday to Sunday from 10 am to 5 pm. Admission is free.

Other Buildings

The administrative buildings on Hallituskatu were designed by Alvar Aalto, the world-famous Finnish architect. There are guided tours of Lappia-talo, a conference centre and theatre, from 24 June to 15 August Monday to Friday at 10 am and 1 and 4 pm.

Pöykkölä

This suburb has two museums and a youth hostel. **Lapin Metsämuseo** is the Lapland Forestry Museum at Metsämuseontie 7, with old buildings and objects used by lumberjacks during the first half of the 20th century. It's open from 1 June to 15 September Tuesday to Sunday from noon to 6 pm. Admission is 10 mk.

The **Ethnographical Museum** is on the eastern bank of the Kemijoki River, 3.5 km south of the town centre. It consists of 18 buildings, most of which have been brought here from various parts of Rovaniemi. Objects connected with salmon fishing, cattle raising and reindeer husbandry form the focus of the collection. The museum is open from 1 June to 31 August daily (except Monday) from noon to 4 pm. Admission is 10 mk.

To get to Pöykkölä, catch a local bus No 6 from Ruokasenkatu. These depart at 10 minutes past the hour until 5.10 pm.

Ounasvaara

Ounasvaara Hill offers both cross-country and downhill skiing. There is a good five km skiing track, which can be used free of charge. The slope is 750 metres long and 110 metres high. Skiing equipment can be rented at the Sky Hotel Ounasvaara, downhill equipment at the Ounasvaara Slalom Centre. There are summer toboggan runs, available daily from mid-June to mid-August from noon to 8 pm. A chairlift ride up and a toboggan run down costs 20 mk.

Places to Stay – bottom end

Ounaskosken leirintäalue (☎ 345 304), along the Ounasjoki River, is open during the summer months, and pitching a tent costs 70 mk for a group and 35 mk for individuals, including the use of showers. Laundry costs extra, as does the sauna.

The *youth hostel* (☎ 344 644) at Hallituskatu 16, also known as Tervashonka, has dormitory accommodation at 50 mk per person. The new kitchen is popular and a terrific improvement but generally the place serves as a 'one night stand' only, due to its basic facilities. Nevertheless, it's the most international youth hostel in Finland.

Places to Stay – middle

Matka Borealis (☎ 342 0130) at Asemieskatu 1, a pleasant old house with 15 rooms near the railway station, gives good value for money. It's clean and friendly, singles/doubles cost 150/220 mk. Nearby, in the bus terminal, *Summer Hotel Pilvenlonka* (☎ 342 4189) has 16 rooms, priced at 170/230 mk.

Outa (☎ 312 474) is a small, smoke-free guesthouse at Ukkoherrantie 16. Singles/doubles are 140/180 mk.

Rovaniemen ammattioppilaitos (☎ 392 651) at Kairatie 75 is a typical school dormitory, used as a hotel from 15 June to 15 August. Singles/doubles are 140/180 mk.

Domus Arctica (☎ 347 950) is another summer hostel open May to August. The office is at Ratakatu 6, and is open Monday to Friday until 4 pm.

Places to Stay – top end

Rovaniemi is a boom town as far as European tourist groups are concerned. There's a wide variety of excellent accommodation in central Rovaniemi.

City Hotelli (☎ 314 501), Pekankatu 9, has 93 rooms and a few popular restaurants, and rents singles/doubles from 290/380 mk.

Hotelli Lapponia (☎ 33661), Koskikatu 23, has 167 rooms, some with a sauna. It's currently the newest hotel in town, featuring an open lobby and a host of services. In summer, rooms cost 390 mk, while at other seasons singles/doubles cost 480/580 mk.

Hotelli Oppipoika (☎ 338 8111), Korkalonkatu 33, is the hotel part of a hotel & restaurant school. In summer it has singles/doubles for 300/380 mk in summer, while at other times they are 350/440 mk.

Pohjanhovi (☎ 33711), Pohjanpuistikko 2, is the oldest hotel in Rovaniemi, and includes a large annex. This legendary hotel includes a legendary restaurant with live music. The hotel has singles/doubles from 370/450 mk.

Hotel Polar (☎ 342 3751), at Valtakatu 32, has 64 rooms in two buildings (occupying a whole street block), two restaurants and two saunas. There are singles/doubles from 250/360 mk to 420/520 mk.

Hotel Rudolf (☎ 342 3222), Koskikatu 41, has 41 rooms, with singles/doubles from 300/380 mk.

Sokos Hotel Vaakuna (☎ 332 211), Koskikatu 4, is probably the finest hotel in town. The hotel has 157 well-equipped rooms, and singles/doubles start from 450/450 mk. The restaurants and nightclub are among the most popular in Rovaniemi.

Sky Hotel Ounasvaara (☎ 346 001) has 69 rooms at the top of Ounasvaara Hill. Singles/doubles cost 450/560 mk.

Hotel Lapinportti (☎ 342 2555), Pohjolankatu 19-21, is actually outside the city centre but closest to the railway station. The hotel has singles/doubles at 310/410 mk.

Places to Eat

Torikeidas, at the unsuccessful market square not far from the railway station, is a small place serving big portions of junk food, or ask for poronkäristys (reindeer casserole).

Kisälli at Korkalonkatu 35 is an unusual restaurant in offering food by the weight, thus making it one of the best deals in town. It is run by the local hotel & restaurant school. The nearby *Oppipoika* is dearer but open longer hours.

Sampo at Korkalonkatu 32 is the most Finnish of Rovaniemi's restaurants and serves inexpensive lunch packages in a huge Sami-style kota (hut). Try the salty tönkkömuikut (fish plate) with a beer in the evening.

Cafés include *Sandwitz* on Koskikatu and *Walentina* on Rovakatu. *Rovaniemen Panimo* on Koskikatu brews its own beer – four types of beer in fact.

Entertainment

Rovaniemi has several nightspots, and you can usually get in before 11 pm. The cover charge is around 30 mk on weekends. *Hotel Lapponia* welcomes anyone over 18 years, whereas *Doris* at Hotel Vaakuna is stricter and more popular with slightly older people. *Hotel Pohjanhovi* features live music for more mature people. There are also places outside the hotel scene. *Pub Roy* at Maakuntakatu 24 and *Boswell* on Kansankatu are two popular places.

Things to Buy

The most popular souvenirs are traditional Sami handicrafts made of reindeer skin and horns, or of Arctic birch. Whole reindeer skins are also a popular buy, but they are hard to transport and may cause troubles with some countries' customs services.

Lauri-tuotteet at Pohjolankatu 25 sells handicrafts and good knives, which can be mail ordered.

J Marttiinin puukkotehdas at Marttiinintie 6 is the most famous knife manufacturer in Finland. The shop is connected to the factory. You can buy *puukkos* cheaper here than in other places, but the same items are available in stores throughout the country.

Getting There & Away

Air There are four to five flights a day between Helsinki and Rovaniemi. Most of them are nonstop, while some go via Oulu. There are also connections to/from Ivalo.

Bus There is a daily bus between Oulu and Rovaniemi. The trip takes 3½ hours. From Kemi, buses run Monday to Saturday. Rovaniemi is the major bus travel hub in Lapland, with long-distance buses departing every morning from the railway station (buses wait for delayed trains) to places in North Lapland and to Norway.

Train There are four trains a day to/from Helsinki via Tampere, Seinäjoki, Oulu and Kemi, two of which are night trains. The trip from Helsinki takes approximately 12 hours.

Getting Around

To/From the Airport Buses meet each arriving aeroplane, and charge 20 mk. Buses depart from the bus station 50 minutes prior to each departure, and from Hotel Vaakuna and Pohjanhovi 40 minutes prior to each departure.

Bus Bus maps and timetables can be obtained from the tourist office. Buses No 8 and 10 go to Napapiiri, bus No 6 to Pöykkölä.

Is Santa Finnish?

In 1995 it happened again. Finland boycotted the international congress of Santa Claus impersonators. This snub is easily explained: if Santa Claus comes from Finland, how could there be so many other Santa Claus pretenders in the world, and why should the real Santa Claus bother to join these fakes?

Santa Claus is big business, with many nations seriously claiming to be the real homeland of the generous Father Christmas. Judging by the hundreds of thousands of letters that the town of Napapiiri (north of Rovaniemi) receives every year, Santa Claus must be from Finland. Millions of children can't be wrong!

The real legend comes from Turkey. A poor peasant, father of three daughters, did not have enough money for their dowries. To ensure that at least two of his daughters could find husbands, the man had to sell the youngest to slavery. One day the man finally decided that the sad deed should be done the next day. The now-famous St Nicholas learned of the miserable situation and filled a sock with golden coins while the family was sleeping. The honour of the family was saved and they lived happily ever after. Since then Santa Nicholas (Claus) has filled socks with presents at Christmas.

In Finland, Uncle Markus (a famous radio voice since the 1930s) established the Finnish legend that Santa Claus lived in Korvatunturi Hill, right at the Russian border. Everybody believed the tale, and Santa Claus (Finnish: Joulupukki) became very well known by all Finns.

The Finnish Tourist Board has utilised the marketing value of Santa Claus. When a Soviet missile landed on frozen Lake Inari in January 1985, Santa Claus appeared on TV sets throughout the world. When a civil airplane was hijacked in Japan 10 years later, a Finnish Santa Claus (on a business trip) was on board, to everyone's astonishment. There is no Santa Claus theme park so far, although countless attempts have been made to set up one. Napapiiri currently fills the Santa niche, and there are related places in various locations, including Savukoski and Pello (both in Lapland) and even Serena (near Helsinki). ■

Car Rental Avis (☎ 362 808) and Europcar-Interrent (☎ 315 645) are at Aallonkatu 2, Hertz (☎ 313 300) is at Pohjanpuistikko 2, and Esso (☎ 344 711) is at Rovakatu 3.

AROUND ROVANIEMI
Saarenkylä

The commercial centre across the bridge includes the monster Citymarket. Three thousand German soldiers who died in Lapland during WWII are buried in the cellar of Norvajärvi Chapel, 22 km from Rovaniemi. The chapel is open in summer.

Napapiiri

The Arctic Circle (see the West Lapland and South-East Lapland maps), nine km north of Rovaniemi on the main Rovaniemi to Sodankylä road, is the home of the **Santa Claus Village**. It consists of several buildings, including Santa's Office and many shops. This is the busiest tourist trap in Finland (in fact, the only one of this magni-

tude), with computerised portraits with you and Santa Claus available while you wait! All letters sent to Finland for Santa Claus are answered here – approximately half a million letters are received annually. Many of the children also send pictures of themselves, and these are all kept in photo albums. **Etiäinen** (☎ 362 528) is the information centre for national parks and trekking regions, with essential information and maps available. The village is open in summer daily from 8 am to 8 pm and in other seasons from 9 am to 5 pm. To get there, take local bus No 8, or one of the long-distance buses from platform No 3 or 4 at the central bus station.

The Arctic Circle is the southernmost line where the midnight sun can be seen. Since all celestial bodies affect each other, the Arctic Circle can shift several metres daily. Groups from the tourist buses have great fun crossing the line painted on the asphalt (supposedly marking the circle) in order to be awarded their Arctic Circle certificates. The actual Arctic Circle is approximately one km from here. Please don't tell them!

Vikajärvi

This road crossing, 30 km north of Rovaniemi (see the South-East Lapland map), includes a shop and a fishing park at the Vikaköngäs rapids. Don't confuse this with Lohiapaja farther south where you catch the fish from ponds.

There are several places where you can stay. *Aittaniemien Maatilaloma* (☎ 732 222), one km north of Vikajärvi, has four superb cottages. *Vikajärven Lomamajat* (☎ 732 227) has 13 small huts near the main road. *Ahosen Lomamökit* (☎ 732 221) farther north has just three cottages but they are luxurious.

Tiainen

Two km north of this small place, 60 km north of Rovaniemi, *Korvalan Rantapirtit* (☎ 737 211) is a cluster of cottages on the shores of a lake. It's open all year and the British owner runs reindeer tours in winter. There are a few saunas and a kitchen, and food is available. Prices vary.

South-West Lapland

Lapland is not just wilderness and fell-walking. The south-west corner of Lapland is usually referred to as Sea Lapland, and is relatively urban, industrialised and prosperous. Kemi is the northernmost port in Finland, with icebreaker cruises available in winter. Tornio at the Swedish border is the main overland entry point to Finland. The region is also dominated by the mighty Kemijoki River.

TORNIO

The twin towns of Tornio (Swedish: Torneå) and Haparanda (Finnish: Haaparanta) are the best known pair of the Finnish-Swedish towns along the long border. These two towns share tourist brochures, and even a golf course. You can't really play golf at midnight anywhere else: if you start from the Finnish side at, say, half past midnight, you can hit the next ball in Sweden, yesterday!

Tornio has 23,200 inhabitants in an area that is 10 times larger than Kemi, but Swedish day-trippers help Tornio to keep busy. It's a nice little town with some fine attractions. Haparanda municipality boasts over 10,000 inhabitants.

History

The area along the Tornionjoki River has been inhabited since medieval times, when it was the centre for Pirkka tax collectors (who worked for the king of Sweden). Tornio was founded in 1621, and the entire Tornionjoki River Valley was administered by Sweden until 1809, when it was incorporated into Finland (under Russian suzerainty). In 1821, Haparanda was founded as a Swedish trading town to replace the loss of Tornio to Russia. After the independence of Finland in 1917, and with continuing friendly relations with Sweden, the twin towns have increased cooperation in all fields.

Information

Tourist Office Tornio's tourist office (☎ 452 733) is at the Green Line Centre at the border. It's open from 1 June to 15 August Monday to Friday from 8 am to 8 pm and on weekends from 10 am to 8 pm. At other times, it is open Monday to Friday only, from 8 am to 4 pm.

Money There's a money exchange facility at the Green Line Centre at the border.

Post & Telephone The post office is at Puutarhakatu 3, 95400 Tornio.

Library The fine public library is in the Rajakartano building at Torikatu 2, next to the Aine Art Museum. It's open Monday to Friday from 11 am to 8 pm and Saturday from 10 am 3 pm. The newspaper room is also open Sunday until 5 pm.

Books & Maps There's a bookshop at Kauppakatu 6.

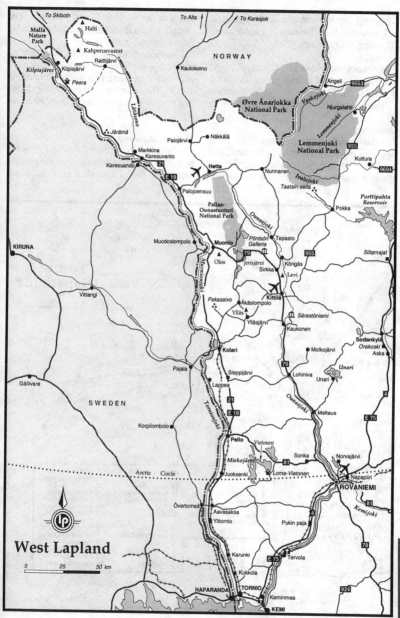

West Lapland

0   25   50 km

Camping Equipment Check Sportia-Settu at Länsiranta 9 or Kesport at Laivurinkatu 10, which also rents bicycles.

Emergency Services In a general emergency, ring ☎ 112. For a doctor, call ☎ 10023. The health centre is at Sairaalakatu 1. There's a pharmacy at Hallituskatu 14.

Churches

The old church of Tornio is one of the most beautiful wooden churches in Finland, and should be of interest for its fine paintings alone. It was completed in 1686 and is dedicated to the Swedish Queen Eleonora. The church is open in summer Monday to Friday from 9 am to 5 pm.

The Orthodox church of Tornio was constructed when Tsar Alexander I of Russia ordered the building of a military church in Tornio. The church is near the border station and is open in summer daily from 10 am to 8 pm.

Maakuntamuseo

The Tornio River Valley Historical Museum at Keskikatu 22 has displays relating to the history of West Lapland. It is an excellent

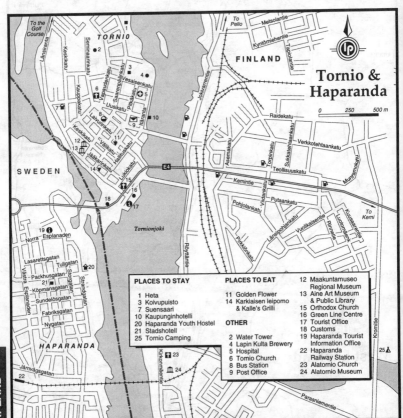

PLACES TO STAY
1 Heta
3 Koivupuisto
7 Suensaari
10 Kaupunginhotelli
20 Haparanda Youth Hostel
21 Stadshotell
25 Tornio Camping

PLACES TO EAT
11 Golden Flower
14 Karkiaisen leipomo & Kalle's Grilli

OTHER
2 Water Tower
4 Lapin Kulta Brewery
5 Hospital
6 Tornio Church
8 Bus Station
9 Post Office

12 Maakuntamuseo Regional Museum
13 Aine Art Museum & Public Library
15 Orthodox Church
16 Green Line Centre
17 Tourist Office
18 Customs
19 Haparanda Tourist Information Office
22 Haparanda Railway Station
23 Alatornio Church
24 Alatornio Museum

LAPLAND

museum and a good introduction to Lapland. The museum is open Tuesday to Friday from noon to 7 pm and on weekends from noon to 5 pm.

Aine Art Museum

This museum at Torikatu 2 features a private collection of Veli Aine, who is a local business tycoon. The collection consists of Finnish art from the 19th and 20th centuries, and the museum also has temporary exhibitions. The museum is open in summer Monday to Friday from 11 am to 7 pm and on weekends from 11 am to 5 pm. There is a voluntary admission charge of 5 mk.

Other Attractions

Tornio has a great number of statues and other monuments around town – ask at the tourist office for details.

The tower, north of the centre, is open in summer daily from 11 am to 8 pm. Admission is 5 mk, and there's a café.

Places to Stay

Tornio Camping (☎ 445 945) on Matkailijantie, 2.5 km east of the town centre, is open from 1 June to 31 August. Camping costs 80 mk, and two/four-bed cottages are 190/220 mk. There are just 15 cottages so get there early. The place also offers tennis, mini golf, bicycles, boats, canoes, and rods, all for a price.

Suensaari (☎ 481 682) at Kirkkokatu 1, one km from the railway station, is the student dormitory turned youth hostel in summer, open from early June to mid-August. It has dormitory beds for 65 mk. There are 72 rooms, and each has access to a kitchen. You can rent a bicycle here.

Koivupuisto (☎ 481 316) at Saarenpäänkatu 21 is in the centre of Tornio. It is a nice, clean place, with 16 singles/doubles for 130/220 mk. Prices include breakfast.

Heta (☎ 480 897) at Saarenpäänkatu 39, some 300 metres from Koivupuisto, is probably not as attractive as Koivupuisto. Singles/doubles are 130/180 mk, but breakfast is 20 mk.

Kaupunginhotelli (☎ 43311) at Itäranta 4, facing mainland Finland near the bridge, is the top establishment in Tornio with 100 rooms, three saunas and so much capacity in its five restaurants that it is here that Finnish tango singers and similar entertainment superstars spend their evenings impressing locals.

In summer, rooms cost 330 mk; at other times they're from 390/490 mk. The price includes breakfast.

Places to Eat

You will find such local specialities as pizza, hamburger or kebab, but anything really good is hard to find. On the other hand, supermarkets, including the wide choice of Haparanda's food stores, are a good option for self-catering.

Karkiaisen leipomo at Länsiranta 9 is the most attractive café in town, with fresh bread, cakes, pastries and coffee directly from the bakery. *Kalle's Grilli* nearby is a hamburger joint, run by a Swedish company from across the border. *Golden Flower* at Eliaksenkatu 8 is a Chinese restaurant.

Getting There & Away

There are two buses a day from Rovaniemi, and buses from Kemi to Tornio run almost hourly. Most of the buses continue to Haparanda in Sweden. There are also frequent buses between Haparanda and Tornio.

AROUND TORNIO
Alatornio

The church in the suburb of Alatornio was originally founded in the 1400s, but it was completely rebuilt and completed in 1797. Today it is the largest church in north Finland, seating 1450 people. It is open from 1 June to 15 August Monday to Friday from 9 am to 3 pm.

The museum, a two-storey former granary beside the church, is open from 15 June to 15 August Monday to Friday from noon to 4 pm and Sunday from 11 am to 1 pm.

Kukkolankoski Rapids

These rapids on the Tornionjoki River, some

15 km north of Tornio along road No 21, are the longest free-flowing rapids in Finland.

In the Middle Ages, Kukkolankoski was already a well-known fishing place, and today it is visited for its natural beauty. The annual whitefish festival is celebrated on the last weekend of July.

At other times, you can eat *siika* (whitefish) in one of the two restaurants, on either side of the river. White-water rafting can also be arranged. On the Swedish side at Kukkolaforsen is a fishing museum, open daily in summer, but there's no bridge across the river here.

KEMI

Kemi is an industrial town that grew around saw and paper mills. Today, a large proportion of the population is still employed in the wood-processing industries. Kemi has a population of almost 25,000, a vast majority of whom elect socialists to the town council. Cartoons, gemstones, icebreaker cruises and snow castles are currently attractions that are associated with this culturally conscious town.

Information

Tourist Office The tourist office (☎ 199 465; fax 199 468) at Kauppakatu 22 is open Monday to Friday from 8 am to 4 pm (in summer to 6 pm). The office is also open in summer on Saturday from 10 am to 2 pm. There's also a summer information point in the town hall.

Post & Telephone The post office is at Asemakatu 12 near the railway station. It's open Monday to Friday from 9 am to 5 pm.

Library There is a well-stocked public library near the market square, opposite the tourist office.

The library is open Monday to Thursday from 11 am to 8 pm, Friday to 6 pm and Saturday to 3 pm.

Books & Maps There's a bookshop at

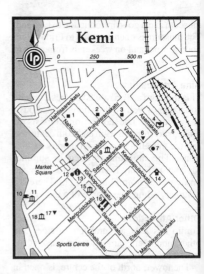

PLACES TO STAY

1	Cumulus
2	Hotelli Merihovi
3	Palomestari
14	Turisti

PLACES TO EAT

2	Ancre Noir
3	Pizzeria Roma
6	Ravintola Meripuisto
10	Café Seilari
17	Raatihuone

OTHER

4	Post Office
5	Railway Station
7	Town Hall & Tourist Information
8	Kemin Historiallinen Museo
9	Public Library
11	Kemin Jalokivigalleria (Gemstone Gallery)
12	Lapponia Safaris
13	Tourist Office
15	Suomen Värimuseo (Colour Museum)
16	Kemi Church
18	Kemin Kostiseutumuseo (Local Museum)

Kauppakatu 13. R-kioski, at Valtakatu 25 and Kauppakatu 18, sells imported magazines.

Top: Rotuaari pedestrian street, Oulu
Left: Museum, Kuusamo
Right: Jyrävä Rapids, Karhunkierros trekking route, near Kuusamo

Top: Hossa, fisher's paradise, south of Kuusamo
Middle: Autumn colours, Lapland
Bottom: Lemmenjoki National Park, Lapland

Travel Agencies Lapponia Safaris (☎ 223 320) at Kauppakatu 22 and Safaris Unlimited (☎ 253 405) arrange icebreaker cruises, winter safaris and trips to the Perämeri National Park.

Kemin Jalokivigalleria

The most famous sight in Kemi is the Gemstone Gallery, in an old seaside customs house. It has an internationally notable collection of over 3000 beautiful and rare stones and jewellery, including a crown that was meant for the king of Finland.

The crown was made in the 1980s by the gallery's founder, Mr Ypyä, who created the 'first and only' crown of the king of Finland from the original drawings. During the recent recession, Mr Ypyä lost his lifetime achievement, and the bankrupt gallery was bought by the town of Kemi.

The gallery is open daily, in summer from 10 am to 8, and at other times until 6 pm. Admission is 25 mk, with discounts available.

Other Museums

The **Kemin Historiallinen Museo** at Sauvosaarenkatu 11 is the historical museum of Kemi. There are no permanent collections, just frequently changing exhibitions. It's open daily from noon to 6 pm. The admission fee depends on the current exhibition.

Suomen Värimuseo at Sankarikatu 12 is a 'colour museum', the only museum in Finland that exhibits industrial paint manufacturing. It's not an interesting museum, but admission is free. It is open daily from noon to 6 pm.

Kemin Kotiseutumuseo is the local museum at the Meripuisto park. The three floors of exhibits include historical items from prehistory to more recent tools and farming equipment. The museum is open from 1 June to 30 September daily from noon to 6 pm, and admission is free.

Työläismuseo and **Kähertäjämuseo** are two museums to the north of Kemi, at Leinosenpolku 10, which display workers' housing, and the history of hairdressing,

respectively. The hairdressing collection is a private achievement and is more interesting. These small museums are open the same hours as the local museum. Admission is free.

Kemi Church

The beautiful 1902 Art-Nouveau church was designed by Josef Stenbäck. It is open from early June to mid-August daily from 10 am to 4 pm.

Town Hall

The top of the imposing town hall at Valtakatu 26 has an observation platform with a café. It's open in summer Monday to Friday from 8 am to 6 pm and Saturday from noon to 6 pm. In winter, it's open on weekdays to 4 pm.

Organised Tours

In winter, you can take the only icebreaker cruise in the world, from Ajos Harbour, 15 km from Kemi (in summer, there's a restaurant).

The icebreaker *Sampo* sails from January to April at noon on Thursday, Friday and Saturday. The four-hour cruise costs a hefty 720 mk per person, including lunch and 'ice swimming' in a survival suit – an experience you will not easily forget.

More interesting is the eight-hour safari that includes a snowmobile ride from Kemi across the frozen sea, and all meals. The price is 1370 mk.

Winter tours to the Kivalo wilderness, east of Kemi, include traditional Lappish experiences, and are arranged by Lapponia Safaris.

The Perämeri National Park on islands west of Kemi is not accessible on regular boat launches. Enquire at the tourist office or travel agencies for information about special arrangements.

Places to Stay

Turisti (☎ 250 876), diagonally opposite the tall town hall at Valtakatu 39, is the cheapest place in Kemi. It has 18 simple rooms, with singles/doubles at 100/180 mk, including breakfast. HI members get a discount.

Palomestari (☎ 257 117), at Valtakatu 12, is the cheapest hotel in the centre. It has 33 rooms, priced at 320/440 mk. Rates are lower on weekends. The restaurant Punainen kukko has inspirational décor and serves a great variety of beer.

Hotelli Merihovi (☎ 223 431) at Keskuspuistokatu 6-8 is the oldest hotel in Kemi. The Art Deco hotel boasts such honourable guests as Russian cosmonaut Yuri Gagarin. The hotel has 71 rooms, the famous restaurant Ancre Noir (aka Ankkuri), and a sauna. Singles/doubles cost 390/480 mk.

Cumulus (☎ 22831) at Hahtisaarenkatu 3 is the largest hotel in Kemi but not exactly very central. The hotel has 185 rooms, two restaurants, a nightclub, three saunas, and a swimming pool. Singles/doubles are 475/550 mk.

Summer Hotel Relletti (☎ 233 541) at Miilukatu 1 is open from 1 June to mid-August. The hotel is two km south of Kemi, and has singles/doubles for 115/185 mk.

Gasthaus Yöpuu (☎ 232 034) at Eteläntie 227 is a motel three km south of Kemi at the main crossing. Singles/doubles start from 220/300 mk.

Places to Eat

There are several restaurants. *Pizzeria Roma* at Valtakatu 12 is in an attractive old building, and serves pizzas; prices are cheaper before 2 pm.

Raatihuone, in the park near Kemin Jalokivigalleria and the local museum, is the finest restaurant in town, set in an old villa that was recently renovated. It serves meals and alcohol.

Café Seilari is a tiny café behind Kemin Jalokivigalleria at the guest harbour. For a typical old-fashioned dance restaurant, check *Ravintola Meripuisto* at Valtakatu 22. It opens at 7 pm, Tuesday to Saturday.

Getting There & Away

All intercity trains in Lapland stop at Kemi's railway station. From the bus station nearby, there are regular departures to Tornio, and some departures to Muonio in the north and Oulu in the south.

KEMI TO ROVANIEMI
Keminmaa

The old church from 1521 in the village of Keminmaa, several km north of Kemi across the Kemijoki River, is a must! You'll see the mummified reverend, Mr Nikolaus Rungius, who died in 1629. He is reported to have said: 'If my words are untrue, my body will rot. If they are true, my body shall not rot'. Well, only the wooden coffin has rotted – it has had to be changed several times. The old paintings date from 1650, and there are medieval sculptures. The church is open in summer daily from 10 am to 6 pm (from mid-August to mid-September to 4 pm). The new church was built in 1827 and is not very interesting.

Near the old church is the local museum, open from mid-June to mid-August Tuesday to Sunday from 11 am to 6 pm (except Saturday, when it closes at 3 pm).

Places to Stay There are two motels at petrol stations in the commercial centre, along the Keminmaa to Tornio road. *Savotan Sanni* (☎ 270 777) near the main road at Autoilijantie 2 is a pleasant roadside motel where rooms in attractive log houses cost 200/300 mk. *Käpylä* (☎ 270 241) at Torniontie 7 is a much older motel, at the back of the petrol station, and has rooms for 160/300 mk.

Getting There & Away All buses between Kemi and Tornio will take you to the motels, but the old church is almost two km from the bus stop; get off right after the river.

Tervola

The 1689 wooden church, across the river from the railway station, is one of the 15 that have survived from the 17th century. Tervola is not a huge metropolis – only 4100 people live in this area, which is larger than Hong Kong. The local museum in Paakkola is open daily in summer from 11 am to 5 pm.

Tervola to Rovaniemi

The main roads, on both sides of the Kemijoki River, offer a scenic ride past a relatively densely-populated area. Although there are few world-class attractions, cheap accommodation is possible during the low season. There are several motels and holiday villages that often advertise loudly; beware of the per person rates for doubles that seem cheap – you have to pay double the rate to get a double room, even if you're alone. Pukin paja, approximately 30 km south of Rovaniemi, is a Santa Claus attraction that provides an excuse for a coffee break.

North-West Lapland

Following road No 21 north from Tornio will take you to two main attractions of Lapland – the mighty Tornionjoki riverside and the highest mountains in Finland. You will have to decide in Tornio; it is either Rovaniemi and the north-east or the river and the north-west.

Both these routes will eventually take you to Norway and – if you like – Nordkapp. Unless you want to try the slow Norwegian route back, both options can be recommended.

YLITORNIO

Ylitornio (population 6100) is a small township at the Swedish border. On the Swedish side of the Tornionjoki River is Övertorneå, Ylitornio's twin town.

Places to Stay

Hotelli Kievari (☎ 571 201) at Alkkulanraitti 67, on the main street, has singles/doubles for 280/340 mk, or less after 9 pm. Above Ylitornio on a hill, *Karemajat* (☎ 571 551) is run by an organisation for retired people.

Getting There & Away

There are buses from Kemi and the north. During the winter holiday season, trains from Helsinki to Kolari stop at Ylitornio.

AAVASAKSA

The main attraction around Ylitornio is Aavasaksa Fell, which has been a popular holiday spot since the turn of the century. It's the southernmost point from which the midnight sun can be seen on 22 June.

Places to Stay

Retkeilymaja Pölkky (☎ 578 102) at Aavasaksa is a small hostel with the cheapest beds. The cottages of *Aavasaksan Aurinkomajat* (☎ 578 150) at the top of Aavasaksa Fell can be rented for 100 mk in summer.

JUOKSENKI

Tuomaan paja is the commercial service for people who want to stop at the Arctic Circle, which runs just south of this small village. There are souvenirs, and an Arctic Circle certificate is available.

ROVANIEMI TO PELLO

There are several places to stay along this route. Some places offer a host of activities.

Sonka

Some 30 km west of Rovaniemi, along the Rovaniemi to Pello road, *Sonkamökit* rents out attractive log cabins near a small lake.

Palojärvi

There are cottages for rent at the lakeside *Palojärven Lomakeskus*, some 40 km west of Rovaniemi along the Rovaniemi to Pello road.

Lake Miekojärvi

This lake, 30 km south-east of Pello, is teeming with fish. At the northern end of the lake is a little fish harbour for anglers. Metsähallitus (the Forest & Park Service) has also built some laavu shelters and a wilderness hut, which can be used free of charge. The village store at Sirkkakoski, six km from the lake, sells fishing permits.

Lake Vietonen

Another beautiful lake near Miekojärvi, Lake Vietonen offers a host of activities if you stay at *Loma-Vietonen* (☎ 546 184). The place is extremely clean and attractive, and you can try reindeer tours, ski safaris and other winter activities. Proceed some 10 km south of the main road, and follow the signs.

PELLO

Pello is another border village with a twin village on the other side of the river. The municipal tourist office is close to the bridge from Sweden. The local museum can be seen if you make enquiries at the nearby library on Museotie. Pello spans several km along the Tornionjoki River. Some 5500 people live in Pello.

The biggest annual event in Pello is the Poikkinainti Festival, held to celebrate the fact that people marry across the border. The festival takes place in July and lasts from Friday to Monday. The wedding ceremony is conducted in the middle of the river.

A French expedition, consisting of eight French scientists and Mr Anders Celsius of Sweden, led by Pierre-Louis Moreau de Maupertuis, did scientific research and measurements on the Kittisvaara Hill north of Pello in 1736. Its scientifically valuable measurements, along with similar ones taken in Peru, proved that Newton had been right about the globe not being perfectly round. A monument can be seen today.

Pentik Pello

This roadside tourist centre north of Pello sells Pentik brand pottery and serves coffee. Downstairs is an excellent playroom for children. The place is open daily between 9 am and 6 pm.

Places to Stay & Eat

The youth hostel *Kittisvaaran hiihto ja leirikeskus* (☎ 586 155), open from 1 June to 15 August, is north of Pello (and the bridge to Sweden). Dormitory beds cost 40 mk for HI members. There are also cottages nearby. *Camping Pello* (☎ 512 494), north-west of the centre on Nivapääntie, has cottages from 100 mk.

Pello also has several guesthouses near the actual village. From south to north they are:

Pellonhovi (☎ 513 991) on Kunnantie, the only hotel in Pello, with singles/doubles for 320/380 (it has a restaurant);

Pellon kestikievari (☎ 512 161) at the Esso petrol station in the main village, with rooms from approximately 100 mk;

Gasthaus Joppari (☎ 512 771) at the Kesoil petrol station near Esso, which provides accommodation in doubles for between 65 and 115 mk per person;

Kartano Rativa (☎ 512 774), almost two km north of the centre, with rooms for 100/140 mk;

Lepo (☎ 512 124) one km north of Kartano Rativa, or one km south of the bridge across the river to Sweden, which has similar prices.

Getting There & Away

There are three daily buses from Kemi (150 km away) via Tornio. The same buses return from Muonio.

SIEPPIJÄRVI

The small village used to be the centre of the Kolari municipality. Now the local open-air museum remains as a prime attraction. The museum is open daily on summer afternoons. Sieppijärvi is some 30 km south of Kolari along road No 21.

LAPPEA

There are rapids worth seeing in Lappea, where the Tornionjoki and Muonionjoki rivers meet. Take road No 938 along the river that runs between Pello and Kolari. Sweden is just across the river.

One of the most unusual things to do in Lapland is a raft tour along the Tornionjoki River (which marks the international border between Sweden and Finland). If you get a group together, you can float down the river on a large raft, fish salmon from the river, prepare your meals aboard and even bathe in a raft sauna. This raft can easily negotiate even the Kukkolankoski rapids farther south! Lappean Loma (see Places to Stay) is the place to contact first.

Places to Stay

One of the best youth hostels in Lapland, *Lappean Loma* (☎ 563 155) has beds from 45 mk. This is one of the places where you can try the delights of a smoke-sauna. The place also arranges a number of activities, including white-water rafting, canoeing and fishing.

KOLARI

The municipality of Kolari (population 4500) is one of the few in Finland that still elects a majority of communists to its local administration. The region is best known for its busy skiing centre of Ylläs.

The village of Kolari has a bank, some supermarkets and a few rows of other retail shops. Kolari is the last stop for the north-bound train, but it only runs during the skiing season. It is also possible to cross the bridge over the Tornionjoki River to Sweden.

The old church of Kolari, across the bridge on an island in the Muonionjoki River, was built in 1818 and is open daily in summer. The municipal tourist office (☎ 561 721) is in Kolari village.

Places to Stay & Eat

Vaattovaaran retkeilymaja (☎ 561 086) is a youth hostel and the only place to stay anywhere near the village proper. Rooms are clean and have a TV. The sauna is free for guests, and there is a well-equipped kitchen. It's a quiet and friendly place, 700 metres from the centre. Dorm beds start at 55 mk, and there are also rooms available.

Nuuskakairan baari on the main street was the only restaurant in Kolari but it closed in 1995. If it remains closed, you have to look for meals at petrol stations along the main road, a few km from the village centre.

Also outside Kolari, on main road No 21 and near the railway station, is *Hotelli Lännentie* (☎ 561 041) with singles from 290 mk in summer.

Getting There & Away

Bus A bus runs between Kolari and Rovaniemi each weekday. There are also two buses a day between Kemi and Kolari.

Train During the winter holiday season, from mid-February to mid-April, there are trains to Kolari from Helsinki. The railway station is approximately three km north-east from Kolari village.

PAKASAIVO

Also called Hell of Lapland, Pakasaivo is a deep forest lake, where Samis used to make sacrifices to the gods. The surface of the lake is some 50 metres below ground level, as the lake is located in a deep recess. To get there, drive 25 km from Kolari towards Äkäslompolo, then turn left and continue 11 km along a forest road. The road to Pakasaivo has signs and can be driven by car all the way to the end.

YLLÄS

Ylläs is the highest fell in Finland to offer the pleasures of downhill skiing. Some 35 km north-east of Kolari, it is also one of Finland's most popular skiing centres. In summer, the village of Äkäslompolo is like a ghost town. There are empty holiday cottages everywhere, restaurants are closed until October and few people can be seen on the road. Ylläsjärvi village at the other side of the mountain is even quieter. Skiing is possible from November to May. Lift passes cost 80 mk per day or 360 mk per week. Renting equipment also costs 80 mk per day or 350 mk per week.

There are plenty of events in winter, and a music festival in July. Mountain biking is a popular summer activity in the Ylläs area.

Places to Stay

Äkäslompolo There are plenty of empty hotel rooms and cottages in summer in Äkäslompolo, so you should be able to find reasonably priced accommodation. In winter, accommodation is more expensive.

Lomakiekerö (☎ 569 104) has 12 cottages from 200 to 500 mk per night.
Äkäshotelli (☎ 569 171) has 40 rooms and 46 cottages with singles/doubles from 230/280 mk.
Hotel Seitapirtti (☎ 569 211) has rooms and cottages with singles/doubles from 150/300 mk.
Hotel Ylläshumina (☎ 569 501) has 24 doubles from 290 mk.
Hotel Ylläskaltio (☎ 569 401) has 72 rooms and some cottages with singles/doubles for 350/595 mk.

LAPLAND

Ylläsjärvi This holiday village south of Ylläs is quieter than Äkäslompolo.

Yllästokka (☎ 565 421) has 12 apartments and 12 cottages near the main road, with rooms from 200/220 mk in summer, or from 220/250 mk during the skiing season.
Ylläsrinne (☎ 565 441) has 50 rooms with doubles from 320 to 520 mk.
Ylläsjärven Tunturihotelli (☎ 565 111) is also near the main road and has 36 rooms with singles/doubles from 300/420 mk.

Getting There & Away
Finnair has package arrangements with local hotels. If you take a train to Kolari, there will be a connecting bus that first goes to Ylläsjärvi, then to Äkäslompolo. A few long-distance buses travel via Äkäslompolo each week. For Ylläsjärvi, catch a post bus that runs between Kolari and Kittilä, Monday to Friday.

KITTILÄ
Kittilä (population 6200) is a large municipality north of Rovaniemi. According to one story, the place was named after Kitti, a daughter of the mighty witch Päiviö, who appears in old fairy tales. Kittilä puts on a traditional market at the beginning of July and attracts people from all over Lapland. Early September sees a marathon race, which is probably the northernmost regularly organised such event in the world.

The centre of Kittilä has 3000 inhabitants and is still one of the main centres of Lapland. The airport is served by regular flights and road connections are good. Most of the places of interest are either in the centre of Kittilä or at the nearby village of Sirkka, 20 km to the north. Sirkka is near Levitunturi Hill, where most of the area's outdoor activities are centred.

Information
The tourist office is in Levi, 20 km north of Kittilä

Church
The old wooden church of Kittilä was designed by CL Engel, one of the most famous Finnish architects, and completed in 1831. It's open from 1 June to 15 August from noon to 8 pm Monday to Friday.

Taidemuseo Einari Junttila
This art museum in central Kittilä commemorates Mr Einari Junttila, who lived in this house. It is open Monday to Saturday from 1 to 5 pm.

Kittilä Museum
The Kittilä open-air museum features old buildings. It's open from 1 June to 15 September daily (except Monday) from 11 am to 6 pm. The museum is three km south-east from the village.

Places to Stay
Kittilän retkeilymaja (☎ 642 238) is conveniently situated in the centre of Kittilä. A school dormitory in winter, it is a youth hostel in summer, with beds from 45 mk.

The most central place, *Gasthaus Kultaisen Ahman Majatalo* (☎ 642 043) has nice, clean singles/doubles for 180/300 mk. In the low season, the price of doubles goes down to 200 mk.

Hotelli Kittilä (☎ 643 201) in the northern end of the village at Valtatie 49 has 37 rooms priced from 380 to 440 mk each.

Places to Eat
In addition to the restaurant at the hotel, you will find simple eateries such as *Leilan Pihvi ja Pizza*, a grilli and a café that serves fresh bakery products.

Getting There & Away
There is a daily flight between Helsinki and Kittilä. Four buses a day run between Rovaniemi and Kittilä, a 2½ to three-hour trip, depending on the route. Buses depart at the K petrol station.

AROUND KITTILÄ
Molkojärvi
This beautiful village, south of Kittilä and 22 km from Lohiniva and the main road No 79, has 100 inhabitants, an old village shop and the excellent *Kittilän Eräkeskus* (☎ 655 323)

with B&B from 130 mk per person in very clean rooms that have their own TV sets. The estate has two small museums (admission is 10 mk) and a café. Activities include fishing, hunting, berry picking, skiing and snowmobile safaris. There are also reindeer.

Lohiniva

This small village south of Kittilä on road No 79 has a post office, a bank, a shop and a restaurant called *Lohihovi*.

Särestöniemi

Visiting this unusual museum is a must for everyone visiting Kittilä. Mr Reidar Särestöniemi, who died in 1981, was the best known painter from Lapland. Except for the years when he studied painting in Helsinki and in Leningrad (now St Petersburg), he always lived in Särestö in Kittilä. Today, his home has been converted into a museum, where his big, colourful paintings are exhibited, together with some drawings and graphic works. You can see Reidar's studio, gallery and remains of the old gallery, and if you're lucky, the home of Reidar Särestöniemi's brother Anton, who still lives in the area. There is also a café. Drive 20 km south of Kittilä to the interesting village of Kaukonen, turn east and proceed nine km. The museum is open from 15 February to 15 October daily from 10 am to 8 pm and at other times of the year from noon to 4 pm. Tickets cost 30 mk for adults, 15 mk for students.

Pöntsö

Another interesting place is the Pöntsön galleria, home of Reijo Raekallio, an artist in the village of Pöntsö. Unlike Särestöniemi, Mr Raekallio is alive and well. To get to the Pöntsön galleria, take road No 79 west of Kittilä and drive some 18 km. The gallery is open Tuesday to Sunday from 10 am to 6 pm. Admission is 15 mk. It may also be possible to stay there overnight, as the family has some rooms to rent out.

Köngäs

This attractive little village eight km north of

Sirkka (and Levi) has several places to stay, including *Kampsumajat* (☎ 653 508) and *Raimo Köngäs*. The youth hostel *Sillankorvan maja* (☎ 653 428) is situated near the river. Each HI member pays 100 mk per night in pleasant cottages. A very special place is Taivaanvalkeat, which can be visited by prior arrangement via Hullu Poro in Levi. It is a meticulously renovated old logging house with fine rooms (and a few other buildings) but it caters to groups only.

A few km east of Köngäs on the road towards Inari, there is a husky farm (☎ 657 111) that arranges winter tours to the wilderness. Two-hour tours with a husky dog team, including a meal at a camp fire, cost approximately 300 mk, but there are also three-day tours with the huskies for 2800 mk, including transport, accommodation, full board, equipment, sauna and a guide. Contact Reijo Jääskeläinen, Box 39, 99101 Kittilä for information.

Tepasto

This small place at a beautiful spot along the Ounasjoki River has plenty of cottages that are rented for approximately 250 mk per day. *Ounasrannan Majat* (☎ 659 414) has several excellent cottages, home-made food, fish and plenty of activities both summer and winter.

Taatsin-Seita

This pillar-shaped stone god, worshipped by the ancient Sami people, is at Lake Taatsi, 13 km from the village of Pokka.

SIRKKA & LEVI

In winter, Levi is a major skiing centre in the village of Sirkka, some 20 km north of Kittilä. In summer and autumn, trekking and mountain bike tours are the main outdoor activities.

Skiing is possible until May. Downhill-skiing tickets at Levitunturi Hill are 95 mk per day or 455 per week. Equipment rental costs 80 mk per day or 350 per week. Ask at the Ski Shop Vuokraamo or Levin Hissit (☎ 641 246). Opportunities for cross-country skiing are also good. There are routes to Aakenustunturi Hill, Särestöniemi (for the museum) and other places. The length of marked walking tracks varies from a few km to several hundred km. On longer ski treks, you can stay overnight in wilderness huts, which have supplies of firewood. Always take a good map and a compass, and listen to weather forecasts before departing.

Information

Tourist information (☎ 648 510), cottage rentals (☎ 643 466) and other arrangements are all taken care of by the roadside Levin Portti tourist office opposite Hotelli Levitunturi. The post office is in the actual village, a bit off the main road.

Canoeing the Ounasjoki River

This long river is one of the best canoeing routes in Lapland. The river runs from Hetta in the north to Rovaniemi in the south, and passes villages like Raattama, Sirkka, Kittilä and Kaukonen. Equipment can be rented at the Levin Safarit (☎ 641 484) at the Kittilä airport. Another company is Pole Star Safaris (☎ 641 688) at the Levin Portti tourist centre.

Places to Stay & Eat

Levi is one of Finland's most popular winter holiday centres. Avoid the busy weeks in February and March when schools are closed for winter holidays.

Hullu Poro (☎ 641 506) is a bit off the main road and has 44 apartments and a popular restaurant, with rooms from 270 to 480 mk.

Levihuvilat (☎ 641 336) has 24 luxurious cottages one km from the village from 390 mk.

Hotelli Levitunturi (☎ 641 301) opposite the tourist office near the main road is a spa with a pool and Turkish bath. This large establishment has a restaurant and 121 rooms from 380/440 mk.

Levin Matkailumaja (☎ 641 126) is a clean guesthouse with slightly lower rates than in regular hotels.

Matkailevi behind the tourist office has excellent rooms with kitchen and bathroom from 370 mk in the high season (from 220 mk in summer).

Sirkantähti (☎ 641 491) is a good hotel with 68 rooms and a restaurant, with singles/doubles from 360/460 mk.

PALLAS-OUNASTUNTURI NATIONAL PARK REGION
Muonio

This small village (population 2750 including outlying areas) offers more commercial services than anything north of here until Norway.

The wooden church in Muonio is from 1817. When the Germans burned the village during WWII, the church was among the few buildings to escape the fire. The local museum is in another building that survived the Germans in 1944. It's open from late June to 31 August on weekdays from 1 to 6 pm.

Muonionjoki River The Muonionjoki River is excellent for canoeing and rafting. The Harrinivan lomakylä (☎ 532 491), south of the village of Muonio, rents out canoes and kayaks. A white-water rafting trip takes approximately one hour and costs 85 mk. After rafting, you will get a 'diploma' and coffee. There are two departures a day in summer. The owner is a lot of fun and speaks good English.

Places to Stay & Eat *Lomamaja Pekonen* (☎ 532 237) is in the centre of Muonio. Hostel accommodation costs 105 mk per person. There are cottages for two/four people at 140/220 mk. See the previous Muonionjoki River paragraph for an alternative at Harriniva.

For meals, check the petrol stations.

Getting There & Away There are two buses a day between Rovaniemi and Muonio. The trip takes approximately four hours. From Kemi and Tornio, there are two buses each weekday and one on Saturday.

Olos

This downhill skiing centre, just east from Muonio, is not a bad place although it isn't as enormous as some of the others in Lapland. *Hotelli Olostunturi* (☎ 536 111) is the only hotel here and will provide you with all assistance. Singles/doubles with breakfast cost 440/590 mk.

Lake Jerisjärvi

This scenic lake has a number of places to stay. At Keimiöniemi, on the northern shores of Lake Jerisjärvi, you will find some fishers' cottages dating from the 18th century.

Places to Stay *Keimiötunturin maja* (☎ 538 515) has a few cottages, priced from 150 to 520 mk per night. Nearby, *Jeris* (☎ 558 511) is a large hotel with 46 rooms; singles/doubles are from 250/350 mk. There are a few other places to the west of here, such as *Torassiepin Loma-Pallas* (☎ 529 144) in the village of Toras-Sieppi, with cottages from 320 mk.

Pallas-Ounastunturi National Park

Pallastunturi Fell is in the middle of the Pallas-Ounastunturi National Park. The park, established in 1938, is one of the first national parks in the country. The main attraction is the excellent 60 km trekking route from the village of Hetta in Enontekiö to Hotel Pallastunturi. The trek takes three to four days, though many people take longer.

In winter, Pallastunturi Fell is a popular place for both cross-country and slalom skiing. The longest slope is two km long, and lift passes cost 85 mk per day or 360 mk per week.

Information At Pallastunturi Fell, there is a good information centre (☎ 532 452) for trekkers that sells maps, makes reservations for locked huts (20 mk per night) and provides facts about the area, and its flora and fauna. It also has slide presentations about the national park, in several languages. The centre is open from 1 June to 30 September Monday to Friday from 9 am to 8 pm and on weekends from 9 am to 4.30 pm.

Trekking Route This route is probably the easiest in the country. One reason for this is that much of the route is treeless – you can see several km ahead. The route is also easy because it is well marked, with poles every 50 metres or so. There are several wilderness huts along the way. The larger huts have a 1:50,000 map on the wall, so carrying a map

is not necessary (but recommended). Unfortunately, the trek is so popular that in some huts (especially Hannukuru hut), there may be up to 60 people there at one time.

Day 1 – At the Hetta end of the trek, you have to cross the lake to get to the national park. There is a boat-taxi system, and you pay according to a fixed tariff – approximately 40 mk. (If you come from Pallastunturi Fell, there is a flagpole at the riverside. Raise the flag, and someone from the Hetta side will come to pick you up.) Walk five km through a forest to Pyhäkero hut. Have a proper meal here and some rest. Start the ascent to the high Pyhäkero, which is part of Ounastunturi Fell. There are hut ruins on the plateau before the highest peak. Seven km from the previous hut is Sioskuru hut.

Day 2 – Walk to Tappuri for lunch and rest. It is mostly treeless plateau with good visibility (and the poles throughout). The day's trek is 10 km from Sioskuru (plus the detour to Tappuri) until you reach Pahakuru. If you can find place here, stay. There is a nice view across the fells. If it's full, continue two km farther to Hannukuru, the 'capital' of the Pallastunturi Fell area. Enjoy a sauna bath in the evening.

Day 3 – There is 14 to 15 km of walking today. The first leg is five km over relatively difficult terrain to a small laavu where you can cook lunch and rest. Another nine km takes you through some impressive views across the mountains to the small hut of Montelli between hills. If it is full, continue one km farther to Nammalankuru, with more capacity.

Day 4 – The last walking day takes you through some magnificent scenery and high mountains. There is only one place to stop, a simple laavu and campfire place just 2.5 km from Nammalankuru. Eat and rest. It is an uphill job from here – 10 km to the hotel. There are only some hut ruins up in the fells where you can find shelter from the weather – nothing else. The scenery between here and the hotel is probably the best along the entire route, with the mighty Taivaskero being the highest peak. A steep descent leads you to Hotel Pallastunturi for comfortable beds and showers. If you start the trek from here, you will have the benefit of visiting the park information centre before the trek.

Places to Stay For trekkers in the Pallas-Ounastunturi National Park, free accommodation is available in wilderness huts. Following is a list of huts from north to south.

Pallas-Ounastunturi
National Park Region

0   5   10 km

LAPLAND

Taukota – This tepee-style kota right at the lakeshore, across from the village of Hetta, gives you shelter from the rain, and you can have a campfire inside. You can even sleep on the floor, if necessary.

Pyhäkero – This hut is five km from the lake. You cannot sleep here, except on the floor, but there is a gas stove, a toilet and a café, open in March and April only.

Sioskuru – Another seven km away, this hut accommodates up to 16 people. There are a few mattresses, a gas stove, a telephone and dry firewood.

Tappuri – A nice hut one km off the main path, this place is visible from both directions, because of the red roof. The hut accommodates six people, and has a gas stove and good water, from a nearby creek.

Pahakuru – This hut is 10 km from Sioskuru. It sleeps up to 10 people, and has a gas stove and a toilet. You'll need to walk a few hundred metres to get water.

Hannukuru – Just two km from Pahakuru, this hut has room for 16 people, but it is often full. There are a few mattresses, a gas stove and a telephone here, as well as plenty of firewood. You can use the lakeside sauna.

Laavu – Some five km farther on, this shelter is useful if it rains, and you can light a campfire.

Montelli – Some nine km farther, across high fells, this nice hut just has a fireplace, and room for five people.

Nammalankuru – Just one km beyond the Montellin autiotupa, this large hut accommodates 16 people. There is a gas stove, a telephone, excellent scenery across the fells and a café, open in March and April.

Laavu – This shelter, just two km farther on, is the last place to rest before the hotel.

If you arrive too late to catch a bus or start a trek, or just want to make shorter day trips, try *Hotel Pallastunturi* (☎ 532 441), just 50 metres from the national park information centre. This hotel looks very impressive; it's up in the fells, and is not nearly as tacky as some newer hotels in Finland. The first hotel in Lapland was built here in 1938, just a stone's throw from the present site. It was blown up in 1944 by German soldiers, to be replaced by the present hotel. Rooms cost 170 mk per person (100 mk if you sleep in your own sleeping bag), including an all-you-can-eat breakfast. During the skiing season, prices are much higher. Buses run up to the hotel, when it is open.

Getting There & Away There is a bus service from Rovaniemi to Pallastunturi Fell every Saturday morning. You can also catch the post bus from Kittilä (3.05 pm) or from Muonio (9.30 am), Monday to Friday.

Hetta

Hetta, previously known as Enontekiö, is the centre of the municipality of Enontekiö (population 2450, of which 400 are Sami), and a good place to start trekking and exploration of the surrounding area. Connections to Norway are good, too. Hetta is not a big place, with just a few dozen houses on either side of the road, but travel services are good. The popular Pallastunturi Trek brings many travellers to the village.

Information There is a municipal tourist office (☎ 556 215) at the crossroads of the Hetta main road and the road to Norway. It's open in June, July and August Monday to Friday from 9 am to 8 pm and Sunday from 9 am to 6 pm. In September, it is open every day from 9 am to 6 pm.

Church Enontekiö Church, in the centre of Hetta, was built in 1952 with the financial help of American churches. The organ was a gift from Germany. The church has a very special altar mosaic, which pictures Christ blessing Lapland and its people.

Sami Museum On the eastern side of Hetta, some three km from the church, there is an interesting Sami museum. It's open every day between Midsummer and the end of August from noon to 8 pm.

Places to Stay & Eat There are several places in Hetta. *Ounasloma* (☎ 521 055) has nine cottages and camping facilities at the river near the tourist office. Across the river, *Ounasmökit* (☎ 521 177) also rents cottages. Behind the church in the village centre, *Hotelli Jussantupa* (☎ 521 101) includes a restaurant, and has rooms from 280/380 mk. Behind these houses, *Hetan Majatalo* (☎ 521 351) has rooms from 170/230 mk. Farther east beyond the actual village,

Hotelli Hetta (☎ 521 361) has singles/doubles from 310/360 mk and some youth hostel beds from 70 mk for HI members. Farther east, not far from the museum, *Lomakylä Paavontalo* (☎ 521 044) has two/four-bed cottages for 150/200 mk.

Karhuntassu between the tourist office and the church prepares large pizzas and has set lunch at reasonable rates.

Getting There & Away Finnair flies to Enontekiö three times a week, twice via Rovaniemi. The airport is a few km southwest of Hetta. There are two buses a day from Rovaniemi to Hetta, one of which continues in summer to Kautokeino in Norway. To get to Kilpisjärvi from Hetta, you have to change buses at Palojoensuu.

NÄKKÄLÄ

This Sami village is approximately 40 km north-east of Hetta. You can drive all the way to Näkkäläjärvi, where the Sami people live in winter. If you want to go on to their summer home at Pöyrisjärvi, 16 km farther west, you will have to leave your car in Näkkälä and walk the rest of the way. The 26 km route from Hetta to Näkkälä is itself a popular trek; you will need the 1:50,000 *Topografinen kartta* map for Enontekiö and Näkkälä.

At Palojärvi, along road No 958 towards Norway, *Galdotieva* (☎ 528 604) has cottages from 100 mk.

KARESUVANTO

Karesuvanto and its twin town, the Swedish village of Karesuando across the Muonionjoki River, form an 'international' centre of 1000 inhabitants. There is a bridge between the two villages, and locals cross it daily to go shopping or to visit friends and relatives. Payments can be made in either currency, and Finnish, Swedish and Sami are spoken on both sides of the river.

The Karesuando Church was built in 1905 to replace a wooden church destroyed by the weather. It was here that the famous preacher L L Laestadius preached. His teachings led to the foundation of the strictest Lutheran sect in Finland.

Places to Stay

Hotelli Ratkin (☎ 522 101) has cottages for three to four people, starting at 180 mk in summer and 260 mk in winter. These cottages have good facilities, including a kitchen. Cottages with a sauna cost more. There are cheaper cottages to the south of Karesuvanto at the riverside, such as *Milin Majat* (☎ 522 191) or *Rantamökit*.

Getting There & Away

The bus from Rovaniemi to Kilpisjärvi will take you to Karesuvanto.

LÄTÄSENO RIVER

In the village of Markkina, the pleasant *Lätäsenon Majat* (☎ 524 602) offers accommodation for 110 to 140 mk in cottages that accommodate two to four people. For 40 mk per day, you can also pitch your tent and use the cooking and washing facilities. The river here is popular for fishing and canoeing.

JÄRÄMÄ

On the way to Kilpisjärvi, about 25 km north of Karesuvanto, there is a fortification area constructed during the war fought against the Germans in Lapland in 1944. After Finland had negotiated a cease-fire with the Soviets, the withdrawal of German troops from Lapland turned into a full-scale war. The Järämä fortification was built during the last phase of the Lapland War and is known as Sturmbock-Stellung. A substantial area has now been renovated. Some of the *korsus* (WWII bunkers) offer shelter from the weather, and you can actually stay overnight, though you should not light fires in the korsus. There is a river nearby.

KILPISJÄRVI

The village of Kilpisjärvi, the northernmost place in the 'arm' of Finland, is right in the 'thumb'. It is a tiny place between Lake Kilpisjärvi and the magnificent surrounding fells. The highest fells of Finland can be seen here. Both Norway and Sweden are next door, and one of the most popular treks reaches the joint border of these three countries. There is nothing else to see in Kilpisjärvi besides the beauty of the countryside, but it is well worth visiting just for that.

Note that Kilpisjärvi consists of two 'villages' – one has two hotels and a shop, and the other has Kilpisjärven retkeilykeskus (the Kilpisjärvi Trekking) Centre and a petrol station. The distance between the two villages is several km.

Information

The Kilpisjärven retkeilykeskus (☎ 537 771) is a central place for all trekkers. There, you can meet up with people, get advice on routes, and buy maps and other equipment. The centre also sells fishing permits and rents those huts that can be rented (35 mk per night per person).

All trekking routes and wilderness huts around the Kilpisjärvi area are clearly displayed on the 1:100,000 *Käsivarsi* map (47 mk). The 1:50,000 *Kilpisjärvi* topographical sheet (25 mk) covers a small area.

Saana

The area around Kilpisjärvi offers a fantastic setting for trekking. Routes range from easy day treks to demanding two-week treks to the mountains. A marked loop route to Saana Fell starts right behind the Kilpisjärven retkeilykeskus. This route takes one full day.

Malla Nature Park

Another very popular day trek is the 15 km route through the Malla Nature Park to the joint border post of Finland, Sweden and Norway. A boat will take you there from the Kilpisjärven retkeilykeskus, across the lake, with departures at 10 am and 2 and 6 pm. Boats wait for three hours before making the return journey. The fare is 50 mk for adults, 10 mk for children. The trek starts from the main road, just before the customs point on the way to Norway – the beginning of the trail is clearly marked. At the border is a wilderness hut, if you want to stay overnight.

Raittijärvi

If you are interested in learning more about the Sami people, make a trek to Raittijärvi, a traditional Sami village. There is no road, so walking is the only way to get there. A path starts at the village of Saarikoski, some 35 km south of Kilpisjärvi, and is approximately 40 km long.

Trekking to Halti Fell

For more experienced trekkers, a one to two-week trip from Saana Fell to Halti Fell, the highest point in Finland (there is snow in June), is a demanding but rewarding trip. The scenery is magnificent, and there are excellent fishing possibilities on the way. You will find wilderness huts at Saarijärvi (to accommodate 10 people), Kuonjarjohka (six people), Meekonjärvi (six people), Pihtsusjärvi (12 people) and Halti (five people). Between Meekonjärvi and Pihtsusjärvi huts, you will have to cross rivers. If you are interested in this trek but are not quite sure of your capabilities, join one of the groups organised by Kilpisjärven retkeilykeskus – there are a few departures every year.

Scenic Flights

There is a heliport at the southern end of the village of Kilpisjärvi. Helicopter or hovercraft flights cost a minimum of 150 to 200 mk per person. For information, call Polar-Lento (☎ 537 810) or Helijet (☎ 537 743).

Places to Stay

Peera (☎ 532 659) is a youth hostel definitely in the middle of nowhere, some 25 km south of the village of Kilpisjärvi. It is a pleasant place by the fell, kept by an older lady. It's open from 25 February to 15 May and from 22 June to 30 September. Dormitory beds cost 35 mk for HI members.

Saanan maja (☎ 537 746) is on the right-hand side of the road on the way to Kilpisjärvi. The place is pleasant, if rather quiet. Four-bed rooms cost 320 mk, and cottages for two are 180 mk. *Kilpisjärven retkeilykeskus* (☎ 537 771) has hotel accommodation at hotel prices. A less expensive alternative is staying in the four-person cottages (280 to 340 mk). If you have your own tent, you can pitch it for 60 mk. *Kilpisjärven Matkailuhotelli* (☎ 537 761) is the best place but is a bit far from the Saana. Singles/doubles start from 240/300 mk.

Places to Eat

At *Saanan maja*, you can get lunch for 43 to 55 mk and meat pies, hamburgers and other small dishes for 10 to 15 mk. *Kilpisjärven retkeilykeskus* serves an all-you-can-eat buffet lunch for 45 mk in the high season.

Whether or not you need to go shopping, visit the local supermarket. All the prices are in both Finnish and Norwegian currencies (sometimes mostly Norwegian), and you can pay in either.

Getting There & Away

There is a daily bus connection between Rovaniemi and Kilpisjärvi via Kittilä, Muonio and Karesuvanto. To get from Hetta to Kilpisjärvi, you have to change buses at Palojoensuu. The road to Kilpisjärvi is excellent, so driving is no problem. Just make sure your car is in reasonably good shape and that you have enough petrol; you certainly won't find anywhere to get your car fixed in the wilderness between Karesuvanto and Kilpisjärvi.

South-East Lapland

Some people do not consider South-East Lapland as 'genuine' Lapland. There is little reason to agree. Historically the area has had a strong Sami influence, although there are few Samis left and no Sami is spoken here. There are fell areas, reindeer and true wilderness.

RANUA

The Ranua Wildlife Park, 85 km south of Rovaniemi, regards itself as the northernmost of all such parks – certainly it offers a chance for you to see a polar bear or a lynx in the wild. The inevitable Santa village is attached. There are daily buses from Oulu and Kajaani, and several daily connections from Rovaniemi.

POSIO

The village of Posio, south-east of Rovaniemi and east of Ranua, has supermarkets, four banks, an Alko store, a post office and a laundry. It is a one km walk from the bus terminal to the main highway. Its population is 5300.

The tourist office (☎ 372 1412) is on Pentikmäki.

Pentikmäki

A bit off the village centre, along the main road, is Pentikmäki, a low hill. It was named after Ms Anu Pentik, a designer of ceramics and clothes. The Pentik factory shop includes a café, and is popular for the discounts it gives on its seconds. There are two museums in the same building. **Muistoja Maalta** is a museum whose name translates as 'Rural Recollections', and it has a large collection of knives, old radios, bottles and almost anything that nostalgic Finns can associate with, collected over 30 years by Mr Arvo Ampiala from Lapua. This collection is worth the 10 mk admission fee, and is open daily whenever the sales exhibition is open, in summer until 8 pm (Saturdays until 6 pm). Downstairs, the unique **Kahvikuppimuseo** (the International Coffee Cup Museum) is open daily until 6 pm (except Saturday, when it closes at 4 pm). It has 2000 cups and plates from all around the world. Admission is 5 mk. In the same area, you can visit an art gallery, or check out the Metsähallitus (Forest & Park Service) information booth.

Places to Stay & Eat

Hotelli Posio (☎ 372 1021) is the local hotel in the village, with rooms from around 150 mk in summer. A lunch buffet is available for 45 mk. Nearby, *Sorrento* is a pizza restaurant with a name that sort of tops the Finnish tackiness. On Pentinmäki, there is a café in the shop, and *Milazzo* ice-cream factory café.

There are a number of places to stay

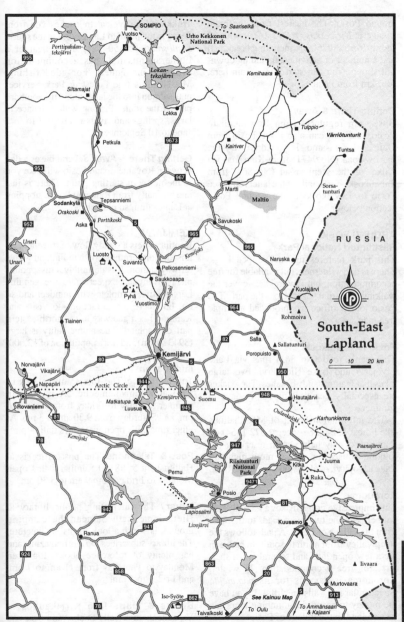

around Posio. The nearest from the main village is *Kirikeskus* (☎ 372 1410) with 22 rooms (for 200/250 mk including breakfast) and a number of activities, including downhill skiing. You can start a trek from here, four km from Posio.

Getting There & Away

Buses run regularly from Rovaniemi to Posio, and you can also reach Posio from Oulu and Kuusamo. If you drive, try the narrow road (No 9471) from Kuusamo via Kitka, or the scenic road (No 863) from Taivalkoski (for details of the latter route, see Posio to Taivalkoski in the Around Posio section below).

AROUND POSIO
Riisitunturi National Park

This park features unusual sloped bogs. There is one wilderness hut available for free accommodation, but few trekkers cover the walking track that leads across the park. The Posio tourist office has produced a simple free map.

Posio to Taivalkoski

The scenic road (No 863) runs via Lake Livojärvi and Lake Hietajärvi, two large lakes that feature sandy beaches. These lakes are especially beautiful on sunny days in summer.

The information booth of Metsähallitus (the Forest & Park Service; ☎ 372 1454) on Pentikmäki may help you in reserving old logging houses for one or more nights at Lake Livojärvi, or along the Livonjoki River.

Korouoma

This impressive gorge makes a natural short cut between the two main roads to the west from the village of Posio. A path follows the steep valley from north to south. In between are a few open huts and several *laavu* shelters, for free accommodation. In winter, Korouoma is famous for its *paannejää* (spectacular ice walls on cliffs). If you have the money to spend, ice-climbing tours can be arranged in the village of Posio.

Trekking

The typical trek takes you from Pernu in the north to Lapiosalmi in the south. *Lapiosalmi* (☎ 350 121), the retreat of a Lutheran mission, has accommodation available on request. For good fishing, Metsähallitus (the Forest & Park Service) puts salmon into the lakes along the southern part of the route. Fishing with a licence in lakes, springs and rivers is allowed from 1 June to 10 September.

Getting There & Away Several buses a day between Rovaniemi and Posio will take you to the northern starting point. There is just one bus daily from Ranua to Posio, stopping at Lapiosalmi, so plan ahead.

KEMIJÄRVI

Kemijärvi gets a steady flow of travellers, as it is the northernmost town in Finland with a railway station. It is definitely a disappointment to anyone expecting to see genuine Lappish life, complete with reindeer and so on, but there are attractions to visit, and Kemijärvi is a gateway to the north-eastern part of Lapland. The municipality is large (3943 sq km) and has a population of 12,000.

Information

Tourist Office The tourist office (☎ 813 777) at Kuumaniementie 2A is open in summer Monday to Friday from 8 am to 6 pm, and Saturday from 9.30 am to 3 pm. At other times, it's open weekdays until 4 pm.

Post & Telephone The post office is at Hallituskatu 5, 98100 Kemijärvi. It's open Monday to Friday from 9 am to 5.30 pm.

Library The interesting public library at Hietaniemenkatu 3, near the camping ground, is worth a look for its architecture. The library subscribes to *Time* magazine, and has plenty of reference books. It's open Monday to Thursday from 11 am to 7 pm, and Friday to 5 pm.

Books & Maps Info Kirjakauppa at Vapaudenkatu 8 sells books, and you can

Kemijärvi

PLACES TO STAY
4 Lohelan Rantamökit
5 Hietaniemi Camping
8 Mestarin Kievari
14 Karppisen Matkustajakoti
17 Sokos Hotel Kemijärvi

PLACES TO EAT
7 Onnimanni
9 Blues Café
10 Casa Mia
15 Kotipizza & Rolls
16 Kahvitupa

18 Auto Grilli Majakka

OTHER
1 Railway Station
2 Local Museum
3 Puustelli Art Centre
6 Public Library
7 Bus Station & Taxis
11 Post Office
12 Kemijärvi Church
13 Bell Tower
16 Book Shop
19 Tourist Office
20 Swimming Pool

find imported magazines and newspapers at
R-kioski at Jaakonkatu 4.

Emergency Services In a general emergency, ring ☎ 112. For a doctor, call
☎ 10023. The hospital (☎ 878 611) is at
Sairaalankatu 9. There's a pharmacy at
Vapaudenkatu 8.

Kotiseutumuseo

The local museum features several old
houses from various time periods. The
museum is open from early June to 31
August weekdays from 10 am to 4.30 pm and
on weekends to 6 pm. Admission is 6 mk, or
4 mk for students.

Kemijärvi Church

The attractive church was built in 1951, but
the old bell tower (1774) remains. The
church is open in summer only, on weekdays
from 10 am to 8 pm and weekends to 6 pm.

Puustelli

The most interesting event in Kemijärvi is
the annual week of woodcarving. Artists
from all over the world attend, and the results
from previous years are on display in this
exhibition. It's open in June and July daily
except Monday from noon to 6 pm. Admission is 10 mk.

There's often an associated exhibition in
Kulttuurikeskus in the library building,
where the Puustelli admission ticket will let
you see more works of art.

Places to Stay

You can pitch your tent at *Hietaniemi
Camping* (☎ 813 640), which is conveniently central considering the fact that it's a
camping ground. You can rent bicycles here.
The cheapest beds in Kemijärvi are at
Lohelan Rantamökit (☎ 813 253), which is a
local youth hostel that charges 80 mk per
person. Also cheap is *Karppisen*

LAPLAND

Matkustajakoti (☎ 813 253) at Hallituskatu 2, with singles/doubles for 80/160 mk.

Mestarin Kievari (☎ 813 577) at Kirkkokatu 9 has 19 rooms from 190/250 mk in summer, including breakfast. *Sokos Hotel Kemijärvi* (☎ 813 841) at Vapaudenkatu 4 is the largest hotel in town. It has 48 rooms and two restaurants, and all rooms cost 320 mk in summer. You can dance to live music in the evenings.

Places to Eat

Kemijärvi has several places to eat, including *Onnimanni* at the bus station. *Kahvitupa* at Vapaudenkatu 6 is a local café with homemade pastries. Torikeskus (the tourist office building) has a café, and *Auto Grilli Majakka* nearby serves hamburgers until late. *Casa Mia* serves pizza, and includes the Falcon Disco upstairs, which opens at 9 pm. *Kotipizza* and *Rolls* compete across the street. Nearby, *Blues Café* at Annaliisankatu 8 is the only restaurant in Kemijärvi to offer the pleasures of live music, and is certainly worth a visit.

The numerous petrol stations have snacks and food until quite late. The best place to dine is reputedly *Mestarin Kievari*. The daily lunch prices start at 34 mk with salad, bread, Nonalcoholic drink and coffee included.

Getting There & Away

Bus The bus terminal is right in the centre of town. There are several buses each weekday to Pyhä (50 km), Sodankylä (110 km), Savukoski (95 km), Salla (71 km) and Kuusamo (160 km). On weekends, buses run infrequently. All trains from Helsinki to Rovaniemi are met by a bus to Kemijärvi. (There is also a bus from Kemijärvi to Rovaniemi prior to train departures for Helsinki.)

Train A direct daily train makes the 14-hour journey from Helsinki to Kemijärvi, arriving in the morning and leaving again after 7 pm.

AROUND KEMIJÄRVI
Suomu

The downhill skiing slopes 42 km from Kemijärvi have had fewer visitors of late, because of the recent recession, but if you go in winter or early spring, you can ski there. The whole place was acquired by a Spanish company in 1995.

Vuostimo

This small place on road No 5 marks the crossing for Pyhä. There are a few landmarks. *JM Tuote* sells handicraft, hot coffee and snacks. *Sarivaara* has a few cottages, and then there's *Kuukiuru* (☎ 882 535) with excellent cottages from 280 mk for a double in summer. The riverside location is scenic and includes a Lappish kota. You can dine here, and it certainly won't hurt to ask about discounts if you need a pleasant place to sleep.

Saukkoaapa

Saukkoaavan retkeilykeskus (☎ 853 402) is 12 km from Vuostimo and three km from the Pelkosenniemi to Pyhä road No 9621. There are 60 beds in this youth hostel, which offers a host of activities.

PYHÄ & LUOSTO

Pyhätunturi National Park, one of the oldest national parks in Finland, is a popular winter sports centre these days, so prices and demand are high from February to May. Summer hikes are recommended between Pyhätunturi Hill and Luosto, as there are fewer people around then and less demand for free accommodation in wilderness huts. Some of the walks in the area are day trips, so even those without proper equipment can reach many of the points of interest.

Information

For accommodation information, you can't beat Pyhä-Luosto Matkailu (☎ 615 200; fax 613 478) at Jäämerentie 9 in the village of Sodankylä. For information on the national park, there is a superb park centre (☎ 882 773) near the Hotel Pyhä, open daily from 9.30 am to 4.30 pm. There is a free English-language slide show to be seen. For an overnight trek, a good map is highly recommended. Karttakeskus has a 1:40 000

Pyhä-Luosto Region

0   2.5   5 km

Luosto-Pyhätunturi map, which can also be purchased in local hotels and resorts. Shorter walks are possible without a map.

Pyhäkuru Gorge

The most notable sight in Pyhätunturi National Park is this steep gorge between the Kultakero and Ukonhattu peaks. If you have only a little time to spend, the 10 km gorge loop is a good hike to choose. There are good signs and paths, and an impressive wooden staircase from the bottom of the gorge to higher slopes.

According to a legend, the small Lake Pyhänkasteenlampi (Lake of Holy Baptism) down the gorge was where EM Fellman, the 'Apostle of Lapland', forcibly baptised the Sompio Samis in the 17th century to convert them to Christianity.

Amethyst Mine

The amethyst mine on Lampivaara Hill started in the early 1990s and is the only such mine in Finland. There's a trekking route of 2.9 km from the car park eight km south of Luosto to the café at the foot of the hill, or you can take a forest road. A staircase leads to the mine.

LAPLAND

Places to Stay & Eat

Cottages As a result of the economic upswing of the late 1980s, a lot of new accommodation was constructed around Pyhä and Luosto. The best guide to rental cottages is the excellent *Pyhä-Luosto Majoitusopas* leaflet, which features over 80 individual options. Prices range from 150 mk per day (four beds) to over 1000 mk per day (up to 18 beds). Call ☎ 615 200 for reservations.

Wilderness Huts It is perfectly possible to arrive at the Pyhä Tourist Centre late on a summer afternoon and walk to the nearest designated sleeping place (laavu or wilderness hut). The morning bus allows you plenty of time for preparations and sightseeing. You are not allowed to stay at *Karhunjuomalampi hut*, some five km from the tourist centre and four km from the Asteli resort, but it is a popular place for preparing a meal. Some two km west, in a gorge, there is the small *Annikinlampi laavu*, with water and dry wood available.

The only hut where you can sleep inside the national park is the clean, modern *Huttuloma hut*. Six people can sleep here, and there are mattresses. Farther west towards Luosto is *Kapusta*, where you can sleep, although it's meant for day-trippers only. *Porontahtoma laavu*, less than two km farther, has dry wood but no water available. About four km north-west, *Rykimäkuru hut* has two beds but half a dozen mattresses, which can also be used by trekkers sleeping under the nearby shelter. There is a gas stove in the hut, and river water is available nearby. A highly recommended place for staying a few nights is *Kuukkeli*. It is a well-equipped, two-room cabin run by the Asteli resort. You can have either room for a mere 20 mk per person, and use of the sauna is free. Kuukkeli is one km from the main road. Some five km from Luosto resort is *Lampivaara hut*, which is only for day use. There are two other huts available, if you plan to walk from Luosto to the main highway, a rough 25 km hike along the Luosto ridges. It is five km from the Luosto resort to the *Torvisen maja* and

another eight km north-west to *Ylä-Luosto hut*, which houses eight people.

Hotels – Pyhä *Hotel Pyhä* (☎ 856 111) is the best hotel in Pyhä, and is worth a look even if you don't stay there. Singles/doubles start at 310/350 mk. There is a good view from the hotel's *Bistro* restaurant, which has lunch at 40 mk. Down the hill and along the road, *Kairosmaja* (☎ 852 126) has rooms at 120 to 170 mk, including breakfast. The nearby Revontulikappeli is the first 'tourist church' in Finland, open daily from 8 am to 10 pm.

A very charming place to stay is *Pyhän Asteli* (☎ 852 141). The Lapinkenttä field has half a dozen Lapp houses as an open-air museum; sometimes you can sleep in one of them free of charge. A dormitory bed costs 110 mk, sauna, sheets and breakfast included. There are also several cottages, of varying quality, size and price. If you stay here several nights, you get one night at Kuukkeli hut for free.

You can rent bicycles (25 mk per day), and canoes (150 mk per day) for use on the nearby Pyhäjoki River. You can also arrange treks to the nearby national park. *Astelin Kide* is the impressive restaurant that offers local specialities and a daily dinner buffet.

Hotels – Luosto *Arctia Hotelli Luosto* (☎ 624 400) has 54 superb cottages. There are two restaurants, and two saunas. Singles/doubles start from 310/370 mk. *Hotelli Luostonhovi* (☎ 624 421) is probably much cheaper once you get there; it has 12 rooms.

Getting There & Away

The easiest connection to the Pyhä Tourist Centre is the 10 am (2.25 pm on Saturday) bus from Kemijärvi. There are buses between Luosto and Sodankylä on school days only (ie Monday to Friday, from mid-August till the end of May). Hitchhiking can be easy, but there aren't that many cars.

SUVANTO

In Lapland during WWII, the Germans got their kicks by burning down anything local people had built. This isolated village survived, however, and is today both preserved and renovated. Now connected to the rest of the world by a bridge, it is easy to visit.

The quaint village doesn't seem to attract many tourists, and this may be the best asset that Suvanto has to offer. Stay two nights here, and try to imagine what Lapland used to look like before WWII.

Approximately 10 houses are inhabited throughout the year, and there are several places you can visit. Across the bridge, **Museolossi** is the old ferry that transported people across the river before the bridge was constructed.

Places to Stay & Eat

Mettiäinen (☎ 854 112) is a local youth hostel with beds upstairs for members from 55 mk (or 15 mk more for nonmembers). It's open all year around. There are also cottages from 300 to 400 mk, coffee and meals. The post office is also here.

Suvannon koulu is the local school building that has a summer café. The school was renovated by the National Board of Antiquities to become a school museum, and has an admission fee.

Getting There & Away

Suvanto is 20 km from Pyhä. There is no public transport. A gravel road from the Sodankylä to Kemijärvi road No 5 starts from the Kokkosniva dam that was about to flood Suvanto. Note the short cut: when driving from Sodankylä, you can cut the trip by visiting Suvanto and then continuing to Pyhä, or vice versa.

SALLA

This large municipality (population 5900) lost quite a piece of territory after WWII, and consequently, its centre has been rebuilt on its present site. The unusual church (1951) is an attractive example of postwar architecture. Locals are watching the border and waiting for it to be opened to travellers. That would increase interest in visits to the Kola peninsula in north-west Russia. There are railway tracks across Salla, all the way to the Russian border, and even now, trips can be

arranged. Meanwhile, Salla offers large areas of untouched wilderness and a host of tourist services. The Sallatunturi Hill Tourist Centre, 10 km from the village, has downhill skiing slopes, and the Sallan Poropuisto (☎ 837 771) has exhibitions, reindeer rides and inexpensive wilderness accommodation for small groups.

Information

The tourist office (☎ 832 141) is called Yrityspalvelukeskus and is on the road to Sallatunturi.

Places to Stay & Eat

Motelli Takkavalkea (☎ 831 801) in the village centre has doubles for 280 to 300 mk. *Hotelli Revontuli* (☎ 831 161) is an imposing edifice at the ski resort, with singles/doubles at 250/360 mk. Also at the ski resort, *Sallatunturin Tuvat* (☎ 831 931) has simple cottages, with singles/doubles at 140/220 mk, and better cottages with a sauna, from 250/320 mk.

Sallan Poropuisto (☎ 837 771), the reindeer park, has simple accommodation in traditional huts from 50 mk per person, and cottages from 200 mk.

Getting There & Away

Buses from Kemijärvi are your best bet, or try hitchhiking, crossing the long causeway from the town of Kemijärvi.

SAVUKOSKI

Savukoski is a genuine wilderness municipality with a declining population – currently 1680, or 0.3 people per sq km. The annual decrease was 2.5% in 1994. The village of Savukoski serves as a base for visits to the isolated attractions around the region, including the eastern part of the Saariselkä area (see the Saariselkä Wilderness/Urho Kekkonen National Park) section in the section of this chapter covering North-East Lapland).

Joulupukin Muorin Tupa

One of the many Santa Claus Land attractions, this place has local handicrafts as well as paraphernalia belonging to Santa Claus' wife. The Finnish tradition places Santa Claus' home at Korvatunturi Fell, an off-limits mountain at the Russian border.

National Park Centre

At the hotel is a superb wilderness exhibition, especially of the Savukoski side of Urho Kekkonen National Park. Ask to see the English slide show, which has excellent photos. The centre is open daily from 10 am to 6 pm. Admission and the slide show are free.

Places to Stay & Eat

The *camping ground* has two huts, with six beds in each. The minimum charge for two people is 160 mk, and additional people pay 50 mk. Pitching a tent costs 30 mk for up to three people. The café sells snacks only.

The top-end choice in Savukoski village is *Samperin Savotta* (☎ 841 351), a superb modern hotel at the Kemijoki River waterfront. Singles/doubles are priced from 180/250 mk.

Getting There & Away

Post buses and Möllärin Linjat buses run daily from Kemijärvi to Savukoski, 94 km away, via Pelkosenniemi. Buses from Salla run only on school days.

MARTTI

The small village of Martti is the last stop for buses running north from Savukoski. In Martti, you will find the K-market Mulari (open daily in summer), a bar that sells snacks only, a petrol station and a telephone booth. There are no petrol sales north of here, until you reach Tulppio.

KORVATUNTURI FISHING AREA

The Kairijoki River has become a popular place for fishing, partly because of the good services provided by *Kairiver* (☎ 841 482). It has excellent cottages for 430 mk and comfortable laavu dormitory beds for 130 mk.

Kairiver also rents canoes and fishing gear, and helps with trekking plans. In winter, snowmobile safaris are arranged. Kairiver sells fishing permits. You'll get a map of the area when you buy the permit. The riverside has several kota and laavu shelters, for free accommodation. The problem with Kairiver is its remote location. Unless you have a vehicle, prepare to stand for several hours when hitchhiking. You can try the unusual *kapulalossi* ferry (you operate it yourself) across the Kemijoki River, from the village of Ruuvaoja, halfway between Martti and Tulppio, then proceed along the gravel roads from there. Do not confuse this fishing area with the better-known fell area at the Russian border (Korvatunturi Hill, Santa's mythical home).

SODANKYLÄ

The village of Sodankylä is a busy commercial centre for the large Sodankylä municipality, which has a population of 10,700, or 0.9 people per sq km. Buses stop here regularly, and there are several attractions. The bus terminal is slightly off the main road, and taxis depart from the same square.

The tourist office (☎ 613 474) at Jäämerentie 9 is open Monday to Friday from 9 am to 5 pm and includes a souvenir sales point.

Churches

Built in 1689, the old church near the Kitinen riverside stands out as one of the few buildings in Lapland to survive the German troops in WWII. It is one of the few 17th century churches that have been left as they originally were. There are mummies below the floor, and the warden will supply you with a torch (flashlight) and help you in locating the dead. The painting is from 1739. It's open in summer daily from 9 am to 8 pm.

The new church nearby is not at all interesting.

Alariesto Galleria

Not far from the church, in the tourist office building near the main road, the gallery displays paintings by this famous Lapp painter. They are colourful, happy images of Sami life. It's open Monday to Saturday from 10 am to 5 pm and Sunday from noon to 6 pm. Admission is 10 mk, but there are discounts.

Museum

The local museum is several km south of the village. There are grey buildings with traditional tools, and the main building from 1906 was rescued from the area that was flooded by the Lokka Reservoir. It's open from 1 June to 30 August daily from 10 am to 5 pm (Saturday from noon to 6 pm). Admission is 10 mk.

Places to Stay

The cheapest place in Sodankylä is *Camping Sodankylä* (☎ 612 181), across the river. It includes dormitory beds at *Lapin opisto* (☎ 611 960) from 55 mk for HI members. It's open from 5 June to 11 August. There are also simple cabins for 180 mk available, and superb apartments from 350 to 450 mk. You can eat and drink at the café.

Majatalo Pohjanpirtti (☎ 611 216) at Ojennustie 19 in the middle of Sodankylä has 10 clean rooms at 100/200 mk. Breakfast costs 25 mk.

Hotel Kultaisen Karhun Majatalo (☎ 613 801) at Sodankyläntie 10 was previously known as Gasthaus. It has 42 rooms from 270/360 mk, and a buffet lunch on weekdays.

Arctia Hotelli Sodankylä (☎ 617 121) at Unarintie 15 has 54 rooms, two saunas and two restaurants, and is close to the bus station. In summer all rooms cost 380 mk, on weekends 360 mk, and at other times 380/485 mk.

About 10 km south of Sodankylä, *Orakoski* (☎ 611 965) is a pleasant riverside camping ground with a large number of cottages, and utilities for campers.

There are a few places as you proceed north from Sodankylä towards Ivalo, mostly providing an overnight option. *Camping Vajusuvanto* (☎ 625 212) in Petkula has cottages three km from the main road. *Peurasuvannon Siltamajat* (☎ 636 711) has very nice cottages near a bridge.

Places to Eat

Sodankylä has several choices, including grillis near the hotels. *Pizza Pirkko* is near the bus station on the main road. Very different is *Seita Baari*, just south of the bus station. Open daily till 10 pm, it offers a selection of inexpensive home-made food, including Lappish specialities such as poronkäristys for 50 mk. In a supermarket building, *Poronsarvi* is a cellar restaurant and pub with a liberal décor. *Revontuli* is a similar place across the road but food here is excellent. *Café Lapponia* sells handicrafts but also serves snacks and coffee. It's open daily until 6 pm.

All petrol stations serve snacks or meals, and there are several of them at both ends of the village.

Getting There & Away

Sodankylä is on the main Rovaniemi to Ivalo road, and a bus from either end costs 70 to 90 mk. Buses from the Rovaniemi railway station depart on the two-hour journey to Sodankylä soon after the train arrives. Walk out of the village if you want to hitchhike.

TEPSANNIEMI

If you're driving on road No 5, see the beautiful lakeside location at Tepsanniemi, on Lake Orajärvi, some 15 km east of Sodankylä. The Tepsa family (☎ 637 208) rents out a traditional, two-room wooden house for 70 mk per person, including sauna. The elderly couple doesn't speak much English, but you can try ringing their daughter in Turku (☎ 251 1716).

North-East Lapland

North-East Lapland offers some of Finland's most rewarding and demanding treks. Here, as in other areas of eastern Finland, the mysterious, virtually sealed Russian border has retained a frontier character. This is the region of the Sami people, the gold rush and the famous Arctic Road, taken every summer by thousands of Europeans on their way to

NORWAY

Nuorgam
Lohiranta
Vetsikko
Pulmankijärvi

NORWAY

UTSJOKI
Kirkkotuvat
Nuvvus

To Nordkapp

Outakoski

Kevo Nature Reserve

Kenestupa

Näätämö   Neiden
To Kirkenes

Iisakkijärvi
Opukasjärvi
Sevettijärvi
Jankkila

Sevettijärvi
Äälisjärvi

To Kautokeino

Karigasniemi
Karasjok

Ruktajärvi

Petsikko
E 75
Iijärvi

971

Kiellatupa
Muotkanruoktu

Kolttamajat

Kiellaroavvi

MUOTKATUNTURIT

Neljäntuulentupa   Partakko

Harakanpesä
Kaamanen

Inarijärvi

Mukkalompolo

Hello Holidays
9553

Ukko

Virtaniemi

INARI
Myössäjärvi
Lapinleuku

Nellim

9681

RUSSIA

Angeli

Njurgulahti

Ukonjärvi

IVALO

See Saariselkä Wilderness Map

To Murmansk

Lemmenjoki National Park

Sallivaara Reindeer Roundup Site

Kuttura

968

Raja-Jooseppi

955

Laanila   SAARISELKÄ
9694
Kiilopää

Taatsin seita

North-East
Lapland

Pokka

Tankavaara

Urho Kekkonen National Park

0   12.5   25 km

Vuotso

Porttipahdan-tekojärvi

955

Lokan-tekojärvi

Kemihaara

E 75
Siltamajat

To Sodankylä

Lokka

Tulppio

the midnight sun of Nordkapp, the northern-most point in Continental Europe.

IVALO

Ivalo (Sami: Avvil) is the undisputed administrative and commercial centre of the huge Inari municipality, but it has little to recommend it. Even its unusually designed church is bleak from inside. With daily flights from Helsinki, Ivalo is the major transport hub in East Lapland, and it has the services you would expect in a small Finnish town. Its population is currently 3500.

Having said this, there are plus sides, too. The library is excellent, food supplies are superb and there is also a unique subculture – gold-panners. Ivalo is the nearest 'big city' for hermits who spend their time and fortune panning the Ivalojoki River sand for gold chips. Hotel Kultahippu is one place where any gold found is traded for booze and where incredible tales are told and new prospects discussed before panners return to where more gold is to be found.

Information
Tourist Office The tourist office is at Neste petrol station along the main street, open in summer daily from 10 am to 6 pm.

Library The beautiful public library has English magazines in the reading room and 1:20,000 maps of the entire Inari municipality in the käsikirjasto section.

Places to Stay
There are no bottom-end accommodation options in Ivalo, although *Näverniemen Lomakylä* (☎ 661 621) just south of Ivalo has cottages from 100 to 400 mk. *Motelli Petsamo* (☎ 661 106), 500 metres off the main road towards Murmansk, has singles/doubles at 175/250 mk. *Hotelli Ivalo* (☎ 688 111) in the south is a fine establishment with singles/doubles for 350/440 mk. *Kultahippu* (☎ 661 825) at the riverside in the north costs 290/340 mk.

North of Ivalo, there are a few top-end places with good locations and terrific services, but you have to book. *Ukonjärvi*

(☎ 667 501) is at the lake of the same name, and has singles/doubles from 100/170 to 340/560 mk.

Lapinleuku (☎ 666 208) is another nice place with heaps of wilderness charm near the Lake Inarinjärvi shore. Singles/doubles start from 230/280 mk.

Places to Eat
There are several places to eat, including Shell, Teboil and Esso petrol stations. *Lauran grilli*, the most popular eatery in Ivalo, stays open till 3 am – its kebabs and poronkäristys taste excellent after a one-week diet of trekkers' food. *Anjan Pizza* and *TL Grilli-Baari*, opposite Lauran grilli, provide an alternative. *Casa Mia* at the bus station is the most typical Finnish restaurant in town. The K-Halli Ylävaara, one of several supermarkets in Ivalo, is open daily from 9 am to 9 pm.

Getting There & Away
There is a daily morning flight from Helsinki to Ivalo, and a few others on weekends. A connecting bus from the airport meets each arriving flight. Buses from Rovaniemi always stop in Ivalo. Hitchhiking to Ivalo is easy, but I found it hard to hitchhike south from Ivalo – start by walking out of the village centre.

Getting Around
Rental companies at Ivalo Airport include Avis, Budget, Hertz and Interrent. Rates are national but negotiable.

TULPPIO

Tulppio is a stepping stone to one of the most interesting natural fishing rivers in Finland, the Nuorttijoki River, which is inside the Urho Kekkonen National Park (see the later Saariselkä Wilderness section). Tulppio used to be a busy logging station before WWI, but little of this legacy remains, as Finnish troops burned down the houses during the Winter War of 1939-40 to prevent the Russians making bases in them.

As the nearby Savukoski wilderness, the south-east pocket of the national park, is attracting more visitors these days, Tulppio is becoming more popular.

Steam Locomotive

The old steam locomotive behind the cottages has plenty of historical significance. As the economic value of the Savukoski forests was discovered in the late 19th century, research was done to find ways to exploit the area. In 1911, a Finnish mechanic was sent to Minnesota to learn how Americans solved the problems of transporting logs. As a result, two steam locomotives were brought to Tulppio via Hanko and Rovaniemi in January 1913. Both locomotives were brought in pieces to Rovaniemi, transported in horse sledges over frozen bogs and forests, with temperatures reaching -30°C. One locomotive is in Rovaniemi, and the other one is here.

Places to Stay & Eat

Tulppio (☎ 844 101) has 19 rooms in cottages with few amenities, but the rooms are clean and can be heated. Doubles start at 200 mk. The café is a popular beer-drinking bar for locals, but there are also meals available (from 39 mk). Poronkäristys can be had for 60 mk.

Getting There & Away

A private vehicle is the easiest way to reach Tulppio, but there are other options. You could take a bus to Martti (south-east of Tulppio), then call the Tulppio cottages (see Places to Stay & Eat) for a lift. Both the Tulppio cottages and the Kairiver cottages (see Korvatunturi Fishing Area in the South-East Lapland section of this chapter) generally charge 1.50 to 2 mk per km for transport, but if you're a paying guest you may get a free lift. Hitchhiking is easiest on weekend afternoons, when people drive to Tulppio for the Tisko, a sort of lumberjacks' disco.

AROUND TULPPIO
Kemihaara

This river confluence (where two rivers join to form the Kemijoki River) some 110 km from Savukoski centre was, until recently, a modern border guard station. Now the quiet location near the national park boundary is a private accommodation and kennel business. *Eräkeskus Kemihaara* (☎ 844 110) has taken over the former border guard station. There are simple dorm beds at approximately 70 mk and proper beds with sauna, sheets and breakfast at 150 mk. A post taxi departs from Savukoski Monday to Friday at 2 pm, and charges what buses would charge.

VUOTSO

Vuotso (Sami: Vuohccu) is on main road No 4 from Rovaniemi to Ivalo. There is a somewhat commercial reindeer village here, where buses stop for 10 or 15 minutes for passengers to have a cup of coffee. If you want to see the pitiful reindeer, ask at the counter for someone to open the door (there is a 15 mk admission fee). The restaurant serves meals.

Vuotson Baari has beer, and there's a shop across the bridge. *Sompio Camping* (☎ 626 146) also has cottages.

TANKAVAARA

Famous for its gold museum and for the annual Gold Panning Competition, Tankavaara, in the northern part of the Sodankylä municipality, is quite a good place to stop during a trans-Lapland tour. Several nature trails around Tankavaara are suitable for short walks. Some routes require waterproof boots.

Kultamuseo

The Gold Museum displays tools and other paraphernalia from Lapland's crazy gold-fever years, described in good English. The museum can be found behind the hotel and restaurant. It's open daily from 9 am to 5.30 pm, and admission is 35 mk.

National Park Centre

The large information centre (☎ 626 251) for the Urho Kekkonen National Park is worth a look, even if you're not planning to visit the park itself. The centre is open in summer from 10 am to 7 pm and in winter 10 am to 4 pm in winter. Admission is free.

Festivals

Several gold-related events are held during the summer, and early August sees the Gold Panning Finnish Open, which should not be missed. The competition itself is short-lived: each competitor's bucket holds a certain number of gold chips (two to 10). Finding the chips quickly means risking the loss of a chip or two, and for each missing chip, five minutes is added. Admission to the area during the competition is 50 mk per day.

Places to Stay & Eat

The hotel, *Korundi* (☎ 626 158), has cottages for 160 to 210 mk, depending on the season, and doubles for 270 to 360 mk. Of the two restaurants, *Wanhan vaskoolimiehen kahvila* is cheaper.

Getting There & Away

Tankavaara is on the main Rovaniemi to Ivalo road. All northbound buses pass the village, stopping on request.

KIILOPÄÄ

Kiilopää, the major trekking centre for the Saariselkä region (see the later Saariselkä Wilderness section), is the best place to start your trek. If you've made the preparations for your trek beforehand, you will probably spend no more than an hour in Kiilopää, but you can also dine well and make most arrangements there and stay overnight. Buy food elsewhere, though, as it is not that cheap in Kiilopää.

Places to Stay & Eat

All accommodation and services are taken care of by the same company, *Tunturikeskus Kiilopää* (☎ 667 101). The cheapest place to sleep is *Niilanpää* dormitory, very similar to wilderness huts, with beds for 85 mk, including sauna. *Ahopää* is the youth hostel where dormitory beds cost 100 mk for HI members. At the hotel, singles/doubles are 210/420 mk and superb cottages cost 420 mk for two people. All prices include breakfast and

sauna. During the winter high season, prices are up to 50% higher. The place rents out mountain bikes, rucksacks, sleeping bags, skiing equipment and much more, sells fishing permits and may provide trekkers with advice. The left-luggage service costs 10 mk per day. Write your name and trekking route in the trekkers book, and don't forget to inform the place as soon as you've completed the trek.

Kakslauttanen (☎ 667 100) on the main Rovaniemi to Ivalo road has 25 luxurious cottages from 290 mk per day. Snacks and beer are also available. There are a few places between Kiilopää and Kakslauttanen, including *Muotkan maja* (☎ 667 104).

Getting There & Away

Kiilopää is six km from the main road. The Matti Malm company has several buses that do the one-hour trip between Ivalo and Kiilopää. If you are travelling by bus from Rovaniemi, you will have to ask whether the bus actually goes all the way to Kiilopää: some do and some don't.

SAARISELKÄ

The village of Saariselkä, with good downhill skiing facilities on nearby slopes, has become synonymous with the entire trekking region, so beware: the village is now one of the busiest yuppie resorts in the whole of Lapland. Real estate prices here are second only to those in Helsinki, big companies have luxurious log houses in the village and hotels are expensive. However, this is not a bad place to start hiking, partly because of the good transport connections and partly because of the good supplies of trekking goodies available in local supermarkets.

Information

Saariselkä Info (☎ 668 122) near Hotelli Riekonlinna provides trekkers with free information, slide shows and a library. The place is open in summer from 1 to 8 pm and at other times from 10 am to 5 pm. Partioaitta sells trekking gear, and Kuukkeli is a general store that sells almost anything else. The post office near the spa is open on weekdays.

LAPLAND

Saariselkä Wilderness (Urho
Kekkonen National Park)

0   5   10 km

RUSSIA

To Murmansk

LAPLAND

To Ivalo

Raja-Jooseppi

Moitakuru

Kaunispää
Fell

Vellin-
särpimä

Kivpää

Rumakuru

Saariselkä

Killopää

Taajosstupa

Luulampi

Rautulampi

Niilanpää

Museum Hut

Tankar-
vaara

Kultamuseo
(Gold Museum)

Reindeer
Park & Café

To Sodankylä
& Rovaniemi

Vuotso

468 m

438 m

546 m

431 m

Suomun-
ruoktu

Gorge

Tammakkolampi

544 m

Sompio Strict
Nature
Reserve

Lankojärvi

Portikoski

Portikoski

Luirojärvi

Luiro

619 m

530 m

Sarvioja

Snelmanninmaja

Kiertämäjärvi

Jyrkkävaara

Ruins & Shelter

Parattiisikuru
(Paradise
Gorge)

678 m

627 m

Muorra-
vaarakka

Lumikuru
(Snow Gorge)

698 m

Sokosti 718

691 m

Hammas-
kammi

Hammaskuru

Karapuljy

Tuiskukuru

Gorge

Karapuljy

Tammikämppä

Old Sokli
Lappish
Field

Ahtarinmukka

Vongoiva
(Kammi)

Gorge

Isitjaannuoktu

Tahvon
Tupa

Peuraselkä

Telephone

Keskihaara

Peskihaara

Häkävaara

Mantto-oja

Mantosselkä

Vieritnarju

Koivatunturi

483 m

Naltiojoki

Reindeer
Roundup Site

429 m

Kamihaara

Tiekasen
Vieritnarju

Protected
Forestry
Area

352 m

Karhuoja

Metto-
palo

Hirvashauta

Kähkeäoja

Majjarova

Sokli

Tulppio

To Savukoski

Fishing

Boat Taxi
from Lokka
Village

Lokka
Reservoir

To Ivalo

Places to Stay

Finnair sometimes has special package tours from Helsinki that include a few nights in the comfortable Saariselkä hotels. Without such arrangements, most budget travellers could not afford to stay in these hotels, although some apartments may be rented at low rates.

Saariselän tunturihotelli (☎ 68111) is the oldest and the cheapest, with singles/doubles at 295/390 mk, including breakfast and sauna.
Kylpylähotelli Saariselkä (☎ 6821) is an enormous spa with a large pool section and a number of activities and other services. Singles/doubles start at 400/570 mk.
Hotelli Riekonkieppi (☎ 668 711) is the smallish hotel area opposite the spa, and has singles/doubles for 360/520 mk.
Hotelli Riekonlinna (☎ 668 601) is the largest edifice in Saariselkä and has singles/doubles from 335/390 mk in summer.
Laanihovi (☎ 668 816), a few km south of Saariselkä, is one of the older hotels, and is not a bad place to begin a trek. Singles/doubles start at 330/450 mk.

Places to Eat

Saariselkä is one of the best places to sample gourmet food, although high-season prices are notorious and some places close during the summer low season. Working from the main road, *Kiekerö* is a down-to-earth eatery with a buffet for 75 mk, or all-you-can-eat soup for 35 mk. *Kelohovi* is finer and more expensive. *Petronella* is probably the finest restaurant in Saariselkä and is good value, although it may be closed in summer. *Pakkasukko* is simpler and serves pizza. *Teerenpesä* is mostly a beer-drinking joint, but it also serves meals.

For an unusual place to eat, climb or drive to the top of Kaunispää, the fell to the north of Saariselkä. Several stuffed birds decorate the restaurant.

Getting There & Away

Each aeroplane arriving in Ivalo is met by a bus to Saariselkä. All northbound buses from Rovaniemi can drop you off at Saariselkä, and some buses make a loop through the village. Timetables in shops give departure times.

RAJA-JOOSEPPI

This border station is a crossing point to Russia for travellers to Murmansk, 250 km away. Many trekkers enter the Saariselkä region from here. If you don't feel like trying to hitchhike, a post taxi departs from Ivalo at 1.55 pm.

SAARISELKÄ WILDERNESS (URHO KEKKONEN NATIONAL PARK)

The Saariselkä region, extending all the way to the Russian border, and including most of the Urho Kekkonen National Park, is by far the most popular trekking region in Finland. It is essentially a network of excellent wilderness huts, with a varied landscape between them, so there is no single trekking path to follow. Most trekkers head to Lake Luirojärvi and, after staying there a night or two, climb Sokosti Fell, or do a circuit near the Russian border. The summer is definitely the low season for Saariselkä, although large groups may be encountered anywhere between the main road and Luirojärvi. In winter, the main activity is centred in the tourist village of Saariselkä. Most people do short day trips on skis in winter, while a number of Finns and Norwegians also engage in some excessive consumption of intoxicating liquids, either as an après-ski activity or their main occupation. The Saariselkä region does not have the greatest downhill skiing, but it is still among the most popular winter resorts in Finland.

If you have walking in mind, come in the summer. The farther you trek away from the village, the more natural beauty you will find and the fewer people you are likely to meet. I walked for three days in the eastern part of the park and saw no-one. The large hut network is one reason for the area's popularity; another is the sheer beauty of the low *tunturi* hills.

Information

Due to the size of the park area, you are likely to visit the information centre that is closest to your starting point. The most established is the one at Tankavaara (☎ 626 251). It has exhibitions and a slide show and sells fishing

The Princess of Itäkaira

After days of lonely trekking in the eastern frontier area of Saariselkä you would be happy to see just a single reindeer. But imagine meeting a woman with little or no clothing on, running around like a fairy tale creature. The story of the Princess of Itäkaira may not be well known but it gave me plenty of fun researching it.

In the solitude of the Tahvon Tupa hut, a lonely man once wrote a long story of a mysterious lady, who might have been the Princess of Itäkaira. He had quite innocently placed an advertisement in a local newspaper, looking for a partner to share a long trek in the eastern part of Saariselkä, also known as Itäkaira. From the plethora of replies, he chose one applicant, a relatively bulky female trekker. He then ordered plenty of parachute cloth from a Pietarsaari factory to ensure enough material for a double sleeping bag. After a lengthy correspondence, and vivid fantasies of this supposedly hairy and enormous lady, he finally had a date.

'See you at the Tahvon Tupa hut, at 6 pm, and do have the sauna heated and your sleeping bag open and warmed'.

After walking for days in excited anticipation of his date, he found himself alone at Tahvon Tupa. He waited but no-one else came.

In the trekkers' book six months later, there was a short note from someone who called herself the 'Princess of Itäkaira': 'Now that I'm here, where are you? I obviously came six months too late.'

Now I was curious. What on earth is going on in this frontier area? And who the heck is the Princess of Itäkaira? During the next few days I found out that this mysterious person had her signature in every book, in every hut or shelter in the region. The entries were a few months apart on average. She also wrote long stories, obviously as bored as the man with the parachute sleeping bag. She wrote in detail about Lapland's nature, as well as how she ran around the wilderness, half naked, sometimes with no clothes at all, chasing ermines and butterflies, and singing songs of joy.

Between all these stories were innumerable comments by lonely male trekkers: 'Where are you, Princess?' or 'Who are you, Princess of Itäkaira?'. And, optimistically, 'When are we going to meet?'.

I soon noticed, by comparing handwriting, that this mysterious lady did sometimes trek with a man, with whom she shared a family name. There was no doubt about it: she was married, middle-aged and had a home near Oulu. Now I know if I see a naked, rather aged lady running around in the wilderness of Lapland, I've only encountered someone who loves Lapland a bit more than the average backpacker. ■

permits. There are also short nature trails in the vicinity, for those who have no time for longer treks. In Savukoski village south of the park (see the Savukoski section in the part of this chapter covering South-East Lapland), there is another modern information centre, catering mostly to those visiting the eastern part of the park. The Kiilopää centre is likely to give valuable practical information on trekking, although it isn't an information centre.

Maps You should not enter the park area without a good map and a compass. There are three maps available for the area. For short treks around the village of Saariselkä, the 1:50,000 *Sompio-Kiilopää* map will do.

The 1:50,000 *Sokosti-Suomujoki* map will take you beyond Lake Luirojärvi. The entire park is shown on the 1:100,000 *Koilliskaira* map.

Zone Division The park is divided into four zones, each with different rules. The basic zone is the area closest to main roads. Camping and fires are only allowed in designated places. In the wilderness zones of Saariselkä (in the west) and Nuortti (south-east, between Tulppio and Kemihaara), camping is allowed everywhere except in certain gorges and on treeless areas. In the Kemi-Sompio wilderness zone (east), camping and fires (using dead wood from the ground) are allowed everywhere.

Things to See

Few trekkers visit the Saariselkä area to see one particular sight. It is the sheer vastness of the virgin wilderness and the physical exercise that make this such a popular area. There are two historical **Scolt fields**, with restored old houses, two km south of Raja-Jooseppi, and two km west of Snelmanninmaja hut, respectively. Another sight near Raja-Jooseppi is a **museum farm**, inside the border zone. Entry is restricted.

There are several natural attractions within the park boundaries, of which the **Rumakuru Gorge**, near the huts of the same name, is closest to the main road. **Lake Luirojärvi** is the most popular destination for any trek, and a hike up the nearby **Sokosti summit** (718 metres, the highest in the park) is something of a must. **Paratiisikuru** (Paradise Gorge), a steep descent from the 698-metre Ukselmapää summit, and the nearby **Lumikuru** (Snow Gorge) are also popular day trips between Sarvioja and Muorravaarakka huts.

Trekking

There are a large number of possible walking routes in the Saariselkä area. Use wilderness huts as bases and destinations, and improvise according to your ability: it is possible to cover three to four km per hour, and up to 25 km per day, but even 20 km on the first day may be too tough. You'll enjoy it more if you walk just a few hours daily and spend more time preparing food and enjoying the quiet and solitude of the wilderness.

Despite its popularity, Saariselkä may be tough going for the less experienced, and there are occasional reports of lost and dead trekkers. Ski safaris in winter are especially dangerous during cold spells. Enter your route information in the trekkers book at Kiilopää, or wherever your starting point is, and write your name and next destination in the visitors books in each hut. This is a voluntary tracking system which seems like a 'Kilroy was here' game but is actually crucial when tracking injured or lost trekkers. Always call the starting point to say you have finished your trek.

Many legs between huts have real paths, some of them almost too wide to seem appropriate in a national park. Some of the narrow paths are actually mere reindeer tracks, which don't lead anywhere near your destination. In fact, most of them don't lead anywhere at all. And the farther east you proceed, the more likely it is that the path will disappear completely. This is the critical point where you will have to start taking note of your surroundings.

I don't want to sound as if I'm giving a lecture on orienteering, but there are several rules which should be observed in Saariselkä. The simplest rule is to look at the peaks. How many do you see? Can you find all of them on your topographical map? If you keep your eyes fixed on a specific gorge while you are walking (in addition to watching your feet, of course), you shouldn't need a compass – at least for some time.

Orienteering in a forest is much more difficult, and there you may just have to set off in the direction of any river, lake or open bog and walk until you bump into it. Following rivers is a simple way to avoid getting lost, but when you leave the river, make sure you know where you are, and where you are intending to end up by taking your chosen direction. One of the highlights of trekking in Saariselkä is the sensation of finding the next hut almost hidden in a deep gorge or in the woods.

A four to six-day loop from the main road to Lake Luirojärvi and back is about the most popular route, and you can extend it beyond the lake. To reach areas where very few have been, take a one-week walk from Kiilopää to Kemihaara, or do the most remote route: with some careful planning and a good map, it is possible to follow old roads and walking routes through the fells all the way from Raja-Jooseppi in the north to Kemihaara or even Tulppio in the south-east.

Unlike in similar parks in Sweden, there is no food available in huts here (except some odd leftovers for emergency). Carry all the food you need and ration it carefully. Any dry food (including protein-rich nuts) will be enjoyable to carry and consume, as will ready-made trekkers' food packs, but a few juicy oranges or other such goodies will help to supplement this boring diet. Water in rivers is drinkable. Carrying water in any form only adds to your burden.

Places to Stay

It is generally possible to arrive at any starting point during the day and walk to the nearest wilderness hut within hours. Note that there is daylight 24 hours a day in June and July. Most huts near the main road have been declared huts for day use only, but I found staying overnight no problem, as there are still bunks inside most of them. On the other hand, more distant huts have comfortable mattresses and better amenities for an overnight stay.

Basic Zone Below is a list of wilderness huts in the basic zone:

Rumakuru – Some six km from Saariselkä village, this is the most popular day cabin in Saariselkä, with over 200 skiing visitors on busy April days. There are bunks for four (no mattresses) and a gas stove, but staying overnight is not encouraged. Some 500 metres east is the old Rumakuru hut, which dates from the turn of the century and easily accommodates two.

Luulampi – Four km from Rumakuru, this is an information centre for tourists. There is even a café in the high season. No sleeping is allowed here, except in an emergency.

Taajostupa – This cosy hut near a river, with two open sides available, accommodates up to 10 people, and has several mattresses to soften the sleep. There are normal facilities, but the sauna burned down in 1990.

Vellinsärpimä – This hut, seven km from Kaunispää/Saariselkä, is supposedly a day cabin, but sleeping is OK. There is space for four. There are normal facilities, with good water available from the river.

Kivipää – Five km from Vellinsärpimä at a small lake, this hut accommodates four people. It's open to anyone from May until the winter comes; at other times, it must be reserved. Even though it is off the beaten path, it gets lots of praise for its thick foam mattresses.

Niilanpää – This Lappish kota-style shelter for five people, only four km from Kiilopää, is seldom used for sleeping. For water, follow the reindeer fence down to a nearby river.

Rautulampi – A popular hut at the northern end of a lake of the same name, Rautulampi hut is for day use only (sleeping is OK, but not encouraged). There is a telephone available, if it's not out of order.

Suomunruoktu – Fifteen km from Kiilopää, at a creek, this hut is usually busy in the high season. It accommodates 10 people in the open side and 10 in the reserved section, with mattresses in both rooms. If the place is full, walk 200 metres upriver and cross the river to the old hut, which gets few overnight visitors. There are no amenities, as it has been declared a wilderness museum, but sleeping is OK.

Tammakkolampi – This small *kammi* (earth-covered hut) three km south of Suomunruoktu hut accommodates only three people, and you have to reserve it in advance. Getting there is not worth the effort.

Lankojärvi – This hut on the western shore of the Suomujoki River has two sides, with 10 places in each. There is a crossing point across the river, to the south of the hut.

Porttikoski – This northern hut is one km from the bridge over the Suomujoki River. The hut sleeps 10 people and has a popular sauna.

Snellmanninmaja – This small hut is on the northern shore of the wide Suomujoki River. It sleeps five people but is out of bounds for most trekkers, due to its location.

Saariselkä Wilderness Zone The hilly Saariselkä region is quite busy during the winter holidays, in August before school starts and during the ruska (autumn) weeks in late September. Most trekkers visit this area, where superb wilderness huts abound.

Tuiskukuru – This popular hut near a creek has two sides, with space for 10 people in the open side and mattresses in both rooms. Gas and firewood are available.

Luiro – There are three lakeside huts at Lake Luirojärvi, each with good facilities (including a gas stove), and a popular sauna. The largest hut was built in 1991. It has space for 12 people in both rooms, but there are no mattresses in the open one. The smaller *porokämppä* ('reindeer hut') accommodates six people. The third hut has to be reserved in advance. Many groups pitch tents near the huts during the summer high season.

Hammaskuru – This hut has two sides. One side is always open, with room for 12 people (but no mattresses). The hut has normal facilities, and good drinking water is available from the nearby creek.

Hammaskammi – Two km south along a good road,

this primitive lakeside shelter for two has a stove inside, and dry firewood.

Siulanruoktu – The dramatic position of this hut, halfway up a ridge, makes it an unforgettable place to stay. Steep stairs lead from the path to the hut, and farther down to the river. There is room for six people, a few mattresses, gas and a stove.

Tahvon Tupa – Six km east of Siulanruoktu hut is this gem among wilderness huts, in a small river valley. There is a good self-service sauna, plenty of firewood and half a dozen mattresses, but relatively few visitors. The small *niliaitta* construction on a pole is used to store empty bottles; take one for extra water if you are heading farther east to the riverless region.

Peuraselkä – This lonely hut, seven km north-east of Tahvon Tupa, and just eight km from the Russian border, has few visitors. It is easy to find with a map and a compass, but getting there is hard, as there are plenty of fallen trees in the area. There is no bridge across the river, but crossing it with long rubber boots is generally OK. The hut accommodates four people, and has mattresses and a gas stove.

Jyrkkävaara – This two-room hut sleeps 10 people in each room. Located at a small lake, it serves mainly those heading south-west from the Raja-Jooseppi starting point. There is a telephone in the hut.

Kiertämäjärvi – This small hut for five people, at the northern shore of a lake, is the first sleeping place for many of those who start their trek from Raja-Jooseppi.

Sarvioja – This hut has two rooms, with 10 places in the open side. Slightly off the beaten track, the hut nevertheless serves as a base for several side trips.

Muorravaarakka – There is a good two-room hut (with 10 beds in the open side, and a telephone) and a small kammi, both of which must be reserved in advance. These huts are in a river valley at the junction of a few paths. There are several popular hikes in the neighbourhood, so expect a few other trekkers to show up by night time.

Anterinmukka – This beautiful hut (also called Keskon mökki) is one of the best ones in the whole park, with a good sauna available for trekkers. The hut accommodates up to 15 people, but its isolated location makes it hard to predict its nightly usage.

Karapulju – An isolated hut south of Lake Luirojärvi, it has room for five trekkers, but there are few reasons to come to this place surrounded by hostile bogs.

Vongoiva – This kammi in an upper river valley has room for two people only, and it has to be reserved in advance. Many trekkers stop here en route between Anterinmukka and Siulanruoktu.

Kemi-Sompio Wilderness Zone This area gets few trekkers – it is a transitional region between two popular areas, the Saariselkä hill region and the Nuortti fishing area. The terrain is flatter than that of Saariselkä, and there is little water available in summer. The narrow spruces are typical of the wilderness which Finns call *kaira*. It is easy walking country, though, and large bogs can be crossed on *pitkospuu* (board walk) paths (if you follow trails, that is). There are several wilderness accommodation options:

Keskihaara – This laavu shelter marks the crossroads of paths between Peuraselkä and Manto-oja huts, and Kemihaara. It is a good place to stop and get water. If it is late, try to sleep under the shelter.

Peskihaara – This small hut, previously a border guard's hut, takes five people. It is a side trip from the main path leading to Kemihaara.

Manto-oja – This hut, a one-day hike from Peuraselkä, is an essential stop along a route across the park. There is room for eight people, and a telephone.

Mantoselkä – If Manto-oja hut happens to be full, this hut, one km north, has six beds in the open side. The Tulppio holiday village has keys for the other side.

Vieriharju – Five km east of Manto-oja, this hut has room for six people, and a sauna.

Other Huts – Very distant huts in this zone include *Härkävaara*, which has a sauna, and *Tammikämppä*, which can be reached if you arrange boat transport from Lokka village across the Lokka Reservoir and enter the park from that side.

Nuortti Wilderness Zone The Nuortti region is popular for fishing, and most visitors come for this reason. Tulppio is used as a starting point for exploring the area. If you plan to trek from here, negotiate a ride from Tulppio to one of three places: Kärkekeoja, Tikkasen vieriharju or Kemihaara. Wilderness huts in the area include:

Kärkekeoja – This hut is the closest to Tulppio, with a gravel road across the river. It is possible to cross the river on foot.

Mettopalo – There are bunks for four people in this hut, a dozen km farther downriver.

Karhuoja – Six people can stay here for free, and there is room for another six in the reserved side.

Naltiojoki – This hut, not far from Kemihaara, accommodates 10 people.

Hirvashauta – There are two rooms in this hut, with room for six people in each. The hut is on the other side of the river, a few km south of Karhuoja hut.

Tikkasen vieriharju – This hut, close to the park boundary and a gravel road, can be reserved in Tulppio for up to four people. There is a sauna, and a natural well nearby provides fresh water.

Getting There & Away

As the park is so vast, it is possible to start the trek from several points.

To/From Kiilopää

There is a regular bus service from Ivalo village, and the morning post bus from Rovaniemi makes the side trip to Kiilopää. You should head first either to the Luulampi information centre or to Niilanpää kota. (See the earlier Kiilopää section for more information.)

To/From Saariselkä

See the earlier Saariselkä section for information on getting to Saariselkä. Start the trek from the south-eastern corner of the village. The first leg will take you to Rumakuru.

To/From Tankavaara

This is not a good starting point, unless you want to visit the Sompio Nature Reserve.

To/From Kaunispää Fell

You have to hitch-hike up to this hill, then descend the downhill skiing slope to a valley. Follow the path down there to your left. The nearest hut is Vellinsärpimä.

To/From Raja-Jooseppi

On weekdays, there is a regular post taxi to Raja-Jooseppi (see that section earlier in this chapter). Failing this, you'll have to hitchhike. This is a good starting point for a trek, as it takes you directly into the real wilderness. The first huts are Kiertämäjärvi and Jyrkkävaara.

To/From Kemihaara

Catch a post taxi from Savukoski (see the earlier Kemihaara section

for times). The park boundary is just one km from Kemihaara. The nearest hut is Peskihaara, but the path leads directly to Keskihaara, where there is a laavu.

To/From Tulppio

See the earlier Tulppio section for information on getting to Tulppio. Negotiate a ride closer to the park boundary, or follow gravel roads to Kärekeoja.

To/From Lokka

Villagers will take trekkers across the large Lokka Reservoir by boat. The nearest hut will then be Tammikämppä.

NELLIM

This small village of 260 people has become a meeting point for two distinctive Sami groups of people, and there is a *tsasouna* of the Orthodox Scolt Lapps, and a small Sami museum. Nellim has a shop and a café, and the *Koskela Nellim* (☎ 666 925) offers rooms from 60 mk.

Nellim is also a gateway to the controversial Kessi wilderness area, seriously threatened by overzealous loggers. If Kessi remains virgin forest, Nellim will be an interesting starting point for exploring one of the most isolated trekking regions in Finland. With some careful planning and good maps, it is possible to follow old roads and walking routes through the wilderness, all the way from Nellim in the south to Näätämö in the north. Consult the *Inarijärvi* map for routes.

Getting There & Away

On weekdays, there are morning and afternoon post buses from Ivalo to Nellim, 43 km away, and Virtaniemi, eight km farther on.

MYÖSSÄJÄRVI

The fishing region of Myössäjärvi, midway between Inari and Ivalo, is one of the places where it is possible to try your luck if you have appropriate fishing permits. If you have a vehicle, it may be a good idea to stop at the souvenir shop. The main tourist attraction is Karhunpesäkivi, or 'Bear Den Rock', a large hollow rock 200 metres from the main road.

The legend goes that a hunter, while looking for a shelter, found a bear in this small cave.

INARI

At 17,321 sq km, Inari (Sami: Anár) is the largest municipality in Finland, just a little smaller than Slovenia. The small village of Inari, inhabited by 550 people, is the main Sami community in the region. Inari has supermarkets, banks and interesting shops scattered along the scenic road which follows Lake Inarinjärvi, and it has three not-to-be-missed, world-class attractions. You will need at least one full day to cover the Inari village attractions. The village can also be used as a base for exploring the northern part of the municipality.

The Inari day trip itinerary includes a morning trek to the wilderness church, a two-hour lake cruise at 2 pm and a visit to the Saamelaismuseo in the evening.

Information

The Inari Info tourist office is open in summer daily from 9 am to 8 pm. In winter it's open until 3 pm. Several maps are available for the large municipality of Inari. The 1:100,000 *Inarinjärvi* map covers the entire Lake Inarinjärvi area.

Saamelaismuseo

The superb Sami Museum of Inari should not be missed: it is one of the best open-air museums in Finland, with unique Sami handicrafts, old buildings and local artefacts on display. For a few mk, you can get a map which might be useful for finding your way through the thick pine forest. It's open daily from 8 am to 8 pm. Admission is 20 mk, with discounts available for children.

Wilderness Church

The *erämaakirkko* of Lake Pielpajärvi can be reached by walking seven km from Inari.

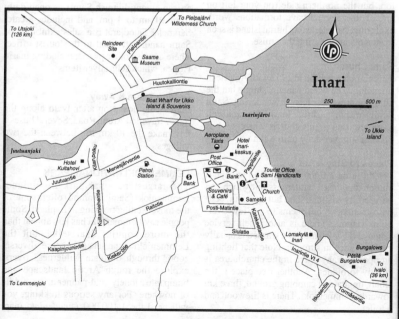

The hike itself serves as an introduction to trekking in Lapland. The track, marked by yellow paint on tree trunks, is of medium difficulty, with several desolate lakes along the route. The church area has been an important marketplace for the Sami over the centuries, with the first church erected here in 1646. The present church was built in 1760, and careful work in 1973-76 restored the original subtle paint of the pulpit. To get to the path, follow the 'Kansanopisto' sign near the Saamenmuseo. It is a five km walk from the parking place.

Ukko

There are regular departures on Lake Inarinjärvi as soon as the ice melts from the lake, usually by mid-June. There are cruises until the end of August daily at 2 pm, with two additional departures in July (10 am and 6 pm), for 50 mk. The destination is the island of Ukko (Sami: Äjjih), sacred to the Sami for at least 1000 years. During the brief (20 minute) stop, most people climb to the top, but the northern side (on your left on arrival) has several cave formations worth exploring. An interesting burial island is seen from a distance during the cruise.

Sami Church

This church was built in 1952 with American financing. The wood panel is simple but the altar painting depicts a wandering Sami family meeting Christ. Inari Sami and Fell Sami are used in this church. The church is open in summer daily until 8 pm.

Places to Stay & Eat

For those on a tight budget, the Pielpajärvi church area has a wilderness hut which can be used by visitors. The hut has four beds with mattresses but seems to get few overnight visitors. There is also a self-service sauna at the lakeside but a warden is usually in attendance in summer. Note that lighting an open fire anywhere in the church area is strictly forbidden. Another free place is the small, unguarded camping ground, three km towards Lemmenjoki. There is firewood and a toilet.

The popular *Kukkula youth hostel* was closed in 1995 and there was no reopening in sight.

Several bungalow villages are to be found to the south of the village. *Lomakylä Inari* (☎ 671 108) is within walking distance of the bus station, with cottages from 120 to 420 mk. Others such as *Pätilä* (from 150 mk) and *Uruniemi Camping* (from 110 mk) are farther south.

Inari-keskus (☎ 671 026) is a local scene with an excellent lunch, beer, a grilli and all kinds of souvenirs for sale. There are several rooms, priced at 145/200 mk.

The top-end choice, *Hotel Kultahovi* (☎ 671 221), a bit off the main road along the Lemmenjoki road, has rooms from 310/400 mk. *Koskikrouvi* bar in the hotel serves siika (whitefish) by weight.

Things to Buy

Inari is one of the centres for *sámi duodji* (Sami handicrafts). Samekki, the studio of Mr Petteri Laiti (who is the most famous artisan among Finnish Sami), is open daily from 10 am to 4 pm, and includes a café. Sápmelaš Duodjarat is a sales exhibition of Sami handicrafts next to the tourist office. There are also other places, including Inarin Hopea, which sells silver items.

Getting There & Away

Inari is the next stop after Ivalo along the much-travelled Arctic Road. Several buses a day make the 40 km trip between the two villages.

LEMMENJOKI NATIONAL PARK

The largest national park in Finland, Lemmenjoki (Sami: Leammi) offers some of the most exciting trekking in Lapland. Some people say Lemmenjoki has less appeal than the more popular Saariselkä, but the Lemmenjoki experience is more diverse: zoom through desolate wilderness rivers, explore the rough Arctic landscape and bump into a lonely gold-panner in the middle of nowhere. For any serious trekking, you will need the 1:100,000 *Lemmenjoki* map,

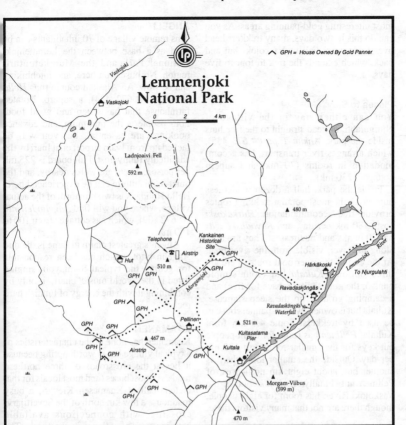

Lemmenjoki National Park

GPH = House Owned By Gold Panner

Vaskojoki

Vaskojoki

Ladnjoaivi Fell
592 m

▲ 480 m

Telephone

Kankainen
Historical
Site

Hut   Airstrip   GPH

510 m   GPH   GPH

Härkäkoski

Morgamjoki

Lemmenjoki River

To Njurgulahti

Ravadasköngäs

GPH   GPH

Ravadasköngäs
Waterfall

Pellinen

GPH   GPH

▲ 521 m

Kultasatama
Pier

GPH   GPH

Airstrip

467 m

Kultala

GPH

GPH   GPH

Morgam-Viibus
(599 m)

▲ 470 m

0   2   4 km

---

available in bookshops. An information hut at Njurgulahti is open in the high season.

Things to See & Do
The Lemmenjoki River is scenic, with its steep slopes. The Ravadasköngäs Waterfall can be seen from the river. You can walk there, and climb the staircase, from Ravadasköngäs hut. The Morgamjoki River is the main gold-panning area, and there are several old huts where gold-panners still sleep in summer.

Much of the Lemmenjoki River and beyond is good for fishing. You can buy

permits (20 mk per day or 60 mk per week) and rent canoes and boats at the Ahkun Tupa in Njurgulahti, and cover the beautiful river route by yourself.

Some 70 km south of Inari, there's a reindeer roundup site at Sallivaara, six km from the main road. The site is protected, and you can sleep overnight in one of the huts.

Trekking All logical trekking routes are within the relatively small area between the Lemmenjoki and the Vaskojoki rivers. The shorter 18 km loop between Kultala and Ravadasjärvi huts takes you to some of the most interesting gold-panning areas. As you can do this in two days, many trekkers head over Ladnjoaivi Fell to Vaskojoki hut and back, which extends the trek to four to five days.

Places to Stay

You can either stay in the village of Njurgulahti, or head straight to the free huts inside the park. *Ahkun Tupa* (☎ 673 435), which arranges river transport, has accommodation in rooms (70 mk) and superb cottages (230 mk).

Inside the park, half a dozen wilderness huts along the most popular trekking routes provide free accommodation. *Härkäkoski* costs 180 mk per day, and *Ravadasköngäs* has 20 bunks and mattresses. They are both along the river, visible from the river boat. At the end of the river-boat route, there are three options: *Kultala* hut (four simple bunks), the kota shelter (space for five) and a camping ground, up the steep staircase. Kultala hut is owned by gold-panners but can be used by trekkers. Some 4.5 km from Kultala, *Pellinen* has room for eight people but keys for the smaller room cost 130 mk per day. Outside the smaller loop, there is another hut, about eight km north-west of Pellinen hut. Finally, *Vaskojoki* hut, at the Vaskojoki River, has room for eight people, though there are not that many visitors there.

Getting There & Away

There are usually one or two post buses daily from Inari to the Njurgulahti village, or Lemmenjoki. If you have very little time, and want to use the river taxi, the afternoon eight-seat bus in the village waits until the boat has made the return trip, then drives back to Inari. The scenic boat tour along the Lemmenjoki River is worth the fare (60 mk one-way, 120 mk return). From mid-June to mid-September, there are daily departures at 10 am and 5.15 pm; from 21 June to 18 August there is an extra departure at 10 am. Departures from Kultala are at 11.40 am and 6.40 pm. You can get on/off the boat at other jetties along the route.

ANGELI

This remote village of 70 inhabitants can be used as a base between the Lemmenjoki National Park and the Muotkatunturit region. No buses run here, and hitchhiking can be slow. An Alaskan couple runs *Hello Holidays* (☎ 672 434), a superb, isolated farmhouse that has sheep and good food. Four people are the minimum, and advance bookings are essential, but you will be picked up from Ivalo airport or at Inari by the admittedly funny host. Full board is 225 mk per person. There are walks nearby, and the quiet Sami culture can be experienced here. Hello Holidays is two km north of the actual village, where you will find *Angelin leirintä* (☎ 672 409), which has cottages from 100 to 150 mk.

Angeli's greatest claim to fame is the duo Angelin tytöt, which has been responsible for getting the typical Sami yoik singing listed in the 'world music' chart, if only by combining it with the energy of Finnish hard rock.

KAAMANEN

Kaamanen has none of the characteristics of a typical village but is worth noting because it lies at the crossroads of three northern roads. All post buses (and most locals for that matter) call at Kaamasen Kievari, a busy roadhouse a few km north of the Sevettijärvi crossing, with connections available between various villages in the north. The Kotipuoti shop has postal services and a fuel station. Some five km north is the Karigasniemi crossing.

Places to Stay & Eat

Kaamasen Kievari (☎ 672 713) has nice riverside cottages for 60/80 mk, or better cottages for 170 to 250 mk. Hotel-style accommodation is available in spring and summer for 320/420 mk, or less at other times. *Jokitörmä* (☎ 672 725) has two-bed cottages for 130 mk, and four-bed ones for 280 mk.

Neljäntuulen tupa (☎ 672 700) is five km north of the Karigasniemi crossing on road No 4 towards Utsjoki. It's an impressive pinewood cabin with a variety of accommodation possibilities; cottages are 80/100 mk, rooms 150/220 mk.

At the Sevettijärvi crossing, *Ahmakulma* (☎ 672 815) has just two cottages from 120 to 160 mk. There's also a café.

MUOTKATUNTURIT

This large fell area, east of Inari, is not very well known. *Muotkan Ruoktu* (☎ 676 900), midway between Kaamanen and Karigasniemi, is run by a Sami family who owns a large number of reindeer. Cottages cost from 120 to 310 mk per night. This is a possible starting point for the little-travelled trekking route across the Muotkatunturi Fells. You can reach the village of Angeli, staying in a few wilderness huts along the way. The three wilderness huts, *Kiellaroavvi*, *Harakanpesä* and *Mukkalompolo* are free, like most huts in Lapland, but you need excellent maps and plenty of skills for this route.

You can also stay at *Kiellatupa* (☎ 676 921), farther west, and 39 km before Karigasniemi. Two-bed cottages cost 150 mk.

KEVO NATURE RESERVE

Probably the most breathtaking sights in Finland (though they are nothing spectacular if you've spent your life in Norway or near the Grand Canyon) can be enjoyed by following the splendid gorge of the Kevo River (Sami: Geävu), which also has some spectacular waterfalls.

The rough 70 km (one-way) trek takes about four days. The 1:100,000 *Kevo* topographical sheet is rather overpriced at 47 mk.

Places to Stay

Kenestupa (☎ 678 531), near the eastern starting point, next to the main road, rents cabins from 110 mk per day. Use of the sauna costs 40 mk.

There also are four free wilderness huts along the north-western path between the two main roads, and a few other shelters. If you plan to walk from hut to hut, up in the fells, you won't have a chance to walk down in the gorge. If you want to cover the entire

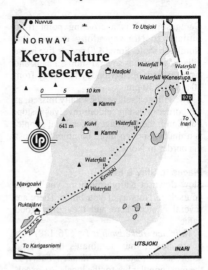

riverside, you'll need a tent, which you can pitch at designated camp sites. The huts along the north-western route, from south to north, are:

Ruktajärvi, at the south end of the gorge route (accommodates eight people and has a telephone and an oven);
Njavgoaivi (10 people, telephone);
Kuivi, inside the park (10 people, oven);
Madjoki (Mad River), inside the park (eight people).

Getting There & Away

If you start from Kenestupa, catch a Nuorgam-bound bus from Inari. It is easier to start from the other end, as the Kenestupa and its sauna can come in handy after a rough trek; you have to catch the Karigasniemi-bound bus from Inari, and get off at the starting point (ask the driver to drop you off at the right place).

Those with a car can leave their vehicle at the Kenestupa, catch the afternoon bus to Kaamanen and change to the Karigasniemi-bound bus. Plan ahead, as there is apparently just one connection that works!

KARIGASNIEMI

The small village of Karigasniemi (Sami:

Gáregasnjárga) is a crossing point from Finland to Norway along the popular Nordkapp route. Some 470 people live in the village, which has several shops, a bank and a post office, open Monday to Friday from 10 am to 4.30 pm.

The village itself can be totally missed, as the border crossing seldom involves a stop. Fell Sami, the language of the local people, is a dialect spoken more commonly across the border in Norway.

Places to Stay & Eat

Slow down at Karigasniemi or you'll find yourself in Norway if you blink. There are several choices here and they offer good value.

Välimäen retkeilymaja (☎ 676 188) is a youth hostel that dominates the village scene, as its restaurant, *Välimäen baari*, is the most popular bar for the locals. An excellent lunch is served from 11 am to 2 pm daily (35 mk, including salad bar, bread, milk and coffee). The youth hostel prices start at 30 mk per bed, but there are also doubles from 80 mk and four-bed huts at 130 mk. An inexpensive sauna bath is available.

Lomakylä (☎ 676 160, 676 136) is the first place you come to on the way into Karigasniemi from Inari. There are 12 cottages from 150 to 200 mk, and four rooms from 150/200 mk. The restaurant *Soarve Stohpu* is the best place to meet old Sami men; this place is currently the only one in Karigasniemi where alcohol is served.

Camping Tenorinne (☎ 676 113) has eight excellent cottages at a pleasant location near the youth hostel. Cottages cost from 160 mk for two people to 230 mk for four people. The best cottages have running water, plates and a small kitchen. The service building also includes a kitchen. The large sauna is complementary for those staying more than a few days.

Loma Karigas (☎ 676 209) is nearest the Norwegian border. There are eight cottages from 140 mk. The café serves sandwiches. Other options include *Lomamajat Napakettu* (☎ 676 232) two km north of Karigasniemi, and *Ylä-Tenon Takkatuvat* (☎ 676 200) some

12 km south along the Karigasniemi to Angeli road.

In Karigasniemi, the *Ailigas* shop serves hamburgers, and the *Tenohalli* shop has a café.

Getting There & Away

Two buses a day travel from Ivalo to Karigasniemi, continuing on to the Norwegian town of Karasjok. Eskelinen even drives to/from Lakselv in summer. An interesting drive along the Teno River is taken twice on Tuesday and Friday by a shared taxi, serving the little Sami villages along this beautiful route. Prices are similar to those charged by buses.

SEVETTIJÄRVI

One of the roads from Kaamanen heads eastwards along the shore of Lake Inarinjärvi to Sevettijärvi (Scolt Sami: Če'vetjäu'rr), in the north-east of the 'head' of Finland. It is mostly inhabited by a distinctive Lappish group called Scolt Lapps *(kolttalappalaiset)*. The women wear typical Russian scarfs, and on special occasions, a hat is worn under the scarf. Some of the Scolts speak Scoltish, Finnish and Russian. The Sevettijärvi region has more lakes per sq km than any other region in Finland. Very few trekkers explore this desolate wilderness, yet it is worth any effort you put into it.

Things to See

The orthodox **tsasouna**, built in 1951, is dedicated to Father Trifon from Petsamo (now part of Russia). The altar has several beautiful icons, some of which were brought from the Soviet-occupied monastery of Valamo. In front of the church is a wooden memorial to the dead who were left in Petsamo. The oldest graves have a wooden *grobu* above them, with a wooden bird attached. The church is open Monday to Friday from 10 am to 3 pm, but you may have to knock first at the warden's door.

Not far from the church, **Perinnetalo** is a small museum devoted to Scolt traditions. It's open weekdays from 9 am to 7 pm.

Organised Tours

The only person who takes tourists on guided tours is a Dutch man, Ernest Dixon. He has guided his 'Lapland Pulka Treks' and 'Lapland Ruska Treks' for over 30 years, and has the best local knowledge in the region. Ernest takes trekkers to local Lappish homes, will locate reindeer herds for photographers and provides food that he prepares over an open fire – he buys fresh salmon from the Lapps!

Write well beforehand to J Ernest Dixon, SF-99930 Sevettijärvi, Finland, or contact Travel North (☎ 31-023 537 7573), Duinlustparkweg 48 A, 2061 LD Bloemendaal, Holland.

Places to Stay

Sevettijärven Lomamajat (☎ 672 215) is right behind the church – follow the sign. The reception is in the private home. There's a lake, with clear water. Doubles are 130 mk, and four-bed huts with cooking facilities are 150 mk. *K-Valinta Nykänen* has one or two rooms for rent.

Farther south from Sevettijärvi are several holiday villages. The modern *Nili-Tuvat* (☎ 672 240), four km to the south, has several huts but is close to the road. There is a food kiosk there.

Some 26 km south of Sevettijärvi, *Kolttamajat* (☎ 673 531) has several modern huts (from 200 mk). There is good fishing in the nearby lake.

Places to Eat

It is advisable to buy your own food and prepare it either in your hut or while you trek. *Sevetin Baari* is the only place that offers meals, snacks and coffee. The only shop in the village, the K-Valinta Nykänen, has the usual selection of the less-expensive Pirkka products.

Getting There & Away

The nearest airport to Sevettijärvi is Kirkenes in Norway. From the airport, first take a bus to Kirkenes (no hitchhiking, as the airport is in a military area). The nearest Finnish airport is in Ivalo.

You can hitchhike from Ivalo, but traffic is sparse beyond the Kaamanen crossing. There is a post-bus connection on weekdays, leaving Ivalo at 3.15 pm and arriving in Sevettijärvi at 6.25 pm.

AROUND SEVETTIJÄRVI

Näätämö

Näätämö (Sami: Njauddám) is the last village before the Norwegian border along the Sevettijärvi route, and a popular Sunday shopping spot for Norwegians from across the border; there are three shops and 70 inhabitants. The village is situated on a bare plateau. You can start your trek south from Näätämö (see the Sevettijärvi section for details). The only place to stay is *Loma-Näätämö* (☎ 672 511). Cottages for one/two people are 130/160 mk. There is a fee for using the shower or the sauna.

Partakko

This small place (Sami: Päärtih) has a nice lakeside location. *Tshiuttajoen lomamökit* (☎ 673 163) has huts from 100 mk. The place rents boats for 50 mk per day. A sauna costs 20 mk per person.

Sevettijärvi Treks

Sevettijärvi to Kirakkajärvi This is the shortest route, and there are two huts along the way. You can walk the route in two days, or set a more leisurely pace and do it in three days. The route takes you across the rocky, hilly region on the other side of Lake Sevettijärvi. Cross the narrow strait just south of the Siitapirtti. Follow the route north-east, and you'll end up on the other side of Lake Sevettijärvi. Use the 1:20,000 map No 4911 for this route. At the other end, preferably at the western side of Lake Kirakka, you'll come to a minor road that will take you to the main road.

Näätämö to Sevettijärvi This exciting route starts at Näätämö and goes via Jankkila, Routasenkuru, Vätsäri, Tuulijärvi and Sollomisjärvi to Sevettijärvi, taking you to an area where very few people go. There are a few huts along the way, all clearly marked on major trekking maps. First head for Näätämö, right at the border. There is a marked path from there south to Jankkila house (14 km). The path is marked on the 1:20,000 map No 4913, as well as on the nature trail (stones piled on rocks etc). From Jankkila, along the Pakanajoki River, there is a path to a large lake, and you have the choice of two routes around the lake. The northern one is easier.

The beautiful gorge, Routasenkuru, is easy to find, as it extends north-south for over five km. You may camp near the camp-fire places, or stay at the border guards' hut, which has shelter for two to three trekkers. The following day, trek south along Routasenkuru Gorge to the Vätsäri Fells, then turn west again. There is no path, so have your compass ready. You'll find a mountain hut to the west of Vätsäri, and another at Tuulijärvi – one route has a path, the other does not. Farther west is *Sollomisjärvi* hut. From the hut, there is another short walk through the wilderness or a slightly longer trek along a path, back to Sevettijärvi.

Sevettijärvi to Nuorgam This is an established trekking route, and the most popular from Sevettijärvi. There are six mountain huts along the route, and you'll need the 1:50,000 maps Nos 4911 and 4913, available for 59 mk at Karttakeskus in Helsinki or Rovaniemi. There are two places to start the trek, the better one just north of Sevettijärvi, at Saunaranta. You'll see a sign reading 'Ahvenjärvi 5', and a trekking sign – 12 km to Opukasjärvi, 69 km to Lake Pulmankijärvi.

The mountain huts and their distances are *Opukasjärvi* (12 km), *Iisakkijärvi* (five km), a nameless hut (14 km), *Tsarajavrrik* (13 km), a nameless hut close to the border (20 km) and Pulmankijärvi (five km). From Pulmankijärvi, you can walk to Nuorgam along a road, or make a phone call from a local home for a taxi to Nuorgam village.

UTSJOKI

It would be misleading to call the village of Utsjoki (Sami: Ohcejohka) an attractive place, but as the northernmost municipality in Finland and with a relatively large Sami population, it has certain interest. There are 1550 people in the municipality, over half of whom are Sami.

Information

In the village of Utsjoki, Utsjoki Info (☎ 686 234) is jointly run by the municipality and Metsähallitus (the Forest & Park Service). There are maps for sale, and you can see the exhibition and browse through the slide collection. The office is open from 1 June to 30 September daily from 10 am to 8 pm. There are two banks, a post office and several shops in the village.

Kirkkotuvat

The Utsjoki Church, six km south from the village, and the *kirkkotuvat* (church huts), across the main road, are worth a look. The huts, old lodging facilities for long-distance visitors to the church, have been restored. Some huts are like museums. In summer, there is a café for the many visitors who stop here. The church itself offers little interest but it's open in summer.

Swimming & Sauna

The indoor swimming pool is generally open in the afternoon, Tuesday to Saturday. Swimming and sauna costs 15 mk.

Places to Stay & Eat

Utsjoki Camping (☎ 677 213), at the southern end of the village, has huts from 200 to 250 mk, and they accommodate four to five people each. There is a kitchen and coin-operated showers. The top-end *Utsjoen Matkailuhotelli* (☎ 677 121), behind the post office, has rooms from 240/340 mk. Lunch is available from 45 mk, all extras included.

For meals, check prices at *Tenohelmi*. *Tšarssi* promises 'pizza, food, café and music' and is essentially a place where young Samis learn to rock'n'roll.

Getting There & Away

The daily post bus leaves Rovaniemi each

morning (with later departures from Ivalo, Inari and Kaamanen) and reaches Utsjoki by 5 pm. There is an earlier bus on weekdays. The same bus returns from Polmak (Norway) and Nuorgam to Utsjoki. There is also a new bridge crossing from Norway at Utsjoki, and occasional shared-taxi transport from Karigasniemi village.

UTSJOKI TO KARIGASNIEMI

The narrow road No 9703 follows the Teno River, and is considered the most beautiful road in Finland. A taxi bus runs along the road on Tuesday and Friday (information is available at both ends), and will take people to places like Outakoski, the most genuine Sami village in Finland, and Nuvvus, with access to the holy Ailigas Fell. There are several places to stay, especially at the Utsjoki end of the route.

NUORGAM

Nuorgam (Sami: Njuorggan) is the John O'Groats of Finland, and that may be its only appeal. Some Finns are attracted to the idea of visiting the northernmost village of Finland. The commercial services, which include a bank, shops and a mail box, are scattered along the narrow main road. The last houses in Finland are tacky discount shops that sell cheap clothes to Norwegians. All prices here are in Norwegian kroner. Population is 200, the majority of whom are Sami.

The main attraction is the Teno River and its salmon. Most fishers gather near Boratbokcankoski and Alaköngäs rapids, some seven km south-west of Nuorgam.

There are also a few minor tourist attractions, such as the Kuninkaan kivi (King's stone – a royal signature from 1766, carved on a rock by the king of Sweden) and the Museotie (Museum Road – a narrow dirt road along the riverside). Nuorgam is also the northern end of a trekking route from Sevettijärvi.

Places to Stay

Holiday villages in Nuorgam and along the river are booming due to good fishing pros-

pects along the Teno River. There are almost 10 possibilities along the road from Utsjoki to Nuorgam. These places have mid-range prices, cater mostly to people fishing the Teno River, and are usually open from June to August only. They are listed here in geographical order from Vetsikko (with the distance from the Utsjoki bridge given in parentheses) to Nuorgam.

Vetsikon lomamökit (☎ 678 803) has 10 four-bed cottages at the riverside in Vetsikko. Huts are 150 to 260 mk. There is a sauna, boats for rent and a canteen (12.9 km).

Vetsituvat (☎ 678 805) nearby has only five huts and they are more expensive, from 240 mk (12.5 km).

Kiviniemi (☎ 678 812) a bit farther has huts at 160 to 280 mk (17.9 km).

Lohiranta (☎ 678 919) is at an isolated place on the hillside, with huts available at similar prices (25.4 km).

Ala-Jalven tuvat (☎ 678 605) is most magnificently located at the popular fishing rapids of Alaköngäs. There are two/four-bed huts at 150/170 mk (35.5 km).

Alaköngäs (☎ 678 612) just nearby is on the hillside but near the food kiosk. Huts are 130 to 180 mk (36.3 km).

Koskipirtit (☎ 678 620) is also in the area of the rapids on the hillside, with huts at 150 mk (36.8 km).

Matkakoti Suomenrinne (☎ 678 306) is a guesthouse in the village of Nuorgam. There are 20 beds, and it is only open from 10 June to 10 August.

Nuorgamin lomakeskus (☎ 678 312) is geographically the top-end business in Finland. There are rooms at 150 mk and four-bed huts from 250 mk. Try to arrive before 9 pm. There are boats, fishing permits and a sauna here.

Places to Eat

Tenon lohikellari is a roadside café (36.6 km east from the Utsjoki bridge) that serves mostly meat dishes, although some fish is available; after all, almost everyone here catches their own fish. In Nuorgam itself, *Staalonpesä* is a very nice restaurant with beer and meals, but it ain't cheap. There's sometimes a dance, and even a sauna.

Getting There & Away

A daily post bus serves Nuorgam from Rovaniemi, with an earlier bus on weekdays. When coming from Norway, it is a two km walk from the Norwegian village of Polmak to the border, and another four km to the village of Nuorgam.

NORDKAPP

Nordkapp (North Cape), a high, rugged coastal plateau at 71°10'21", is Europe's northernmost point. There are few visitors to Lapland who don't dream of extending their visit to Finnmark in northern Norway, and quite a few undertake the long journey to the top of Europe.

Finland is the choice of most bus tours from Europe for the transit journey. Reasons for this are obvious. Finland has good, well-maintained roads. There are no mountains, no tunnels, no serpentine roads, no expensive ferries across fjords. Norwegians themselves whisk through Sweden and Finland on their way from southern Norway to Finnmark. Prices are generally lower in Finland than in Norway, and there are good hotels and roadhouses along the way.

A visit to Nordkapp is certainly one of the current crazes among central Europeans. Queues for the ferry are long and the whole place is sometimes simply too crowded to be appreciated.

Nordkapp hallen is the touristy complex with exhibits, eateries, souvenir shops and a post office. An entry fee of 130 kr is payable (there's a discount if you arrive before 6 pm). Champagne, caviar and a midnight buffet are served at very steep prices.

Getting There & Away

Nordkapp can be visited in 30 hours from Rovaniemi. Depart from Rovaniemi at 11.20 am, change buses at Lakselv (Norway) at 7.15 pm and arrive just before midnight at Nordkapp. After 75 minutes at the northernmost fog in Europe, you'll be happy to return with the same bus. This bus route is only run from early June to mid-August. For approximately 500 kr, you will get a return ticket from the Finnish border, including ferry trips.

From Karigasniemi, you can drive via Karasjok (the Sami centre) and Lakselv, a small settlement on the shores of the Arctic Sea. From Hetta (in Enontekiö), you can drive via Kautokeino (another Sami centre) and Alta (which features rock paintings and an excellent museum, and several hotels).

Glossary

You may encounter some of the following terms and abbreviations during your travels in Finland. See also the Language section at the end of the Facts about the Country chapter, and the Food section in the Facts for the Visitor chapter.

aapa – open bog
Ahvenanmaa – Åland
aitta – small wooden storage shed in a traditional farmhouse, used for accommodating guests
Ala- – Lower, in place names, as opposed to Yli-, or Upper
ämpäri – bucket
asema – station

baari – simple restaurant serving light lager and some snacks (also called *kapakka)*
bruk – early ironworks precinct (Swedish)

erämaa – wilderness

feresi – old Karelian dress worn daily by working women, now used in North Karelia tourist traps

grilli – small hamburger stand or other junk-food outlet

halla – soil frost, typically a night frost in early summer that often destroys crops or berries
hämärä – twilight
hankikanto – springtime snow-cover solid enough to walk on
harju – ridge or esker, formed during the Ice Age
havupuu – evergreen coniferous tree.
heinä – hay
hiidenkirnu – literally 'devil's churn'; a round-shaped well formed by water and small rocks and the dramatic force of moving ice during the late years of the Ice Age
hilla – highly appreciated orange Arctic cloudberry, which grows on marshlands (also *lakka* or *suomuurain)*
honka – pine

ilmavoimat – Air Force

jää – ice
jääkausi – Ice Age; prehistoric period, some 10,000 years ago, when all of Finland was covered by a thick ice layer
jäätie – ice road; a road across a lake in winter
jäkälä – lichen
järvi – lake
joiku – sung lyric poem, *yoik* among Samis
jokamiehenoikeus – right of public access
joki – river
joulu – Christmas
joulupukki – Santa Claus
juhannus – see *Midsummer*
juoksuhauta – wartime trench

kaamos – twilight time, the period of darkness over the Arctic Circle when the sun doesn't rise at all
kahvila – café
kahvio – cafeteria, usually simpler than a *kahvila*
kaira – wilderness
kala – fish
Kalevala – the national epic of Finland; *Kalevala* combines poetry, runes and folk tales with various personalities and biblical themes, such as creation and the fight between good and evil
kalmisto – old graveyard, especially pre-Medieval or Orthodox
kämppä – wilderness hut, cabin
kansallispuisto – national park
kantele – traditional Karelian string instrument, similar to a harp (also *kannel)*
kapakka – see *baari*
katu – street
kauppa – shop
kauppahalli – indoor market
kaupunki – town or city

kaura – oats

kelirikko – season of bad roads after the snow has melted

kelo – dead, standing, barkless tree, usually pine

kioski – small stand that sells sweets, newspapers and food items

kirkonkylä – any village that has a church

kokko – bonfire, lit during Midsummer festivals

köngäs – rapids, waterfall

korpi – wilderness

korsu – log bunker used as accommodation by soldiers during WWII

koski – rapids

kota – traditional Lappish hut, resembling a tepee or wigwam (from the Finnish *koti*)

kotimaa – 'home country'

koulu – school

kruunu – crown, krone (Scandinavian currency)

kuksa – Lappish cup, carved from a burl, gnarl or burr

kunta – commune or municipality, the smallest administrative unit in Finland

kuntopolku – 'fitness path'; jogging track in summer, skiing track in winter

kuusi – spruce

kylä – village

laakso – valley

lääni – province

laavu – permanent or temporary open-air shelter used by trekkers

lahti – bay

laituri – pier

lakka – cloudberry

lama – recession

lampi – pond, small lake

lappalainen – a Sami person

Lappi – Lapland

lappilainen – Laplander, either Finn or Sami

lehtipuu – deciduous tree

lestadiolaisuus – a strict Lutheran sect in north Finland

liiteri – shelter for firewood

linja-autoasema – bus station

lintu – bird

lohi – salmon

lossi – a small ferry for travel across a strait

luontopolku – nature trail

luppokota – see *kota*

maa – country, earth, land, area

maakunta – a traditional region, with tribal or cultural rather than administrative ties as opposed to a *lääni*

mäki – hill

mänty – pine tree, the most common of Finnish trees

majoitus – accommodation

makuupussi – sleeping bag

marja – berry

markka – Finnish unit of currency (plural *markkaa*, abbreviation *mk*)

Matkahuolto – bus station (name of the national bus line of Finland)

matkakoti – guesthouse, inn

matkustajakoti – guesthouse, inn

metsä – forest

Midsummer – (or *juhannus)* the longest day of the year, celebrated at the end of June on Friday evening and Saturday

mökki – cottage

mono – skiing shoe (plural *monot)*

muikku – vendace, a typical lake fish

mummonmökki – 'grandma's cottage'

museo – museum

mustikka – blueberry

nähtävyys – tourist attraction

niemi – cape

niliaitta – a small store on a pole

nuoska – wet snow

nuotio – campfire

ohra – barley

öljy – oil

opas – guide (person) or guidebook

opastuskeskus – information centre, usually of a national park

opiskelija – student

Oy – abbreviation for Osakeyhtiö, often seen after company names (the equivalent of Limited in English); in Swedish it's Ab, short for Aktiebolag

pää – head, end

paja – workshop

pakkanen – below-freezing weather

pelto – cultivated field
petäjä – pine
peura – deer
pihlaja – rowan (tree)
pikkujoulu – 'Little Christmas', an informal party arranged by companies or schools
pirtti – small room in a traditional Finnish farmhouse
pitäjä – see *kunta*
pitkospuu – boardwalk constructed over wetlands or swamps
pitopöytä – large buffet table
polku – path
polttopuu – firewood
poro – reindeer
poroerotus – reindeer roundup, held annually in designated places around Lapland
poronhoitoalue – reindeer herding area
poronkusema – Lappish (slightly vulgar) unit of distance: how far a reindeer walks before relieving itself
Praasniekka – also *Prazniek*; Orthodox religious festival that sometimes includes a *ristisaatto* to a lake, where a sermon takes place
pubi – pub serving strong alcohol and very little food
puisto – park
pulkka – boat sledge
puomi – boom
puro – stream
puu – tree, wood
puukko – sheath knife (a useful tool on treks)

rakovalkea – log fire
ranta – shore
räntä – wet snow (snowing)
rauhoitettu – protected
ravintola – restaurant which also serves as a bar
reppu – backpack
retkeilymaja – youth hostel, hostel
retki – excursion
revontulet – Northern lights, literally 'fires of the fox'
riista – game
rinkka – rucksack
ristinsaatto – an annual Orthodox festival

to commemorate a regional saint, involving a procession of the cross
roskakori – rubbish bin
rotko – gorge
routa – ground frost, causes *kelirikko*
ruis – rye
runo – poem
Ruotsi – Sweden
rupla – rouble (Russian)
ruska – period in autumn (fall) when leaves turn red and yellow
ruukki – early ironworks precinct (see also *bruk*)

sää – weather (also *säätila)*
saari – island
sääski – mosquito (in Lapland)
sähkö – electricity
Saksa – Germany
salmi – strait
salo – island
sauva – skiing stocks
savotta – logging site
savusauna – traditional Finnish smoke sauna with no chimney, just a small outlet for smoke
seita – holy idol or shrine in Lapland
selkä – lake
sieni – mushroom
sora – gravel
sota – war
sotilasalue – military area
SRM – Suomen Retkeilymajajärjesto, or Youth Hostel Association of Finland
suo – swamp, bog, marsh
suomalainen – Finnish, Finn
Suomi – Finland
suomu – gill

taajama – modern village centre, or any densely populated area
taisteluhauta – trench
taival – track, trail
takka – fireplace (inside a house)
talo – house or building
tanssilava – dance floor or stage
Tapaninpäivä – Boxing Day
teltta – tent
tervas – old pine tree stump with a high tar content and a distinctive smell; it burns so

well, Finnish trekkers use it to light fires, even in wet weather (also *tervaskanto*)

tie – road

tori – market square

tsasouna – small prayer hall used by the Orthodox faith all over Finland (also *tšasouna*)

tukki – log

tulva – flood

tunturi – fell, a hill in Lapland

tuohi – birch bark

tupa – the largest room of the main building in a traditional farm

turve – peat

uimahalli – indoor pool

uistin – lure (in fishing)

uitto – log floating

vaara – danger, or wooded hill (typical in North Karelia)

vaellus – trek (verb *vaeltaa*)

vaivaisukko – a pauper statue outside many of the old wooden churches used as a receptacle for church donations

valaistu latu – illuminated skiing track

valtio – state, or government

vandrarhem – youth hostel (Swedish)

vehnä – wheat

Venäjä – Russia

vero – tax

vesi – water, sometimes lake

vilja – grain

virasto – state or local government office building

vuori – mountain

vyöhyke – zone

yliopisto – university

yö – night

Appendix – Alternative Place Names

The following place names are listed alphabetically according to the Finnish:

Finnish-Swedish

Ahvenanmaa – Åland
Häme – Tavastland
Hämeenlinna – Tavastehus
Hamina – Fredrikshamn
Hanko – Hangö
Helsinki – Helsingfors
Hiittinen – Hitis
Houtskari – Houtskär
Inkoo – Ingå
Järvenpää – Träskända
Jepua– Jeppo
Karjaa – Karis
Kaskinen – Kaskö
Kemiö – Kimito
Kirkkonummi – Kyrkslätt
Kokkola – Karleby
Korppoo – Korpo
Kristiinankaupunki – Kristinestad
Kruunupyy – Kronoby
Kustavi – Gustavs
Lappeenranta – Villmanstrand
Lapinjärvi – Lappträsk
Lapväärtti – Lappfjärd
Linnamäki – Borgbacken
Lohja – Lojo
Loviisa – Lovisa
Maalahti – Malax
Maksamaa – Maxmo
Mustasaari – Korsholm

Mustio – Svartå
Naantali – Nådendal
Närpiö – Närpes
Nauvo – Nagu
Oravainen – Oravais
Pännäinen – Bennäs
Parainen – Pargas
Pernaja – Pernå
Pietarsaari – Jakobstad
Pinjainen – Billnäs
Pohja – Pojo
Pohjanmaa – Österbotten
Pori – Björneborg
Porvoo – Borgå
Pyhtää – Pyttis
Raasepori – Raseborg
Raippaluoto – Replot
Rauma – Raumo
Siipyy – Sideby
Sipoo – Sibbo
Siuntio – Sjundeå
Sulva – Solf
Taalintehdas – Dalsbruk
Tammisaari – Ekenäs
Tampere – Tammerfors
Tenhola – Tenala
Tiukka – Tjöck
Turku – Åbo
Uusikaarlepyy – Nykarleby
Uusikaupunki – Nystad
Uusimaa – Nyland
Vaasa – Vasa
Vöyri – Vörå

Index

MAPS

Air Routes, Domestic 105
Åland Province 163

Ferry Routes, International 101
Finland 13
    Central Finland 289
    Eastern Finland 314
    Finland Provinces 27

Häme 256
Hämeenlinna 258
Hamina 236
Hanko 145
Heinävesi, Around 338
Helsinki 116-17
    Helsinki, Around 136
    Helsinki Central 124
Hossa 454

Ilomantsi, Around 383
Imatra 249
Inari 515

Joensuu 357
    Joensuu, Around 361
Jyväskylä 291

Kainuu 440
Kajaani 443
Kaskinen 411
Kemi 480
Kemijärvi 497
Kevo Nature Reserve 519

Kokkola 422
Kotka 230
Kristinestad 408
Kuhmo 447
Kuopio 344
Kuusamo 456
Kymi River Valley 234

Lahti 301
Lapland
    North-East Lapland 504
    South-East Lapland 495
    West Lapland 477
Lappeenranta 244
Lemmenjoki National Park 517
Lieksa 366
    Lieksa, Around 368
Loviisa 159

Mariehamn 166
Mikkeli 329

Naantali 194
North Karelia 355
Nurmes 379

Oulu 430
    Oulu, Around 435
    Oulu, Province 429
Ox Road (South Häme) 266

Pallas-Ounastunturi National
    Park Region 490

Pietarsaari 416
Pohjanmaa 392
Pori 213
Porvoo 155
Punkaharju 322
Pyhä-Luosto Region 499

Rauma 221
Route 66 (North Häme) 283
Rovaniemi 471
Ruka & Karhunkierros 459

Saariselkä 508
Savonlinna 316
    Savonlinna, Around 321
Seinäjoki 399
Suomenlinna 134

Tammisaari 148
Tampere 270
Tornio 478
Turku & Pori Province 184
Turku 186
Turku Region 193

Uusikaupunki 209
Uusimaa 143
    West Uusimaa 151

Vaasa 394
Vammala 226

TEXT

Map references are in **bold** type

Aalto, Alvar 31-2, 123, 137,
    219, 250, 288, 290, 292, 294,
    303, 398, 400, 404, 405, 472
Äänekoski 298
Aavasaksa 483
accommodation 71-5
    wilderness huts 84-5, 453, 455,
    458, 464-5, 488-9, 491, 493,
    500, 509, 512, 514, 518, 519
activities 81-91
    see also canoeing, cycling,
    rafting, rowing, skiing,
    trekking

Agricola, Mikael 15, 35
Ahmovaara 377-8
Ähtäri 298
Ahvenanmaa, see Åland
Ahveninen 360
Ahvenkoski 233
Ainola 141
air travel
    to/from Finland 92-6
    within Finland 105-6, **105**
Airisto 200
Äkäslompolo 485
Ala-Vuokki 453
Alajärvi 405
Åland 162-182, **163**

Alatornio 479
Alavus 404
Älgö 149
Alikartano 160-1
Ameriikka 353
Ämmänsaari 451-2
Änäkäinen 371-2
Anár, see Inari
Anderson, Amos 206
Angeli 518
Angelniemi 205
Anjala 239
Anjalankoski 239-40
Aquatic Nature Trail, see
    Vesiluontopolku Route

architecture 31-2, 123, 237, 240, 292, 303
Arwidsson, AI 18
Asikkala 306-7
Askainen 198-9
Askola 161
Asterholma 179
Astuvansalmi 334
Aulanko 259-60
Aurajoki River 185
Avvil, *see* Ivalo

Bear's Path 370
Bengtskär 144
Bennäs 416
Bergö 413
Billnäs 152
birds 26, 284, 437
birdwatching 26, 137
    Hailuoto Island 434
    Heinolan Lintutarha 308
    Herrön 175
    Lake Kutajärvi 305
    Lake Sysmäjärvi 360
    Linnansaari National Park 324
    Lumijoki 438
    Puurijärvi & Isosuo National Park 220
    Rääkkylä 363
    Salo 204
    Siikalahti 253
    Svanvik 144
    Valtavaara 462
Björköby 398
Björneborg, *see* Pori
boat travel, *see* ferries
boating 112, 370
    see also canoeing, rafting, rowing
Bomarsund 177-8
books 35, 62-3, 80
    history 62-3
    travel guides 63
border crossings
    to/from Norway 97-8
    to/from Russia 98-9
    to/from Sweden 96
Borgboda 176
Brahe, Per 16, 183, 185, 243, 315, 333, 365, 407, 425, 440
Brahelinna 334
Brändö 179
Bullerås 397-8
bus travel
    to/from Norway 98
    to/from Russia 99
    to/from Sweden 97
    within Finland 106
business hours 57-8

canoeing 88-90
    Central Finland 89
    Jongunjoki River 372
    Kainuu 89
    Karstula 299
    Kitkajoki River 461
    Kuusamo & Lapland 89-90
    Lake Koitere 390
    Lappea 485
    Lätäseno River 492
    Lemmenjoki River 517
    Muonionjoki River 488
    North Karelia 89
    Oulankajoki River 461-2
    Ounasjoki River 488
    Pankasaari Route 372
    Pohjanmaa 89
    rentals 88
    river routes 88
    Ruunaa 370
    Saramojoki River 381
    Savo 89
    south Finland 88-9
    Tjöck 410
    Ulpukka 326
    Vaikkojoki River 378
    Vesiluontopolku Route 335
car & motorbike travel 109-11
castles & forts
    Borgboda Fort 176
    Brahelinna 334
    Fort Elisabeth 231
    Fort Slava 231
    Fortress of Honour 231
    Häme Castle 257
    Hamina Fortress 237
    Hiidenvuori 242
    Kajaani Castle 442
    Kastelholm Castle 176-7
    Kuusisto Fort 199-200
    Linnavuori 328
    Olavinlinna Castle 315, 317
    Rapolan Linnavuori 263
    Raseborg 150
    Retuutti 242
    Rosen Fort 159
    Svartholm Fort 159-60
    Turku Castle 185
    Ungern Fort 159
Central Finland 288-312, **289**
churches 122, 156, 158, 175, 178, 179, 180, 187, 207, 211, 235, 260, 271, 295, 296, 326, 345
cinema 36-7
climate 24
Crown Park 250
culture 37-42
currency 54

customs 54
cycling 85-7, 133, 282
    Åland 86
    east Finland 86-7
    Pohjanmaa 86
    south Finland 86

Dalsbruk 206
dance 35
Dånö Island 173
deer 450, 451
Degerby 181
Degersand 171
design 33
Djävulsberget 177
Dragsfjärd 206
drinks 76-8

Eckerö 169-72
economy 28-30
education 31
Ekenäs Archipelago National Park 149
Ekenäs, *see* Tammisaari
electricity 62
electronic mail services 61-2
Elimäki 238-9
Ellivuori 227-8
embassies 52-3
Engel, Carl Ludvig 31, 113
Enklinge 180
Enonkoski 325
entertainment 78-9
Eräjärvi 278
Espoo 135-6
Eura 219
European Union 23
Evijärvi 420

Fagervik 153-4
fax services 61
ferries 100-4, 112, 132
    international routes 100-4, 132, **101**
    to/from Estonia 103-4
    to/from Germany 104
    to/from Poland 104
    to/from Russia 104
    to/from Sweden 100-3
    within Finland 112
festivals 58-60, 124, 214, 223, 232, 275, 300, 310, 318, 346, 358, 363, 367, 380, 384, 393, 398, 402, 420, 448, 480, 484, 507
Finlandia 35
Finlandisation 11, 22
Finström 172

fishing 90
  Änäkäinen 371
  Halti Fell 493
  Hossa 453-55
  Korvatunturi 502
  Kylmäluoma 455
  Lake Hoikan Kylkeinen 387
  Lake Miekojärvi 483
  Lappea 485
  Lätäseno River 492
  Lemmenjoki River 517
  Molkojärvi 486
  Myössäjärvi 514
  Peurajärvi 382
  Ruunaa 370
  Syöte 464
  Syväjärvi 449
  Tjöck 410
  Uittotupa 332
  Vilkaharju 327
  Yli-Vuokki 451
Fiskars 152
Fladalandet 149
flora & fauna 25-6, 68, 69, 324
Föglö 181
food 75-77
forestry 29
Forssa 267-8
Fort Elisabeth 231
Fort Slava 231
Fortress of Honour 231
forts, see castles & forts

Gallén-Kallela, Akseli 34, 136,
  214, 225, 257, 284-5
Gallen-Kallela, Jorma 214
Galtby 201
genealogy 90-1
geography 24
Geta 172-3
Getabergen 173
gipsies 41
Godby 172
golf 90
government 26-8
Gustav Vasa 15, 113

Haapamäki 296-7
Haaparanta, see Haparanda
Haihara 273
Hailuoto Island 434-6
Hakoinen 261
Halikko 204-5
Halikonlahti Bay 204
Halti 493
Halti Fell 493
Haltiala 122-3
Häme 255-87, 256
Häme Castle 257

Hämeenkyrö 278-9
Hämeenlinna 255-60, 258
Hamina 235-8, 236
Hamina Fortress 237
Hammarland 173-4
Hamnö 182
Hanko 142-7, 145
Haparanda 476
Harjavalta 217, 218
Härkätie, see Ox Road
Härmä 403-4
Hartola 308-9
Hatanpää 273
Hattuvaara 386-7
Hauensuoli 144
Hauho 260
Haukipudas 436
health 64-9
  insurance 64-5
  medical problems & treatment
    66-9
  medical services 118
Heinävesi 337, 338
Heinola 307-8
Heinolan Harju 308
Heinolan Lintutarha 308
Heinoniemi 364
Hellsö 182
Helsinki 113-41, 116-17, 124,
  136
  architecture 123
  churches 122
  getting around 132-3
  getting there & away 131-2
  history 113-14
  information 114-18
  museums 118-22
  places to eat 127-30
  places to stay 124-7
  Senate Square 113, 123
  shopping 130-1
  tours 123-4
Helsinki parish area 139
Helsinki Square 223
Helvetinjärvi National Park 285
Hepoköngäs 451
Hetta 491-2
Heureka 138
Hiidenvuori 242
Hiittinen 207
hiking, see trekking
Himanka 424
Himos 296
history 12-24
  Civil War 19
  Continuation War 21
  Crimean War 18, 158, 162, 177
  Great Northern War 17, 154,
    162, 178, 208

  Gustavian Wars 18
  independence 19-20
  Kekkonen years, the 22-3
  Russian Rule 18
  Swedish Rule 15
  Winter War 21
  WWII 20-1
hitching 111-12
Högholmen 149
Högsåra 207
holidays, see public holidays
Hollola 304-6
Hossa 453-55, 454
Houtskär 201-2
Hyrylä 140
Hyrynsalmi 450-1
Hytermä 327
Hyvinkää 154-5

ice hockey 277
icebreaker cruises 476, 480-1
Ii 436
Iisalmi 350-2
Iittala 261
Iitti 241-2
Ikaalinen 279-80
Ikaalisten Kylpylä 279
Ilmajoki 402
Ilomantsi 382-90, 383
Imatra 248-51, 249
Imatrankoski 250
Inari 466, 515-16, 515
Ingbyberget 174
Iniö 202
Inkoo 153-4
Irjanne 215-16
Iso-Palonen 450
Isojärvi National Park 311
Isokyrö 402-3
Ivalo 505

Jaala 242-3
Jakobstad, see Pietarsaari
Jalasjärvi 407
Janakkala 261-2
Jansson, Tove 35, 272
Järämä 492
Järsö 167
Järvenpää 139
Jeppo 415
Jepua, see Jeppo
Joensuu 356-60, 357, 361
Jokioinen 268
Jomala 174
Jongunjoki River 372
Joutsa 310
Julma Ölkky 463
Juntusranta 453
Juoksenki 483

Jurmo 179
Juuka 375-6, 378
Juuma 460
Juva 335-6
Jyväskylä 288-95, **291**

Kaamanen 518-19
Kaapelitehdas 121
Kaarina 199-200
Kainuu 439-55, **440**
Kajaani 439-44, **443**
Kajaani Castle 442
Kajaaninjoki River 442
Kalajoki 424-5
Kalanti 211
Kalevala 18, 35, 62, 285, 354
Kalevala (theme park) 448
Kalevala Forum 364
Kallenautio 284
Kalliojoki 450
Kangasala 280
Kankaanpää 216-17
Karelia, *see* North Karelia, South Karelia
Karesuvanto 492
Karhunkierros Trekking Route 458-60
Karigasniemi 520
Käringsund 170
Karjaa 151
Karjala, *see* North Karelia
Karkali Nature Reserve 153
Karkku 227
Karleby, *see* Kokkola
Karstula 299
Karvio 337-8
Kaskinen 410, **411**
Kaskö, *see* Kaskinen
Kasnäs 206-7
Kastelholm Castle 176-7
Kastelli 426-7
Kasurila 349
Kattby 173
Kauhajoki 406
Kauhava 404
Kaunisnurmi 240-1
Kaunissaari 231
Kaupunginlahti Bay 208
Kausala 242
Kaustinen 420-1
Kauttua 219
Käylä 461
Kekkonen, Urho K 22, 441
Kelvänsaari 375
Kelvenne Island 306
Kemi 480-2, **480**
Kemijärvi 496-8, **497**
Keminmaa 482
Kempele 436-7

Kerimäki 326-7
Kerma 338
Kesälahti 364-5
Keuruu 296
Kevo Nature Reserve 519, **519**
Kiekinkoski 450
Kiilopää 507
Kiiminki 437
Kilpelänkangas 450
Kilpisjärvi 492-4
Kimito 203, 205-6
Kimo 414
King's Road 142, 203, 235
Kirkkonummi 137-8
Kitee 363-4
Kitkajoki River 461
Kittilä 486
Klaus Kurjen tie 282
Klobbskat 398
Koillismaa 455-65
Koivusuo Nature Reserve 387
Kökar 181-2
Kokemäenjoki River 212, 217-18, 220, 227
Kokemäki 217
Kokemäki River 216
Kokkola 421-3, **422**
Kolari 485
Koli 374-5
Koljonvirta 352
Kolkanlahti 299
Kolovesi National Park 326
Köngäs 487
Konginkangas 300
Korkeakoski 284
Korkeasaari 122
Korouoma 496
Korpikylien tie 381, 450
Korpilahti 311-12
Korppoo 201
Korsholm 393, 397
Korsnäs 412
Korvatunturi 502
Koski 202
Kotka 229-33, **230**
Kotkansaari 229
Koukkela 212
Kourukoski 382
Kovjoki 415
Kouvola 240-1
Köyliö 219-20
Kristiinankaupunki, *see* Kristinestad
Kristinestad 407-9, **408**
Kronoby 416
Kruunupyy, *see* Kronoby
Kuhankuono 192
Kuhmo 446-9, **447**
Kuhmoinen 310-11

Kuivajärvi 451
Kukkolankoski 480
Kukouri 231
Kullaa 216
Kullaanjoki 216
Kumlinge 179-80
Kuopio Town 343-49, **344**
Kuortane 404-5
Kurikka 406-7
Kuru 282
Kustavi Archipelago 207-8
Kustavi Island 202
Kuusamo 455-8, **456**
Kuusisto Fort 199-200
Kuusisto Island 200
Kvarnbo 175-6
Kvevlax 398
Kylmäluoma 455
Kymi River Valley 229-43, **234**
Kyrkoby 171-2
Kyröskoski waterfall 279

Laajalahti 137
Lahti 300-4, **301**
Laihia 401-2
Laitila 211-12
Lake Hoikan Kylkeinen 387
Lake Jerisjärvi 488-9
Lake Koitere 390
Lake Kutajärvi 305
Lake Lohjanjärvi 152
Lake Luirojärvi 511
Lake Miekojärvi 483
Lake Mujejärvi 382
Lake Näsijärvi 274-5
Lake Päijänne 300-12
Lake Pieksäjärvi 336
Lake Pielinen 373-82
Lake Pitkälampi 252
Lake Puurijärvi 220
Lake Pyhäjärvi 219, 242, 274
Lake Rautavesi 227
Lake Stortträsket 149
Lake Sysmäjärvi 360
Lake Syväjärvi 449
Lake Vietonen 483
Lake Viinijärvi 362
Lake Virmajärvi 387
Lammala 206
Långbergsöda 176
Langinkoski 231
language 12, 18, 43-51
    courses 123
    Fell Sami 469
    Finnish 43-7
    Inari Sami 469-70
    Sami 469-70
    Scolt Sami 470
    Swedish 43, 47-51

Lapinjärvi 161
Lapinjoki River 219
Lapinlahti 349-50
Lapland 466-524
  north-east Lapland **504**
  south-east Lapland **495**
  west Lapland **477**
Lappea 484-5
Lappeenranta 243-7, **244**
Lappfjärd 410
Lappi 219
Lappo 179
Lappohja 144
Lapua 403
Larsmo 415-16
Lätäseno River 492
Lauhavuori National Park 405-6
Laukaa 294-5
laundry 62
Leammi, *see* Lemmenjoki
  National Park
Lehmäsaari 231
Leineperi 216
Leiviskä, Juha 32, 240
Lemi 248
Lemland 174-5
Lemmenjoki National Park
  516-18, **517**
Lemmenjoki River 517
Lempäälä 280
Lemu 198
Lenin, Vladimir 19, 268
Lentiira 449
Lentuankoski 449
Leppävirta 340-1
Levi 487-8
libraries 57
Liedenpohja 286-7
Lieksa (region) 367-73, **368**
Lieksa (town) 365-7, **366**
Liesjärvi National Park 265
Liljendal 161
Liminka 437
Liminka Bay 437
Linnamäki 156
Linnansaari Island 324
Linnansaari National Park 324-5
Linnavuori 328
Lintula 339
literature 35
Lohiniva 487
Lohja 152-3
Lohtaja 423-4
Lönnrot, Elias 12, 18, 35, 441
Loppi 262
Louhisaari 198
Loviisa 158-60
Lövö 178-9
Luhanka 310

Lumijoki 438
Lumparland 175
Luonnonmaa 196
Luostarinmäki 185-7
Luosto 498-500
Lusto 320-3
Luumäki 247
Luvia 216

Maakalla 425
Maalahti, *see* Malax
Maksamaa, *see* Maxmo
Malax 412-13
Malla Nature Park 493
Mannerheim, CGE 19, 20, 119,
  198, 262, 328
Mäntsälä 160-1
Mänttä 297
Mäntyharju 332-3
maps 63
Mariehamn 165-9, **166**
Martinselkonen 453
Martti 502
Marttila 202
Masku 198
Maxmo 413
media 63-4
Meekonjärvi 493
Merimasku 199
Messilä 304-5
Midsummer 60
Mikkeli 328-32, **329**
Modermagan 149
Möhkö 388
Molkojärvi 486-7
money 54-5
  bargaining 55
  costs 54-5, 66
  taxes 55
  tipping 55
Moomin World 195
motorbike travel, *see* car &
  motorbike travel
Mouhu 333
Muhos 438
Munsala 415
Muonio 488
Muonionjoki River 488
Muotkatunturit 519
museums 118, 122, 134-6, 139,
  149, 152, 160, 165, 167, 185,
  187-8, 206, 245, 257, 262,
  268, 272-3, 290, 365, 393,
  397, 431-2
music 35-6
Mustila 238
Mustio 153
Mutalahti 389

Muumimaailma 195-6
Muurame 294
Mynämäki 207
Myössäjärvi 514-15
Myyrmäki 138

Naantali 194-8, **194**
Näätämö 521
Naisvuori 330
Näkkälä 492
Näkkäläjärvi 492
Napapiiri 475-6
Napue 403
Närpes 410-12
Närpiö, *see* Närpes
Näsby 201
national parks & wilderness
  areas
  Crown Park 250
  Ekenäs Archipelago National
    Park 149
  Helvetinjärvi National Park 285
  Isojärvi National Park 311
  Karkali Nature Reserve 153
  Kevo Nature Reserve 519
  Koivusuo Nature Reserve 387
  Kolovesi National Park 326
  Lauhavuori National Park 405-6
  Lemmenjoki National Park
    516-18
  Liesjärvi National Park 265
  Linnansaari National Park 324-5
  Malla Nature Park 493
  Nuuksio National Park 137
  Oulanka National Park 458
  Päijänne National Park 306
  Pallas-Ounastunturi National
    Park 488, 489, 492
  Patvinsuo National Park 369
  Petkeljärvi National Park 388-9
  Puurijärvi & Isosuo National
    Park 220
  Pyhä-Häkki National Park 299
  Pyhätunturi National Park 498
  Ramsholmen Natural Park 149
  Ranua Wildlife Park 494
  Riisitunturi National Park 496
  Rokua 438
  Saariselkä Wilderness (Urho
    Kekkonen National Park)
    508-14, **508**
  Seitseminen National Park 282
  Torronsuo National Park 267
Nauvo 200-1
Nellim 514
Niirala 363
Nokia 280-1
Nordkapp 483, 524
Norrby 175, 202

North Karelia 354-90, **355**
Nousiainen 198
Nunnanlahti 377
Nuorgam 523-4
Nurmes 378-81, **379**
Nurmi, Paavo 20
Nurmijärvi 371-2
Nuuksio National Park 137
Nuutajärvi 264-5
Nuvvus 523
Nykarleby 414-15
Nyland, see Uusimaa
Nystad, see Uusikaupunki

Olavinlinna Castle 315-17
Olos 488
Onkiniemi 309
Önningeby 174
Oravainen, see Oravais
Oravais 414
Orimattila 161
Orivesi 282-4
Orrdals Klint 162, 176
Österbotten, see Pohjanmaa
Ostrobothnia, see Pohjanmaa
Otaniemi 137
Oulanka National Park 458
Oulankajoki River 461-2
Oulu Town 428-34, **430**, **435**
Oulu Province 428-65, **429**
Oulujoki River 438
Ounasjoki River 488
Ounasvaara 473
Outakoski 523
Outokumpu 360-2
Överby 172
Överö 181
Ox Road 202-3, 265-8, **266**

Paalasmaa 376-7
Paateri 373
Padasjoki 310
Päijänne National Park 306
Paimio 203
Paimionjoki River 202
painting 33-5
Pakasaivo 485
Paljakka 451
Pallas-Ounastunturi National
  Park 488-92, **490**
Pallastunturi Fell 489
Palokki 338-9
Paltaniemi 444-5
Panelia 219
Pankasaari Route 372
Pännäinen, see Bennäs
Papinniemi 254
Parainen 200
Parattula 202

Parikkala 252
Pattijoki 426
Patvinsuo National Park 369
Pello 484
Pentikmäki 494
Perinnekylä 286
Pernå, see Pernaja
Pernaja 158
Perniö 205
Petäjävesi 295-6
Petkeljärvi National Park 388-9
Petsamo 467
Peurajärvi 382
photography 64
Pieksämäki 336-7
Pielisjoki River 360
Pietarsaari 416-18
Pietilä, R & R 32
Pihlajavesi 297
Pihtsusjärvi 493
Piikkiö 203
Piippola 439
Pirkanmaa 278-82
Pirkka people 466, 476
Pohja 151-2
Pohjanmaa 391-427, **392**
Pohjataipale 339
Polvijärvi 362
Pöntsö 487
population 30
Pori 212-15, **213**
Porkkala 138
Porras 267
Portus tavastorum 204
Porvoo 155-7, **155**
Posio 494-6
postal services 60-1
Postimäki 158
Pöyrisjärvi 492
Prästö Island 178
provinces **27**
public holidays 60
Pudasjärvi 463-4
Puijo 345
Pulkkilanharju Ridge 306
Punkaharju 320-4, **322**
Punkaharju Ridge 320
Puolanka 451
Putikko 323
Puurijärvi & Isosuo National
  Park 220
Pyhä 498-500, **499**
Pyhä-Häkki National Park 299
Pyhäjoki 425
Pyhämaa 211
Pyhäniemen Kartano 305
Pyhäranta 211
Pyhätunturi National Park 498
Pyhtää 235

Qvidja Gård 200

Raahe 425-6
Rääkkylä 363
Raate Road 452
rafting 456
  Juuma 460
  Käylä 461
  Kukkolankoski 480
  Lappea 484
  Lentuankoski 449
  Muonionjoki River 488
  Rovaniemi 472
  Ruka 462
  Ruunaa 370
Raisio 192-4
Raittijärvi 493
Raja-Jooseppi 509
Ramsholmen 149
Ramsholmen Natural Park 149
Rantasalmi 324
Rantatie Route 140-1
Ranua 494
Ranua Wildlife Park 494
Rapolan Linnavuori 263
Raseborg 150
Rauhalahti 346
Rauma 220, 222-3, 225
reindeer 25, 446, 451, 468, 476,
  483, 487, 521
reindeer rides 501
Reksaari 223
religion 42-3
Renko 265
Replot 397-8
Reposaari 215
Retretti 320
Retuutti 242
Right of Public Access 71, 81
Riihimäki 262-3
Riisitunturi National Park 496
Ristiina 333-5
Road of Wilderness Villages, see
  Korpikylien tie
Rödjan 149
Rokua 438
Rönnäs 158
Rosala 207
Rosen 159
Route 66 282-7, **283**
Rovaniemi 470-6, **471**
rowing 88-90
  Central Finland 89
  North Karelia 89
  Savo 89
  south Finland 88-9
Ruissalo 192
Ruka 462-3
Runeberg, JL 156, 416, 418

Runni 352
Ruokolahti 251
Ruotsinpyhtää 233-5
Ruovesi 285
Ruukki 439
Ruunaa 369-71
Ruunaan Koskikierros 370
Ruuvaoja 502
Rymättylä 199

Sääksmäki 263-4
Saarenkylä 475
Saari Park 265-7
Saarijärvi 298-9, 493
Saarikoski 493
Saarinen, Eliel 31-2, 114, 137,
    303
Saariselkä 507
Saariselkä Wilderness (Urho
    Kekkonen National Park)
    509-14, **508**
safety 69-70
Saimaa marble seal 324
Salla 501
Salo 203-4
Saloinen 426
Salonsaari Island 227
Saltvik 175-6
Sami people 466-9
    Scolt Samis 467
Sammatti 153
Sandö Island 179
Santa Claus 475
Santa Claus Village 475
Saramo 381-2
Saramo Jotos 381
Saramojoki River 381
Särestöniemi, Reidar 487
Särkänniemi 273-4
Särkisalmi 252
Satakunta 212-28
sauna 38, 123, 191, 274, 309
Saunajärvi 450
Savo 313-53
Savonlinna 315-20, **316**, **321**
Savukoski 501-2
Säynämö 339
Säynätsalo 294
Seglinge 180
Seinäjoki 398-401, **399**
Seitseminen National Park 282
Serlachius Art Museum 297
Sevettijärvi 520-1
shopping 79-80
Sibelius, Jean 35, 139, 141, 158,
    188, 257, 374
Sideby 407
Sieppijärvi 484
Siikajoki 438

Siikalahti 253
Siilinjärvi 349
Siipyy, see Sideby
Sikosaari 157-8
Simanala 326
Simskäla Island 179
Sipoo 155
Sirkka 487-8
sisu 40
Siuntio 153
Sivakka 450
Skag 172
Skarpkulla 152
Skarpnätö 173-4
Skata 417
ski jumping 87, 302
skiing 87-88
    Himos 296
    Lahti 303
    Messilä 304
    Olos 488
    Ounasvaara 473
    Pallastunturi Fell 489
    Ruka 462
    Saariselkä 507
    Saariselkä Wilderness (Urho
        Kekkonen National Park) 509
    Siilinjärvi 349
    Sirkka 487
    Suomu 498
    Syöte 464
    Ukkohalla 451
    Ylläs 485
snakes 69
Snappertuna 150-1
snowmobile safaris 481, 487,
    502
Sodankylä 502-3
Soisalo Island 340
Solf 397
Somero 267
Sonck, Lars 32
Sonka 483
Sonkajärvi 352
Sotkamo 445
Sotkuma 362
Sottunga 182
South Karelia 243-54
sport 78-9, 277
Ståhlberg, KJ 20
Storby 170-1
Stubben 415
Sulkava 327-8
Summassaari 299
Sund 176-8
Sundom 397
Suolahti 298
Suomenlinna 133, **134**
Suomu 498

Suomussalmi 452
Suonenjoki 341-2
Suuraho 339
Suvanto 500-1
Svanvik 144
Svartholm Fort 159-60
Svartsmara 172
Svartvik 138
Sveitsi Park 154
Swedish Coast 407-13
Syöte 464-5
Sysmä 309-10
Syväjärvi 449

Taipale 342
Taitajan taival 389
Taivalkoski 463
Taivassalo 207-8
Täktom Road 144-6
Tammela 265
Tamminiemi 120-1
Tammio Island 237
Tammisaari 147-50, **148**
Tampere 268-78, **270**
Tankari 422
Tankavaara 506-7
Tapiola 137
Tapion taival 387
Tarvaspää 136-7
Tavastehus, see Häme
Tavastland, see Häme
taxes 55
taxis 109
Teijo 205-6
telephone services 61
Teljä 216-17
Tenala 150
Tepasto 487
Tepsanniemi 503
Tervajoki 403
Tervakoski 261
Tervasaari 237
Tervola 482
Tiainen 476
Tiensuu 367-9
Tikkakoski 295
Tikkurila 138
Tjöck 410
Toriseva 285
Tornio 476-9, **478**
Tornionjoki River 466, 476
Torp 171
Torronsuo National Park 267
tourism 29-30
tourist offices 56-7
tours 112
    husky tours 487
    reindeer tours 476, 483
    snowmobile safaris 481, 487, 502

train travel
  to/from Russia 99
  to/from Sweden 97
  train passes 108
  Trans-Siberian Railway 99-100
  within Finland 107-9
Treaty of Friendship, Coopera-
  tion & Mutual Assistance 21
Treaty of Nöteborg 354
Treaty of Tartu 20, 467
Treaty of Tilsit 18
Treaty of Uusikaupunki 17, 354
trekking 81-5
  Central Finland 83
  Eastern Finland 83-4
  Hossa 453-5
  Isojärvi 311
  Korouoma 496
  Kuivajärvi 451
  Kuusamo & Lapland 84
  Kylmäluoma 455
  Lake Mujejärvi 382
  Lauhavuori National Park 405
  Martinselkonen 453
  Peurajärvi 382
  Pyynikki Ridge 274
  Ruunaa 370
  Saana 493
  Saariselkä Wilderness (Urho
    Kekkonen National Park)
    508-12
  Sevettijärvi 521
  Sirkka 487
  south Finland 83
  Syöte 464
  trekking equipment 80
  Vilkaharju 327
trekking routes
  Bear's Path 370-1
  Hetta to Näkkälä 492
  Iso-Palonen 450
  Karhunpolku 83
  Karhunkierros Route 84,
    458-60, 459
  Kevo Gorge Nature Reserve 84
  Kiilopää 507
  Korpikylien tie 381, 450
  Kuhankuono 192
  Lemmenjoki National Park 517
  Maakuntaura trails 83
  Malla Nature Park 493
  Näätämö to Sevettijärvi 521-2
  Pallas-Ounastunturi National
    Park 489-92
  Pirkan taival 83
  Raittijärvi 493

Ruunaan Koskikierros 370
Saana Fell 493
Saariselkä 507
Saramo Jotos Trek 381
Sevettijärvi to Kirakkajärvi 521
Sevettijärvi to Nuorgam 522
Susitaival 83
Taitajan taival 84, 389
Tapion taival 387
UKK Route 83, 449-50, 464
Tulppio 505-6
Turkansaari Island 432
Turku 183-94, 186, 193
Turku & Pori Province 183-228,
  184
Turku Castle 185
Turunmaa 194-99
Turunmaa Archipelago 199-202
Tuusula 139-41
Tyrnävä 438

Uimaharju 360
Uittotupa 332
UKK Route 449-50, 464
Ukko Island 516
Ukkohalla 451
Uleåborg, see Oulu
Ulkotammio Island 237
Ulpukka Route 326
Ulvila 212, 216
Ungern 159
Untamala 211
Urajärven Kartano 306
Urho Kekkonen National Park,
  see Saariselkä Wilderness
Urjala 264
Urpola 330
Utajärvi 438
Utsjoki 522-3
Uukuniemi 253-4
Uusikaarlepyy, see Nykarleby
Uusikaupunki 208-11, 209
Uusimaa 142-61, 143, 151

Vääksy 307
Vaala 438-9
Vaasa 393-8, 394
Vaikkojoki River 378
Vakka-Suomi 207-12
Valamo Monastery 339-40
Valkeakoski 264
Valtavaara 462
Vammala 225-7, 226
Vanajanlinna 260
Vanha Raitti 260
Vantaa 138-9

Vårdö 178-9
Vargata 178
Varissaari 231
Varistaipale 340
Varistaival 340
Varkaus 341-3
Värtsilä 363
Vasa, see Vaasa
Västanfjärd 206
Vehmaa 207
Vehmaanniemi 225
Velkua 199
Verla 242
Vesilahti 282
Vesiluontopolku Route 335
Vihanti 427
Viinijärvi 362
Viitalahti 340
Viitasaari 299-300
Vikajärvi 476
Vilhelm, Johan Vilhelm 19
Vilkaharju 327-8
Vinkkilä 207
Virrat 285-6
Virtaa 309
visas 52-3
Visavuori 263
Visulahti 331
Vörå 413-14
Vöyri, see Vörå
Vuohensaari Island 204
Vuokatti 445-6
Vuokko 377
Vuoksi River 250
Vuonislahti 372-3
Vuorikoski 325
Vuostimo 498
Vuotso 506

Wäinö Aaltonen Museum 188
walking, see trekking
whitewater rafting, see rafting
wildlife, see flora & fauna
women travellers 69
work 70, 340, 341
WWII 20, 371, 452, 455, 467,
  470, 475

Ylämaa 247-8
Yli-Vuokki 451
Ylistaro 403
Ylitornio 483
Ylivieska 427
Ylläs 485-6
Ylläsjärvi 485
Yyteri 215

LONELY PLANET JOURNEYS

JOURNEYS is a unique collection of travellers' tales – published by the company that understands travel better than anyone else. It is a series for anyone who has ever experienced – or dreamed of – the magical moment when they encountered a strange culture or saw a place for the first time. They are tales to read while you're planning a trip, while you're on the road or while you're in an armchair, in front of a fire.

JOURNEYS books will catch the spirit of a place, illuminate a culture, recount a crazy adventure, or introduce a fascinating way of life. They will always entertain, and always enrich the experience of travel.

ISLANDS IN THE CLOUDS
Travels in the Highlands of New Guinea
Isabella Tree

This is the fascinating account of a journey to the remote and beautiful Highlands of Papua New Guinea and Irian Jaya. The author travels with a PNG Highlander who introduces her to his intriguing and complex world. *Islands in the Clouds* is a thoughtful, moving book, full of insights into a region that is rarely noticed by the rest of the world.

'One of the most accomplished travel writers to appear on the horizon for many years . . . the dialogue is brilliant'

– Eric Newby

LOST JAPAN
Alex Kerr

Lost Japan draws on the author's personal experiences of Japan over a period of 30 years. Alex Kerr takes his readers on a backstage tour: friendships with Kabuki actors, buying and selling art, studying calligraphy, exploring rarely visited temples and shrines . . . The Japanese edition of this book was awarded the 1994 Shincho Gakugei Literature Prize for the best work of non-fiction.

'This deeply personal witness to Japan's wilful loss of its traditional culture is at the same time an immensely valuable evaluation of just what that culture was'
– Donald Richie of the Japan Times

THE GATES OF DAMASCUS
Lieve Joris
Translated by Sam Garrett

This best-selling book is a beautifully drawn portrait of day-to-day life in modern Syria. Through her intimate contact with local people, Lieve Joris draws us into the fascinating world that lies behind the gates of Damascus.

'A brilliant book . . . Not since Naguib Mahfouz has the everyday life of the modern Arab world been so intimately described'

– William Dalrymple

SEAN & DAVID'S LONG DRIVE
Sean Condon

Sean and David are young townies who have rarely strayed beyond city limits. One day, for no good reason, they set out to discover their homeland, and what follows is a wildly entertaining adventure that covers half of Australia. Sean Condon has written a hilarious, offbeat road book that mixes sharp insights with deadpan humour and outright lies.

'Funny, pithy, kitsch and surreal . . . This book will do for Australia what Chernobyl did for Kiev, but hey you'll laugh as the stereotypes go boom'

– Andrew Tuck, Time Out

LONELY PLANET TRAVEL ATLASES

Lonely Planet has long been famous for the number and quality of its guidebook maps. Now we've gone one step further and in conjunction with Steinhart Katzir Publishers produced a handy companion series: Lonely Planet travel atlases – maps of a country produced in book form.

Unlike other maps, which look good but lead travellers astray, our travel atlases have been researched on the road by Lonely Planet's experienced team of writers. All details are carefully checked to ensure the atlas corresponds with the equivalent Lonely Planet guidebook.

The handy atlas format means no holes, wrinkles, torn sections or constant folding and unfolding. These atlases can survive long periods on the road, unlike cumbersome fold-out maps. The comprehensive index ensures easy reference.

- full-colour throughout
- maps researched and checked by Lonely Planet authors
- place names correspond with Lonely Planet guidebooks
  – no confusing spelling differences
- legend and travelling information in English, French, German, Japanese and Spanish
- size: 230 x 160 mm

Available now:
Thailand; India & Bangladesh; Vietnam; Zimbabwe, Botswana & Namibia

Coming soon:
Chile; Egypt; Israel; Laos; Turkey

LONELY PLANET TV SERIES & VIDEOS

Lonely Planet travel guides have been brought to life on television screens around the world. Like our guides, the programmes are based on the joy of independent travel, and look honestly at some of the most exciting, picturesque and frustrating places in the world. Each show is presented by one of three travellers from Australia, England or the USA and combines an innovative mixture of video, Super-8 film, atmospheric soundscapes and original music.

Videos of each episode – containing additional footage not shown on television – are available from good book and video shops, but the availability of individual videos varies with regional screening schedules.

Video destinations include: Alaska; Australia (Southeast); Brazil; Ecuador & the Galápagos Islands; Indonesia; Israel & the Sinai Desert; Japan; La Ruta Maya (Yucatán, Guatemala & Belize); Morocco; North India (Varanasi to the Himalaya); Pacific Islands; Vietnam; Zimbabwe, Botswana & Namibia.

Coming soon: The Arctic (Norway & Finland); Baja California; Chile & Easter Island; China (Southeast); Costa Rica; East Africa (Tanzania & Zanzibar); Great Barrier Reef (Australia); Jamaica; Papua New Guinea; the Rockies (USA); Syria & Jordan; Turkey.

The Lonely Planet TV series is produced by:
Pilot Productions
Duke of Sussex Studios
44 Uxbridge St
London W8 7TG UK

Lonely Planet videos are distributed by:
IVN Communications Inc
2246 Camino Ramon
California 94583, USA

107 Power Road, Chiswick
London W5 UK

Music from the TV series is available on CD & cassette.
For ordering information contact your nearest Lonely Planet office.

PLANET TALK

Lonely Planet's FREE quarterly newsletter

We love hearing from you and think you'd like to hear from us.
When...is the right time to see reindeer in Finland?
Where...can you hear the best palm-wine music in Ghana?
How...do you get from Asunción to Areguá by steam train?
What...is the best way to see India?

For the answer to these and many other questions read PLANET TALK.

Every issue is packed with up-to-date travel news and advice including:

- a letter from Lonely Planet founders Tony and Maureen Wheeler
- travel diary from a Lonely Planet author – find out what it's really like out on the road
- feature article on an important and topical travel issue
- a selection of recent letters from our readers
- the latest travel news from all over the world
- details on Lonely Planet's new and forthcoming releases

To join our mailing list contact any Lonely Planet office.

Also available: Lonely Planet T-shirts. 100% heavyweight cotton (S, M, L, XL)

LONELY PLANET ONLINE

Get the latest travel information before you leave or while you're on the road

Whether you've just begun planning your next trip, or you're chasing down specific info on currency regulations or visa requirements, check out the Lonely Planet World Wide Web site for up-to-the-minute travel information.

As well as travel profiles of your favourite destinations (including interactive maps and full-colour photos), you'll find current reports from our army of researchers and other travellers, updates on health and visas, travel advisories, and the ecological and political issues you need to be aware of as you travel.

There's an online travellers' forum (the Thorn Tree) where you can share your experiences of life on the road, meet travel companions and ask other travellers for their recommendations and advice. We also have plenty of links to other Web sites useful to independent travellers.

With tens of thousands of visitors a month, the Lonely Planet Web site is one of the most popular on the Internet and has won a number of awards including GNN's Best of the Net travel award.

http://www.lonelyplanet.com

LONELY PLANET PRODUCTS

The Lonely Planet list covers every accessible part of Asia as well as Australia, the Pacific, South America, Africa, the Middle East, Europe and parts of North America. There are eight series: *travel guides* – covering a country for a range of budgets, *shoestring guides* – with compact information for low-budget travel in a major region, *walking guides, city guides, phrasebooks, audio packs, travel atlases* and *travel literature*.

EUROPE

Austria • Baltic States & Kaliningrad • Baltic States phrasebook • Britain • Central Europe on a shoestring • Central Europe phrasebook • Czech & Slovak Republics • Dublin city guide • Eastern Europe on a shoestring • Eastern Europe phrasebook • Finland • France • Greece • Greek phrasebook • Hungary • Iceland, Greenland & the Faroe Islands • Ireland • Italy • Mediterranean Europe on a shoestring • Mediterranean Europe phrasebook • Poland • Prague city guide • Russia, Ukraine & Belarus • Russian phrasebook • Scandinavian & Baltic Europe on a shoestring • Scandinavian Europe phrasebook • Slovenia • St Petersburg city guide • Switzerland • Trekking in Greece • Trekking in Spain • Vienna city guide • Walking in Switzerland • Western Europe on a shoestring • Western Europe phrasebook

NORTH AMERICA & MEXICO

Alaska • Backpacking in Alaska • California & Nevada • Canada • Hawaii • Honolulu city guide • Los Angeles city guide • Pacific Northwest USA • Rocky Mountain States • San Francisco city guide • Southwest USA • USA phrasebook

CENTRAL AMERICA & THE CARIBBEAN

Baja California • Central America on a shoestring • Costa Rica • Eastern Caribbean • Guatemala, Belize & Yucatán: La Ruta Maya • Mexico

SOUTH AMERICA

Argentina, Uruguay & Paraguay • Bolivia • Brazil • Brazilian phrasebook • Buenos Aires city guide • Chile & Easter Island • Colombia • Ecuador & the Galápagos Islands • Latin American Spanish phrasebook • Peru • Quechua phrasebook • Rio de Janeiro city guide • South America on a shoestring • Trekking in the Patagonian Andes • Venezuela

ALSO AVAILABLE:

Travel with Children • Traveller's Tales

AFRICA

Arabic (Moroccan) phrasebook • Africa on a shoestring • Cape Town city guide • Central Africa • East Africa • Egypt & the Sudan • Ethiopian (Amharic) phrasebook • Kenya • Morocco • North Africa • South Africa, Lesotho & Swaziland • Swahili phrasebook • Trekking in East Africa • West Africa • Zimbabwe, Botswana & Namibia • Zimbabwe, Botswana & Namibia travel atlas

MAIL ORDER

Lonely Planet products are distributed worldwide. They are also available by mail order from Lonely Planet, so if you have difficulty finding a title please write to us. US, Canadian and South American residents should write to Embarcadero West, 155 Filbert St, Suite 251, Oakland CA 94607, USA; European and African residents should write to 10 Barley Mow Passage, Chiswick, London W4 4PH; and residents of other countries to PO Box 617, Hawthorn, Victoria 3122, Australia.

NORTH-EAST ASIA

Beijing city guide • Cantonese phrasebook • China • Hong Kong, Macau & Canton • Japan • Japanese phrasebook • Japanese audio pack • Korea • Korean phrasebook • Mandarin phrasebook • Mongolia • Mongolian phrasebook • North-East Asia on a shoestring • Seoul city guide • Taiwan • Tibet • Tibet phrasebook • Tokyo city guide

Travel Literature: Lost Japan

MIDDLE EAST & CENTRAL ASIA

Arab Gulf States • Arabic (Egyptian) phrasebook • Central Asia • Iran • Israel • Jordan & Syria • Middle East • Turkey • Turkish phrasebook • Trekking in Turkey • Yemen

Travel Literature: The Gates of Damascus

ISLANDS OF THE INDIAN OCEAN

Madagascar & Comoros • Maldives & Islands of the East Indian Ocean • Mauritius, Réunion & Seychelles

INDIAN SUBCONTINENT

Bengali phrasebook • Bangladesh • Delhi city guide • Hindi/Urdu phrasebook • India • India & Bangladesh travel atlas • Karakoram Highway • Kashmir, Ladakh & Zanskar • Nepal • Nepali phrasebook • Pakistan • Sri Lanka • Sri Lanka phrasebook • Trekking in the Indian Himalaya • Trekking in the Nepal Himalaya

SOUTH-EAST ASIA

Bali & Lombok • Bangkok city guide • Burmese phrasebook • Cambodia • Ho Chi Minh city guide • Indonesia • Indonesian phrasebook • Indonesian audio pack • Jakarta city guide • Java • Laos • Lao phrasebook • Malaysia, Singapore & Brunei • Myanmar (Burma) • Philippines • Pilipino phrasebook • Singapore city guide • South-East Asia on a shoestring • Thailand • Thailand travel atlas • Thai phrasebook • Thai audio pack • Thai Hill Tribes phrasebook • Vietnam • Vietnamese phrasebook • Vietnam travel atlas

AUSTRALIA & THE PACIFIC

Australia • Australian phrasebook • Bushwalking in Australia• Bushwalking in Papua New Guinea • Fiji • Fijian phrasebook • Islands of Australia's Great Barrier Reef • Melbourne city guide • Micronesia • New Caledonia • New South Wales & the ACT • New Zealand • Outback Australia • Papua New Guinea • Papua New Guinea phrasebook • Queensland • Rarotonga & the Cook Islands • Samoa • Solomon Islands • Sydney city guide • Tahiti & French Polynesia • Tonga • Tramping in New Zealand • Vanuatu • Victoria • Western Australia

Travel Literature: Islands in the Clouds • Sean & David's Long Drive

THE LONELY PLANET STORY

Lonely Planet published its first book in 1973 in response to the numerous 'How did you do it?' questions Maureen and Tony Wheeler were asked after driving, bussing, hitching, sailing and railing their way from England to Australia.

Written at a kitchen table and hand collated, trimmed and stapled, *Across Asia on the Cheap* became an instant local bestseller, inspiring thoughts of another book.

Eighteen months in South-East Asia resulted in their second guide, *South-East Asia on a shoestring*, which they put together in a backstreet Chinese hotel in Singapore in 1975. The 'yellow bible' as it quickly became known to backpackers around the world, soon became *the* guide to the region. It has sold well over half a million copies and is now in its 8th edition, still retaining its familiar yellow cover.

Today there are over 180 titles, including travel guides, walking guides, language kits & phrasebooks, travel atlases and travel literature. The company is one of the largest travel publishers in the world. Although Lonely Planet initially specialised in guides to Asia, we now cover most regions of the world, including the Pacific, North America, South America, Africa, the Middle East and Europe.

The emphasis continues to be on travel for independent travellers. Tony and Maureen still travel for several months of each year and play an active part in the writing, updating and quality control of Lonely Planet's guides.

They have been joined by over 50 authors and 155 staff at our offices in Melbourne (Australia), Oakland (USA), London (UK) and Paris (France). Travellers themselves also make a valuable contribution to the guides through the feedback we receive in thousands of letters each year.

The people at Lonely Planet strongly believe that travellers can make a positive contribution to the countries they visit, both through their appreciation of the countries' culture, wildlife and natural features, and through the money they spend. In addition, the company makes a direct contribution to the countries and regions it covers. Since 1986 a percentage of the income from each book has been donated to ventures such as famine relief in Africa; aid projects in India; agricultural projects in Central America; Greenpeace's efforts to halt French nuclear testing in the Pacific; and Amnesty International.

Lonely Planet's basic travel philosophy is summed up in Tony Wheeler's comment, 'Don't worry about whether your trip will work out. Just go!'

LONELY PLANET PUBLICATIONS

Australia
PO Box 617, Hawthorn 3122, Victoria
tel: (03) 9819 1877 fax: (03) 9819 6459
e-mail: talk2us@lonelyplanet.com.au

USA
Embarcadero West, 155 Filbert St, Suite 251,
Oakland, CA 94607
tel: (510) 893 8555 TOLL FREE: 800 275-8555
fax: (510) 893 8563
e-mail: info@lonelyplanet.com

UK
10 Barley Mow Passage, Chiswick,
London W4 4PH
tel: (0181) 742 3161 fax: (0181) 742 2772
e-mail: 100413.3551@compuserve.com

France:
71 bis rue du Cardinal Lemoine – 75005 Paris
tel: 1 44 32 06 20 fax: 1 46 34 72 55
e-mail: 100560.415@compuserve.com

World Wide Web: http://www.lonelyplanet.com